EXPERIMENTAL PHOTOGRAPHY

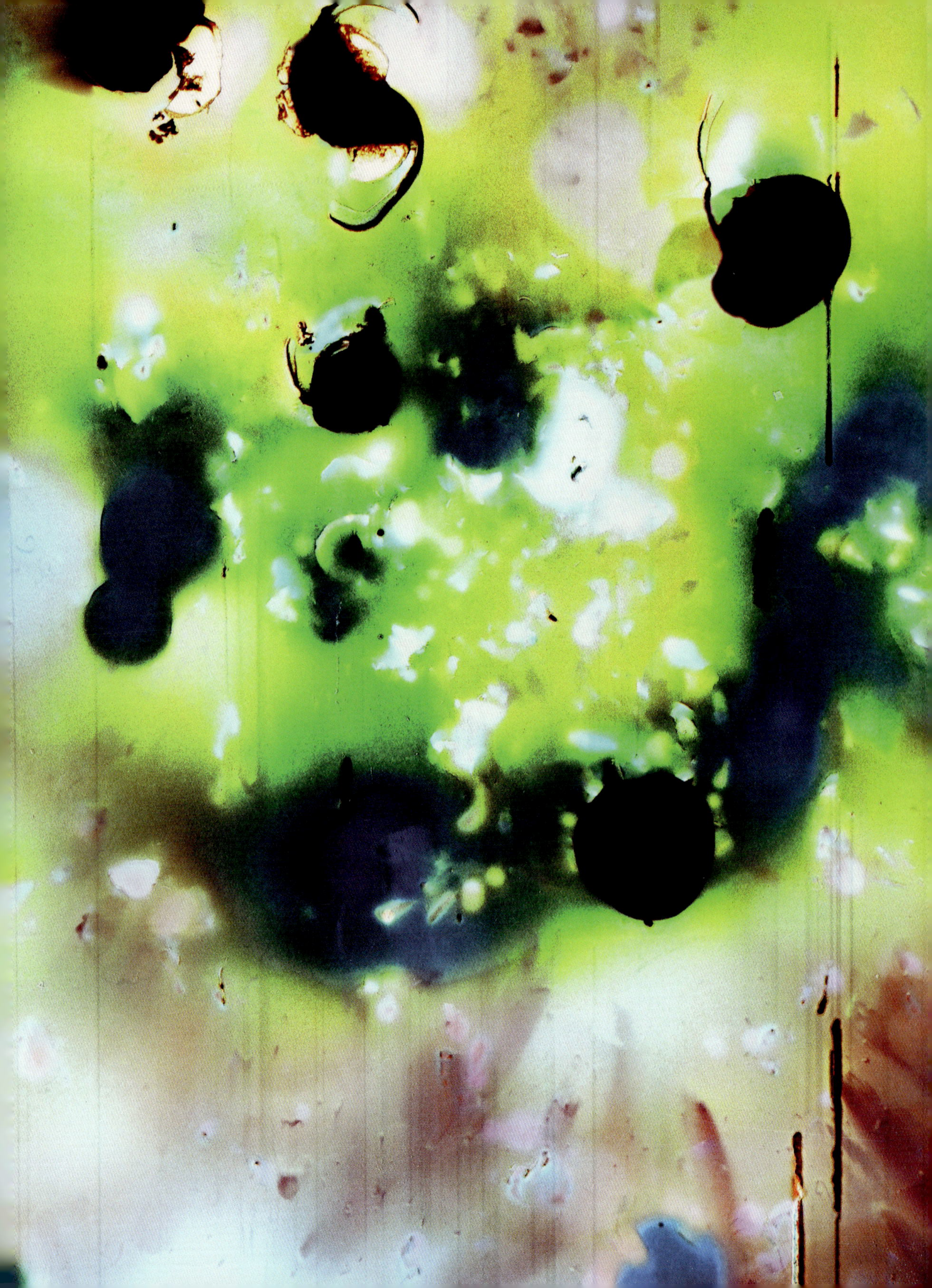

EXPERIMENTAL PHOTOGRAPHY

A HANDBOOK OF TECHNIQUES

With over 600 illustrations

MARCO ANTONINI

SERGIO MINNITI

FRANCISCO GÓMEZ

GABRIELE LUNGARELLA

LUCA BENDANDI

EDITED BY LUCA BENDANDI

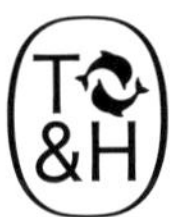

ON THE COVER:

FRONT Ruth Erdt and Eva Vuillemin, *Cyanotypes 16–22*,
cyanotypes, 2011. Courtesy the artists.

BACK Taras Perun, *Untitled*, CMY gum bichromate print, 2013.
Courtesy the artist.

FRONTISPIECE
Drew Kunz, *Untitled*, scan from distressed colour film with
holes, 2008.

First published in the United Kingdom in 2015 by
Thames & Hudson Ltd, 181A High Holborn, London WC1V 7QX

First published in the United States of America in 2015 by
Thames & Hudson Inc., 500 Fifth Avenue, New York,
New York 10110

Reprinted 2024

Experimental Photography © 2015 SHS Publishing,
www.shspublishing.com

Designed by Luca Bendandi, SHS Publishing
Texts by SHS Publishing, unless otherwise credited
Step-by-step photography by Cristóbal Pereira and
Gabriele Lungarella
Alternative printing processes by Francisco Gómez
and Barbara Ghidini at Taller Milans, Barcelona

British Library Cataloguing-in-Publication Data
A catalogue record for this book is available from
the British Library

Library of Congress Control Number 2014944633

ISBN 978-0-500-54437-2

Printed and bound in China by Toppan Leefung Printing Ltd

Be the first to know about our new releases,
exclusive content and author events by visiting
thamesandhudson.com
thamesandhudsonusa.com
thamesandhudson.com.au

Be Safe

Whenever you work with chemicals you need to be aware
of the hazards and safety measures associated with them.
When the symbol ⚠ appears on project equipment lists,
you should refer to the appropriate entry in the Chemical
Safety Information on pp. 226–29. The safety information
provided in this book is only a starting point and does not
supersede the manufacturer's safety instructions, which
you should consult in all circumstances before beginning
work. It is always recommended that you wear protective
gloves, goggles, and a lab coat (or similar form of protective
clothing) as basic precautions. Additional protective
measures may be necessary depending on the chemicals
involved.

Reasonable effort has been made to review and verify the
information in this book. Neither the Authors, SHS
Publishing, Thames & Hudson, nor its publishing partners
assume responsibility for completeness and accuracy of
the information, or for its interpretation. The reader is
responsible for making appropriate decisions and taking
appropriate care with respect to the safe use of specific
materials, work practices, equipment and regulatory
obligations.

The techniques suggested in this book should not be used
by anyone under 18 years of age. To the extent permitted by
law, no liability is accepted by SHS Publishing, the Authors
or Thames & Hudson for any loss, damage or injury arising
as a consequence of attempting the processes described
in this book.

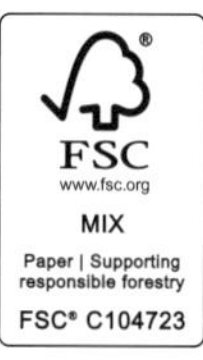

2 Handmade, Toy and Disposable Cameras

3 Operative Hacks

5 Post-Printing Experimentation

Appendix

Introduction: The Paradox of Photography

Modern photography has a central paradox. Never before has it been so easy to take a picture, yet the more photography becomes widespread and readily available, the less we understand how the process works. Today we can take pictures with our mobile phones, tablet computers, hand-held cameras and SLRs. The easier it becomes to take a picture, the more complex is the technology behind it and the more difficult it is to distinguish the individual photographer's touch. Today everyone is a photographer; every event, from birthday, to sports game or concert, is documented in rich detail. It would seem that reality has never been so accurately represented. But is this truly the case?

In a world ever-more dominated by images, this paradox of photography has brought us to a homogenization of visual culture. A small number of camera manufacturers produce all the equipment that we use to photograph our reality. Even in the case of analogue photography, a handful of processes have become the industry standard. Although there is infinite variety in the subjects of our photographs, out of the estimated billions (trillions?) of photos snapped each month, all are taken with roughly the same equipment, and, if printed, developed and processed in the same ways. Yet in its original and purest form, photography requires only a straightforward combination of a few basic ingredients: light, an aperture of some kind, and a medium to record the resulting image. Within this simple recipe, the possibilities for experimentation and variation are nearly endless.

This book speaks to those who consider photography first and foremost as a craft, rather than as an elevated artistic gesture on the one hand or mere technical process on the other. For them photography is a journey of exploration, from initial inspiration through capture of the subject-matter, and finally to the subtle decisions to be made in choosing and manipulating printing techniques. The projects, interviews and artist profiles in this volume celebrate not only the flexibility of photography as a medium but, above all, the role of the photographer as a visual pioneer, rather than simply a reporter of the visible world.

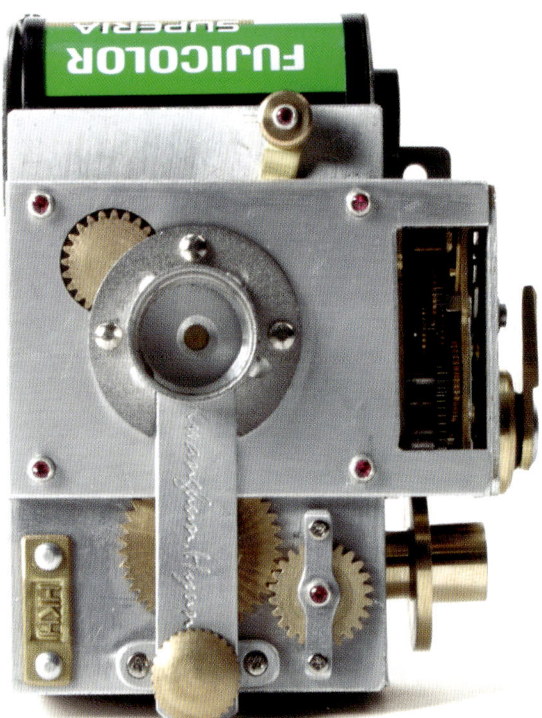

LEFT

Kwanghun Hyun
Obscura VII, gear 3,
handmade pinhole
camera with watch-style
movements, aluminium,
brass, 0.3 mm pinhole,
82 × 66 × 39 mm (3¼
× 2⅝ × 1½ in.), 2010

Many of the photographers featured here are also avid camera-makers.
Their work sheds revealing new light on the mechanical devices that
we use to capture images, deconstructing them, reconstructing them,
and extending the definition of what we consider a camera – assuming
that we even need a camera in the first place. Some of the techniques
described in this book push the boundaries of conventional photographic
technology so far as to require no camera at all. From egg whites to
beetroot, flowers or complex chemicals, the possibilities for developing
images are endless, compelling the photographer to become at once
both botanist and chemist, artist and magician, and theoretician and
builder. The photography that is reproduced in these pages therefore
wholly transcends conventional ideas of beauty, redefining it with every
experimental process.

Cameraless

A camera can be optional in photography.
These techniques bridge the divide
between photography and painting,
expanding on the basic concept
of light sensitivity.

1

CAMERA OBSCURA

The earliest method for capturing an image, camera obscura (Latin for 'dark room'), works on the principle of rectilinear propagation of photons. Light travels unobstructed through a hole in a wall (or the side of any box-like structure) and is reflected upside-down on the opposite surface, preserving colour and perspective. Lenses can be added to focus the image, as with a traditional camera, and a prism or mirror can turn it right-side up. The ancient technique was described by Aristotle, and sketched by Leonardo da Vinci (see below), who, like many artists of his time, projected camera obscura images onto paper as a drafting aid. Contemporary artists have recently rediscovered camera obscura, using it to create gallery projections or combining it with other processes to obtain printed images.

Turn a room into a camera obscura

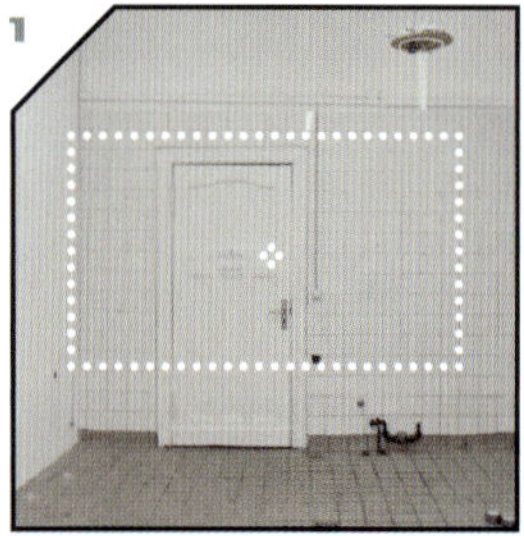
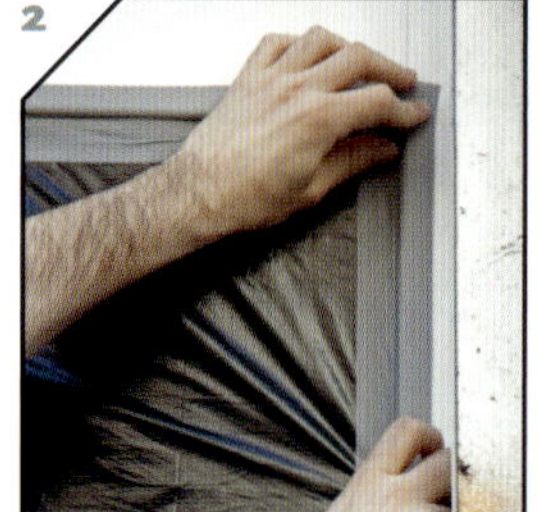
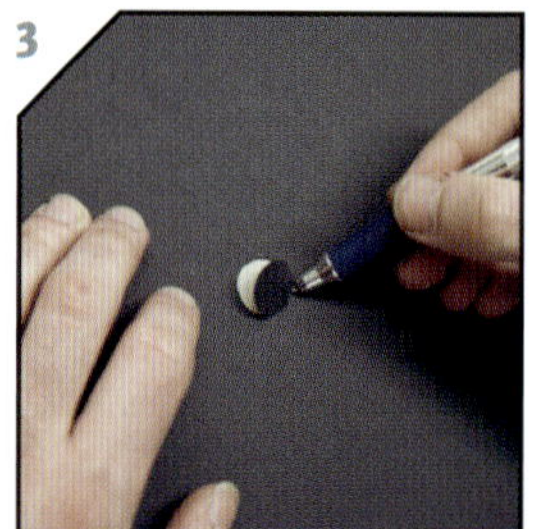
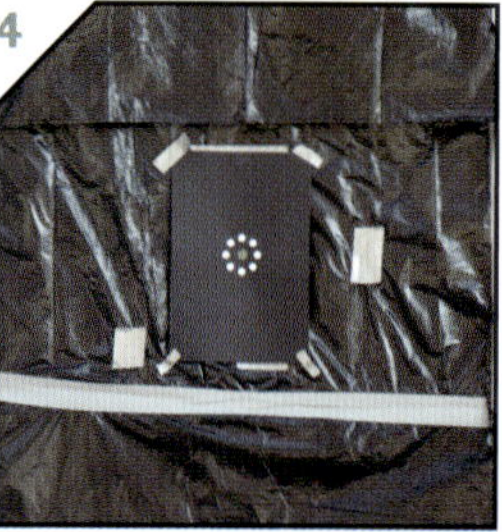

What you need:
- ☐ room with a window
- ☐ white wall, curtain or projection screen opposite the window
- ☐ black plastic sheeting
- ☐ duct tape
- ☐ art knife
- ☐ heavy black paper
- ☐ converging lens and PVC tube or cardboard toilet roll (optional)

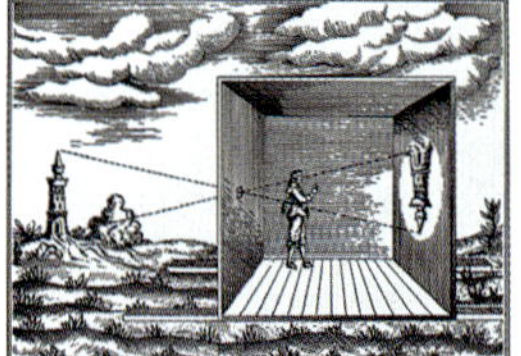

Choose the right room

1 The room should have a central window opposite a bare white wall.

Darken the room

2 Use black plastic sheeting to cover the windows. Apply duct tape around the edges to block out any remaining light.

Cut a hole in the centre

3 For an average-sized room, a hole of 1–2 cm diameter cut in the centre of the central window covering will suffice.

4 To improve sharpness, use the art knife to cut a smaller hole into a piece of heavy black paper, and tape it over the opening in the plastic sheeting. This will restrict the amount of light passing through, but the resulting image will be sharper.

View and refine the image

Wait for a sunny day. If the room is dark, the image will appear, upside-down, on the wall opposite the window (see opposite, top). To improve sharpness (optional; not pictured), set a converging lens in the far end of a PVC tube or cardboard toilet roll, position the tube over the hole, and tape the base to the black paper surround. The lens's focal length should be roughly equal to the distance between it and the opposite wall. You can buy a lens from an optician, using this formula to convert focal length to diopters: $D = 1/FL$ (D = diopters; FL = focal length of the lens in metres). For example, a converging lens with focal length of 4 m has a power of +0.25 diopters ($D = \frac{1}{4}$). ('+' indicates a converging rather than diverging lens.)

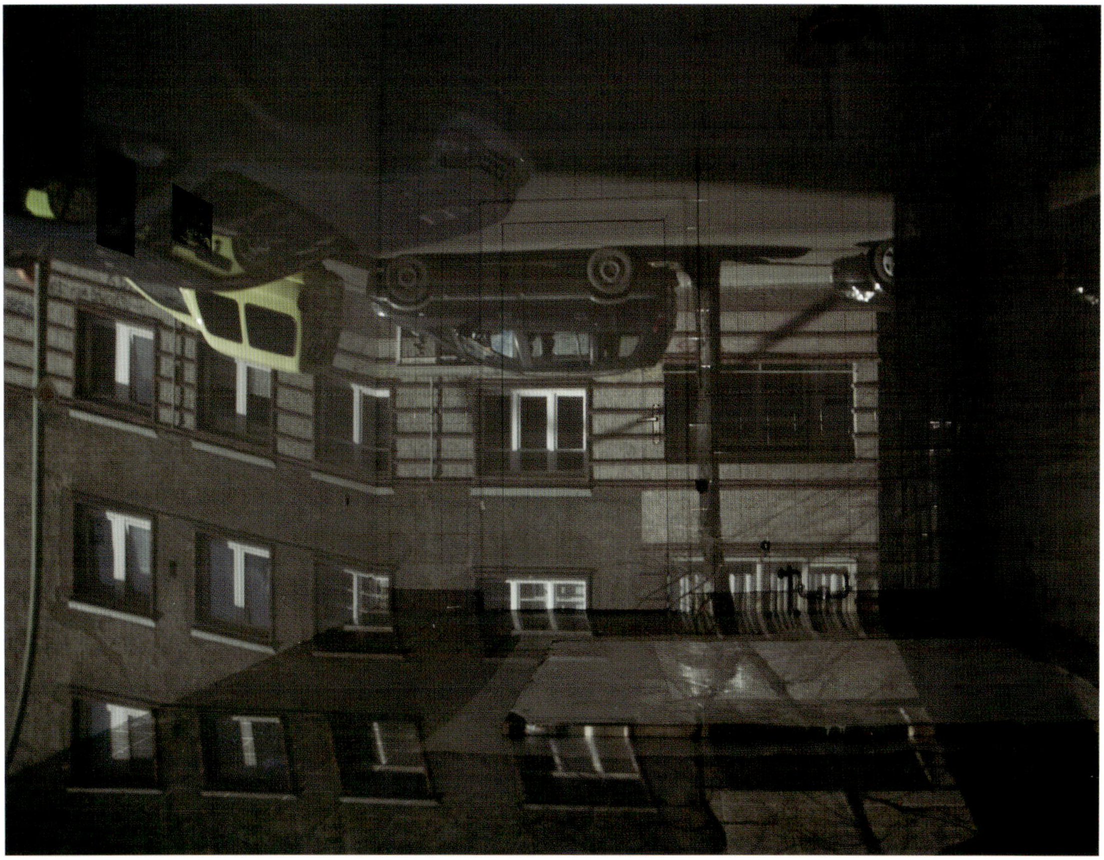

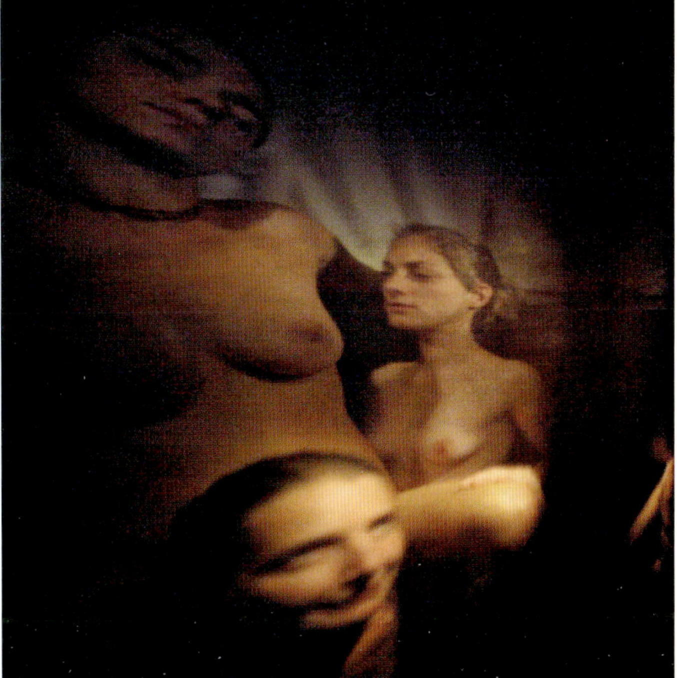

ABOVE
Sample camera obscura image
projected at Frankfurt am Main
Galerie, Berlin, 12 May 2014

LEFT
Ctibor Bachratý
Orthographe performance
through camera obscura,
Divadelna festival, Nitra, Slovakia,
2008

Italian theatre company Orthographe often
incorporates photographic techniques into its
performance pieces. Its members have designed and
built an 'Optic Stage', consisting of both a camera
lucida ('light room') and a camera obscura. The first
is set up in a room where the performance takes
place; the latter reveals the image to the audience
seated in a separate room. Alessandro Panzavolta,
who formulated the concept, explains its origins:
'Intrinsically this principle is as old as the Platonic
myth of the cave. Cinema itself is a large camera
obscura in which images previously shot and cut
are shown for viewers. What happens on our Optic
Stage is simply the vision of projected images,
"acted" and cut in real time.'

ABELARDO MORELL

*Profile by
Marco Antonini*

Abelardo Morell has established himself on the international art scene as a photographer who understands the creative potential of his medium, adapting traditional tools and techniques such as camera obscura in unconventional ways to produce amazingly immersive visual experiences.

Cuban-born artist Abelardo Morell, who moved to the United States in 1962, has been active as a photographer for more than thirty years. Grounding his formative work in domestic experiences and observations, Morell first experimented with large-format photos of household objects and scenes of childhood. Inspired by classroom demonstrations he conducted while teaching at the Massachusetts College of Art, he then grew increasingly fond of camera obscura. He now uses large-scale camera obscura installations to create temporary 'sets', which he then photographs. Physical details of the room, such as the furniture and personal objects left in place, create an unexpected overlap of indoor and outdoor elements that the artist describes on his website as a 'weird yet natural marriage'. After working in all sorts of domestic interiors, including his own home, Morell extended his practice to include a wider range of settings, using larger, custom-built portable camera obscura devices. These tent-like structures (see illustration on p. 20) allow him to project images of a landscape onto other parts of the same landscape, creating compositions that

RIGHT
View of Landscape Outside Florence in Room With Bookcase, camera obscura, dimensions variable, 2009

OPPOSITE
View of Landscape Outside Florence Looking East toward where Galileo Died in Exile, camera obscura, dimensions variable, 2009

OVERLEAF
View of Central Park Looking North, Spring, Fall, Winter, Summer, camera obscura, dimensions variable, 2008–13

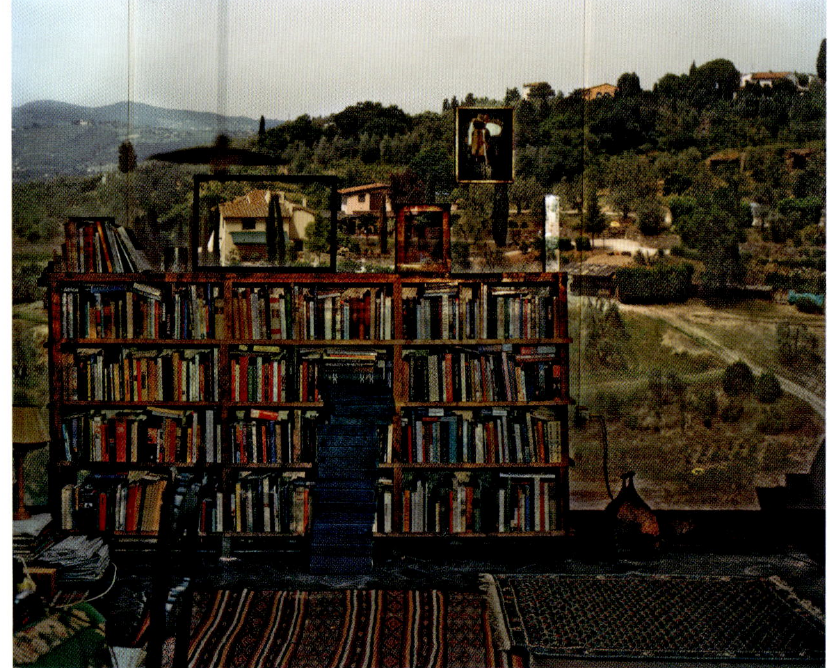

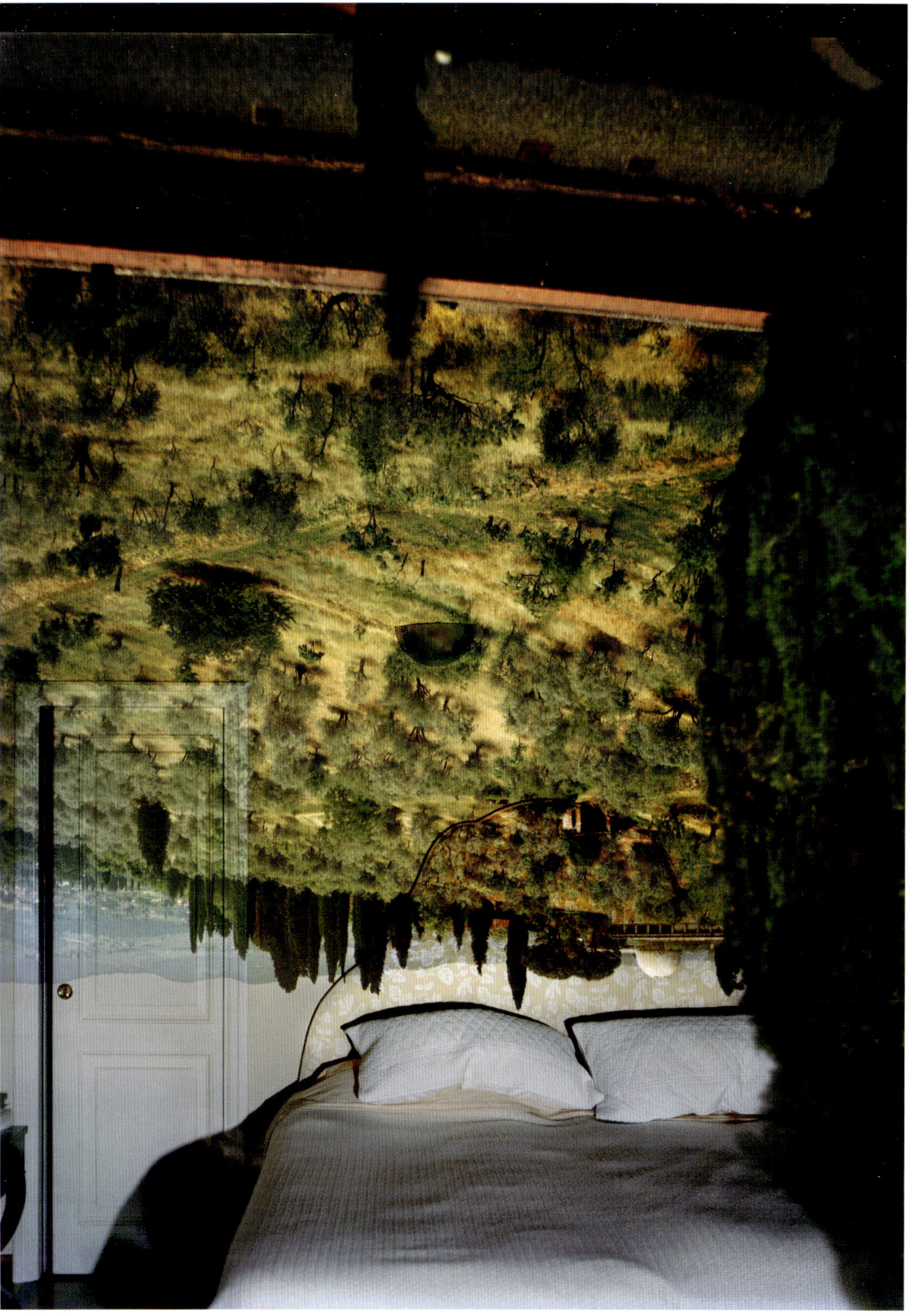

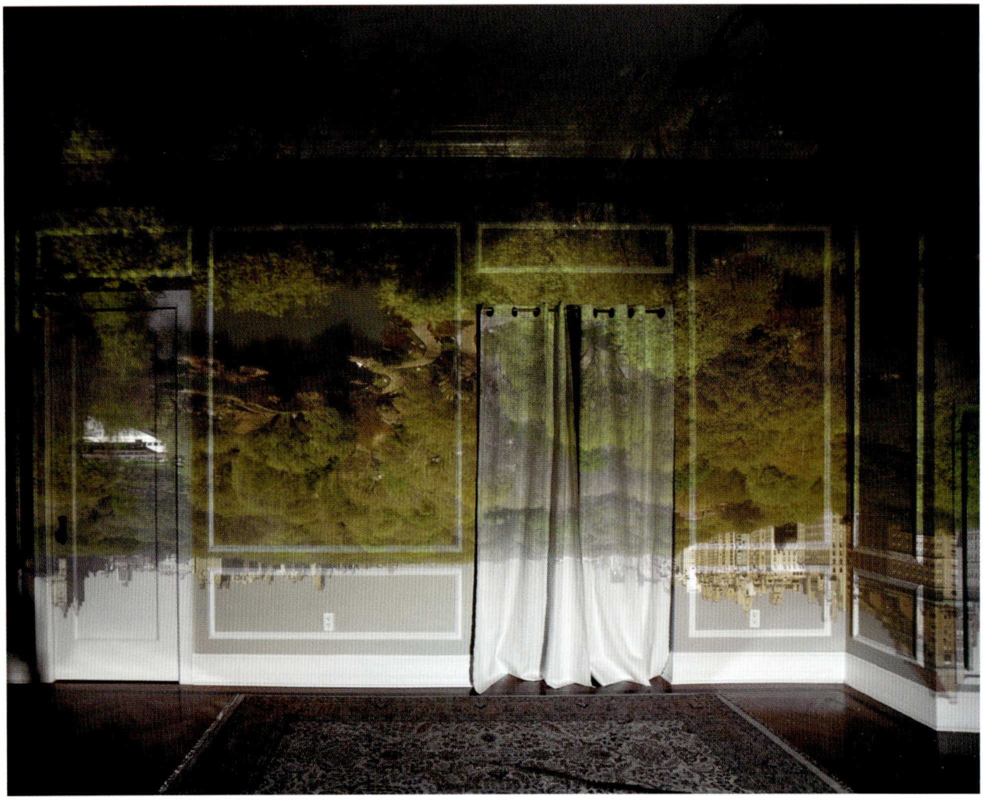

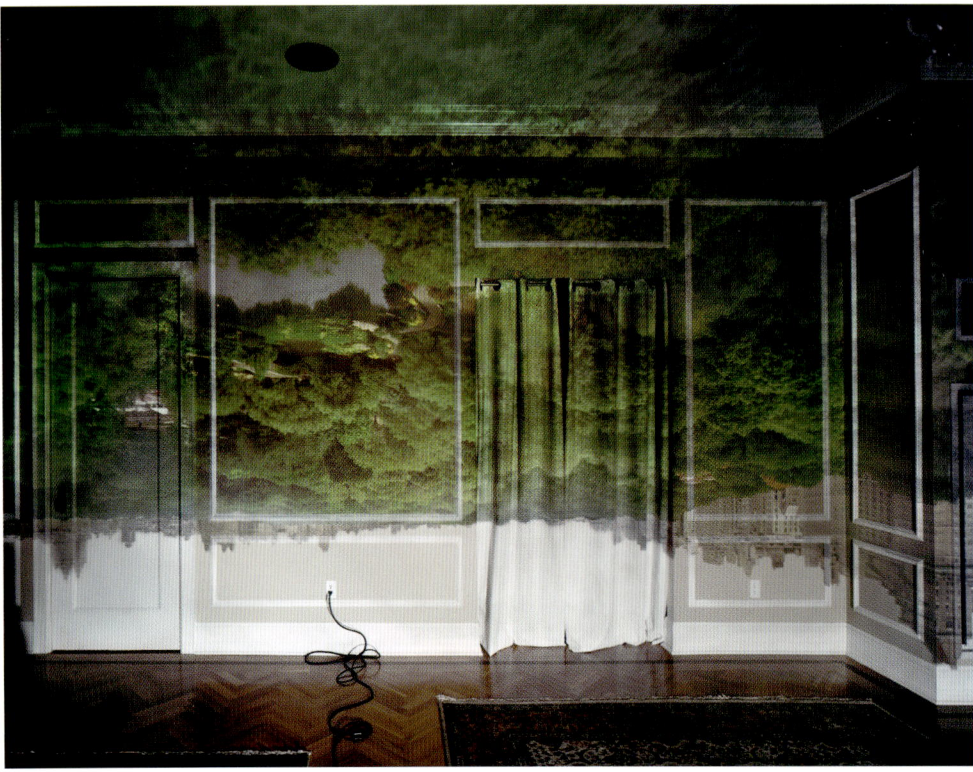

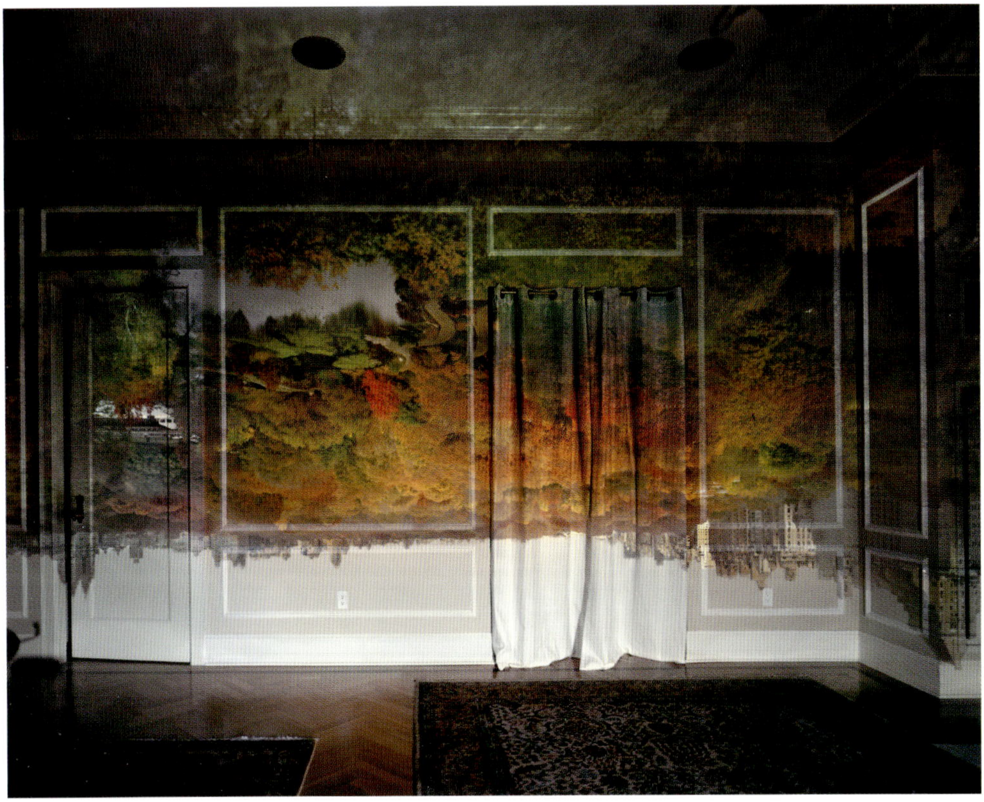

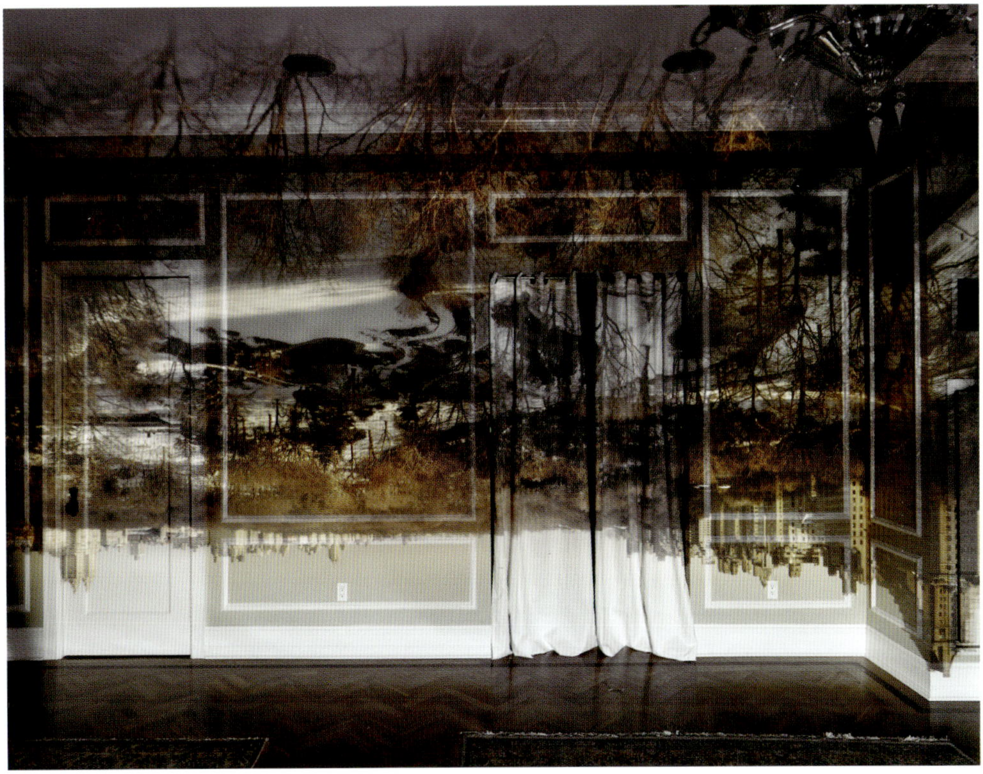

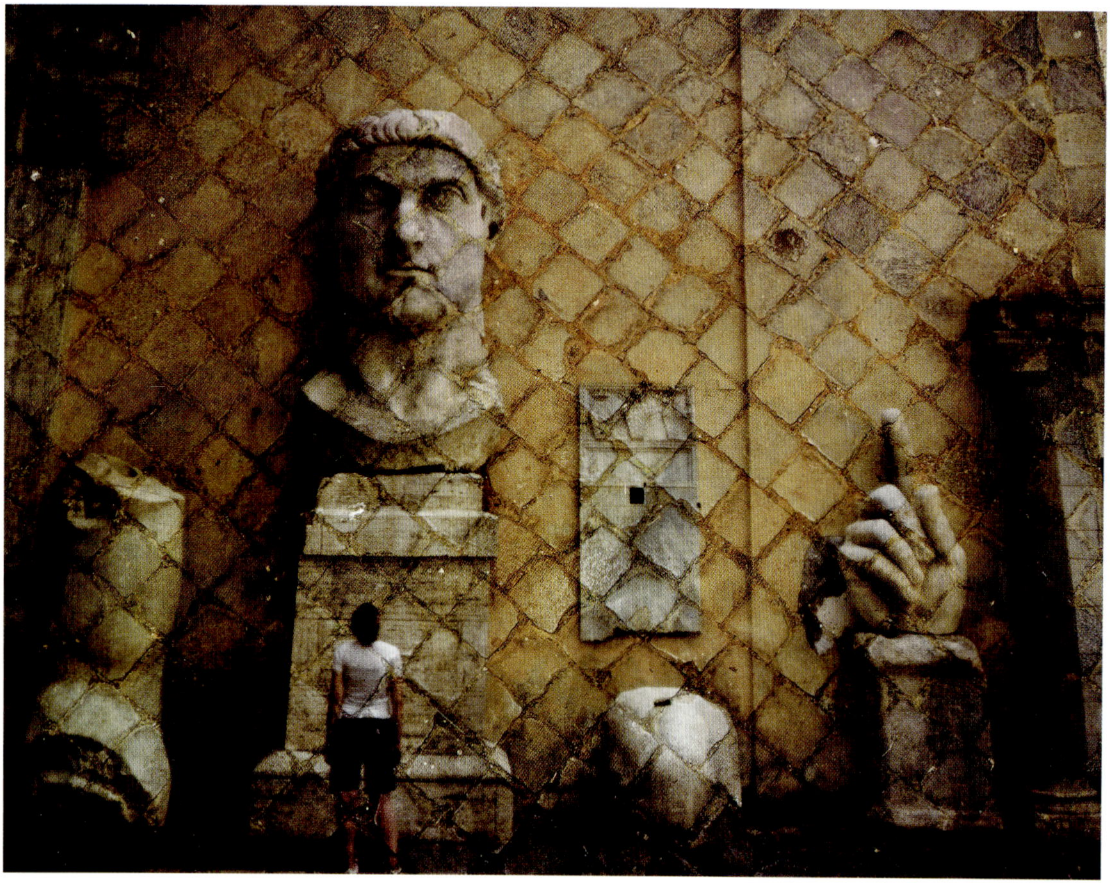

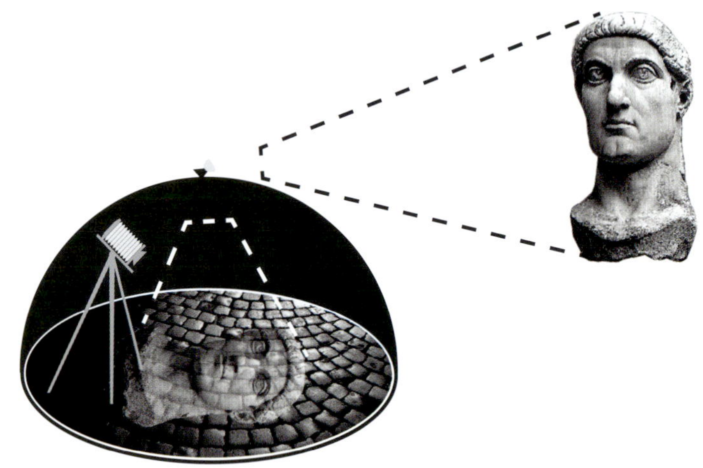

ABOVE

*Tent-Camera Image on the Ground:
View of Roman Sculpture in
Palazzo dei Conservatori*, camera
obscura, dimensions variable,
2010

RIGHT

A schematic representation
showing how Morell set up his
camera obscura tent to produce
the images on these pages.

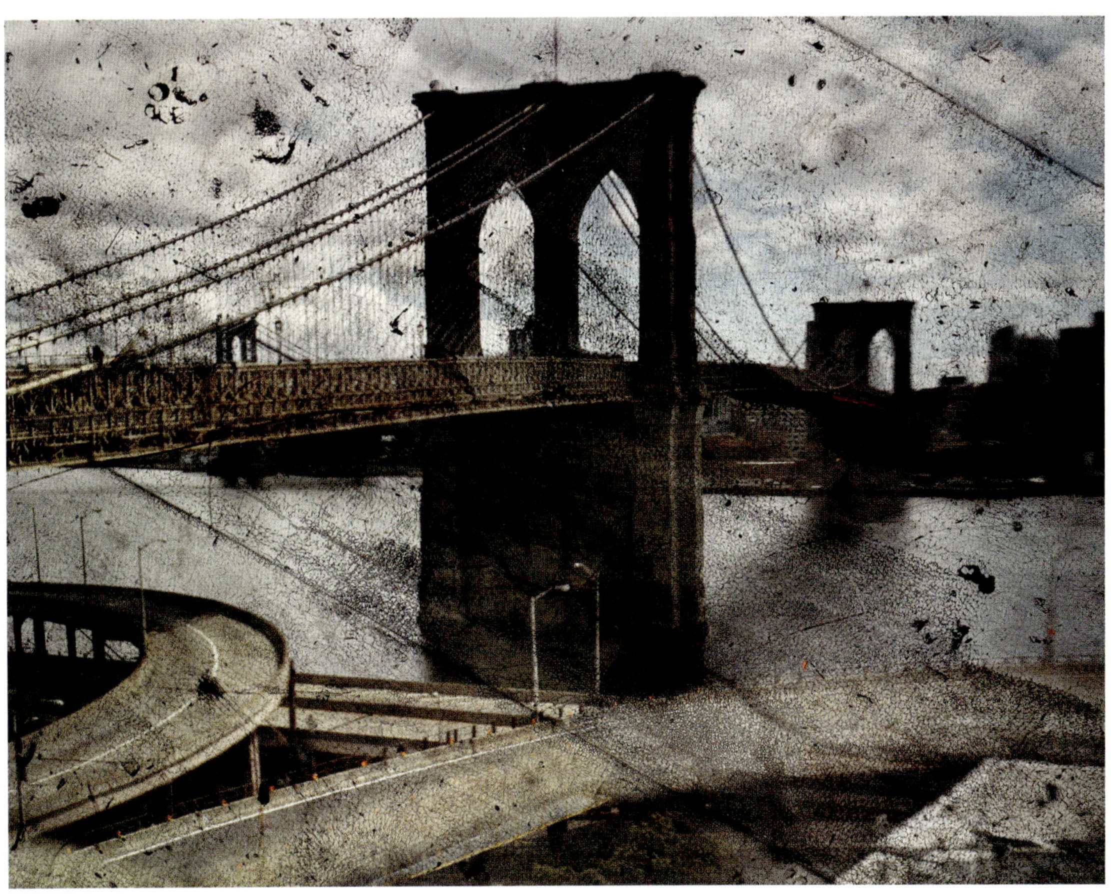

Tent-Camera Image on the Ground: Rooftop View of the Brooklyn Bridge, camera obscura, dimensions variable, 2010

emphasize the harmony and connectedness of the two different layers of imagery. Throughout his career Morell has alternated these experiments with more traditional series, switching between black-and-white and colour photography, and analogue and digital cameras, in order to explore the full range of the medium. His recent series include experiments with photograms and cliché-verre, producing largely abstract works that bring the handmade and machine-made together in the same way that his camera obscura works conflate indoor and outdoor scenes into a single, uncanny image.

DARKROOM

What you need:
- ☐ enlarger
- ☐ timer
- ☐ easel
- ☐ safelight
- ☐ printing tongs
- ☐ processing trays
- ☐ thermometer
- ☐ graduated glassware
- ☐ bottles
- ☐ funnel
- ☐ print squeegee
- ☐ all-purpose tape
- ☐ photographic paper
- ☐ cutting board
- ☐ art knife
- ☐ loupe
- ☐ disposable gloves

A good darkroom – that is, a room to experiment in subdued light or total darkness – is very simple to set up. The basic requirements are: complete darkness; satisfactory ventilation; access to water facilities; and enough space to hang and dry prints. If you want to use an enlarger, you will also need an electrical supply. The space doesn't have to be permanent – some photographers temporarily adapt a bathroom or a spare room into a darkroom whenever they need to develop and print. If running water isn't available, it is also possible to make do with a bucket of clean water and a 'waste' bucket. With sufficient space and time, however, nearly any room can be transformed into a very well-equipped and efficient darkroom, with a wet side and a dry side, an effective ventilation system and various kinds of safelights, all without spending a fortune.

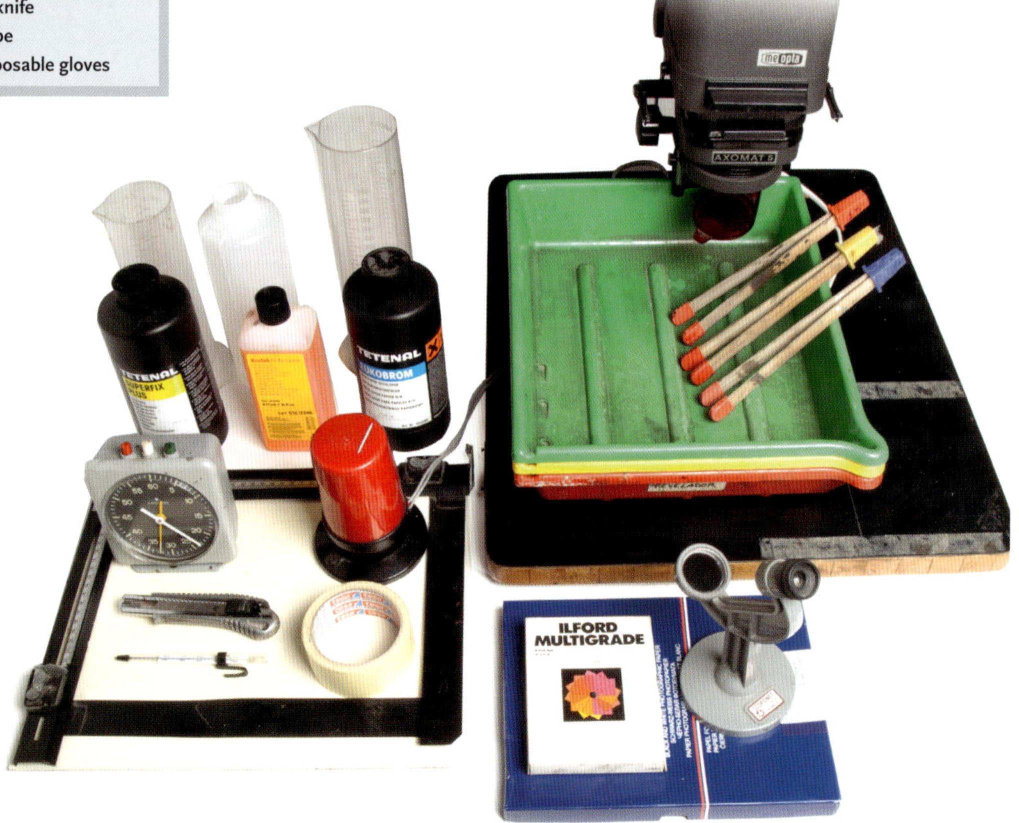

Constructing and equipping a darkroom

Space

As obvious as it may seem, darkroom space must be well organized, as things can get messy when you are working under a tight timeline and in darkness. Make sure to allocate space for all small tools (tongs, scissors, thermometer). Consider installing shelves and/or drawers, and a wall-mounted or table-top dispenser for paper towels (essential for cleaning up spills). Work tables should be at a comfortable height.

Allocate wet and dry areas

Keep wet and dry areas separate in case of spills and to prevent accidents. Locate your wet area near your sink and the dry area near the electrical socket. The wet area is for storing and mixing chemicals, washing prints, and bath processes (to minimize splashes, select trays that are larger than the maximum intended print size). The dry area is for drying prints, for using the enlarger or other electrical equipment, and for storing paper, negatives and the timer.

Lightproof the room

Block out any windows with black plastic sheeting. Landscaping rolls are optimal; use one or two layers depending on thickness. If you wish to use the room for other purposes, fasten the window covering to a detachable wooden frame to allow quick set up and removal. Light leaks are hard to see if your eyes are not accustomed to the dark, so close the door, darken the window and wait 5–10 minutes to find them. Felt weather strips are great for filling small cracks, but larger gaps will need to be covered with additional plastic sheeting or black cardboard.

Running water

A normal-sized sink will do for a basic darkroom, but the best solution is to install a plastic sink, big enough to hold water-bath trays and still have space to rinse prints.

Ventilation

Chemical fumes can be lethal, so good ventilation is crucial. You can leave open a window or door, covering it with a thick curtain to block out light, but the ideal solution is to install a range-hood extraction fan (preferably close to the wet area) or a conventional extraction fan.

Safelight

There is always a compromise between visibility and paper sensitivity. Red bulbs are safest, although most techniques in this book are not hyper-sensitive to light, and will probably work fine with orange bulbs. Turn the bulb towards the ceiling to avoid shadows, which can hinder visibility.

Enlarger and timer

An enlarger is a small projector used to produce photographic prints from film or glass negatives. (If working exclusively with contact-printing techniques, however, you will likely just use a contact-printing frame (see p. 134).) Enlargers are obsolete equipment for most photographers so there is a good chance you can find one cheaply or for free. For any operation that requires careful timing, an analogue timer with a bell is preferable to a mobile phone, as its illuminated LCD screen can damage light-sensitive prints.

Trays

Developing trays do not need to be specific to photography: dishwashing tubs will work. They need to be at least 10–15 cm deep but not much wider than your maximum print size to avoid wasting excess solution.

Print-drying rack

An upright rack with several slots for prints ensures quick drying and is ideal. A clothesline is a cheaper but messier alternative. See the list opposite for other basic equipment that will be needed.

EXPOSURE TEST STRIP

Several factors affect the exposure time when making a print. If you are exposing under sunlight, then the weather, cloud coverage and altitude are all variables to keep in mind. Similarly, UV lamps vary in strength and brightness, and tend to lose brightness with age, so they are equally inconsistent. The distance of the lamp from the paper is also a factor, both in contact-printing and when using an enlarger. Finally, there is the speed and sensitivity of the emulsion and the photographic paper. To take all of these varying factors into consideration, test strips are made to determine exactly how much time is needed to expose a picture.

How to make an exposure test strip

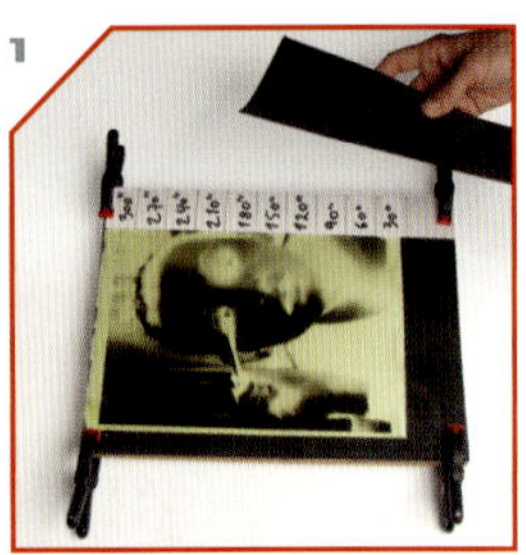
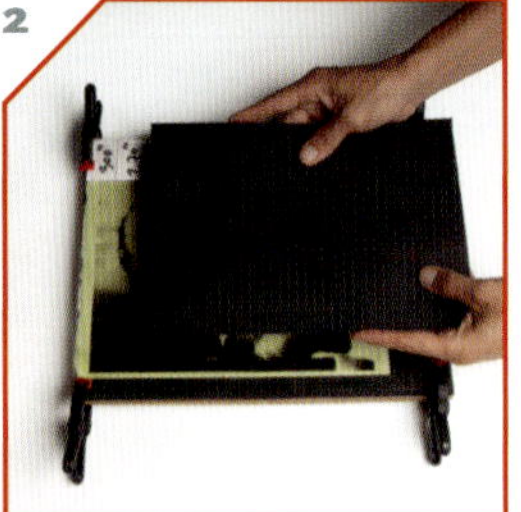
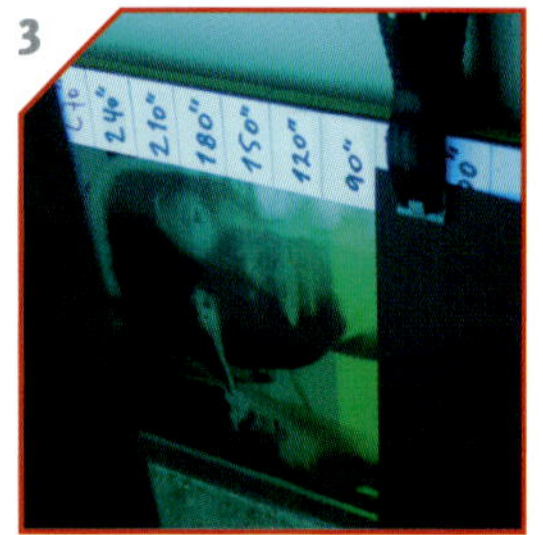
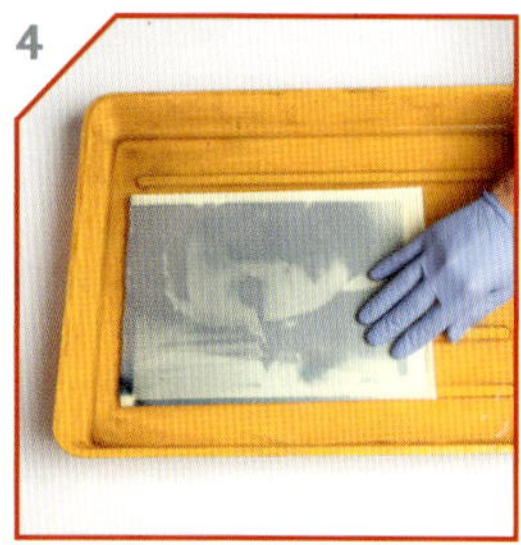

What you need:
- ☐ photographic paper
- ☐ ordinary white paper
- ☐ UV lamp or other light source
- ☐ contact-printing frame
- ☐ negative
- ☐ heavy black paper
- ☐ timer
- ☐ developing trays and solutions ⚠

Preparing paper and timing guide

1 Start by preparing the darkroom and materials as you would for ordinary printing. Cut a strip of ordinary white paper and number it in seconds from 30 (at the bottom) to about 300 (at the top). Mark it in 30-second intervals, approximately 2 cm apart, as shown opposite. Take a piece of photographic paper from the stock on which you plan to print and place it on the contact-printing frame, below your light source. Place the negative on top of the paper, choosing an area that represents the widest tonal range. Align your timing strip beside the negative.

Mask the light

2 Cover the print with a sheet of black paper that is thick enough to block light. Align the top edge of the black paper with the 300-second mark on the timing strip.

Exposure

3 Switch on the lamp and start the timer. Every 30 seconds, move the top of the black sheet down to the next mark on the timing strip.

Development

4 Develop, wash and dry the test strip normally for the technique you are testing.

Evaluating the test strip

5 Once it is dry, examine the test strip in ordinary light and determine which time slot looks best; this will be your exposure time. As long as both position and intensity of the light remain constant, this strip can be used as a continuing reference for the process and paper. Test strips can also be used to determine how long to burn-in light areas such as sky, and how long to dodge ('hold back') to maintain detail in shadowy areas.

! light-sensitive step

⚠ Review chemical safety for your chosen solutions

5

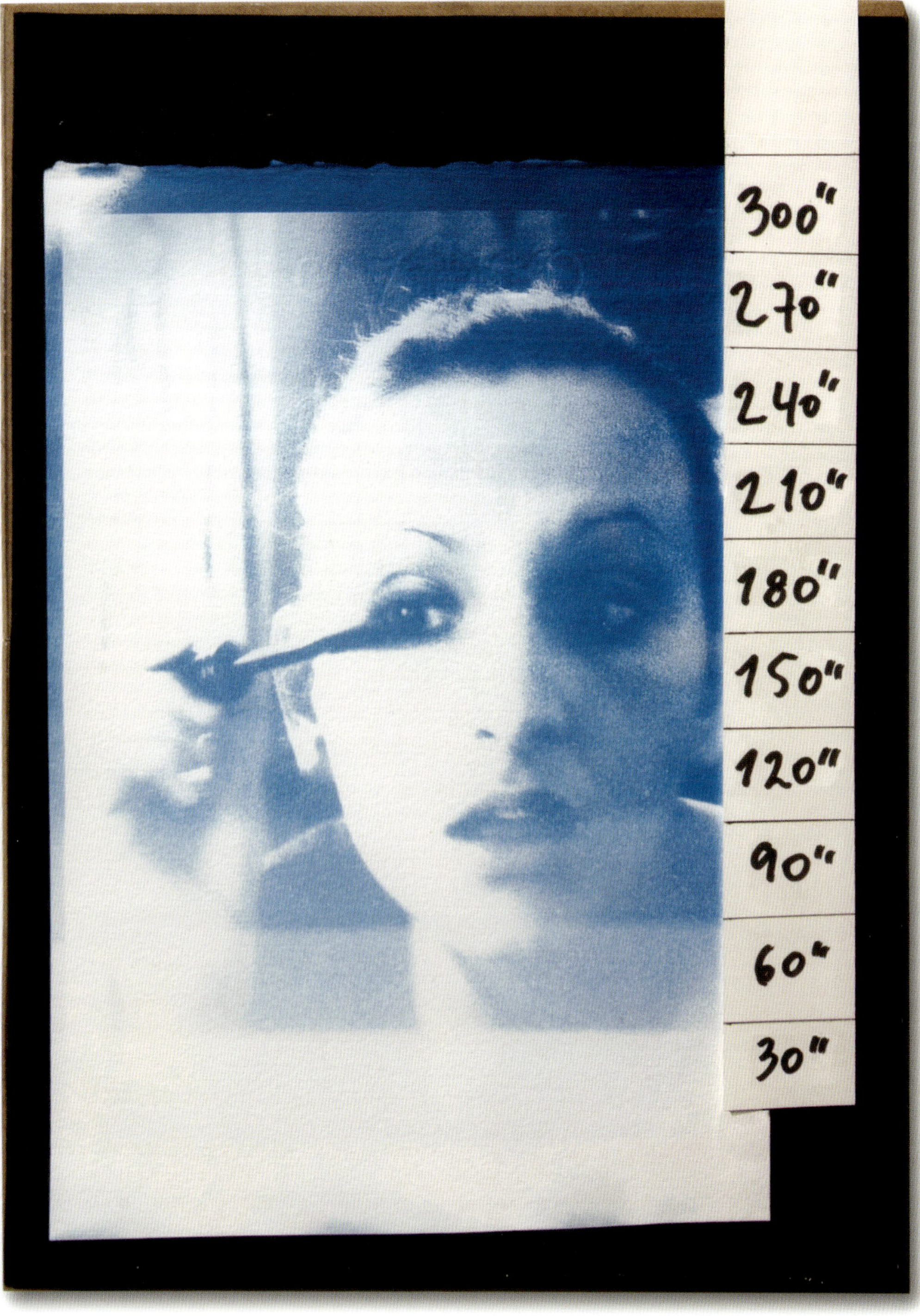

PHOTOGRAMS

Photograms are made through a simple cameraless process that dates back to the earliest photographic experiments. Pioneering nineteenth-century photographer W. H. Fox Talbot developed this technique for his 'shadowgrams', but it was Man Ray who popularized it, using it to make creations that he called 'rayograms'. This technique produces a shadowy negative image that is obtained by placing objects directly on photographic paper or other light-sensitized surface in the darkroom and then exposing it to light, often using an enlarger.

The photogram process

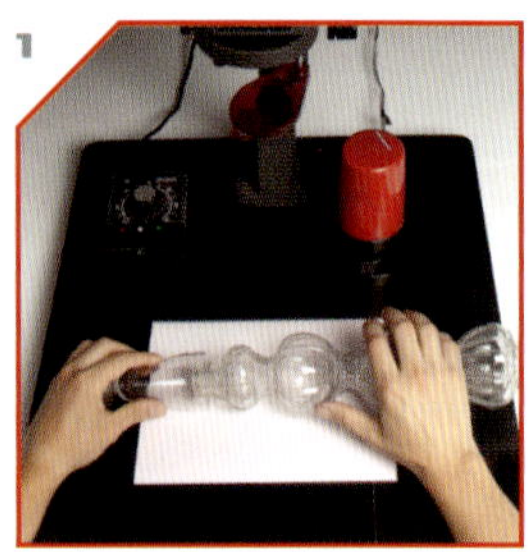 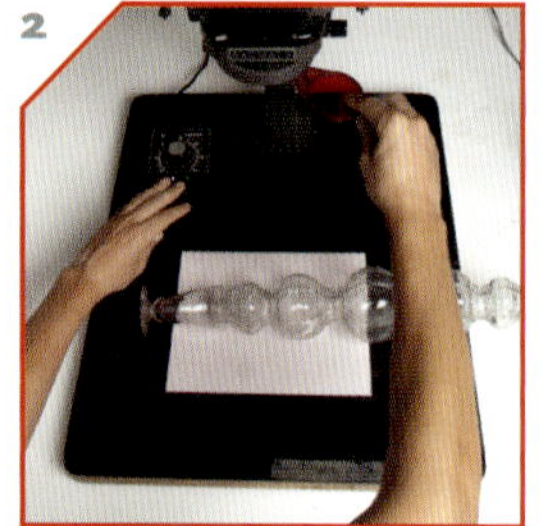 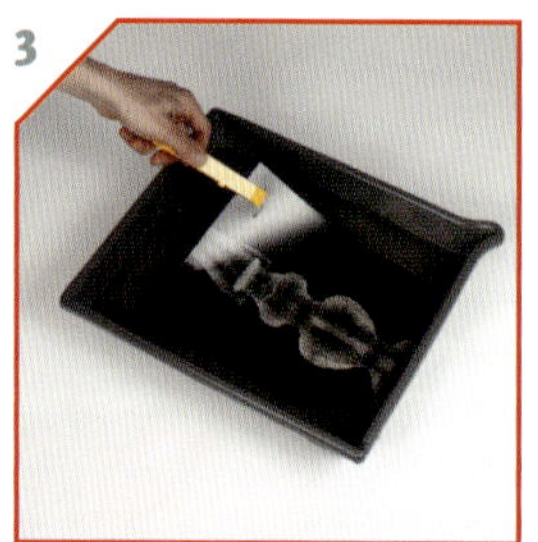 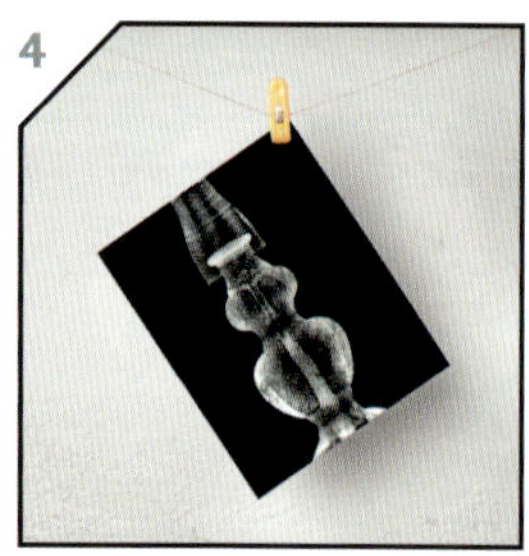

What you need:

- [ ] any transparent, semi-transparent, or opaque objects
- [ ] light source
- [ ] photographic paper
- [ ] darkroom
- [ ] developer, stop bath and fixer ⚠
- [ ] enlarger with red filter (optional)

1 Composition

While working under safelight conditions, position your objects on the photographic paper as desired. Keep in mind that the resulting image will have a two-dimensional appearance if the object is opaque and in close contact with the paper, and three-dimensional if it is less opaque or further away.

2 Expose

Turn on the light, or, if working with a red-filter enlarger, remove the filter to expose the photogram. Exposure time will vary, so you will need to perform an exposure test on a small sample of the paper beforehand (see pp. 24–25).

3 Develop

Develop the print according to the developer solution and paper you are using (this typically takes around 2 minutes).

Transfer the print to a stop bath for a minimum of 30 seconds, and then fix it thoroughly.

4 Wash and dry

Once the print is fixed, wash it for at least 10 minutes (longer for fibre-based papers), then hang it up to dry.

OPPOSITE
Francisco Gómez
Untitled photogram, 27 × 21 cm (10⅝ × 8¼ in.), 2013

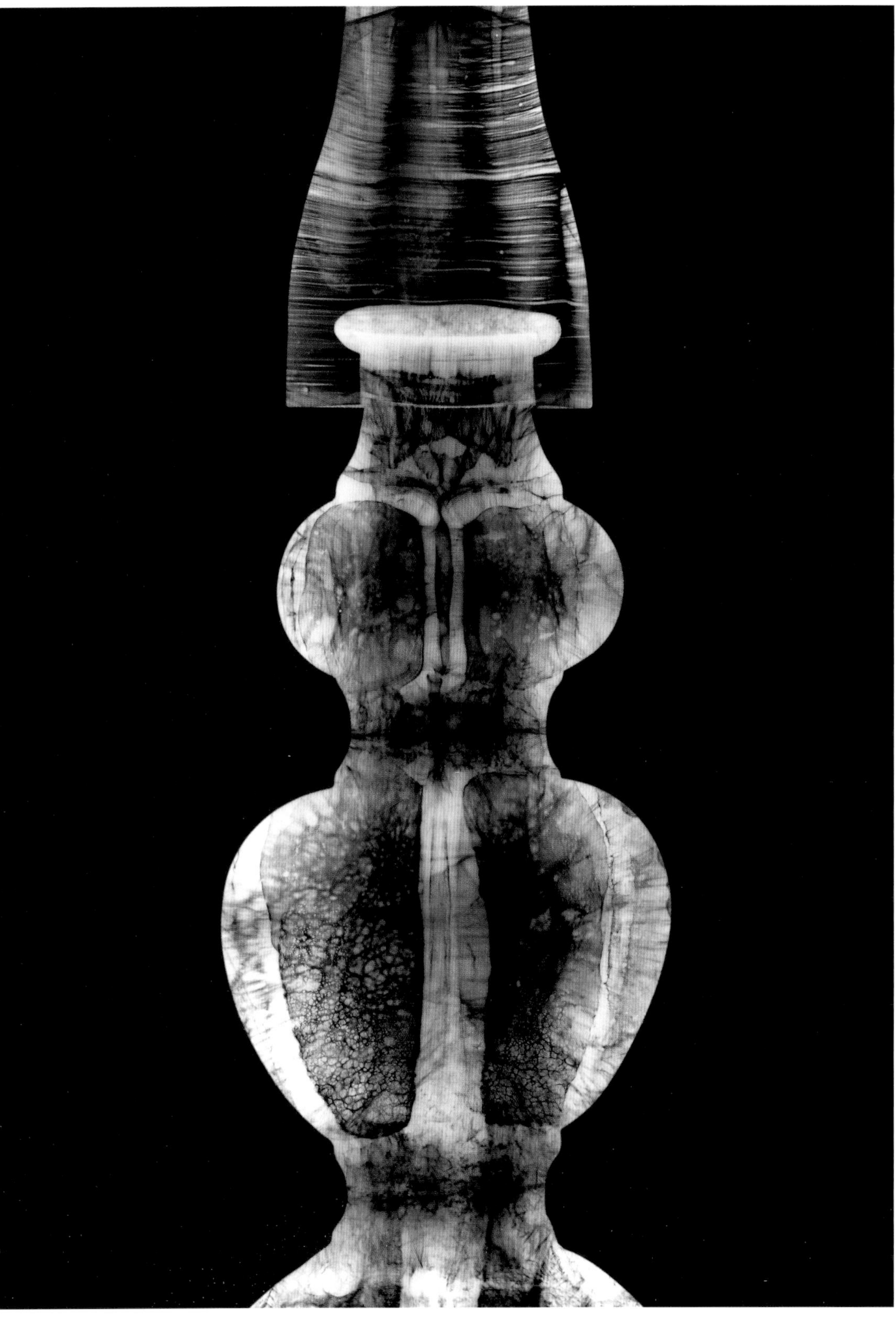

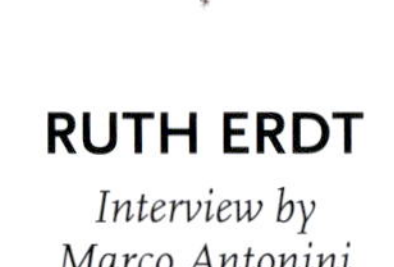

RUTH ERDT

*Interview by
Marco Antonini*

The Swiss artist specializes in life-sized photograms and stresses the importance of chance happenings in creating work through cameraless photography.

What technical, formal or conceptual concerns inspired you to work with large-format photograms? Tell us a little more about your technique: what materials and tools are used, and how you set up your studio and darkroom.

The photogram, along with many other analogue techniques and associated equipment, is already vanishing. There are fewer and fewer people using these techniques. I see the shift to digital more as a question of philosophy. It's not only a technological issue, or a trend – it's also a change of perception, of mindset, of feelings towards the image. As an artist, I'm interested in this change, along with researching what we'll gain and what we'll lose. Digital equipment gives the photographer a firm control over every setting; I find this boring. Photograms represent a graphic limitation, a way of working with radically simplified forms in which random chance is a part of the composition. I first started working in a large darkroom studio as a student. My intent was to print life-sized images, in order to show things as big as they actually are. This technique only required light and developing paper, no negatives. I used a big

RIGHT

Artist's studio in Zurich, showing the set-up for one of her photograms, 2009

OPPOSITE

The Gun, photogram on colour print paper, 2009

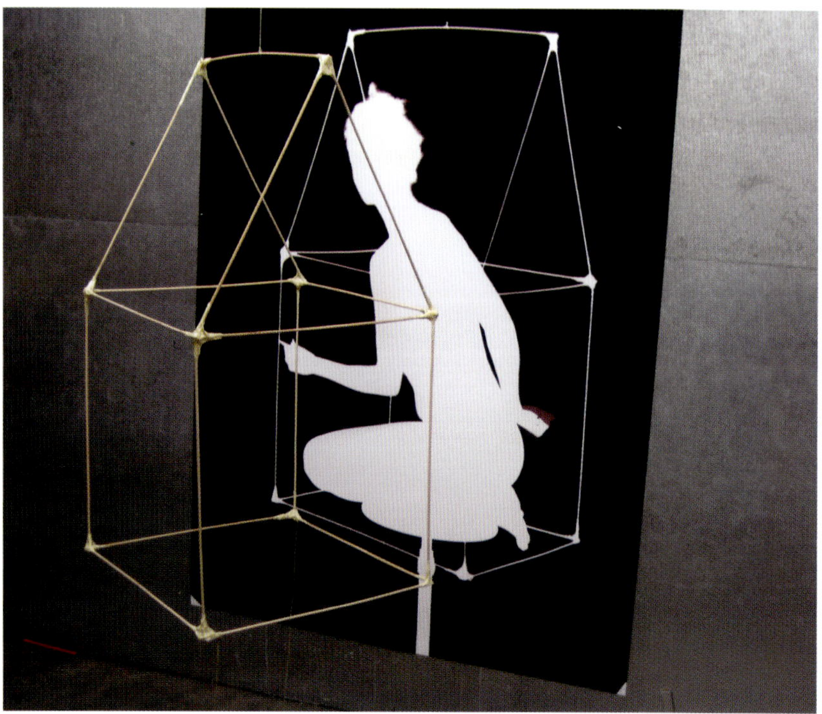

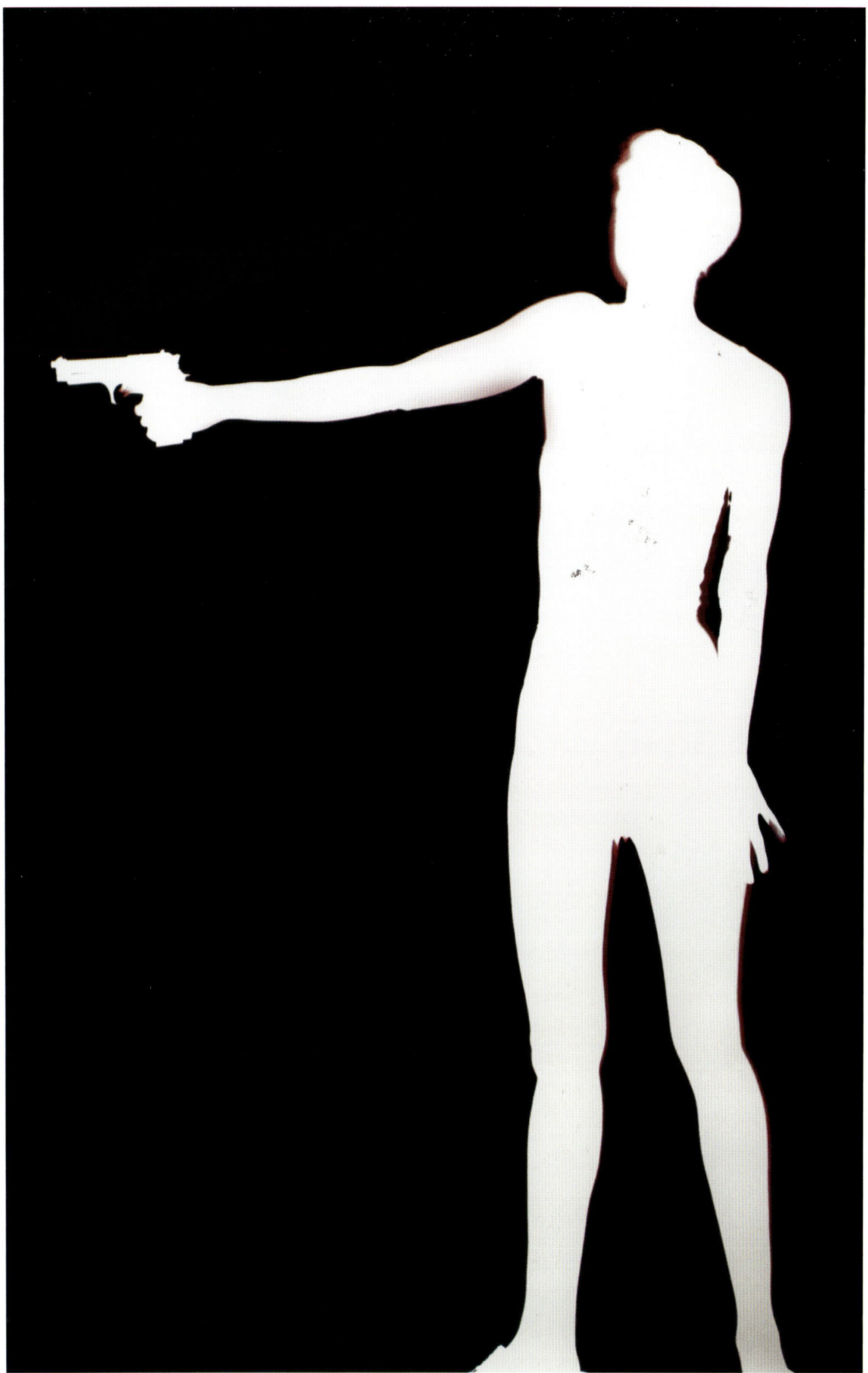

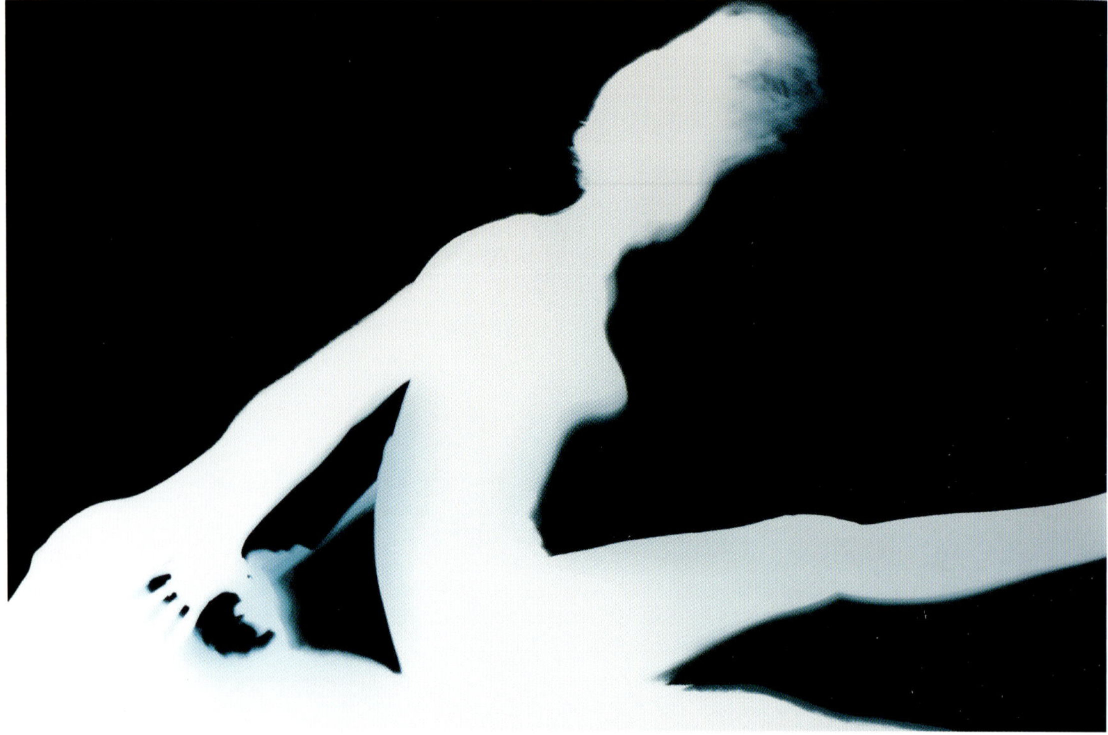

The Gun, photogram on colour print paper, 2010

roll of colour analogue photo paper, more than one metre in width, and very sensitive to light. Since I could not even use red light, I was blind, working in absolute darkness. I first tried working with models, but preparing and directing them in total darkness proved too cumbersome. So I switched to 'self-portraits' and object photography, hanging things from the ceiling.

Do you or other collaborators/models 'perform' the photograms or are they entirely composed in advance?

For some of the works we first did a dry run with the light on. I showed the models what I had in mind, and they re-created the scene, but in the dark it was not so easy to find the paper and the right position again. The room was approximately 10 × 10 m (33 × 33 ft) in size. When I switched to self-portraits I soon found out how hard it was: I first needed to lay out the large developing paper roll. Then I would take off my clothes and assume the right position. Finally, pulling a string mechanism (with my mouth) I would turn on the lights and the enlarger. Some photos required an exposure of several minutes, during which I needed to lie completely still. It was more than just a click.

What kind of subject/object relationships are you most interested in? When and in what context did sculpture emerge in your practice?

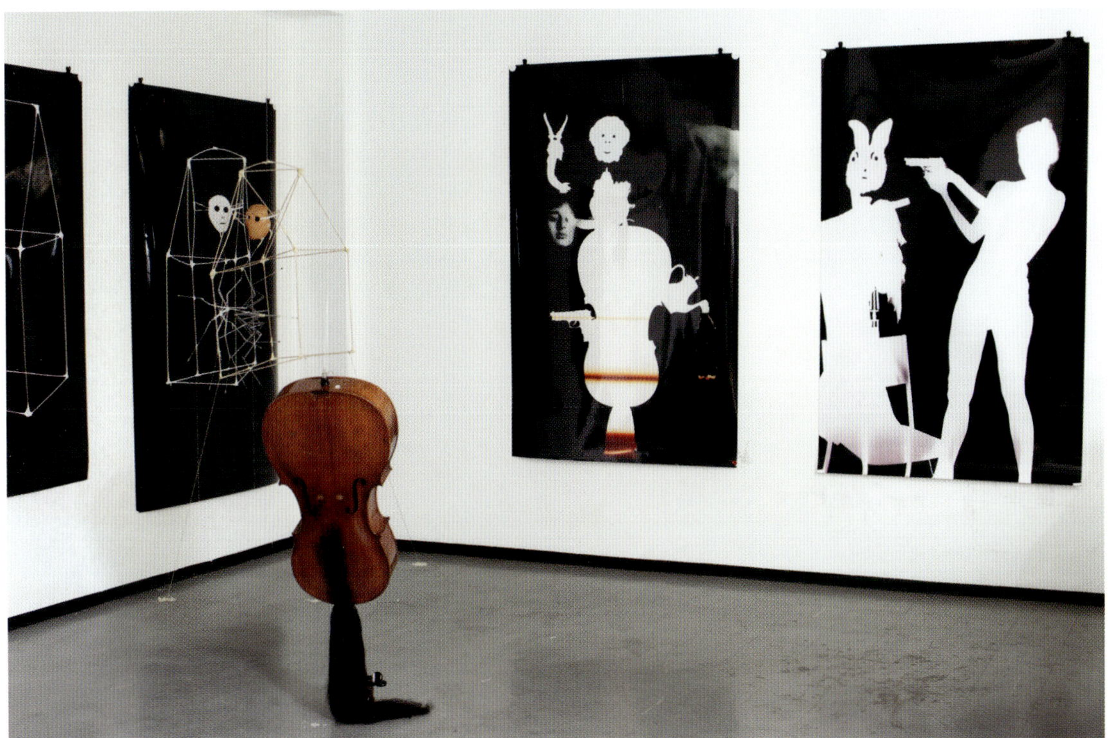

Over the years I filled up my studio, collecting objects randomly, with no specific concept in mind. The first compositions focused more on the surface and form of the objects, without a definite perspective. I wanted to use the shadow of the objects to claim the two-dimensionality of my art. A different issue was my obsession with the gun shape. A gun is a recognizable and meaningful symbol and worked perfectly with the photogram technique. The question of perspective was more central in my *The Naked House* exhibition (above). A house is such a common shape that we are automatically drawn to it, whatever the perspective.

A large part of your work comprises photographic images that you claim were formed in your own consciousness at an early age, even before acquiring a camera. How has your relationship to photography changed over the years?

I was a pretty rebellious teenager; I fought a lot with my parents and against the system in general. I learned from a very early age how to build my own view of things. The imaginary camera was one way to do this. When I finally got a real camera the transition was easy. Sometimes I feel like I'm still taking the same picture I was taking in my mind when I was fourteen. The advent of digital changed it all. The immediacy, the knowledge you can do things over and over again gives a new sense of security, but also takes a lot out of your imagination. My artistic research focuses on ways to photograph without 100% control.

The Naked House, mixed media, exhibition view, Neuropa – The Modern Institute, Zurich, 2010

CLICHÉ-VERRE

Cliché-verre, literally 'glass-picture', is a nineteenth-century technique that involves covering a sheet of glass with ink or soot from a burning candle and then drawing an image on the clouded side. The drawn plate is then applied to a photosensitive sheet of paper and exposed. Nineteenth-century French painters such as Camille Corot and Jean-François Millet were among the first artists who made extensive use of this process, using it to create drawings on glass that could then be reproduced at will. With recent advancements in digital technology the cliché-verre process will surely continue to evolve in new and exciting directions. This recipe uses a thin layer of black paint or ink to coat the glass, as a quicker and tidier alternative to the traditional soot.

The cliché-verre process

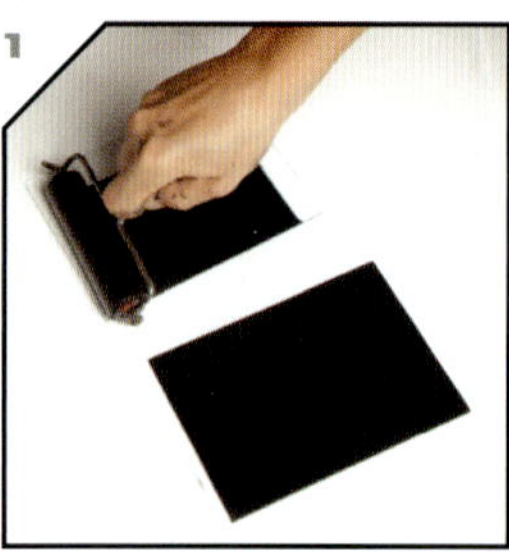
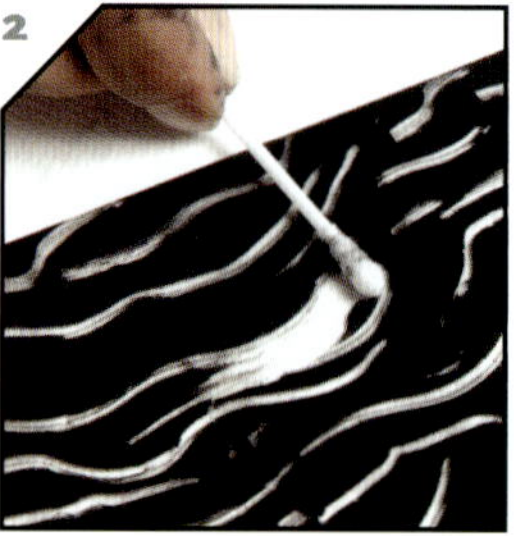
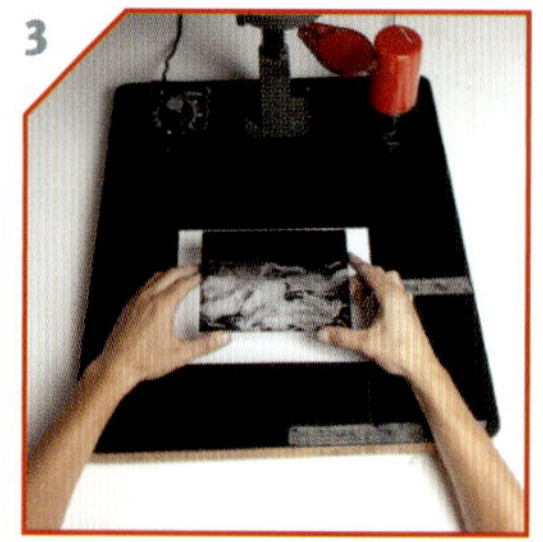
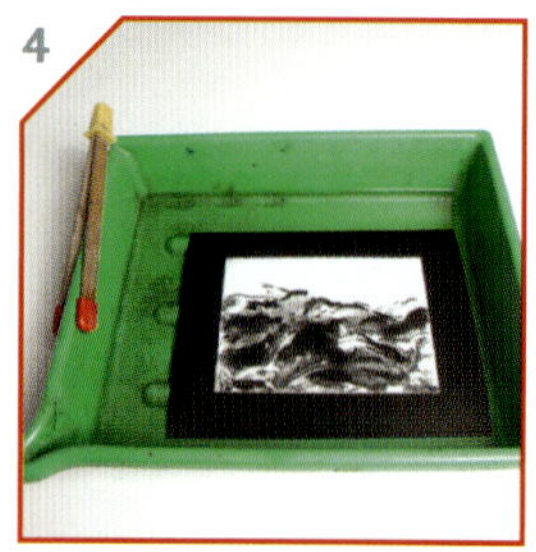

What you need:
- ☐ sheet of glass
- ☐ black paint or ink
- ☐ art roller
- ☐ brush or cotton swab
- ☐ enlarger
- ☐ photographic paper
- ☐ developer, stop bath and fixer ⚠

Darken the glass

1 Take a blot of paint or ink and use an art roller to spread it evenly on one side of the glass. You can use an art brush but the brushstrokes will be visible in the final result.

Draw on the glass

2 There are endless techniques for drawing on the glass: drawing, etching, scratching, rubbing and daubing with a brush, cotton swab or other implements are all acceptable options. Take time to experiment. You can always repaint the glass black if you need to start over.

Expose the painted glass

3 Once you are satisfied with your painted glass plate, it can be used as a negative for contact-printing or exposed using an enlarger, as shown. Determine the exposure time by making a test strip (see p. 24).

Develop

4 Develop, stop, fix and wash as you would normally for a black-and-white print, then hang the print to dry.

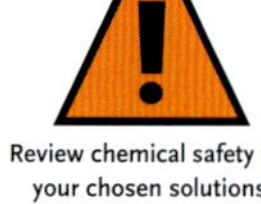

OPPOSITE
Francisco Gómez
Cliché-verre, 27 × 21 cm
(10⅝ × 8¼ in.), 2013

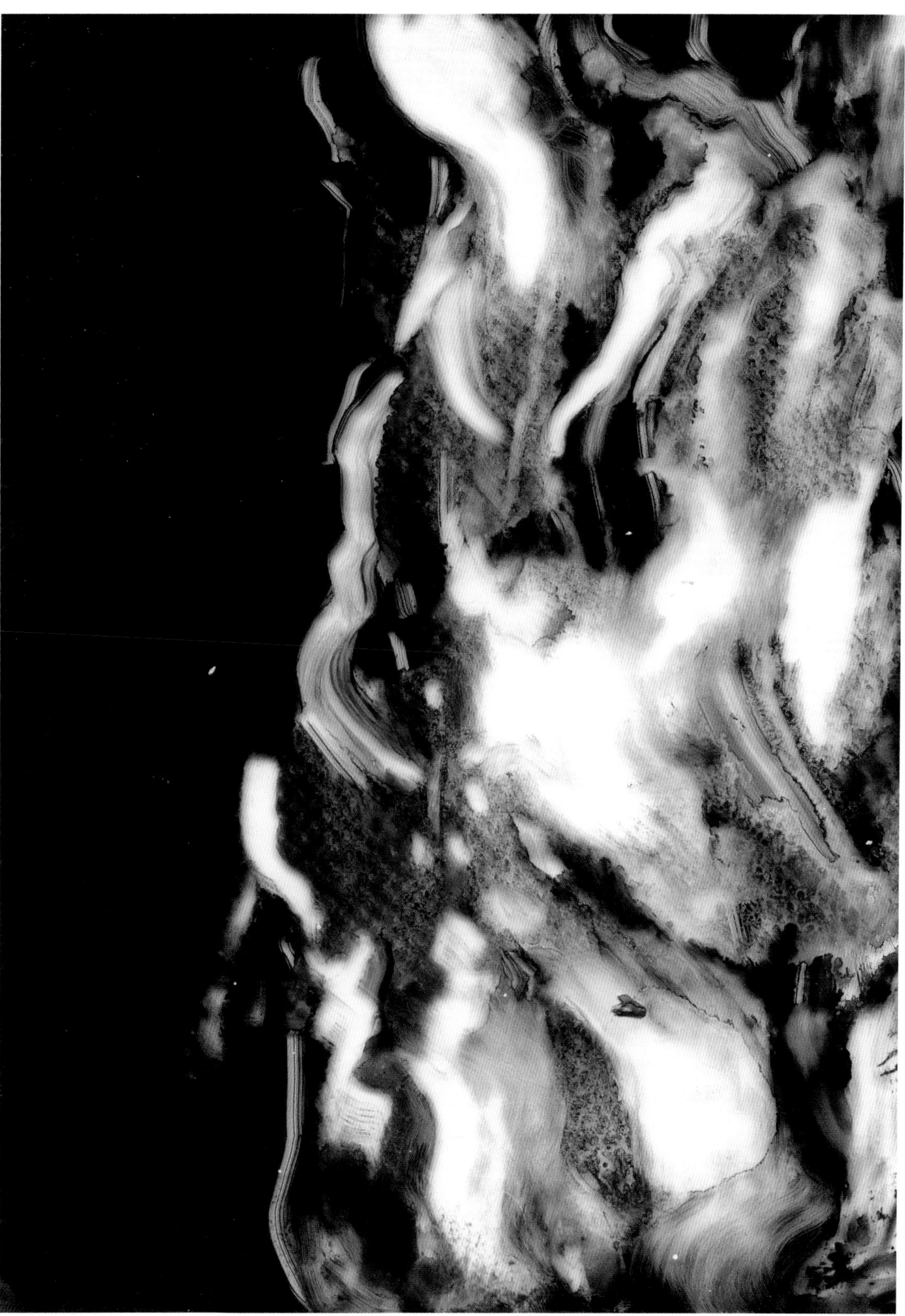

LUMEN PRINTS

Lumen prints have a transparent, glowing appearance like photograms, but a darkroom is not necessary, and the prints are fixed, rather than fully developed. This technique results in an image that changes its colour. The only specialist equipment required is photographic paper (preferably black and white), over which objects – often plants – are laid, and then given lengthy exposure to sunlight. If the paper is past its use-by date, its fogginess and fading can add additional atmosphere. Be aware that some flowers and plants are easier to print than others. Those with thin petals and leaves may shrivel in the sun or let in too much light, whereas very thick ones may require longer exposure to achieve sufficient detail.

The lumen print process

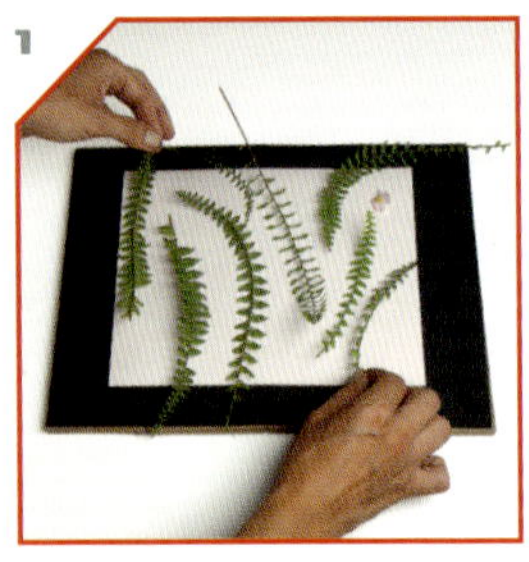
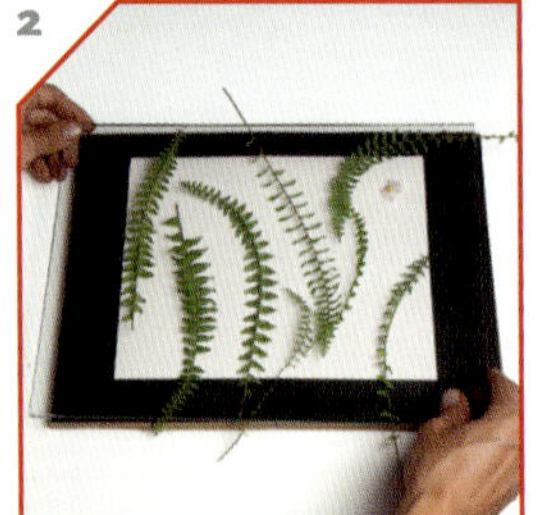
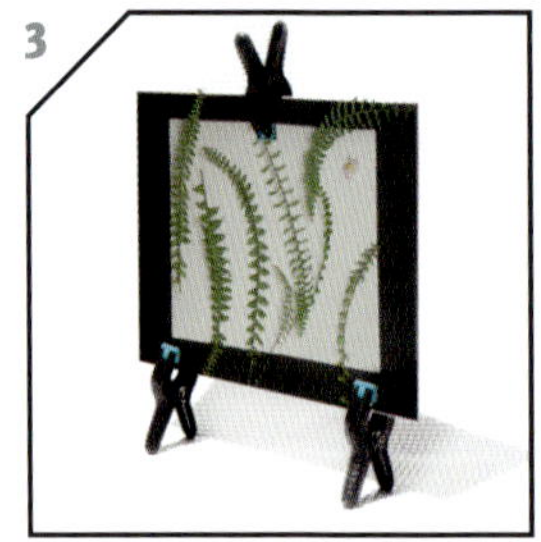
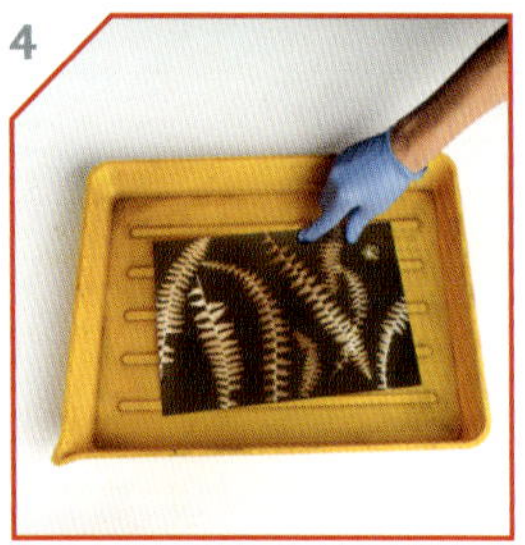

What you need:

- [ ] contact-printing frame, or piece of glass, board and clamps
- [ ] photographic paper
- [ ] plants
- [ ] fixer bath (ammonium thiosulfate, 5% to 8% dilution) ⚠

Composition

1 Working indoors, in subdued light, position plants, flowers or other flattenable material on top of a piece of photographic paper, and adjust to produce the desired composition.

Set up contact-printing frame

2 Sandwich the photographic paper and plants or flowers between a piece of glass and a board, and clamp in place; alternatively, use a hinged contact-printing frame (to build your own, see pp. 134–35).

Expose

3 Expose the contact-printing frame under a UV lamp or allow it to solarize in sunlight. Exposure time can vary from half an hour to several days depending on the type of paper (see examples on p. 37) and strength of the sunlight, but as a rough starting point, most require 4–8 hours.

Fix the image

4 Once exposure is complete, remove the photographic paper from the contact-printing frame and wash in water for 2 minutes. Transfer the print to a fixer bath for a further 2 minutes; during this time the tone of the print will change. Once fixed, give the print a final wash and then hang it up to dry. You can also experiment with toning and bleaching the print before rinsing and drying (see pp. 210–11).

light-sensitive step

!

SEE PAGES 226–29

OPPOSITE
Francisco Gómez
Lumen print, 27 × 21 cm
(10⅝ × 8¼ in.), 2013

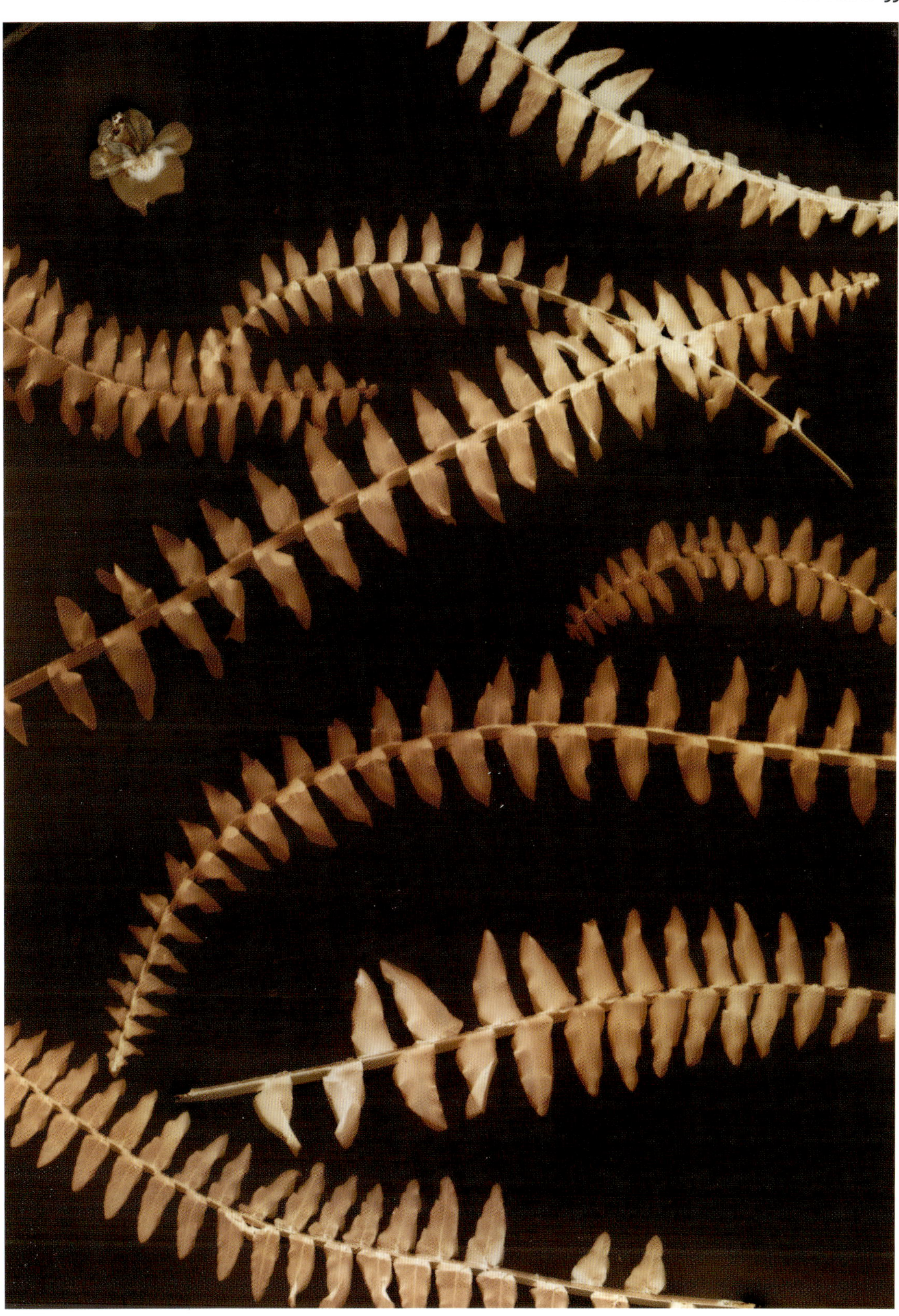

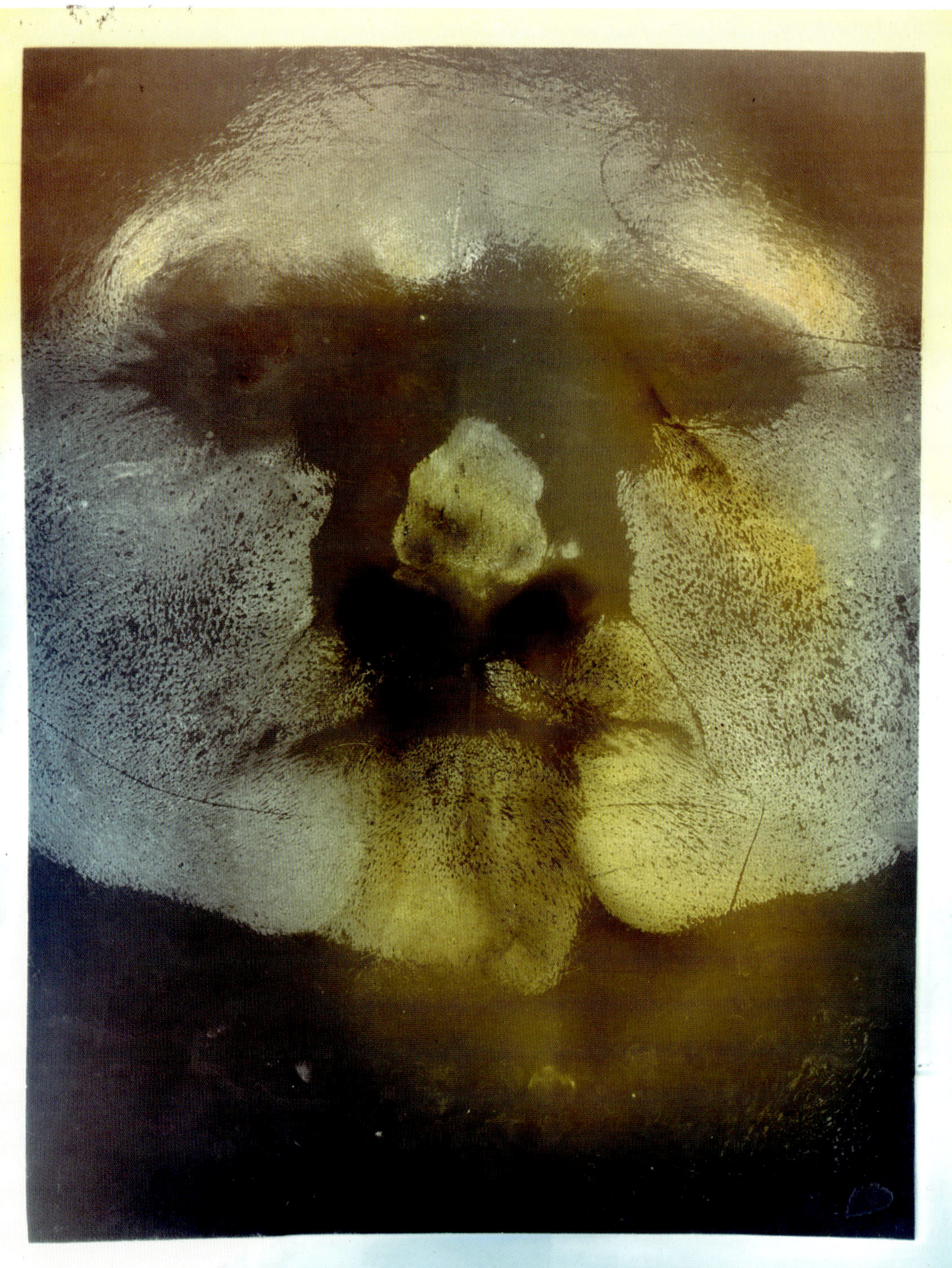

ABOVE
Ky Lewis
Lumen Face 4bss, Lumen Shrouded
series, lumen print, 29 × 21 cm
(11½ × 8¼ in.), 2012

'I used Grade 1 Ilford paper and got my subjects [all wearing sun cream] to start on one side of their faces and roll the paper to the other, much like the cloth would be if draped over a face. These were then put out into the sun for 4 hours under glass. The images were stronger before fixing; this is the strongest of them and it's mine.' *Ky Lewis*

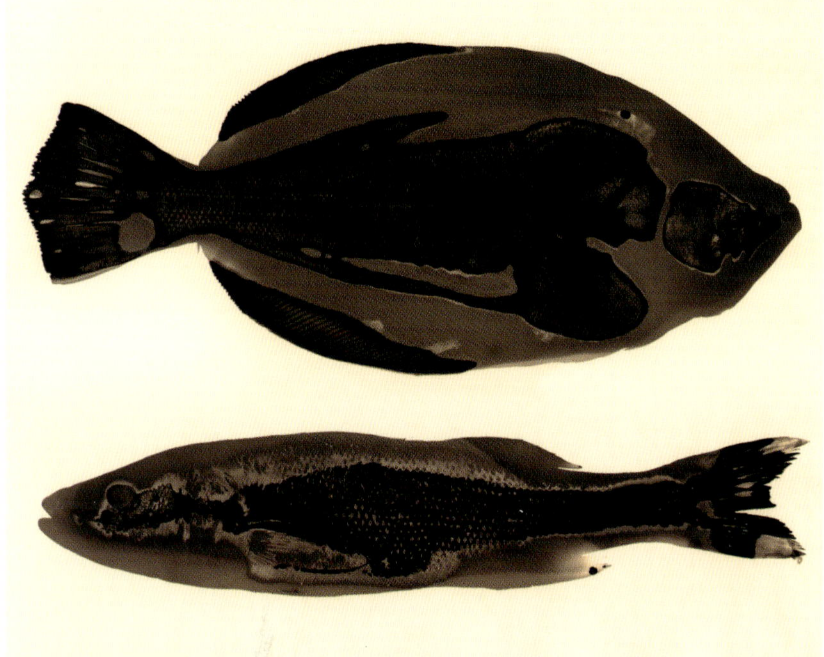

LEFT
Michael Mendez
Bottom Feeder (For Gunter Grass), lumen print, 40 × 80 cm (15¾ × 31½ in.), 2013

BELOW
John Dearing
Comparison of different paper brands for lumen prints, all featuring an oakleaf hydrangea leaf and exposed to afternoon sunlight for between 4 and 8 hours. Top row, left to right: Kodak Polymax RC paper; Oriental VC FB Warmtone paper; Bergger Prestige Variable CB paper; Arista VC FB paper. Bottom row, left to right: Kodabrome II RC F3 paper; Bergger Prestige Variable NB FB paper; Kodak Elite Fine Art S3P FB paper; Agfa MC Classic FB paper.

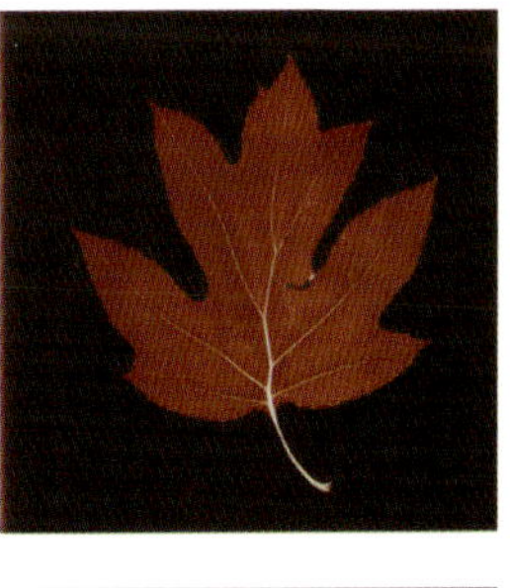
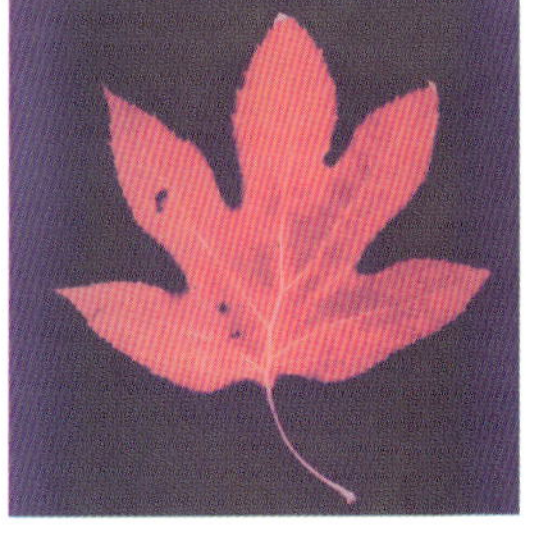
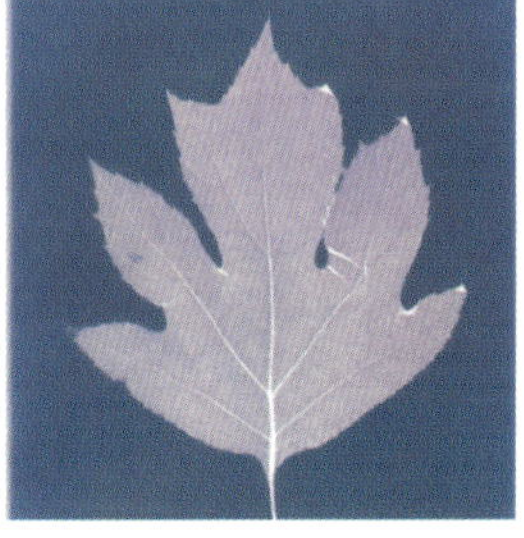
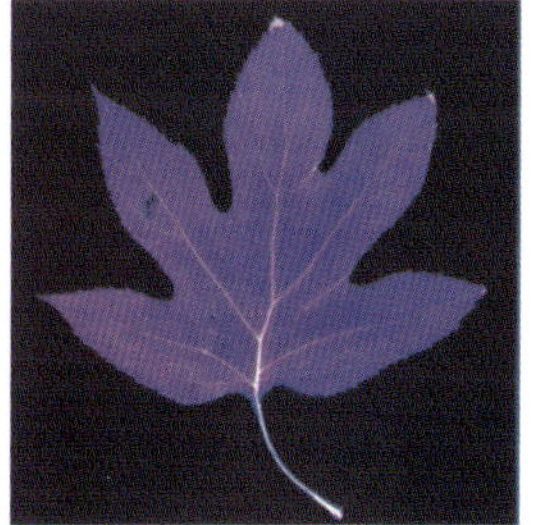
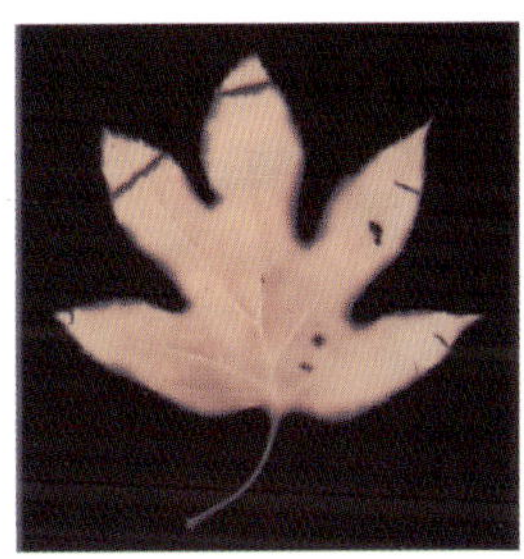
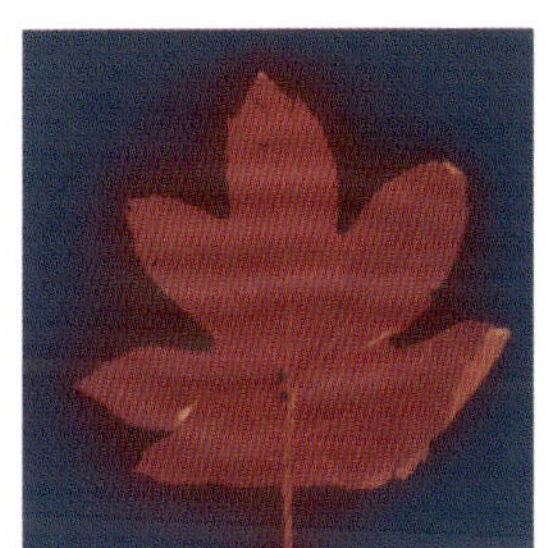
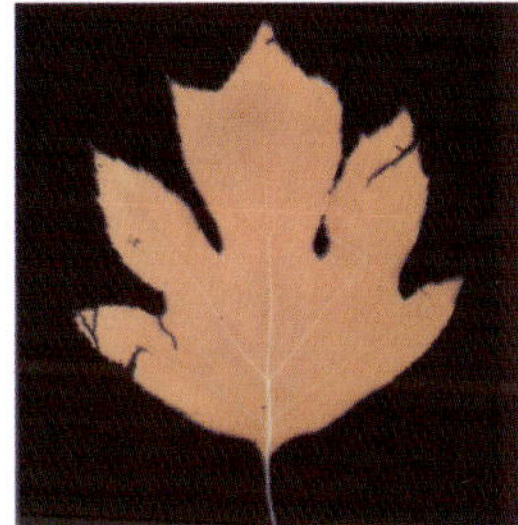
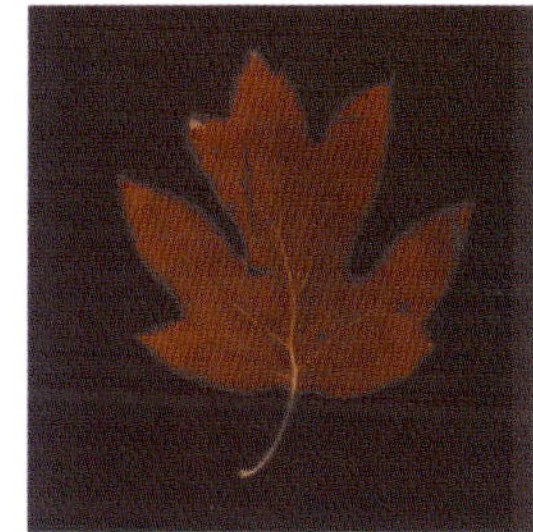

MULTIPLE EXPOSURES

Prior to the advent of digital photography, multiple exposure was widely used to create hoax and composite images. Offering a wide array of possibilities for manipulating, superimposing and adding or removing objects in a photograph, this technique essentially involves layering two or more different exposures to create a single image. This can be achieved either by winding back the film and shooting the same frame twice on an analogue camera, or by the cameraless process outlined here, in which two separate analogue and/or digital exposures are combined in the darkroom. The resulting composite image can subsequently be rephotographed so it appears even more seamless.

The multiple exposures process

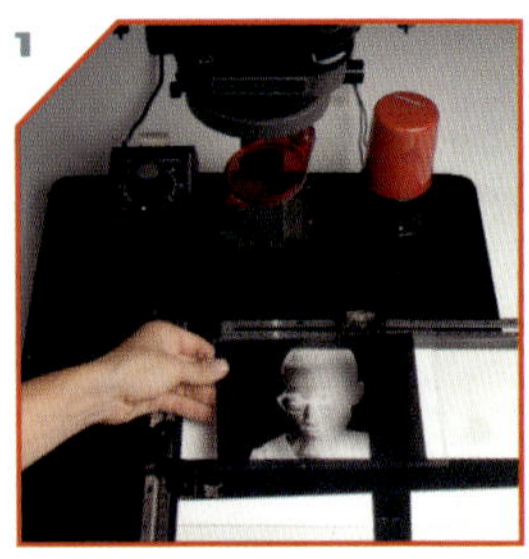 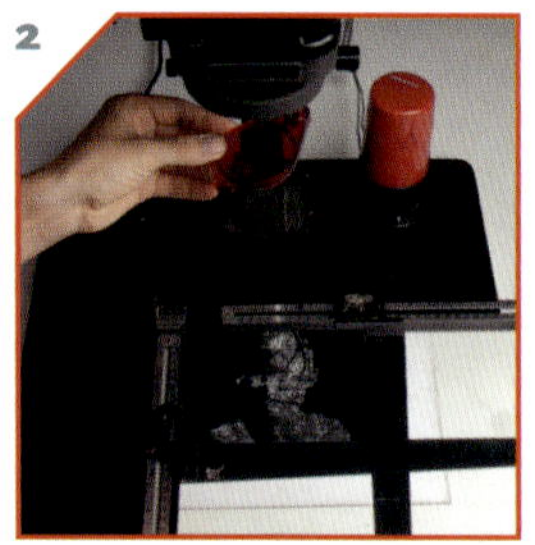 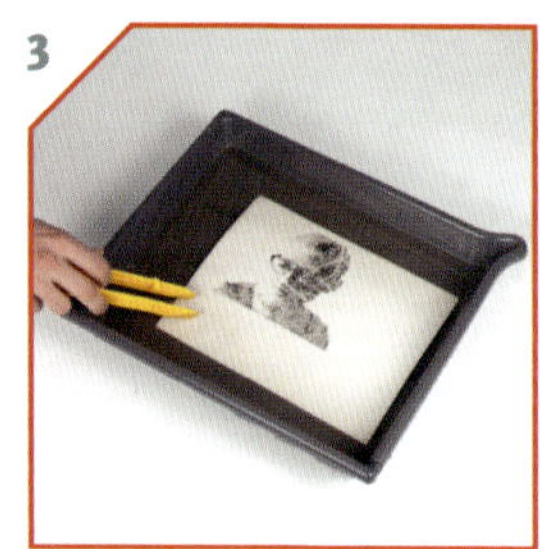 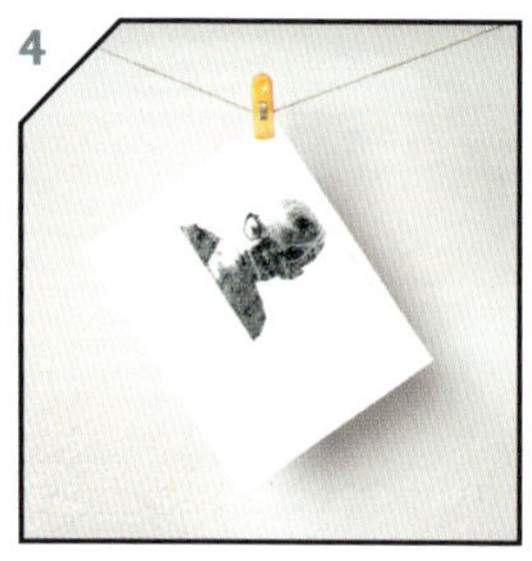

What you need:
- ☐ enlarger with red filter
- ☐ photographic paper
- ☐ two negatives
- ☐ developer, stop bath and fixer ⚠

First negative

1 Working in the darkroom under safelight, place a sheet of photographic paper under the enlarger and your first negative on top of the paper. Here we used a large-format negative for the first image (the portrait; see pp. 132–33 for how to generate large-format negatives from both analogue and digital images) and a 35 mm negative for the second image (the leaves), but there are many other possible combinations.

Second negative

2 Place the second negative in the enlarger holder and adjust its position to achieve the desired composite image. When ready, remove the red filter on the enlarger and make a test strip to determine the exposure needed to print the two negatives together. You can also expose each negative separately in succession. This will improve the end result if the negatives have very different contrast levels, and it enables you to adjust the exposure for each one independently, making one darker and another lighter, for example. However, this also makes it harder to determine the overall exposure that is needed.

Develop

3 After you have made the exposure(s), develop, stop and fix the print, then wash it thoroughly.

4 Hang to dry.

Review chemical safety for your chosen solutions

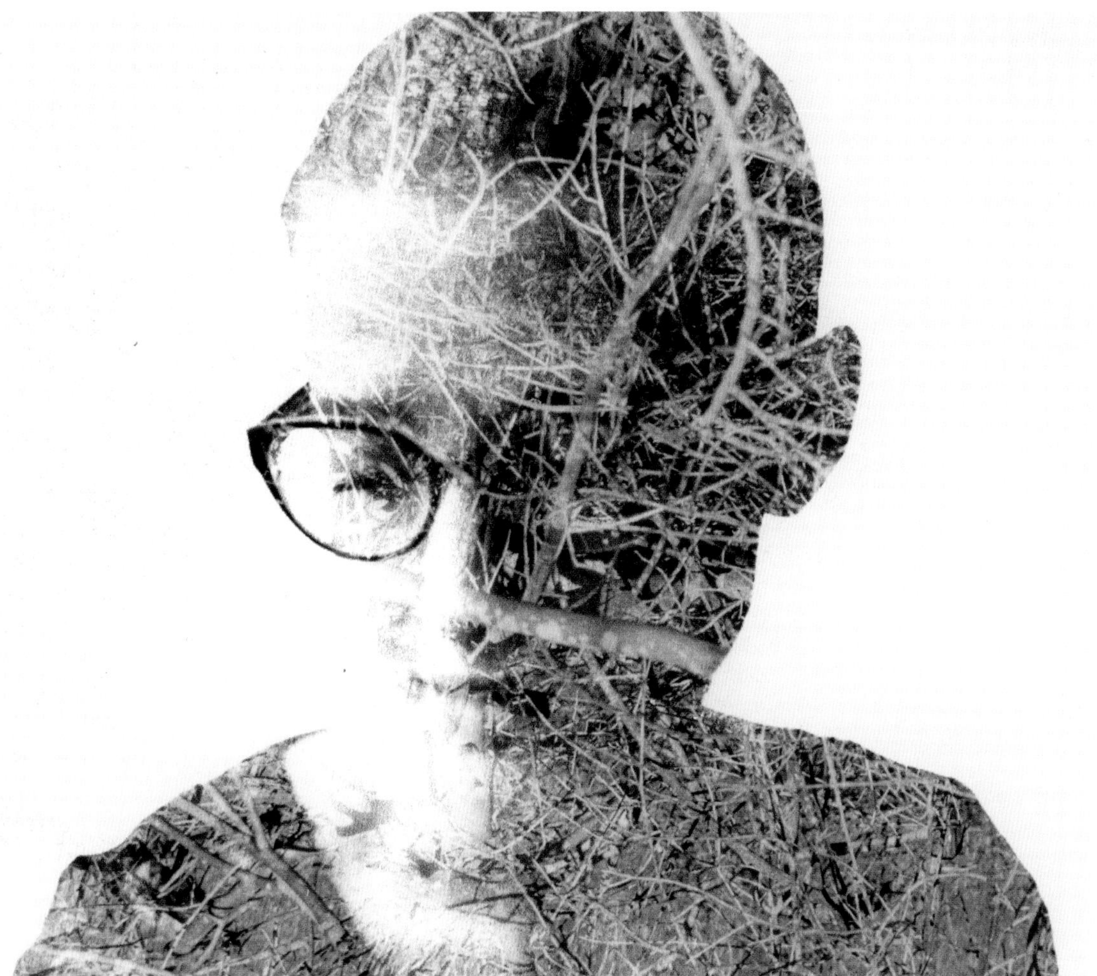

ABOVE
Brembo
Muratori nel Giardino, gelatin silver
print with double exposure, 21 × 21 cm
(8¼ × 8¼ in.), 2013

Handmade, Toy and Disposable Cameras

These handmade and inexpensive cameras are easy to use and offer boundless opportunities for experimentation, image manipulation and creating vintage effects.

2

MAKING A PINHOLE CAMERA

A pinhole is the most basic device for capturing an image on film. Despite their simplicity, pinhole cameras have some interesting benefits. They have a virtually infinite depth of field, which means that everything in the image, no matter how close or distant, is always in focus. Long exposure times are a staple requirement of pinhole photography, creating atmospheric visual effects and intriguing imperfections in the image. Pinhole photography offers an exciting way to explore the basic mechanics of capturing images and to experiment with exposure, lighting and timing. For aspiring camera builders, making a pinhole camera is often the first step in learning to build or hack more complex devices.

How to build a matchbox pinhole camera *by Alan E. Cooper*

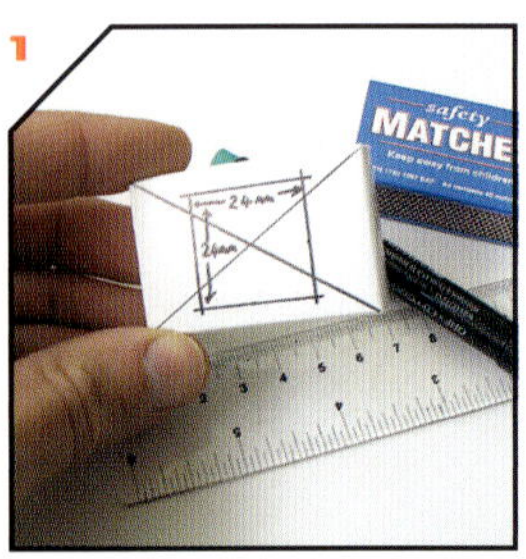
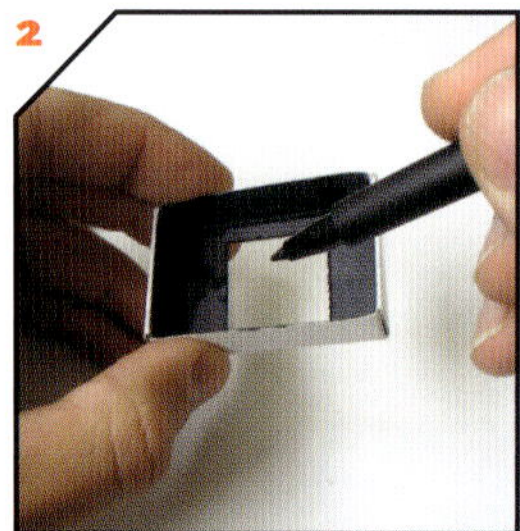
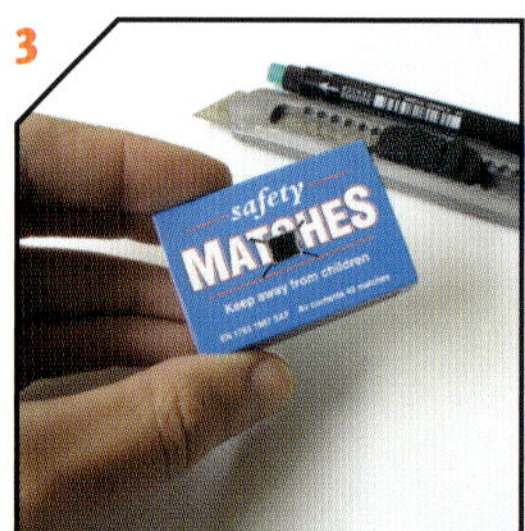
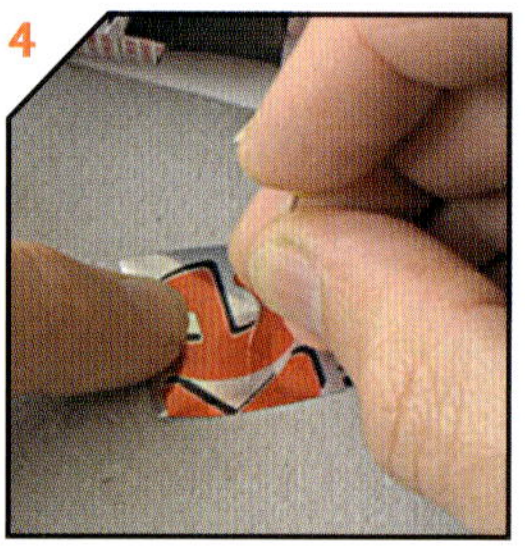

What you need:
- [ ] rectangular matchbox
- [ ] roll of 35 mm film and its box
- [ ] empty roll of 35 mm film with at least 1 cm stub of film sticking out
- [ ] black electrical tape
- [ ] scissors
- [ ] fine needle or pin
- [ ] black permanent marker
- [ ] aluminium soda can
- [ ] plastic comb-binding
- [ ] ruler
- [ ] art knife

The box

1 Remove the match tray (the inner part of the matchbox), and mark out a 24 mm square in its exact centre. Alternatively, if you want rectangular photos (some photo labs will find these easier to print), mark out a 36 mm × 24 mm rectangle. Carefully cut out the frame shape with a sharp knife, keeping the edges as neat as possible – or deliberately irregular if you prefer! Any rough edges and cardboard fibres will appear around the edges of each photo.

2 To reduce internal reflections in the camera, colour in the inside of the tray with a black felt-tipped pen. If possible, also colour the inside front of the matchbox sleeve black.

3 Mark out a 6 mm square in the exact centre of the front of the matchbox sleeve. Carefully cut out this square, again keeping the edges as neat as possible to avoid any stray fibres obscuring the image.

Making the pinhole

4 Cut out a piece of aluminium about 15 mm square from the can. Place the aluminium over a piece of thick cardboard and gently press a fine sewing needle or sharp pin into the centre of the metal. Twist the pin between your fingers while doing this so that it slowly drills a hole through the aluminium; don't push down so hard that the pin punches straight through. Use a drilling motion to produce a very small hole with clean edges. The ideal diameter of the pinhole is about 0.2 mm; a smaller hole is fine, but a larger hole will result in images that are less sharp. Once you have finished making your hole, colour the back of the aluminium plate black to help reduce internal light reflections in the camera.

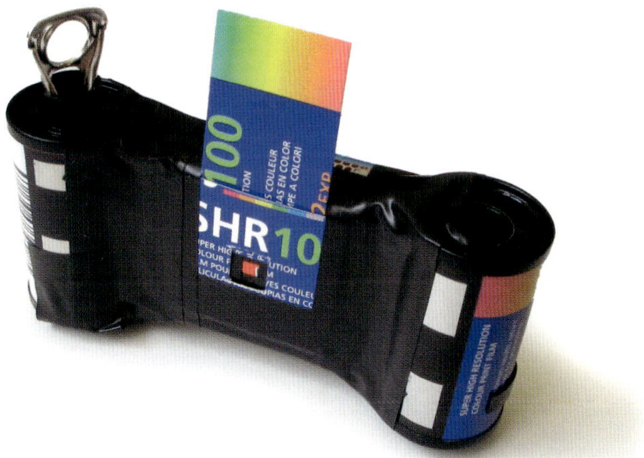

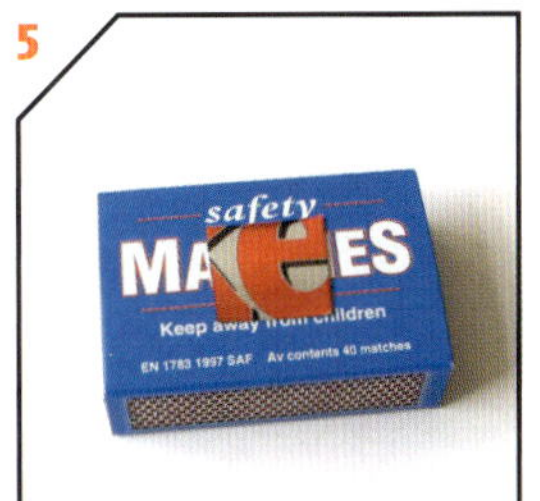

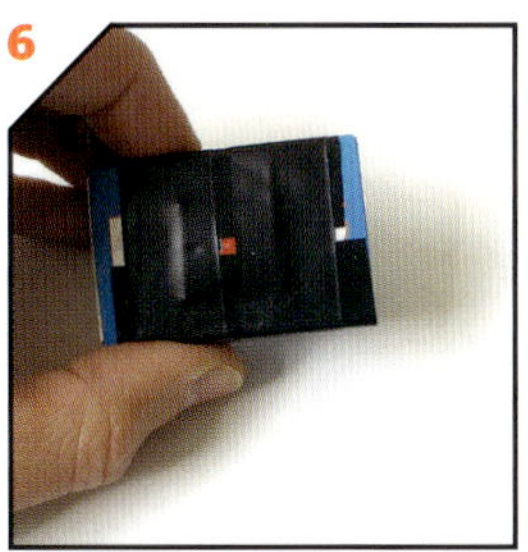

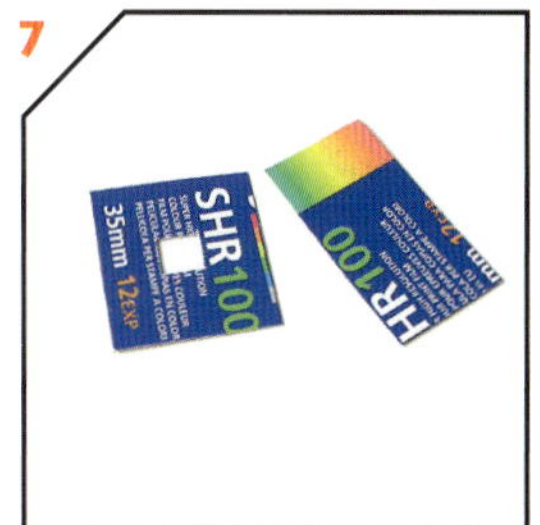

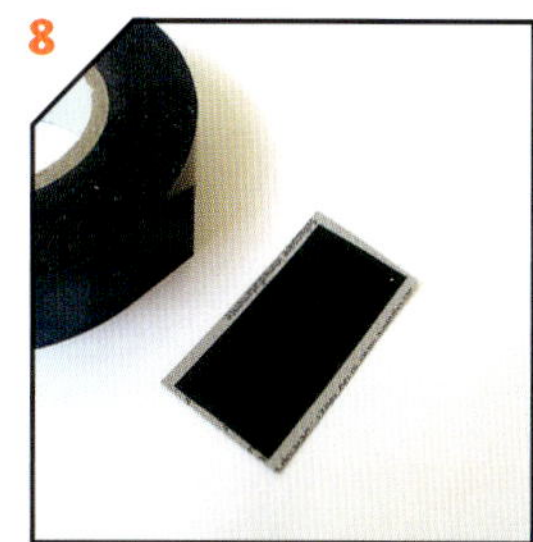

5 Place the aluminium pinhole plate over the square hole already cut in the top of the outer matchbox, making sure that the pinhole is exactly in the centre of the square.

6 Tape the pinhole plate to the top of the box using black electrical tape, securing all four sides to prevent light leaks.

Adding a shutter

7 The simplest shutter mechanism for your camera is a piece of electrical tape over the pinhole that can be unfastened for the desired exposure time. A cardboard sliding shutter is, however, more convenient.

To construct one, cut two pieces of thin cardboard from the empty film box: a square about 32 mm × 32 mm, and a rectangle about 25 mm × 40 mm. Cut a 6 mm square hole in the centre of the square piece.

8 Cover one side of the rectangular piece with black electrical tape to help prevent light leaks.

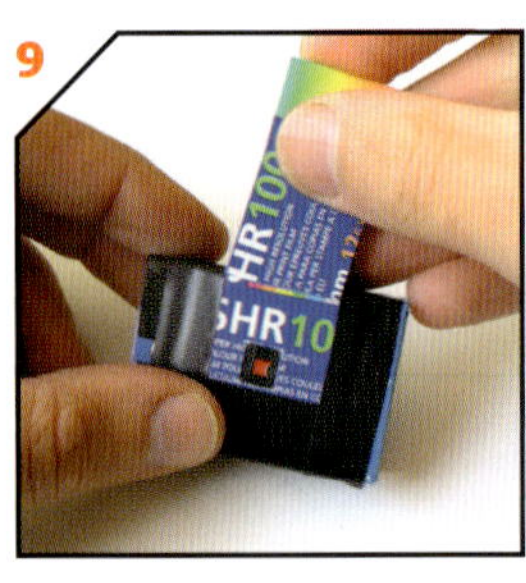
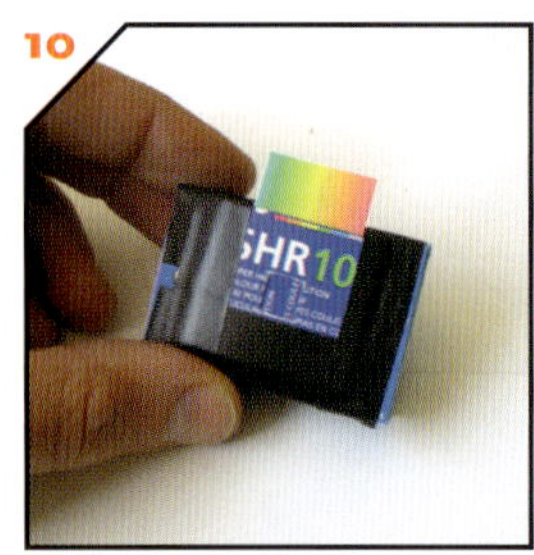
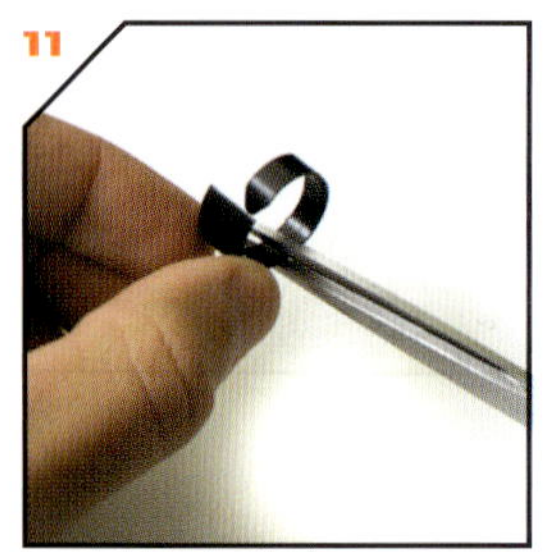
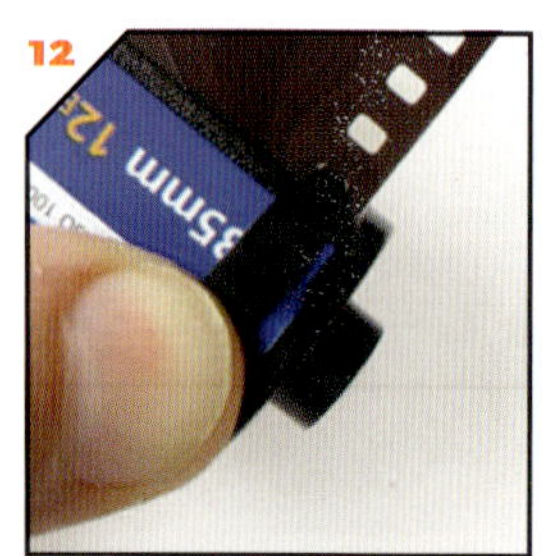
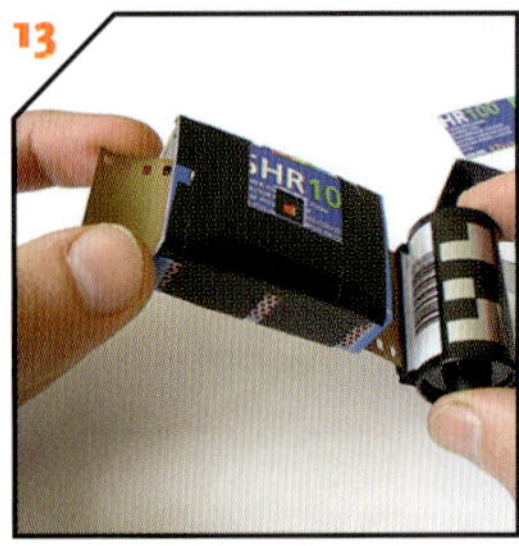
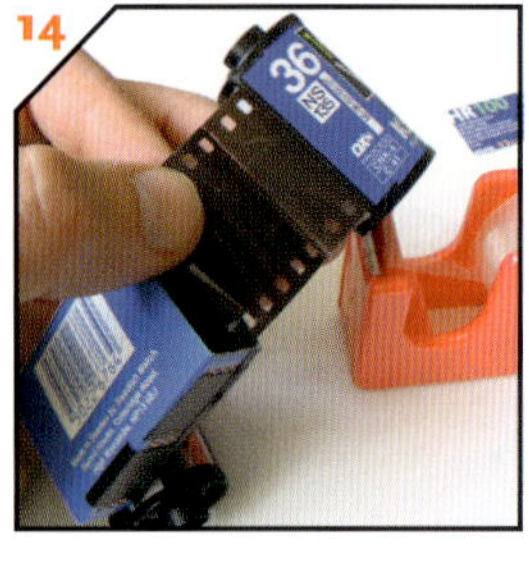
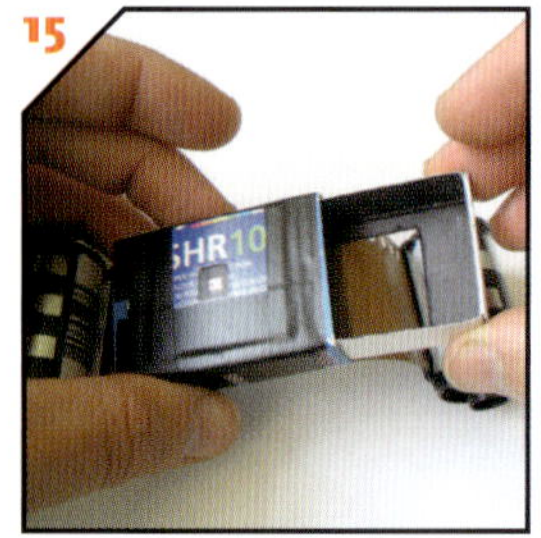
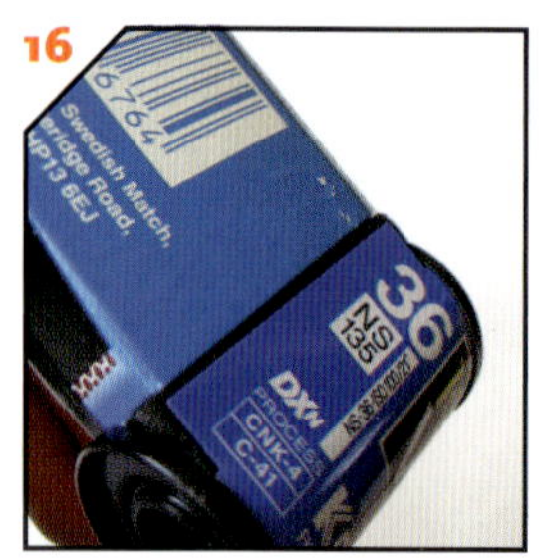
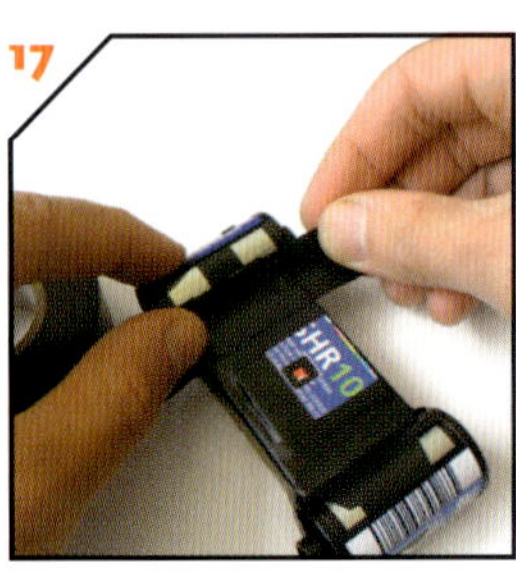
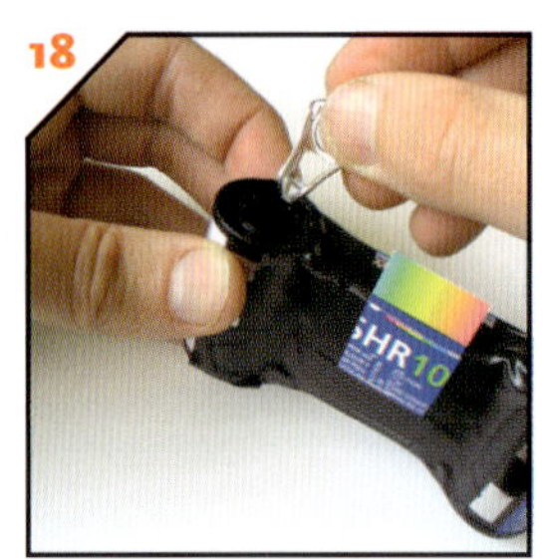
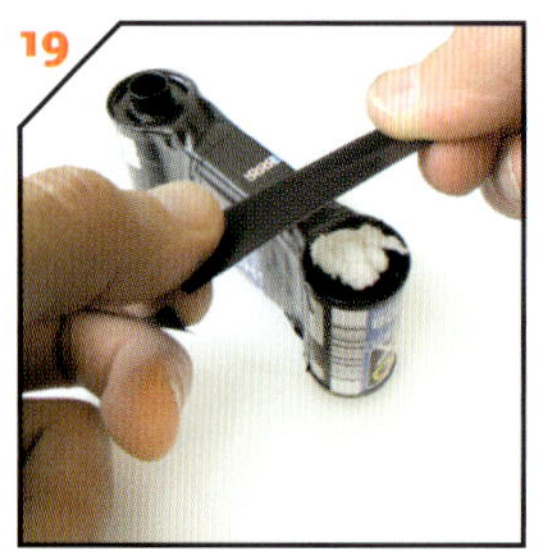
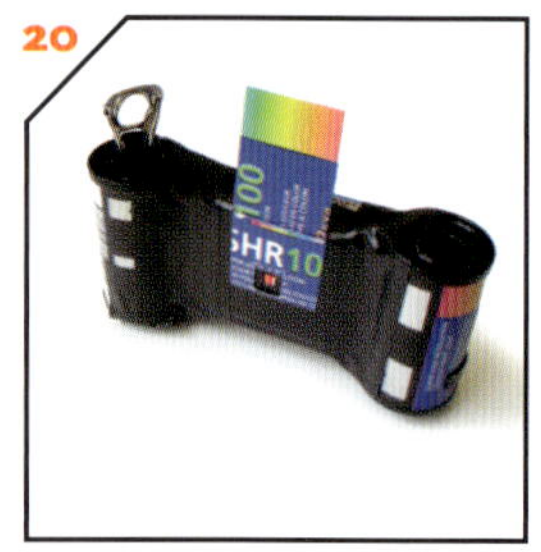

9 Place the square piece of card over the pinhole and tape it down on three sides, leaving a gap at the top into which the rectangular shutter-card can slide.

10 Check that the rectangular piece of card can be pushed down far enough to cover the pinhole completely.

Film advance

11 Judging how far to wind the film between each photo can be a bit tricky. Winding on too far wastes film; winding on too little produces double exposures. To avoid this problem, you can make a film-advance 'clicker' to measure the film accurately. First, cut off one of the loops of the plastic comb-binding.

12 Place the pointed end of the plastic loop so that it just enters one of the sprocket holes of the film in the new canister.

Tape the plastic securely to the film canister. Test the clicker by gently pulling out some film. The clicker should ride smoothly across the back of the film and make a click as it drops into the sprocket holes. If not, remove the tape, wind the film back into the canister and try again after repositioning the clicker slightly.

Loading the camera

13 First, trim the leader off the film, cutting the edge as squarely as possible. If the film stub from the empty canister is not cut squarely across, trim it square too, so it will splice neatly. Pull out a little more film from the new roll and thread it through the matchbox. Make sure the emulsion (non-shiny side) of the film is facing the pinhole.

14 Using some clear sticky tape, splice the ends of the two rolls of film together as neatly as possible. Try to make sure the edges are lined up together so the film can pass easily into the empty canister. Tape both sides and make sure the joint is secure.

15 Slide the match tray back into the matchbox, so that the frame you cut out in Step 1 is against the film. Turn the spindle of the empty film caniser so that the slack film is wound into it.

16 Make sure the edges of each film canister are pushed up tight to the matchbox and no film can be seen. The film is now loaded, but needs to be made light-tight.

Lightproofing

17 It's important that the only light getting into the camera comes through the pinhole. Use black electrical PVC tape to make your camera light-tight. The most important places to seal are between the film canisters and the matchbox. Place strips of tape down the front on both sides, using two layers and making sure it is stuck down firmly. Pay attention to the ends of each film cassette, adding more tape and trimming around the spindles so the tape doesn't prevent the film being wound on. Again, use a couple of layers of tape and check the joints to make sure they are totally sealed. The cardboard of the matchbox will also leak a small amount of light, especially in bright conditions. This will likely give your photos a mottled red effect. If you don't want this, tape the back and sides of the box so no card is showing.

Winder

18 To make it easier to wind the film on, insert the ring-pull from the can into the top of the empty spool. Alternatively, you could use a large paperclip.

19 As you wind the film on, the film in the take-up spool will tend to keep springing back. To keep some tension on the take-up spool, tape a small wad of tissue paper over its base. Don't make this too tight or it will be difficult to wind the film on.

Using the camera

20 To make an exposure, raise the card shutter for the desired exposure time, then lower it and wind the film on. Use your film-advance clicker to determine how far you need to wind the film. The precise number of 'clicks' you need to wind will depend on the size of your frames: use six clicks if you are using a 24 mm × 24 mm frame size, or 8 clicks for a 36 mm × 24 mm frame. The Matchbox Pinhole camera has an aperture of approximately $f/90$ (assuming a 0.2 mm pinhole). There is no need to be very accurate about exposure times, but the following can be used as rough guidelines for ISO 100 or 200 film.

Outdoors, sunshine: 1 or 2 seconds
Outdoors, cloudy conditions: 5 seconds
Indoors, normal lighting: 5–10 minutes

Unloading and reloading

When the film can't be wound on any more, it's time to unload it. You can just cut the box open, remove the film, and discard the camera, but if you want to reuse it, first carefully push back the tape to find the end of the clicker plastic, grasp the clicker with a pair of pliers, and remove it. This prevents the clicker tearing the film as it is rewound. Seal the tape back down again, and wind the film back into the original canister. Remove the black tape carefully from around the canister and cut across the film stub, leaving enough to splice your next roll as in Step 14.

FRANCESCO CAPPONI

*Interview by
Sergio Minniti*

A self-defined 'non-photographer' committed to reviving the magic of taking pictures, Italian artist Francesco Capponi's whimsical, sculptural pinhole cameras transform photography from automatic gesture to entertaining performance.

Your body of work includes sculptures and photos, encompassing numerous genres. How did you progress artistically from sculpture to photography to camera-making?

It was never a linear path. I studied sculpture and during the final years of my course I started to incorporate lenses, darkrooms and projectors into my work. I also spent most of my time in the photo lab. I was both fascinated and bored by photography. I especially enjoyed experimenting in the darkroom, solarizations, negative superimpositions and other experimental techniques. Then I started playing with Polaroids and mistreating them: crunching the prints, or washing them. I loved the aesthetic indeterminacy that I could obtain. I wanted to write my final-year dissertation on Polaroid cameras but I was told that the subject had little relevance to sculpture. Almost as a challenge I began building my stenopeic objects that became as much a part of the work as the photos they took; installations halfway between sculpture and photography. I eventually graduated, defending a thesis on pinhole photography. To this day, my work, including my sculpture, is heavily influenced by that research.

The top-hat pinhole, undoubtedly surreal and dramatic, performs a magic trick: a rabbit appears inside the cylinder; the photographic act becomes magical, like in the early days of photography when the new technology made it an amazing visual spectacle. So would you call yourself a visual illusionist or an entertainer?

I want to fascinate, amuse and intrigue the audience. The top-hat camera is one of my favourite pieces because of this power it has to amaze. I am very attracted by the 'magical act' that forms the basis of photography. The cylinder and rabbit trick represents this: say 'Abracadabra', and the rabbit is in the hat, represented on film. For me it's magic. So yes, I suppose I'm a visual illusionist.

We can look at photography, especially (though not exclusively) at the popular level, as a medium in which the craft is hidden from the practitioner: he or she pushes a button and the photo is done. There is no need for technical knowledge where the 'Kodak Philosophy' prevails. While on one hand this has helped to extend the medium beyond all expectations, it has also closed off a wide array

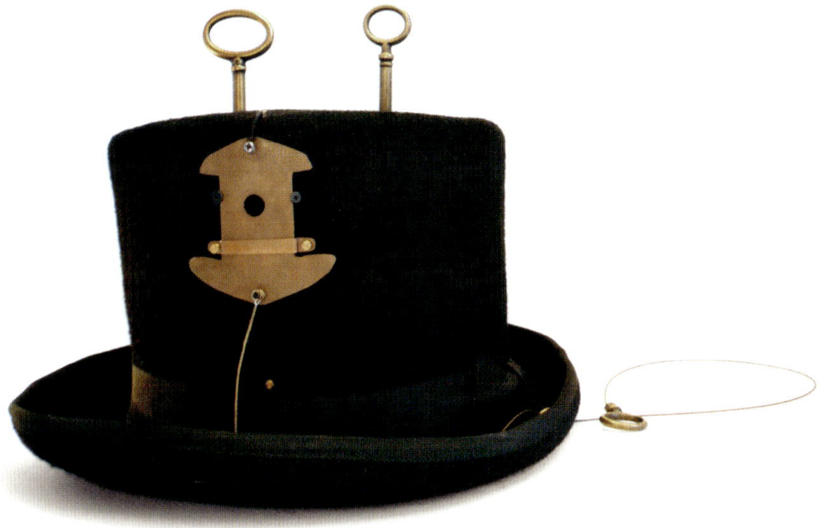

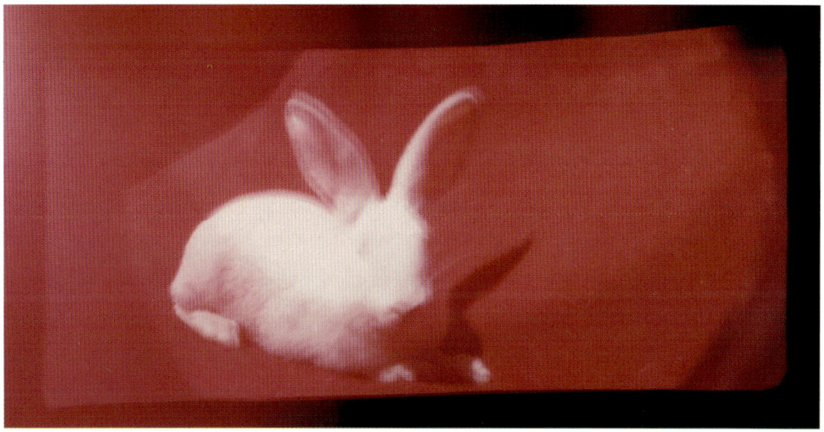

of expressive and creative possibilities. Do you think that photography can or should recover its earlier identity as an 'opaque medium' that requires technical knowledge and hands-on experience with development processes?

The 'You press the button, we do the rest' approach doesn't work for me. I want to keep as much control over the process as possible because I think that the quality of the journey affects the end result. Photography has completely changed since its beginnings; it is now available to everyone. While this has opened myriad new possibilities, at the same time it has also left photography devoid of a large part of its original magic. Taking pictures has become a daily and often repetitive gesture, and today most photos are taken with a phone. If there is no emotion in the creative act, then we can't expect to find it in the

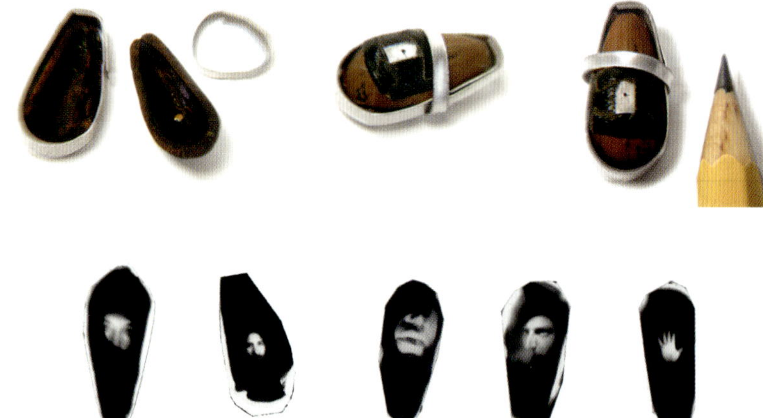

image that is created. Look at passport and ID-card pictures, for example. Photographic technology has advanced dramatically, but the portrait that should most represent our identity is getting worse and worse. My grandfather had his taken by a photographer with a big camera, the right lighting, wearing his Sunday suit and all groomed. He probably travelled to town especially for the occasion and was thrilled to have his picture taken; it was a rare thing. Over time, we have gone from this to Photomatic cabins, which still took four nice black-and-white pictures, each slightly different, to the digital photobooth, where you see yourself projected on a screen, choose the shot, correct and print it; delete the others. There's no more waiting in anticipation while the machine dries the prints, wondering if you came out alright. And when I recently renewed my electronic identity card, my photo was taken by an employee of the Registry in a dark room with a poor-quality webcam. The result: my grandfather looked handsome on his ID card; I look like a monster. I can't think of this as progress.

Why did you start building cameras?

Initially I started out of curiosity. I was surprised that I could capture light and convert it into images. Then, when I started to show my cameras, what I loved most was the wonder and surprise in the eyes of those who saw them. People couldn't believe that I could take a picture with a walnut or a pinenut; in order to understand how it worked, they had to envisage the process behind it. The answer is unsettling in its simplicity: light travels in a straight line, and since only one line can be drawn between two distinct points, images can therefore be transported. The act of stripping all the traditional casing from the underlying mechanism, revealing it in all its banality and intuitive simplicity, helps me to understand what appears to be complex.

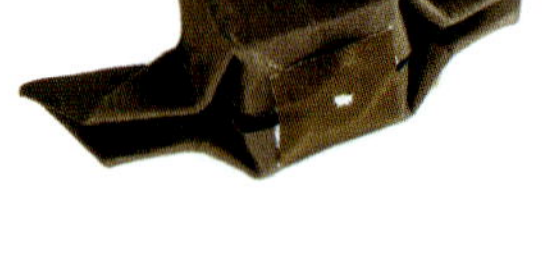

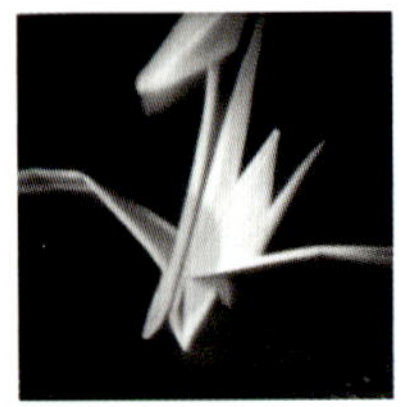

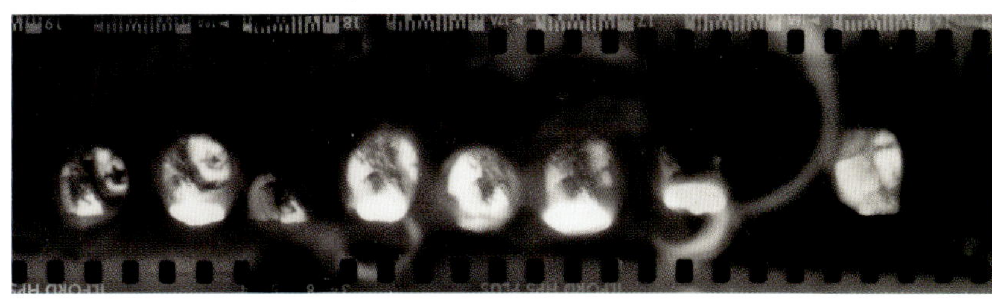

Stenopeic Piano, 2007
The Stenopeic Piano (below left) incorporates thirty-seven shutters and pinholes. It prints on regular 35 mm film (top). Each piano key corresponds to a shutter that opens the pinhole as the piano is played. The shutter will open according to the pressure and/ or frequency with which the key is played. The result is a series of small portraits (below right) of the person who is playing the music; Capponi calls this a 'photophony'.

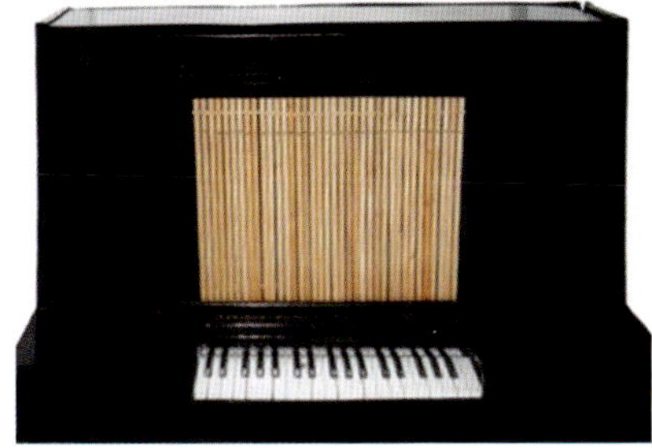

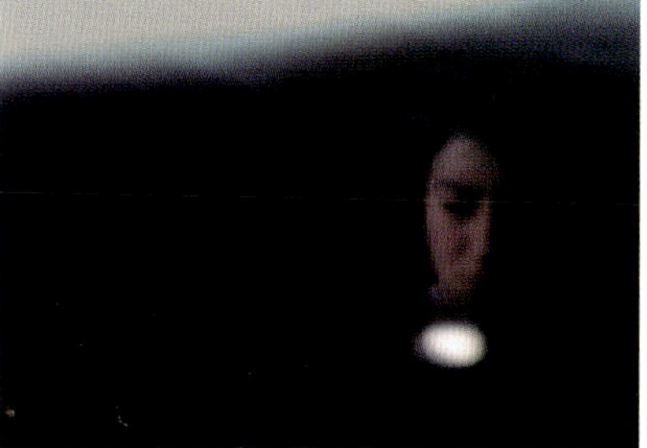

So maybe we should have the guts to throw away our cameras in order to reacquaint ourselves with the medium. Is this why you call yourself a 'photographer without a camera'?

I have always tried to destroy photography – yet ended up being considered a photographer. There was a time when I didn't have a real camera – my equipment consisted only of various pinholes, toy cameras and maybe an old 35 mm SLR – but people still kept asking me to take their portraits or wedding photos! I literally try to 'photo-graph', that is, to write with light. And one doesn't necessarily need a camera for that. I've used camera obscuras, mirrors and lenses in my photographic work. As I said, I'm often bored by photography; there are way too many pictures around. So my reaction is to abuse it, destroy it. I look for deformations and try to accentuate these flaws. This process re-creates photography in my mind, making it interesting again, and less trivial, at least for me. From the outside, most people notice only the final products of this process, so they call me when they need a photographer. Yet I don't consider myself one, at least not in the usual meaning of the word.

You 'photo-graphed' music with your Stenopeic Piano. A sort of communion between music and photography, or 'photophony' as you called it. Each time you open the shutter, it is as if the music itself impresses the film through the pinhole. Does your aesthetic research force the camera to represent the invisible?

I either adapt cameras or purposely create them out of scratch in order to represent an idea. In this case, an idea as invisible as music. The aesthetic

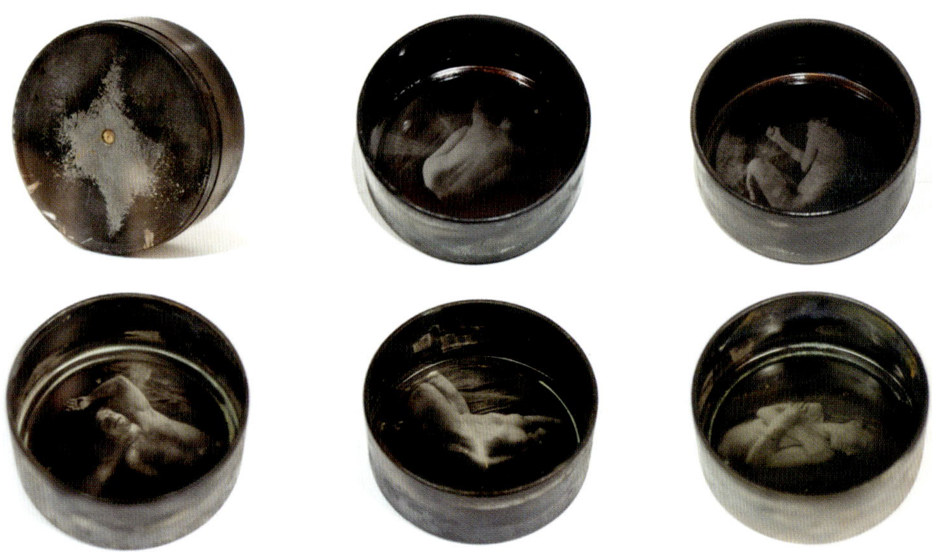

Chair en Boîte, wet-plate collodion tintypes in pinhole cameras constructed from candy tins, 4 cm (height) × 10 cm (diameter) (1½ × 4 in.), 2013

relevance of 'photophony' isn't important; it's an image that varies with the music played. A melody is theoretically unphotographable, but I did not want to accept this fact, and I couldn't resist trying to overcome this paradox in my own way.

All your camera projects have a close connection with the photographic subjects they shoot. Do you believe in a kind of shamanic power of the photographic device?

My cameras are usually built to tell a story about their specific subjects. I shoot rabbits with the Abracadabra top-hat camera, and a chess game with the pawn-camera. Once that object shows me what it wants, the camera has run its course and I usually don't reuse it. I prefer to tell a story, a fable, instead of mechanically stating the truth. I'm looking to establish a magical, dreamlike, maybe miraculous relationship between my cameras and my photos, but not shamanic. I try not to take myself too seriously. That's why I think there should always be an ironic side to my work as well.

Time is very important in classic photography. What does time represent for a 'non-photographer' like you?

When you work with stenopeic cameras, time is a concept that you deal with continuously. You have to engage the subject in a completely different way, and stop and look at it for the entire duration of the exposure. It can be considered almost a Zen exercise: you need to observe, not just see. Maybe a bit

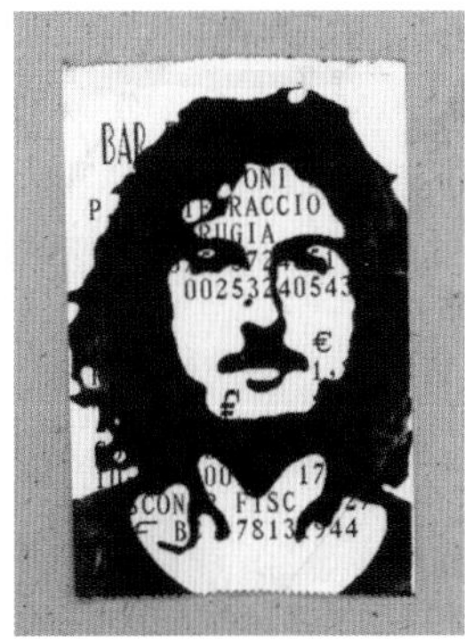

ABOVE
Fiscal Self-Portrait, PoGo print
on thermoactive receipt paper,
7 × 5 cm (2¾ × 2 in.), 2009

pretentiously, this consideration inspired me to try to photograph another seemingly impossible paradox: the 'space-time' dichotomy. I walked along a street holding the camera, leaving the shutter open the whole time. The result was a blurry silhouette with streaks of light, conceptually representing the street in the time it takes to walk it.

Let's talk about your experiments with the PoGo printer. Were you aiming again at a process of deconstruction of technology? Were you playing more with the camera or with the image?

A PoGo printer is essentially a printer aimed at becoming the digital version of the Polaroid system. I started making portraits with receipt rolls, since it uses the same heat-transfer principle as normal Zink photo paper. I also manipulated PoGo printed images through image transfer. For me, a digital reflex was a powerful yet very cold tool, I couldn't conceive making art with it. But when I discovered PoGo, I realized it could give me back the 'hands-on' feeling that I had previously with camera obscuras and Polaroids. My friend and videomaker Francesco Bicchieri helped me in the experimentation and filming the process. The video had an unexpected success and watching people emulate our photo manipulations was very satisfying.

What is your intent when you take pictures and build cameras?

I choose to keep random chance in my work because I feel it generates emotion. Often, a small inaccuracy, error or unexpected reaction gives a feeling to a piece and makes it unique. I am also aware that everything works according to the parameters that I establish, so the more I have to control the process, the more I try to counter-balance it with a little touch of randomness. I believe this warms up my pictures; it gives them flavour. I don't feel I have any special mission in photography, though I do realize that I belong to a large spontaneous movement of people who are trying to re-think photography after the sea-change that came with digital technology.

KWANGHUN HYUN

*Interview by
Sergio Minniti*

Korean metalwork artist Hyun is a new-generation camera builder who strives for both beauty and mechanical perfection in his craft: Swiss-clockwork precision cameras.

Do you consider yourself an artist, or a camera builder? What is the role that photography plays in your daily life?

I am not only an artist working with metal; I also consider myself a designer. I make handmade cameras and watches, as well as lamps using camera lenses. I was into photography as a hobby in my younger years, and always carried around a camera, but now I like building cameras better than taking good pictures. I also collect classic cameras, as they are naturally connected to my work.

How did you get into photography?

I started taking pictures with my father's old analogue camera when I was in high school. I love the entire act of shooting a picture with a reflex-winding, focusing through the viewfinder and pressing the shutter. I felt that it was a very magical experience. But I never felt that when I was using an automatic or digital camera.

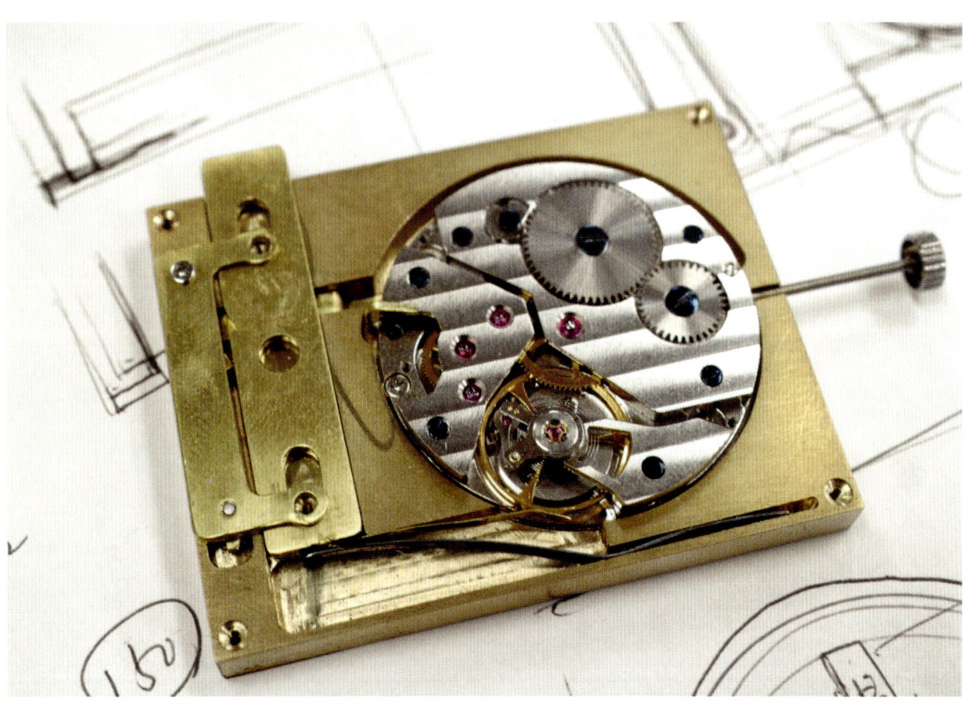

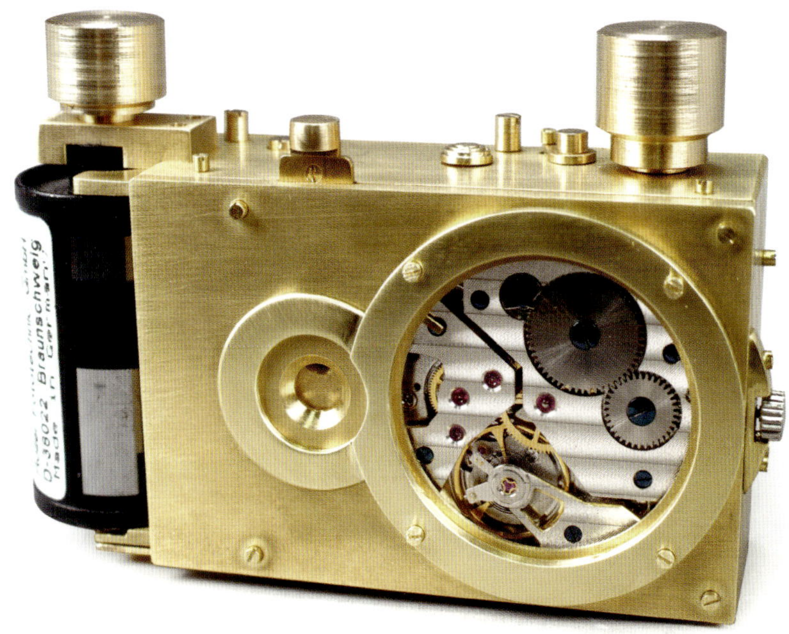

How did you have the idea of combining metal craftsmanship and photography?

I received a bachelor and a master's degree at Hongik University in Seoul, majoring in metal art and design, and produced my first pinhole cameras and watches as coursework. During my undergraduate years, I took general photography classes because I was fascinated with cameras and photography. One of the assignments was to build a pinhole camera out of paper. It was then that I got the idea to make a pinhole camera with metal. Combining my metalwork major with this newfound interest, I started building my cameras.

What distinguishes your work from that of other camera makers is that you make your own cameras from watch movements. There has been a connection between watch- and camera-making in the past – I remember, for example, the Jaeger LeCoultre Compass camera and the Robot cameras designed by German watchmaker Heinz Kilfitt. What does it mean for you to rediscover this mechanical connection in the digital age?

I always try to focus my artistic work on the camera's mechanism and re-interpret it from my own perspective. A pinhole camera, for instance, is a

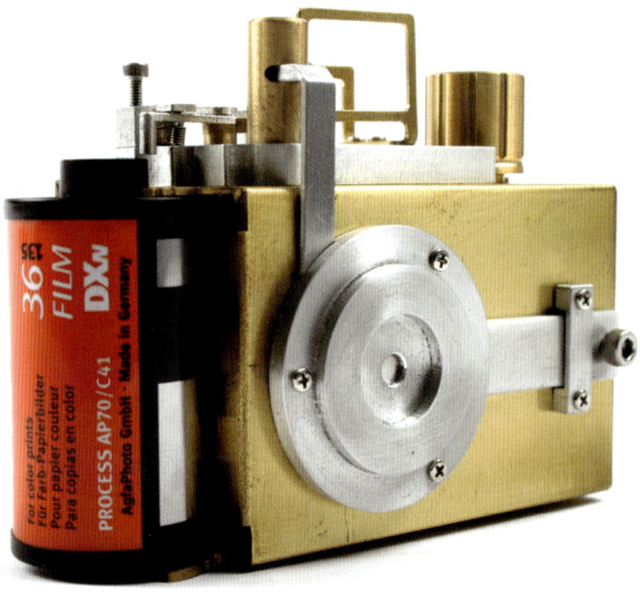

machine that is very close to the primitive principle of the camera obscura. An automatic clock movement is also an amazing device. Although people can buy unerring precise electronic watches, many still think that only a watch with a mechanical automatic movement can be a masterpiece. Likewise, I believe that my pinhole camera will be a unique example of a primitive light-capturing box in a sea of high-resolution cameras.

Clocks and cameras both changed the world. What else do they have in common?

Cameras are tools for capturing light: light that is reflected from a subject and then triggers a chemical reaction on the surface of film inside a box. In other words, through film we are able to see invisible particles of light. Likewise,

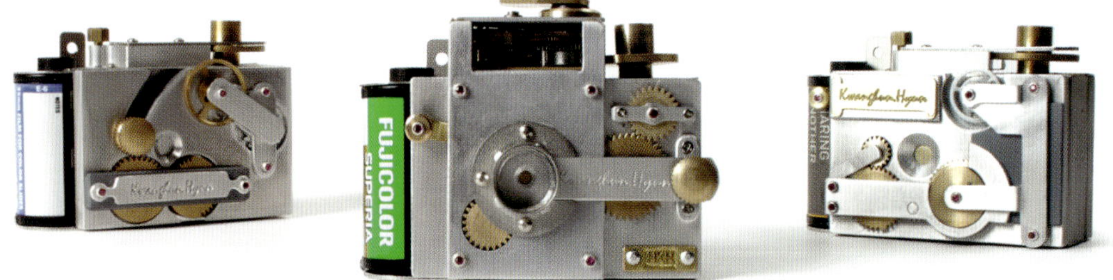

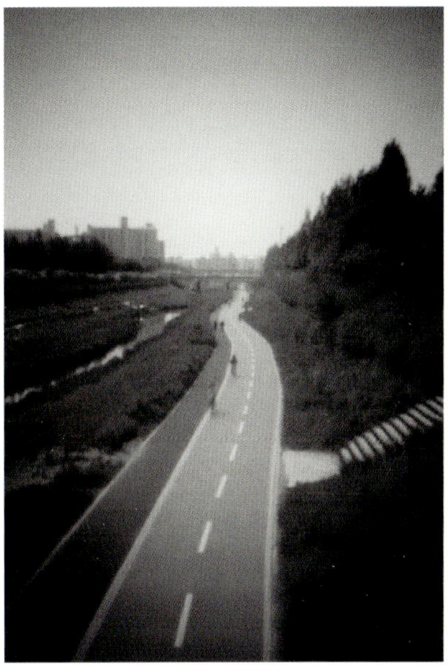

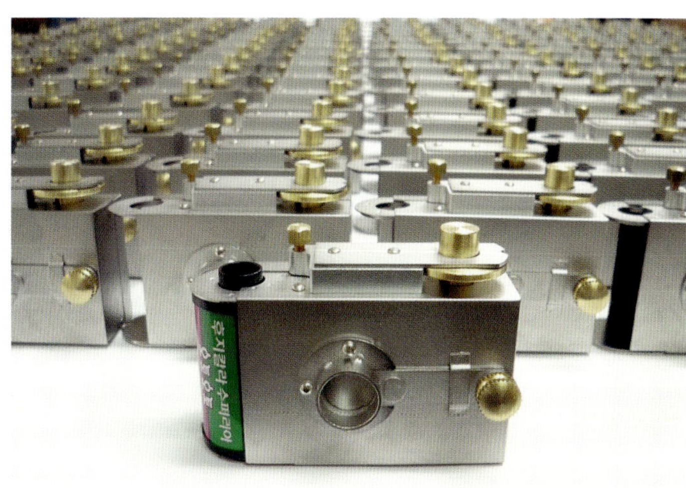

ABOVE LEFT
A picture taken with Hyun's
Heartbeat II model.

ABOVE RIGHT
Obscura VII.1, stainless steel,
brass, 0.3 mm pinhole, 61 × 82 ×
32 mm (2⅜ × 3¼ × 1¼ in.), 2008

through their two hands, clocks allow us to see time, another otherwise invisible phenomenon.

There is something paradoxical – and intriguing – in your hybridization of cameras and watches: the mechanical precision of watch movements is also used to make pinhole photography, which is considered the most imprecise way to take photographs. How do you solve this paradox?

People usually think that the pinhole camera is a low-grade camera made of paper or empty cans, but I am trying to make a perfect pinhole camera in terms of the appearance and function of the clock movement. My goal is to make a high-end, flagship pinhole camera. I am practising metal processing techniques in order to make more precise and accurate the clock movement parts, rather than using ones recycled and adapted from existing clocks.

SOLARGRAPHY

Solargraphs (or solarigraphs) are obtained by loading simple pinhole cameras with black-and-white photosensitive paper, fixing them in position outdoors, and leaving them to expose for days, weeks, months or even years, producing surreal images that record the sun's daily trajectory across the sky. Curiously, there is no record of cloudy days. The technique does not require any chemical processes since the picture appears by direct darkening. Solargraphs are neither developed nor fixed: the resulting negative needs to be scanned and inverted using image software in order to obtain a permanent positive image.

How to make a pinhole camera for solargraphy *by Diego López Calvín*

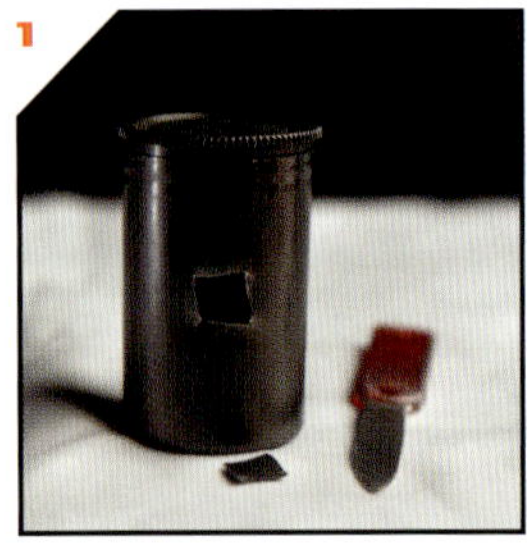

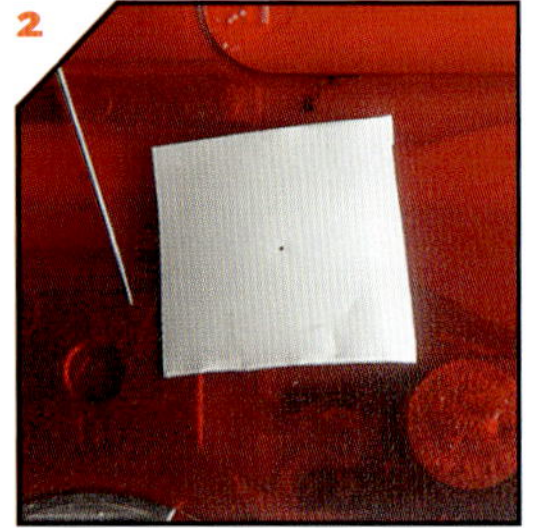

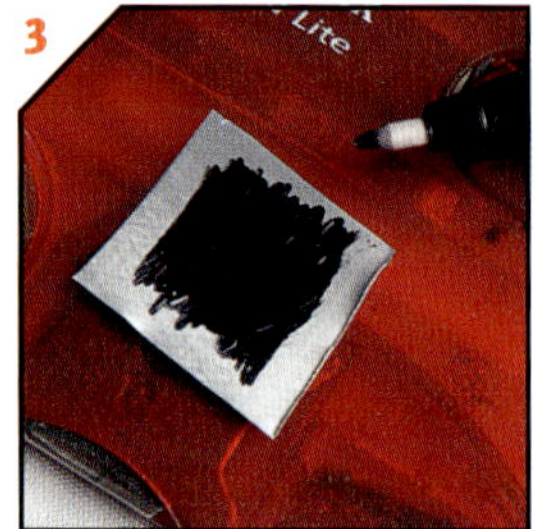

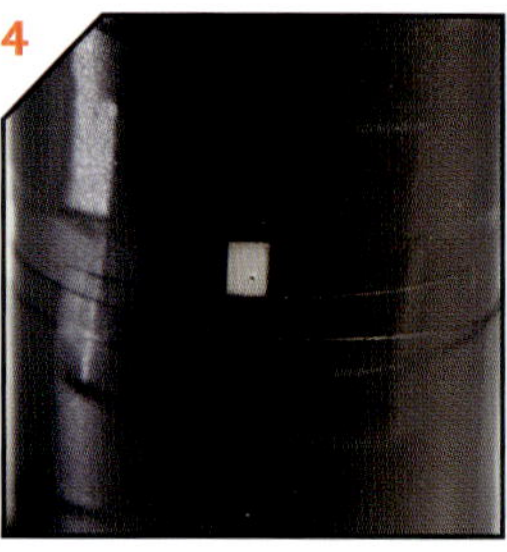

What you need:

- ☐ opaque plastic 35 mm film canister
- ☐ black electrical tape
- ☐ scissors
- ☐ craft knife
- ☐ fine needle or pin
- ☐ black permanent marker
- ☐ aluminium soda can
- ☐ photographic paper
- ☐ thin cardboard
- ☐ cellophane tape
- ☐ silicone glue or plastic cable ties

A camera for solargraphy is essentially an ultra-wide-view pinhole camera with cylindrical projection and field coverage of 160° horizontal and 120° vertical. Although it is a black-and-white technique, over prolonged exposure periods additional free silver is liberated and colours start to appear: first yellow, then shifting gradually to sepia, red-brown and finally slate-grey. This technique was developed in 1999 by photographers Diego López Calvín, Sławomir Decyk and Paweł Kula in Szczecin, Poland, for their project Solaris.

Preparing the camera

1 Use the craft knife to cut a square window measuring approximately 10 × 10 mm in the centre of the curved side of the opaque film canister.

2 Make a pinhole plate measuring about 20 × 20 mm from the aluminium soda can, using the process outlined on p. 43, Step 5.

3 Use a permanent black marker pen to colour the pinhole plate black. This will help prevent internal reflections.

4 Attach the pinhole plate over the hole you cut into the plastic film canister. Use black electrical tape, making sure to seal the edges securely to avoid light leaks.

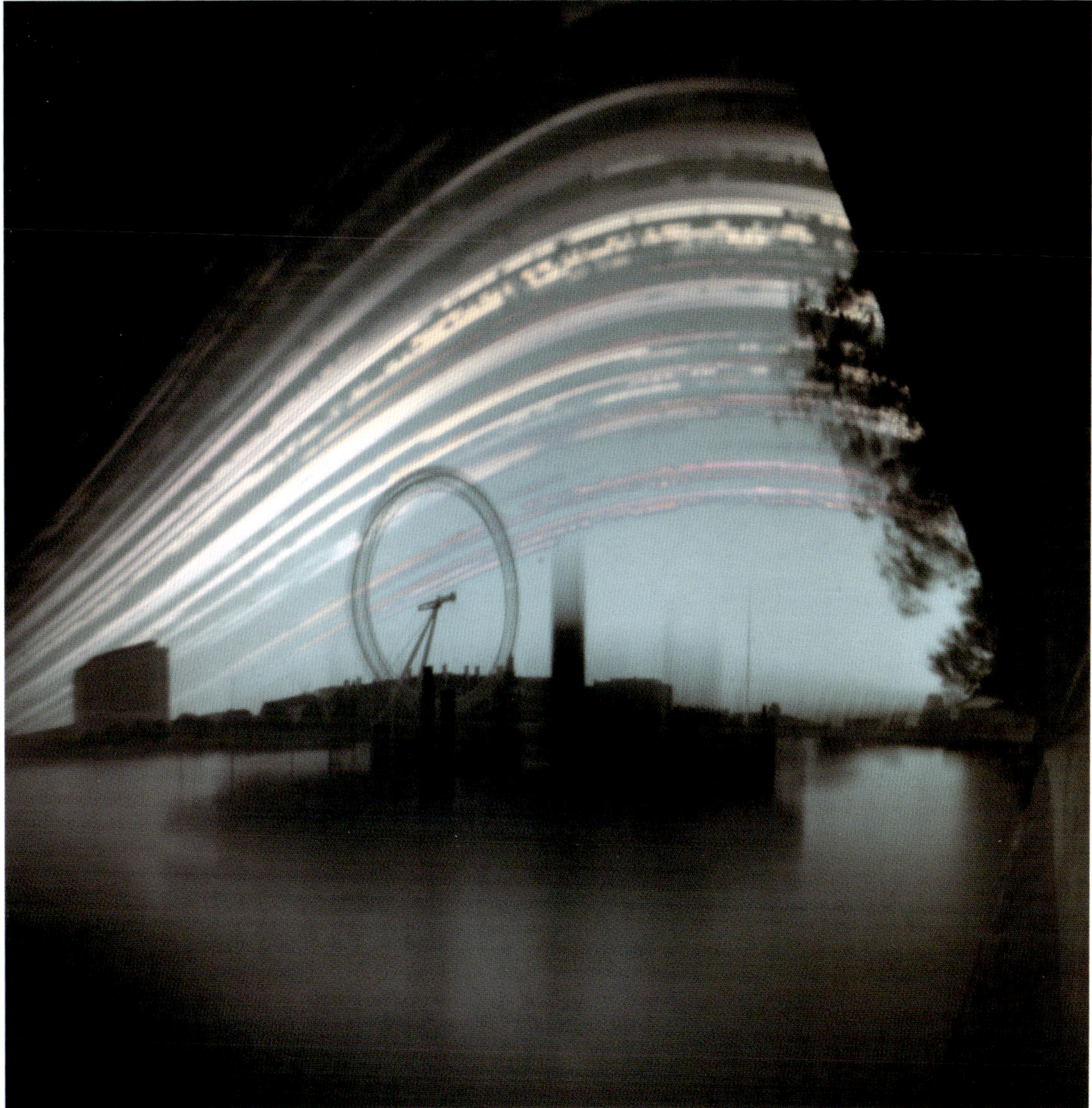

Diego López Calvín
London Eye, taken with a pinhole
camera made from a soda can,
loaded with Ilford photosensitive
paper, exposed 10 August–2
December 2008

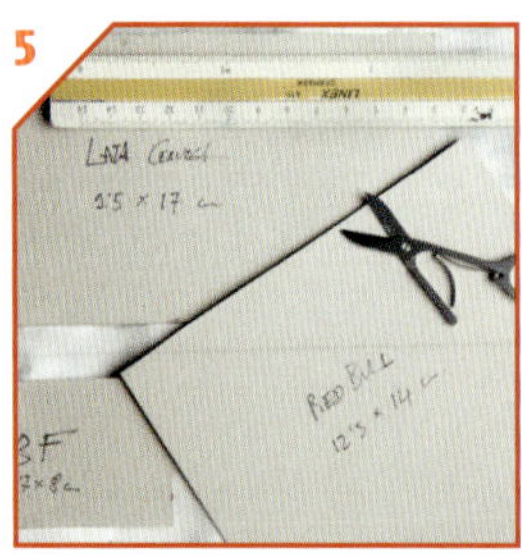

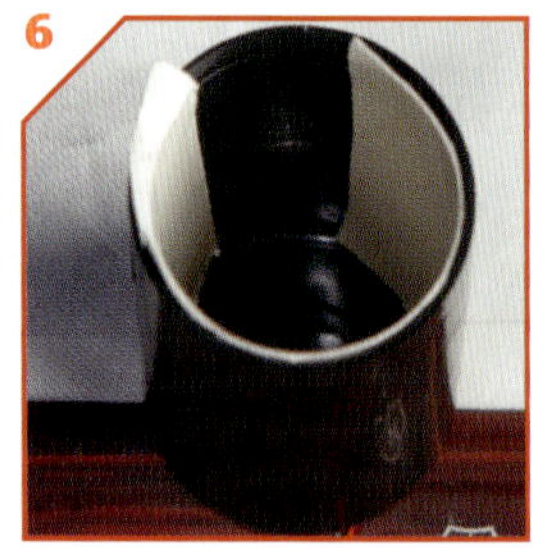

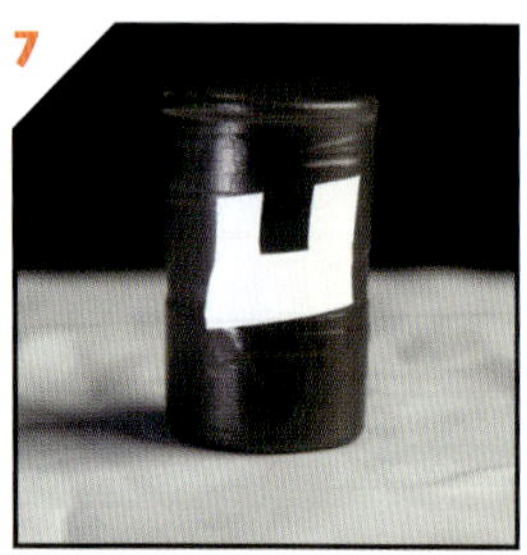

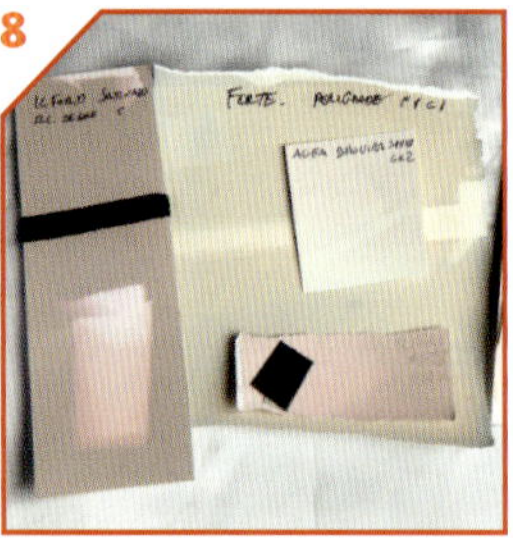

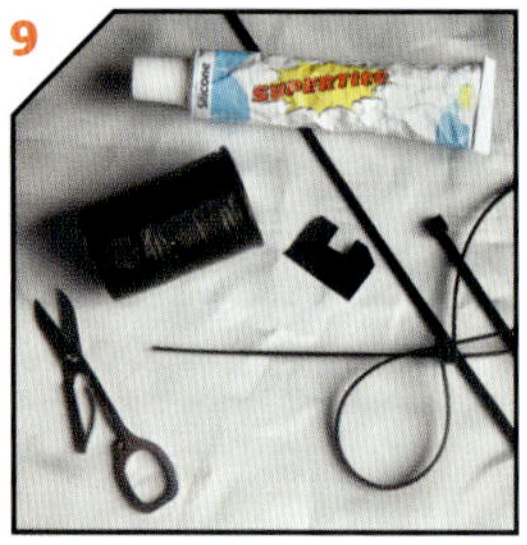

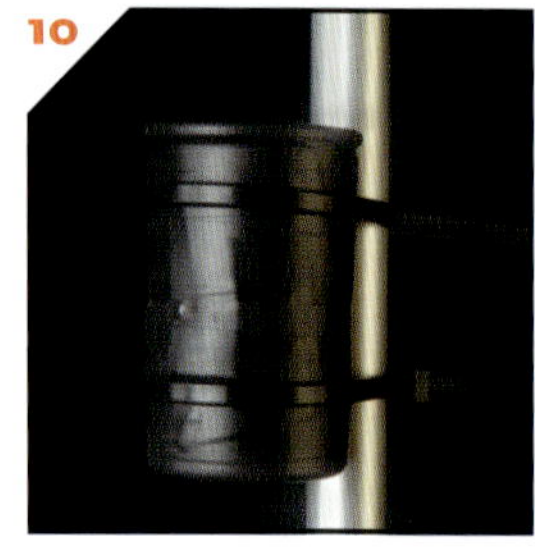

For more information about the technique, see these websites:

Paweł Kula
http://pawelkula.blogspot.com.es

Sławomir Decyk
http://www.galeriaff.infocentrum.com/2005/decyk/decyk_a.htm

Diego López Calvín
http://solarigrafia.com

Tarja Trygg (global project)
http://solargraphy.com

Loading the camera

5 Measure the canister's depth and circumference (subtracting 1 cm from the latter for the pinhole) and cut a rectangular template from thin cardboard. Then, working under safelight in the darkroom, use your card template to cut a piece of photographic paper of the same size.

6 Still working in subdued light, load the photosensitive paper into the camera, making sure the pinhole is not obscured, and fix it to the edges of the canister with transparent tape.

7 Seal the top of the canister with black electrical tape. Fasten a piece of tape over the outside of the pinhole as a temporary shutter until the camera has been positioned outdoors.

Preparing for long exposure

8 The sensitivity of the paper needs to be tested inside the camera to estimate exposure time. Ideally, the test should approximate the exposure time of the intended photograph, but if this is not practical, a test of one full day should reveal any serious overexposure, which is the main danger. Should overexposure be a problem, try a slower (less sensitive) paper.

Since it can be hard to tell exactly what the camera is pointing at, you can test the approximate camera angle and position as part of the exposure test, bearing in mind that it will be impossible to reproduce the exact position for subsequent exposures.

9–10 To shoot the solargraph, the camera needs to be fixed in place outdoors in a quiet place where it won't be interfered with. Silicone glue works best on irregular surfaces; or cable ties can be used to fix the camera to a pole. Once the camera is securely in place, remove the shutter and start the exposure.

Processing the negative

When the exposure is complete, replace the shutter, return the camera to subdued lighting and remove the paper. Scan the paper negative and invert using image-processing software (see p. 132, Steps 1–3) to produce a positive image.

! light-sensitive step

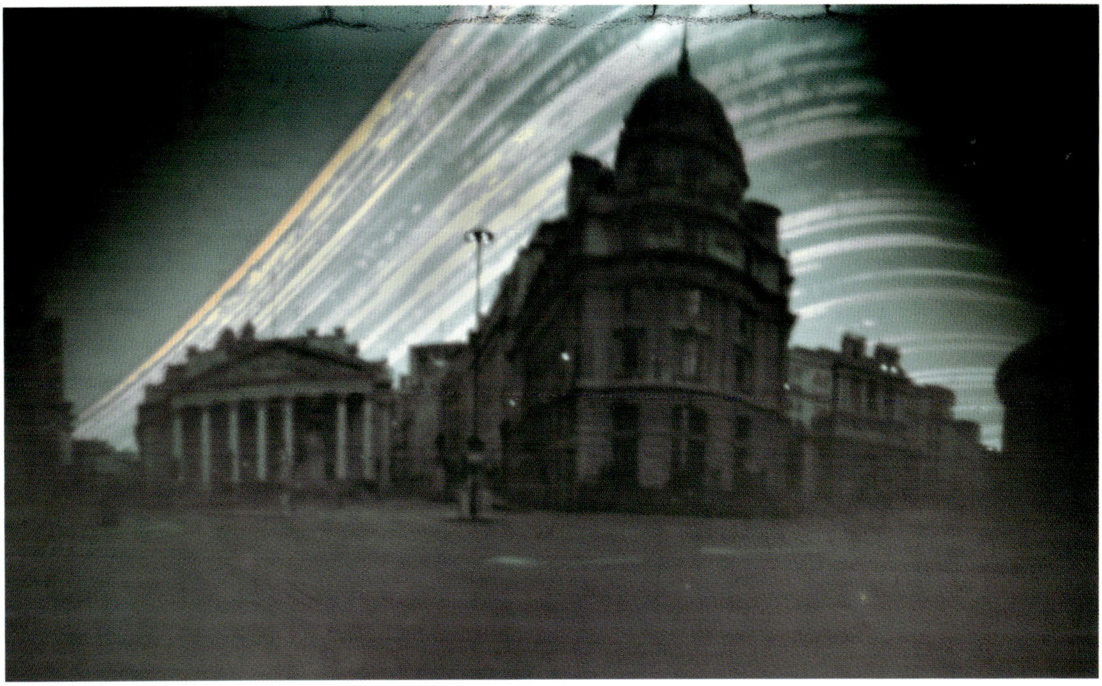

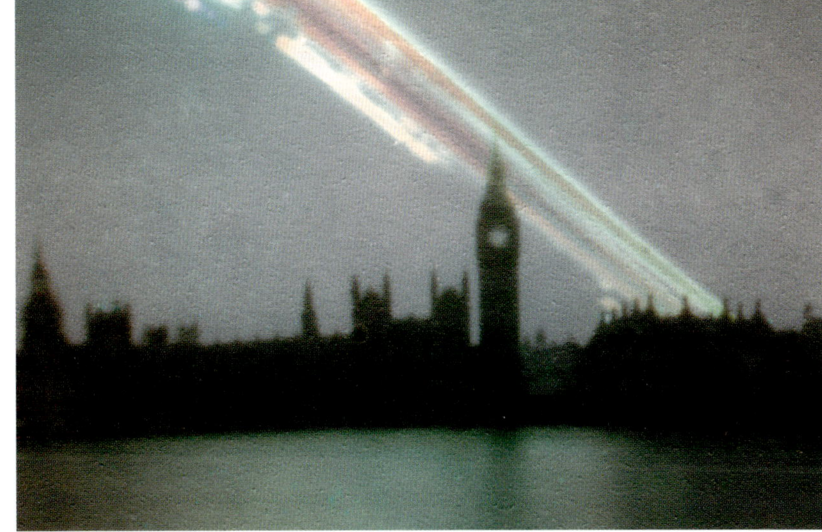

Diego López Calvín
Bank, London, taken with a pinhole
camera made from a 35 mm
film canister, loaded with Ilford
photosensitive paper, exposed
10 August–2 December 2008

Diego López Calvín
Big Ben, London, taken with a
pinhole camera made from a
35 mm film canister, loaded
with Ilford photosensitive paper,
exposed 21 February–3 March
2008

**WAYNE
MARTIN
BELGER**

*Interview by
Sergio Minniti*

Machinist, dive master, musician and artist Wayne Martin Belger designs and crafts unconventional pinhole cameras. Each camera he creates is used to photograph a specific subject. The result is a study in the relationships implied by the photographic process itself.

Your creative process starts with the conception of the camera, linked to a specific subject. How did this process develop, and how do you approach each project?

My approach really begins with my desire to learn, and I have found over the years that I learn best through experience. Creating a camera project based on the subject I wish to learn about builds a bridge between myself and the subject, giving me first-hand insight and a core learning experience. Using artefacts and materials sourced directly from my subject deepens that experience and fortifies the bridge of understanding that the camera becomes. I have never taken a photography class, nor had any formal art instruction. I come from a long line of engineers and toolmakers. In the 1940s and 50s my grandfather was an engineer at a secret air base in the Mojave desert. A lot of the planes he designed and built were essentially tools for the first experiments in breaking the sound barrier, and he was close to the pilots who flew them. For me, as for my grandfather, a tool – in my case a camera – is an extension of myself, designed to bring me into a deeper relationship with my subjects. Having not approached this work from the perspective of an artist, I feel this work is just the natural evolution of my desire to create tools that enrich my understanding of the subjects I am passionate about.

OPPOSITE
Untouchable Camera, 4" × 5" camera made from aluminium, copper, titanium, acrylic and HIV+ blood, 2006
'The blood pumps through the camera; in front of the pinhole it becomes my #25 red filter. The camera was designed to shoot a geographic comparison of people with HIV.'

RIGHT
Bloodworks, 16 (right) and 35 (far right), C-prints shot with the Untouchable Camera, 91.4 × 76.2 cm (36 × 30 in.), 2006

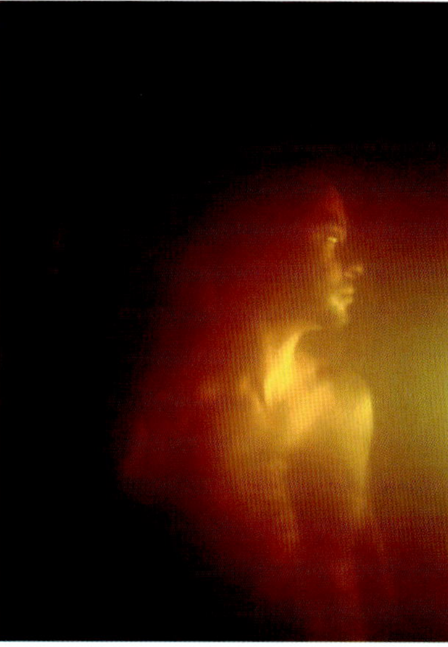
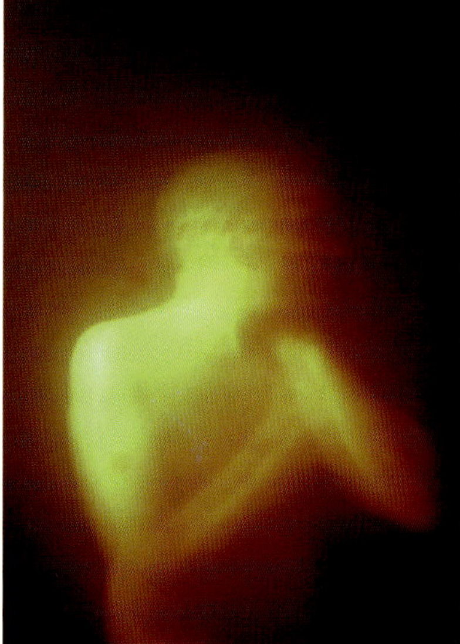

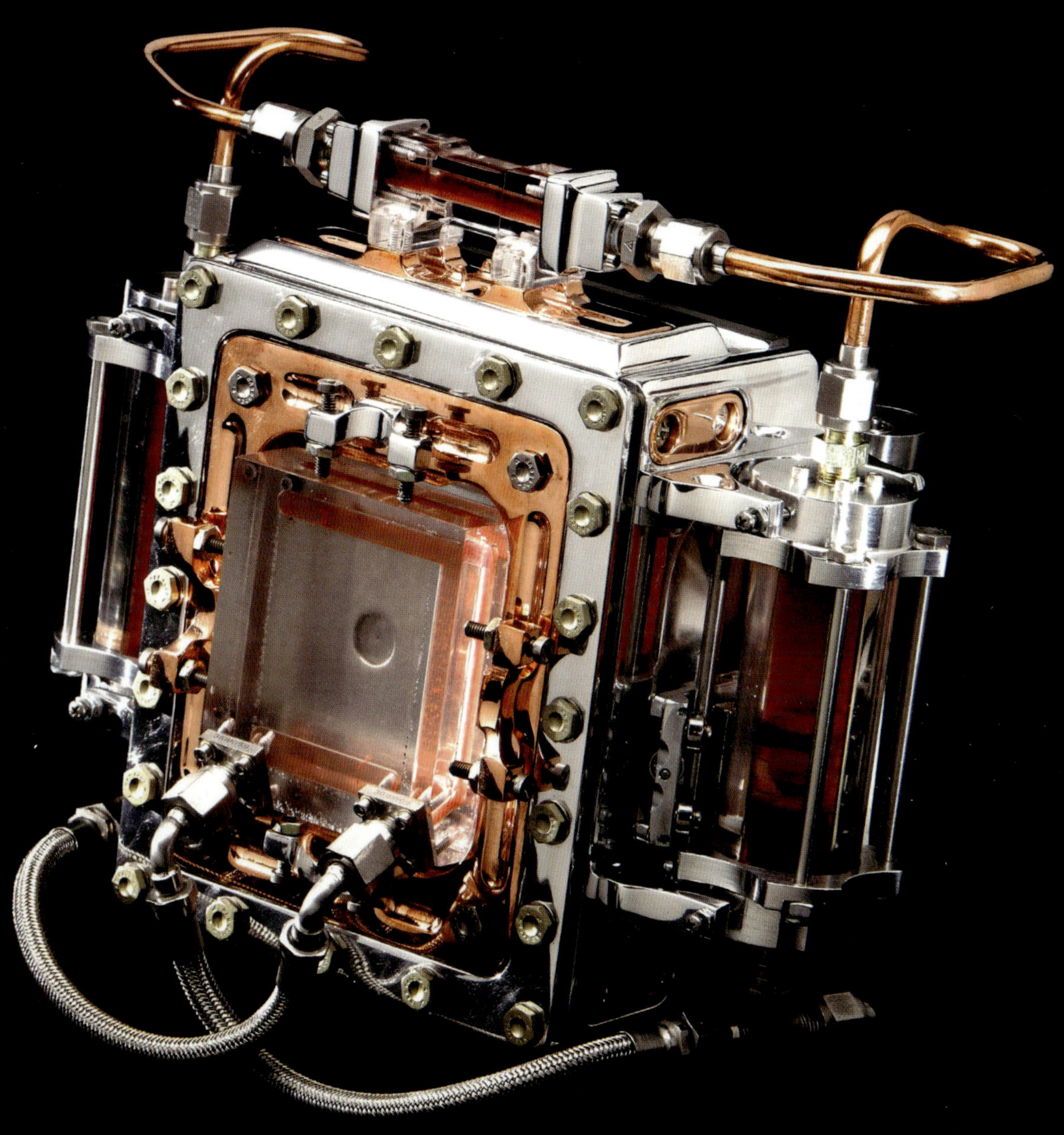

What role does the pinhole play in your conception of photography? Why is this type of photography 'far more real than others'?

Fifteen years ago, my first camera was a pinhole camera. Being a physics fanatic, I found the process of recording unedited and unmodified light and time on film intriguing. I like the fact that the air that touches my subject can pass through the camera and touch the film emulsion. Because of this, I feel that an image taken through a pinhole is a truer representation of the subject and the moment than it would be if taken through lenses and filters.

Your subjects themselves are used as materials for cameras: a skull becomes a camera obscura; circulating blood is used as a filter; pinhole eyes produce stereo photographs that later can be viewed through the skull itself – it seems that your work treats photography as a genuinely organic process, with tools that can properly be called 'camera bodies'. Would you say this is indeed the case?

It is an organic process, from the conception of a project, through its development and continued employment in the world (I have an arrangement with my collectors that I can borrow back any camera to do further shoots if I feel inspired). The camera bodies do have a presence – almost a consciousness – of their own.

BELOW
Yama camera, detail of pinhole
'Yama's eyes are cast from bronze and silver with a brass pinhole in each. A divider runs down the middle of the skull creating two separate cameras. A finished contact print mounted on copper is inserted into the back of the camera, allowing the viewer to see what Yama saw in 3D.'

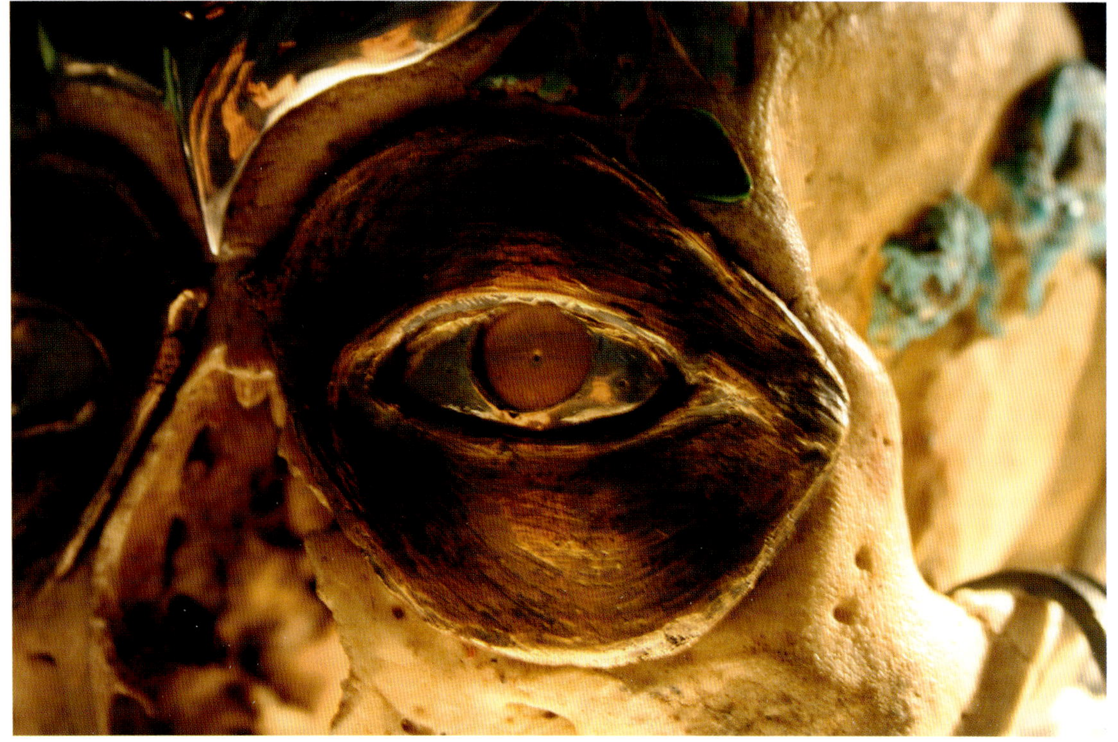

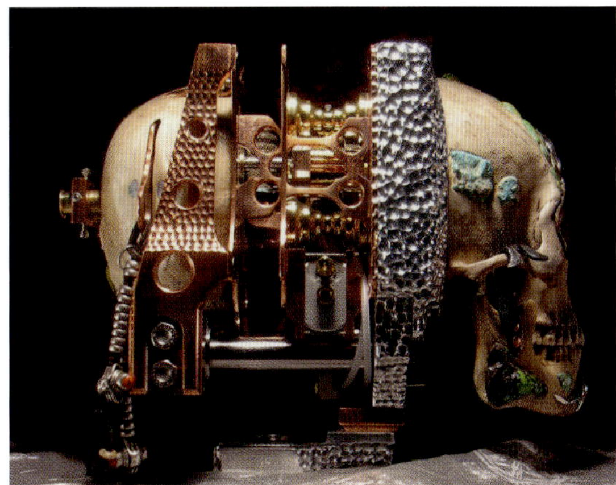

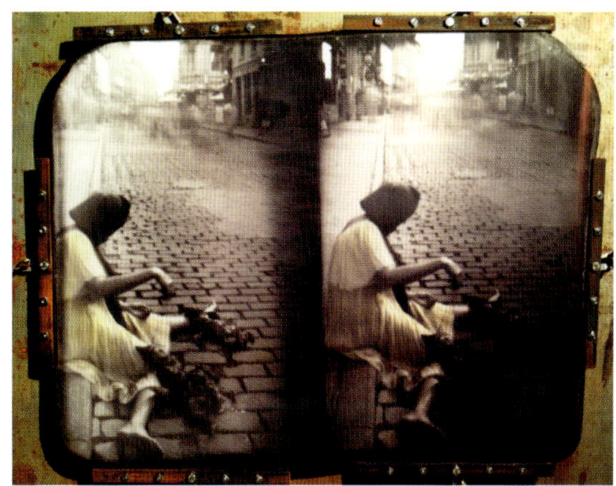

Yama, for example, is made from the 500-year-old remains of a Tibetan monk. The skull came to me in a very natural, organic way, as did all the other elements that came together to create the camera as it now exists. In Tibetan Buddhism, Yama is the God of Death who will see all of life. Yama was designed for two different photo series: one exploring modern incarnations of South East Asian deities; another photographing in the Tibetan refugee cities of India in association with a Tibetan legal organization – it will be a homecoming seen through the eyes of a 500-year-old-Tibetan. The skull was blessed by a Tibetan Lama for its current journey. I feel I have a relationship with that camera as an individual, almost living being, as well as with that unknown energy that conspired to help it come into existence through me. This is true of every project I undertake.

Even your most sensitive projects employing human body parts are handled with grace and sincerity. Did anyone ever feel upset about them?

I've had mixed responses to my work, and they always seem to be at extremes. There's not much middle ground. The vast majority of people have been deeply touched and grateful for what they learn through my explorations. I have received numerous letters from HIV support organizations as well as from individuals sharing personal experiences of growth through the Untouchable Camera project, for instance. That said, I have also been told I am going to hell by various fundamentalist Christian groups for using human remains in my work, as well as for working with homosexuals and Muslims. Somehow I find that encouraging...

You have said: 'I don't even own a camera that wasn't made by me.' Why is handmaking cameras so important to you?

LEGOTRON

The Legotron is a medium-format camera constructed almost entirely from Lego® building blocks, incorporating a sanded Plexiglas ground glass and a used 127 mm lens.

Cary Norton is an American photographer based in Birmingham, Alabama. In 2009 he started toying with the idea of building a camera out of Lego blocks and used camera parts. He built a prototype and blogged about it, and the response was so overwhelming that he decided to perfect the device. Today, the finished Legotron Mark 1.1 is a marvel of several hundred building blocks, comprising a main box, an internal box, a 4" × 5" film holder, a Plexiglas ground glass slot (below right) and a lens board mounted with a used 127 mm f4.7 Kodak lens. The internal box (bottom right) is slid forwards or backwards to focus the image. The original focal range was limited to 0.5–1 m, confining its use to portraiture, but the new set-up works from roughly 40 mm to infinity. The lens board can be changed to accommodate a different lens or a pinhole board. The custom tripod mount makes it easy to set up the Legotron on any standard tripod.

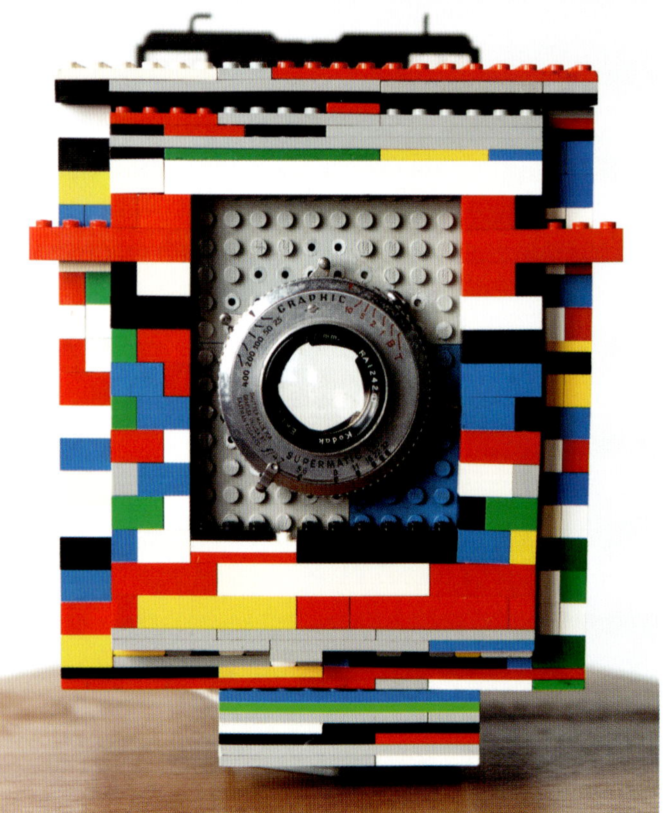

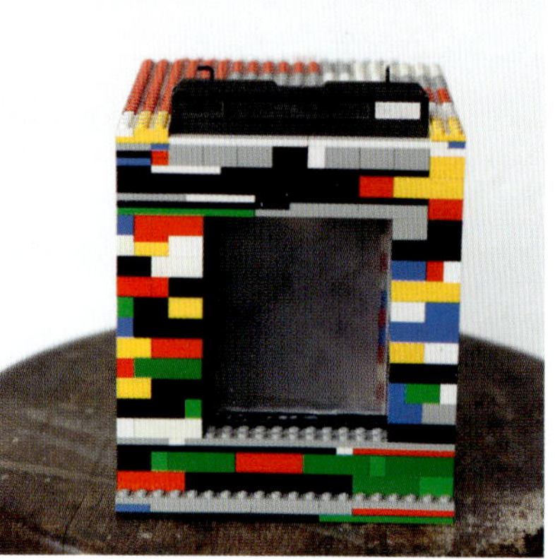

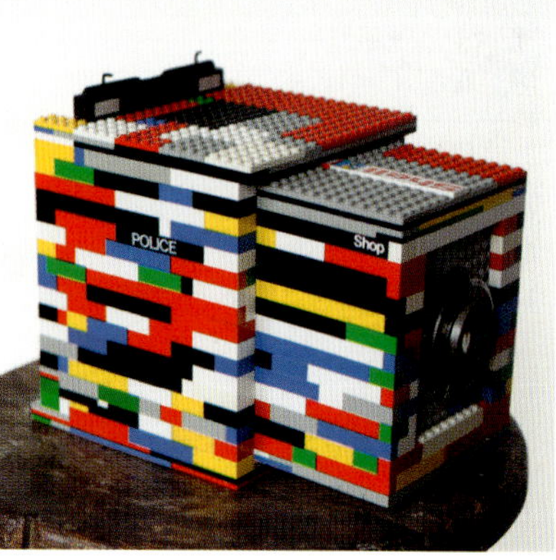

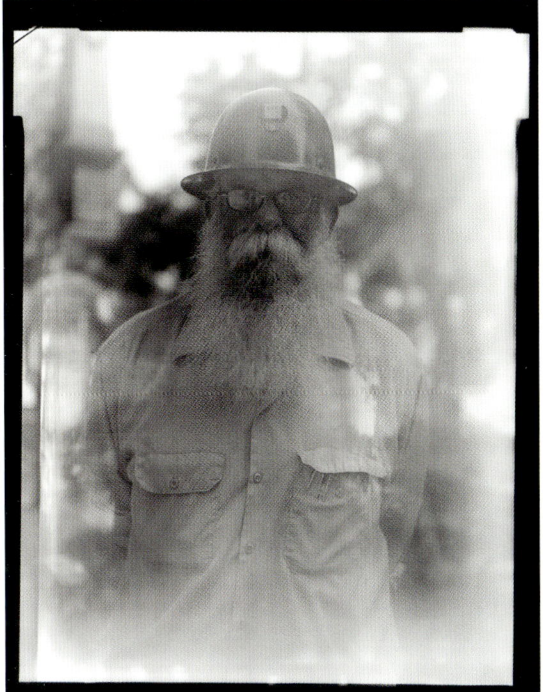
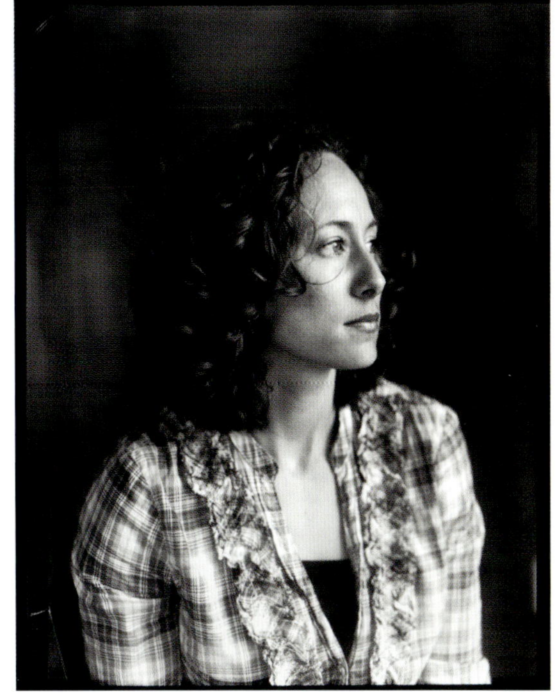
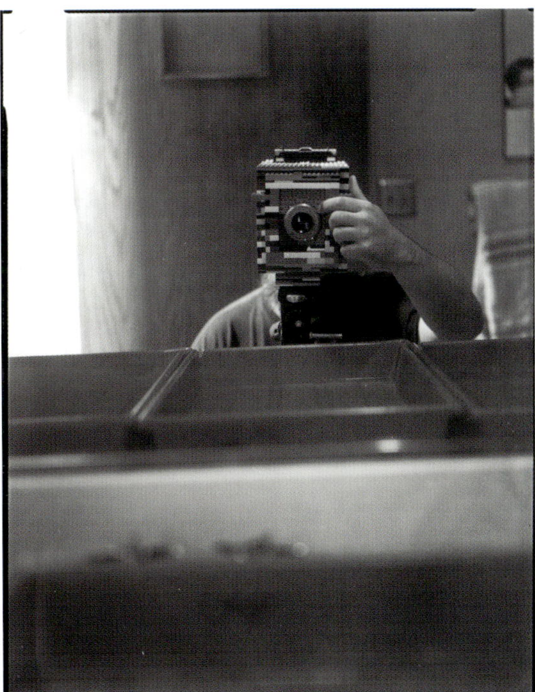
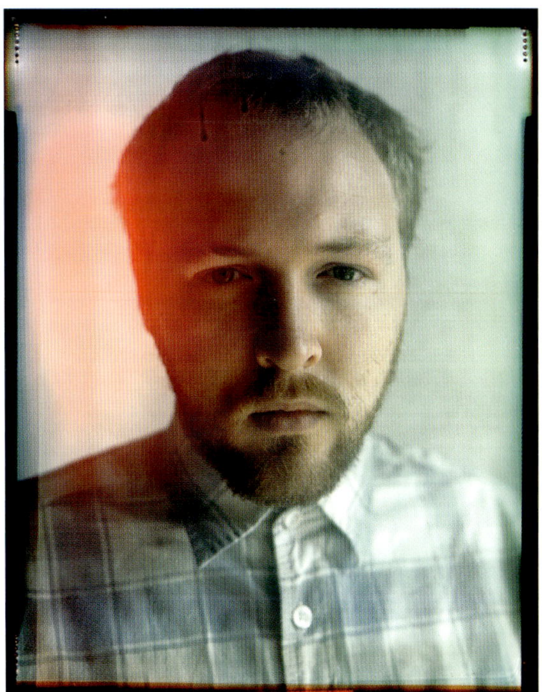

Portraits shot with the Legotron, clockwise from top left: Todd Kiscaden, 2012; Ashley Johnson, 2011; Branden Lower, 2011; self-portrait in bathroom/makeshift darkroom, 2013. All 12 × 9 cm (4¾ × 3½ in.).

MULTICELL GENESIS II

Irish photographer and camera maker James Guerin conceived and built the Genesis II, a multicell lensed camera that creates unique tiled images. It comprises twenty-five lensed sub-cameras, or cells, arranged in a 4 × 5 grid, and is intended primarily for taking portraits.

Guerin first conceived a simple shoebox pinhole camera arranged in a 5 × 5 grid of twenty-five separate light-tight cells, each with its own pinhole. The Genesis II is the lensed version of that design, incorporating twenty 150 mm simple plastic double-convex lenses. Due to the nested box design, the focal range goes from 300 mm (the distance at which there is 1:1 image magnification) to approximately 550 mm. At 300 mm each cell lines up with its neighbour, creating a standard image, but at greater distances the lens coverage overlaps, distorting the image and creating the peculiar tiled effect.

Accurate focusing is achieved with the aid of a simple ground glass (made from Perspex and cellophane tape) and the shutter is a simple sliding sheet of MDF. Other features include focus lock, focus scale, a back for film holders, linear slides for smooth focusing and a tripod mount in the base. The aperture is changed by placing custom 'aperture plates' that slide in front of the lenses.

BELOW

The Genesis II, 2012
Clockwise from top left: camera without shutter board or aperture plate; camera with aperture plate and without shutter board; camera back with ground glass screen; camera back on its own. Below, far right: image (of a globe lamp) as it appears on the ground glass at a distance greater than 300 mm (12 in.).

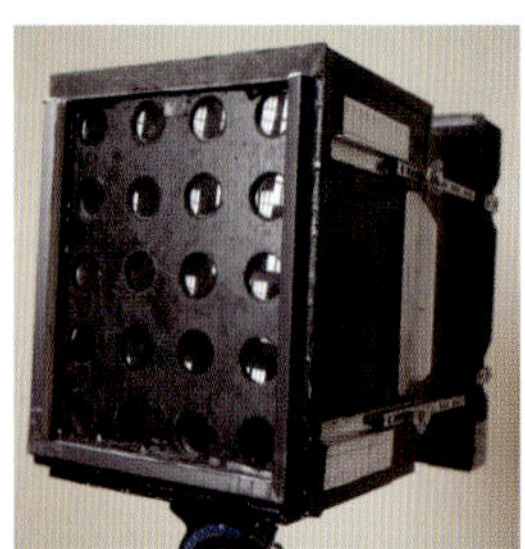
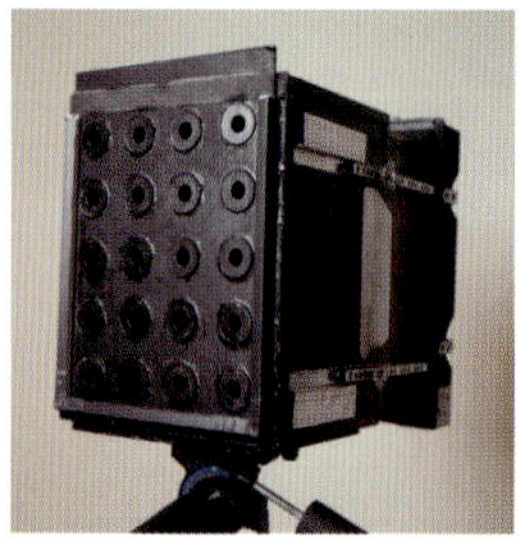
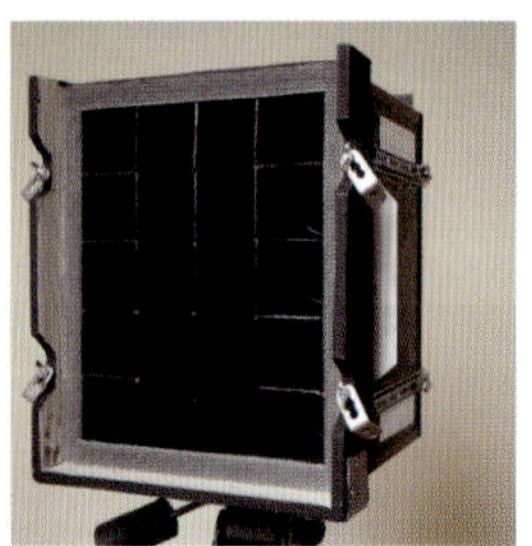
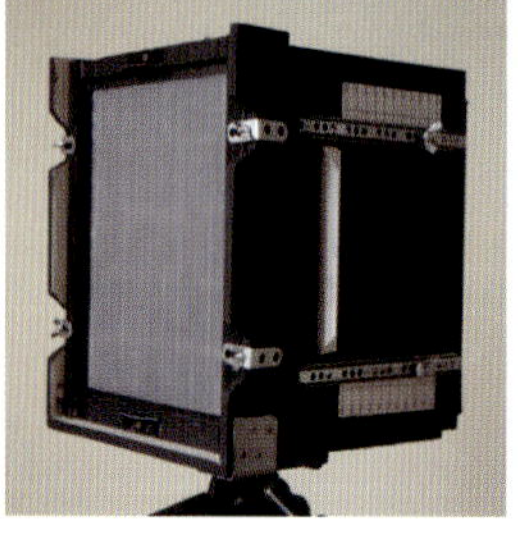
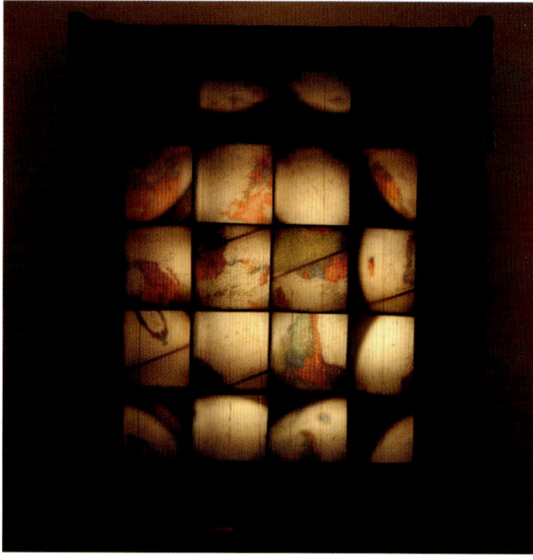

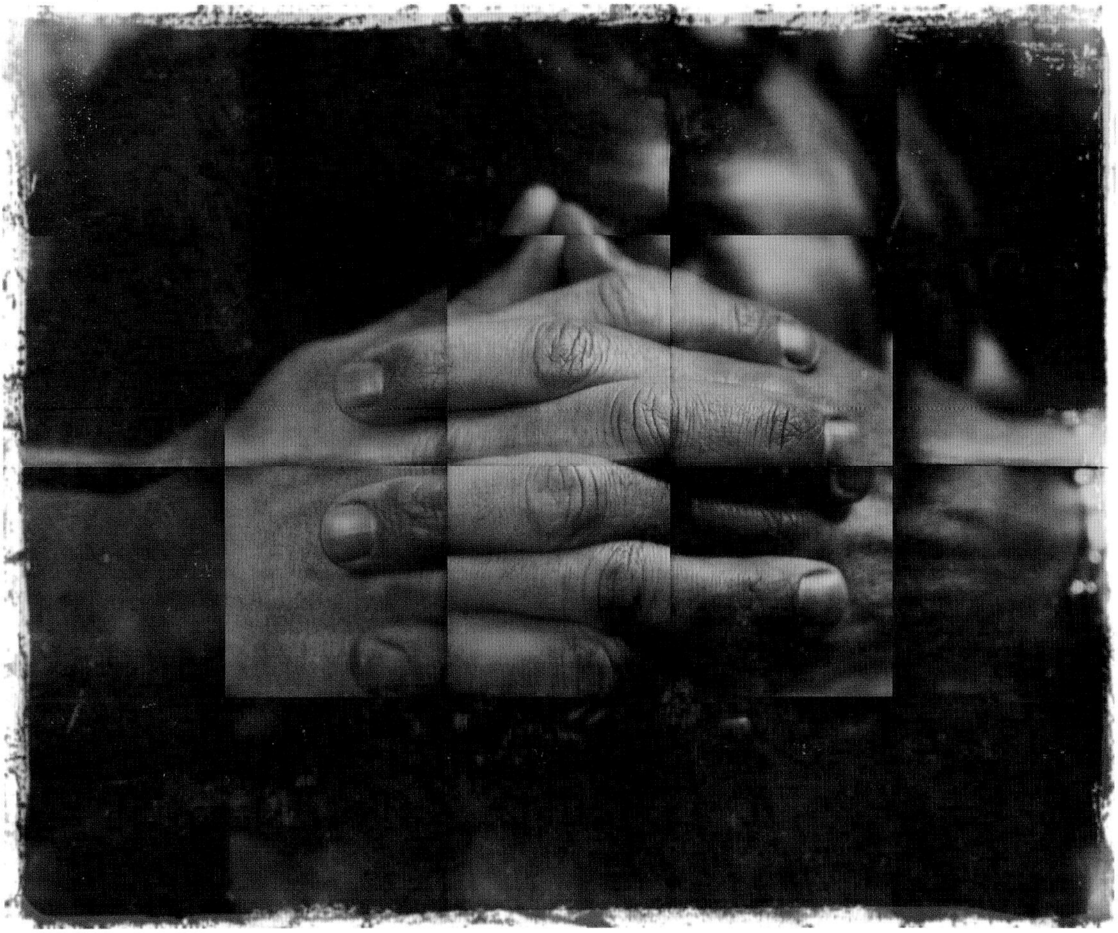

Photos taken with the Genesis II,
20 × 25 cm (7⅞ × 9¾ in.), 2013

'Composition isn't easy as each
image on the ground glass is
back to front and upside-down
and it's hard to align. When I
scan the negative I transpose the
cell in Photoshop to create the
final image. Most of the photos
I've taken with it so far have been
on photographic paper and I've
only just started to use X-ray film.'
James Guerin

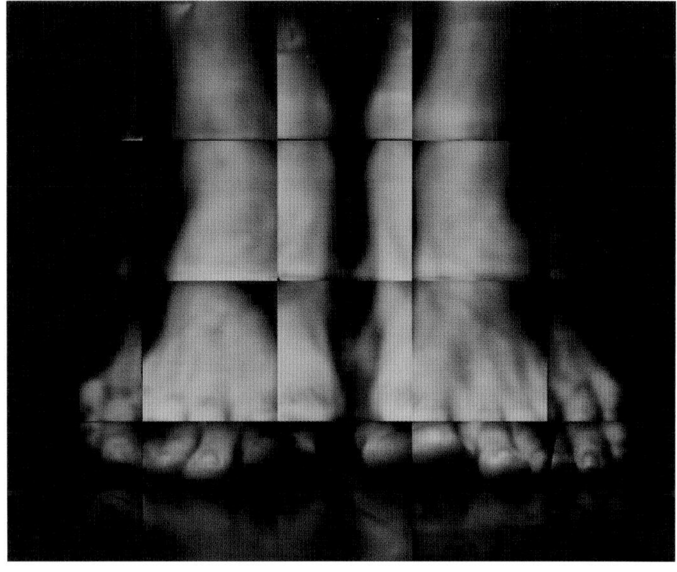

TAIYO ONORATO & NICO KREBS

*Interview
by Marco Antonini*

This eclectic Swiss duo marks the centre of their artistic research as a process-oriented and aesthetic view of the camera as both tool and object.

Your work is decidedly multidisciplinary; did you both study photography?

We both studied photography at the University of Arts in Zurich. After a while we started to add different media to our practice, as it seemed a natural development. Our photography has always included custom-built props, choreography and performance. Installation and film photography are also important, and always have their roots in an initial picture.

Your collection of variously altered and/or composed road-trip pictures, The Great Unreal, *is a good example of your creative approach to the limits of photo-verité… but it's interesting to note how other series actually limit your ability to alter the final image; for instance, your direct-to-positive prints.*

Every technical approach has its own characteristics that you can bend, play with and use to explore ideas. For example, positive paper has a distinctive nineteenth-century look, a very low light sensitivity and a high chance of unpredictable imperfections. The long exposure times led us first to work with objects and still lifes and then with movement and kinetic sculptures. Physical limitations can be a huge source of inspiration.

BELOW
Armadillo, sculpture,
30 × 35 × 30 cm
(11¾ × 13¾ × 11¾ in.),
2012

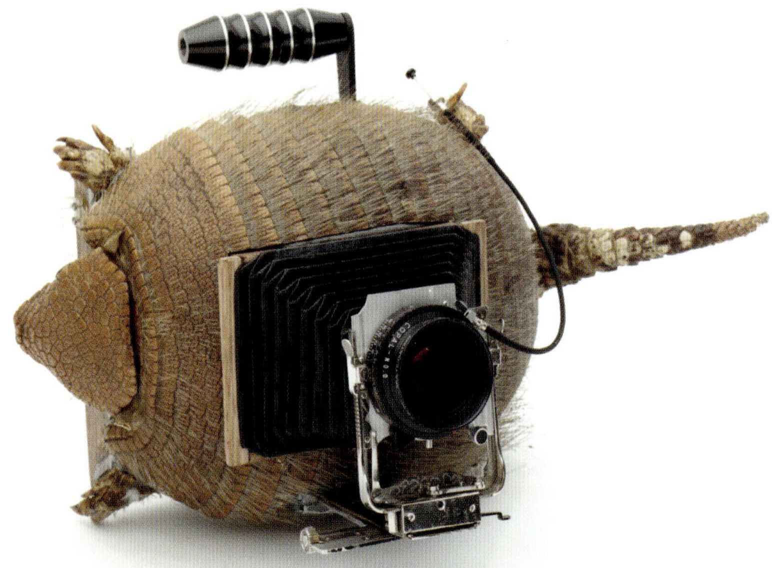

OPPOSITE
O4 (magenta yellow), C-print,
95 × 70 cm (37⅜ × 27½ in.), 2012

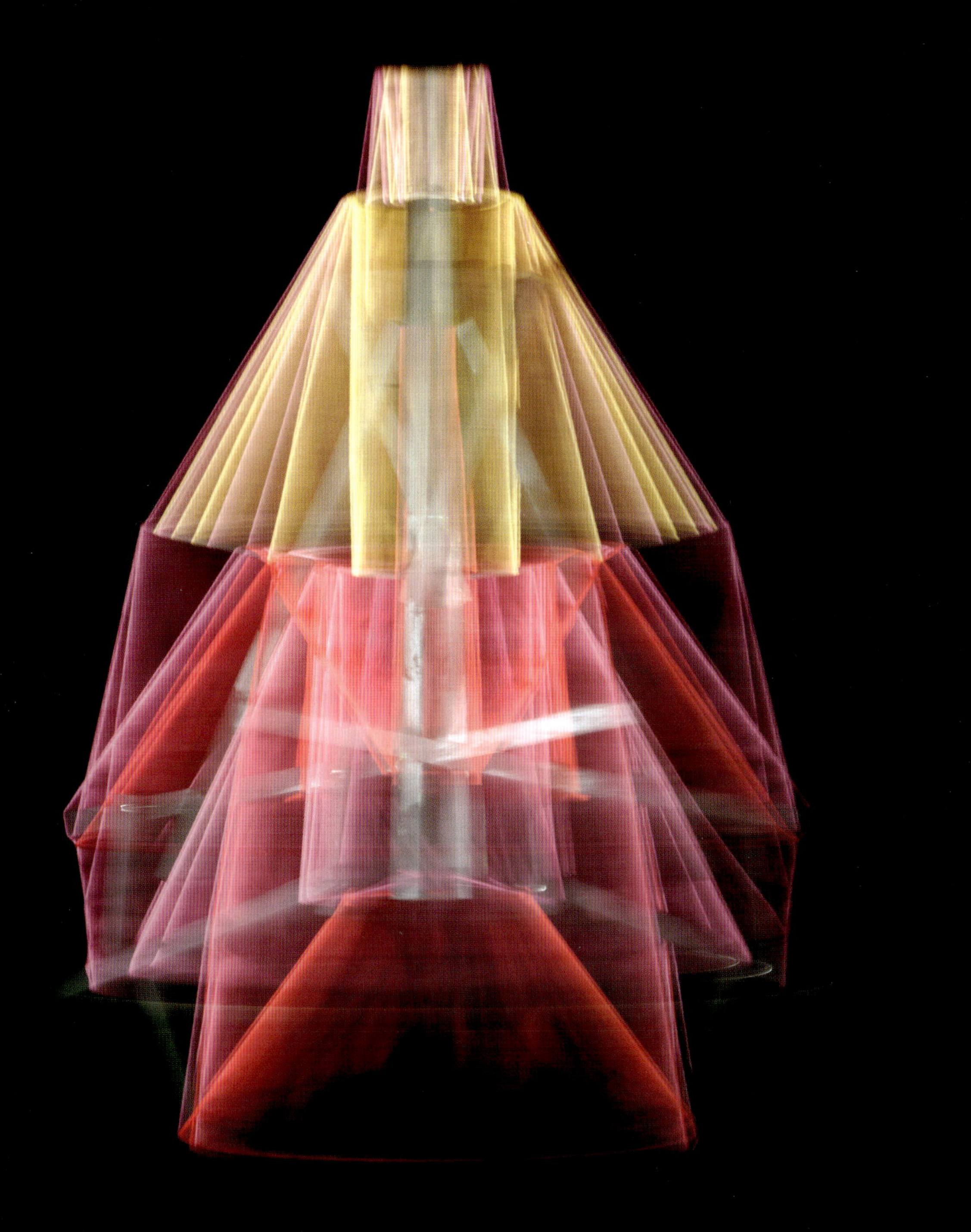

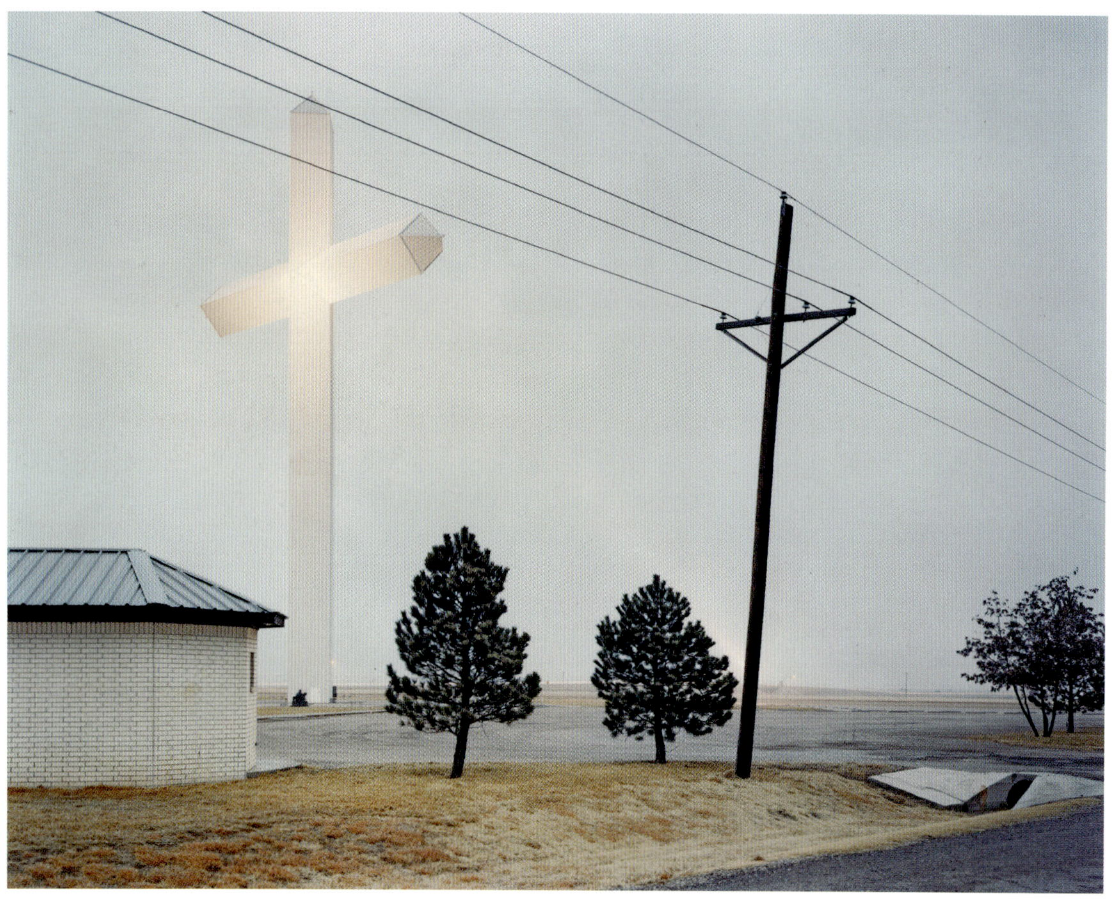

What inspired you to create the surreal custom photo equipment for your As Long As It Photographs... *series? Do all the cameras work? Were they primarily created to take photographs or was their design dictated by conceptual concerns?*

Our work is very process-oriented, which means that the road we travelled to assemble and create our cameras was long, with many detours. Each camera began with radically different objectives. After we got in contact with the internet camera community (while seeking advice for technical problems), we started to become interested in basic questions around the tool that can be seen as the very centre of the medium. All the cameras are functional, as this was a prerequisite when we started to build them. However, they were always thought of more as objects, as stimulating sculptures, rather than as functioning tools.

Biggest Cross in Texas, C-print, 39 × 50 cm (15⅜ × 19¾ in.), 2005

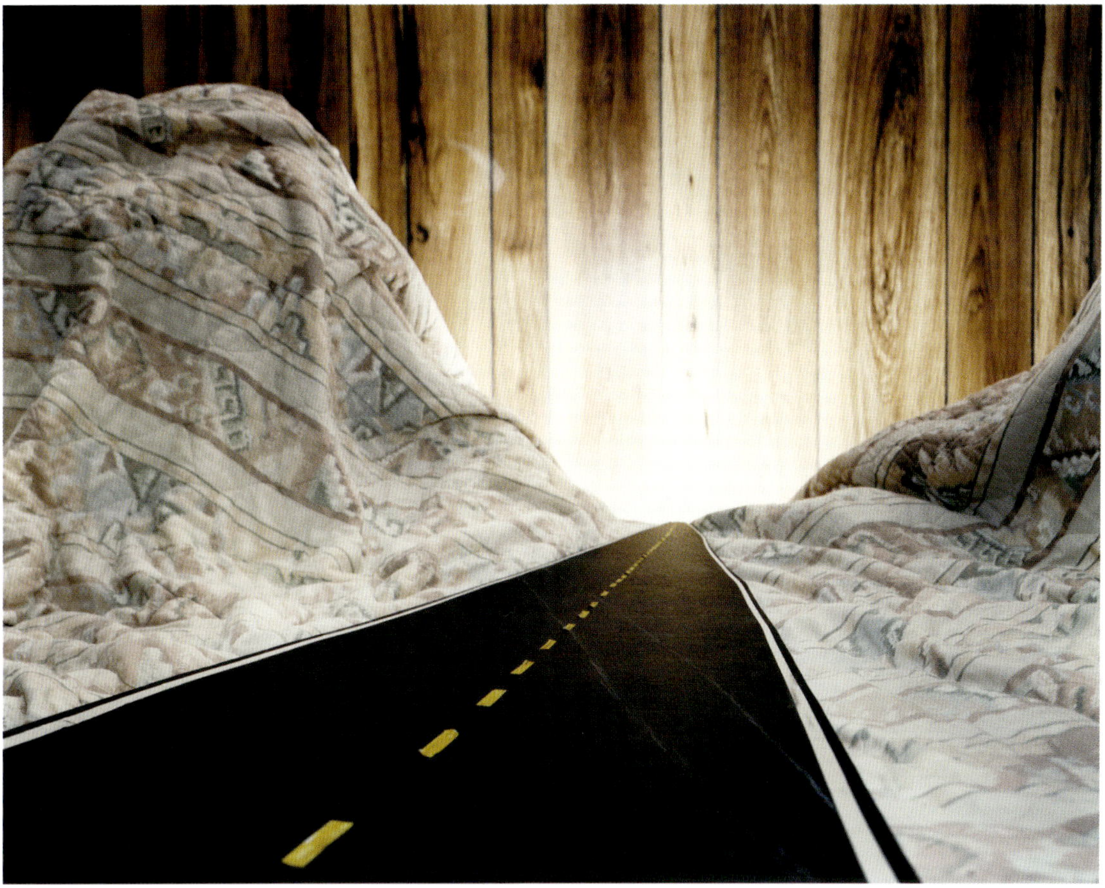

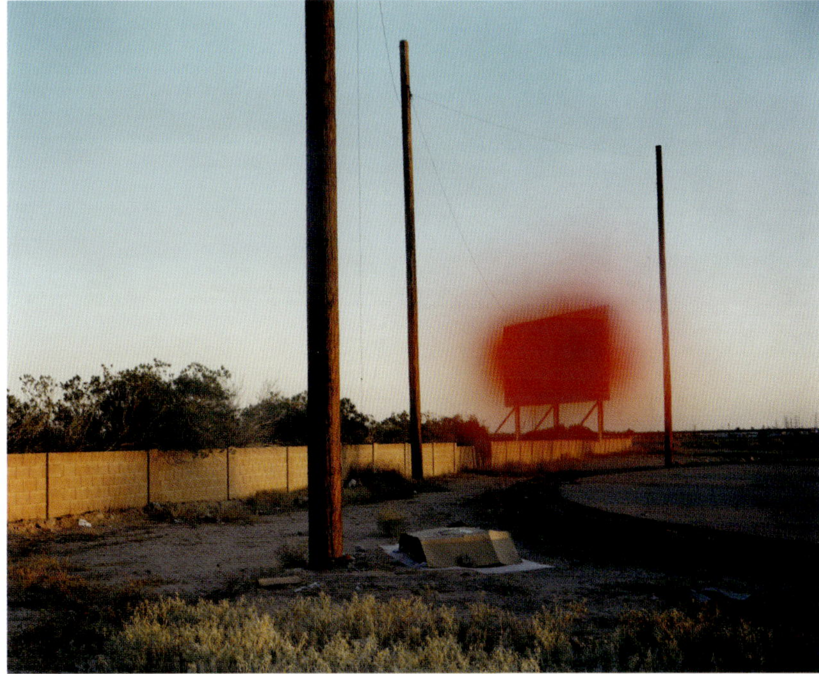

ABOVE
Bed Street, C-print, 46 × 55 cm
(18⅛ × 21⅝ in.), 2006

LEFT
Red Glow, C-print, 94 × 120 cm
(37 × 47¼ in.), 2006

Some of the pictures shot with your custom-built cameras show evident flaws, almost to the point of acquiring a sort of camera-specific graphic signature, like the rows of light present in the Book Cam *prints. Did you leave that to chance or was it possible to test, control and/or tweak the outcome of each camera?*

Every camera has flaws, even brand-new ones straight from the shop. In our case, it was much more interesting to think about what these self-built cameras represent than about what they are able to mechanically reproduce.

Ontologically speaking, what is photography to you? How do you think the nature and purpose of the medium has changed in response to both technical developments and the changing awareness of the public?

Photography is a very exciting tool, a magic door, an interpreter, storyteller, poet, encryptor. The nature and purpose of photography are constantly changing; they always have. Technical developments have opened wider access to photography and more people are using it than ever, also more thoughtlessly and aimlessly than ever, but that's just another step in the ever-changing shapeshift of the medium.

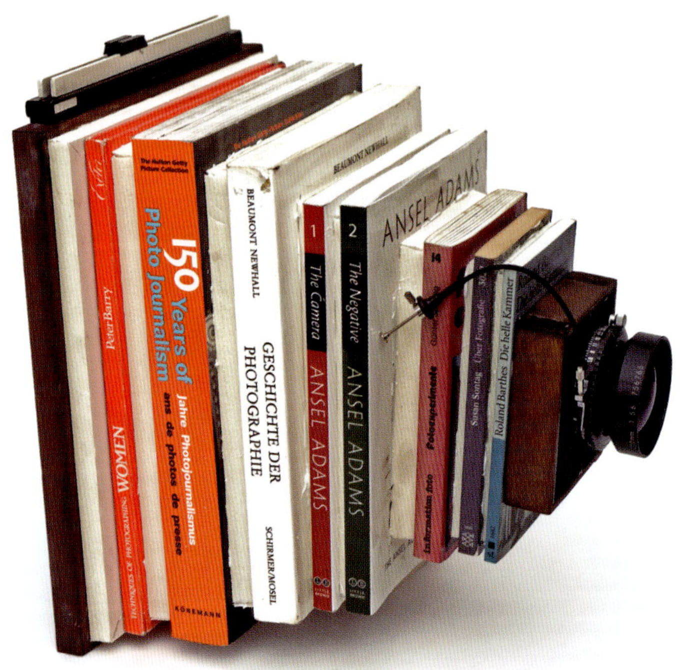

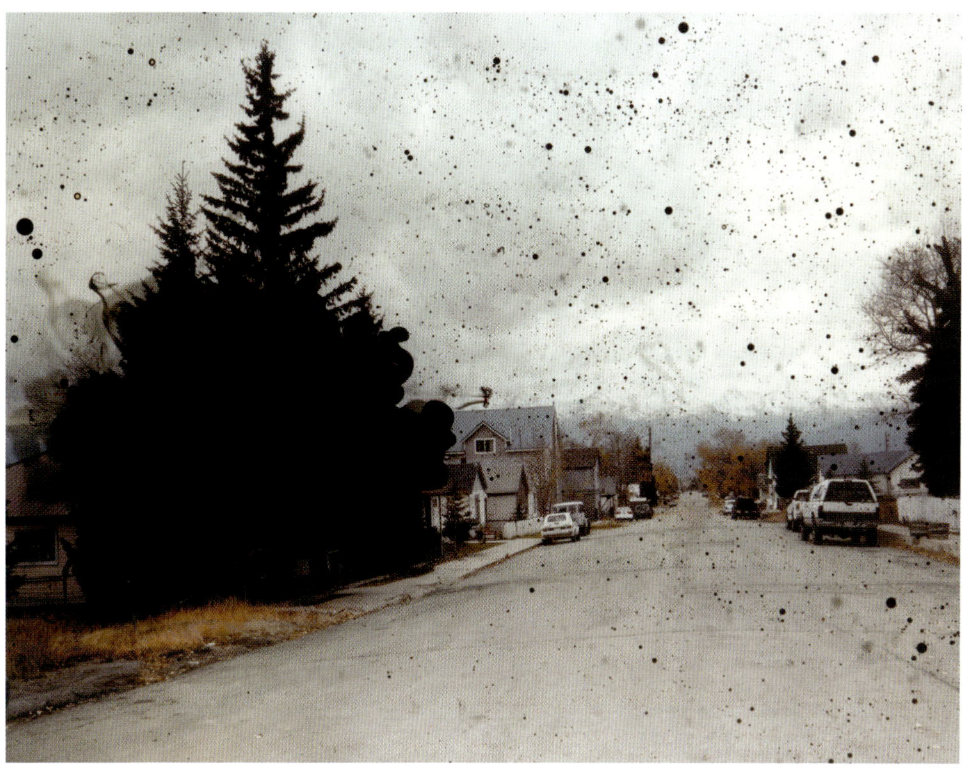

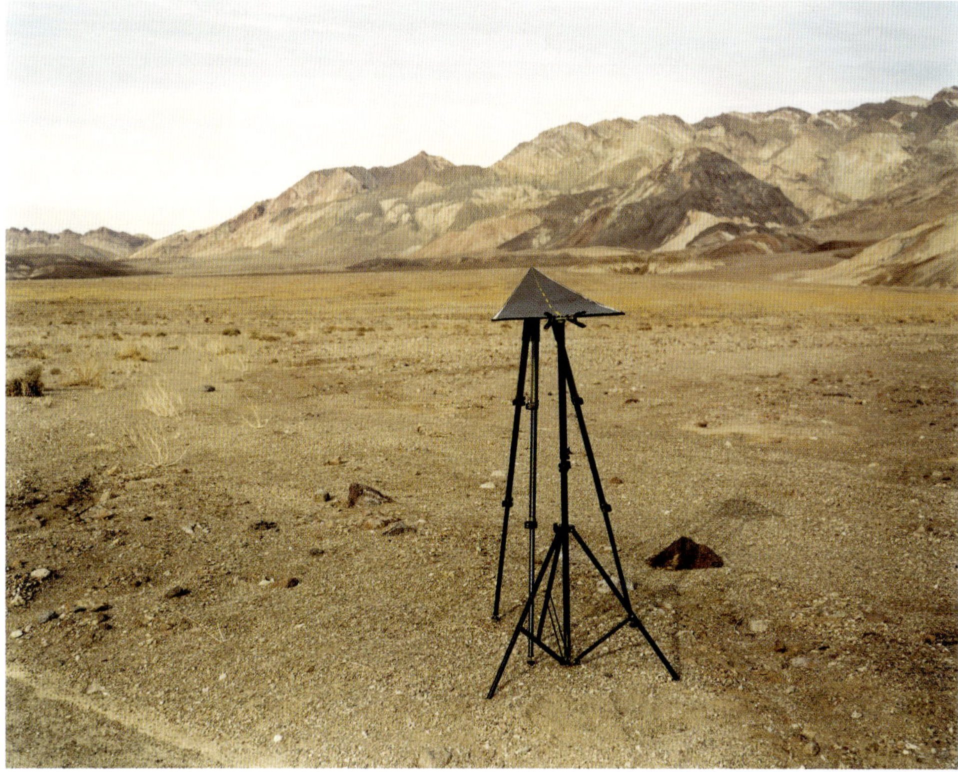

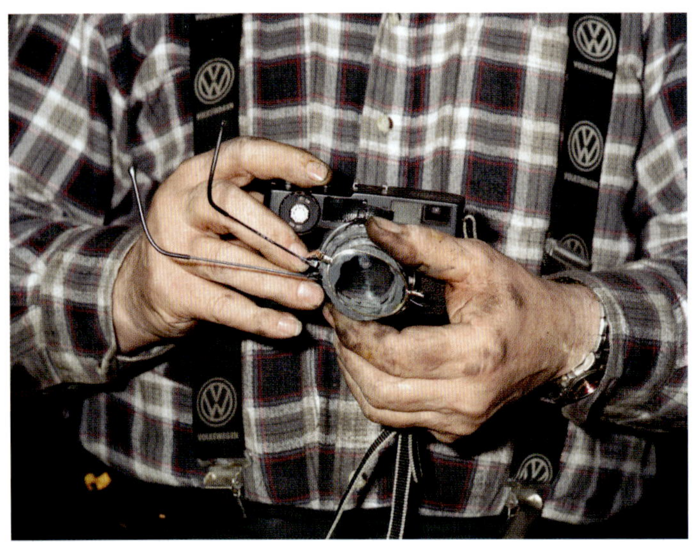

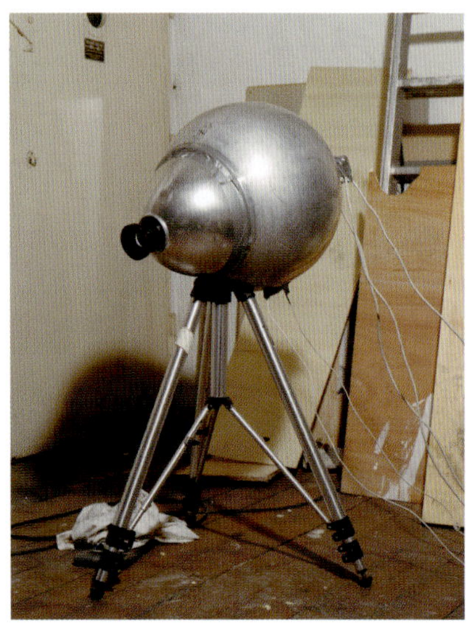

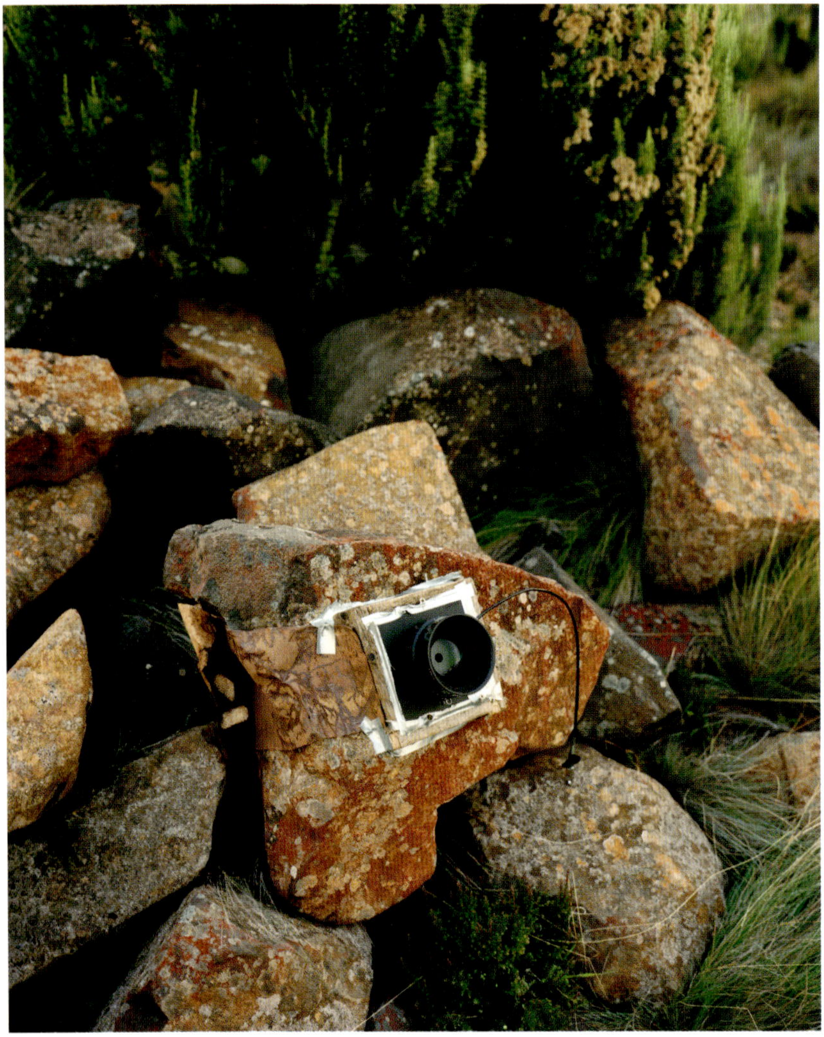

Taiyo Onorato & Nico Krebs
Creator, C-print, 26 × 33 cm
(10¼ × 13 in.), 2011

Taiyo Onorato & Nico Krebs
Kugel Camera, C-print,
27 × 22 cm (10⅝ × 8¾ in.),
2011

Taiyo Onorato & Nico Krebs
Stone Camera, C-print,
19.5 × 25.3 cm (7¾ × 10 in.),
2010

Taiyo Onorato & Nico Krebs
O5 (blue), C-print, 95 × 70 cm
(37⅜ × 27½ in.), 2012

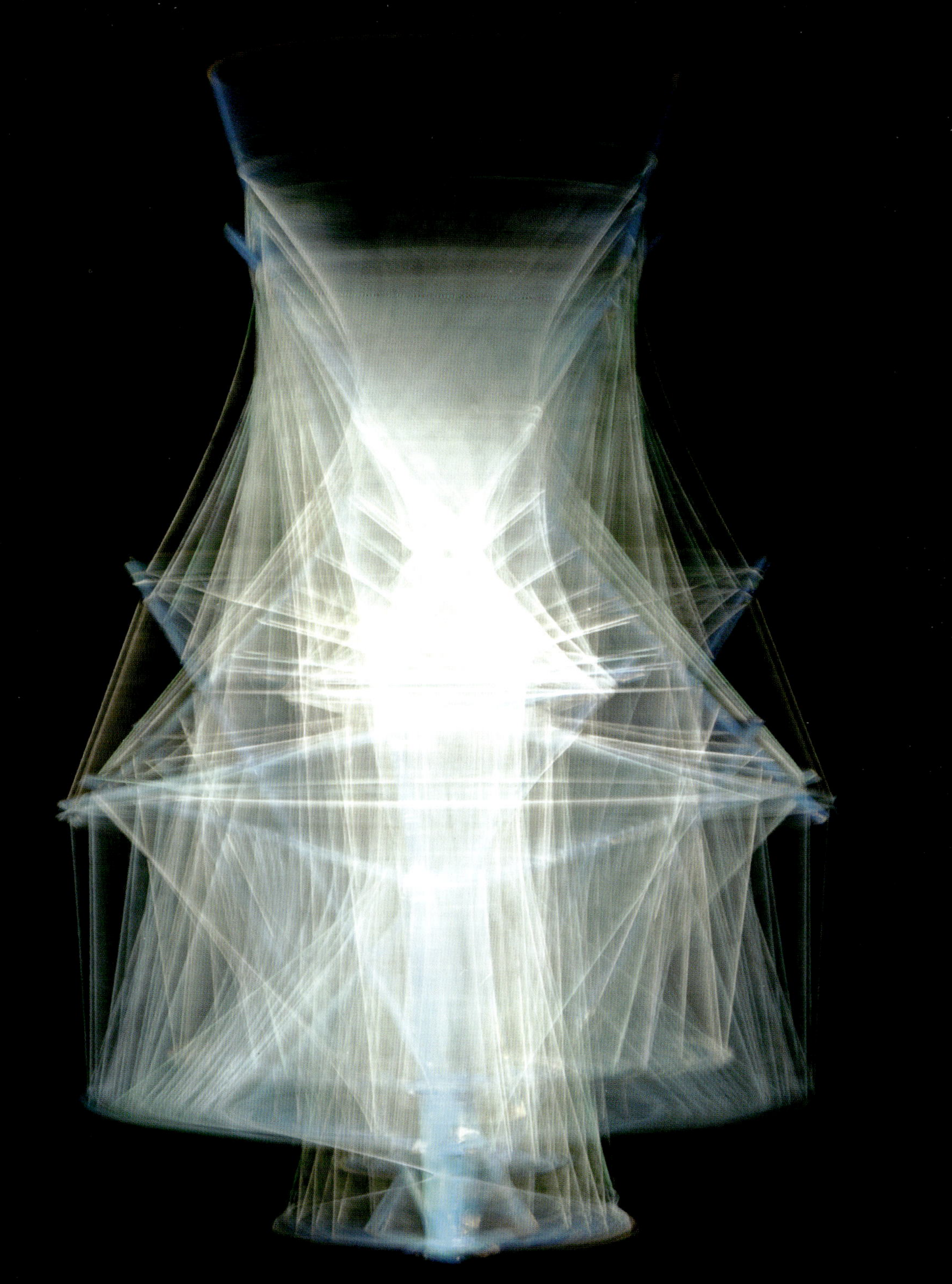

LOMOGRAPHY

This mass response to the growing despair at digital homologation uses simple, inexpensive cameras that date back to the Soviet era and produce beautiful low-fi imagery.

Lomography began in the early 1990s when a group of Viennese students visiting Prague found a used Lomo Kompakt Automat in a shop. The Lomo LC-A was a Soviet-made compact camera, very different from anything they'd ever seen. It produced wonderful, saturated images with vibrant colours and vignettes framing every shot. The students brought it back to Vienna, where interest in the Lomo grew quickly, encouraged by the analogue photography community that was blossoming online at the same time. Initially, the Lomo could only be bought new in Russia, and was about to be discontinued, but anticipating the low-fi vintage photo trend, the Lomography founders flew to St Petersburg and worked out a contract for the worldwide distribution and production of the camera. Lomography has since become an international movement for reviving analogue photography, and the focus of numerous exhibitions, installations, conventions and websites. In addition to the LC-A, other Soviet-era models, including the Holga, the Diana and the Lubitel, are used by fans, both as vintage originals and as modern reproductions. The LomoWall, consisting of thousands of Lomo snapshots stuck to a physical or virtual wall, remains the movement's distinctive mode of display.

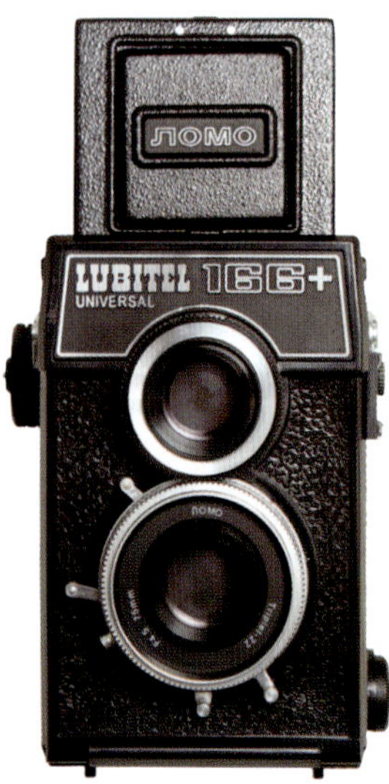

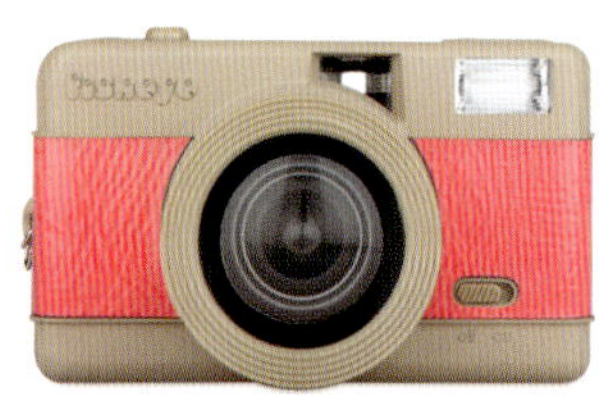

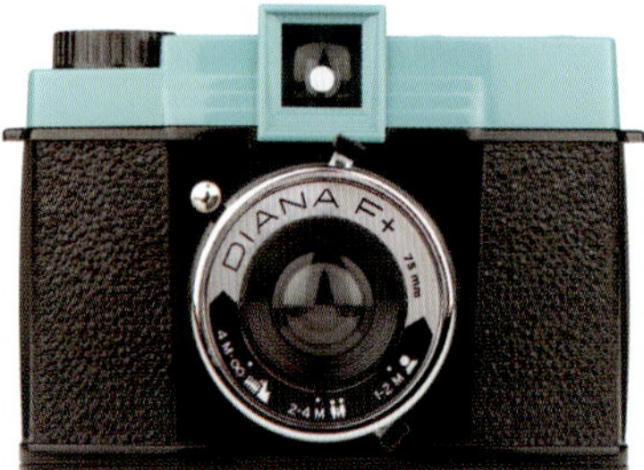

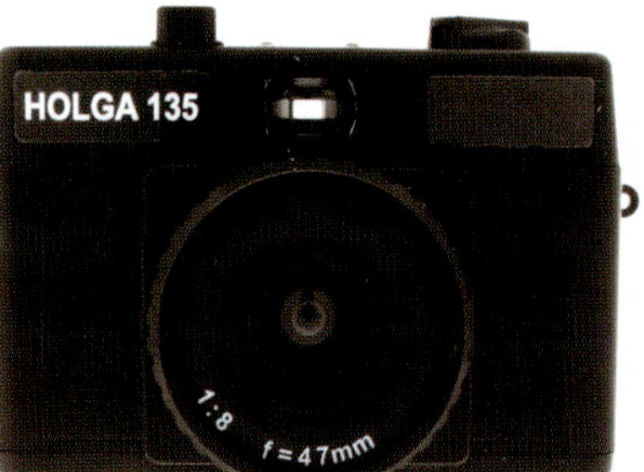

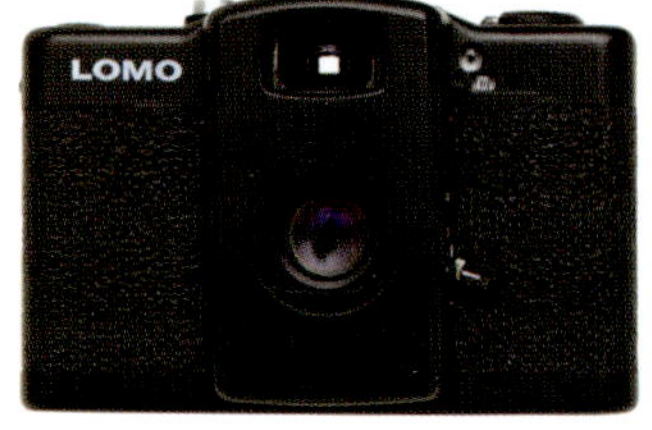

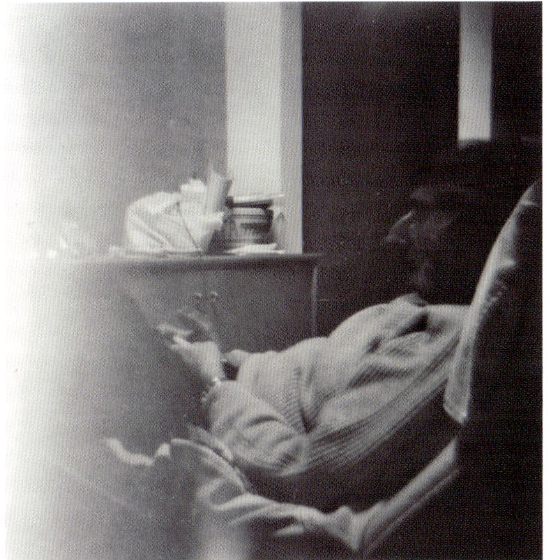
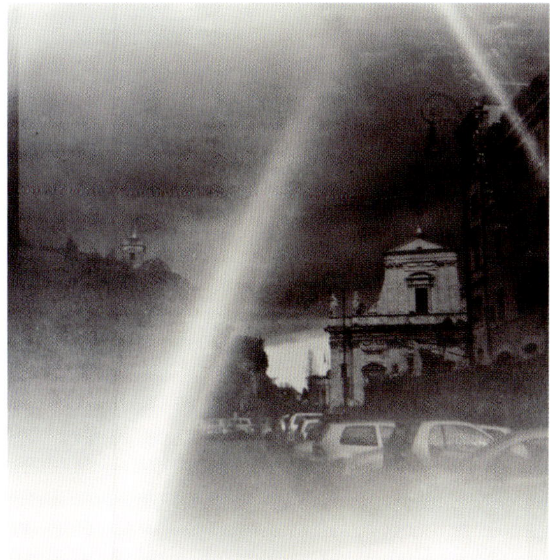
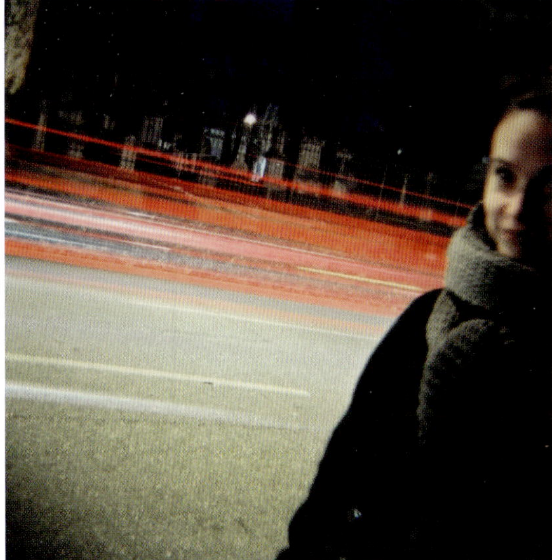
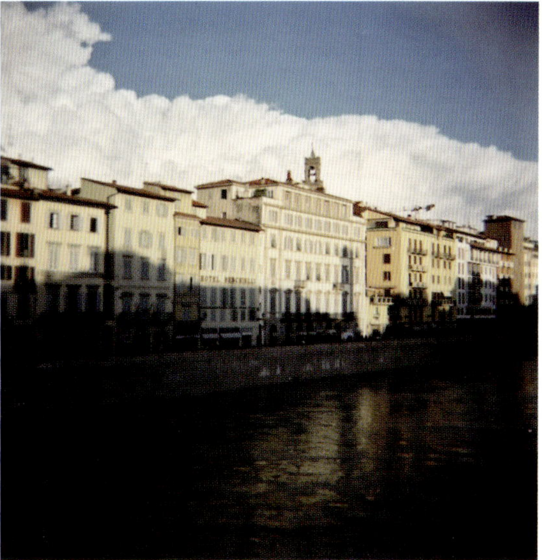

Clockwise from top right: Holga 135;
Lomo LC-A+; Diana F+; Lomo Lubitel
166+ U; Fisheye One

Aaron Kossmann
Images shot on a Diana F+

From top to bottom: Diana Mini;
Fisheye No. 2; Fisheye One

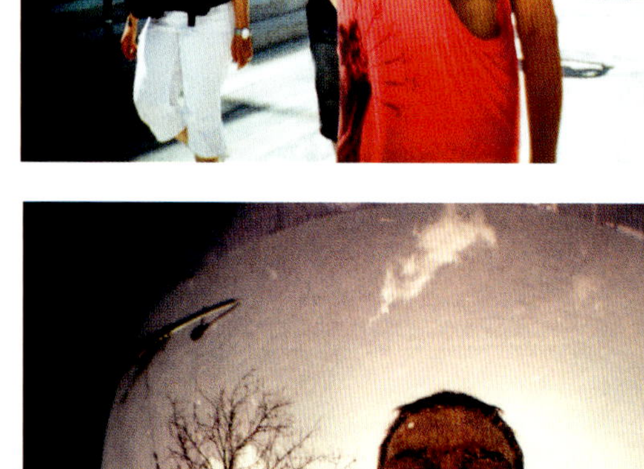

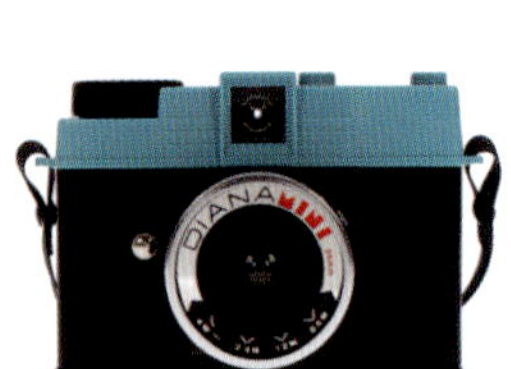

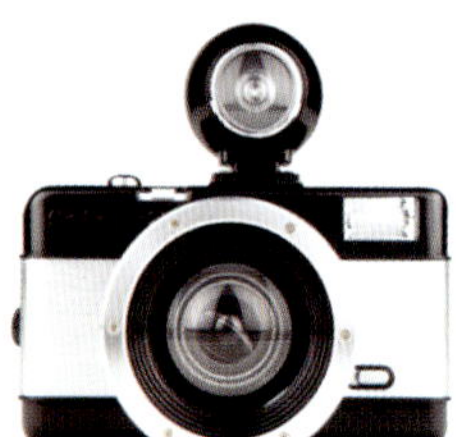

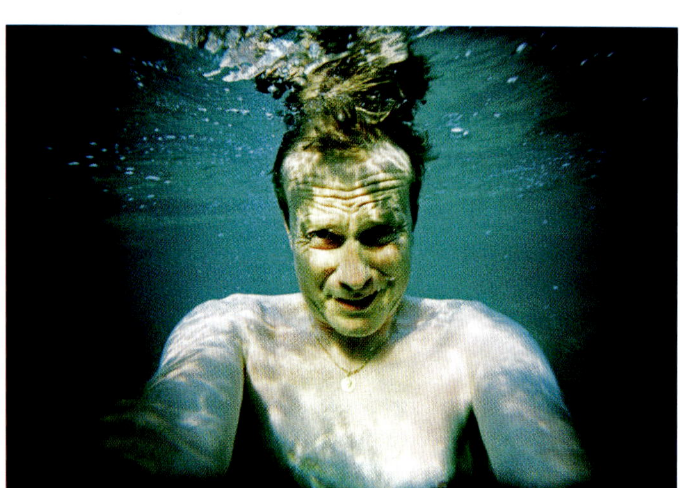

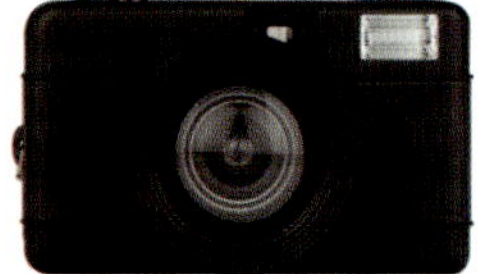

From top to bottom: Konstruktor;
Horizon Kompakt; SuperSampler

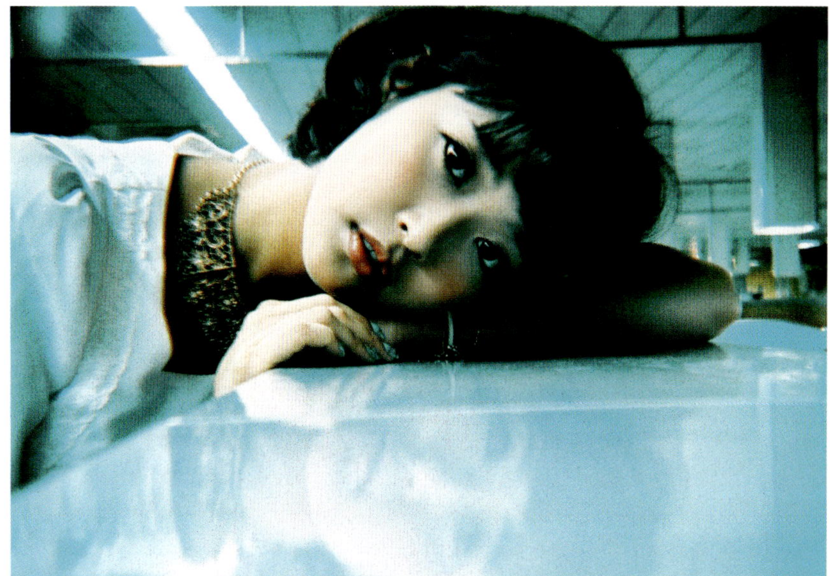

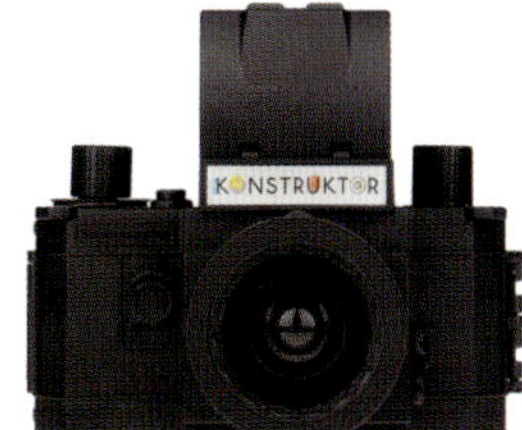

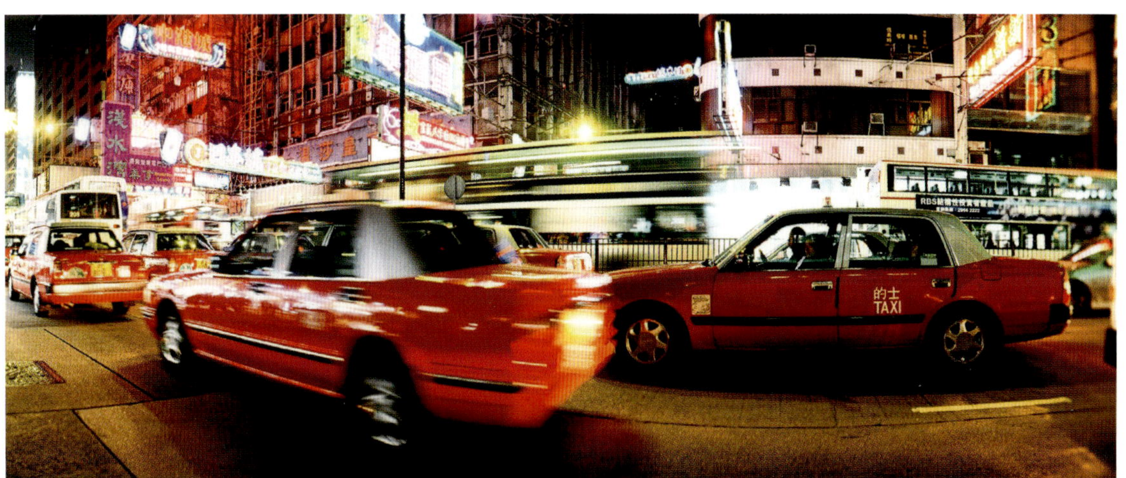

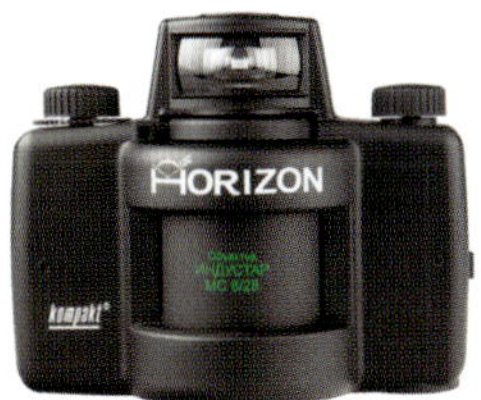

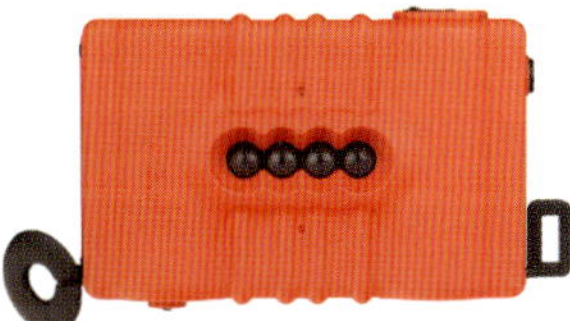

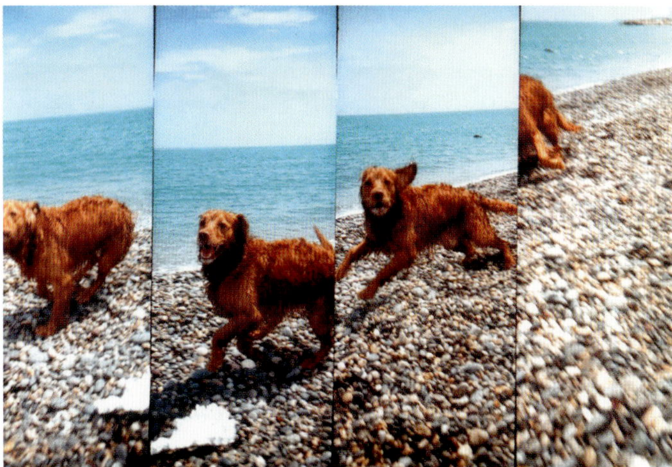

DISPOSABLE CAMERAS

Thanks to their low cost and widespread availability, disposable cameras open up many possibilities for experimentation, from hacking to collective projects and underwater photography.

A disposable or single-use camera is a simple box camera usually made out of cardboard or plastic and equipped with a fixed-focus lens. The earliest mass-market model was the Utsurun-Desu produced by Fujifilm in 1986; more recent models have incorporated integrated flashes and waterproof or shock-resistant housing. Affordable prices and simple operation make disposable cameras ideal for hacking, with applied filters, lens alterations or other changes. They are also great for collective projects involving members of the public. One example is the Disposable Camera Project (DCP), an interactive and dynamic global photo album that profiles places through the eyes of the people who share them. Organizers Mark Serrano and Michaelangelo Yambao, based in Toronto, and Nick Hill and Paul Nuestro, based in Vancouver, explain how it works: 'We leave a disposable camera with attached instructions in several popular locations. People either intentionally find them through our social media hints, or by chance. They use the camera, then put it back. We come to pick it up when the roll is done and put the photos on the website. In less than four months the project has spread globally and is now in six countries and nine cities with over eighty albums available online. A stolen kiss, a daring selfie, sunrises and sunsets, couples, groups, babies & dogs: we've seen it all, from around the world.'

The Disposable Camera Project
All the images opposite were taken in 2013 with disposable cameras left in public spaces in Toronto, Vancouver, Los Angeles and Brooklyn.

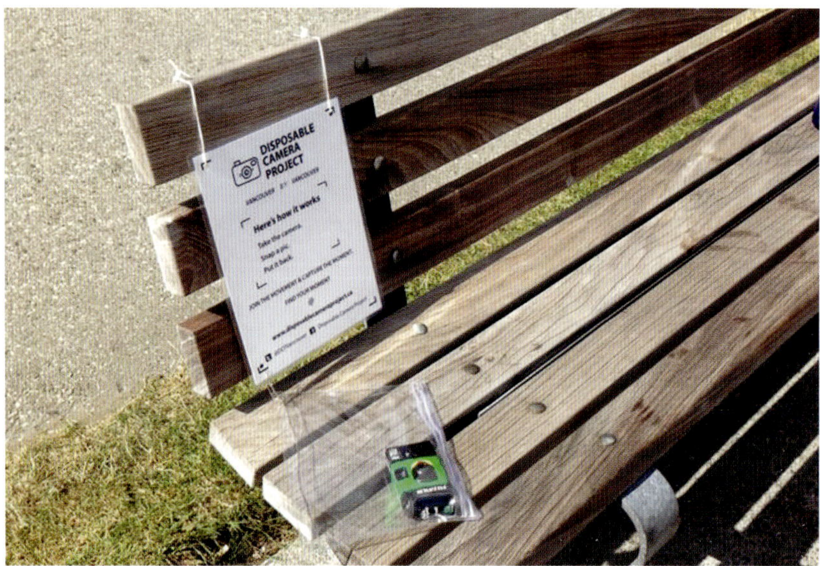

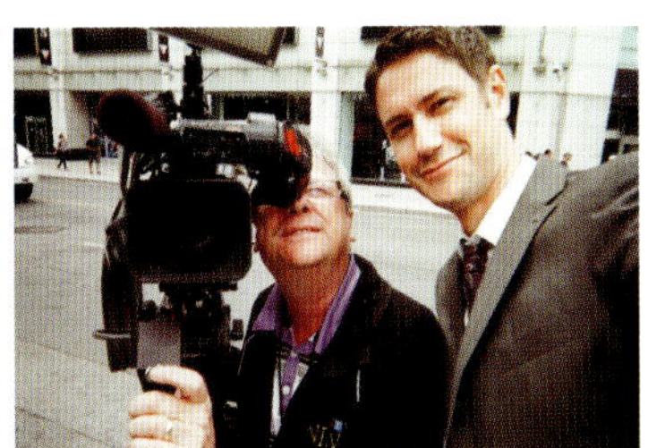
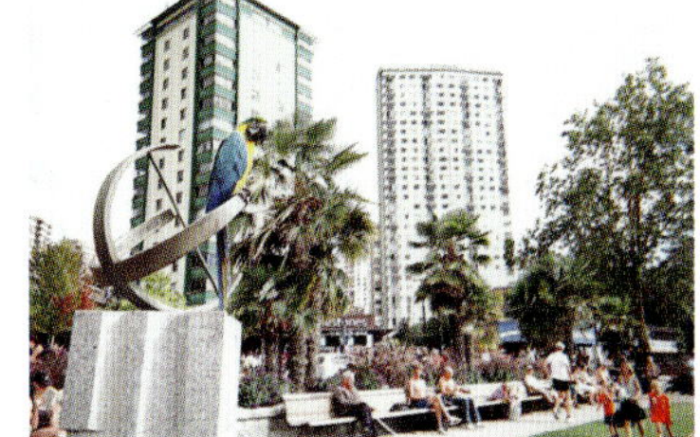
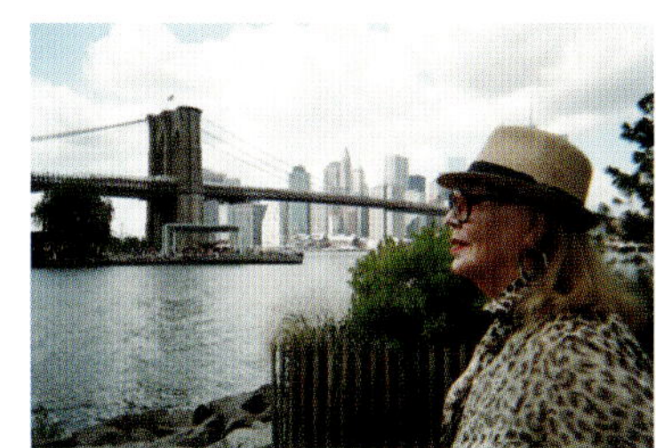
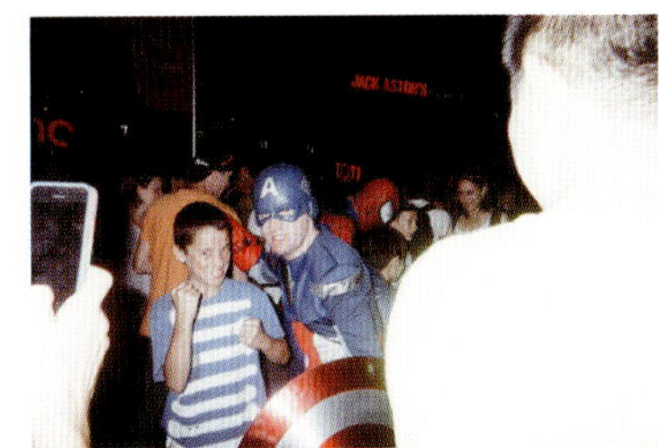
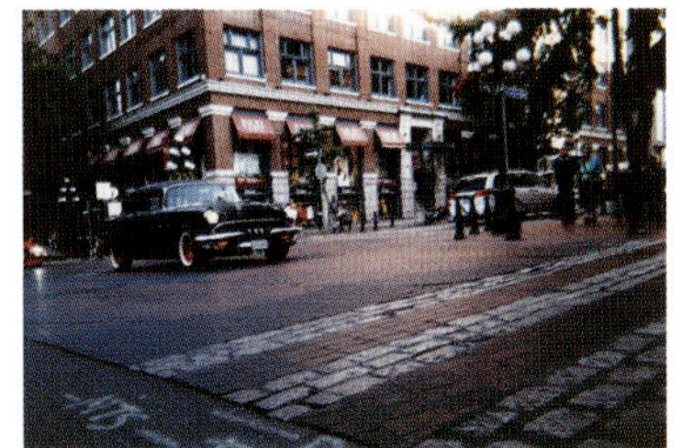
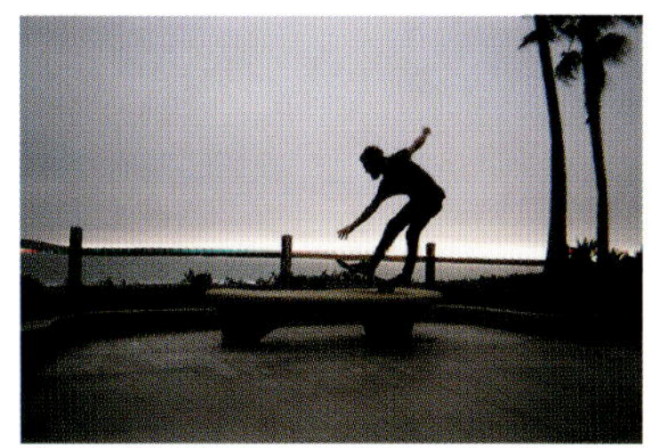
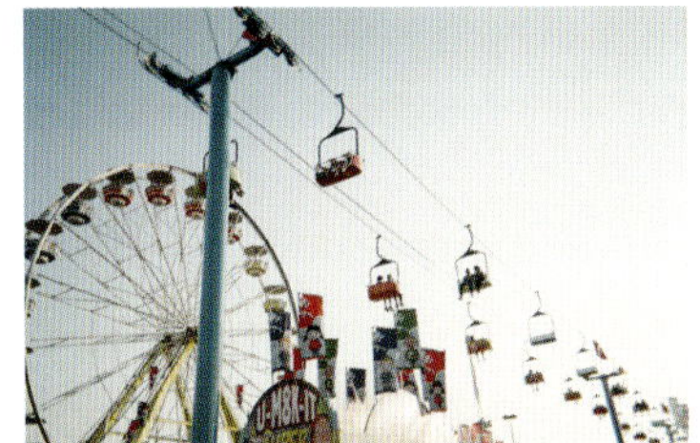
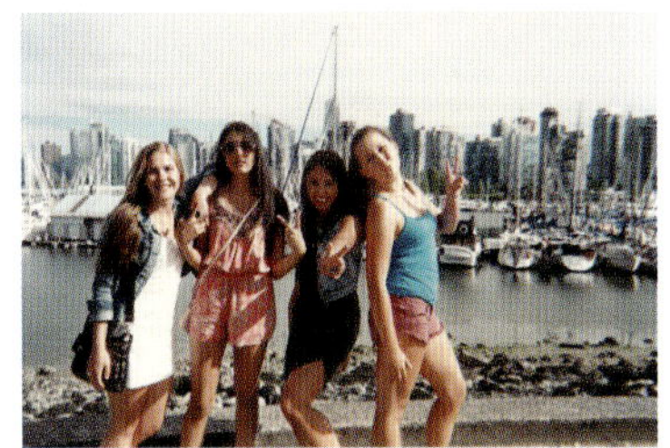
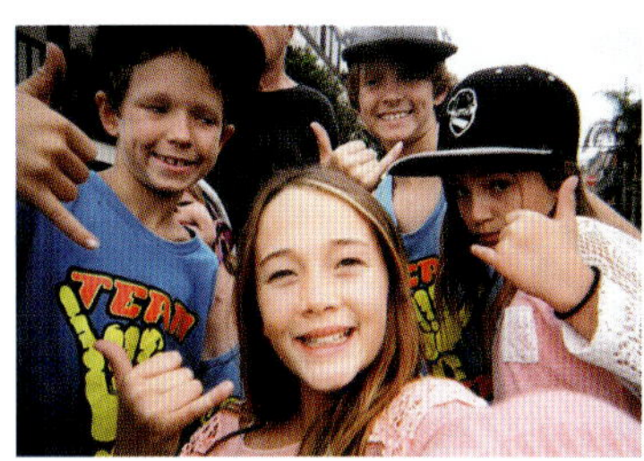
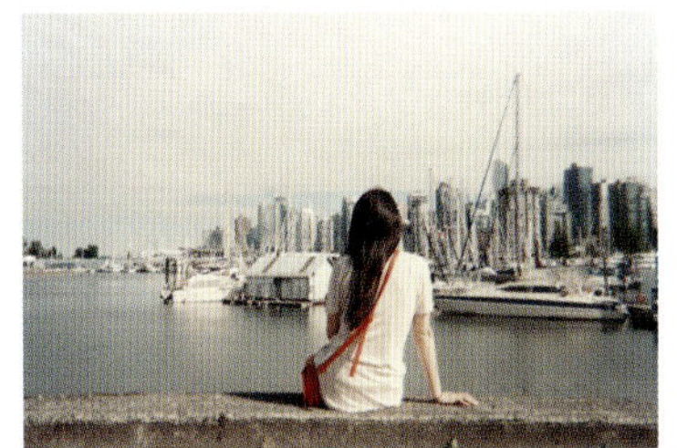
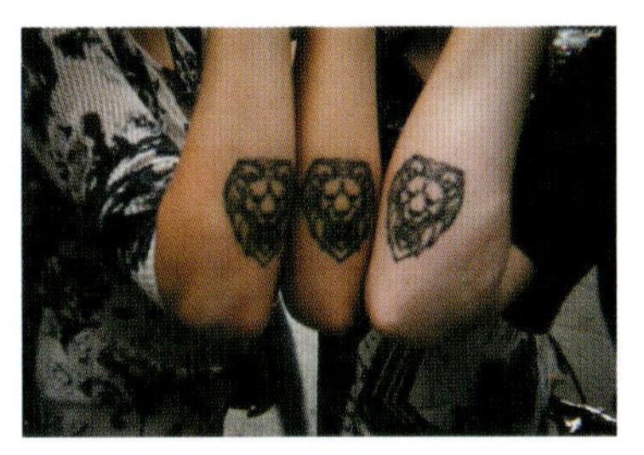
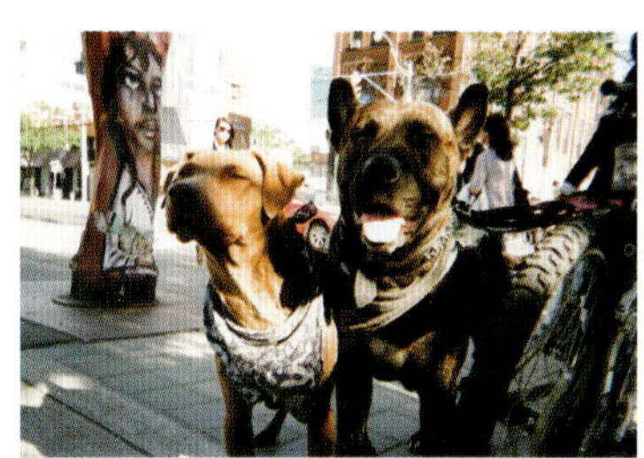
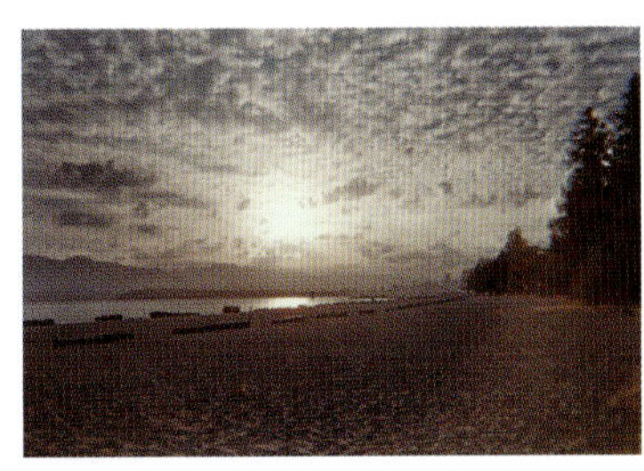
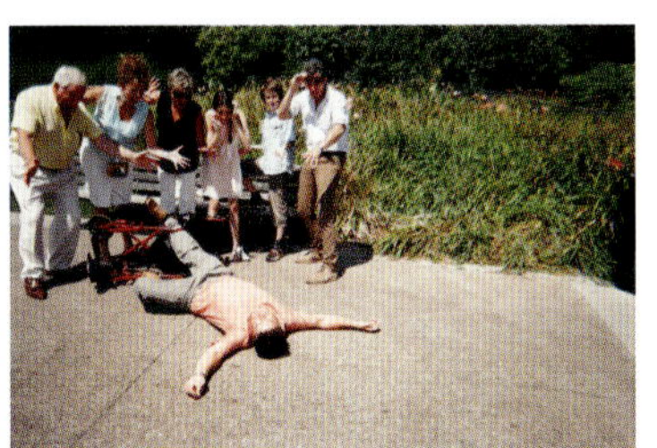
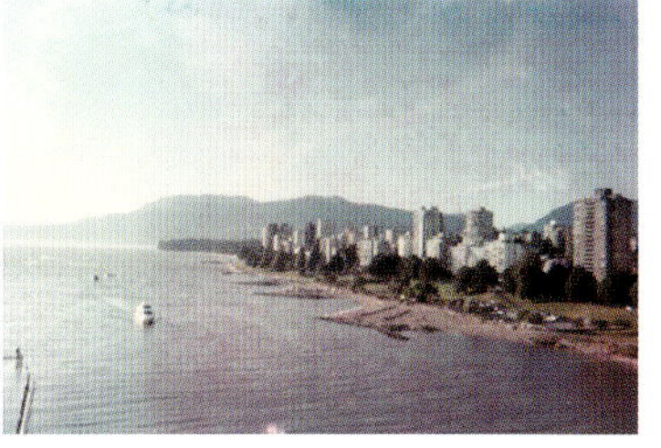
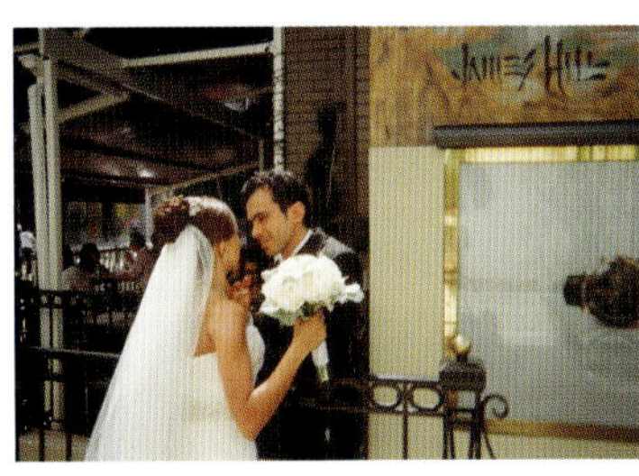
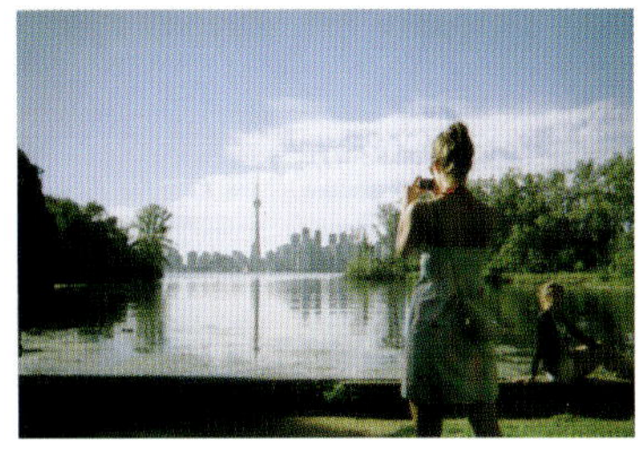
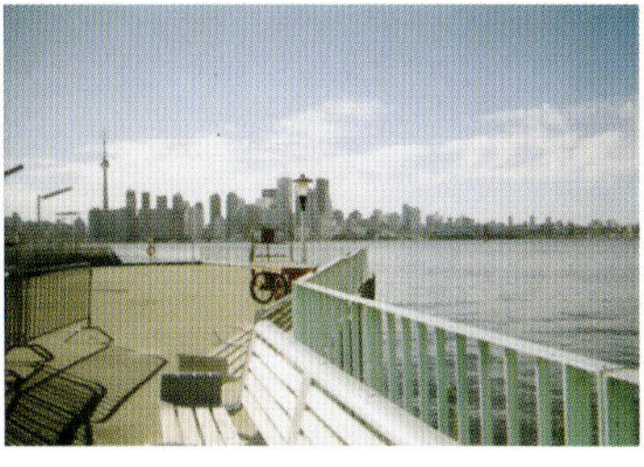

JNO COOK
*Interview by
Beth Horning**

Photographer, sculptor, filmmaker, art critic and self-defined 'aesthetic investigator', Dutch-born American Jno Cook is a legendary figure in alternative photography who has elevated the construction and hacking of cameras and optical equipment to an art form.

There are more and cheaper ways to take a picture than the companies that manufacture cameras would lead you to believe, the Chicago photographer asserts, and the cameras he has constructed from apartment-door peepholes, cookie tins, cardboard boxes, and various used spare parts prove his point. The prints that result are noteworthy too: not only are they beautiful, but they show how much sheer aesthetic freedom is possible for those who refuse to passively accept whatever pricey, touch-me-not technology the photo industry dishes out. With degrees in electrical and industrial engineering, Cook is naturally more intrepid than most about taking technology into his own hands. But he insists that other people could do the same things he has done as long as they're willing to invest a little time and effort. 'Cameras and lenses date from the thirteenth century, and the principles of their operation can be summed up on the back of an envelope,' he has written. 'In building or modifying my equipment I have not used any knowledge that could not be found in high school texts on geometry and physics.' To inspire others to educate themselves and embark on experiments of their own, he exhibited his funky, odd-looking homemade cameras at the Randolph Street gallery in Chicago and at the List Visual Arts Center at MIT. As all this suggests, Cook's approach to both technology and art is thoughtful, original and, especially, humanistic.

Jno Cook
Sketch of the 16" × 20" Backyard Camera, reclaimed materials: process camera, aerial lens, packard shutter, toilet flush handle, red wagon and small boy, 99 × 53.4 × 61 cm (39 × 21 × 24 in.), 1990

*A longer version of this interview originally appeared as 'Radically Recycled Cameras' in *Technology Review Magazine*, August 1990.

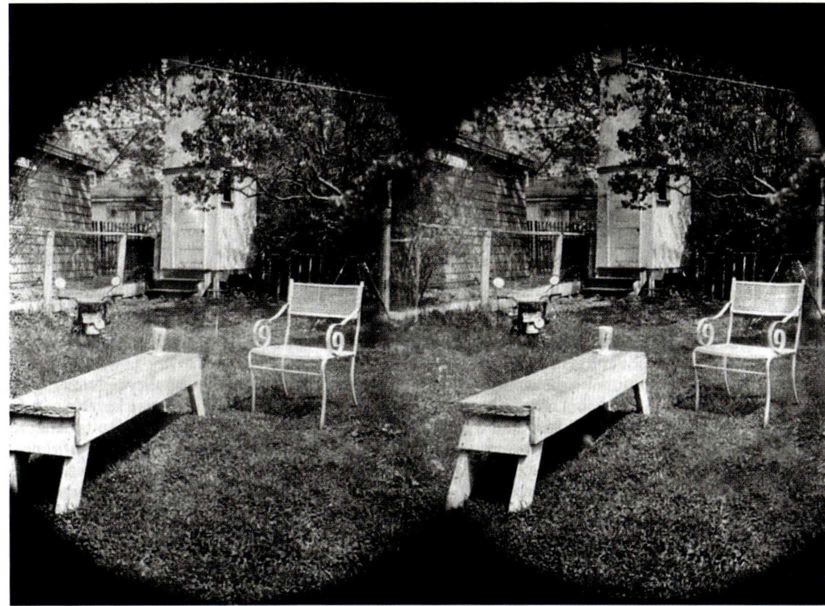

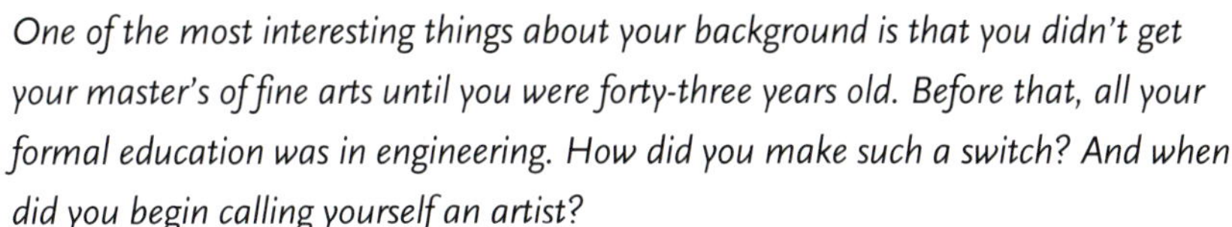

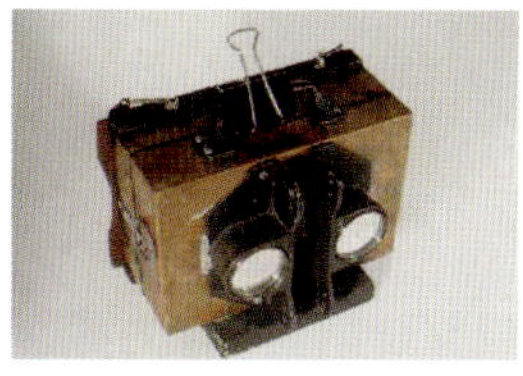

Photos taken with the 5" × 7"
Stereo Camera, 1984

ABOVE RIGHT
5" × 7" Stereo Camera, reclaimed
materials, 16.5 × 21.6 × 15.2 cm
(6½ × 8½ × 6 in.), 1984

*One of the most interesting things about your background is that you didn't get
your master's of fine arts until you were forty-three years old. Before that, all your
formal education was in engineering. How did you make such a switch? And when
did you begin calling yourself an artist?*

First of all, calling yourself an artist is something you just have to get used to. It
takes a while before you can do it without wincing. But it was clear to me early
on that I couldn't stand the jobs I was getting with my engineering degrees. I
worked mostly in management, either for the Chicago Transit Authority or the
State of Illinois, and I kept quitting because I was too bored. For example, I was
very efficient at what I did for the State of Illinois, so I would be through with
everything 15 minutes after I got to the office and there would be nothing to do
the whole rest of the day. I'd still have to hang around, though – just in case
the phone might ring. It drove me nuts. Anyway, during the 1970s, when I was
continually taking these furloughs from the business world, my father died. One
of the things that made it especially sad was that since this happened only a year
after he'd retired, he'd never had a chance to pursue his interest in sculpture
the way he'd planned to. So I decided I had to do it myself, and I began to take
courses with the Clay People, who ran what was probably the largest unaccredited
clay school in the country. That was some of my first exposure to artists and their
way of looking at the world. A woman I knew there would get totally interested in
things like 'granularity' – I helped her move once and some of the stuff I had to
carry were bags of wood shavings and curlicue pieces of metal that had come off
a lathe. She also used to plant fluorescent tubes in the ground just to have them

BELOW
Sketch of the 120 Panoramic
Camera, reclaimed materials:
cookie tin, coffee can, lazy
susan, DC gearmotor, lens,
mirror, 17.8 × 28 × 22.8 cm
(7 × 11 × 9 in.), 1988

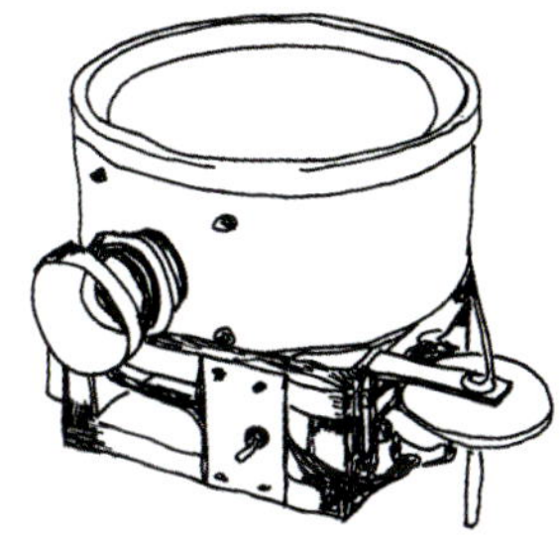

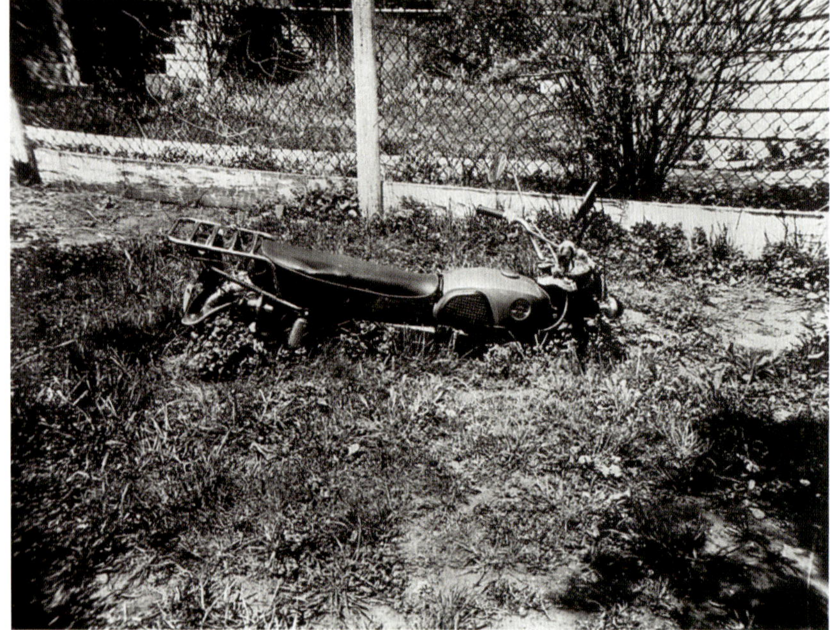

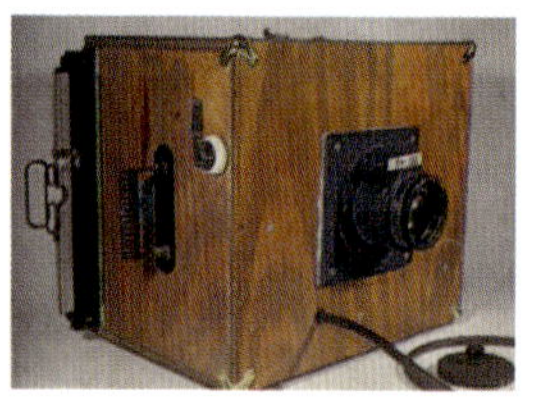

stick up into the air. Well, I didn't quite understand any of this. But I slowly came to appreciate it, and what I realized, I think, is that one of the things you're allowed to do as an artist is simply play around. You get to have fun. So there was that very basic but crucial lesson, and then there were lessons in technique, too, some of which had to do with photography, another hobby that I was involved with around that time. A friend of mine who had seen a show of my photos at a café told me, 'You don't know how to print,' and I resolved that I would find out, which led me to take some introductory photography courses at Columbia College here in Chicago. By the time I got through with those I knew how to print. The last course I took at Columbia was called 'Generative Systems,' where the emphasis was on expression rather than on the mechanics and pyrotechnics of photography. It was the sort of class where the students were calling themselves artists and their work art. And at that point I met a woman who was about to enroll in the MFA program at the School of the Art Institute of Chicago and she said, 'Hey Cook, why don't you apply, too! Then we can both play for a couple of years.' So I did, almost on a lark. I suppose what it boils down to is that engineers just have a different perspective. Let me give you an example. Artists who see an exhibit of my cameras seem to marvel at the fact that these objects look as if I assembled them from odds and ends I picked up off the floor. They apparently have this image of me walking around in my basement saying things like, 'Yes! This could fit here! And let's see now … that hinge would be appropriate … there.'

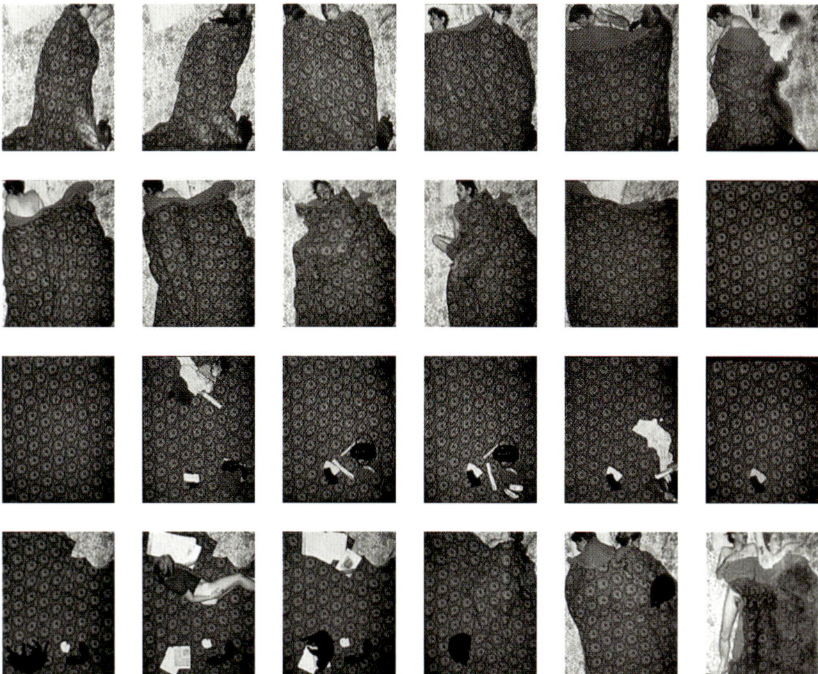

Photos taken with the Half-Frame Motor Driven Camera, 1978

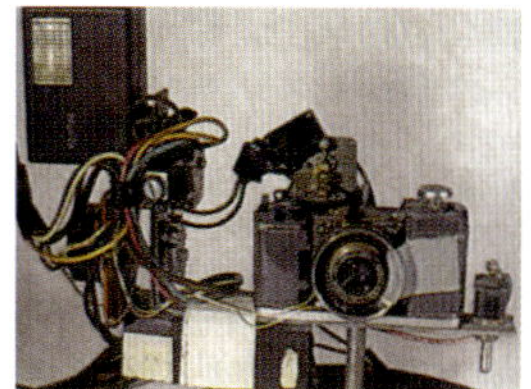

ABOVE LEFT
Photos taken with the Half-Frame Motor Driven Camera, 1978

ABOVE RIGHT
Half-Frame Motor Driven Camera, reclaimed materials, 22.9 × 25.4 × 10.2 cm (9 × 10 × 4 in.), 1978

Whereas you don't work that way at all.

Well, to tell you the truth, that really is the way I work a lot of the time. But I'm also capable of assembling apparently unlikely parts in a very methodical way without any particular recourse to intuition, which I suspect has something to do with my engineering background. Because friends of mine who are engineers will have a much more matter-of-fact response to the very same exhibit, even if they like it. They'll simply see the cameras as the only logical assembly of available parts that would accomplish a specific design purpose. What strikes me is that even if engineers do find themselves using intuition, they often limit themselves because they don't necessarily value it or take it seriously – while artists focus on intuition almost exclusively and go out of their way to cultivate it. Sometimes a bit too far out of their way, in my opinion. I get impatient with artists who take an intuitive approach when a rational solution would do as well and give results more quickly. I have other attitudes that come directly from four years in engineering and natural sciences and remain unadulterated. To be specific, I am intolerant of work that passes itself off as broadly metaphorical, or that presumes to mythologize. And I usually dismiss work that is based on a shallow understanding of materials or subjects. Few artists object so strenuously to anything anyone else is doing. For the most part, they're quite generous with one another – it's something you learn in art school. But I myself cannot see creating without a purpose.

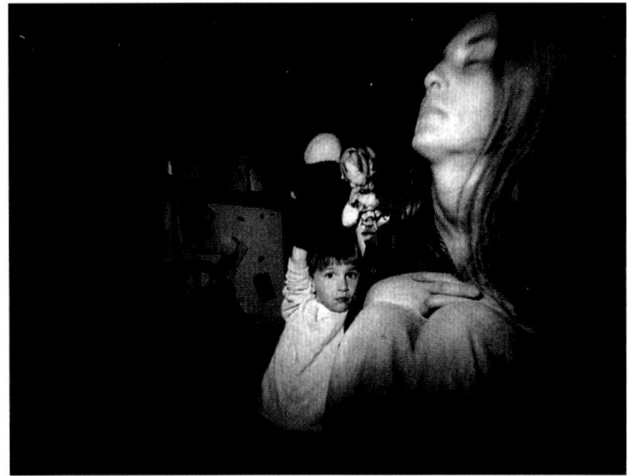

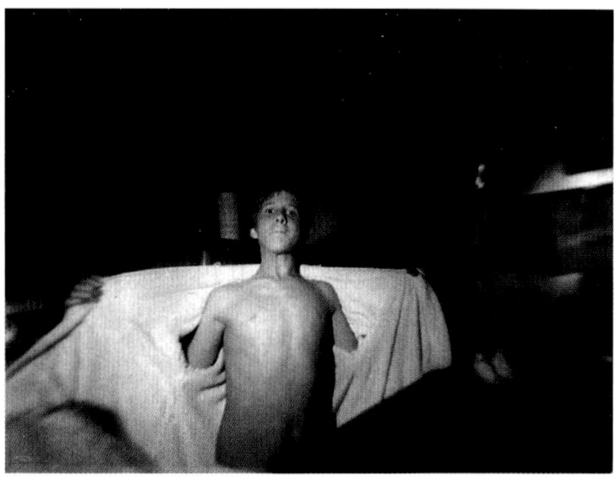

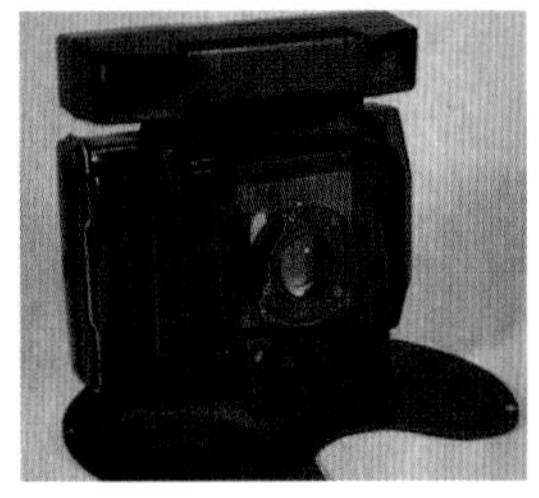

ABOVE
Modified Polaroid Pack-Film
Camera, reclaimed materials,
modified tripod socket,
30.5 × 26.6 × 20 cm
(12 × 10½ × 8 in.), 1983

TOP LEFT AND RIGHT
Photos taken with the Modified
Polaroid Pack-Film Camera, 1983

BELOW
Sketch of the Slow Zoom
8 mm Camera, reclaimed
materials, 45.7 × 47 × 45.7 cm
(18 × 18½ × 18 in.), 1991

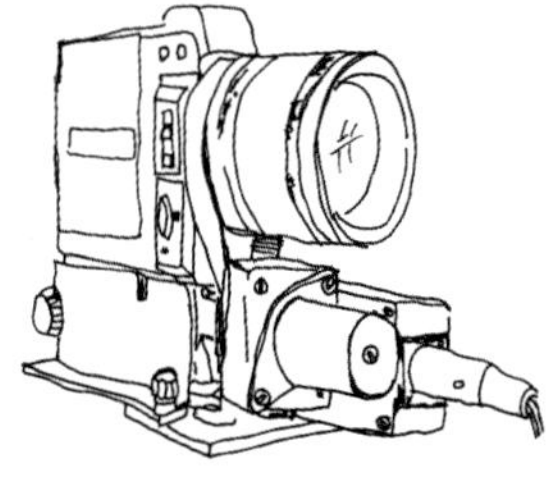

Some of your interest in the workings of the brain seems to come through in the cameras you make; for instance, your 'stereo' camera, which gives you pictures with two identical but slightly overlapping images. When I first saw it, I thought, 'Oh, I know what this is. He's wondering what the world would look like if somehow we couldn't integrate the information coming in from our right eye with that coming in from our left eye.'

Well, that's going too far. I've never made cameras as psychological studies or interpretations of biology or inquiries into what it would be like to be cross-eyed – which is why I use deadpan titles that just give the size and use. In fact, building these devices is a completely secondary activity: it's the photographs I can take with the cameras that interest me, not the cameras themselves, which often fall into a state of total disregard and dismantlement once I've got whatever results I'm after. It near even crossed my mind to display them until the Randolph Street Gallery in Chicago asked me to, and when that happened I had to go into my workshop and start finding things in boxes and putting parts back together again.

If you have such a casual attitude towards your cameras, how could you go along with the idea of exhibiting them? I know that demystifying technology is important to you and that your shows are a way of telling people, 'If I can do this, you can, too.' But as long as works of yours are sitting in a gallery, some people are inevitably going to look at them as art in themselves – as sculpture – regardless of your didactic intent. Are you comfortable with that?

Yes I am. I've come to accept the cameras as sculpture, even though they weren't initially intended that way. I understand, also, their appeal as sculpture. They clearly reveal an attitude, and what's especially nice about them is that the steps I went through to make them show clearly: at the base level, art is always

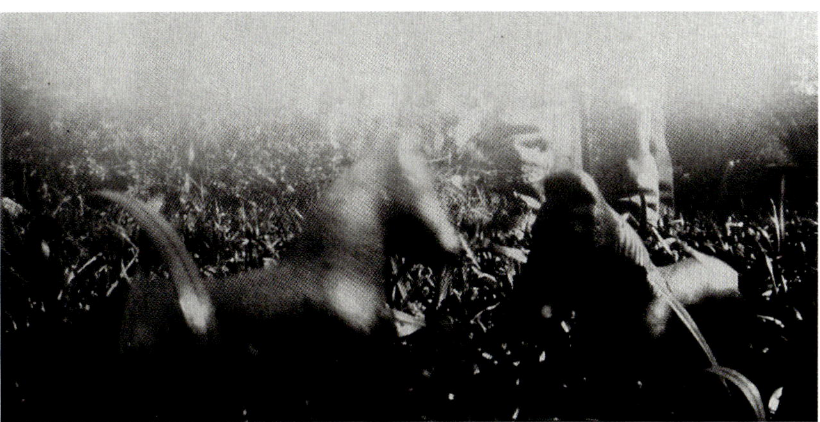

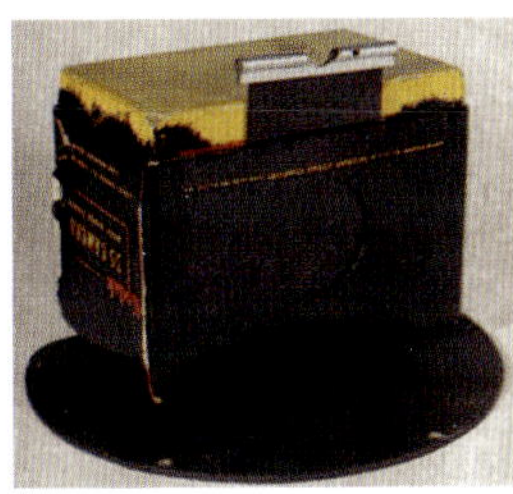

about the process of making art and anything that strikes home reveals its process in the final product. The point is that you can almost tell by looking at these cameras how I work, which is very opportunistically, using materials I acquire through serendipity or through this bizarrely detailed visual memory I have of where I've seen what in hardware stores. Sometimes I'll go for months or years without doing anything on a camera and then suddenly a part I need for it will turn up out of nowhere. And some of my ideas come from the cameras themselves: they simply ask to be made into this or that. Also, these cameras, when they're on display in a gallery, assume a life of their own. Partly it's because they have this potential of taking pictures – of being image-makers – but they're not in use; they've become objects of contemplation. They're all sitting on pedestals or shelves or whatnot. Another interesting aspect of the cameras is that I'm asking the viewer to take a conceptual leap between image and image-maker – a leap similar to the one I had to take to build the cameras in the first place.

In much of your work, you seem to be preoccupied with the 'candid camera'. You set up cameras that take pictures every hour no matter what, even when people are eating or sleeping or making love. What draws you to that approach?

Partly it's data collection. I've chosen the hour interval because our lives are run by hours that continue even when we defy them by engaging in an activity where we lose track of time. I get the pictures, arrange them in sequence, and leave viewers on their own to draw a conclusion or just delight in the research, as I do myself. There's an aesthetic at work, too, although it's not the kind that's crafted as in painting. The idea is that the world has an inherent beauty that will become clear if you let it. All you have to do is set up some parameters, like the hour interval, and the thing goes by itself – the aesthetic is out there in ordinary physical reality like everything else.

Operative Hacks

The operation and construction
of existing cameras can be
manipulated in many different
ways by the experimental
photographer.

3

DISTRESSING NEGATIVES AND FILM

The negative is at the heart of analogue photography, and its alteration can create dramatic and unexpected effects. In addition to the techniques demonstrated here, negatives can be 'abused' by washing them, spilling liquids or gum onto them before (or during) development, putting a diffusing layer between the light source and the negative, or sandwiching two or more negatives together. Although these techniques can be applied to 35 mm or other film sizes, large-format negatives are easier to manipulate. Additionally, as in the examples produced by Drew Kunz (opposite), a roll of film can be punctured or partially exposed before use. Light leaks in the camera can also produce interesting results, as can deliberately using film that is long past its expiration date.

Techniques for distressing negatives

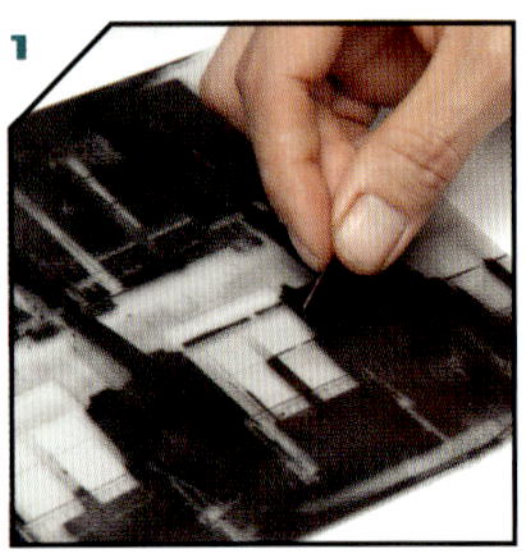 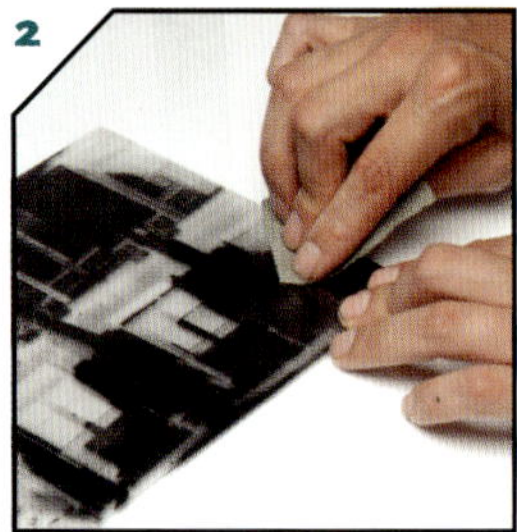 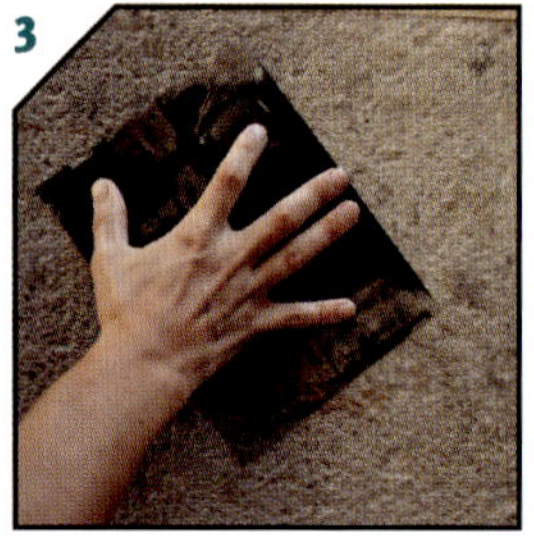 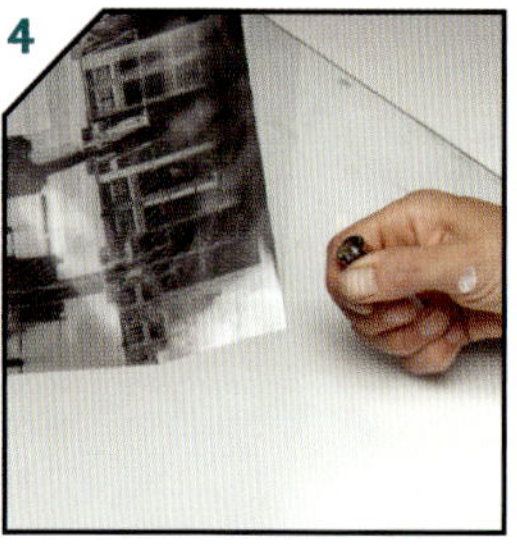

What you need:
- [ ] negative
- [ ] needle
- [ ] sandpaper
- [ ] rough surface, such as a concrete or brick wall
- [ ] cigarette lighter or candle
- [ ] protective gloves
- [ ] container of water

Needle

1 Scratching the black parts of the negative with a needle will produce transparent scratches. These will translate into thin black marks when the negative is printed.

Sandpaper

2 Lightly rubbing a negative with sandpaper produces larger transparent scratches than using a needle. It can also be used to create semi-transparent areas (depending on the amount of pressure applied) that will appear 'foggy' on the finished print.

Rough surface

3 Rubbing a negative across a rough surface, such as a concrete or brick wall, will produce a random pattern of small scratches across the entire image.

Burning

4 Parts of a negative can be burned carefully using a candle or cigarette lighter. This will produce holes, melted emulsion and other distortions. Beware that cellulose is very flammable, however, so this is something best done with protective gloves and a nearby container full of water into which you can drop the burning film if necessary.

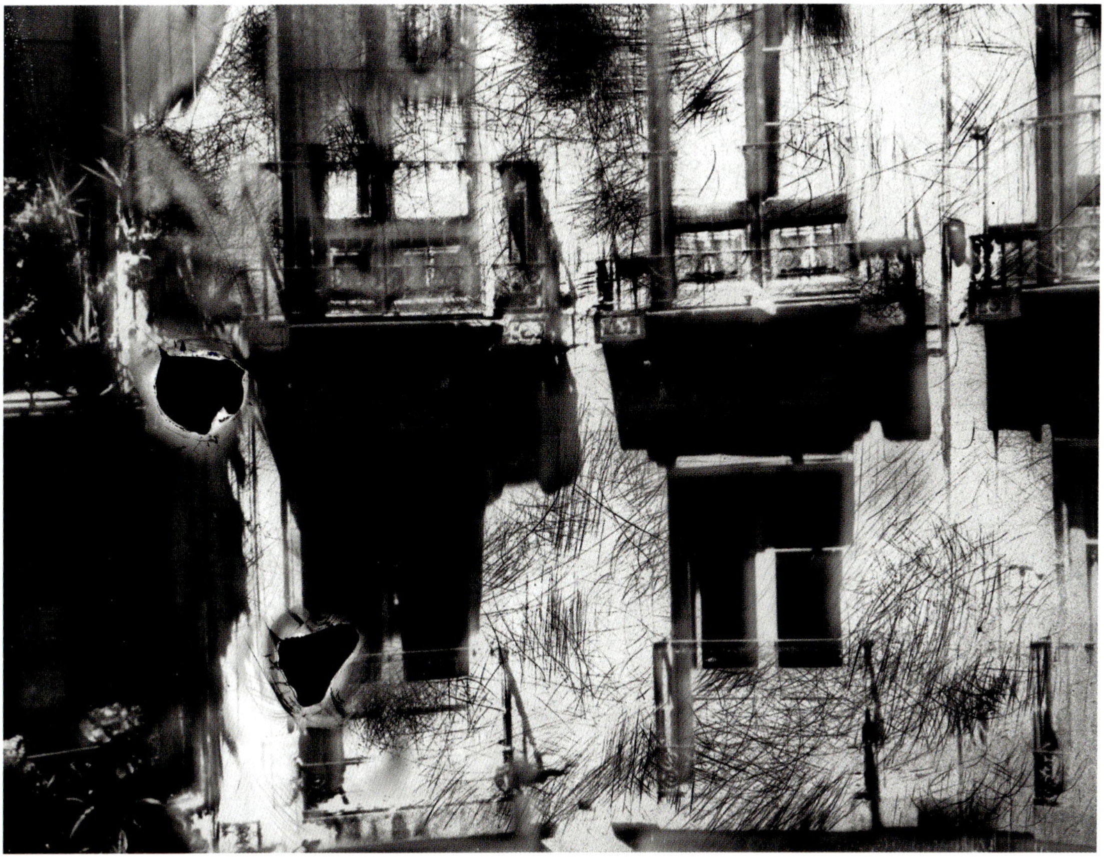

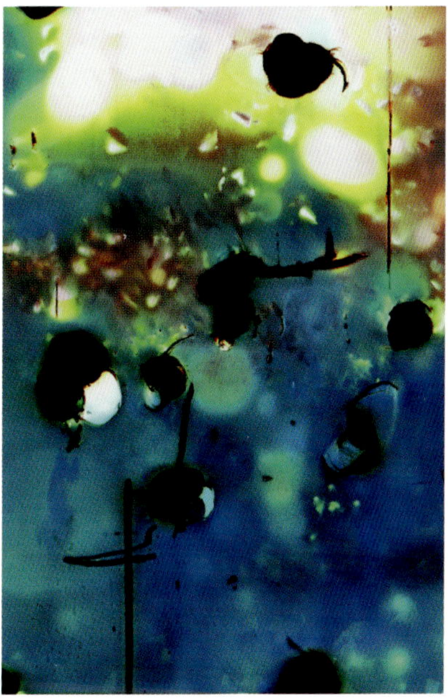

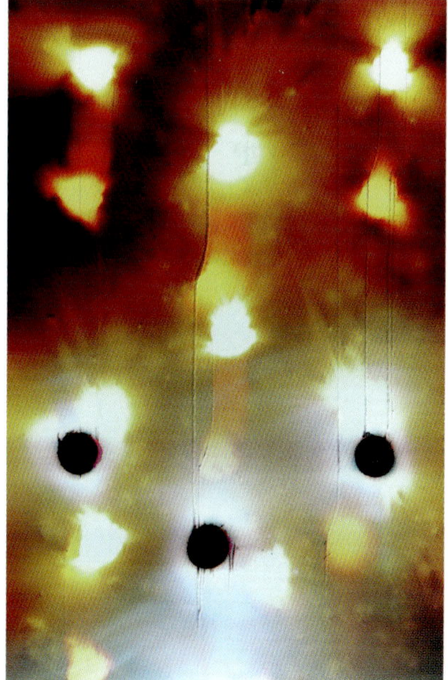

Francisco Gómez
La Plaza, black and white silver
gelatin print from a distressed
negative 16.6 × 21.6 cm
(6½ × 8½ in.), 2013

Drew Kunz
Untitled, distressed colour film
with holes, each 36 × 24 mm
(1½ × 1 in.), 2008
To make these images, Kunz
drilled several holes into a roll of
35 mm colour film and exposed
it to light. Additional distress to
the film was caused with the tip
of a small nail. The film was then
developed successively with two
separate processes: the first was
a coffee developer and sodium
carbonate; the second was a
standard C-41 process.

SLIT-SCAN CAMERAS

Through a simple modification of a camera, this hack results in warped images and a psychedelic array of colours and shapes. 'Slit-scan', or 'linear strip' photography is a technique in which an image is created while the film moves past a narrow slit in the back of the camera. Consequently, a slit-scan image is made up of many narrow slices, assembled side by side, rather than a single exposure. The image does not record a single instant in time, as in conventional photography; instead, it creates a timeline of events occurring in the same position over a slightly longer period of time.

Medium-format slit-camera hack *by Tony Kemplen*

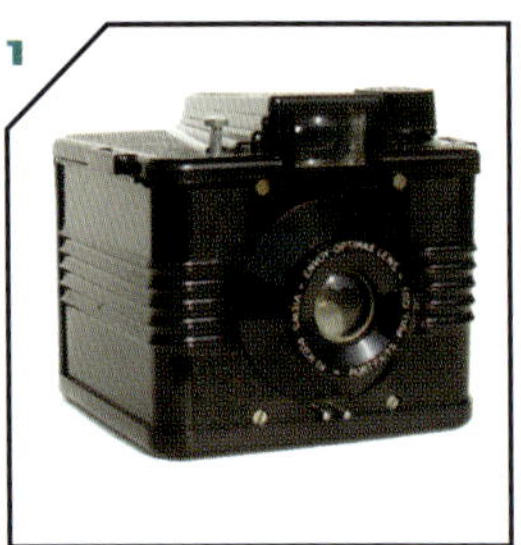

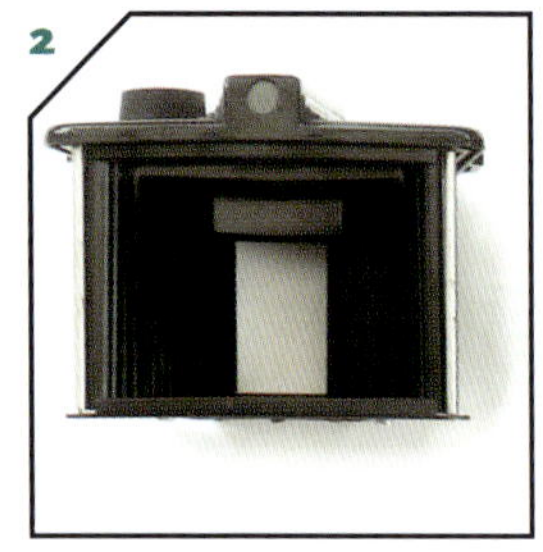

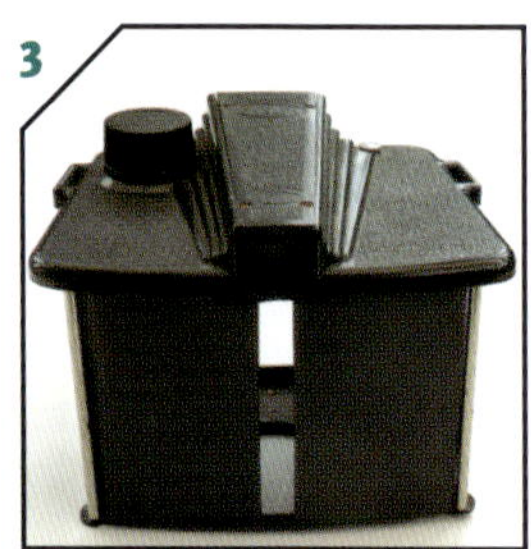

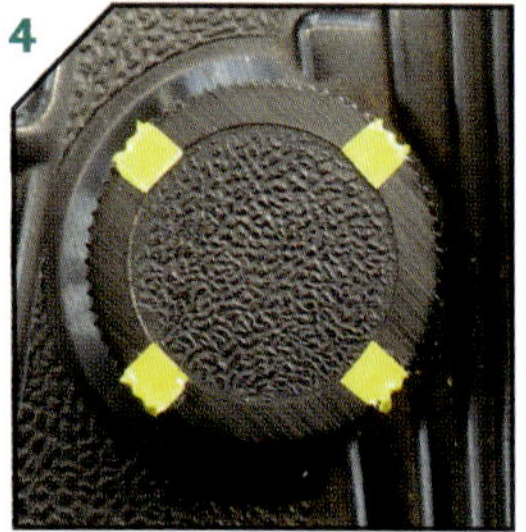

What you need:
- medium-format camera
- black card
- black tape

Select the camera

1 The ideal camera for this hack is one that takes medium-format roll film (120 or 220 format). Look for a model that allows you to easily make multiple exposures and has a B (Bulb) setting so you can hold the shutter open indefinitely; many vintage box-style cameras are ideal for this.

Hacking for slit-scan

2–3 Open the camera and tape two pieces of black card inside the back to create a 5 mm slit at the centre of the frame.

Mark the winder

4 Applying marks to the winder can be helpful if you want to prevent your images from overlapping (see Multiple Exposures on pp. 38–39) or keep the different exposure strips as close together as possible for a more homogenous result.

Using the camera

The camera can now be used to make multiple thin exposures on a single roll of film. A disjointed and abstract-looking panorama can be achieved by winding the film, making an exposure, panning the camera slightly (to adjust the area of the scene being photographed), and then making another exposure. Repeating this process will allow you to photograph as broad or as narrow a view as you choose, creating a final image that is made up of multiple 'slit shots' (as shown opposite above). Note that the direction you pan the camera is very important: if the winding knob is on the left of the camera, then you should pan from right to left; otherwise your slices will appear in reverse order.

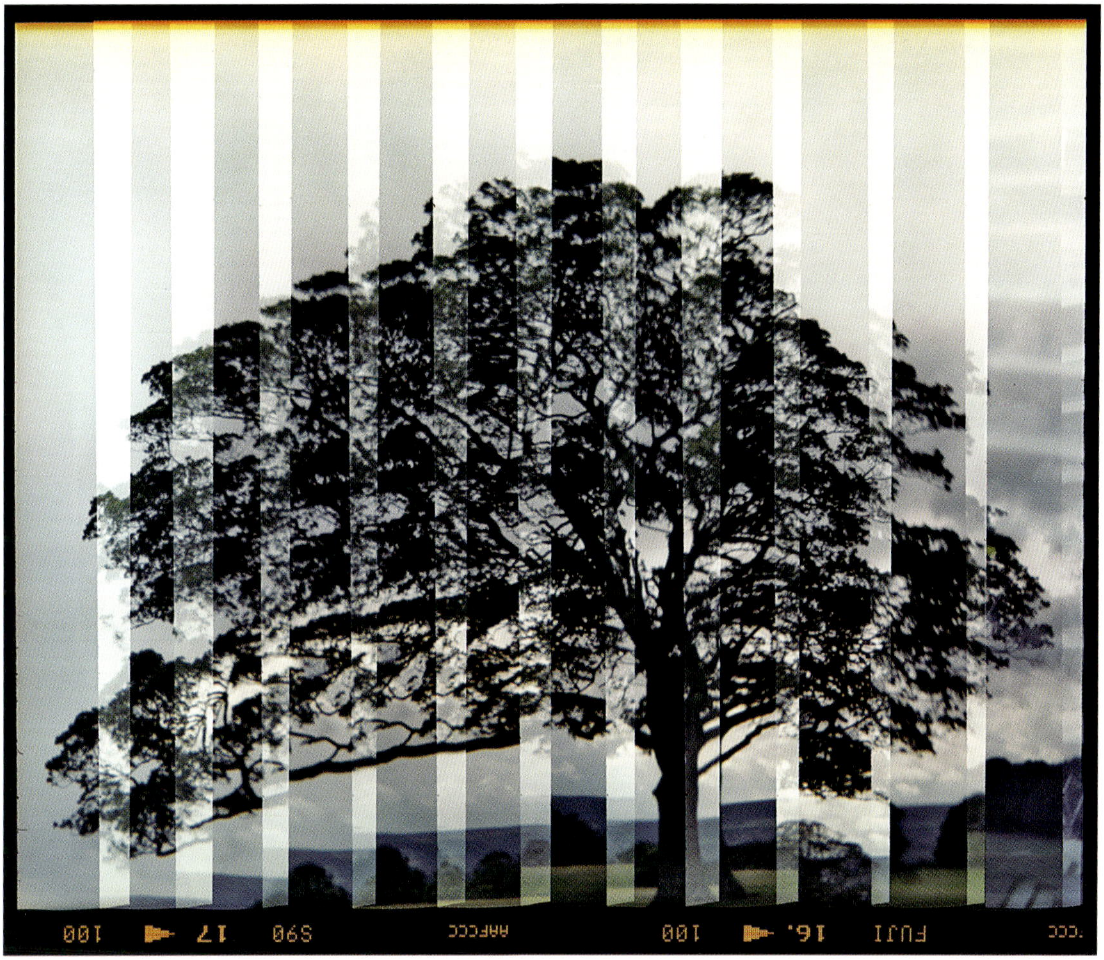

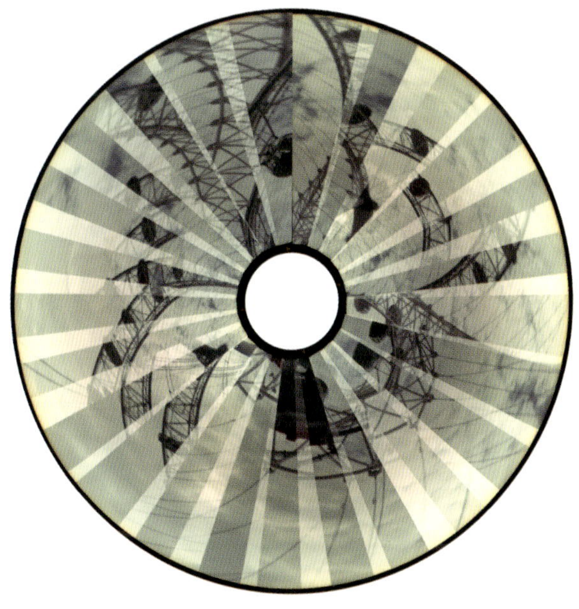

ABOVE

Tony Kemplen
Sliced Sycamore, slit-scan
negative, 24 × 36 mm
(1 × 1½ in.), 2013

RIGHT

Tony Kemplen
London Eye, polar slit-camera
photograph, 20 × 20 cm
(7⅞ × 7⅞ in.), 2013
The film was advanced by
⅛ turn after each exposure,
producing minor slit overlap at
the beginning of the film and no
overlap at the end. The final result
was processed using the polar
coordinates filter in Photoshop.

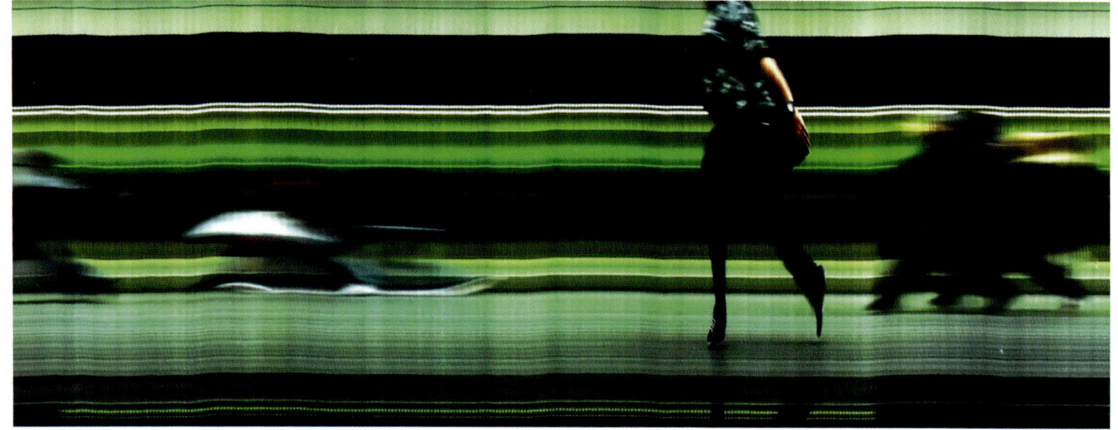

35 mm compact camera slit-scan hack *by Tony Kemplen*

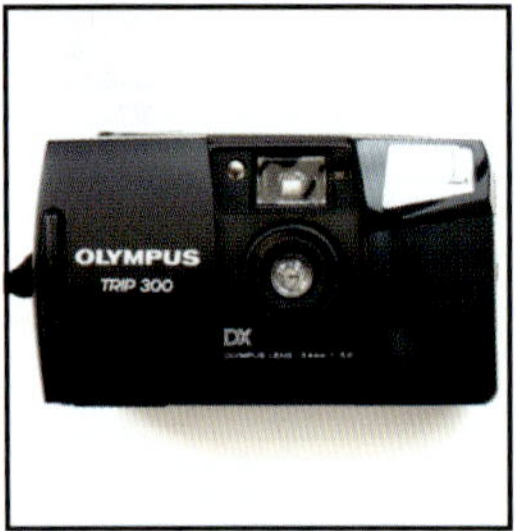

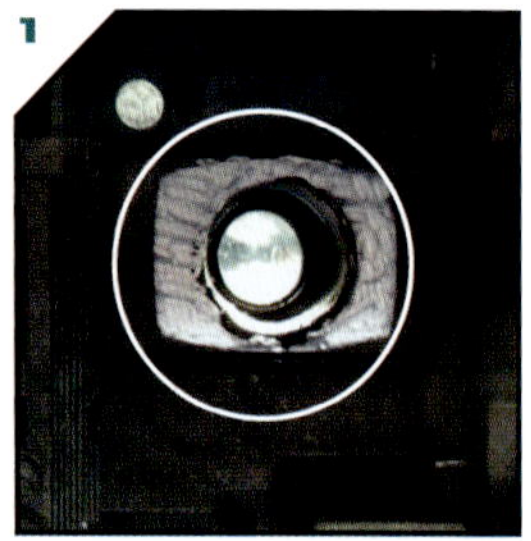

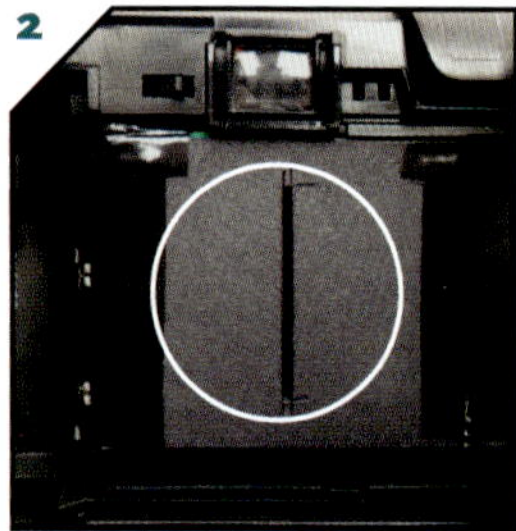

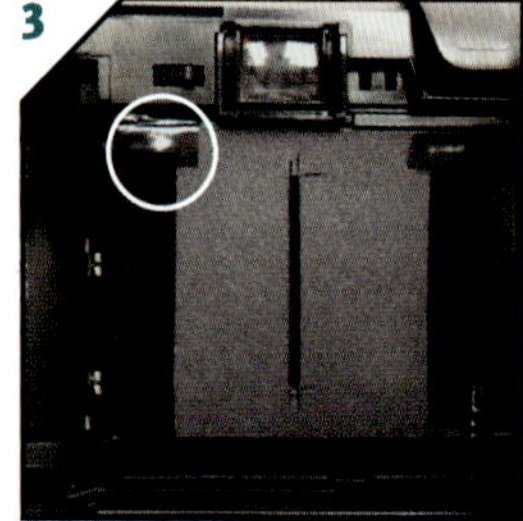

What you need:
- ☐ 35 mm camera
- ☐ plastic tube
- ☐ Blu-Tack (or similar adhesive putty)
- ☐ black cardboard
- ☐ black tape

The camera

For this hack we're using a point-and-shoot 35 mm camera to make a slit-scan device. The key difference between this modification and the previous slit camera is that here the image is a result of the film moving across the slit for the duration of the exposure time. The camera used is an Olympus Trip 300, which is ideal for the technique as it features automatic film winding and a sliding lens cover that can be applied between exposures.

Hacking the camera

1 The shutter needs to be wedged open so the lens is constantly exposing the film to light. To do this insert a short length of plastic tubing surrounded by adhesive putty.

2 Cut a 1 mm slit into a piece of black card, and tape the card into the back of the camera at the film plane. This forms the slit.

Fooling the automatic film wind

3 For the film to move across the slit and make an exposure, you need to fool the camera's automatic winding system so it will keep running each time the shutter release is pressed. To achieve this, you need to tape over the cog-wheel that normally engages with the sprockets on the film.

The film will now run for about 4 seconds each time the shutter-release button is pressed. As the film is transported 60 mm per second, this means the 1 mm slit gives an exposure time equivalent to 1/60 sec. The lens has a fixed aperture of $f/5.6$, so this exposure is just right for an overcast afternoon using ISO 200 film.

Tony Kemplen
Pedestrians, slit-scan photograph taken with modified Olympus Trip 300, 10 × 20 cm (4 × 7⅞ in.), 2013

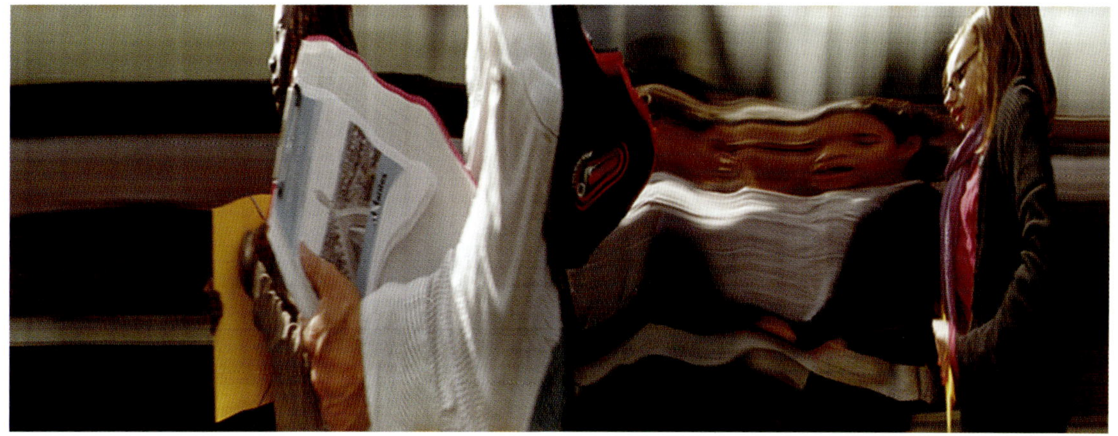

35 mm SLR slit-scan camera with electronic speed control *by James Guerin*

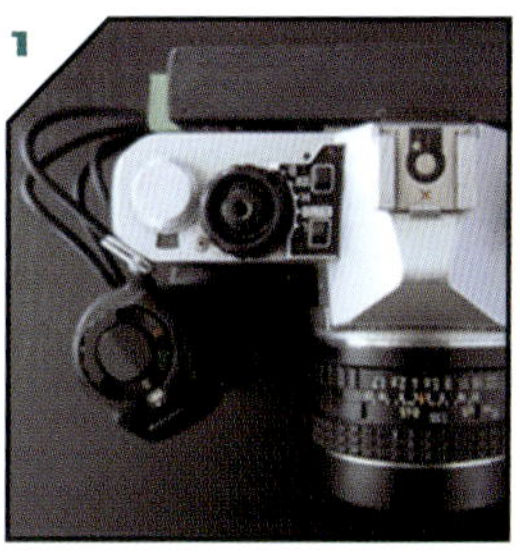

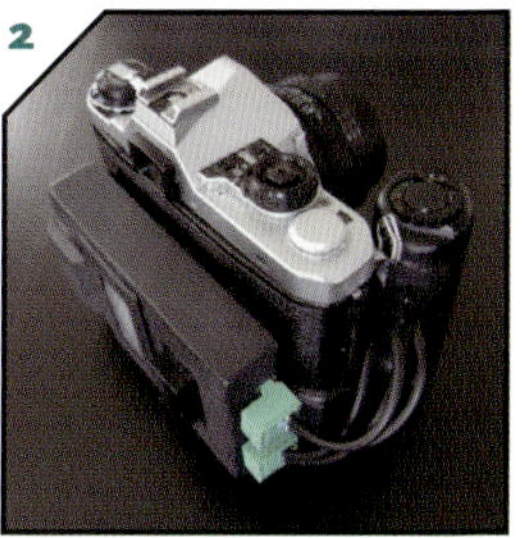

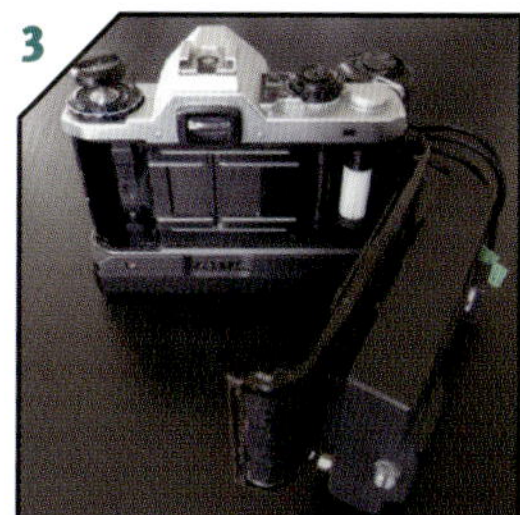

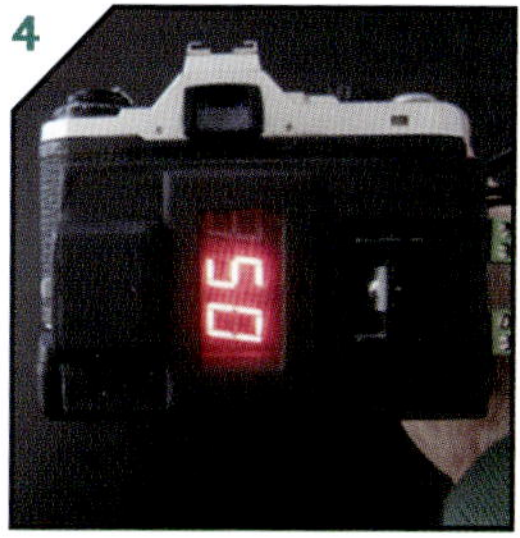

What you need:
- ☐ 35 mm SLR camera
- ☐ power winder
- ☐ speed control circuit

TOP

James Guerin
Slit-scan photograph, 10 x 20 cm
(4 × 7⅞ in.), 2013
'This image was shot at a busy
tram station. I used a wide-angle
lens (19 mm) that allowed me to
shoot from 1–2 m away and still
get an entire person in the frame.
I prefocus at 1 or 2 m (usually
at $f/8$–$f/16$) and shoot with the
camera at waist level. The speed
the film moves at is quite slow, so
the motor is almost silent. People
are not aware I am taking photos
as they walk by. If they stood still
in front of the camera they would
be indistinguishable blurs!'

The camera

1, 2 This is a very sophisticated example
of a slit-scan camera, adapted from an old
Pentax ME Super 35 mm SLR. The camera
is heavily modified to include an electronic
speed control circuit wired into a power
winder. This allows the speed of the film
transport to be matched to the speed of
a moving subject, so the subject appears
(relatively) sharp in the final image. Since
the modifications require a high level of
technical camera knowledge to execute,
these instructions give only an overview.

Hacking the camera

3 To make the camera, the shutter is removed
and remade into a 0.5 mm slit at the film
gate. The wind-on system is modified to
allow continuous winding with a compatible
Pentax power winder. The mirror is also
modified so it is 'right-side-up', and a push-
button added to slide the mirror down.

Adding speed control

4 Finally, a speed control circuit (with
an LED readout) is wired into the
Pentax power winder, which allows the
photographer to control the speed at which
film is pulled across the slit. At 100%
power, the winder runs at the maximum
speed for which it was designed, effectively
transporting film across the slit at a rate of
100 mm/sec. The speed can, however, be
reduced to as little as 30% to slow the film
transport down to a rate of approximately
15 mm/sec. The formula for determining
the speed required is:

film transport speed =
(focal length of lens × subject speed) /
(distance between camera and subject)

PAOLO GIOLI
Interview by
Aaron Kossmann

Italian artist and filmmaker Paolo Gioli is renowned for his experimental work, and was one of the first to use slit-scan camera techniques in art photography.

How did you create these images of strip photography (for La linea transparente*)?*

These images were created using slit-scan cameras, a popular technique that is usually employed in science photography or at sport events to determine who arrived first at the finish line. Many artists have also made strip photographs, though with less sophisticated cameras. I started using this technique not out of simple artistic curiosity, but because it was strongly related to my other creative experiments with pinhole cameras.

What is the technical rationale behind the series?

The starting point is the pinhole: it is a luminous dot, which in the slit-scan technique then becomes a line. The shutter, redundant for my purposes, is substituted with a metal plate into which I cut a line. In successive experiments I have multiplied the lines and cut the luminous slit, thin as a pencil mark, in the shape of an angle or of a semi-circle. Many artists just rewind the film in the camera, rolling it along one single [slit]. This gives them images that are more or less deformed, but out of context, with no background. My 35 mm reflex cameras have been hacked to remove all inner workings; I also add one or two cranks in order to advance or rewind the film when I'm shooting.

OPPOSITE ABOVE
I segni dell'Etrusco, strip photograph using a negative image of an Etruscan tombstone as the slit, black and white print, 40 × 50 cm (15¾ × 19¾ in.), 1995

OPPOSITE BELOW
Volto attraverso, strip photograph using the negative of an image of a hornet's nest as the slit, black and white print, 40 × 50 cm (15¾ × 19¾ in.), 2001

RIGHT
Volto attraverso, strip photograph using the negative of Lodovico Sforza's signature photograph as the slit, black and white print, 30 × 40 cm (11¾ × 15¾ in.), 2000

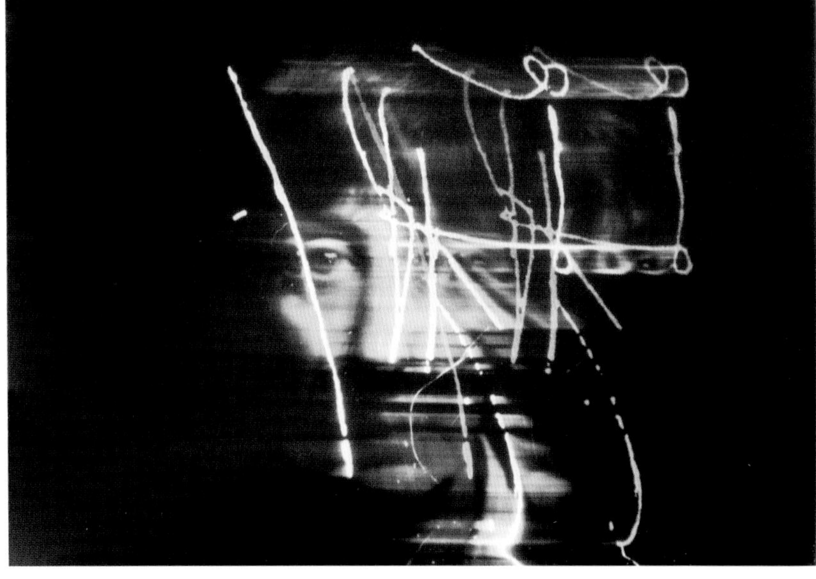

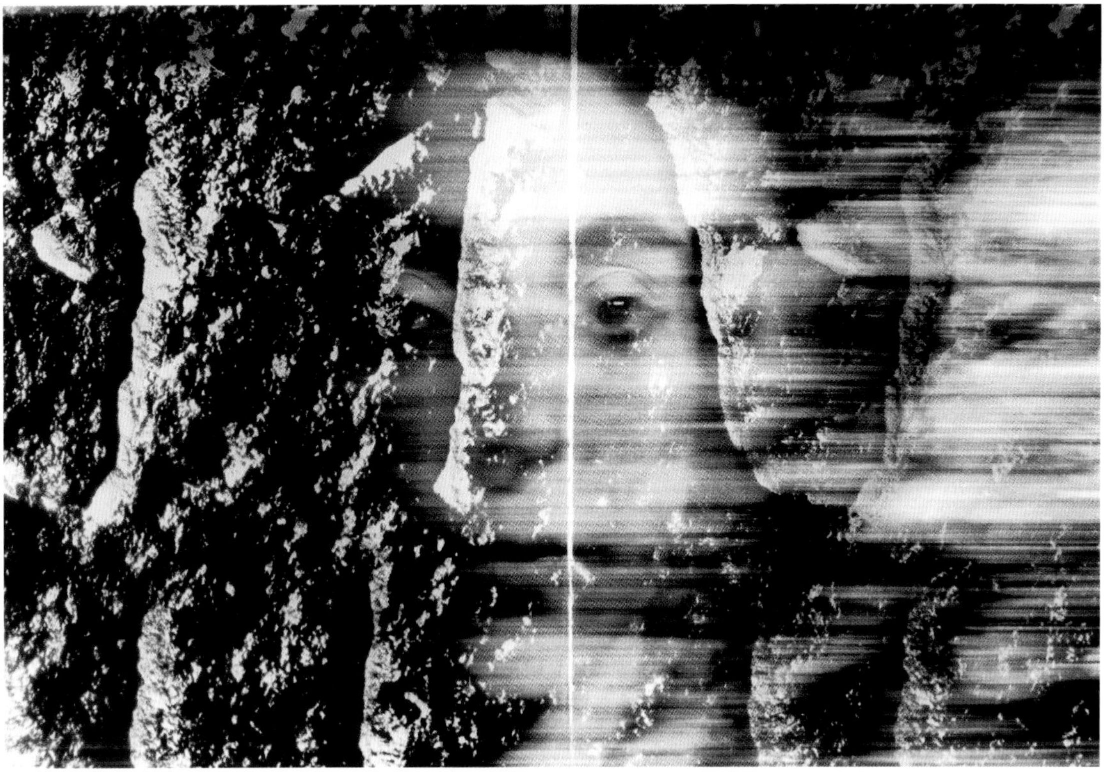

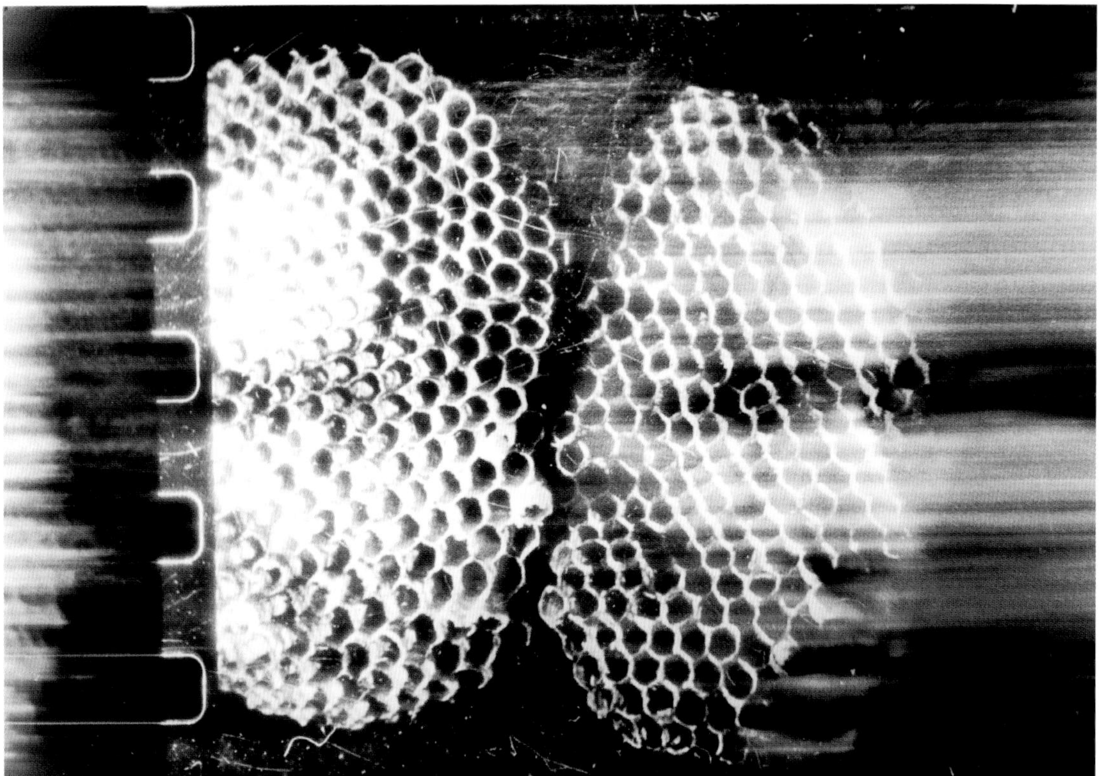

Volto attraverso, strip photograph using a negative image of pubic hairs as the slit, black and white print, 40 × 50 cm (15¾ × 19¾ in.), 2001

Volto attraverso, strip photograph using the negative of a photograph of the fingers of a hand as the slit, black and white print, 40 × 50 cm (15¾ × 19¾ in.), 1996

Volto attraverso gli occhi di Pasolini, strip photograph using a negative image of Pasolini's eyes as the slit, black and white print, 30 × 40 cm (11¾ × 15¾ in.), 1995

What sort of images can you shoot with that set-up? Is image deformation still the main characteristic?

I aim for my figures not to be deformed but to undergo a process of composition and de-composition on perfectly natural-looking backgrounds. The results are odd double figures without any mirror-like effects. I move the camera as if I were shooting a film. I emulate proto-cinematic shooting techniques, and this allows me a very wide-angle field, even a 360-degree view. The frenetic shooting times are dictated by the model. The sudden stops, the changes of speed and direction [in winding the film] can only be creative if done manually, carefully focusing on the speed at which I wind the film and shift the camera, and the movement I ask of the models.

What are your favourite subjects to shoot using the slit-scan technique? Is it accurate to say you prefer photographing actions and movements rather than models?

Actions are scenes filled with rhythm and movement. I divide them into two categories. The first comprises unpredictable scenes, such as a car or a person passing by in an urban context. The second is orderly gestures, executed by or on the models, as if they were actors in a psychodrama. My intention is to discover, in the ordinary gestures of everyday life, moving figures that have never before come to light: a sort of an unearthed world.

Do you think this technique can still surprise us in the future?

Certainly! This process is at the same time both creative and quasi-scientific. It is very complex and there is still a lot to discover and experiment with. But when [the slit-scan technique] is not approached seriously, it is frequently reduced to a charming, superficial game.

Front and back view of the modified camera used by Paolo Gioli to shoot the strip-photograph series opposite

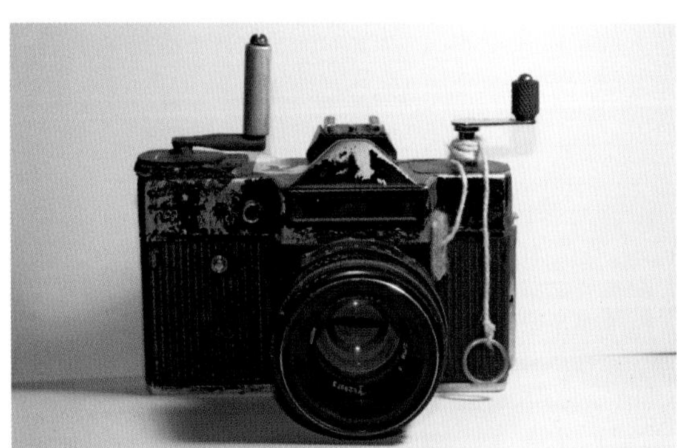
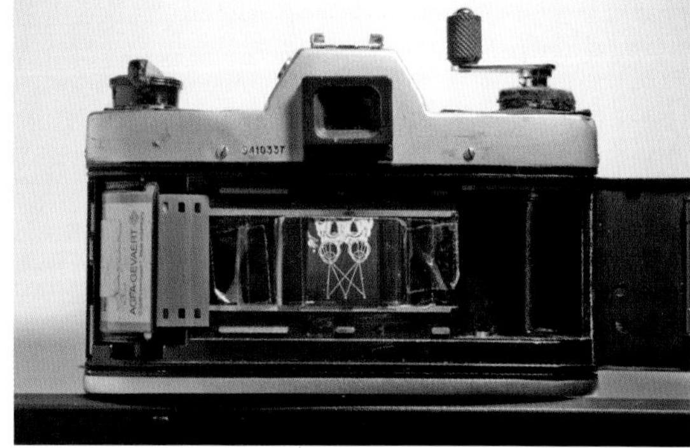

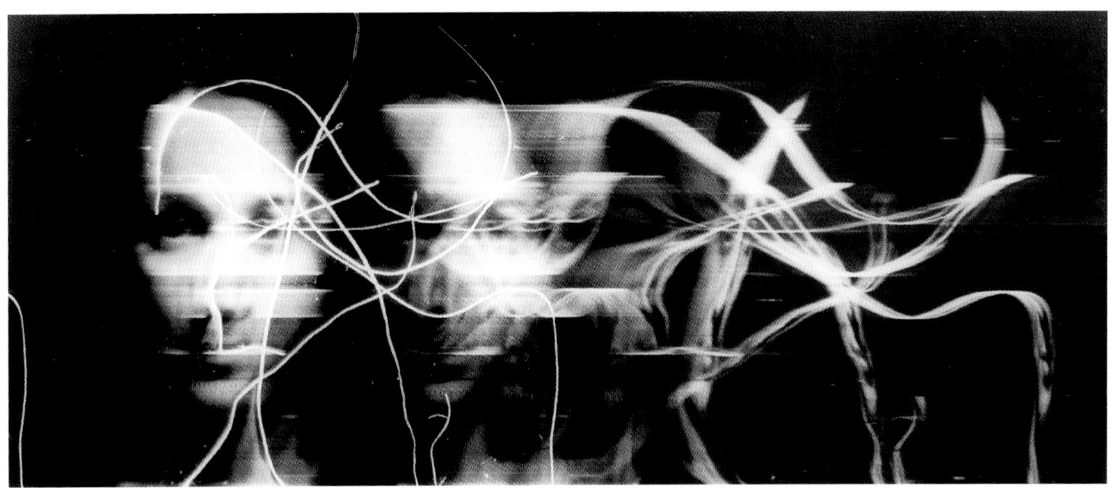

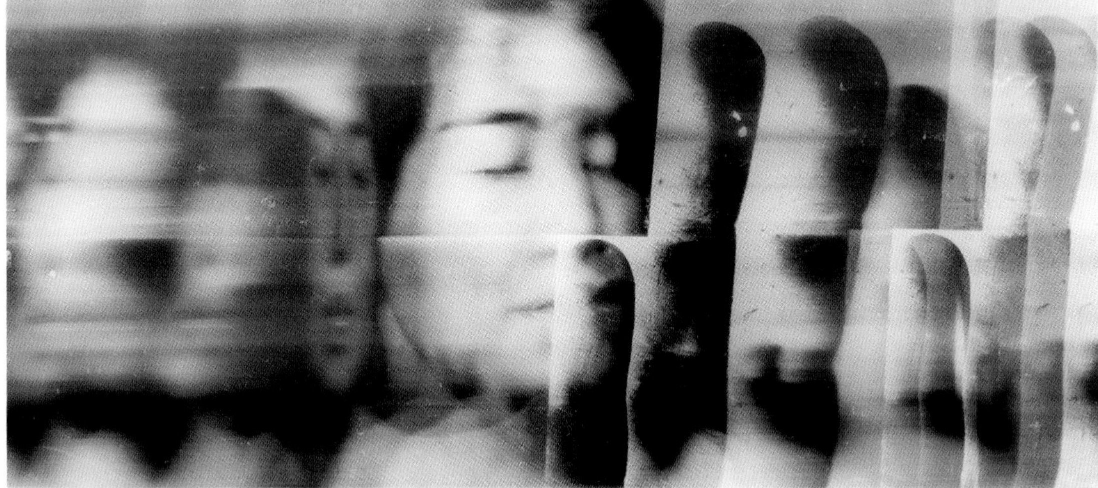

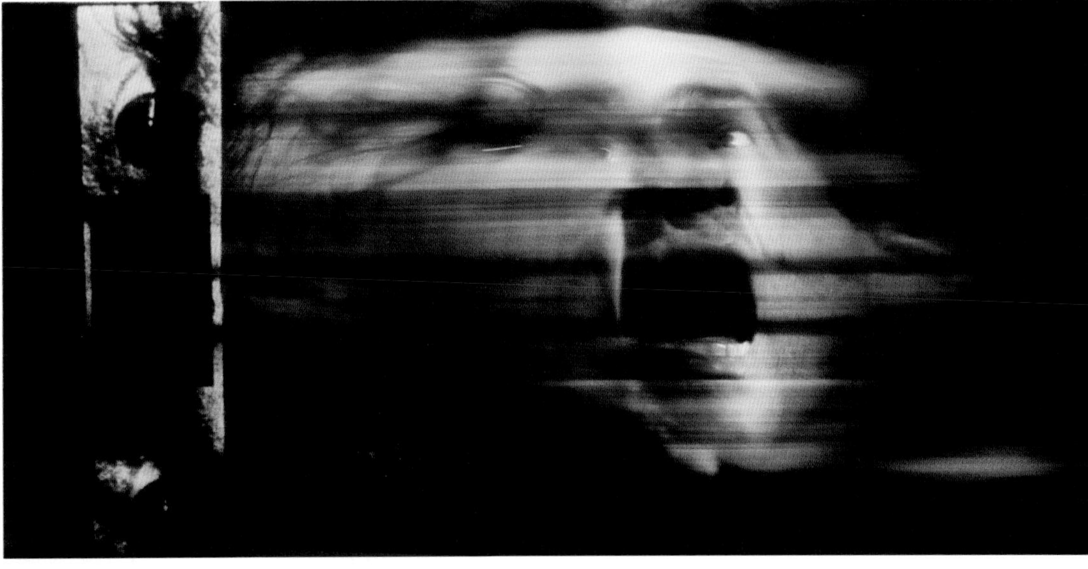

CESARE FABBRI

*Interview by
Luca Bendandi*

Magnesium flashes were one of the first artificial lighting aids used in photography. Italian photographer Cesare Fabbri rediscovers this forgotten technique and applies it to colour photography at distances unthinkable for a normal flash.

Can you briefly explain this lighting technique?

A magnesium flash is a controlled explosion that is unusually bright relative to the force of its detonation. It was invented shortly after photography itself, allowing early practitioners to shoot in low-light conditions with materials that were not very sensitive. The most famous early examples of this technique are the albumen prints of the Paris catacombs made by Nadar in 1861, and the photos of Nevada miners underground taken by Timothy O'Sullivan in 1868.

How did you come to discover this technique, and what technical complexities did you encounter in refining it?

In 2009 I was working with Orthographe, a theatre company in Ravenna (see p. 15), on their play *Controllo Remoto*. Alessandro Panzavolta, Marco Amadori and I decided to investigate magnesium flashes, as we were curious to hear the sound they produced. We eventually found a 1924 edition of a Lumière Brothers

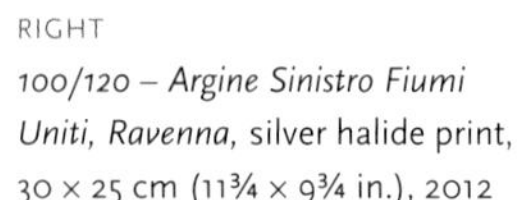

RIGHT

100/120 – Argine Sinistro Fiumi Uniti, Ravenna, silver halide print, 30 × 25 cm (11¾ × 9¾ in.), 2012

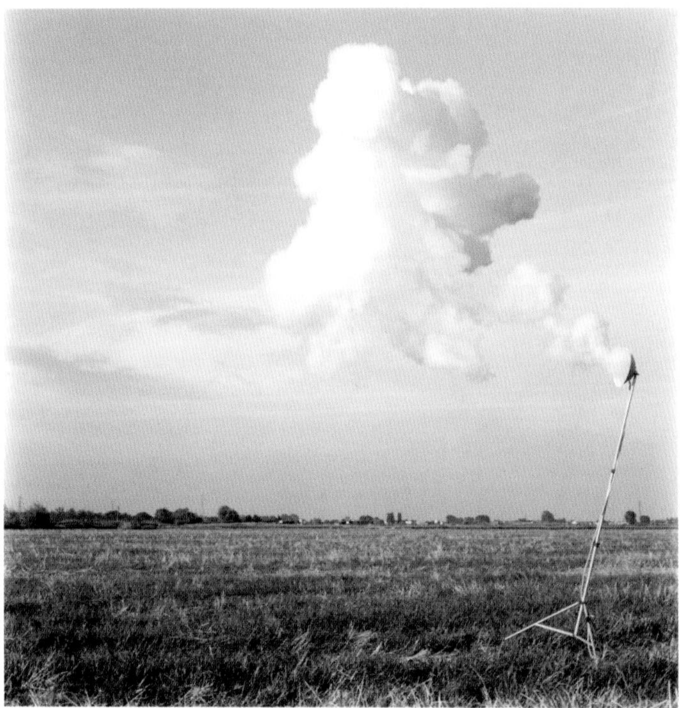

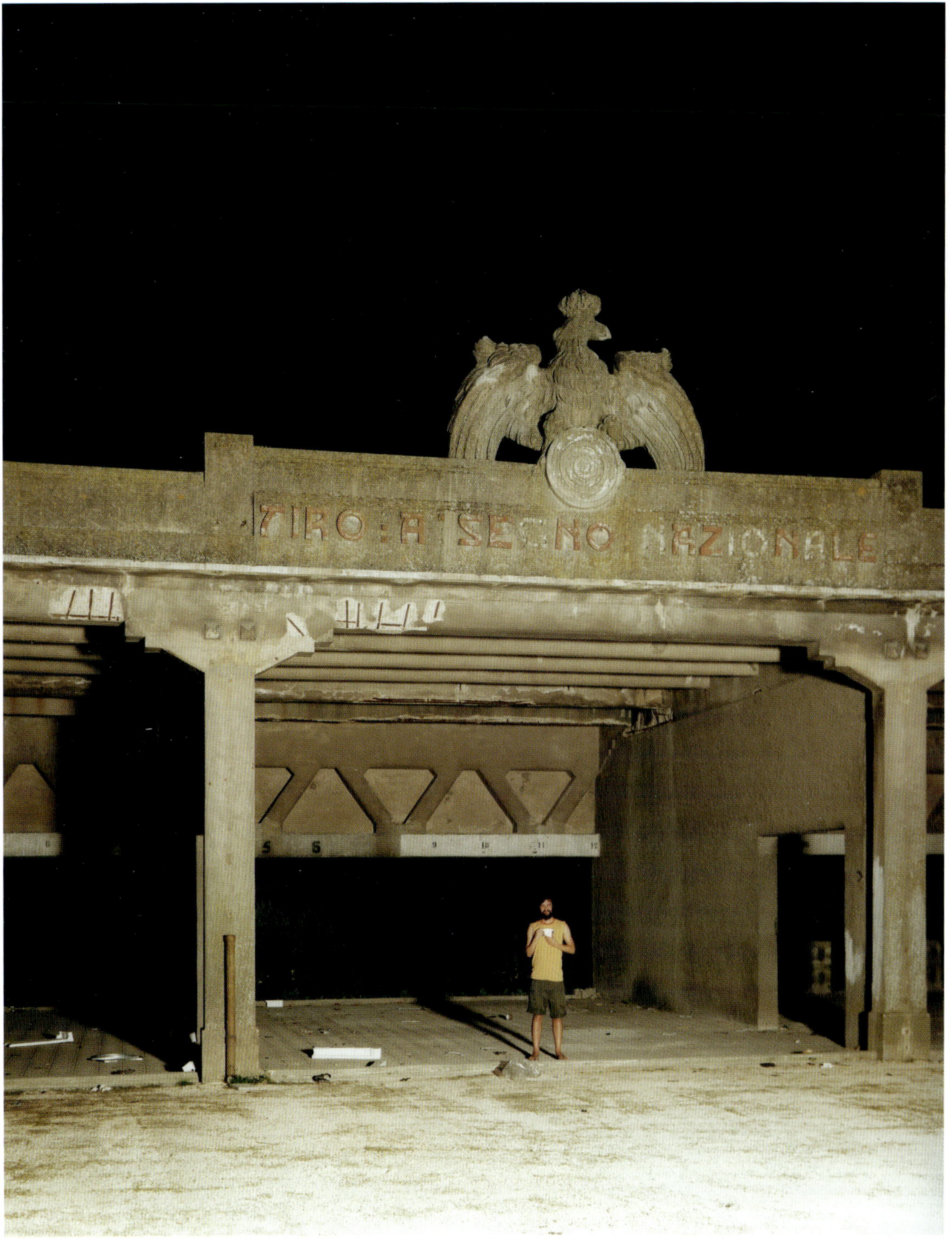

ABOVE

*2582 – Poligono Regio, Darsena di
città, Ravenna,* C-print, taken with
magnesium flash, 30 × 24 cm
(11¾ × 9½ in.), 2010

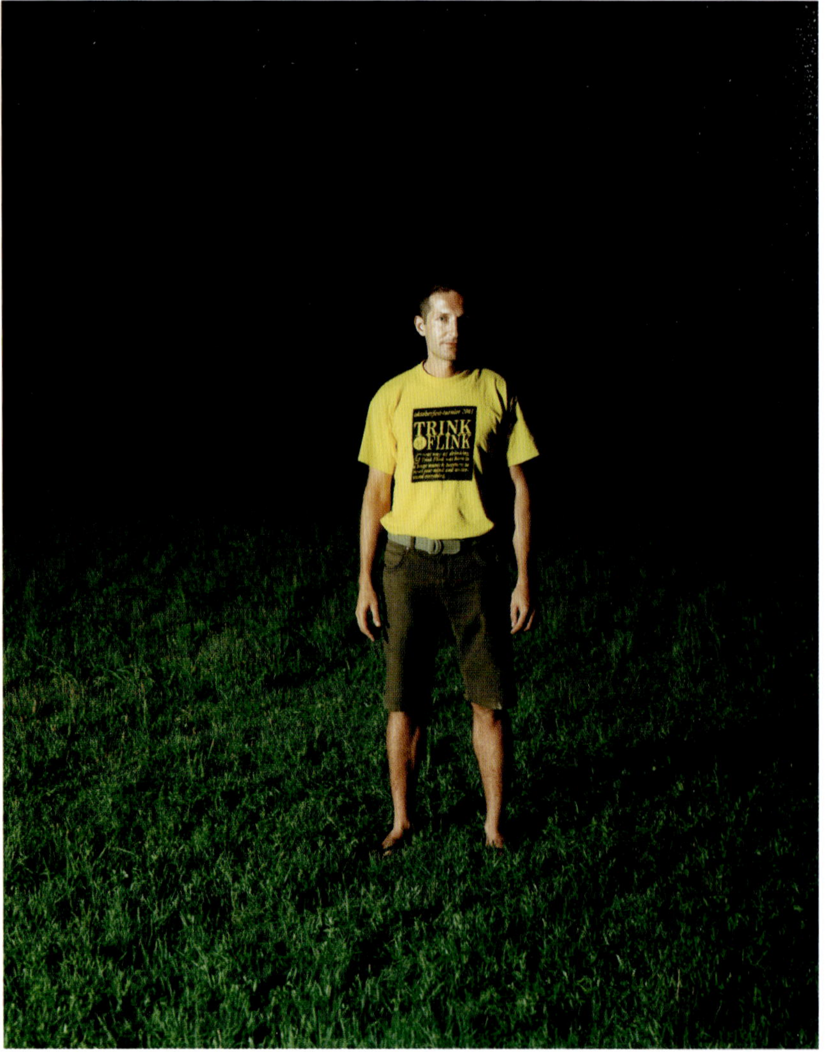

book, which contained the original formulas for magnesium powder. This partly overcame the difficulty of sourcing ready-mixed powder and storing and transporting it safely, although the individual ingredients are still highly flammable. Our first tests were relatively simple; the hard part was then calibrating the formulas so they worked reliably and finding a detonator suitable for use in photography. Determining exposure times was also a challenge that required much trial and error.

What are the visual qualities of the resulting images? What differences do you see in comparison with contemporary artificial lighting techniques?

From a photographic point of view, it is very interesting to see the results of this lighting technique applied to colour photography, since (to my knowledge) no

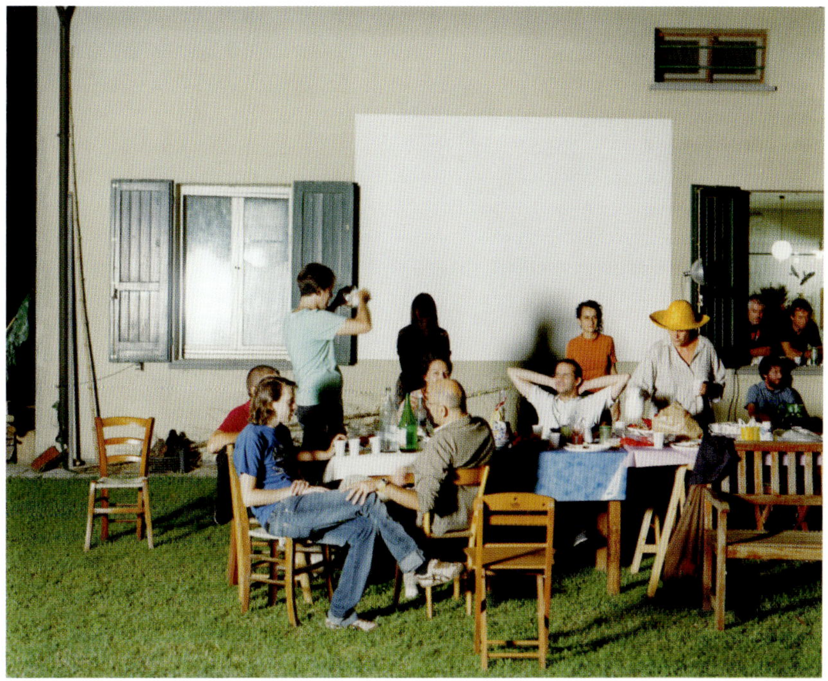

one had ever tried it before, since colour photography hadn't been invented
when magnesium flashes were last in current use. The colourimetric result can
be compared to that of a photo taken with an ordinary sodium-based light
source (e.g. streetlights). However, the lumen produced by the reaction is
astonishing. It is so strong that it allows you to work with non-standard
apertures at night and in low-light conditions. The performative effect is also
exciting: the tension as the flash is prepared; the hot 'breath' it blasts onto the
subjects, not to mention the boom and the smoke cloud afterwards. It is no
coincidence that we decided to experiment with this technique while rehearsing
for the theatre!

*Although magnesium flash is an old technique, would you like to see a
widespread revival of its use to explore its new creative possibilities?*

I can confidently say that these flashes are not for everyone, but I believe they
have great potential for unconventional applications, especially when used
by a team of photographers. In the past, the flash was meant to speed up the
exposure of the slow photosensitive materials used for portrait photography,
or to allow pictures to be taken indoors and in dim lighting. But magnesium
flashes also allow the modern practitioner to photograph subjects in nearly
total darkness at distances of 80–200 m, thus opening up very interesting
possibilities for night landscape photography.

CHRIS McCAW

Interview by
Marco Antonini

Exploring the paradox of time through the movement of the sun, American artist Chris McCaw elevates sunburn photography to an art form.

Can you tell us something about the photographic process behind your Sunburn *series? How do you typically set up a shoot for one of these images, and what are the technical issues you encounter?*

The process for the sunburn pieces is actually very basic and simple. There are no major secrets. A large-format camera is set up with black-and-white enlarging paper loaded in the film holder instead of film. A composition is made, anticipating the apparent path of the sun through the sky, and the film holder is put into the camera. Most of the lenses' shutters are disabled to allow for long exposures, so the lens cap is simply removed for the desired length of time. Once the exposure is done, I take the holder home and in the darkroom I develop it as I would any black-and-white print: developer, stop bath and fixer. There is no Sabattier effect happening during development (as in Man Ray's rayographs); instead, the reversed image tone of the paper negative is achieved through extreme overexposure to light, known as solarization. So it really requires only the basic elements of photography: lens, light, time and a photosensitive receiver (in this case photographic paper).

The more unusual issues are things like modifying, or building from scratch, cameras that are able to support the unusually massive optics I use. Also, as the burning process occurs within the camera, I need to vent off the resulting smoke in order to retain contrast in the image; I use a solar-powered computer exhaust fan for this. With direct unique pieces the ash tends to get everywhere, making a mess of the mat boards when I frame them. As time goes on, a small pile of ash collects at the bottom of the frame, which I rather enjoy seeing. Sometimes the cooked gelatin in the paper becomes gluelike and getting the paper out of the film holders can be challenging. Processing a 30" × 40" with a giant burn that goes completely through the paper base is nerve-wracking and often results in damaged or destroyed pieces.

What led you to explore the concept of the passage of time through photography?

It started when I was documenting my grandfather's workshop with my homemade 7" × 17" view camera. The images were exposed only by the natural light coming through the cobweb-covered skylights and the cracks in the wood of the shed. At $f/64$, to get any kind of depth of field, the light meter suggested

Sunburned GSP#226 (Monterey Bay), unique gelatin silver paper negative, 35.6 × 29.7 cm (14 × 11¾ in.), 2008

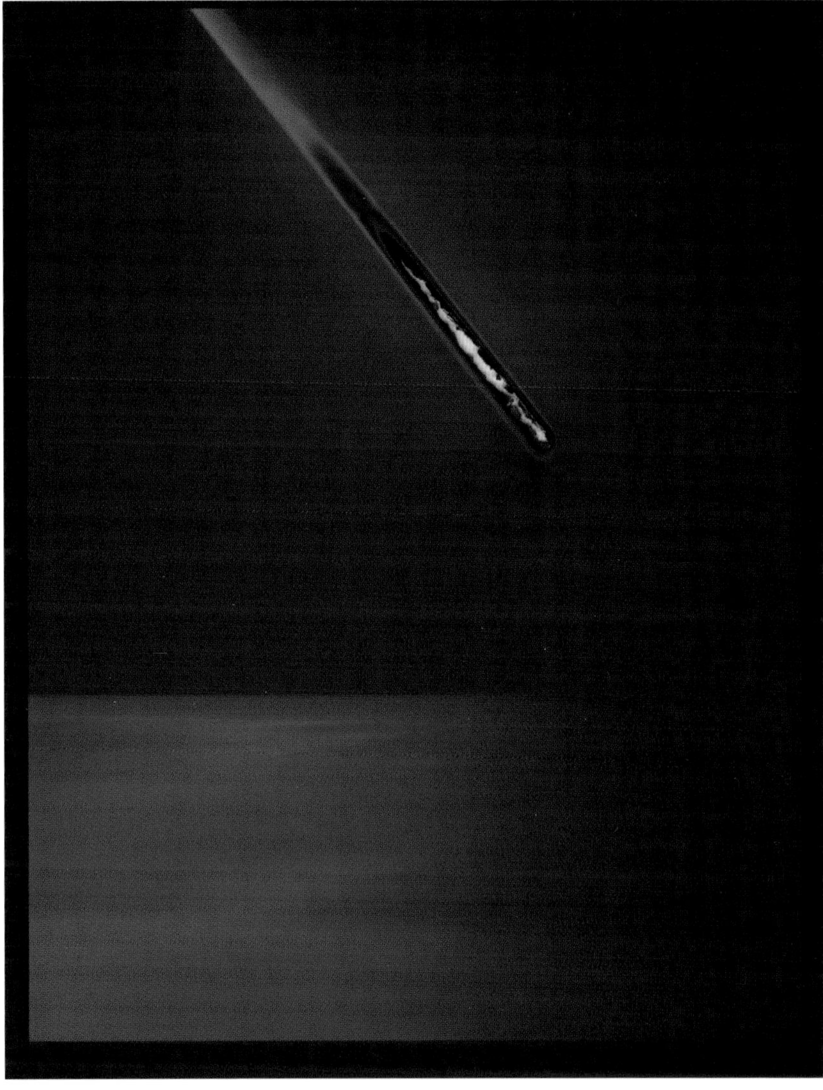

an exposure of 2 minutes, but it was probably tricked by the uneven lighting; I knew through testing that I needed to expose the film for 1.5–2 hours. During this time the sun would move, causing a smoothing of the dim shadows. It was not unlike doing time-lapse exposures of the night sky on camping trips, which is how I eventually discovered the sunburn process: when I failed to close the shutter before sunrise, the rising sun not only destroyed the night's exposure, but was also so powerful that it physically changed the film.

Where do you find the materials and equipment to build your own cameras? Did you hack existing camera models or did you have to work from scratch to achieve what you wanted?

Sunburned GSP#322 (Pacific Ocean/30 Minutes), unique gelatin silver paper negative, 60.9 × 50.8 cm (24 × 20 in.), 2009

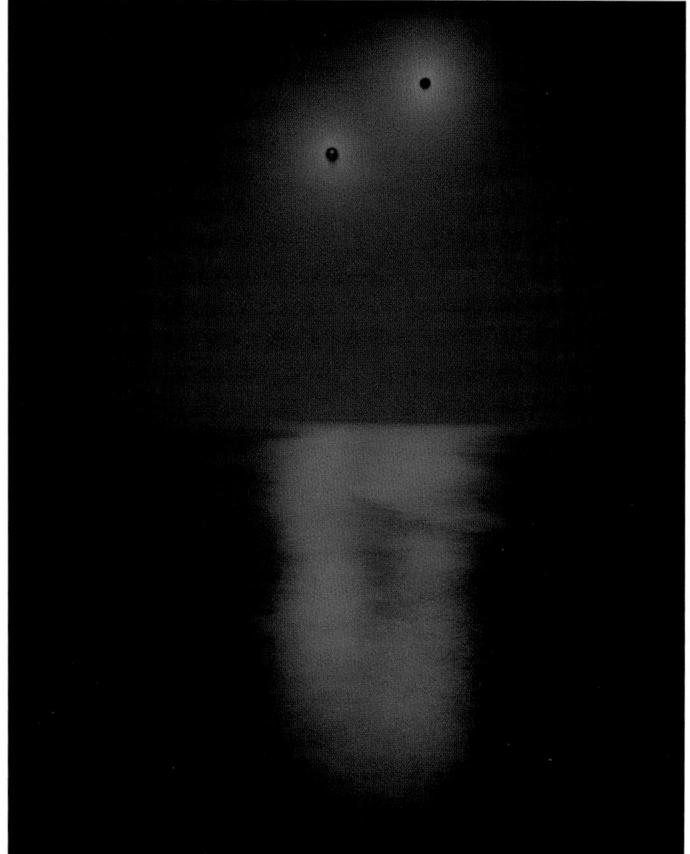

The act of building cameras started strictly out of poverty. I had recently graduated from college and had been using my almost 100-year-old 7" × 17" and was frustrated by the rickety antique. To make ends meet, I decided to sell the camera, and kept just the film holders. I reinvested about $150 building a completely homemade camera, complete with hand-folded bellows that I made from scratch (the hardest part of the process). I would gladly have paid the thousands of dollars for a brand-new modern banquet camera, but I was just your classic starving artist. So I had to find a way to make a camera. This was in 1995, when the internet was just something you'd hear about; I wish I'd had Google back then. The camera was built around the film holders. I used photographs of modern designs of view cameras as much as I could but I also improvised. I used stacked hacksaw blades as spring steel for the film back. (My grandfather once built a giant saw that ran off the belt of a straight six-cylinder engine welded to a homemade trailer; I like to think I got my building sense from him!) The main lesson was that function should be the primary consideration. I didn't care about brass hardware, red leather bellows or kiln-dried mahogany. Over the years I have built many other cameras that could be considered

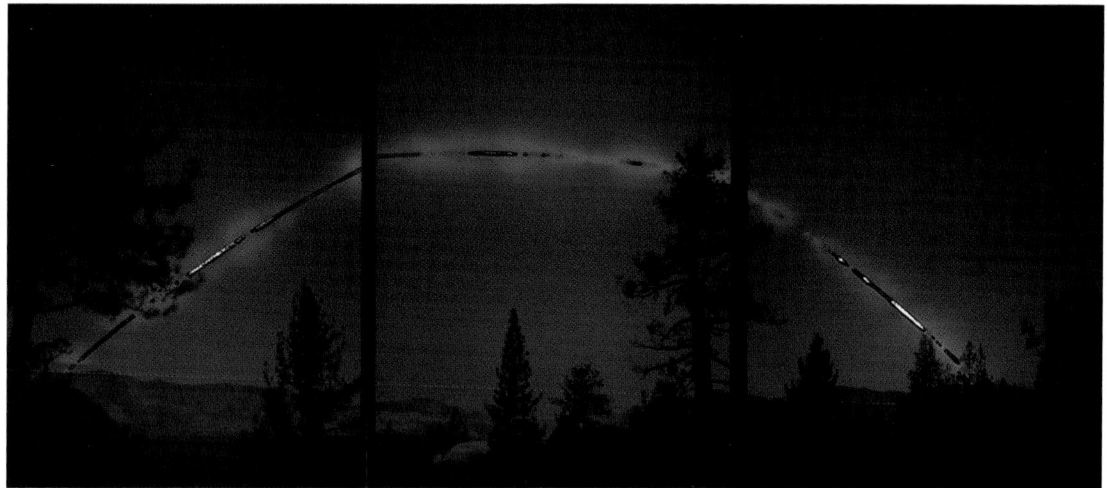

Sunburned GSP#469 (Full Day/ Serrias), three unique gelatin silver paper negatives, each 35.5 × 27.9 cm (14 × 11 in.), 2011

'frankencameras': a mix of pieces from broken cameras and my own woodwork. I first learned of military aerial reconnaissance optics (as well as the effects of solarization) in 1994 during a daguerreotype class taught by Jerry Spagnoli. In the days before the internet, I remember seeing these exotic but practically unrealistic lenses at the annual camera swaps that used to happen. But now eBay and Craigslist have proven to be a great source to find pretty much all the materials I have needed.

What is the merit of working with analogue techniques in our days? What is the difference between creating something via commercially available instruments (and standard processes) versus custom-made ones?

The craft of photography has always been important for me. I do feel strongly about the magic of the meeting between chemistry and light, and I like the feeling of getting my hands wet in the darkroom. A handmade print has a totally different feel. In a world where folks are selling digital prints and saying 'If it gets damaged, I'll just print you a new one,' where's the meaning in the object? I don't really know how to answer this but it makes me uncomfortable and unsatisfied.

ÉDOUARD DECAM

Interview by
Luca Bendandi

French photographer Édouard Decam uses long-exposure techniques to express the relationship between space, time and architecture in industrial landscapes such as seaports and astronomical observatories.

Tell us about the project Port de Barcelona.

In collaboration with architect Sebastian Khourian, I started *Port de Barcelona* in early 2010. The project consists of a photographic investigation of the city's industrial port. It is aimed at collecting the details that describe the port in its social, legal, economic, urban and architectural aspects. The long exposure technique brings out the temporal dimension, and the projection of space in time, capturing the very essence of the site. I used two cameras placed strategically at the entrance of the port. Each camera was custom-built according to the needs of such long exposures, and I went on to use them in all my successive long-exposure work.

What is the rationale behind such long exposure times?

After observing the harbour for months it seemed to me that in addition to capturing the landscape, my photographs needed to record the invisible dimensions that surround us, such as time, the permanence of architecture or the physical relationships and the emotions contained in these places. The long-exposure methodology that Sebastian had used to photograph a number of architectural works presented a way of creating accurate reflections of the passage of time, and illustrating relationships between static architecture and moving elements in the landscape.

How did you come to the idea of using long exposures in the context of your project Le quatrième continent? *How do the landscapes or observatories relate to the subject of your research?*

Astronomical observatories are like islands where temporality is omnipresent. The idea of a conceptual *mise en abyme* was central: I photograph observatories, which in turn photograph the stars, which reflect our own past. My research was devoted to capturing the telescopes' temporality and their relationship to light; trying to understand the permanence of their landscapes and architecture. The recorded movement of the antenna is our reflection; architecture is the tie that binds us to landscape, stars and the earth itself. Through long exposures I've tried to create a way to express this physical connection to our environment.

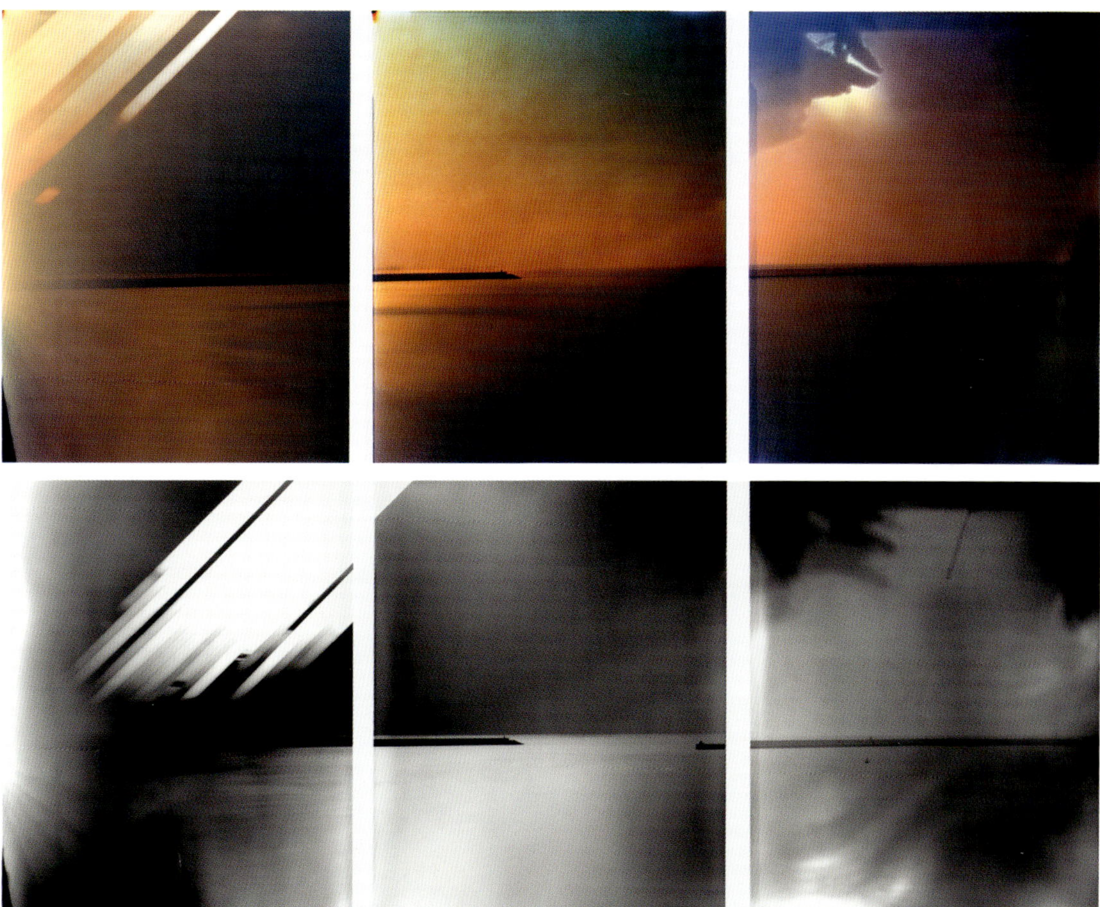

Can you explain the techniques used for Le quatrième continent?

Most of the test shoots were done in Barcelona. During these trials I adjusted exposure times, chose the right film and fine-tuned the cameras we built. But the biggest issue was that classic large-format cameras are not made for such long exposure times. I had to get creative and hack the cameras in order to get them to leave the shutter open for so long. I think photographic research progresses through working with unknown components, creating both successful images and failures. Both are important to the final result of my work.

Pico Veleta | 6 h 25 min, from the series *Le quatrième continent*, Lambda print, 125 × 156 cm (49¼ × 61⅜ in.), 2013

Le Pic | 3 h 30 min, from the series *Le quatrième continent*, Lambda print, 125 × 156 cm (49¼ × 61⅜ in.), 2013

Yebes | 4 h 23 min, from the series *Le quatrième continent*, Lambda print, 125 × 156 cm (49¼ × 61⅜ in.), 2013

Ceberos | 5 h 33 min, from the series *Le quatrième continent*, Lambda print, 125 × 156 cm (49¼ × 61⅜ in.), 2013

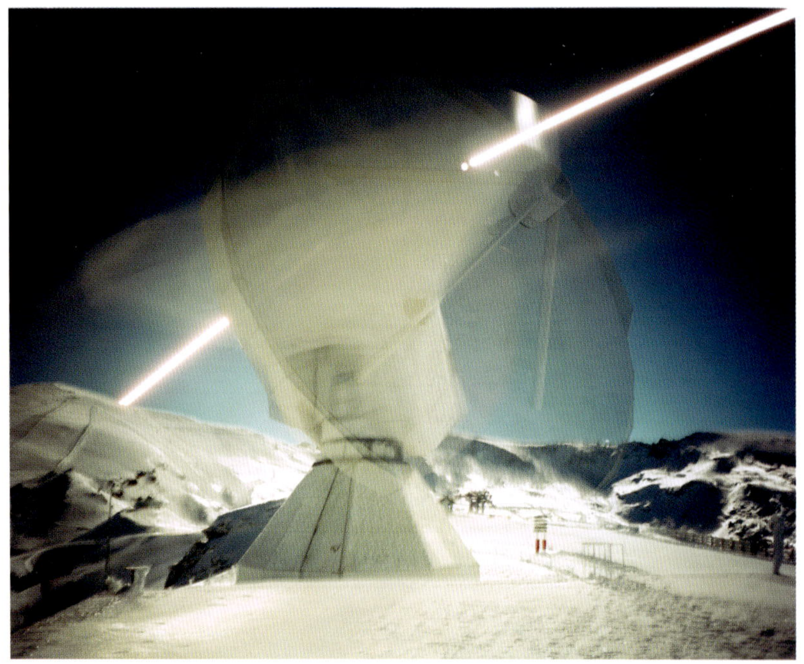

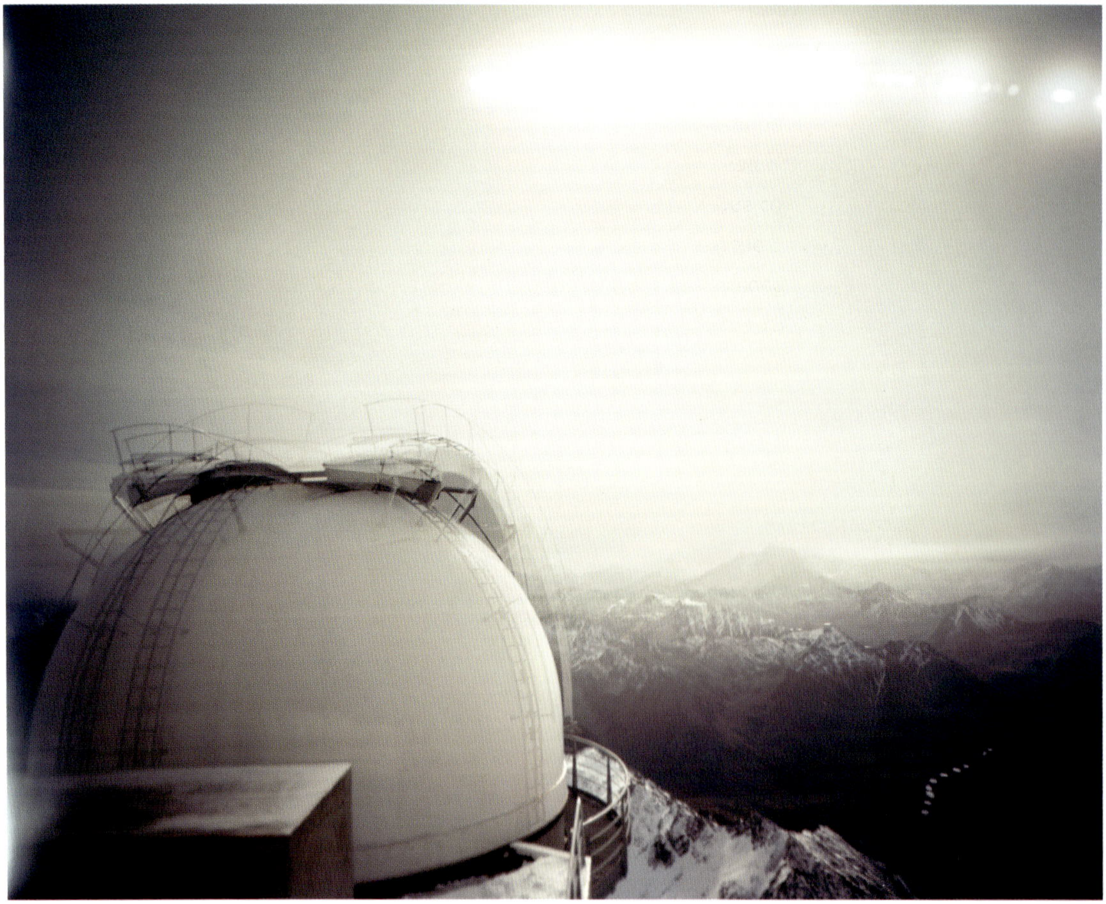

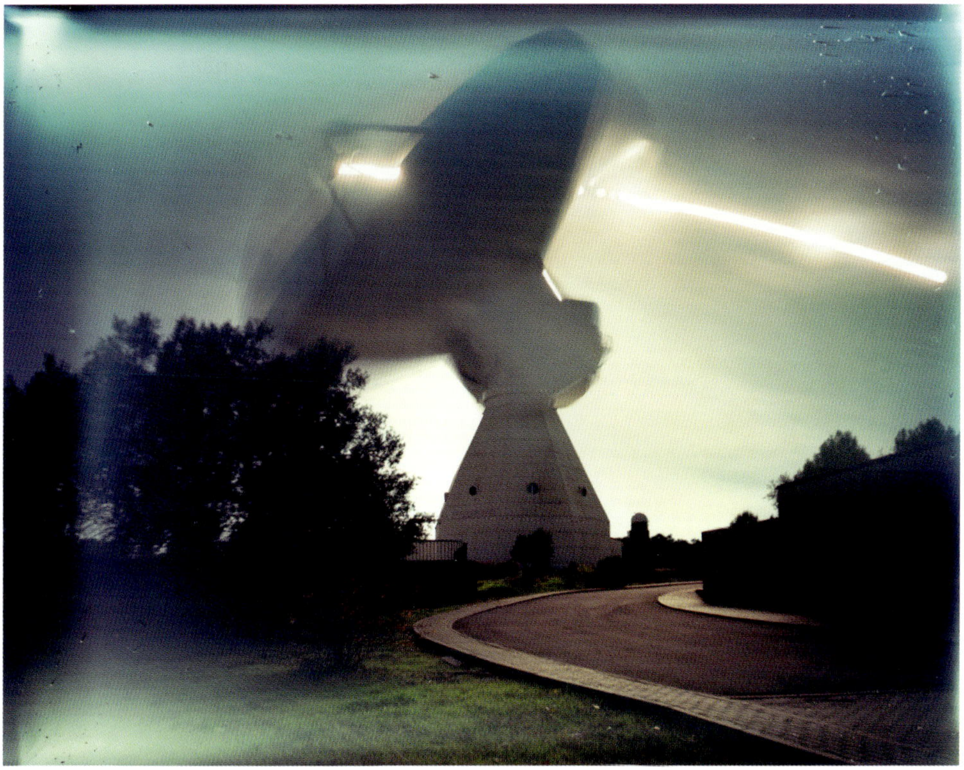

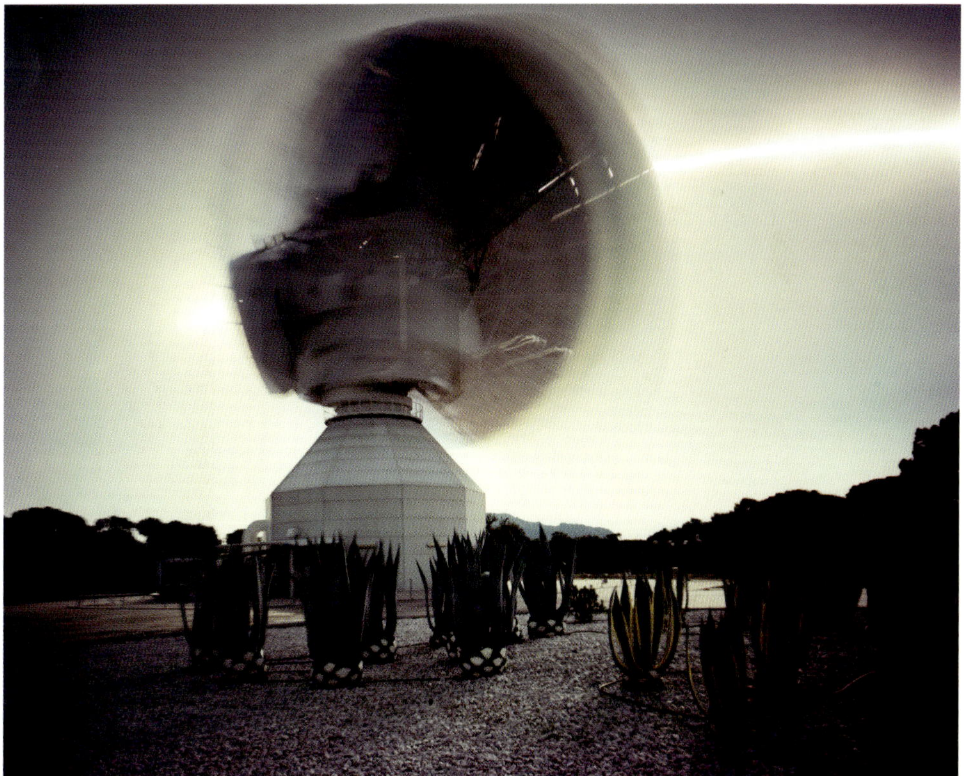

BRANA VOJNOVIC

Interview by Sergio Minniti

Serbian artist Brana Vojnovic's mastery of the art of reclaiming, repairing and upcycling obsolete photographic equipment makes his work unique.

How did you get into photography, and how would you describe your current practice?

At sixteen I started taking pictures to document my youth art group's work. I was initially intrigued by sculpture, but gradually progressed to photography as the focus of my art. There are now three main threads in my work: research related to photography; constructing and upcycling cameras; and actually shooting photos. The end result is always a photograph, but it is a cumulative result of all three activities happening in parallel.

Constructing and upcycling the equipment is an important part of your creative process. When, and why, did you begin building and modifying cameras?

The first camera that I built was a bellows camera, back in 1979. It was an 8" × 10" but I did not have an adequate lens and a cassette to make it work properly. So this one was not functional, but it deserves mention since it was my first attempt. I regained interest in upcycling and building cameras about four years ago. I finally had very concrete ideas of what kind of photo equipment I would need to achieve the effects I wanted, but it was not possible to buy it. At the same time, I realized that old and nonfunctioning cameras and lenses were available for sale in abundance, for low prices, and that I had the skills to make them work again. But simply repairing them was not enough. Upcycling actually allows you to mix and match the parts for improved quality, and often for a whole new purpose. I find it extremely rewarding to be able to give new life and relevance to fine equipment. For me the ultimate satisfaction is in preserving beautiful and precious pieces of human craftsmanship. My photos often also depict old things that are not in use any more.

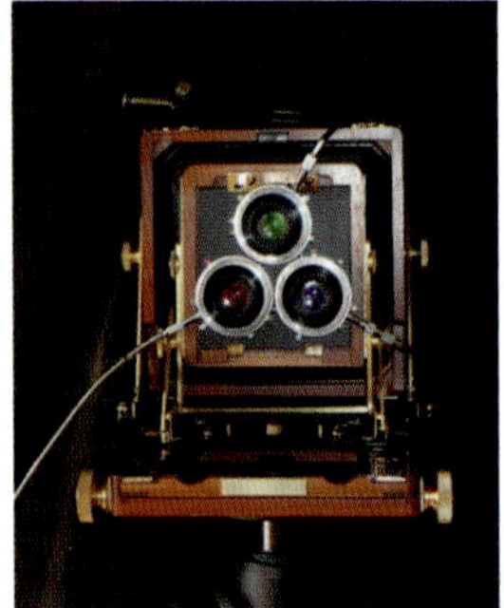

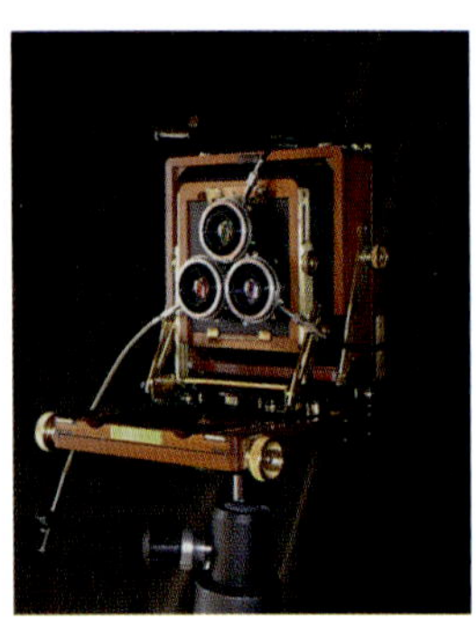

ABOVE
Tri-colour 4" × 5" film camera, three T22 Lomo 75 mm F4.5 lenses with RGB filters inside, 2012

OPPOSITE
Psiha, 4" × 5" Ilford FP4 and RGB GEVA filters, PMK Pyro film developer, 12 × 9 cm (4¾ × 3½ in.), 2012

How does this relate to your conception of photography? Do you think that photographers should pay more attention to how cameras are made and work?

I feel that photography is very similar to painting. Just as a painter has to prepare his or her canvas and sketch before starting to paint, I do a lot of preparatory work in order to get a good photo. First I decide whether I'll be using a wet-plate, film, scan or other technique, and only then do I start thinking about the

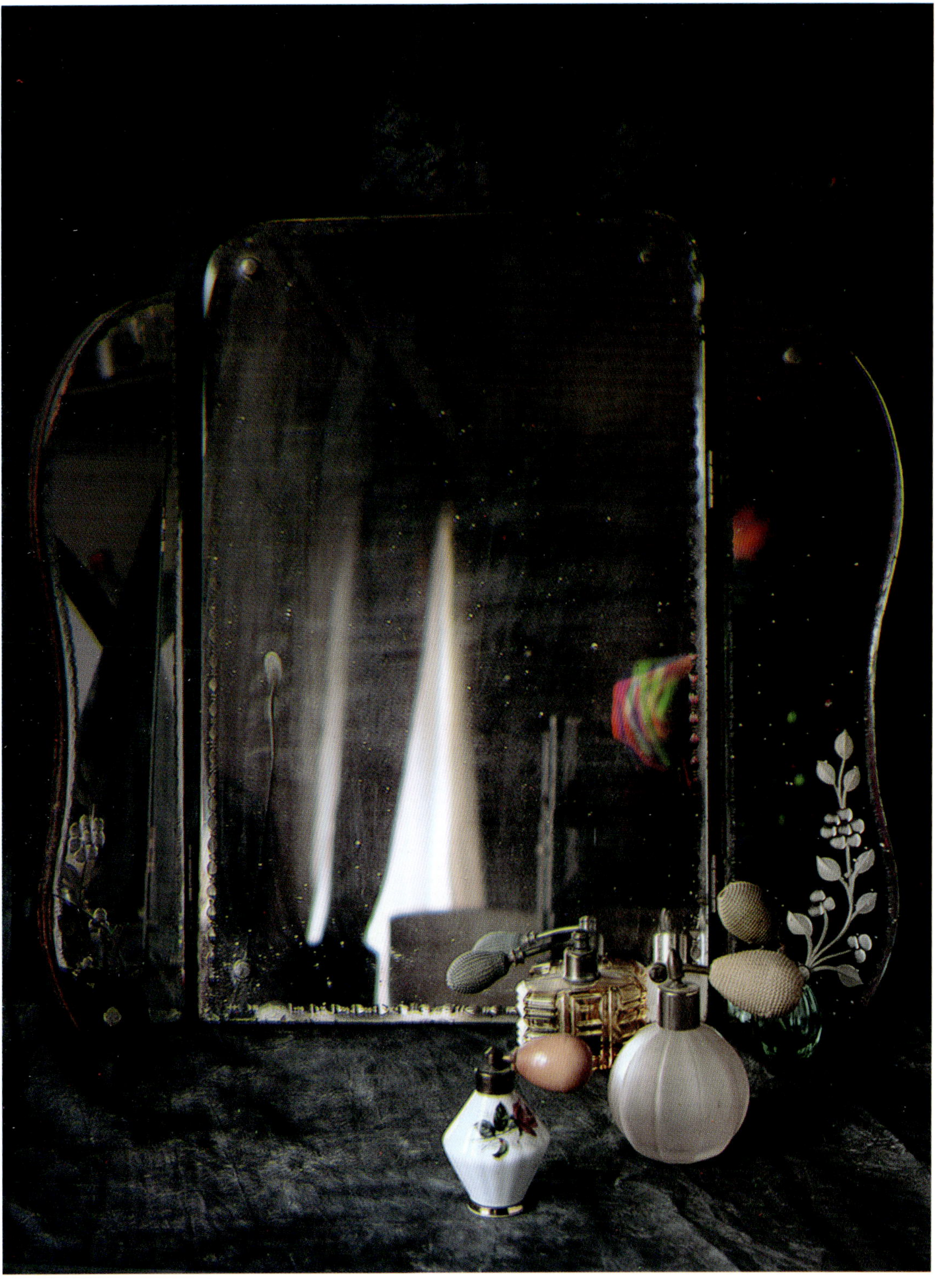

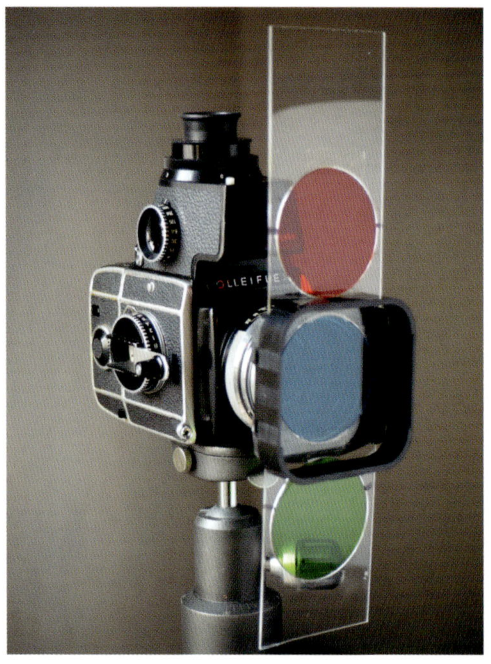

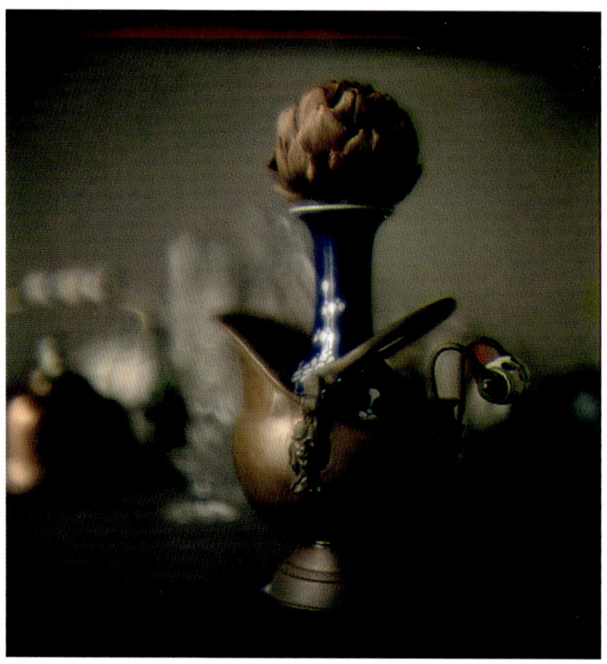

equipment. I find the best lens for the purpose and adapt it to fit to the body of the camera I have chosen. Mixing and matching cameras and lenses is an art in itself. I enjoy this very detailed preparation process because it reminds me more of painting than of simply 'clicking' to produce a photo like many of us do when using digital cameras. Nowadays, cameras are built in a way that makes photographers think less about the process behind the photo; the emphasis is on finding subjects and catching them. With modern high-performance digital cameras all photos are of excellent quality. There is no challenge involved: anyone who has enough money to buy the camera can be a good photographer. Moreover, digital photo retouch software shifts the focus towards post-production to create an ever-more standardized ideal of perfection. I do think it's possible to be a great photographer without really understanding how the camera works. There are wonderful artists who use digital cameras, or even smartphones. But I do think that all photographers should be aware of the value of things in general and we should all think about how we can preserve, adapt, use and reuse, instead of buying new equipment and throwing the old one away. Even if I might use more recent camera bodies, I always use very old lenses, usually early twentieth-century: Rodenstock casket lenses, Goerz or Boyer Paris Saphir. I'm not against digital technology, although I am not thrilled by the fact that it is possible to mimic wet-plate or old-style photos just by changing the options on your phone. I am also not a recycling artist or green activist; I am just a photographer who loves to know how things function, especially in reclaiming old cameras.

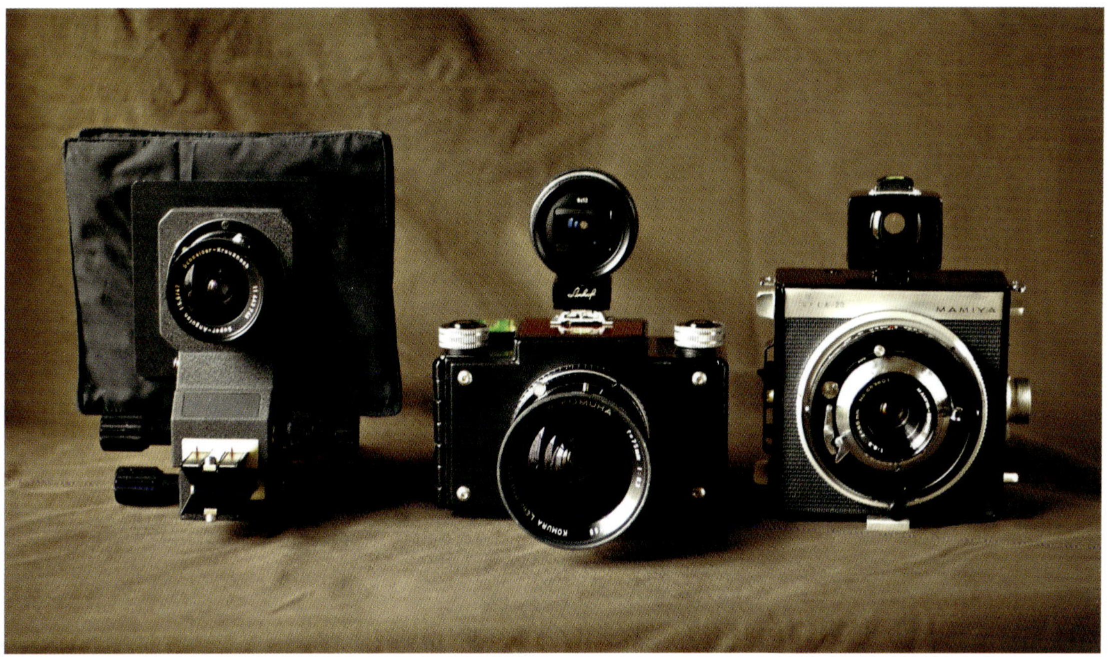

*What is the relationship between the subjects of your photographs and
the cameras you use to capture them?*

My cameras are the tools for my work and very often also the subjects of my
images. Sometimes I build a camera for the specific needs of the subject I have
to photograph. For example, I built the panoramic camera to shoot photos of
old towns. The idea came to me in the island of Cres in Croatia. I wanted to
photograph the long and narrow streets of the old town, so I used a panoramic
camera vertically. I would say that the interaction between my handmade cameras
and the objects is what makes the story; for instance, when the camera I am
using is older than the subjects I am photographing.

*Let's talk about your Scannercameras. Why did you start turning flatbed
scanners into giant digital cameras?*

I started building Scannercameras a few years back, experimenting with CCD
and CIS sensors. I had a strong leaning towards black and white photography
at the time and the CIS sensors were perfect for my needs due to their size,
resolution and tonal range. My Scannercamera 200 is the second camera that I
upcycled from a Canon CanoScan LiDE 200. It is 5" × 7" format, with a compact
body and a 165 mm Tessar objective with built-in focus. When I first started
constructing it, I was just curious about combining old and new techniques
and equipment.

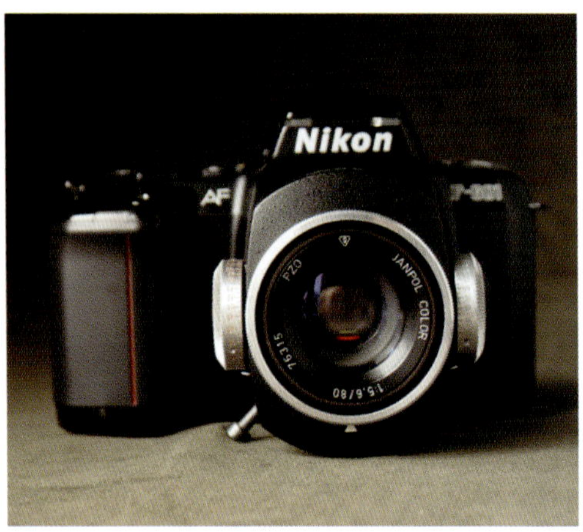 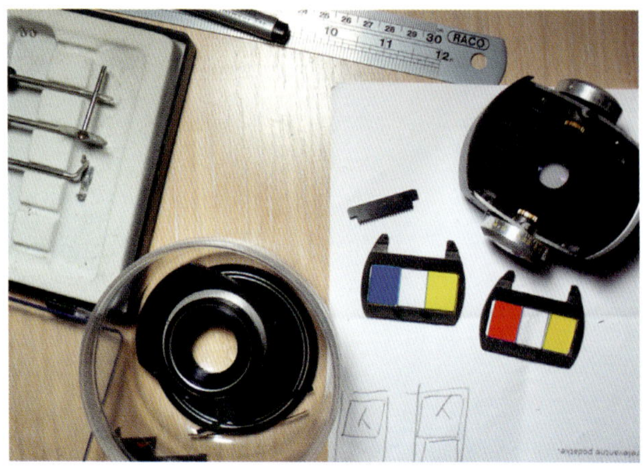

ABOVE
Nikon F601 with PZO tri-colour lens, 2011 (left), and inserting the filters into the PZO casing (right).

BELOW
Portable Scannercamera, Tessar 165 mm 5" × 7" camera with a focusing helicoid and Canon CanoScan LiDE 200, 2009 This set-up was Vojnovic's first (and still favourite) Scannercamera.

People use Scannercameras to obtain a sort of 'scanning movement' effect. Yet you have used all of your Scannercamera models – including the Episkopscan 8 × 10 (using the body of a projector) and the Tri-colour 4 × 5 Scannercamera – for portraits, landscapes and still lifes.

When I started working on Scannercameras my key aim was to obtain high-resolution and large-format photos. With my first portable Scannercamera I tried to capture movements and shoot portraits of myself and my family. Let's say that the subjects weren't impressed with the results! Having always been an admirer of old painters, I then started trying to make still lifes with my Scannercamera equipment. My 'studio' was my home and kitchen, so fruit and kitchen utensils were readily available subjects. Working with Scannercameras was a wonderful opportunity to work with large formats, incorporating weird colours and tiny movement traces. Even when the objects are perfectly still, the light changes and some kind of movement is inevitable, since Scannercamera exposures can take up to 20 minutes. The 'ghosts' in the photos, i.e. the lines that appear, are a

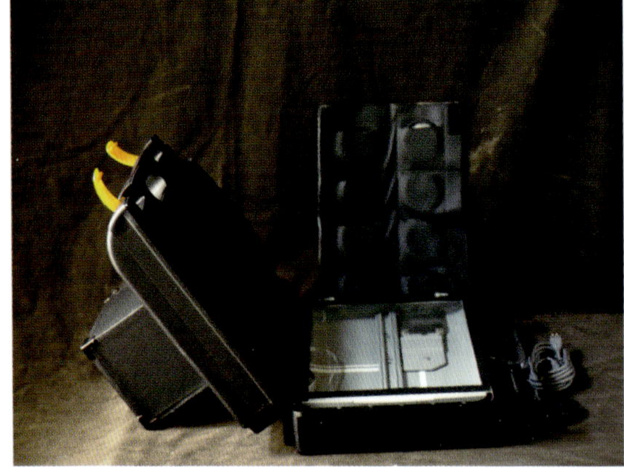 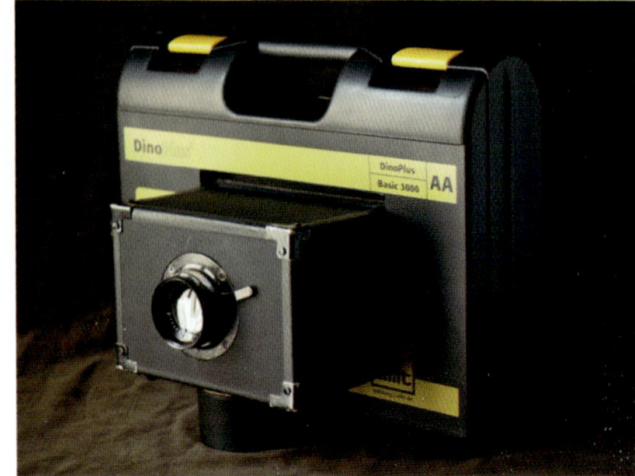

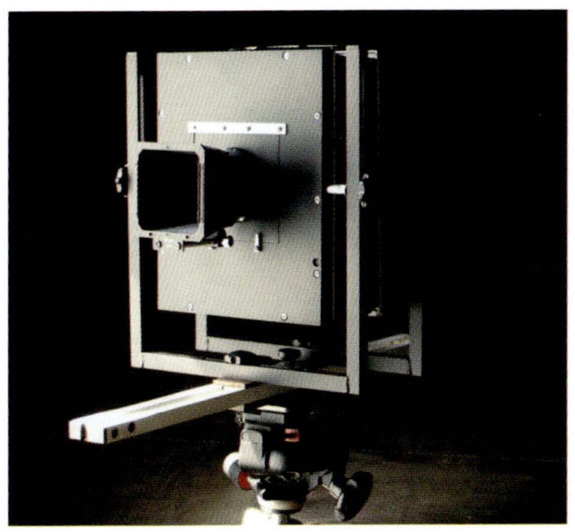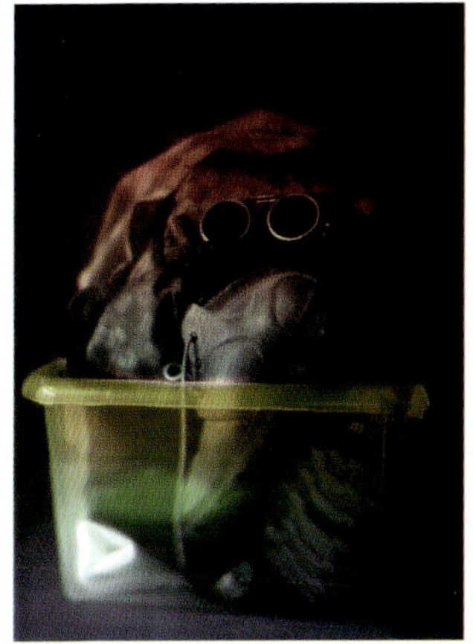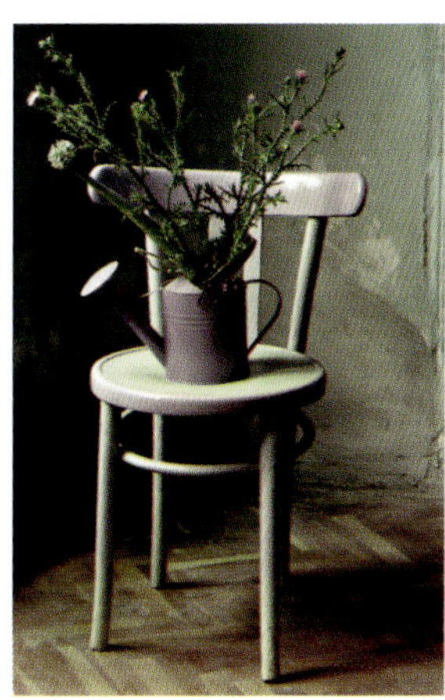

distinctive feature of Scannercamera photography. Preparing for the photo is a process as important as shooting itself: I make drawings of the objects and how I want them to be positioned; I wait for the specific time of the day and if the weather changes quickly I postpone the shoot.

Your experiments are also focused on the trichromy process. Why did you choose the trichromy field to work in?

For the last thirty years I almost exclusively used black and white film because the main colour film brands were too artificial and bright for my taste. So creating the softer colours I preferred was another challenge for me. I started researching the origins of colour photography and colour film. RGB trichromy was an obvious choice, and gave me yet another 'reclaiming' mission. RGB layers that make up a trichromic picture are so soft and transparent, so distinctive in comparison to other processes. They remind me of the palettes of the early Flemish painters. The pioneering colour photography of Sergey Mikhaylovich Prokudin-Gorsky was also of great inspiration to me.

Tell us about your unconventional three-colour Scannercamera process.

The concept is essentially the same as standard trichromy. Every Scannercamera that I have made has a CIS black-and-white sensor, so in order to take colour photos it is necessary to photograph the subject three times, each using a different RGB filter: red, green and blue. The whole process takes approximately 15 minutes with a resolution of 600 DPI (5 minutes for each colour). The three photos then need to be merged with the aid of digital retouching software, but I never use the software for anything else.

POLAROID CAMERA FOR WET-PLATE COLLODION

This is a simple, non-permanent hack that allows you to use a Polaroid camera as a wet-plate collodion camera. Although regular medium- and large-format film cameras can be adapted for wet collodion use with special wet-plate holders, there is a small chance that the collodion can damage the inner mechanism, so it is best to avoid using very expensive modern equipment for this purpose. The turn-of-the-century large-format cameras that were expressly made (and are still usually employed) for this technique are also very expensive. For a cheaper alternative to both, any Polaroid camera that uses instant-pack film can be repurposed for wet-plate collodion use. The low-cost 100–400 series cameras are ideal.

Hack a Polaroid instant pack for wet-plate collodion

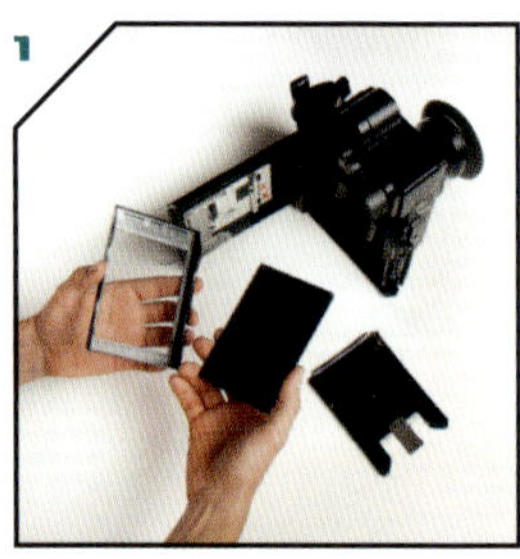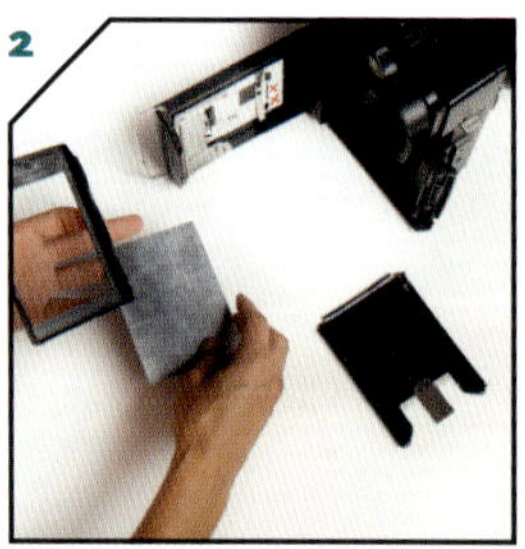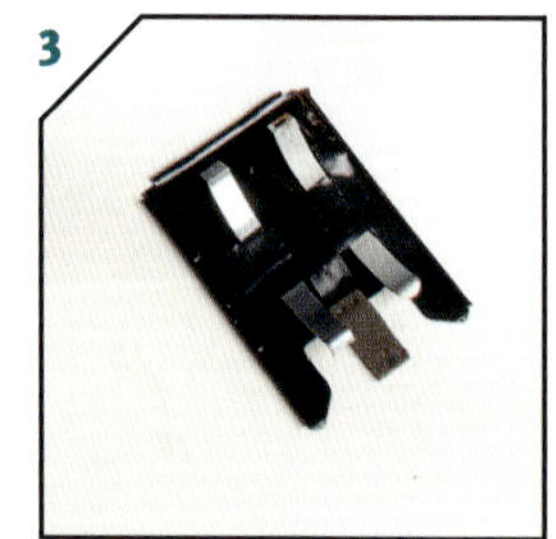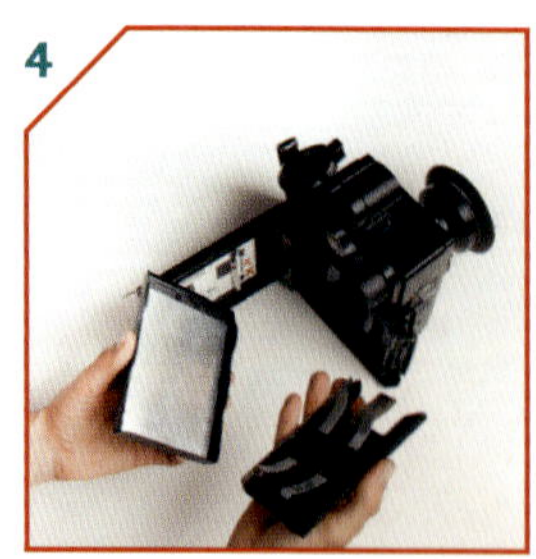

What you need:
- ☐ Polaroid camera
- ☐ Polaroid instant film pack (empty)
- ☐ black adhesive tape
- ☐ thin metal or plastic curved bands, approximately 1 cm wide, 2 mm thick and 5 cm long, from any source
- ☐ collodion plate (aluminium or glass) (see pp. 190–98)

Francisco Gómez
Mickia Brangman, ambrotype taken with hacked Polaroid, 10.7 × 8.8 cm (4¼ × 3½ in.), 2013

! light-sensitive step

Disassemble the instant pack

1 Instant-pack film magazines are made up of three parts: a frame, a film container and a back plate.

2 Disassemble the instant-pack film magazine by pressing the sides gently and lifting the back plate. You should be able to do this with your hands – do not use a screwdriver or other tools as you could damage the pack. Discard the film container.

Hack the pack to hold a collodion plate

3 Attach one or two thin metal bands that will act as springs to press the plate and keep it in place during the exposure. The bands can be taped or glued to the picture frame.

4 Under subdued lighting, take your coated collodion plate and fit it into your holder.

The plate should have been cut to the exact size of the picture frame (see p. 192 for how to cut the glass) and prepared with collodion as outlined on pp. 190–98. Reassemble the film pack, pressing the sides of the frame to lock the back plate in place. Load the film pack into the camera, and it can be taken into the light, ready to be used.

Trick the automatic exposure meter

When it comes to making an exposure, most Polaroid cameras have an automatic exposure metering system, which uses a light-sensitive cell positioned close to the lens. However, even in broad daylight, wet-plate collodion needs an exposure in the order of minutes. To make this possible, cover the camera's metering cell with a piece of black tape so you can make long exposures by pressing and holding the shutter release.

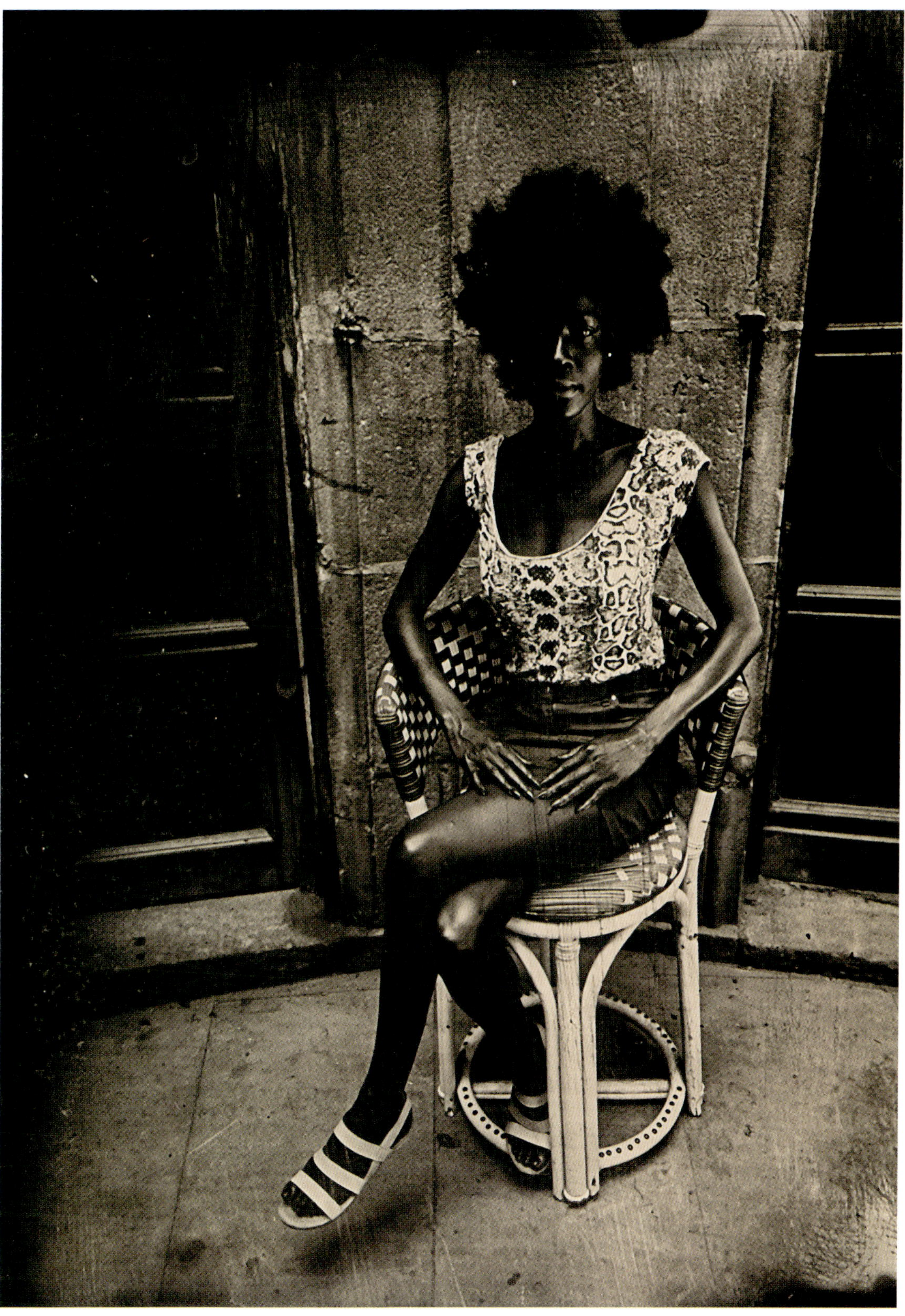

35 MM SLR FOR WET-PLATE COLLODION MICROTYPE

It is easy to hack a 35 mm SLR camera so that it can hold a wet collodion plate made out of an ordinary glass microscope slide. In addition to allowing you to use modern equipment for your shots, an SLR camera will be easier to carry than a large-format model, while sensitizing the small plates (often referred to as 'microtypes') will be quicker and more economical. Here, the hacked 35 mm SLR is used to shoot a miniature ambrotype – that is, a 'positive' image (actually an underexposed negative) on glass – but the process can easily be adapted to produce miniature tintypes. To prevent damage to the camera, avoid leaving the prepared collodion plate inside it for more than 10 minutes.

35 mm SLR camera hack for wet-plate collodion microtype

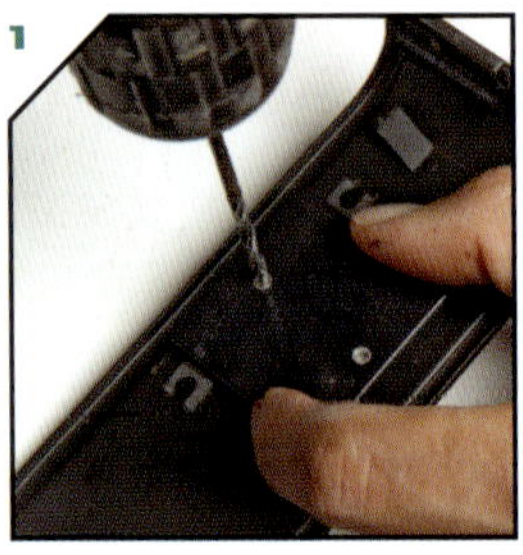
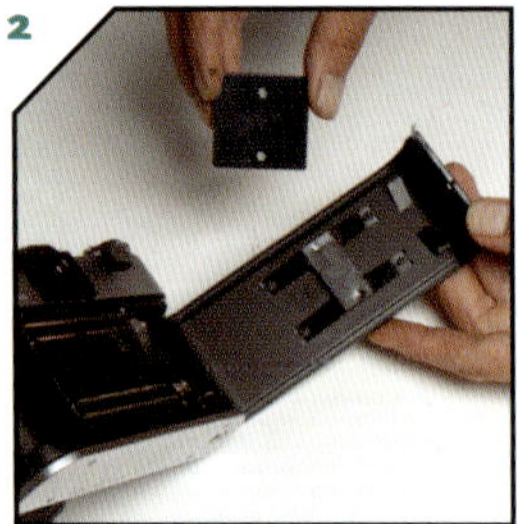
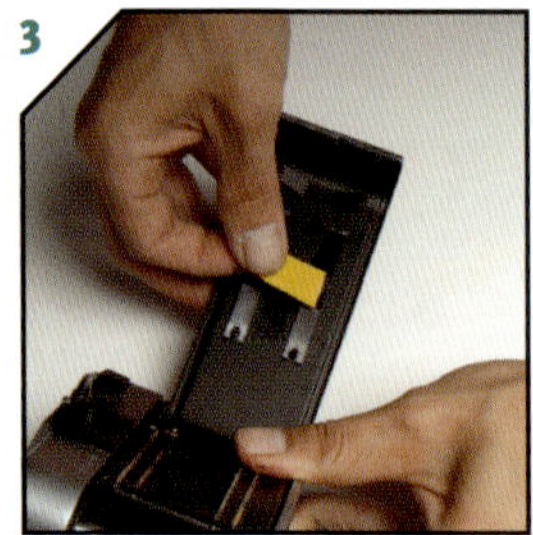
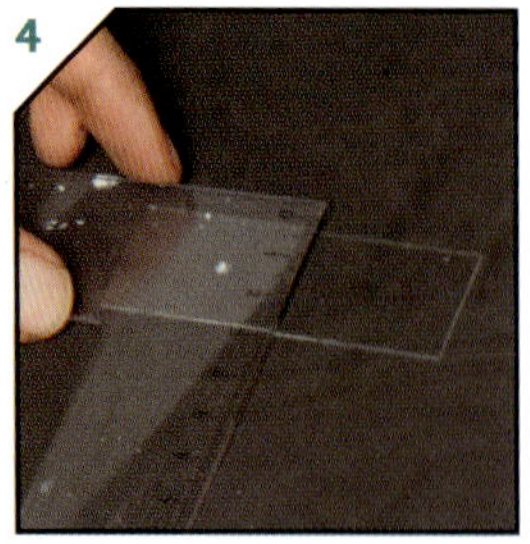

What you need:

- [ ] 35 mm SLR camera
- [ ] drill
- [ ] double-sided adhesive tape
- [ ] microscope slides
- [ ] ruler
- [ ] glass cutter
- [ ] collodion sensitizing, developing and fixing solutions ⚠ (see pp. 190–98)

Hack the back of the camera

Open the rear film door of the camera. Most 35 mm reflex cameras have a pressure plate, which is a square or rectangular piece of metal mounted on two metal band springs. This plate is used to keep the film in place on the film plane, but for this hack it needs to be removed.

1 In most cases some very light drilling will be required to remove the rivets holding the plate in place, but be extra careful not to drill too deep!

2 Remove the pressure plate.

3 Cut a strip of double-sided adhesive tape and stick it onto the spring assembly behind the pressure plate. This tape will be used to hold your microtypes in place.

Cut the microscope slide

4 The image area for a 35 mm frame is 36 × 24 mm, so you will need to cut your microscope slides to size. Usefully, a regular microscope slide measures approximately 75 × 25 mm, so you can simply cut it in half to make two microtype plates. Start by measuring the slide with a ruler to divide it into two parts.

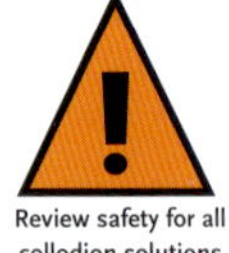

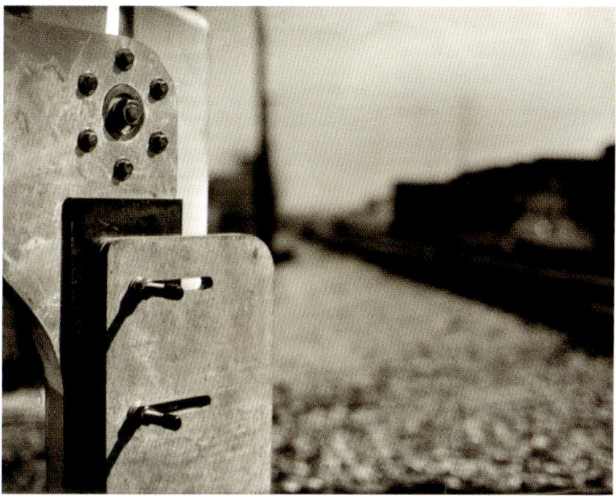

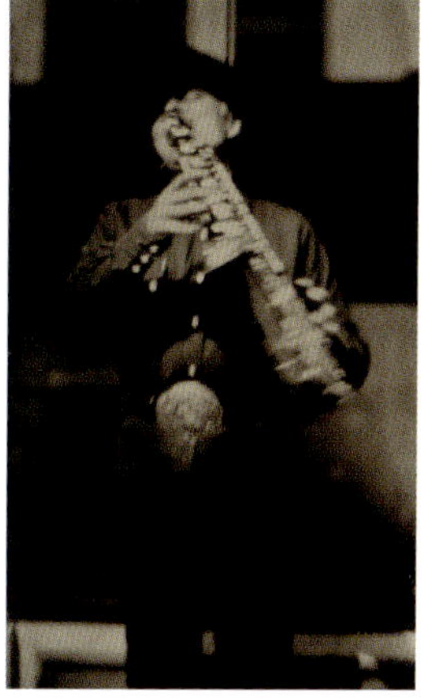

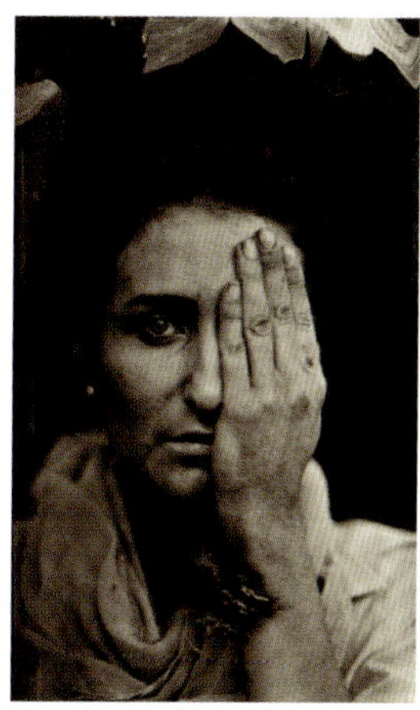

ABOVE LEFT
Gerald Figal
Bolted, 35 mm ambrotype, 2013

ABOVE CENTRE
Gerald Figal
Street Sax, 35 mm tintype, 2013

ABOVE RIGHT
Gerald Figal
Hundful, Eyeful, 35 mm
ambrotype, 2013

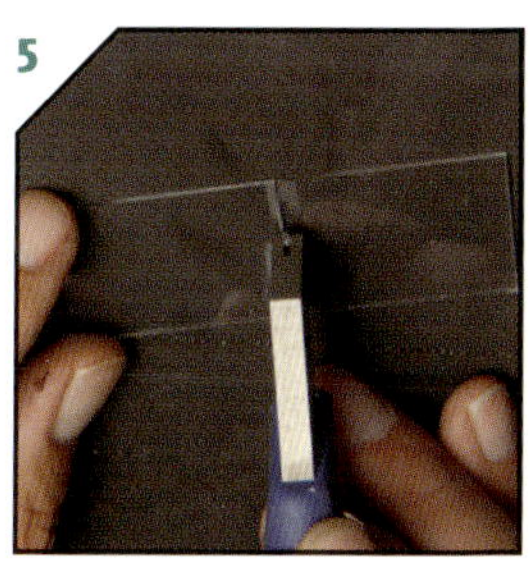

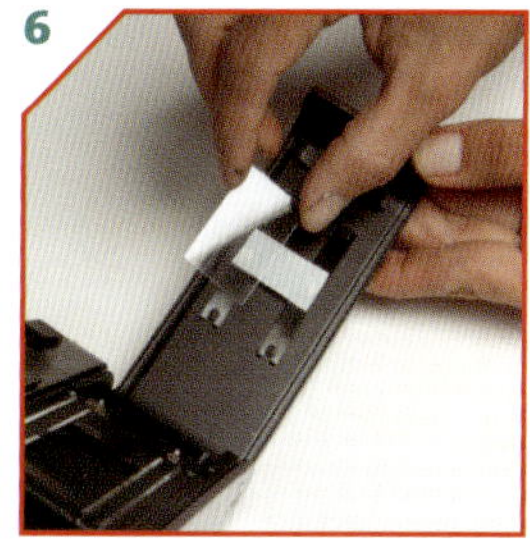

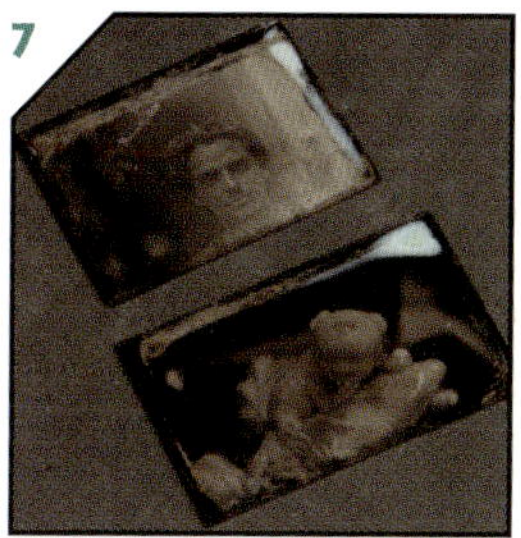

5 Use a glass cutter to cut the microscope slide in half.

Prepare, load and expose the plate

6 Under subdued lighting, sensitize the microscope slide plate (see p. 193). Then load it into the camera, taking care to centre it on the double-sided tape you attached in Step 3. Note that there is very little tolerance between the frame area (36 × 24 mm) and the half microscope slide you are using (c. 37.5 × 25 mm). Once the plate has been loaded, close the back of the camera. Mount the camera on a tripod and use the Bulb (B) setting to hold the shutter open. A cable release will help reduce camera shake during the long exposure time needed for collodion.

Develop and finish

7 When the exposure has been made, remove the wet plate and develop and fix it according to the instructions on p. 198; then varnish and apply a dark backing as per pp. 194–95.

35 mm tintypes

You can use the same procedure to make miniature tintypes (rather than ambrotypes) by wrapping the cut glass slide in several thicknesses of aluminium foil and then blackening the foil with black acrylic paint. Allow the paint to dry, then prepare, load and expose as usual. Be aware, however, that conservation can be an issue as the foil tends to peel off the slide over time.

TREVOR PAGLEN

*Interview
by Marco Antonini*

American artist Trevor Paglen melds science, photography and journalism in his work, including two projects for which he adapted telescopes and radio equipment to photograph invisible radar surveillance systems and classified military installations.

In your photographic work, images show very little of what they promise, and a somewhat romantic, eerie sense of grandiose emptiness prevails. What are your main sources of inspiration for your lens-generated images?

My main sources of inspiration in purely formal terms come primarily from abstract painting and some conceptual art. From a purely formal and imagistic standpoint I spend the most time looking at artists like J. M. W. Turner, Agnes Martin, Ad Reinhardt, as well as more conceptual artists like Hanne Darboven. On the photography side, it's mainly Eadweard Muybridge. Having said that, I'm intellectually more stimulated by people from the Dadists and Situationists through contemporary people like Sean Snyder. I've been really interested in Hans Haacke's early *Systems* work as of late.

Can you describe some of the most interesting hacks and/or trial-and-errors you had to perform on your equipment to produce the results you had in mind?

I'm not sure there are really any 'hacks' in the sense of shortcuts. All the equipment I use has been pieced together through a lot of research and trial-and-error. Often, I'm doing things that the equipment I'm using isn't really designed to do, so flaws in it emerge quite quickly. I spent about a year trying to figure out how to deal with secondary reflections inside a folded mirror (reflector) telescope coupled with a Barlow lens. The solution involved finding an alternative to that particular lens. That's a pretty technical example of a problem that wouldn't have arisen if you were using the equipment for the purpose it was designed for. Most examples of similar problems would be pretty technical and not really even legible to someone who wasn't familiar with the same equipment.

Where do you shop for the telescopic equipment you use? Is it all commercially available or do you need customization?

It's all commercially available, but everyone seems to have their own way of doing things. Fortunately, amateur astronomers are some of the nicest people in the world, so I've had a lot of help in figuring out solutions to various problems.

'The Fence' is the colloquial name for a vast and extremely powerful radar system surrounding the United States. It is an electromagnetic border that extends far into space from transmitters in Alaska, California, Texas, Massachusetts, Greenland and the United Kingdom. The Fence is designed to track spacecraft overflying the United States and to serve as an early warning system to detect ballistic missile launches. This photograph was produced in cooperation with an amateur radio astronomer in Texas. Because The Fence's microwave frequencies are invisible to human eyes (The Fence is made out of the same electromagnetic waves we call light, but is in frequencies lower than what our eyes can see), its emissions had to be shifted up into a visible spectrum in these images.
Trevor Paglen

The Fence (Lake Kickapoo, Texas),
C-print, 127 × 101.6 cm (50 × 40 in.),
2010

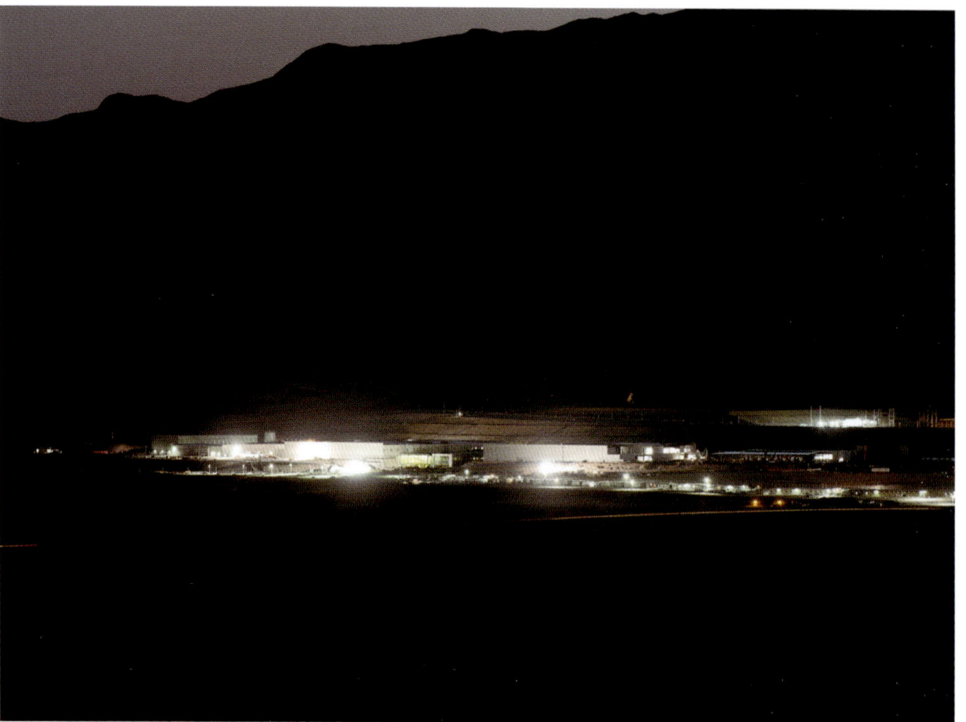

Classified military bases and installations are located in some of the remotest parts of the United States, hidden deep in western deserts and buffered by miles of restricted land. In order to produce images of these hidden landscapes, unorthodox viewing and imaging techniques are required. Limit-telephotography employs high-powered telescopes with focal lengths ranging between 1300 mm and 7000 mm. At this level of magnification, hidden aspects of the landscape become visible.

The process closely resembles astrophotography, a technique that astronomers use to photograph objects in outer space. In some ways, however, it is easier to photograph the depths of the Solar System than it is to photograph the recesses of the military industrial complex. Between Earth and Jupiter (500 million miles away), for example, there are about 5 miles of thick atmosphere, but more than 40 miles of thick atmosphere lie between a civilian observer and the sites depicted in this series.
Trevor Paglen

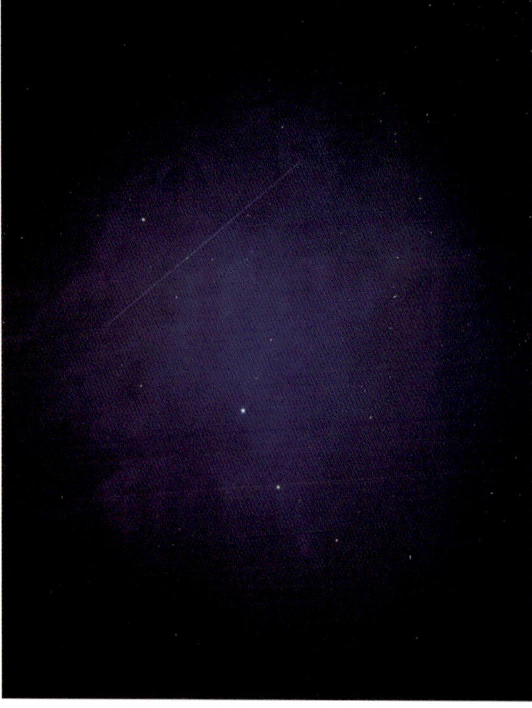

A guy who owned a telescope store in San Francisco used to let me go up on the roof of his shop and experiment with all the equipment.

Can you talk about your project The Fence? *How were you able to capture microwaves via photographic equipment?*

That image was created with the help of an amateur radio astronomer, and it's something that I recently started revisiting. I spent a good chunk of the summer trying to get my own system up and running. It's a complicated set-up: it's not photographic equipment per se, as the image was shot using radio receivers. I used a tuned antenna instead of a CCD or emulsion to collect photons and make an image. It's the same basic idea that radio astronomers use to 'look' at celestial objects like pulsars.

You point the camera at sites and equipment that the powers-that-be strive to conceal from the public. Did you ever experience legal problems because of this approach?

I'm really careful about not breaking any laws with the work that I do. I know exactly where the metaphorical and sometimes literal 'lines' are, and I'll walk right up to them but am careful not to cross them. Some of the work I've done has made certain people upset, but that goes with the territory.

Print Experimentation and Techniques

Some of the greatest opportunities for experimentation lie in the printing processes that transform the latent photographic image into a tangible object.

4

CAFFENOL

Photographic developer is a chemical agent that reduces the silver halides in the emulsion on your film or paper, revealing the latent image. It is usually a toxic and expensive product, but a surprisingly effective eco-friendly alternative can be made using instant coffee. Tea and coffee are both rich in phenolic acids (tannins), which have the potential for supporting development, but coffee also contains caffeic acid, which behaves like the conventional developing agent pyrogallol. The addition of ascorbic acid (Vitamin C) improves contrast and development times, while washing soda is used to turn the solution alkaline and to activate the developing agents.

Make your own Caffenol developer

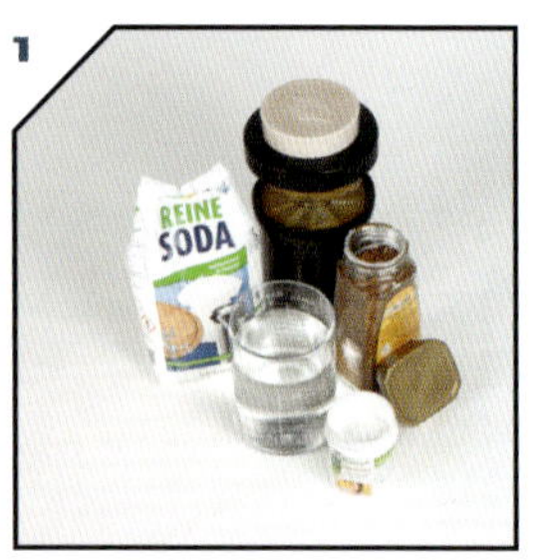
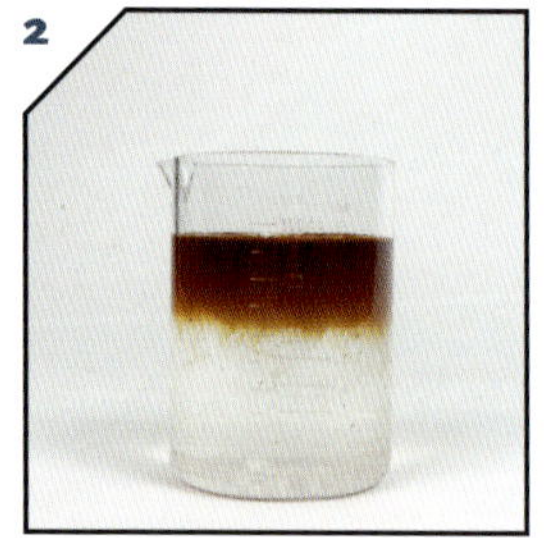
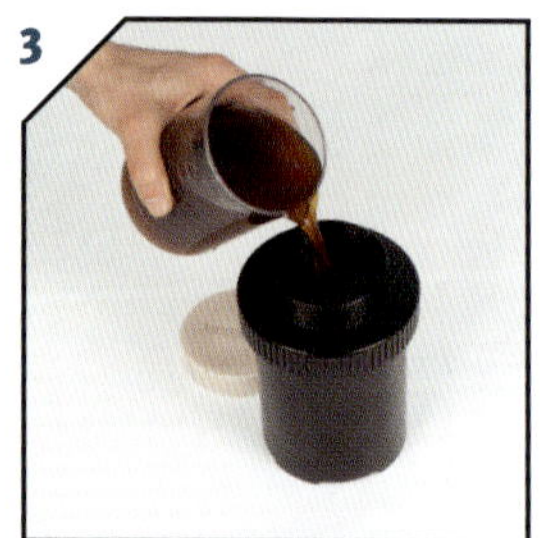
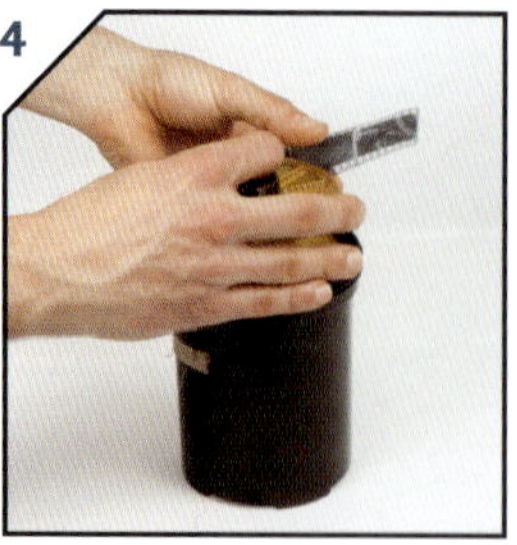

What you need:
- [ ] 1 l water
- [ ] 54 g washing soda (sodium carbonate) ⚠
- [ ] 16 g ascorbic acid (Vitamin C) crystals ⚠
- [ ] 40 g instant coffee
- [ ] 1 g potassium bromide ⚠ or 10 g iodized table salt (optional)
- [ ] developing tank
- [ ] fixer ⚠

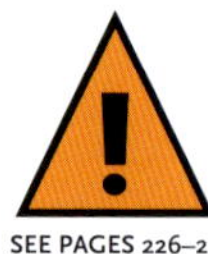

SEE PAGES 226–29

Assemble the ingredients

1 Washing soda is available from swimming-pool suppliers and supermarkets (where it is sold as a laundry aid), while ascorbic acid crystals (not tablets, and not the citric acid form of Vitamin C) can be found in health-food and baking supply stores. Potassium bromide is an optional ingredient that can be used to reduce fogging in high-speed film, but it is only available from chemists (iodized table salt can be substituted at 10x strength).

Make up two solutions. For solution A, mix 54 g washing soda with 300 ml water in a jar. For solution B, mix 16 g ascorbic acid and 40 g coffee (and 10 g salt or 1 g potassium bromide, if using) with 700 ml water. These quantities will make 1 l of developer, but 300–350 ml should be enough to develop one roll of 35 mm film. Excess solution cannot be reused, so adjust accordingly.

Combine the solutions

2 Mix the two solutions in a beaker, and stir until the crystals have dissolved completely.

Develop

Working in darkness, or using a film-changing bag, load the film onto the reel ('spiral') of the developing tank. Slide the reel onto the spindle, insert it into the tank (being careful not to touch the film) and close the tank. You can now work in daylight.

3 Pour in the Caffenol solution and develop for 15 minutes, agitating the tank three times per minute. Rinse the film with water several times to remove the coffee, and then fix as normal.

4 Wash the film thoroughly, remove it from the tank and hang it up to dry. You can then print it using your desired process.

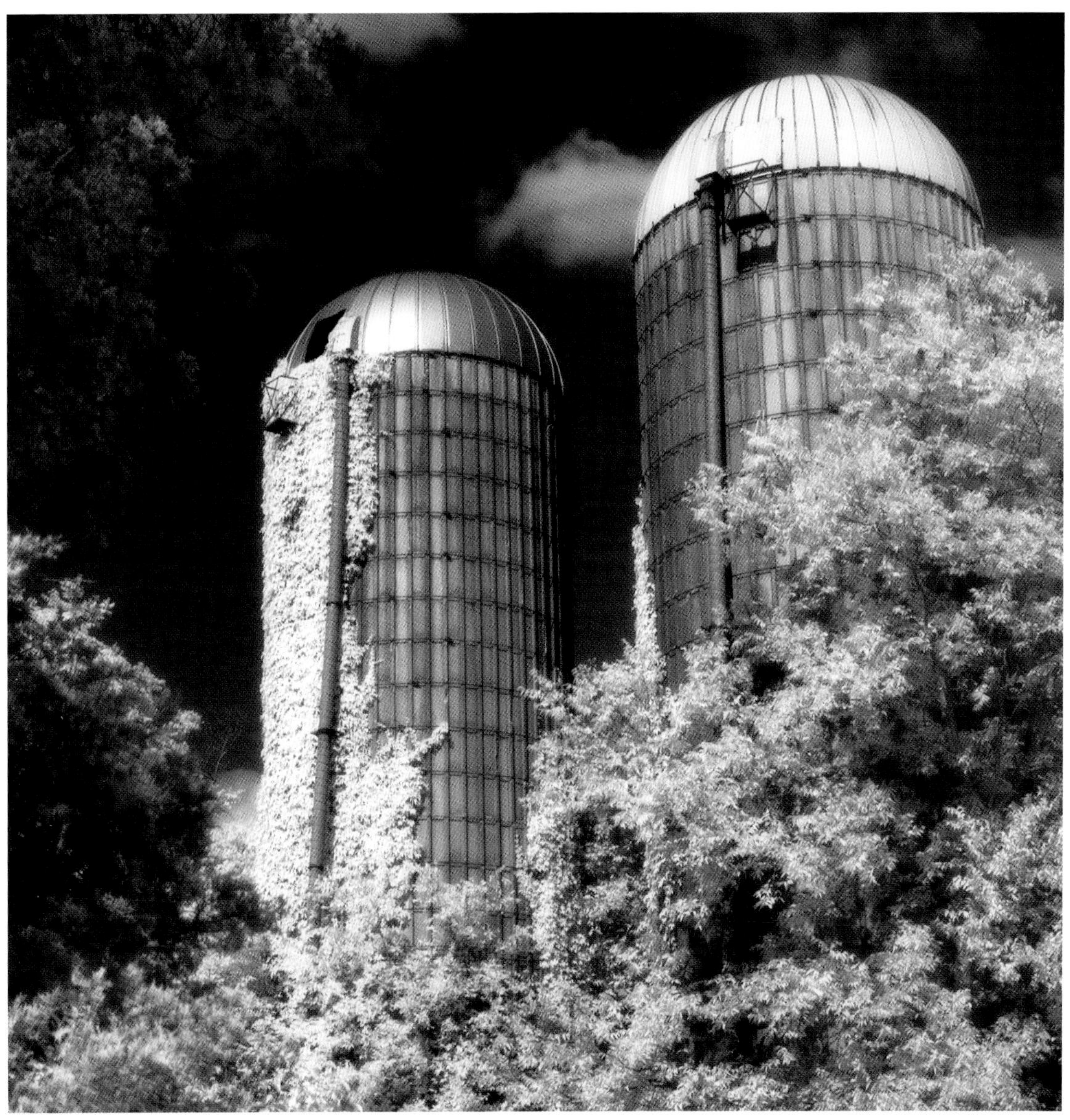

Gerald Figal
Post Agriculture, 4" × 5" Efke
820 IR film, stand developed in
Caffenol C-L for 70 minutes, 2011

LARGE-FORMAT NEGATIVES FOR CONTACT PRINTING

Contact-printing techniques yield images that are the same size as the negative used, so unless you work with a large-format film camera, digital negatives are the most practical solution for making large-scale prints. Using image-editing software and an inkjet or laser printer, digital files can be used to create custom-sized negatives on transparency film, bridging digital and traditional photographic processes. As well as starting directly from a digital photograph, you can scan and enlarge 35 mm and other small-format film negatives. Reproducibility is also a great advantage of working this way: if a digital negative gets ruined you can quickly and easily print another one, allowing you to experiment more freely.

Preparing a digital negative

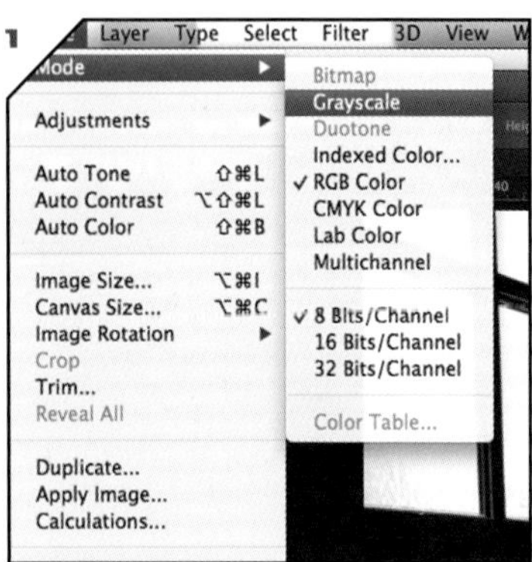
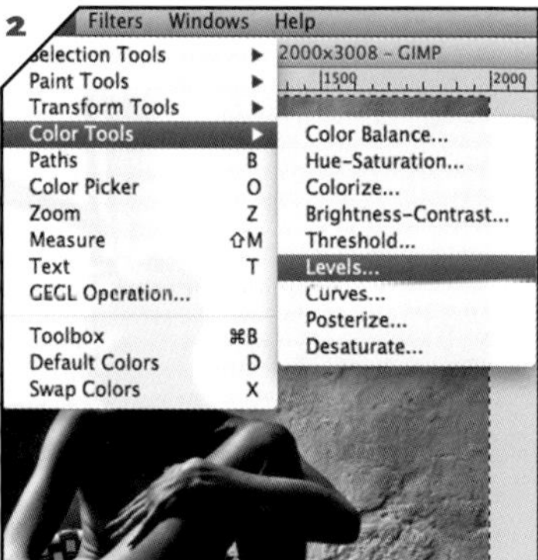
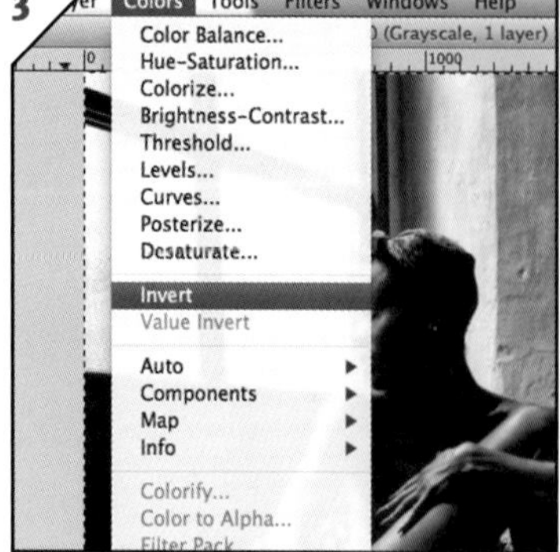

What you need:
- [ ] digital photograph or scanned negative
- [ ] image-editing software
- [ ] inkjet or laser printer
- [ ] transparency film for inkjet or laser printer

The negative-making process consists of two basic steps: preparing the image for the process you wish to use, and then printing the digital negative onto transparency film. For this project we're using GIMP, which is a free open-source image-editing program, but the process is the same in Adobe Photoshop® or Photoshop Elements®.

to increase the contrast to create a high-contrast digital negative (for anthotypes or photosynthesis, for example), or reduce the contrast to make a negative with a wide tonal range (for albumen and salt prints, for example). Make notes of the settings you use so you can refer to them later: tests and experience will teach you a lot.

Convert to monochrome
1 Open your image, and if it is in colour, choose Image > Mode > Grayscale to convert it to black and white.

Adjust the contrast
2 Select the Levels tool (Tools > Color Tools > Levels). Depending on the print process you intend to use you may need

Invert the image
3 Select Colors > Invert to convert your positive image into a negative.

Print the negative
You will need to experiment with your printer settings to get the best results. Most inkjet printers have a transparency setting, but sometimes it can be better to

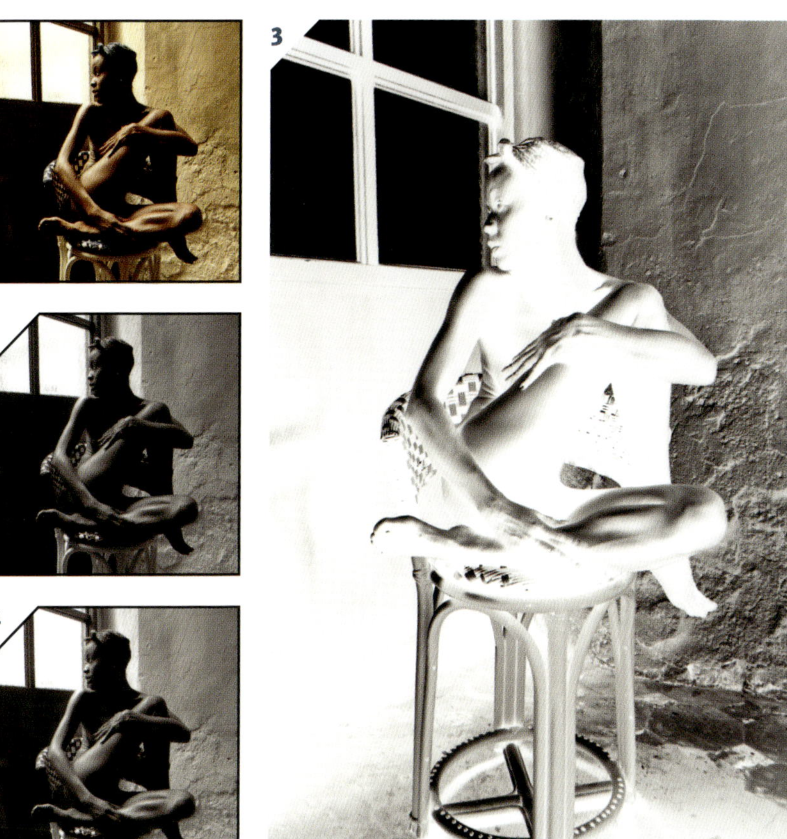

ABOVE
The results you should achieve following the steps described in the instructions opposite. Top left: the original; centre left: converted to monochrome after Step 1; bottom left: with contrast adjusted after Step 2; right: the inverted image ready to print as a negative after Step 3.

use a glossy paper setting as it will give denser ink coverage.

Acetate can be used with a laser printer, but the density of the print can be an issue, as laser printers don't produce particularly strong blacks. Dense black areas are crucial in obtaining a good result, so you may need to print two (or more) acetate negatives and sandwich them together to build up the overall density.

CONTACT-PRINTING FRAME

A contact-printing frame is an indispensable tool for any process that uses contact printing (when the negative is exposed while in contact with the printing paper). The frame must maintain maximum contact, preventing any movement between the frame itself, the printing paper and the negative. A simple contact-printing frame is a fun and easy woodworking project. It consists of a hard transparent layer (glass or clear acrylic) that allows light through to the negative, a spongy support that allows for greater compression and a firm backing board. This 'sandwich' is then locked together using spring clamps, with hinges in the backing board allowing the frame to be opened to check exposures.

Make a contact-printing frame

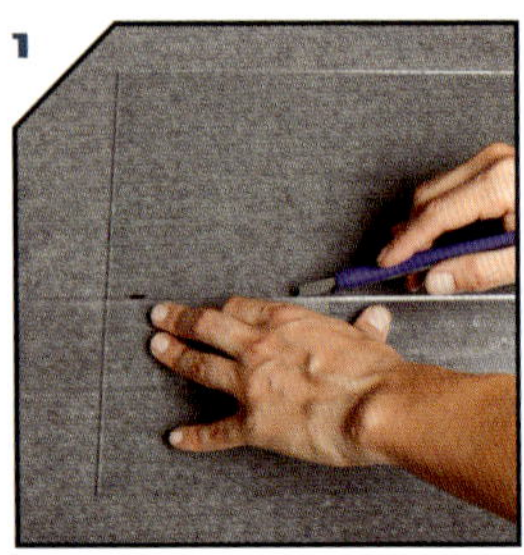 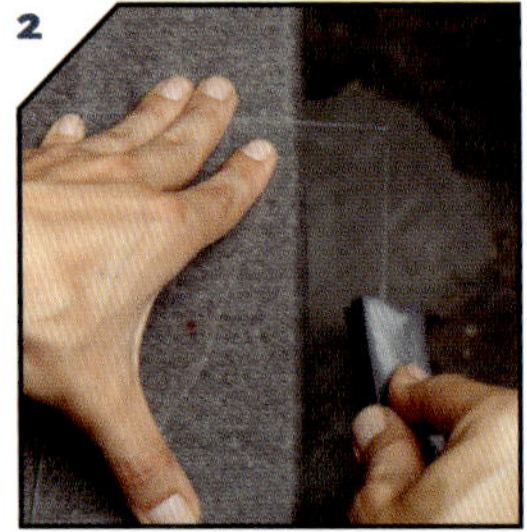 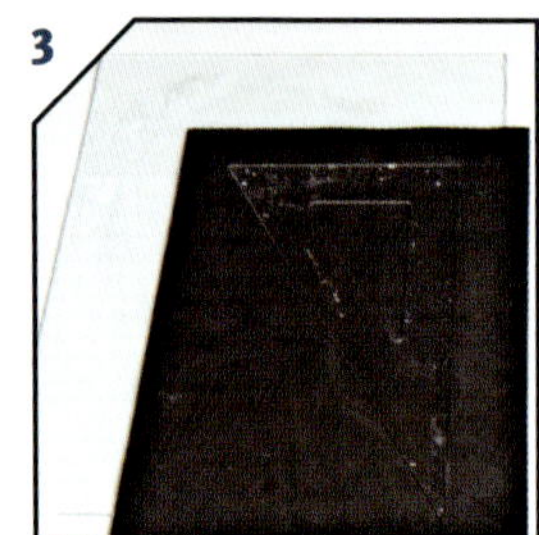 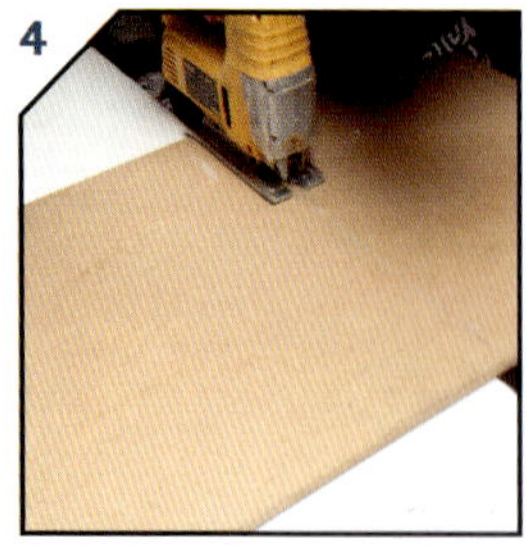

What you need:
- [ ] glass or clear acrylic sheet cut to size
- [ ] rubber (2–3 mm thick) or similar soft material
- [ ] MDF, plywood or similar board
- [ ] 4 spring clamps
- [ ] 2 small hinges
- [ ] 8 screws (for the hinges)
- [ ] tools: ruler, jigsaw and screwdriver
- [ ] glass cutter and rubbing stone (optional)

! light-sensitive step

Prepare the glass

1 To print photos up to 30 × 40 cm, you will need a contact-printing frame that is at least 35 × 45 cm so there is a margin around the edges to which the spring clamps will attach. Recycling a piece of glass from a picture frame is one option (cutting it to the right size if necessary), or you can buy a pre-cut piece of glass from a glazier. Alternatively, you can use clear acrylic (or similar), which will be easier to cut, but can be slightly more expensive.

2 If you are using cut glass, use a rubbing stone to smooth the edges – cut glass can be incredibly sharp if it is not sanded.

Prepare the rubber

3 A sheet of 2–3 mm thick rubber (or similar material) will help to achieve perfect contact between the glass, the negative, the printing paper and the back of the contact-printing frame. Use a sharp craft knife and a ruler to cut the rubber sheet to the same size as the glass.

Prepare the backing board

4 MDF and plywood are inexpensive and easy to find, and both materials are ideal for making a backing board for the contact-printing frame. Buy the wood pre-cut or use a jigsaw to cut it to the desired size.

Install the hinges

5 The backing board needs to be hinged so you can check your exposures without losing the registration between the negative and the printing paper. Start by marking a line along the centre of the backing board.

6 Use a jigsaw to cut the backing board along the marked line.

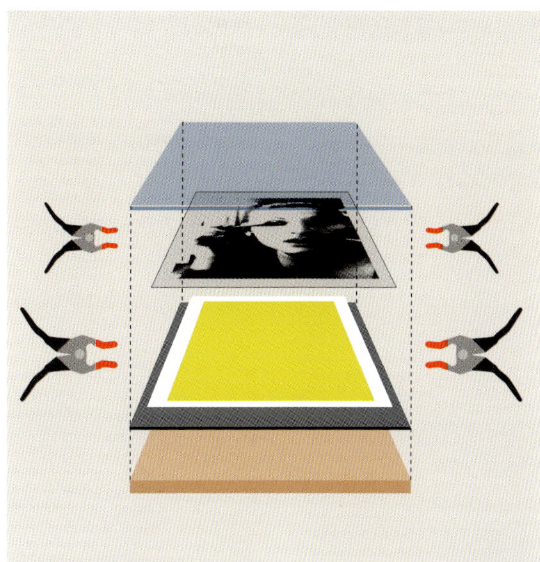

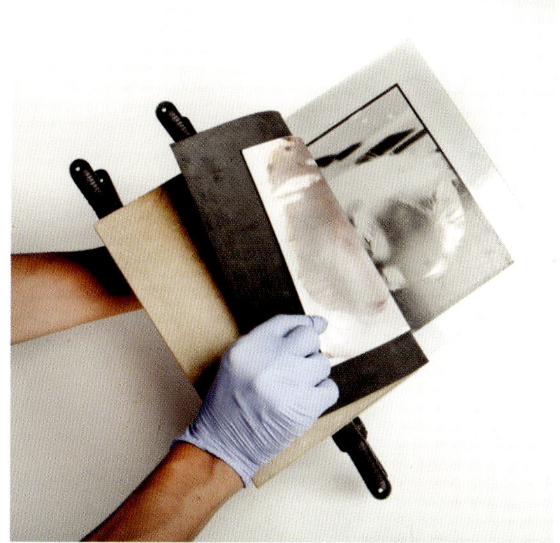

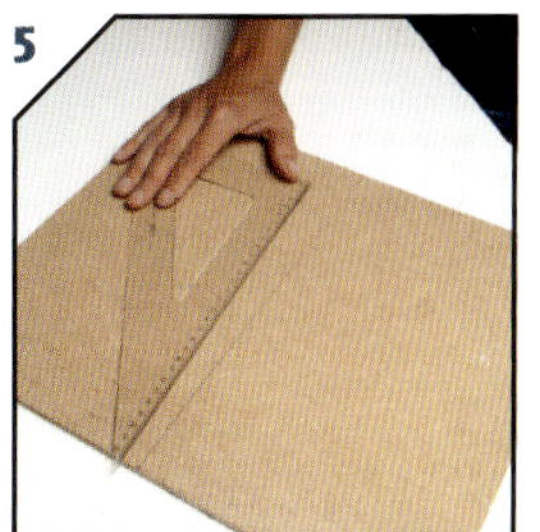

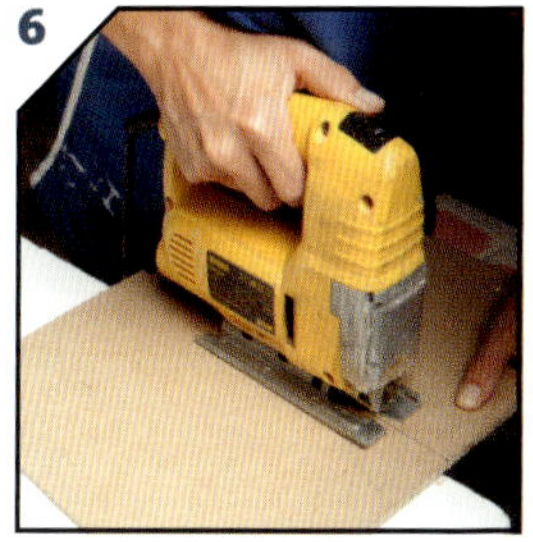

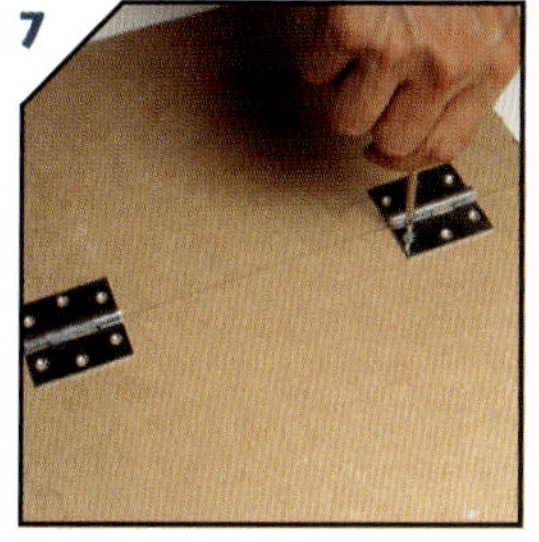

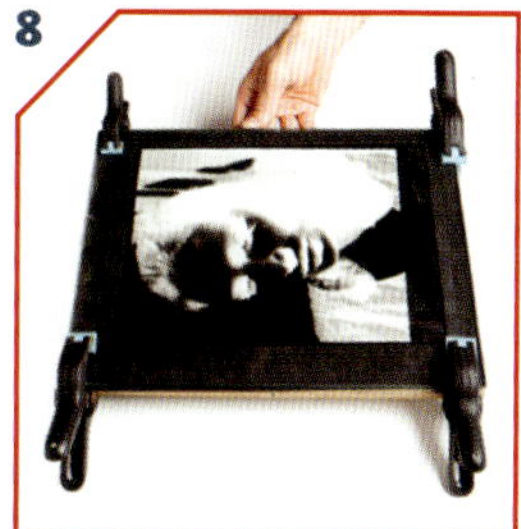

7 Attach hinges to the two halves of the backing board, so you have a single, hinged sheet. Position the hinges about 5–6 cm in from the edges, making sure that the screws you use are shorter than the thickness of the backing-board material.

8 Your contact-printing frame is now ready to use. For most processes it will need to be loaded in a darkroom. Place the rubber on the backing board, followed by the printing paper (sensitive side upwards), the negative and then the glass or clear acrylic board, as illustrated above. Use spring clamps to hold the 'sandwich' together at each corner, positioning the clamps so they don't obscure the negative.

CYANOTYPE

The cyanotype printing process relies on the light sensitivity of iron salts, creating blue-tinted images. It was developed by the pioneering English chemist and photographer John Herschel in 1839–42, and became popular as a simple and cheap process for creating large-scale copies of engineering plans (hence 'blueprints'), but it can also be used for photographic subjects. Although the technique has some disadvantages (primarily long exposure times and a short chemical shelf life), it is a great process for beginners due to its relative simplicity and low cost. You can buy ready-made cyanotype solutions, but it is not too difficult to mix your own.

The cyanotype process

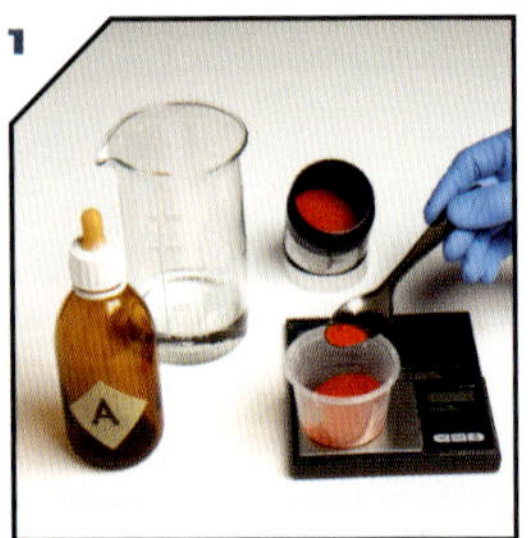

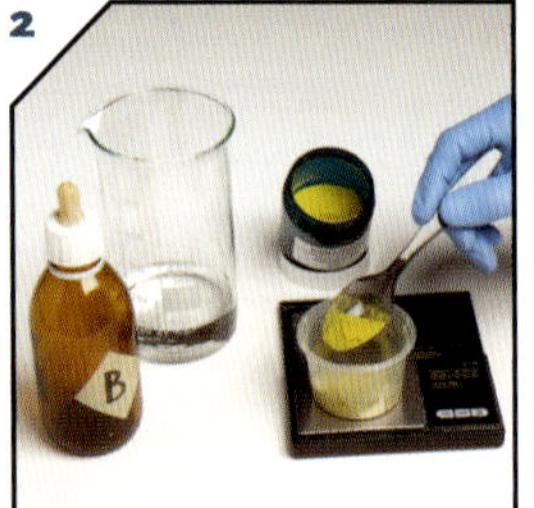

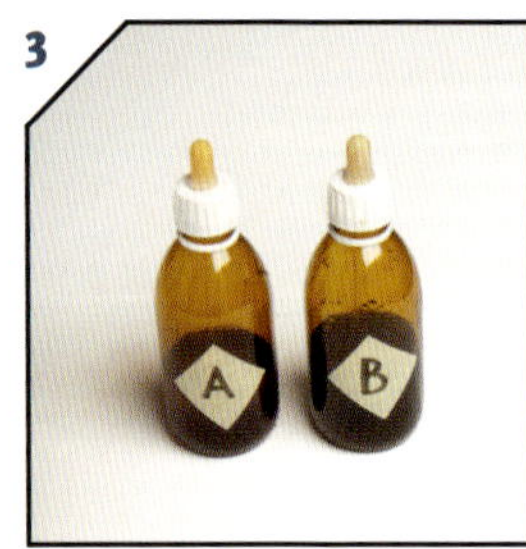

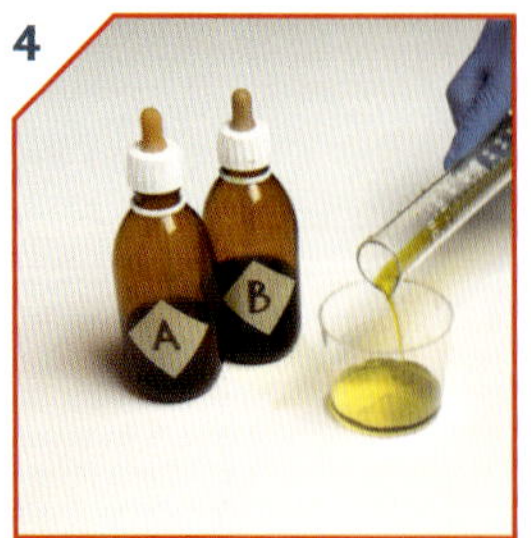

What you need:
- [ ] 25 g ferric ammonium citrate ⚠
- [ ] 10 g potassium ferricyanide ⚠
- [ ] hydrogen peroxide ⚠
- [ ] distilled water
- [ ] beaker (500 ml)
- [ ] gloves
- [ ] scales
- [ ] 2 brown bottles
- [ ] non-metallic brush or glass rod (for coating)
- [ ] contact-printing frame
- [ ] large-format negative
- [ ] watercolour paper
- [ ] UV lamp (optional)
- [ ] trays for processing

Make up the two solutions

1 For solution A, mix 10 g potassium ferricyanide with 100 ml distilled water.

2 For solution B, mix 25 g ferric ammonium citrate with 100 ml distilled water.

3 Store each solution in a labelled brown bottle. The uncombined solutions have a shelf life of several months if you keep them in a cool, dark place.

Combine the two solutions

4 In subdued lighting, mix equal parts of solutions A and B. The resulting cyanotype solution is light-sensitive and will be an intense yellow colour.

OPPOSITE
Barbara Ghidini
Dancer, cyanotype, 27 × 21 cm
(10⅝ × 8¼ in.), 2013

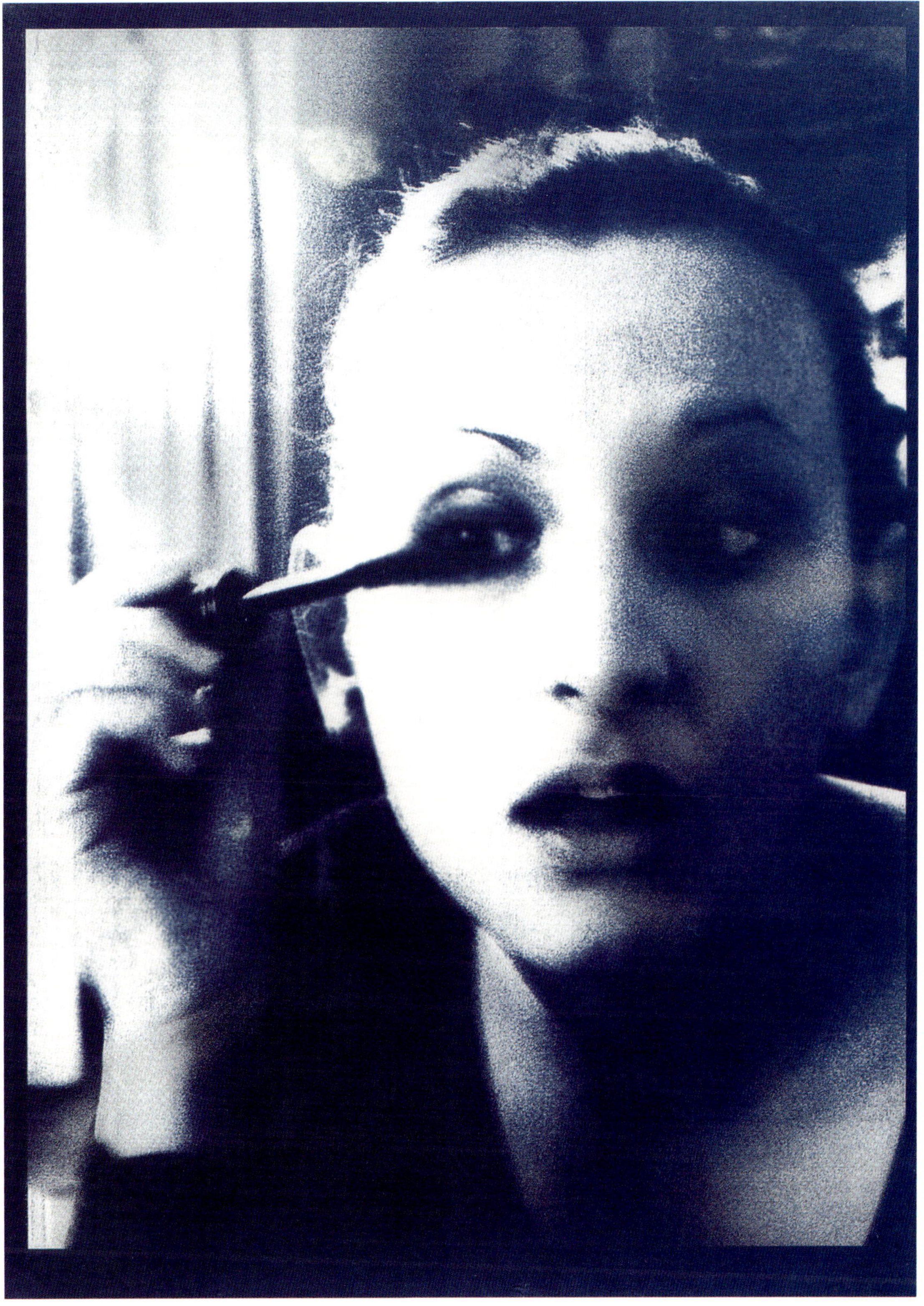

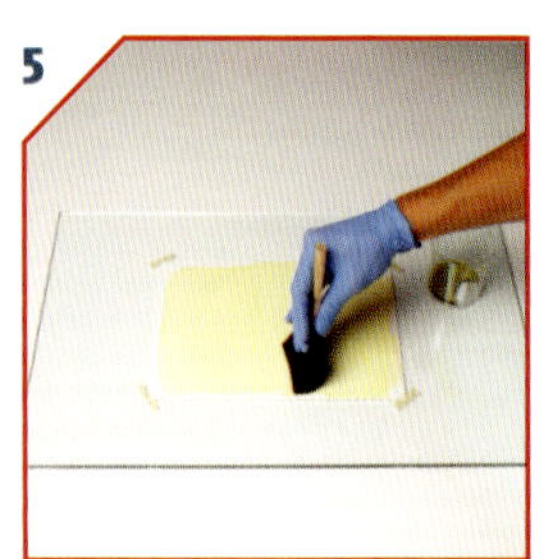 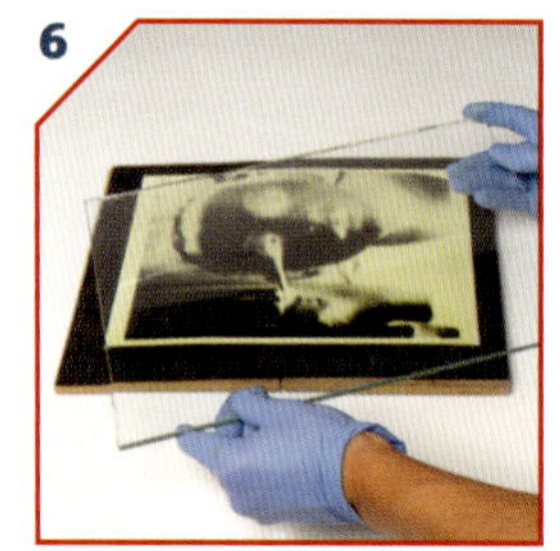 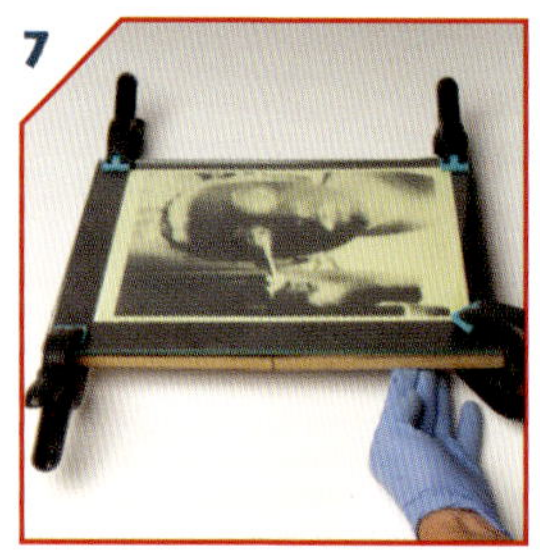 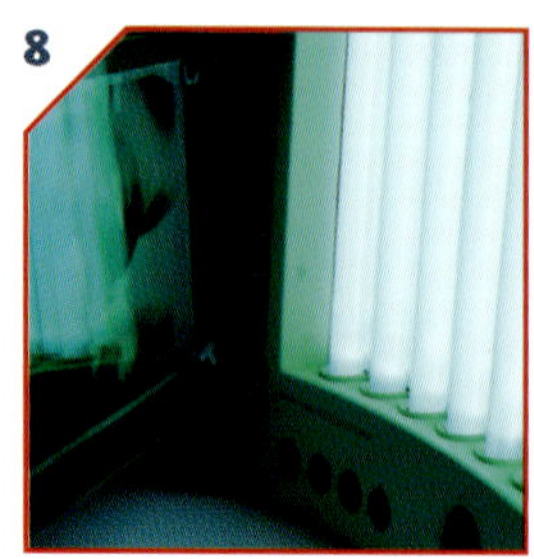

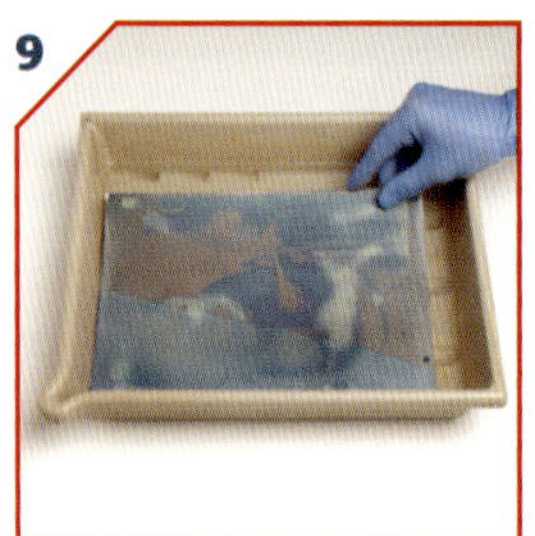 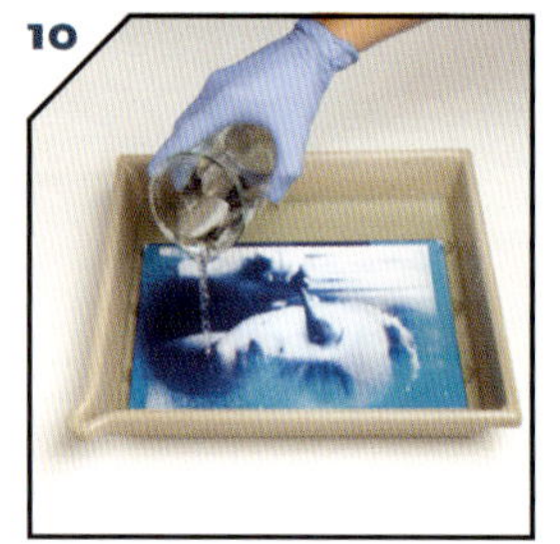 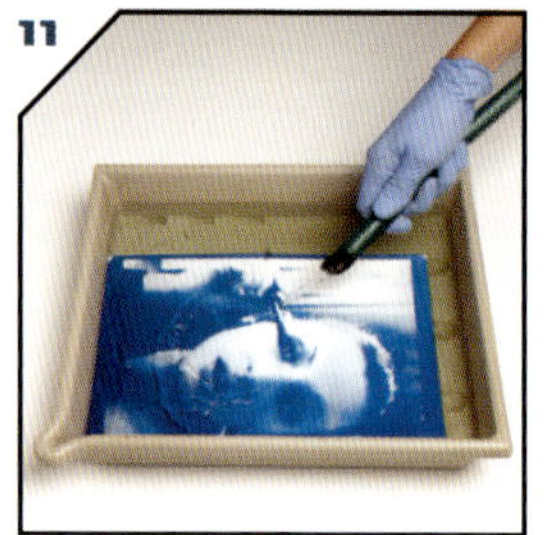 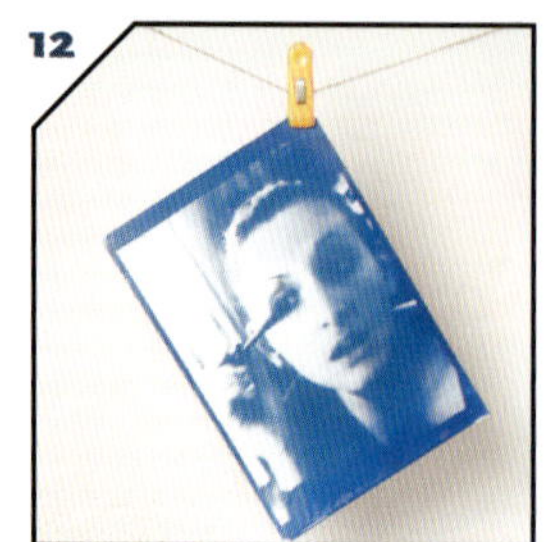

Coating the paper

5 Tape the paper to a table or similar rigid support and brush it with the cyanotype solution until the printable surface is covered with a thin but uniform coating. To ensure even coverage, apply brushstrokes first horizontally, then vertically. Leave the coated paper to dry in the dark. For especially porous paper stocks, a second coat can be applied once the first is completely dry. Sizing (see box on p. 148) is not required prior to coating unless you are printing onto alternative substrates such as fabric or wood. The coated paper can be stored in a light-tight box or opaque plastic envelope (of the type used for standard photographic papers), and it is possible to coat a large batch of paper to use for further printing.

Loading

6 & 7 Cyanotype is a contact-printing technique, so the final result will be the same size as the negative you use (see pp. 132–33 for details on preparing digital negatives). Load the negative and the coated cyanotype paper into a contact-printing frame (see pp. 134–35 for how to build one, if needed), making sure there are no creases in the negative.

Exposure

8 Cyanotypes are exposed using UV light. It is possible to expose them through direct sunlight, but this is not constant or controllable, and it generally entails longer exposure times.

To achieve better control over this essential part of the process, UV exposure units are the best choice, but a cheaper alternative is a UV tanning lamp. These lamps are readily available and easy to find secondhand.

Exposure times will vary depending on the ambient temperature, paper type and the strength of the UV light source, but you can check exposure visually by opening one half of the back of the contact-printing frame. Alternatively, if you are using a UV lamp or exposure unit you can make a test strip (see pp. 24–25) to determine the exposure time beforehand.

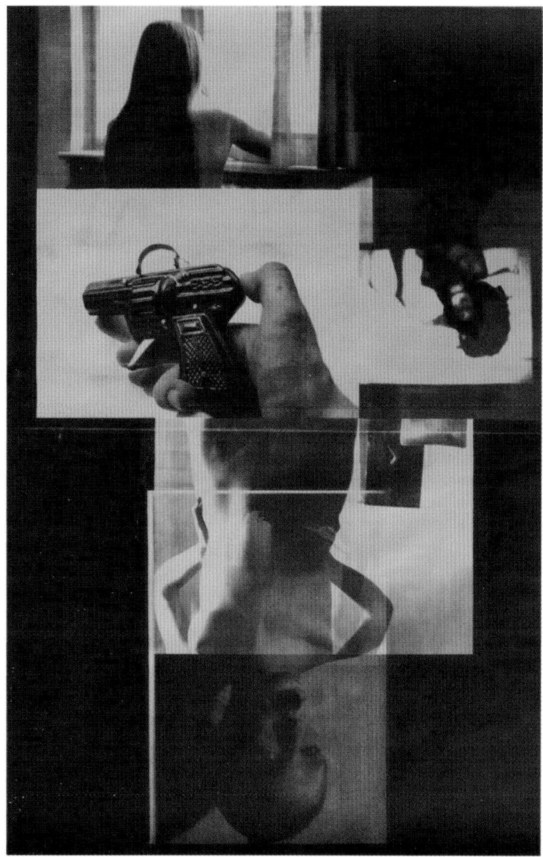
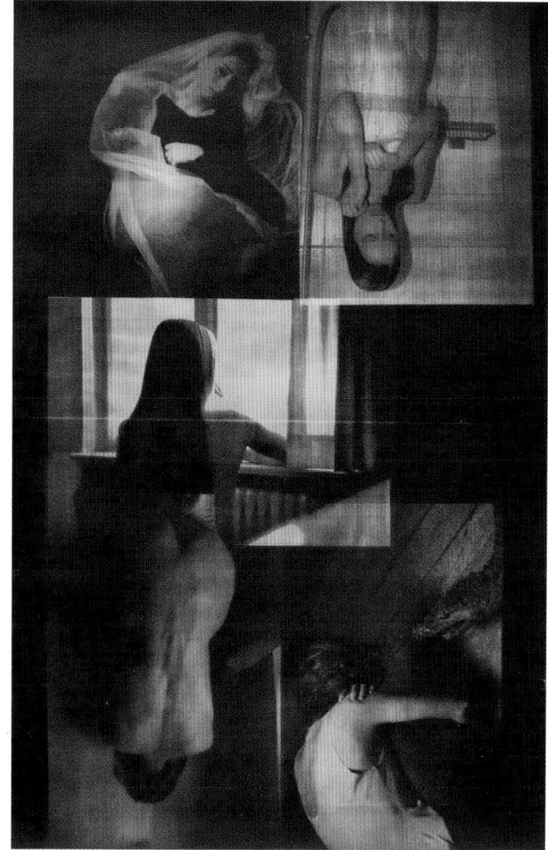

Ruth Erdt and Eva Vuillemin
Cyanotypes 16–22, mixed subjects
with self-portraits of the artists
aged 16–22, cyanotypes, 2011

Development

9 Once exposed, the cyanotype print
is developed using simple water baths
(changing the water twice or more).
Distilled water is preferable, and a gentle
running flow of water is also acceptable.

Toning (optional)

10 In order to achieve a darker tone of
cyan, a light solution (1–2%) of hydrogen
peroxide and distilled water can be used.
Pour the solution into a tray and wash
the print until the cyan darkens to your
liking. Alternative methods and colours
for cyanotype toning are described on
pp. 206–7.

Wash and dry

11 Once you are happy with the result,
wash the print under running water for
at least 15 minutes. The yellowish stain
of the cyanotype sensitizer should clear
completely from unexposed areas.

12 Finally, hang the print in a well-
ventilated area until it is dry.

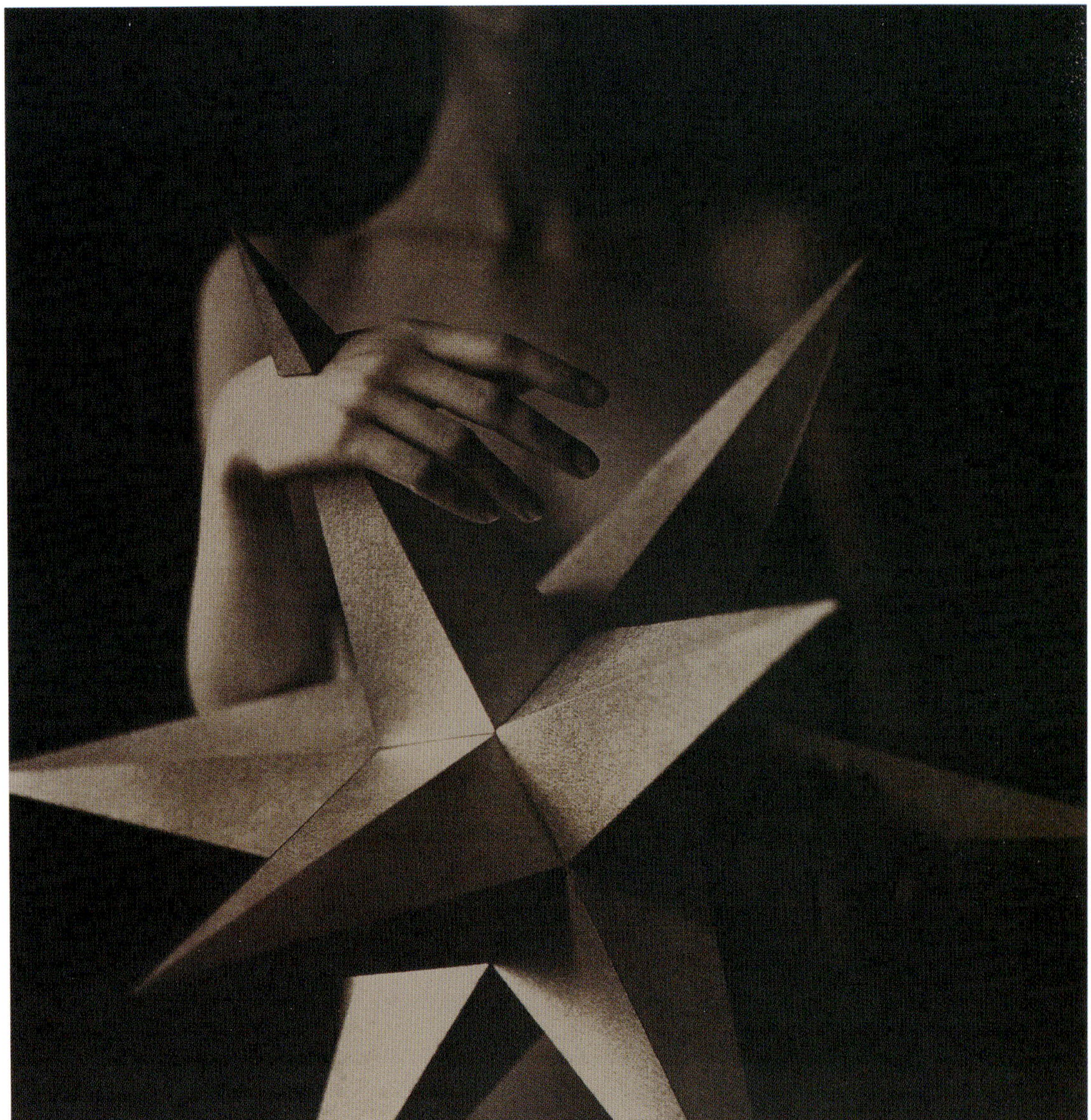

Anton Senkov

Greed, *Pride*, *Envy* and *Gluttony* from the
series *Seven Deadly Sins*, toned cyanotypes,
each 40 × 40 cm (15¾ × 15¾ in.), 2013

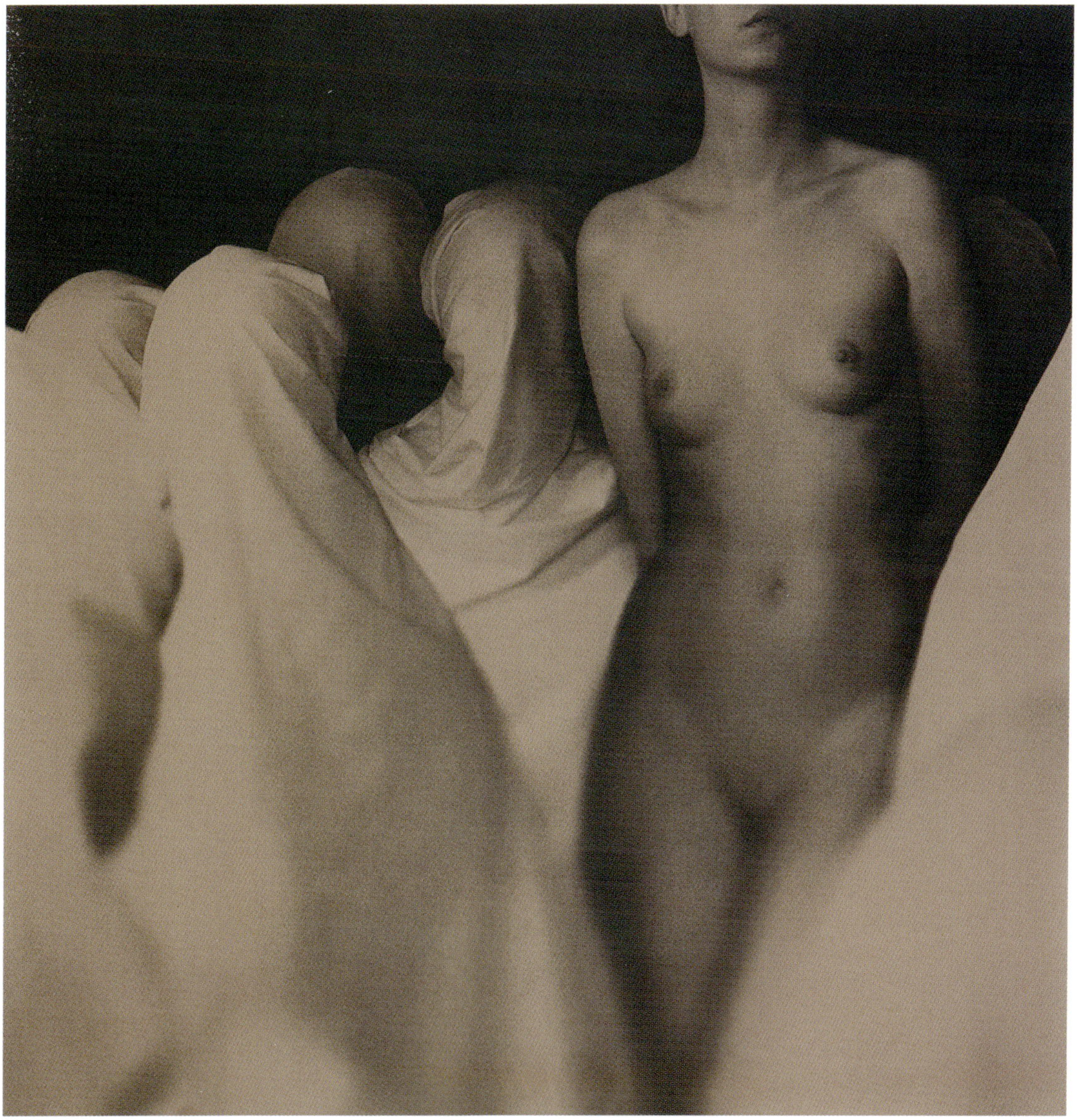

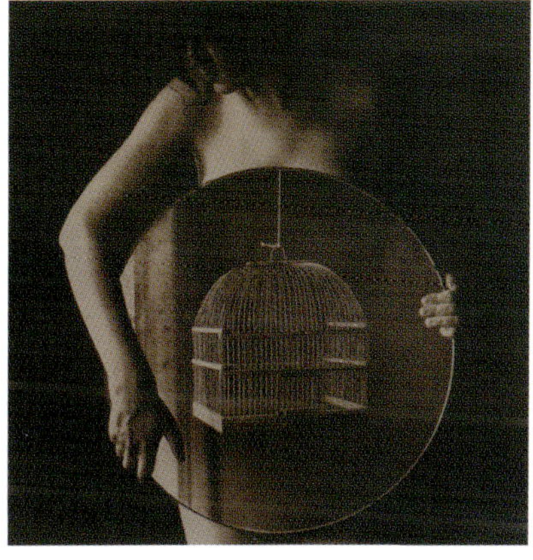

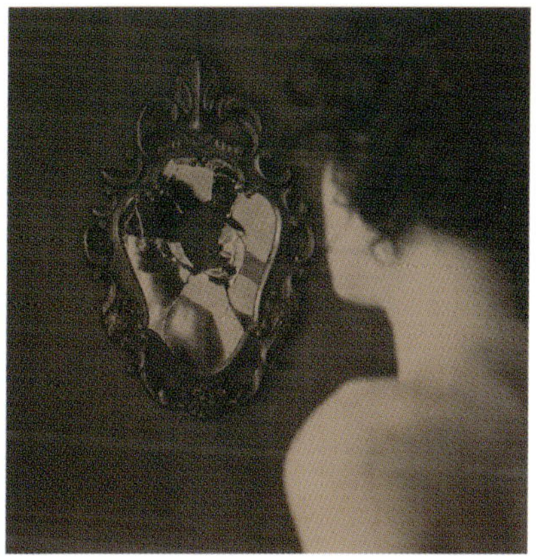

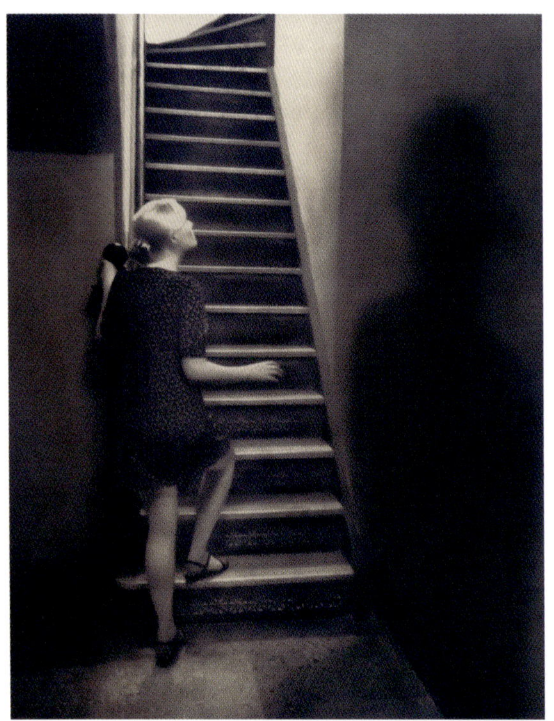

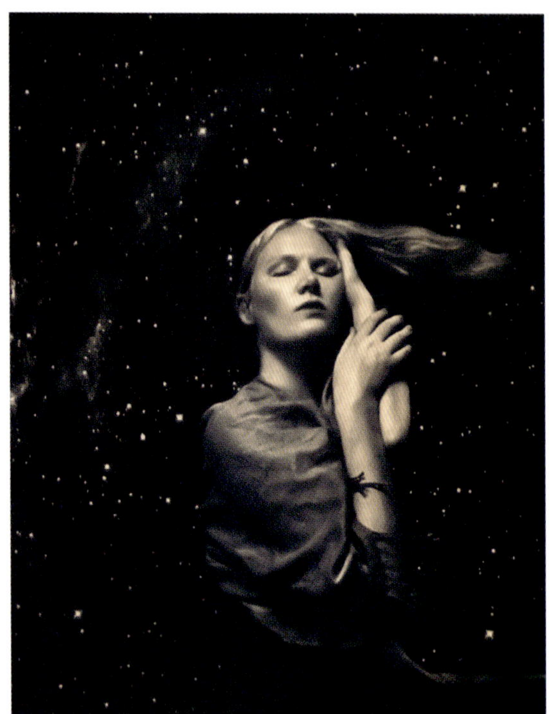

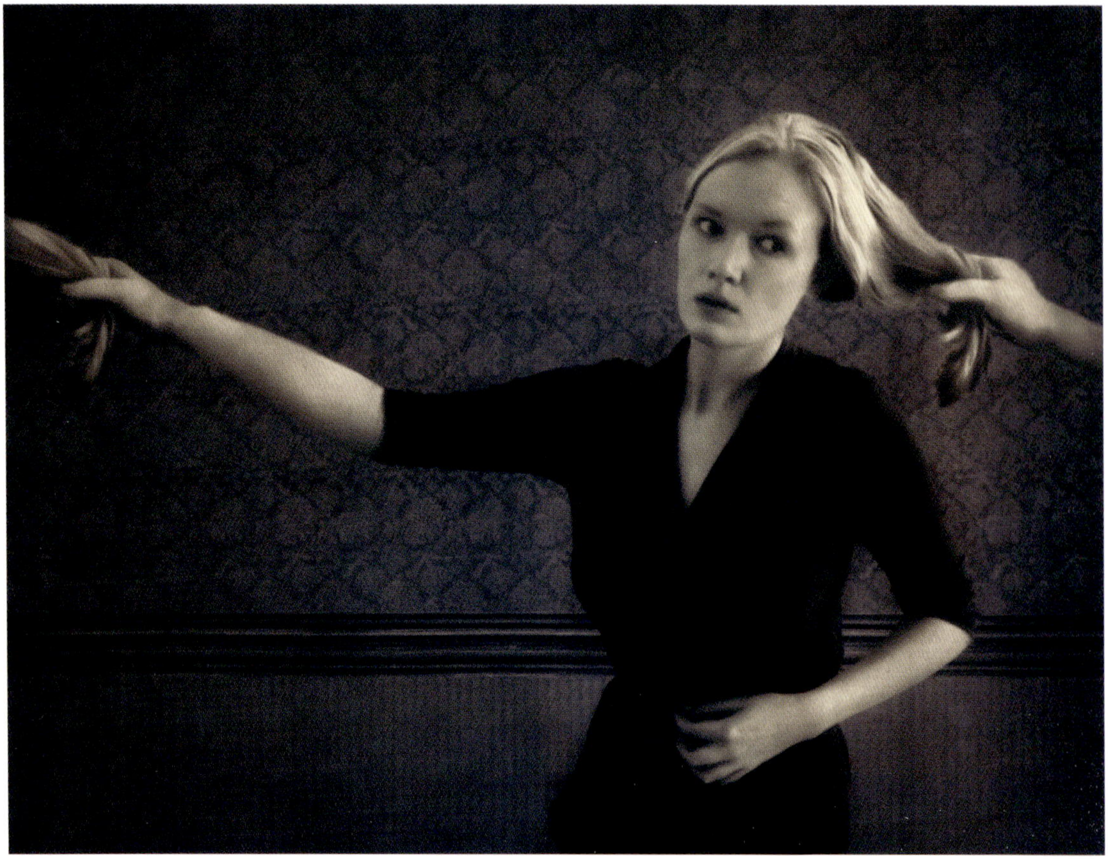

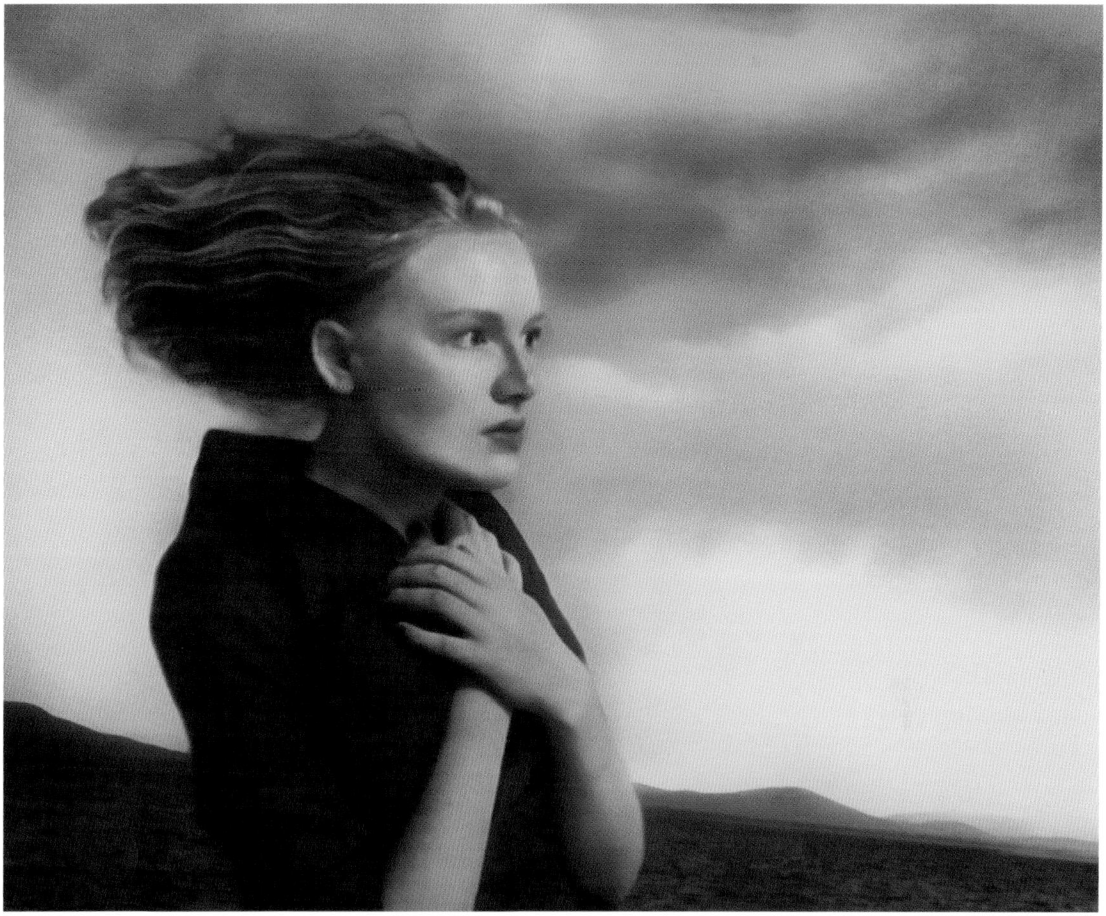

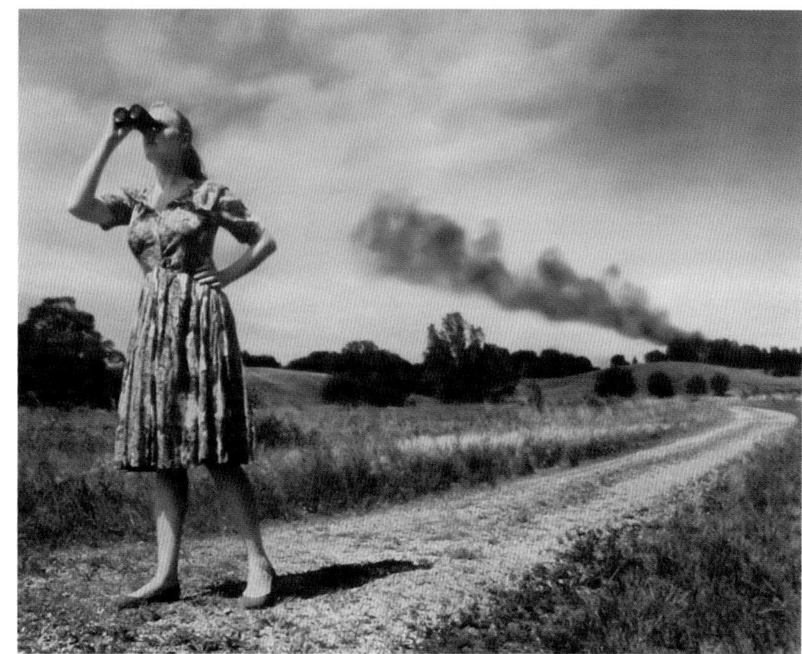

Emma Powell
Against the Storm, *Where there Is Smoke*, *Captive*, *Ascend* and *Oblivion*, from the series *In Search of Sleep*, cyanotypes from digital negatives, each 28 × 35.5 cm (11 × 14 in.) or 35.5 × 28 cm (14 × 11 in.), 2012
'The cyanotype process, with its distinctive blue tones, visually traverses the distance between waking and sleeping. These images are also toned with tea and wine to both dull the blues and add warmth. Tea, wine, cyanide – all three of these substances relate to different levels of consciousness that often mirror the mental states evoked by my photographs.'

CYANOTYPE ON FABRIC

The cyanotype process is incredibly versatile and can be adapted to print on many types of substrate. Printing on fabric is especially fun: the process is essentially the same as printing on paper, although printing on fabric uses approximately five times the amount of sensitizer required for printing on paper and the exposure times are longer. The fabric type also influences the final result: 100% cotton reproduces images reliably, but synthetic fabrics will need to be tested first. The colour of the fabric will affect the colour and intensity of the cyanotype print; for this reason, light colours are usually preferred.

Cyanotype on fabric

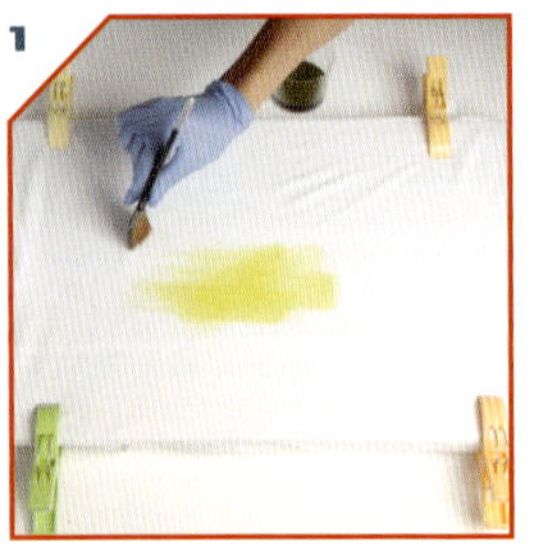 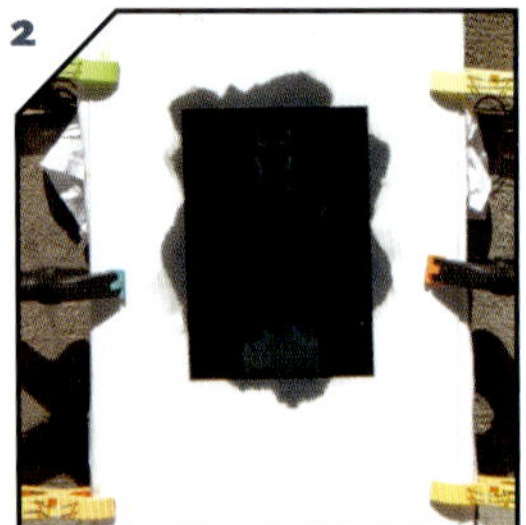 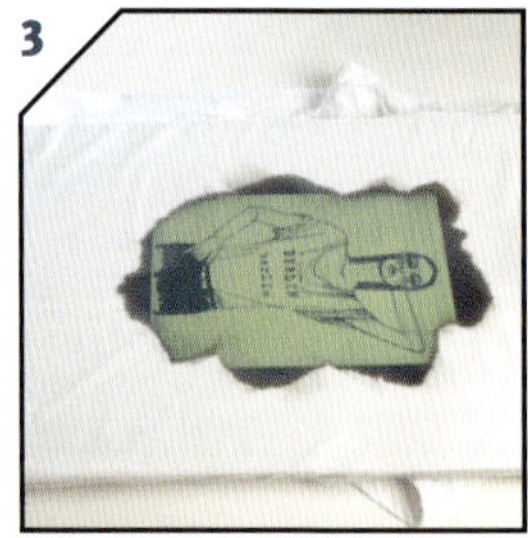 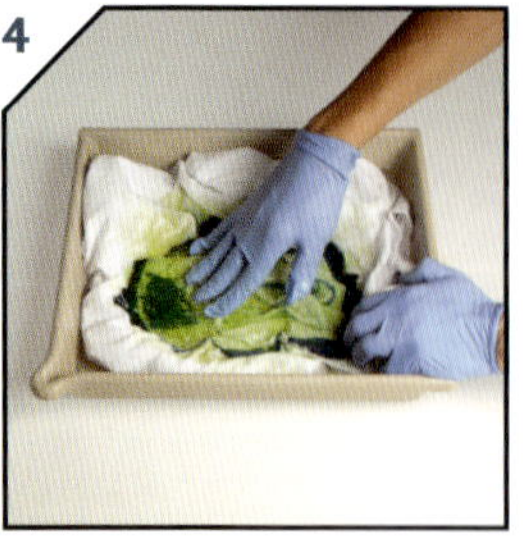

What you need:

- ☐ 500 ml cyanotype sensitizer (see p. 136) ⚠
- ☐ non-metallic brush (for coating)
- ☐ gloves
- ☐ contact-printing frame
- ☐ large-format negative
- ☐ fabric for printing
- ☐ UV lamp (optional)
- ☐ trays for processing (optional)

Preparing the fabric

As a general rule, the fabric you want to print on must be washed several times in water and then air-dried, before printing. This is to remove all traces of oils and any other treatments or chemicals that might affect the print.

Coating

1 Make up a cyanotype sensitizer using solutions A and B as outlined on p. 136. (500 ml of sensitizer should be enough to print at least two T-shirts, allowing for a few mistakes.) Under subdued lighting, brush the fabric with the cyanotype solution until the area you want to print on is covered. (It may be helpful to stretch the fabric across a piece of cardboard or glass and fix it in place with clamps or clothespins while you do this.) Leave the fabric to dry in the dark.

Loading and exposing

2 Load the fabric and negative into the contact-printing frame (see pp. 134–35). Expose the fabric to UV light; visually check the exposure by opening one half of the contact-printing frame.

Development

3 & 4 Once the image has sufficiently exposed, remove the fabric from the contact-printing frame and develop the print using water. You can either use water baths (changing the water twice or more) or develop the print under a gentle flow of running water.

Wash and dry

Once it has been developed, wash the fabric under running water for at least 15–20 minutes and hang in a well-ventilated area until it is dry.

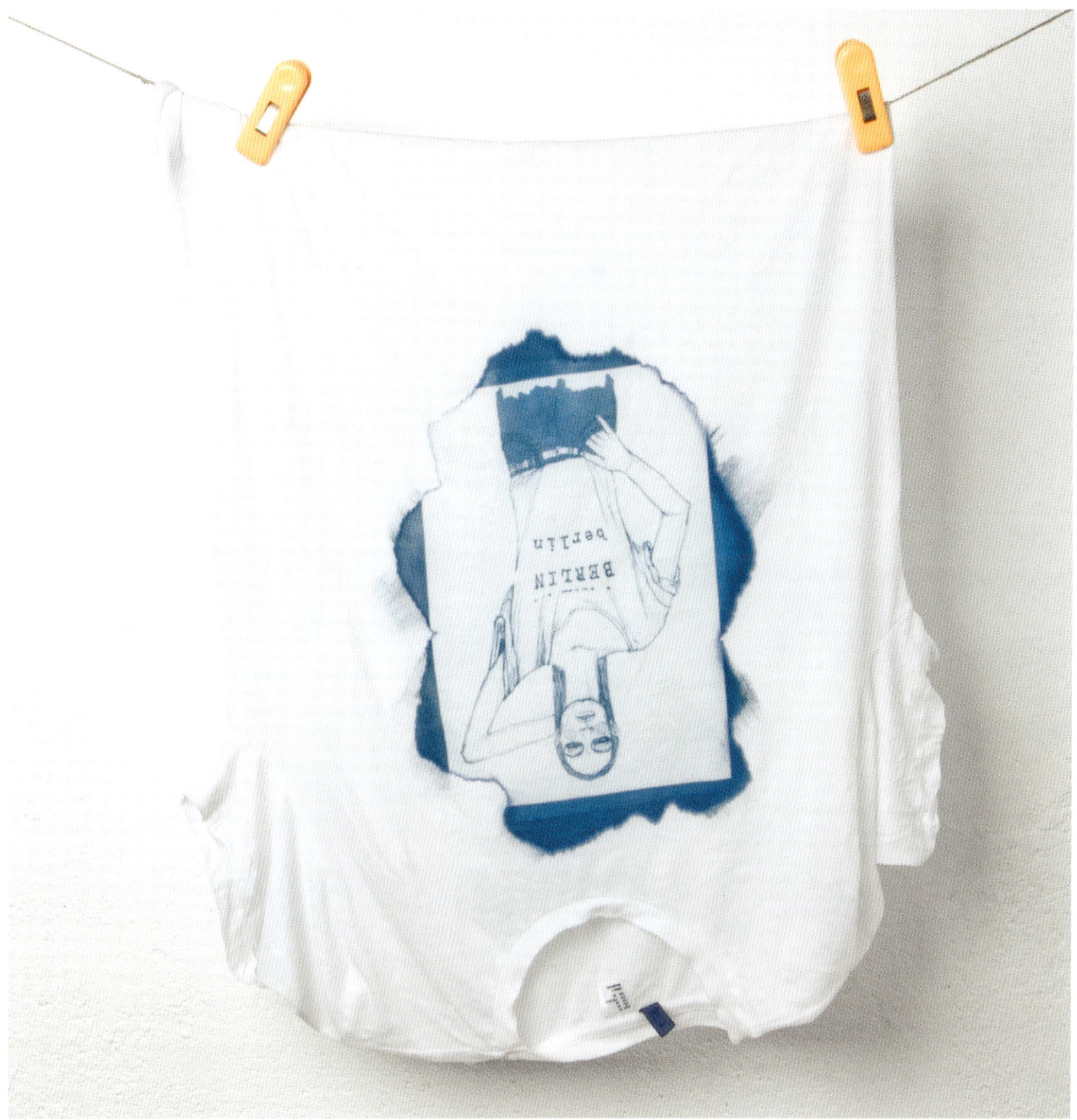

ABOVE

Loreto Binvignat Streeter
Berlin, cyanotype on cotton
T-shirt, image 27 × 21 cm
(10⅝ × 8¼ in.), 2013

Aftercare

A cyanotype on fabric will not be
as durable as a screen-printed
or commercially printed fabric.
Cyanotypes are especially susceptible to
phosphates, bleach or sodium, so it is
a good idea to avoid using detergents
if you do wash the fabric after it has
been printed. Cyanotypes can be ironed
using a dry iron. The colour will change
slightly while warm and will return to
the original colour as it cools.

VANDYKE

Like cyanotypes, the Vandyke process is another iron-based contact-printing method invented by John Herschel in 1842 (although the formula for 'Van Dyke Brown' was first patented by Arndt & Troost in Germany in 1895). The process was named for the Flemish Baroque painter Anthony van Dyck, as it produced earth tones of black, sepia and rich brown reminiscent of his palette. It is based on the Argentotype. A simple solution of ferric ammonium citrate (green), silver nitrate and citric acid is used to sensitize watercolour paper, which is dried, exposed to UV light, washed, fixed and air dried. Since the process offers only limited control over contrast levels, contrast must be adjusted in the negative itself before the image is printed.

The Vandyke process

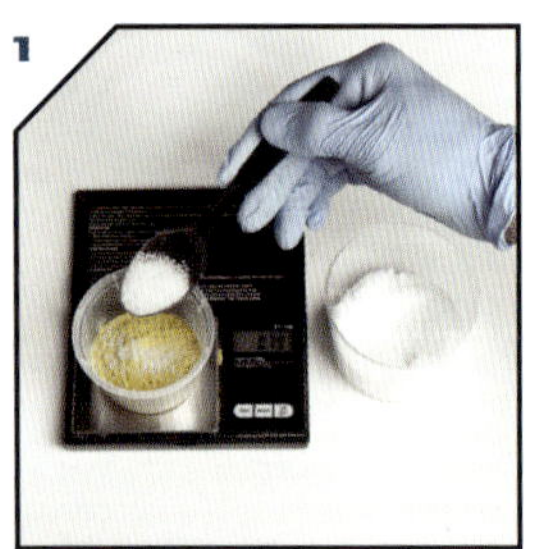 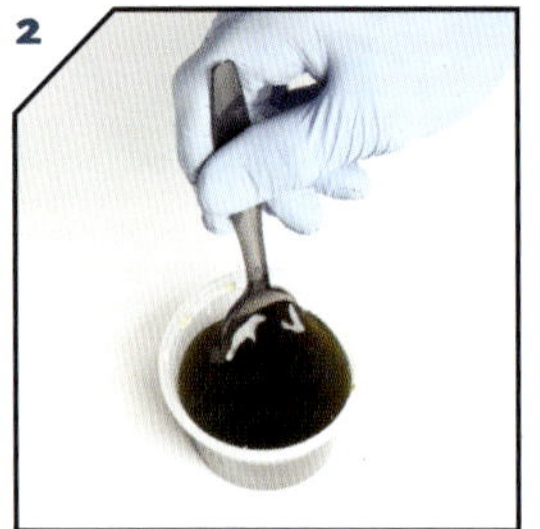 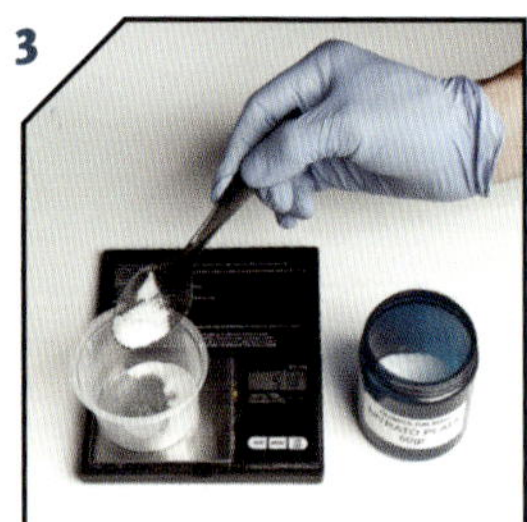 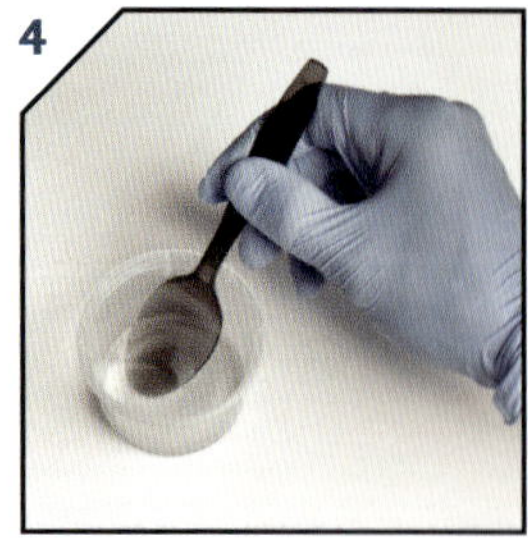

What you need:

- ☐ 20 g ferric ammonium citrate (green) ⚠
- ☐ 5 g citric acid ⚠
- ☐ distilled water
- ☐ 5 g silver nitrate ⚠
- ☐ sodium thiosulfate ⚠
- ☐ beaker (500 ml)
- ☐ contact-printing frame
- ☐ large-format negative
- ☐ watercolour paper
- ☐ UV lamp (optional)
- ☐ gloves
- ☐ scales
- ☐ non-metallic brush or glass rod (for coating)
- ☐ brown bottles
- ☐ trays for processing

Preparing the solution

As with cyanotypes, the Vandyke process involves the preparation and successive mixing of two separate solutions.

Solution A

1 Solution A is made up of 20 g ferric ammonium citrate (green), 5 g citric acid and 50 ml distilled water.

2 Mix together well and transfer to a labelled brown bottle.

Solution B

3 Solution B is made up of 5 g silver nitrate and 25 ml distilled water.

4 Again, mix well and then transfer the solution to a labelled brown bottle.

SEE PAGES 226–29

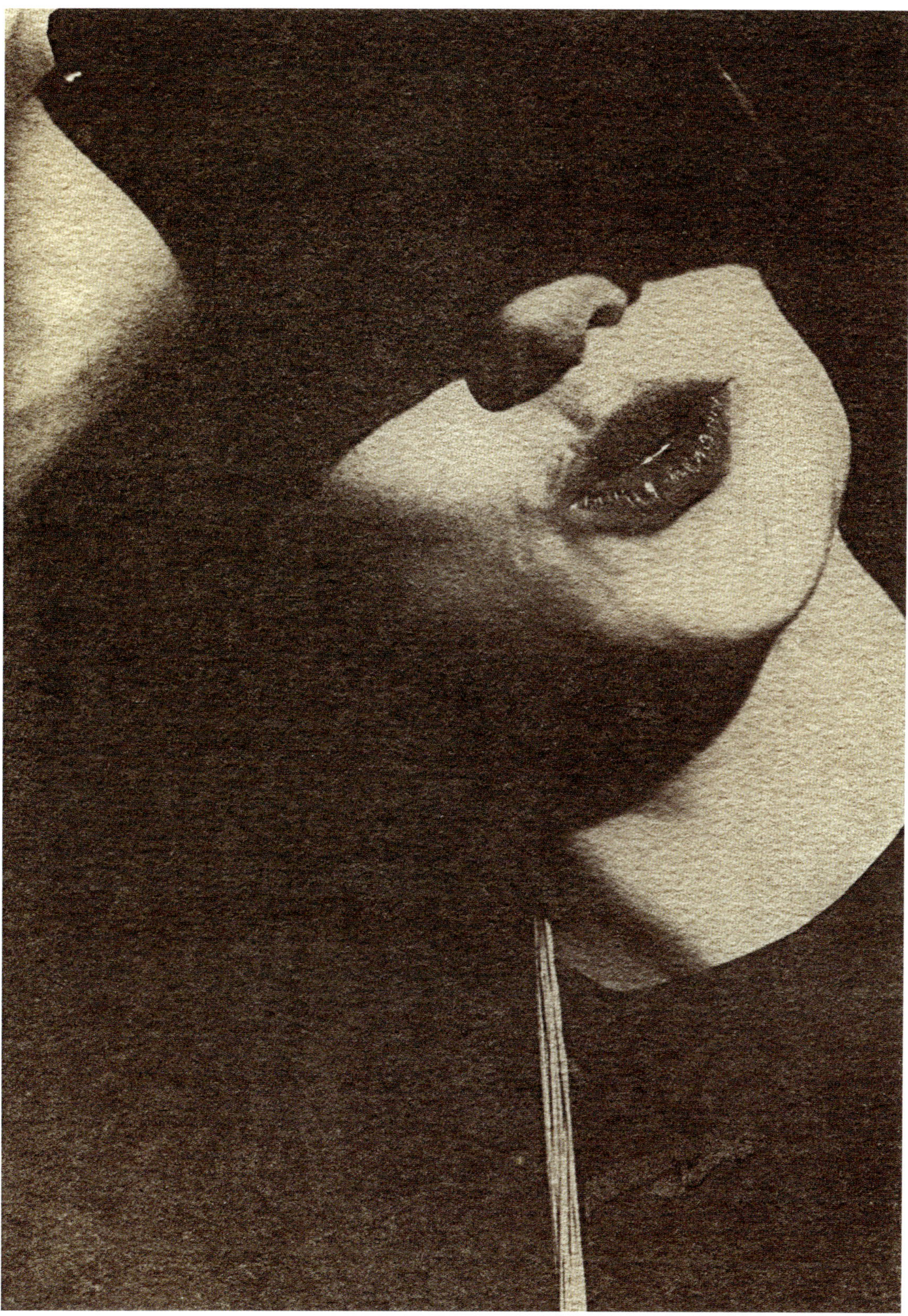

5 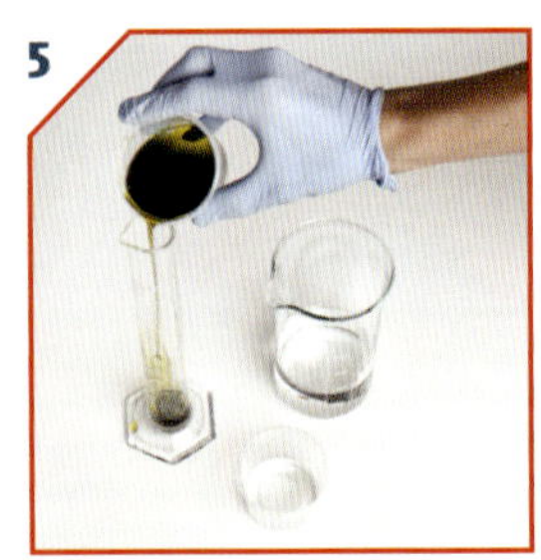
6 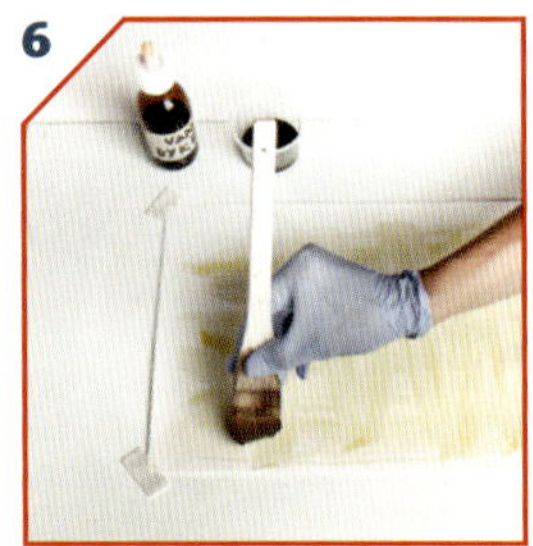
7 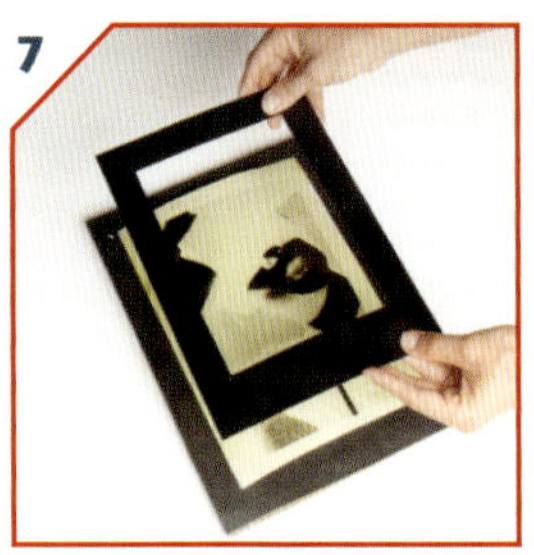
8 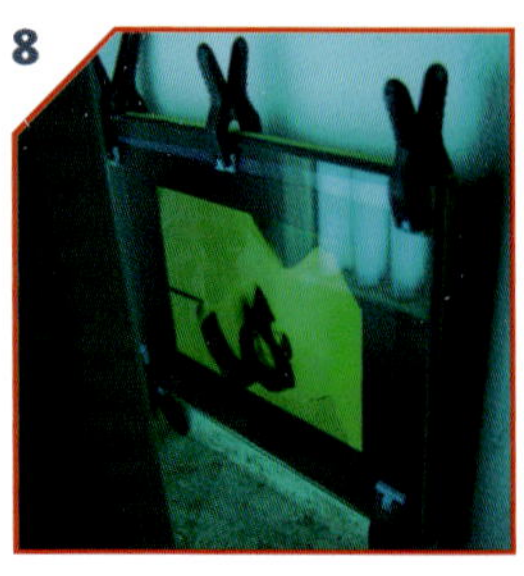

9 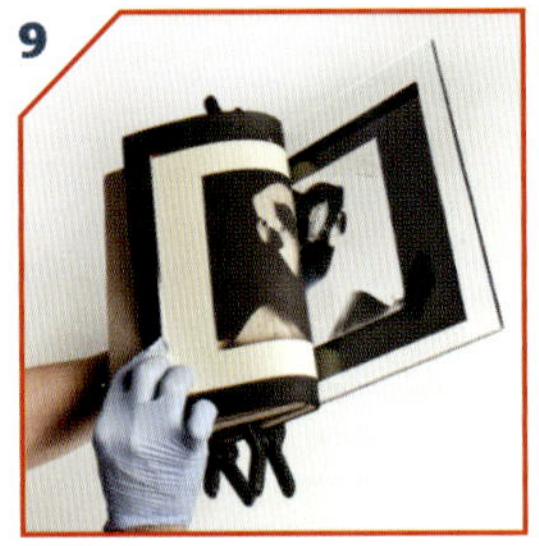
10 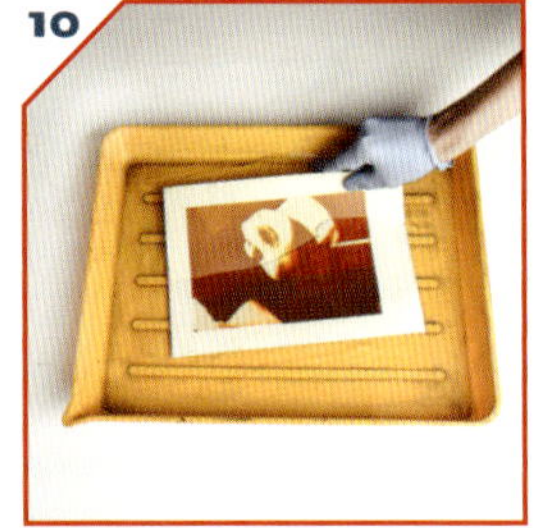
11 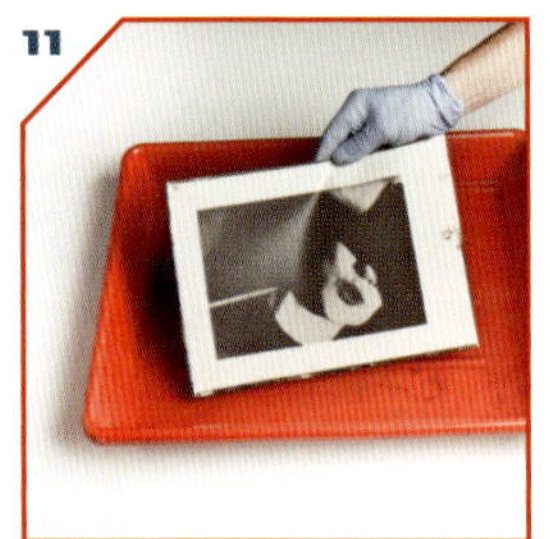
12 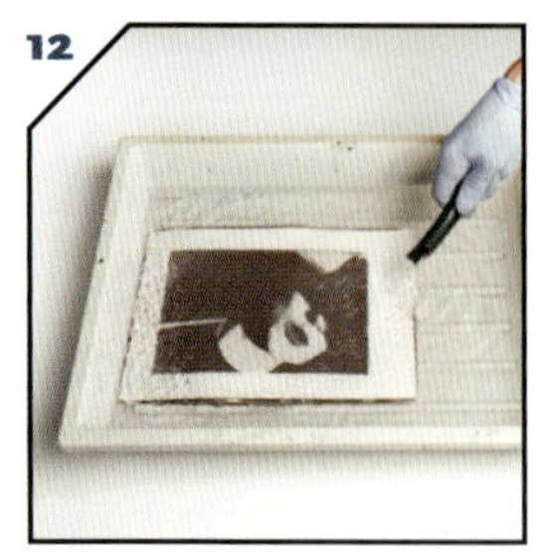

Sizing and salting paper

Although smooth paper stocks generally work best with any technique that requires coating, photographers sometimes experiment with rough, heavy or porous stocks. On their own, these papers will yield low-contrast prints because they absorb sensitizing solution too deeply within their fibres. 'Sizing' the paper – that is, coating it with a solution of gelatin, casein, arrowroot or cornstarch before the photosensitive coating is applied – solves the problem by reducing absorbancy. A 0.2% (2 g/l) solution of gelatin and distilled water is the most common sizing recipe. The sizing can be applied either with a brush or by simply immersing the paper in a tray of solution for a few seconds. The sized paper must dry completely before the photosensitive coating is applied.

! light-sensitive step

---

5 Mix solution A and solution B together and make the resulting sensitizer up to 100 ml with distilled water. As soon as they are mixed, the two solutions become light-sensitive, so be sure to do this in subdued lighting conditions. Note that the solution also needs to settle for a couple of days before it can be used, during which time it must remain in the dark.

Sizing

Sizing is not usually necessary, unless you are printing on particularly rough or absorbent paper stock. If that's the case, size the paper (as described in the box at left) before coating it.

Coating

6 If you are using paper, pin or tape it to a support or to your work table. An A4-size print will require approximately 2 ml of sensitizing solution. Pour the solution into the centre of your paper and then brush it gently with a non-metallic art brush or draw the sensitizer across the paper with a glass rod (the two methods will create subtly different results).

To obtain maximum density (DMax) it can be useful to double coat your paper. Allow the first coat to dry, then apply a second coat, diluting the sensitizer 1:1 with a 5% solution of citric acid (5 g citric acid / 100 ml of water).

Drying

Leave the paper to dry flat for 5 minutes after sensitizing, then hang it up to dry thoroughly. The paper needs to be dry to the touch before you use it, but do not force-dry it with heat, as this may cause fogging and reduce the reflective DMax.

Exposure

7 Load the paper in the contact-printing frame (see pp. 134–35). If you want to avoid printing the ragged brushstroke ends of the coating, a black cardboard frame can be added on top of the negative and sensitized paper in the contact-printing frame to create straight edges.

8 Expose to UV light. The exposure time will vary, depending on many factors, so consider making an exposure test strip (see pp. 24–25) before your final print.

9 Alternatively, you can visually check the exposure by opening up half of the contact-printing frame's backing board.

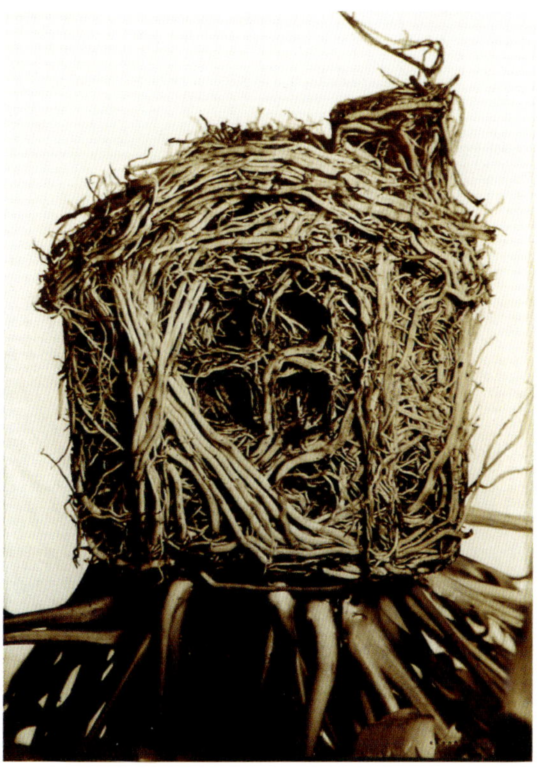

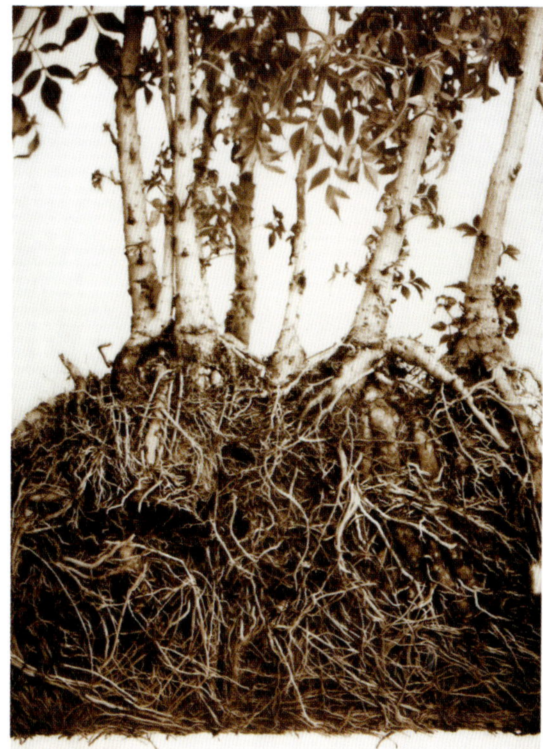

Francis Baker
Containment – Ambition, from the series *The Everyday Garden*, Vandyke print on Wyndstone vellum, 76.2 × 61 cm (30 × 24 in.), 2005

Francis Baker
Containment – Space, from the series *The Everyday Garden*, Vandyke print on Wyndstone vellum, 76.2 × 61 cm (30 × 24 in.), 2006

Developing

10 Once the exposure has been made, the print is developed in a water bath for 3 minutes. The water bath should be slightly acidic, so use a 0.1% solution of citric acid. This will help prevent the iron later oxidizing the silver and fading the print.

Fixing

11 Fixing is done in a bath containing a 5% solution of sodium thiosulfate. Rock the tray for 3 minutes, then drain the used fixer and replenish the bath with fresh, solution. Wash the print under running water while you replace the fixer, then fix for a further 3 minutes in the second bath.

Clearing

12 After fixing the print, place it in a 1% solution of sodium thiosulfate for 2 minutes. Kodak Hypo Clearing Agent or a similar ready-made solution can also be used. These are alkaline clearing baths that will help the paper's long-term conservation.

Wash and dry

To finish, wash the print in running water for at least 5 minutes and then hang it up until it is completely dry.

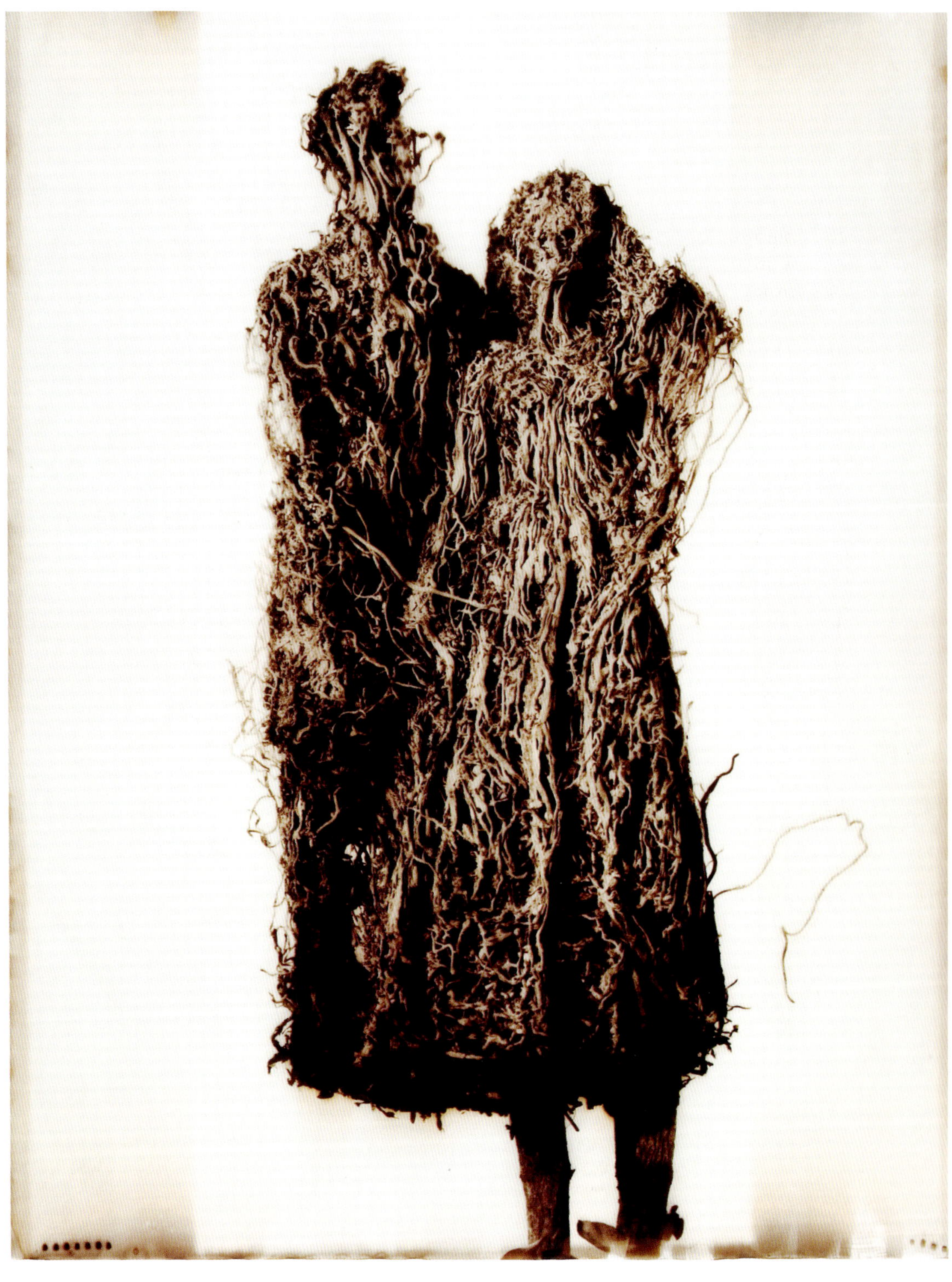

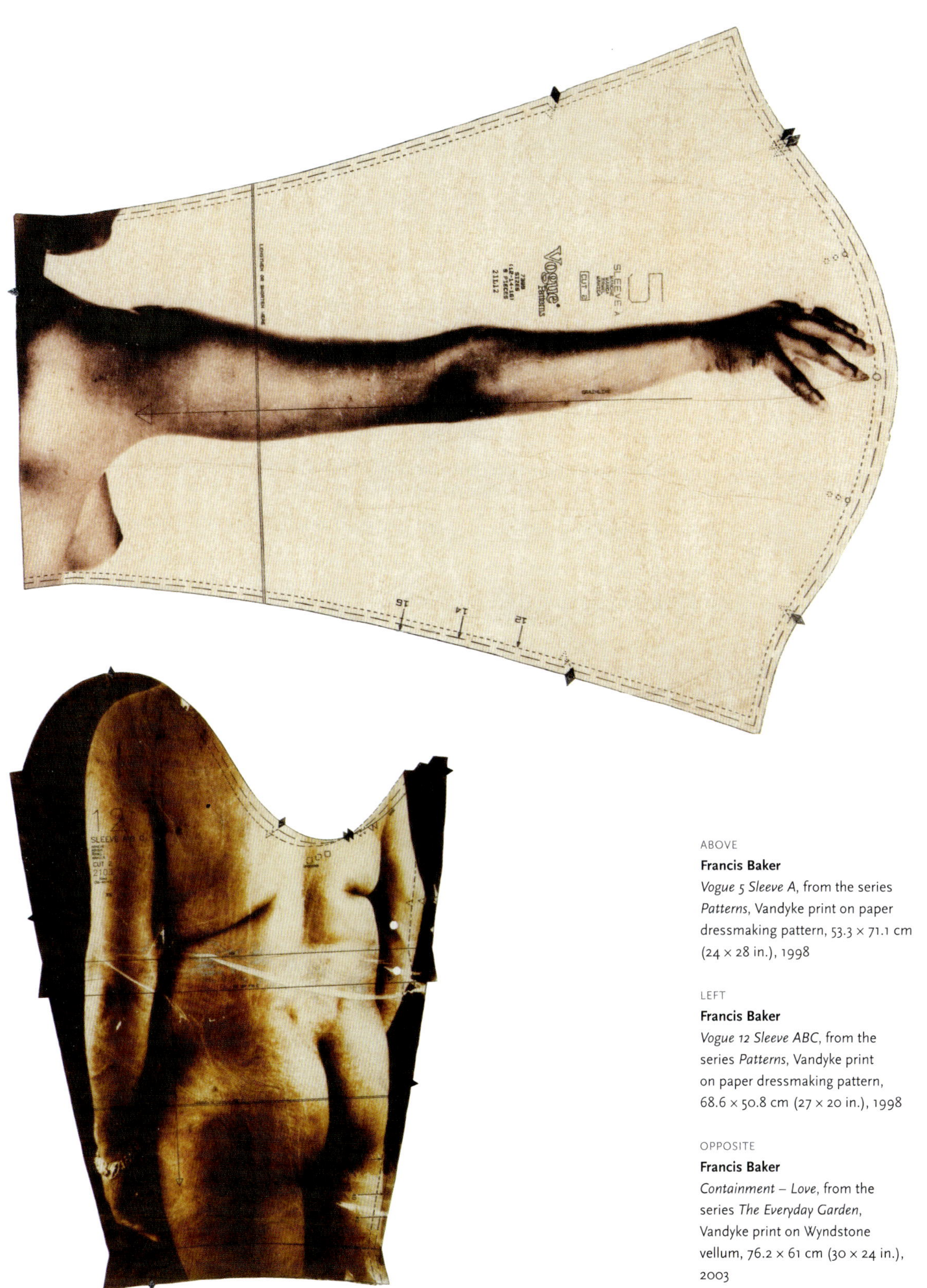

ABOVE
Francis Baker
Vogue 5 Sleeve A, from the series
Patterns, Vandyke print on paper
dressmaking pattern, 53.3 × 71.1 cm
(24 × 28 in.), 1998

LEFT
Francis Baker
Vogue 12 Sleeve ABC, from the
series *Patterns*, Vandyke print
on paper dressmaking pattern,
68.6 × 50.8 cm (27 × 20 in.), 1998

OPPOSITE
Francis Baker
Containment – Love, from the
series *The Everyday Garden*,
Vandyke print on Wyndstone
vellum, 76.2 × 61 cm (30 × 24 in.),
2003

ARGYROTYPE

Argyrotype is a simple iron- and silver-based contact-printing process that yields brown-tinted images in much the same way as a Vandyke or argentotype. However, the Vandyke and argentotype processes require both expensive and toxic ingredients, and the results can be unstable: residual ferric iron will oxidize (bleach) silver, eventually fading the image. Argyrotype, a modern process developed by experimental photographer Mike J. Ware, avoids these problems by using silver sulphamate, a silver salt with a non-oxidizing anion, which is easy to make, inexpensive and relatively non-toxic. The result is a 'brown print' technique that achieves the results and permanence of a gold-, platinum-, or palladium-toned Vandyke print, but without the extra work and cost.

The Argyrotype process

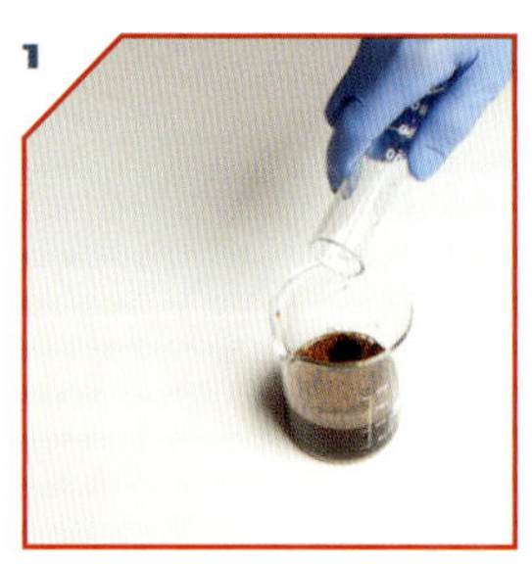

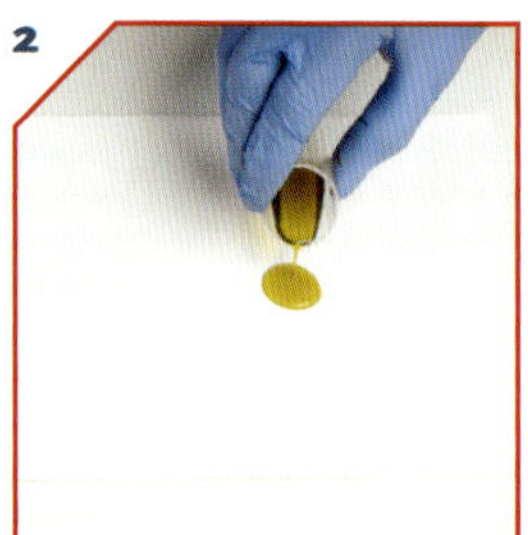

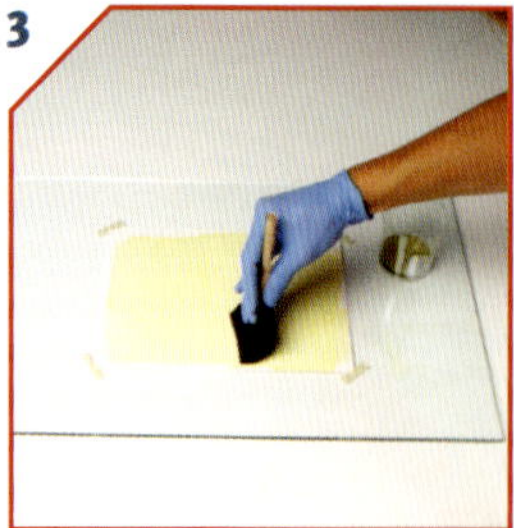

What you need:
- [ ] 7 g sulfamic acid ⚠
- [ ] 7 g silver(I) oxide ⚠
- [ ] 22 g ferric ammonium citrate (green) ⚠
- [ ] distilled water
- [ ] beaker (500 ml)
- [ ] contact-printing frame
- [ ] large-format negative
- [ ] watercolour paper
- [ ] UV lamp (optional)
- [ ] scales
- [ ] non-metallic brush or glass rod (for coating)
- [ ] 2% solution sodium thiosulfate ⚠
- [ ] trays for processing

light-sensitive step

⚠ SEE PAGES 226–29

Sensitizer

1 The argyrotype sensitizing solution should be prepared in subdued lighting conditions as follows:

Heat 70 ml distilled water to 50–60°C and add it to 7 g sulfamic acid. Remember always to add acid to water, and never water to acid – acid interacts very vigorously with water, in a highly exothermic reaction. Add 7 g powdered silver(I) oxide to the solution while it's still warm. Stir until it is dissolved fully. Add 22 g ferric ammonium citrate (green) a little at a time. Stir well and allow to cool down. Add distilled water until you reach a final volume of 100 ml. The solution should be an olive-green colour, and free of all precipitates. Filter it if necessary. Once mixed, the solution has a shelf-life of several months if it is stored in a brown bottle, away from light and at room temperature. Filter any precipitates that might form.

Coating

2 Pin or tape your paper to a board or your work table. Pour a small amount of sensitizing solution into the centre of the paper – an A4-size print requires approximately 2 ml of sensitizer.

3 Brush the sensitizing solution gently with a non-metallic art brush or use a glass rod to spread it evenly across the paper.

Drying

Leave the paper flat and allow it to dry for 5 minutes after it's coated, so that the sensitizing solution soaks in. Then hang the paper to dry. The paper can be used once it is dry to the touch. Drying can be accelerated by using a hairdryer.

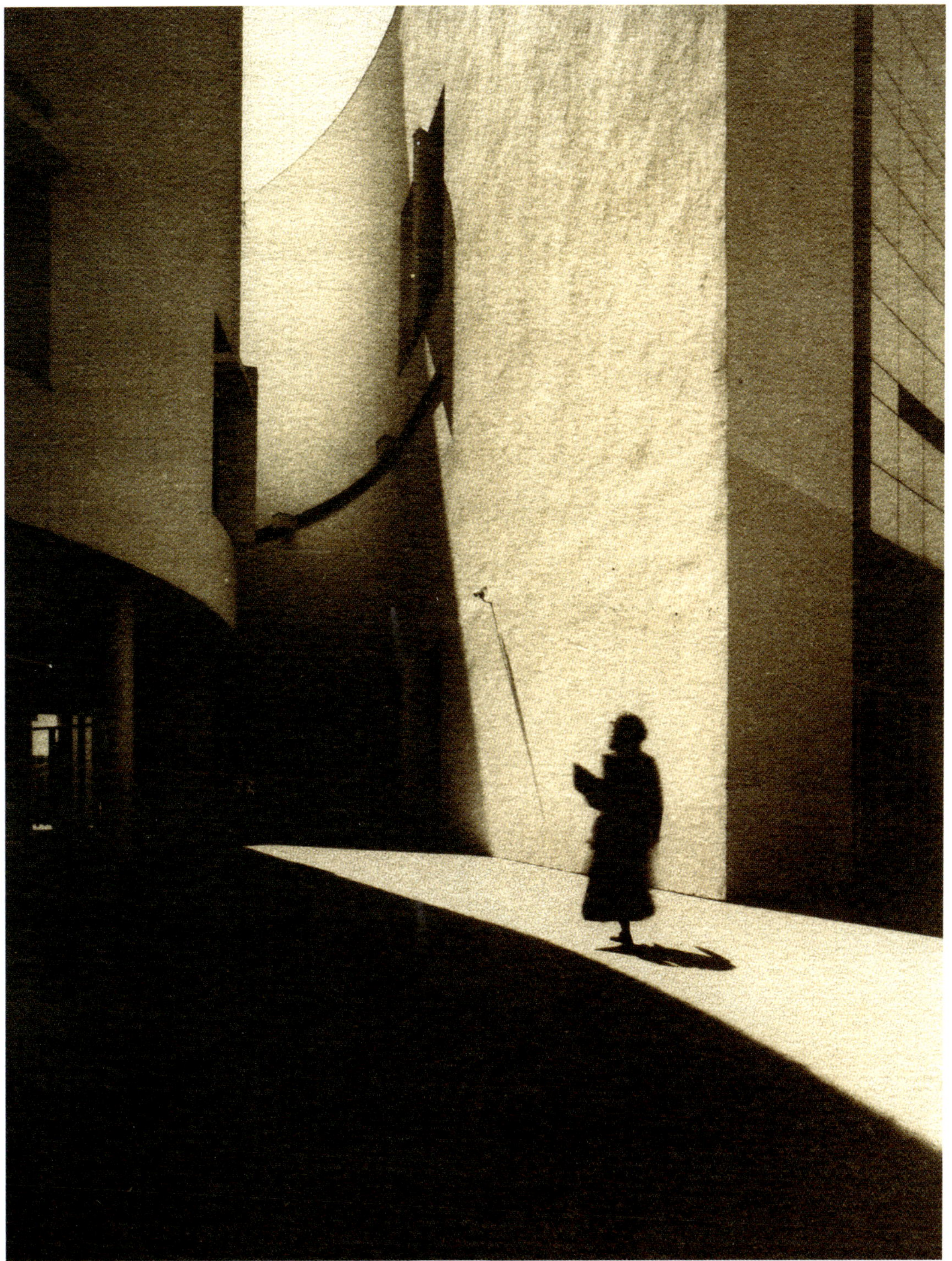

ABOVE
Davide Pellegrini
Untitled, argyrotype, 27 × 21 cm
(10⅝ × 8¼ in.), 2013

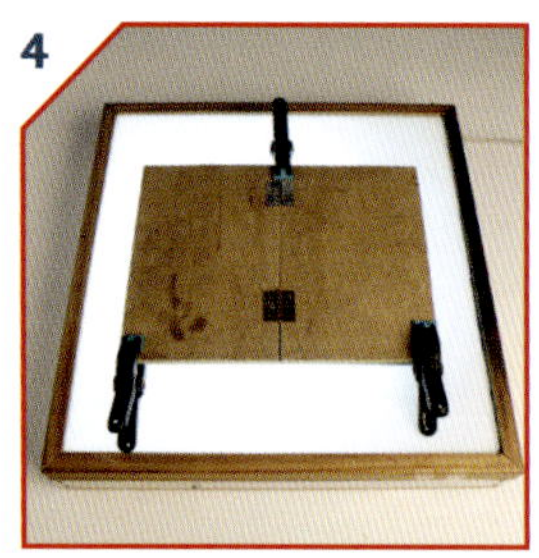 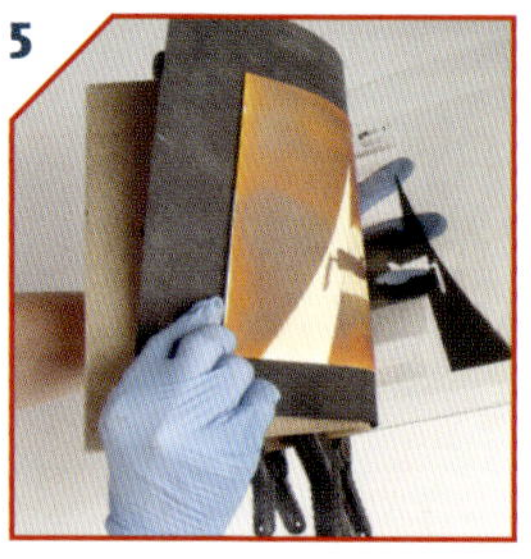 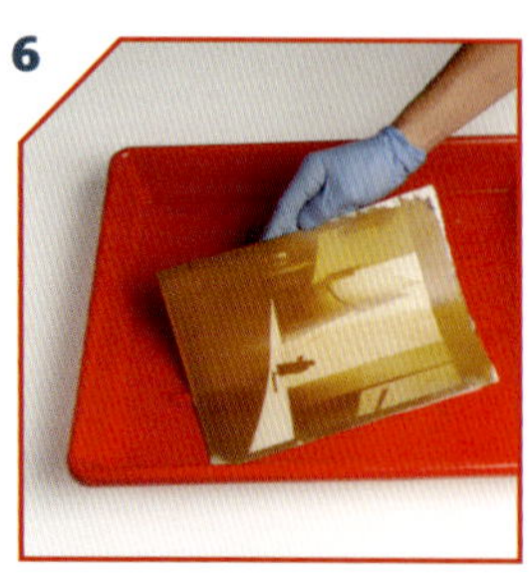

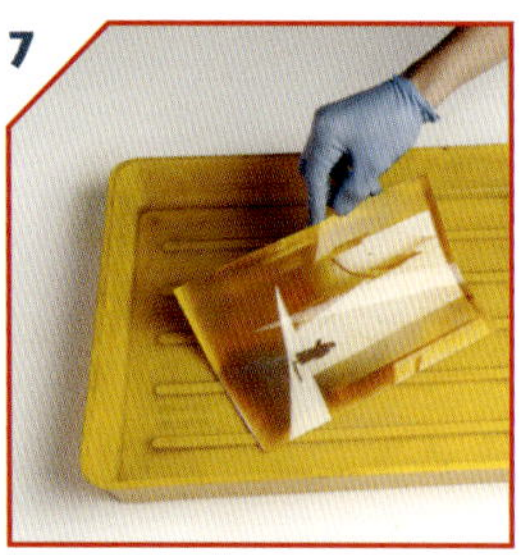 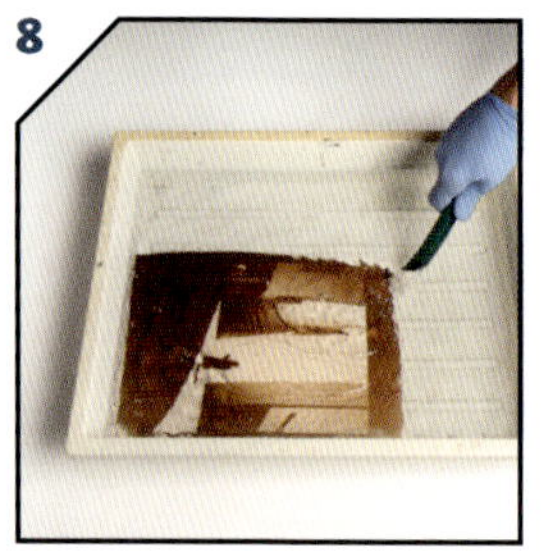 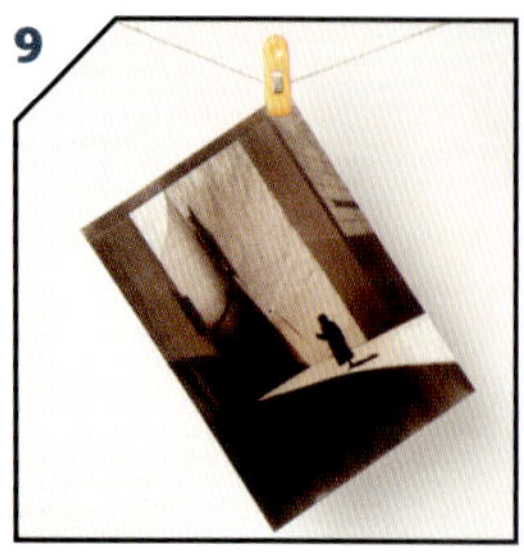

Loading

Load the paper into your contact-printing frame, adding a black cardboard border on top of the negative in the contact-printing frame if you want to obtain a picture with straight edges. Make sure the negative has no creases or wrinkles, then close the contact-printing frame and secure it with clamps.

Exposure

4 Expose to UV light.

5 You can determine the exposure time by first creating a test strip (see pp. 24–25); alternatively, you can carefully open half of the back of the contact-printing frame to assess the image visually.

Development

6 Once the print has been exposed, wash it in a water bath for 5 minutes. If the tap water is particularly chlorinated use distilled water instead. The yellow stain of the sensitizing solution should be washed out completely.

Fixing

7 Fixing is done in a 2% solution of sodium thiosulfate. Rock the tray for 3 minutes and then replenish the bath with fresh fixer. Wash the print for about 1 minute under running water while you change the fixer, and then fix in the second bath for another 3 minutes.

Wash and dry

8 Wash the print under running water for 20 minutes.

9 Hang until dry.

OPPOSITE

Barbara Ghidini

I (top) and *II* (bottom), from the series *Gravity*, argyrotypes, each 13 × 18 cm (5⅛ × 7 in.), 2013

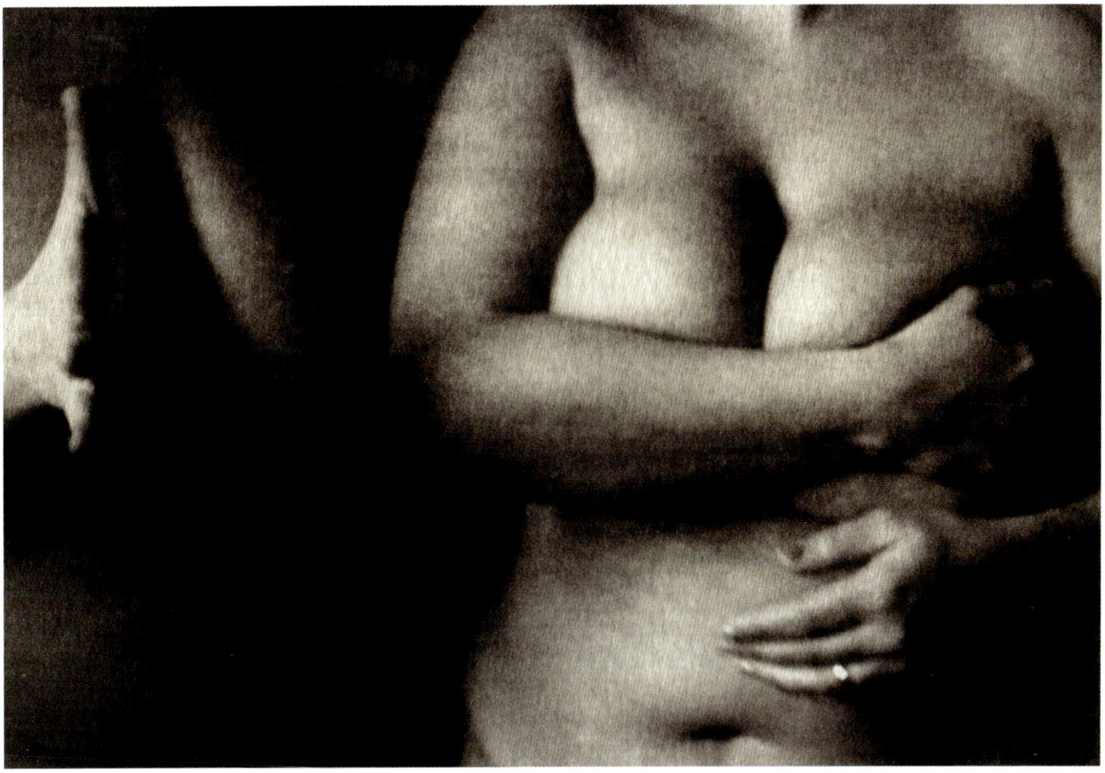

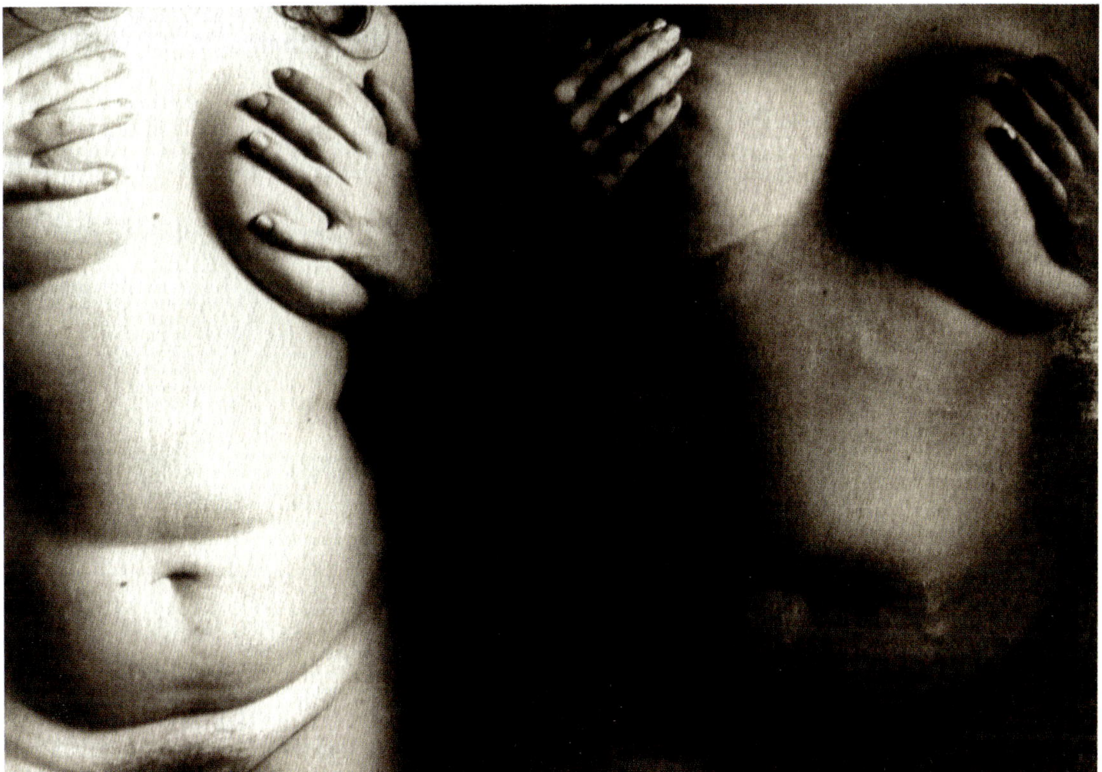

SALT PRINTS

Salt-printing was originally devised by W. H. Fox Talbot, and became the dominant paper-based contact-printing process from 1839 through to the 1860s. It obtains strong, contrasting images from simple table salt (or seawater) and is a very effective and economical way of producing positive prints from large-format negatives. Paper is first coated with a salt solution; once dry, it is sensitized with silver nitrate. The chemical reaction produces silver chloride, which is highly sensitive to light. The emerging picture is usually brown with a red tint, although the intensity of the palette depends on paper type, sizing technique and thickness and the precise formula used. A dark silver colouration, for example, can be achieved by printing on bromidic silver baryta papers.

The salt-print process

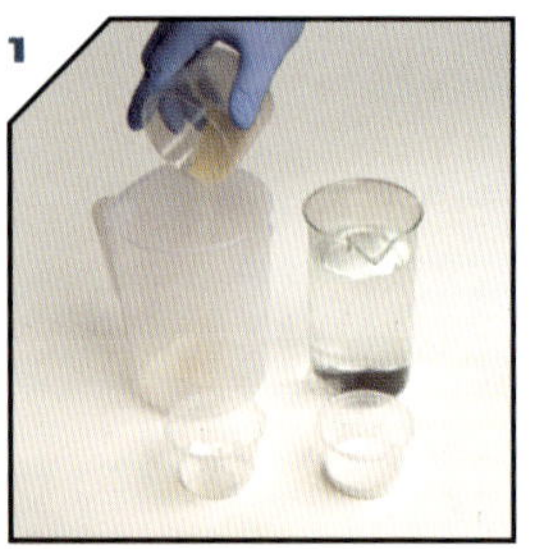
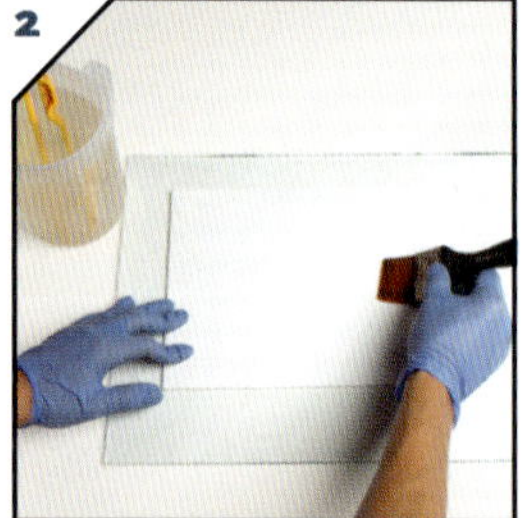
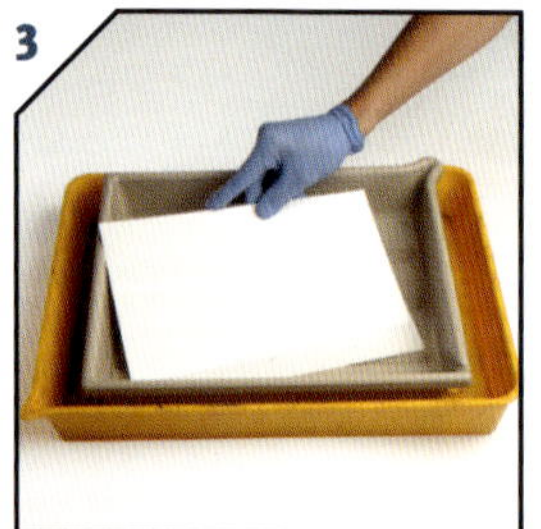
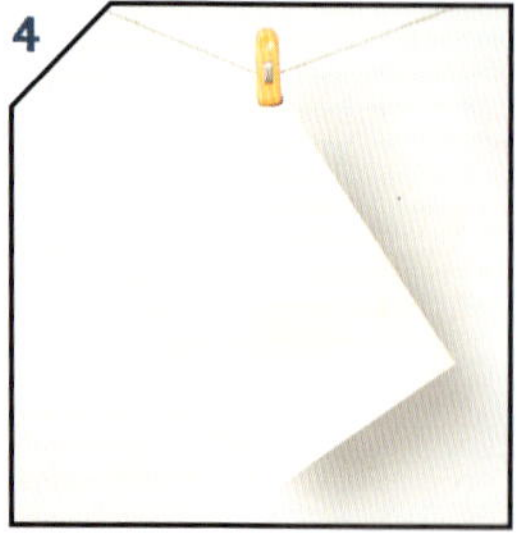

What you need:
- [ ] 2 g gelatin
- [ ] 20 g table salt
- [ ] silver nitrate ⚠
- [ ] sodium thiosulfate ⚠
- [ ] distilled water
- [ ] trisodium citrate or potassium citrate (optional) ⚠
- [ ] contact-printing frame
- [ ] large-format negative
- [ ] heavy watercolour paper
- [ ] UV lamp (optional)
- [ ] beakers / measuring cylinders
- [ ] scales
- [ ] gloves
- [ ] non-metallic brush or glass rod (for coating)
- [ ] trays for processing

Prepare the salting/sizing solution

In the salt-print process, sizing and salting solutions are usually mixed together and applied in one step.

1 To make a salting/sizing solution, measure 2 g gelatin and 20 g salt. Add distilled water to make the solution up to 1 litre. If the gelatin doesn't dissolve, warm the solution slightly. The addition of a neutral citrate (trisodium or potassium) at this stage will enhance the density of the image and increase its reddish tone – experiment with the amount you add, starting at around 20 g.

Coating the paper

2 The paper can be coated by brushing a layer of salting/sizing solution across it, first horizontally and then vertically.

3 Alternatively, since salt and gelatin are inexpensive, the paper can be coated by immersion, which will also prevent the edges from curling. If coating by immersion, the paper needs no more than 30 seconds floating in the solution to be salted. Beware of oversoaking, as this will remove the paper's original coating and may lead to cloudy results.

4 Make sure that no bubbles remain on the surface and hang the paper up until it is dry.

SEE PAGES 226–29

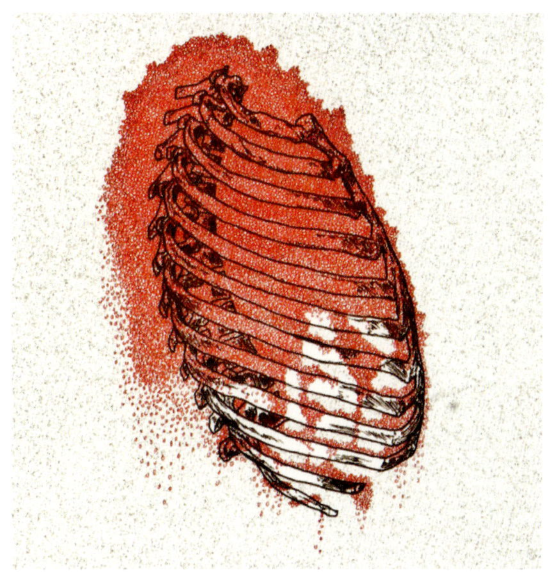

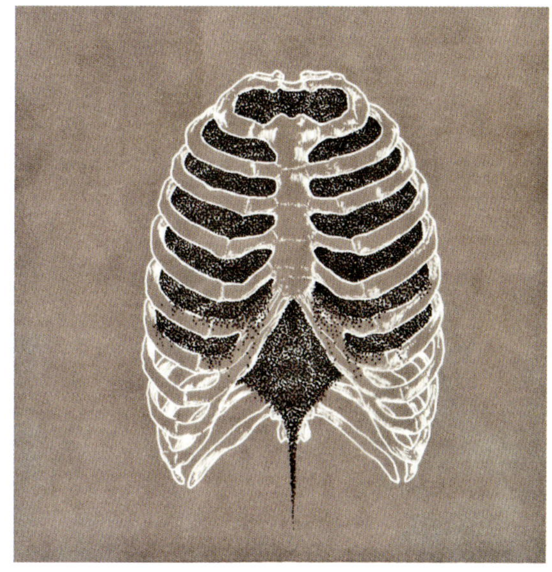

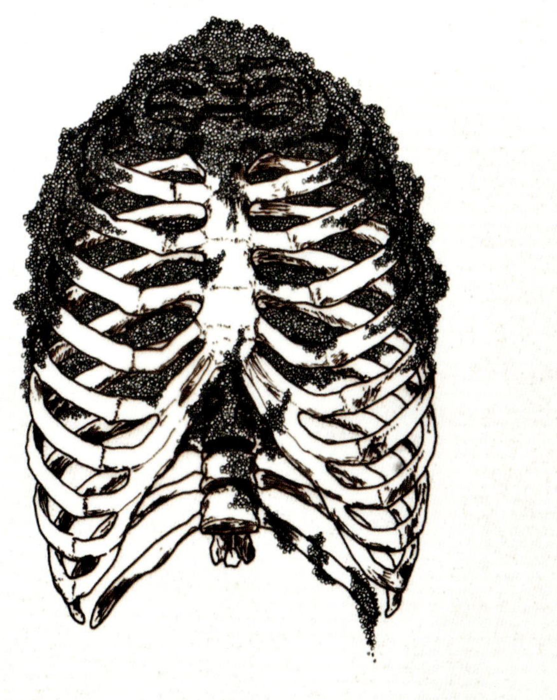

Ellen Krebs
Case Study #17, from *The Human Studies* series, salt print with red ink, 21 × 21 cm (8¼ × 8¼ in.), 2013

Case Study #9, from *The Human Studies* series, salt print with black ink, 21 × 21 cm (8¼ × 8¼ in.), 2013

Case Study #7, from *The Human Studies* series, salt print with black ink, 21 × 21 cm (8¼ × 8¼ in.), 2013

Contact-printing techniques can be used for illustrations and graphics, as well as photographs. You can either create a digital negative from the drawing (as outlined on p. 132) or draw the image directly onto the acetate sheet you will be using as your negative. In these works the artist also applied red and black ink to the finished salt print.

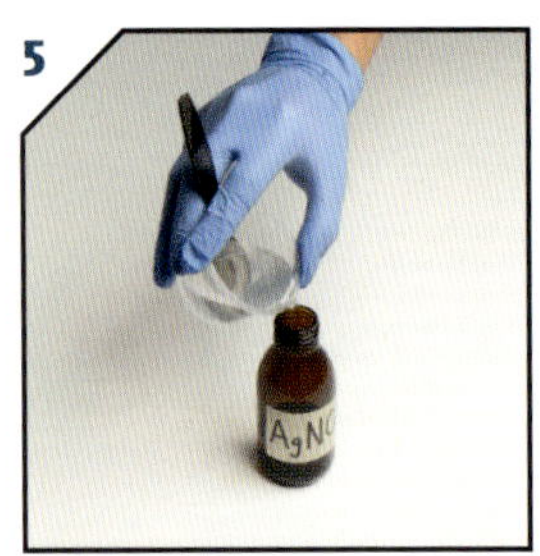

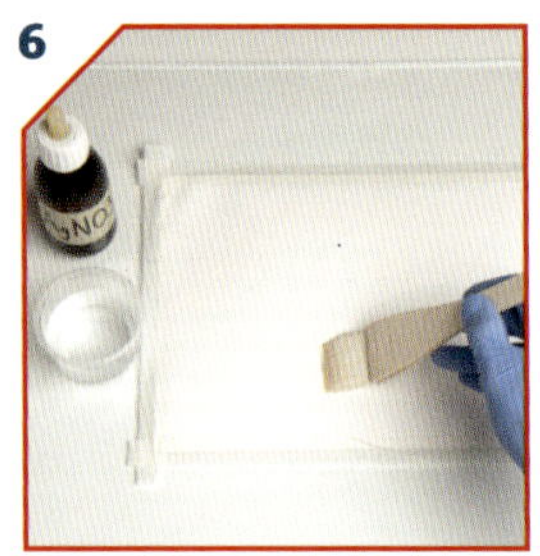

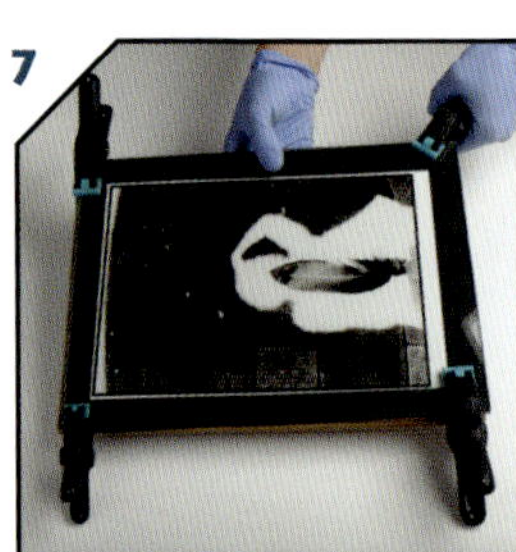

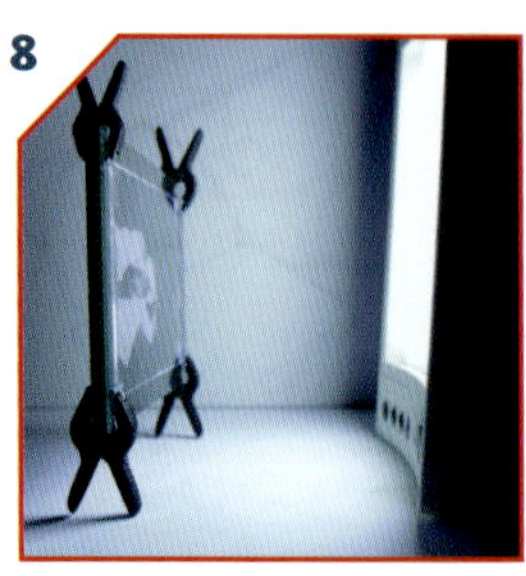

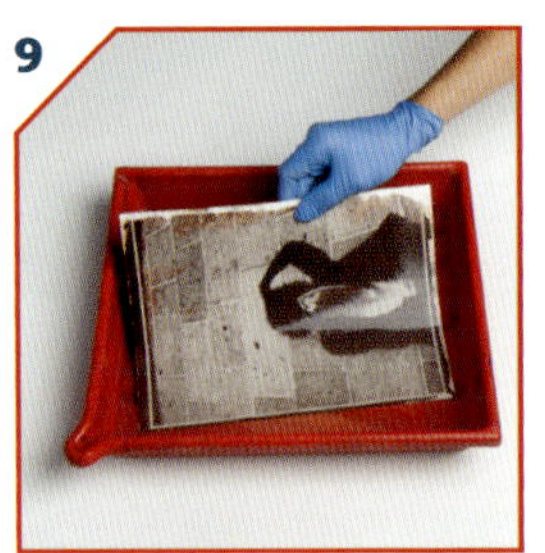

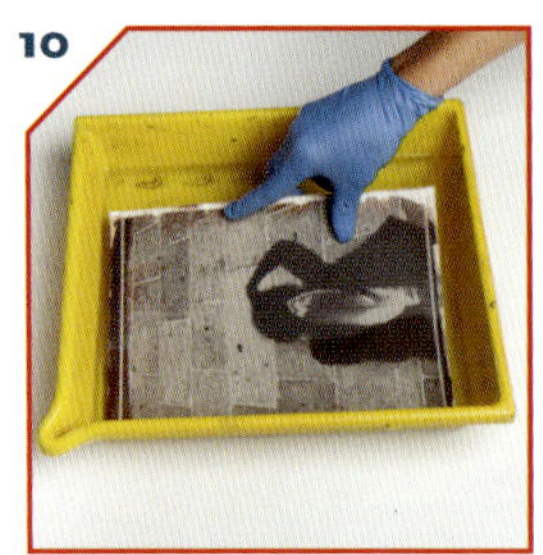

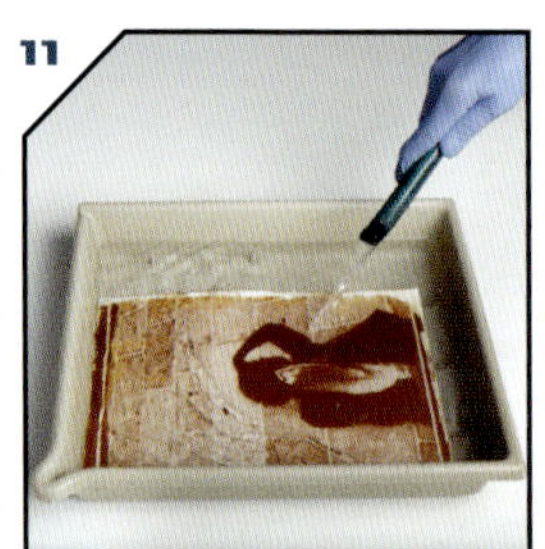

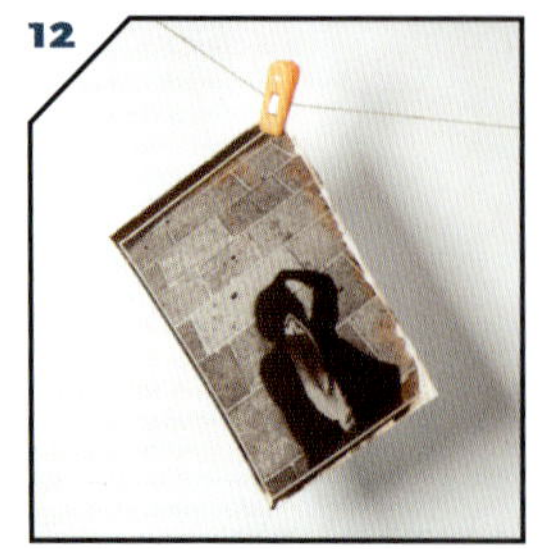

OPPOSITE
Cristóbal Pereira
Feather, salt print, 27 × 21 cm
(10⅝ × 8¼ in.), 2013

Sensitizing

5 Working under safelight conditions, make a sensitizing solution of 10% silver nitrate and distilled water (10 g silver nitrate to 100 ml water).

6 Pin or tape the salted paper to a rigid support and pour a small amount of sensitizing solution into the centre (an A4-size print requires approximately 2 ml of sensitizing solution). Brush it with a non-metallic brush, or spread it across the paper using a glass rod. Leave the paper to dry flat for 5 minutes after coating, then hang until dry to the touch.

Exposure

7 Load the paper into a contact-printing frame, along with the negative, as described on pp. 134–35.

8 Expose to UV light. You can create a test strip to determine exposure time before you begin (see pp. 24–25) or open one half of the back of the contact-printing frame to check exposure visually.

Development

9 Salt prints are developed in water for 1–2 minutes. The excess silver chloride will be washed away in the solution, so don't be alarmed if the print turns cloudy white.

Fixing

10 Fixing is done in a 10% solution of sodium thiosulfate. A 0.2% addition of sodium carbonate is optional, but will help to minimize fading. Rock the tray for 3 minutes and then pour out the fixer and replace it with fresh solution. Wash the print for about 1 minute under running water before immersing in the second fixer bath for 5 minutes more.

Wash and dry

11 Immerse the print in water for at least 30 minutes after the second fixer stage to ensure you remove all of the fixer solution.

12 After this time, wash the print under running water for a further 5 minutes, before hanging it to dry.

! light-sensitive step

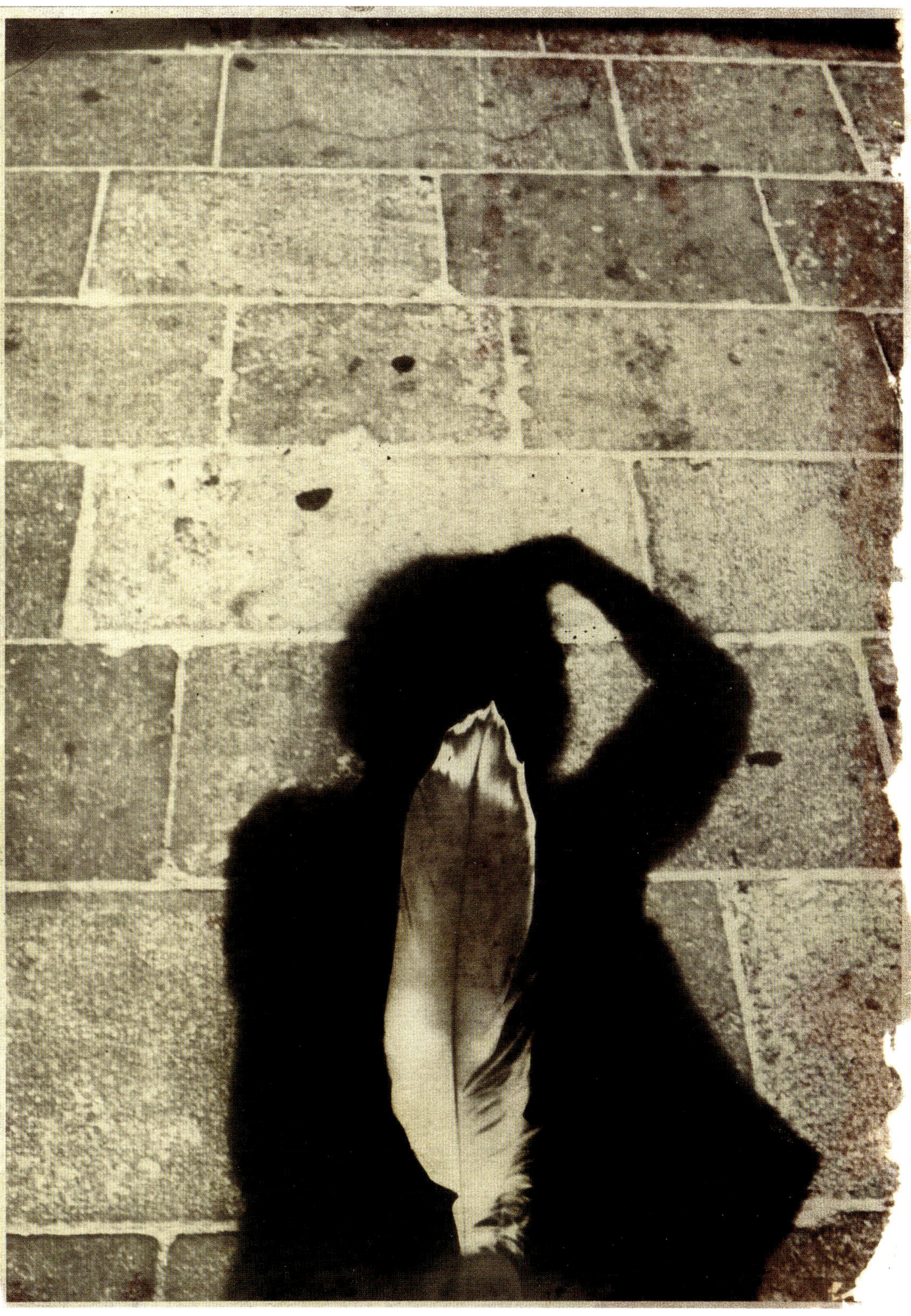

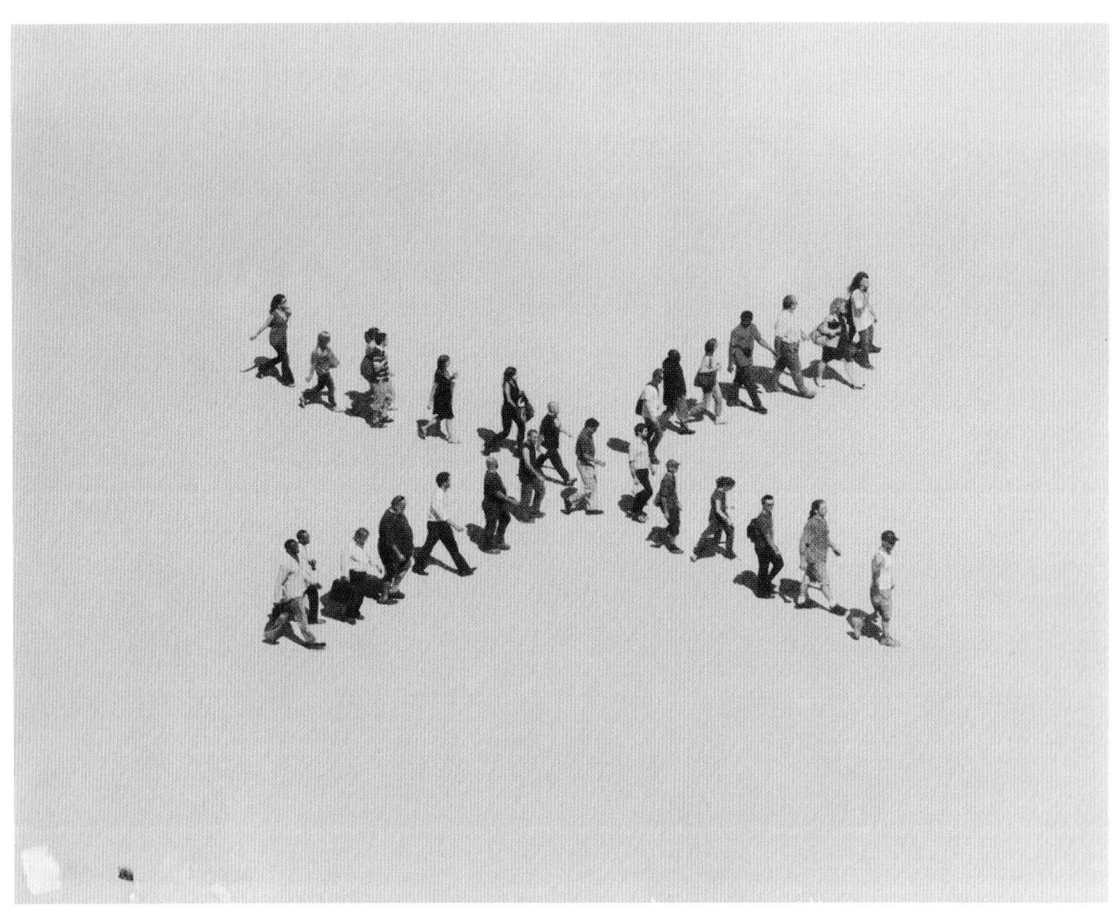

Andrew B. Myers
Untitled, from the series *Xing*,
20.3 × 25.4 cm (8 × 10 in.), 2010

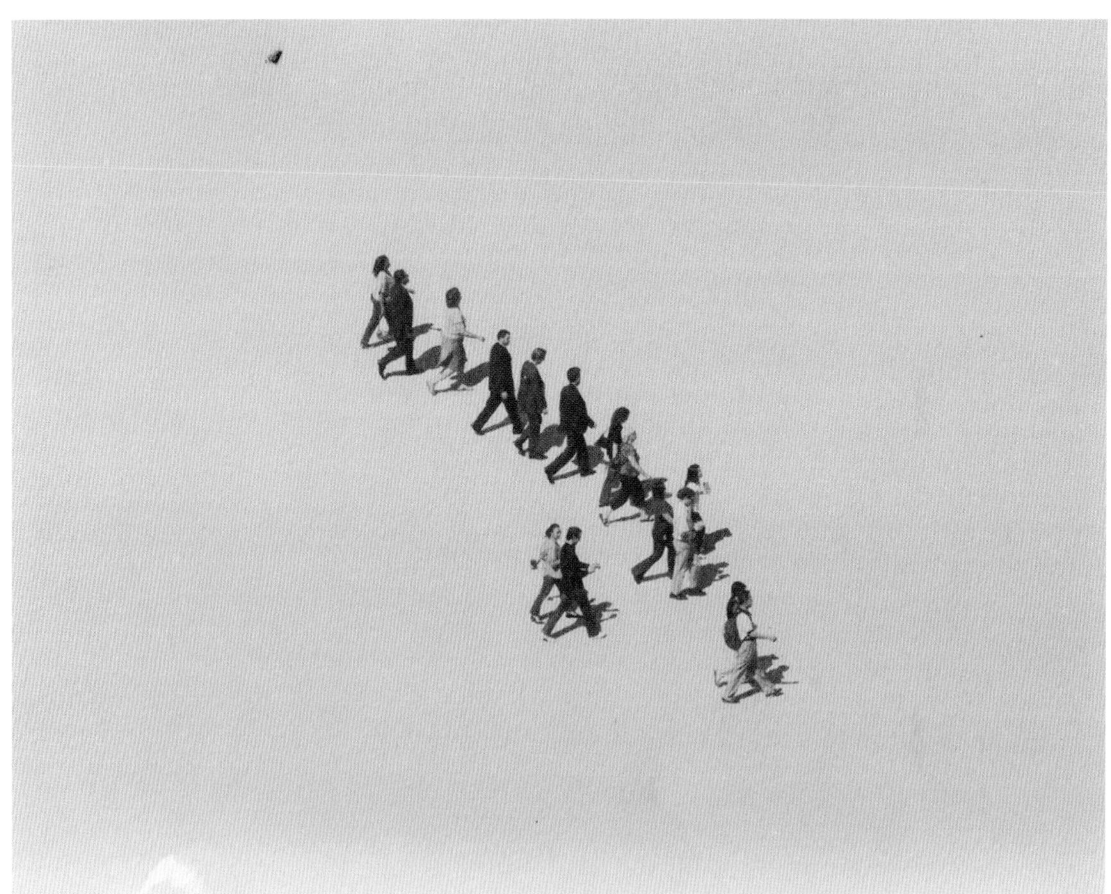

Andrew B. Myers
Untitled, from the series *Xing*,
20.3 × 25.4 cm (8 × 10 in.), 2010

ALBUMEN PRINT

Albumen printing was one of the first effective and commercially available printing methods, utilizing the protein contained in egg whites to bind the sensitizer. It was invented in 1850 by Louis Désiré Blanquart-Evrard and was a natural evolution of the salt paper process, producing intense red-brown images. Quick and inexpensive, it rapidly became the preferred method of printing a picture on paper from a negative. Unlike salt prints, the resulting image is not embedded in the fibres of the paper, but sits instead on the albumen layer. This allows for more intense blacks and greater brilliance and contrast than does the salt print process.

The albumen process

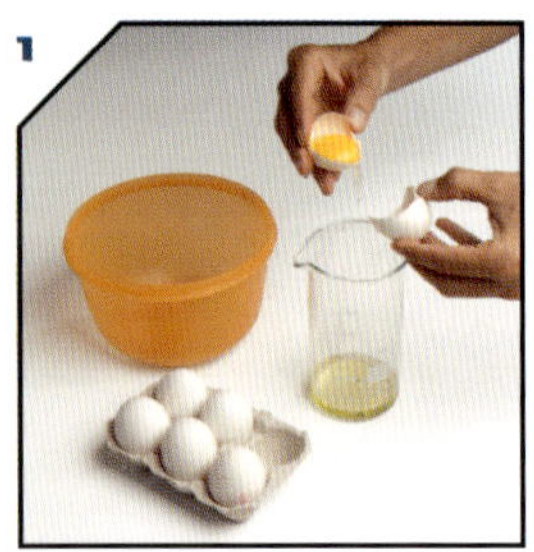
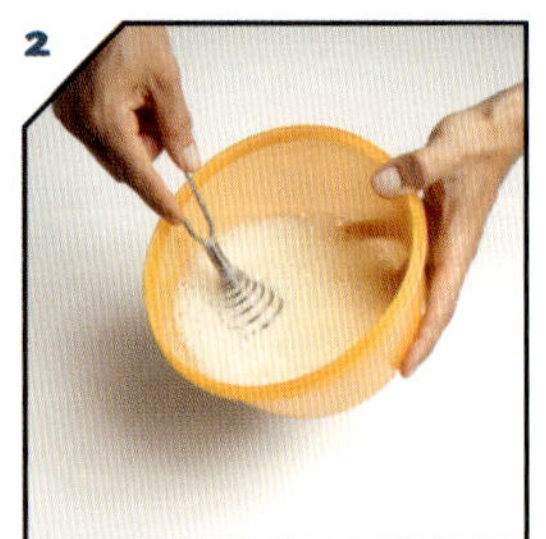
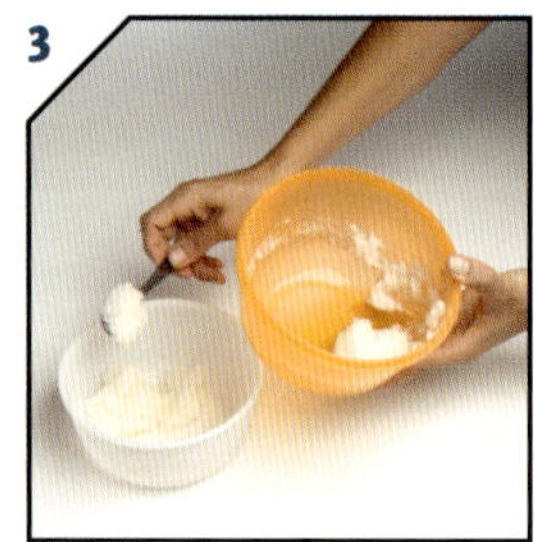
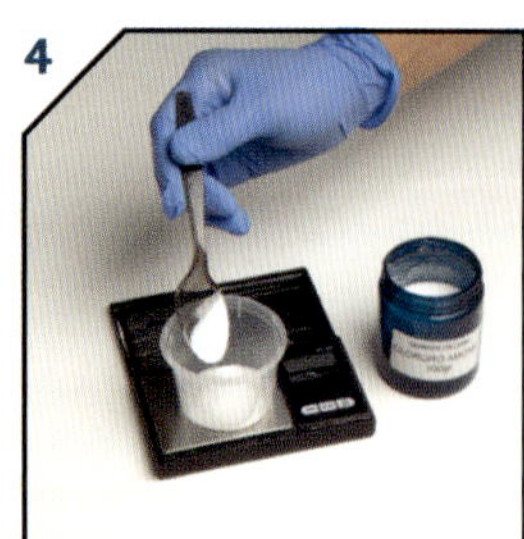

What you need:

- ☐ 12–15 eggs (for 500 ml egg white)
- ☐ whisk or electric beaters
- ☐ mixing bowls
- ☐ 15 g ammonium chloride ⚠
- ☐ distilled water
- ☐ 2 ml 28% acetic acid (optional) ⚠
- ☐ coffee filter
- ☐ needle
- ☐ isopropyl alcohol ⚠
- ☐ salt / ammonium chloride ⚠
- ☐ silver nitrate ⚠
- ☐ sodium thiosulfate ⚠
- ☐ potassium dichromate 6.5–7% solution (optional) ⚠
- ☐ contact-printing frame
- ☐ large-format negative
- ☐ watercolour paper
- ☐ UV lamp (optional)
- ☐ beakers / measuring cylinders
- ☐ scales
- ☐ gloves
- ☐ non-metallic brush or glass rod (for coating)
- ☐ trays for processing

Preparation

1 Start by separating the whites of the eggs from the yolks, taking care not to drop any bits of eggshell or yolk into the albumen. Depending on the size of the eggs you are using you will need 12–15 eggs to produce approximately 500 ml of egg white.

2 Transfer the egg whites into a larger bowl and beat them until frothy – you can use electric beaters to speed up the process.

3 Cover the bowl and place it in a refrigerator for 24 hours. After settling, the albumen liquid will separate from the froth, which needs to be removed.

4 Weigh 15 g ammonium chloride.

SEE PAGES 226–29

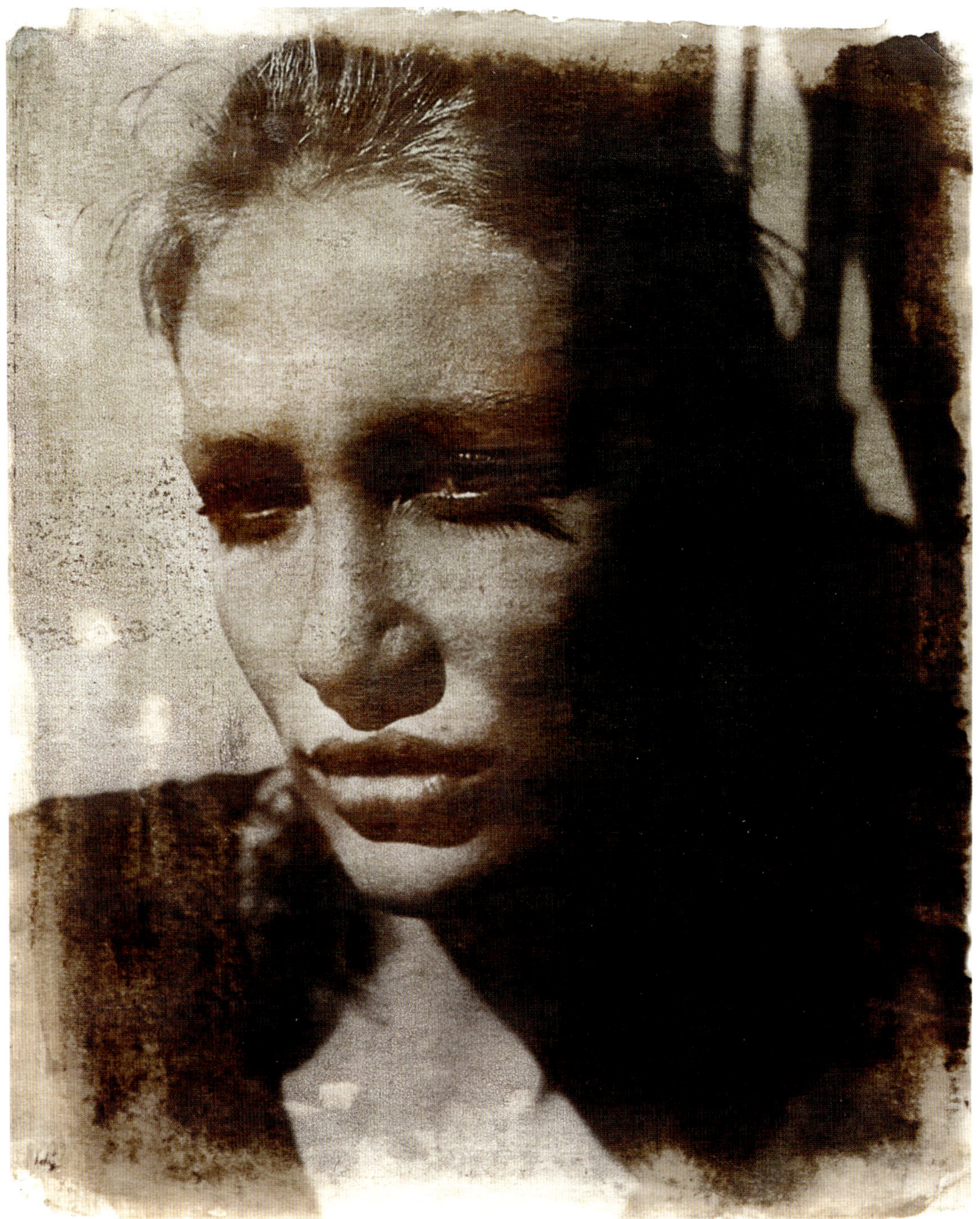

Brembo
Luisa B., albumen print, 27 × 21 cm
(10⅝ × 8¼ in.), 2013

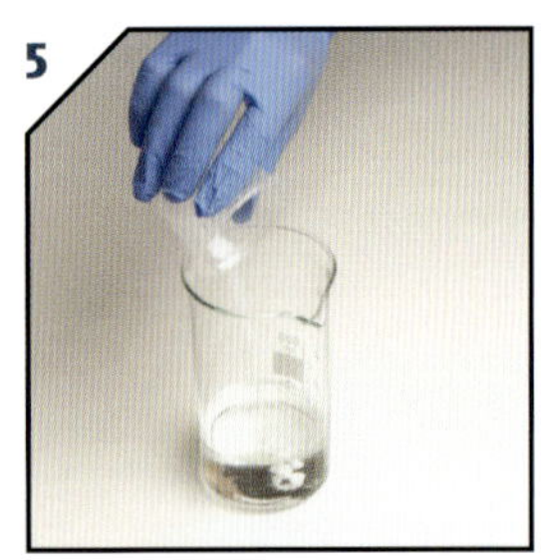 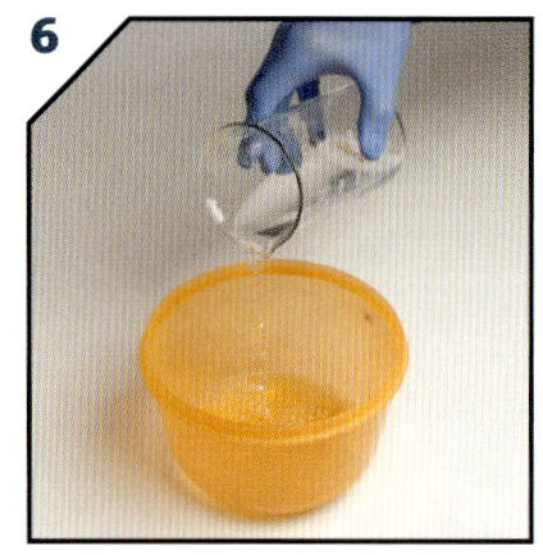 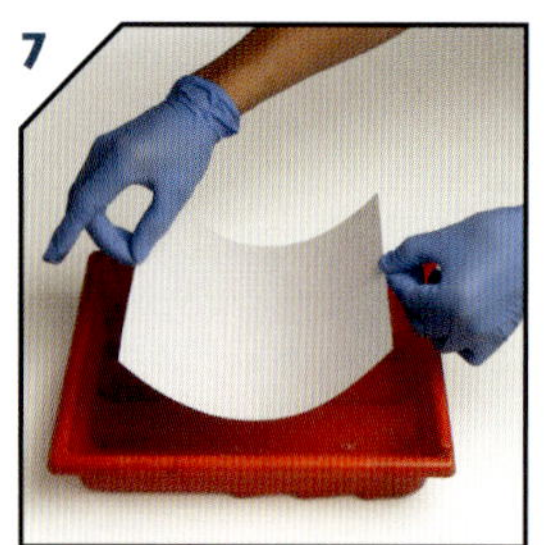 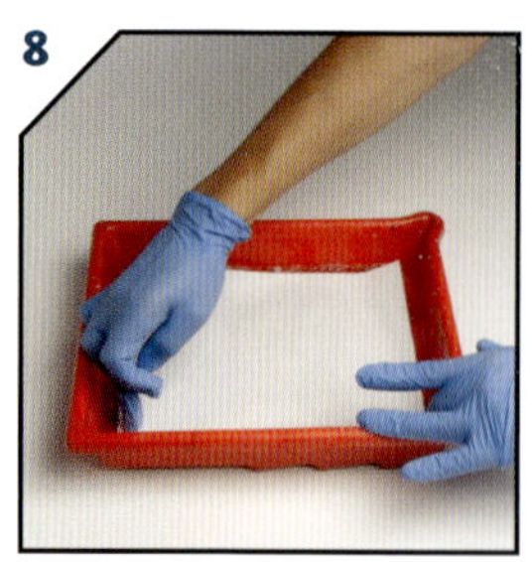

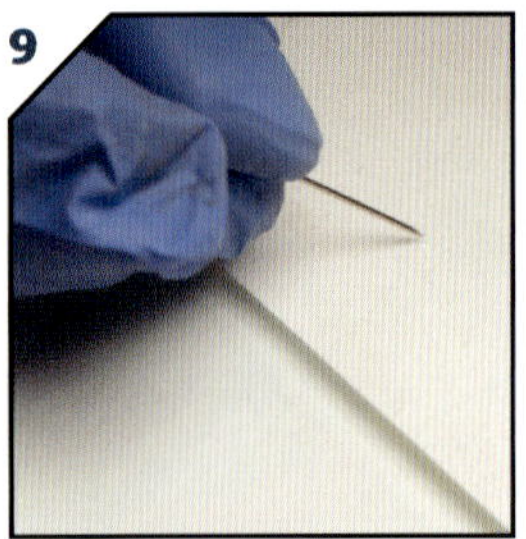 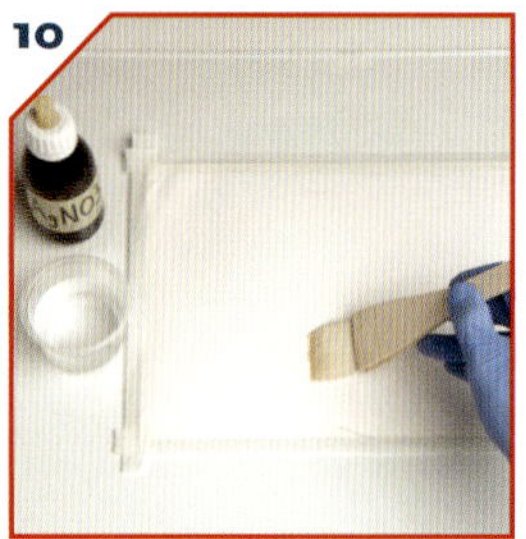 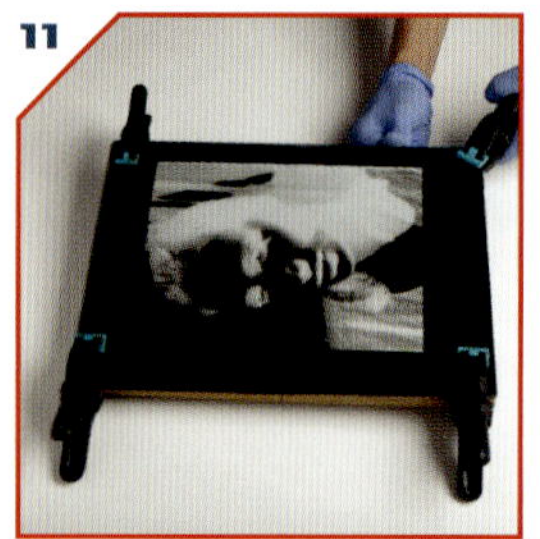 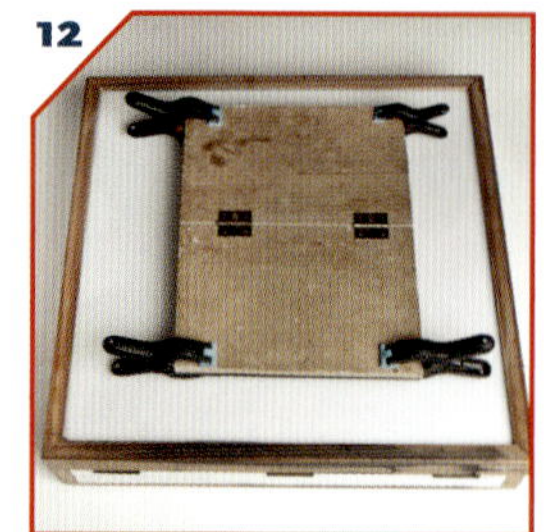

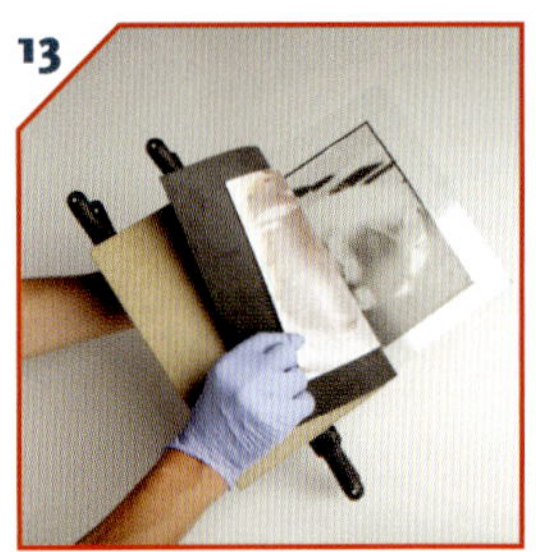 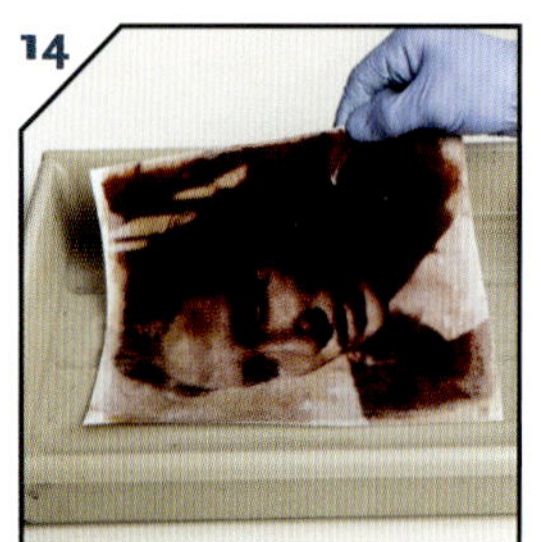 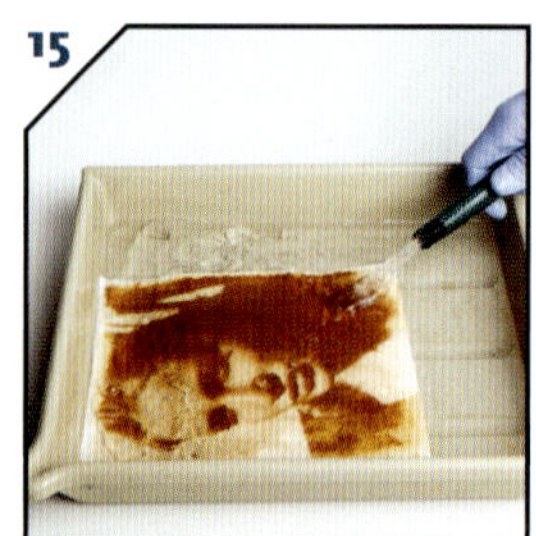 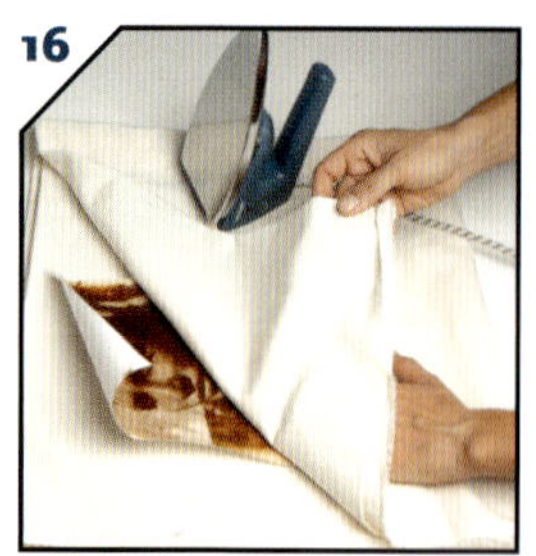

!
light-
sensitive
step

5 Mix the ammonium chloride with 15 ml of distilled water.

6 Add the ammonium chloride solution to the albumen and mix thoroughly. To prolong the permanence of the albumen you can add 2 ml of 28% acetic acid at this stage. Filter the solution through a coffee filter (with or without the acetic acid) and place this back in the fridge for at least a week.

Coating

7 Pour the albumen solution into a tray and gently place your paper on top. Allow the paper to float, making sure that its entire surface is in contact with the albumen solution.

8 If the corners of the paper curl upwards apply gentle pressure to push them down. Be careful to avoid getting any albumen on the back of the paper, as this will cause the image to print on the reverse of the paper, as well as the front. Leave the paper to float for about 3 minutes, then lift it carefully by one corner and allow the excess albumen to drain off it.

9 Remove any blots or lumps of albumen with a thin needle, popping any bubbles that may have formed. Hang the paper from its longer edge, and when it is almost dry, remove any excess albumen that has formed at the bottom of the paper.

Double coating

Double coating (not shown) is an optional step, but it is strongly recommended as it will coat the paper more evenly, produce glossier prints and achieve greater density of the image. The first albumen coat needs to be hardened before the second is applied; otherwise, the second coat will simply wash away the first. To harden the albumen, wait until the first coat is completely dry.

Then, prepare the hardening solution by adding 3% ammonium chloride/salt to a 70% solution of isopropyl alcohol. Use the solution immediately, as the isopropyl alcohol is highly volatile and evaporation will concentrate the solution. Immerse the paper for 15 seconds in the hardener and lift it rapidly using tongs. Wait for the alcohol to evaporate completely, then repeat the coating procedure described in Steps 7–9.

Hang the paper to dry. To minimize curling, hang from the edge opposite that used in drying the first coat. If the paper is subsequently too curled for sensitizing, flatten it between two (heavy) books or under a similar flat, heavy weight.

Sensitizing solution

Make a sensitizing solution (not shown) of 15% silver nitrate and distilled water (15 g silver nitrate for 100 ml water). Print contrast can be increased by adding a drop or two of 6.5–7% (2 g/30 ml) potassium dichromate to the sensitizing solution. Potassium dichromate is extremely toxic, however, so wear protective goggles, a face mask and full skin and respiratory protection while handling.

Sensitizing

10 Pin or tape the paper to a support or to your work table. An A4-size print requires approximately 2 ml of sensitizing solution. Pour the solution into the centre of the paper and then brush it outwards with a non-metallic art brush or use a glass rod to coat the paper. Allow the sensitized paper to dry thoroughly (in darkness).

Exposure

11 Load the paper into the contact-printing frame and secure the glass to the backing board with clamps.

12 Expose the sensitized paper to UV light.

13 You can either make a test strip to determine the exposure (see pp. 24–25) or check the exposure visually by opening the back of your contact-printing frame.

Development

14 After exposure, wash the print in a water bath for 2–3 minutes. The water will cloud at first as the unexposed silver washes out, and the print will quickly shift from bluish-purple to an orange-brown colour as rinsing continues. Do not be tempted to stop development if this colour shift happens before the wash time is up – the silver nitrate should be washed out thoroughly.

Fixing

Fixing is done in two consecutive baths of a 2% solution of sodium thiosulfate. Rock the tray for 5 minutes and then change the bath for fresh fixer, washing the print for about a minute under running water while you do this.

Washing

15 Finish the process by washing the print in water for 20 minutes, then hang it up until it is dry.

Ironing

16 Albumen prints will inevitably curl, but they can be flattened by ironing them. Place the print between two pieces of thick natural fabric, such as heavy cotton towels or canvas, and iron at a low temperature for 1 or 2 minutes. Repeat the process if needed.

Variations

An albumen print can be toned using expensive gold or platinum salts or with cheaper alternatives such as tea or coffee. Toning will also protect the print from early ageing as the albumen degrades, which would be seen as a distinct yellowing of the highlights.

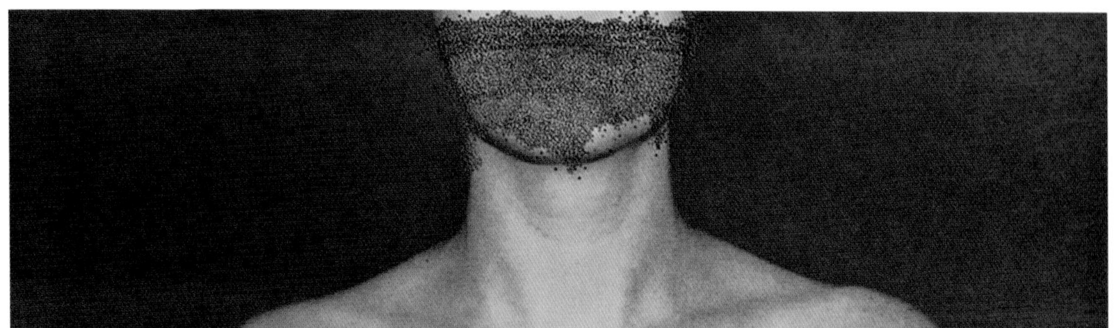

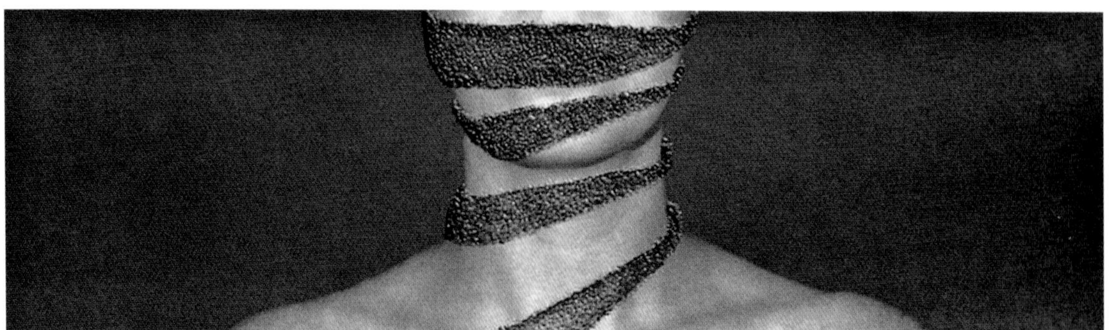

Ellen Krebs
The Beginning 2, from the series
One Thousand Words, matte
albumen print with burned
surface marks, 8.4 × 29.7 cm
(3¼ × 11¾ in.), 2013

Ellen Krebs
The Beginning, from the series
One Thousand Words, matte
albumen print with wax and black
ink, 8.4 × 29.7 cm (3¼ × 11¾ in.),
2013

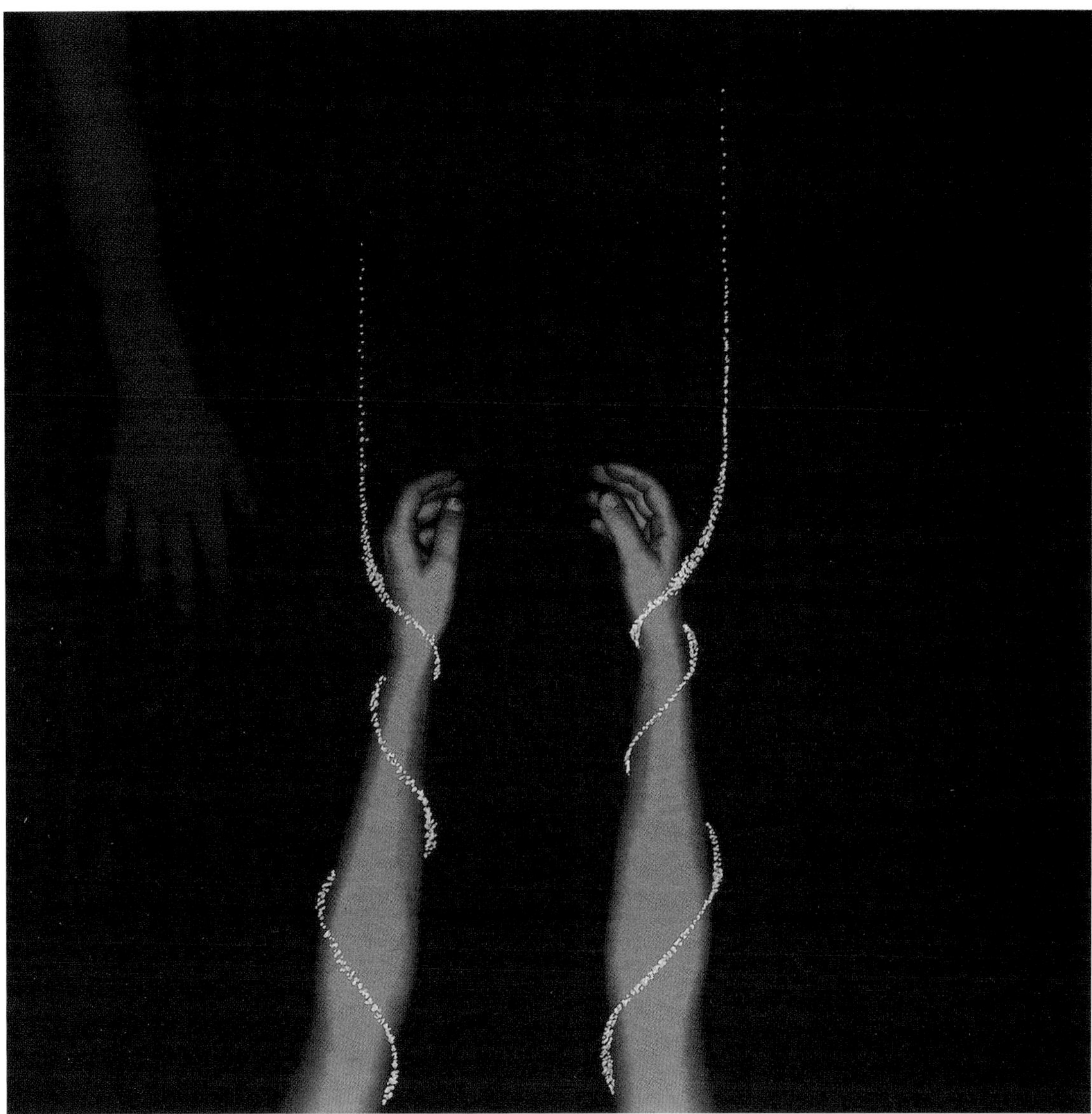

Ellen Krebs
Searching for a Thread, from
the series *Limbs: Yours, Mine
and Ours*, matte albumen print
with white ink, 21 × 21 cm
(8¼ × 8¼ in.), 2013

GUM BICHROMATE

Gum printing is a flexible and relatively simple contact-printing process that utilizes the light-sensitivity of gum dichromates to create colour prints (which are, confusingly, known as gum bichromates). The process was invented by pioneering Scottish photographer Mungo Ponton in 1839, but not commercialized until 1894; it then became popular among turn-of-the-century pictorialist artists such as Alfred Stieglitz. Gum printing allows multiple layers to be combined on the same print. The results, which often resemble pastel or charcoal drawings, are usually broad in tone, high in contrast and reduced in level of detail. For the tri-colour (CMY) printing process shown here, the negative must first be colour-separated using image-editing software.

Part I: Colour separations

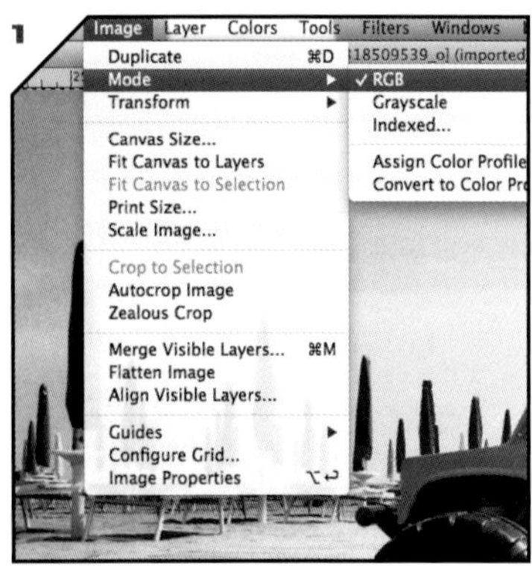
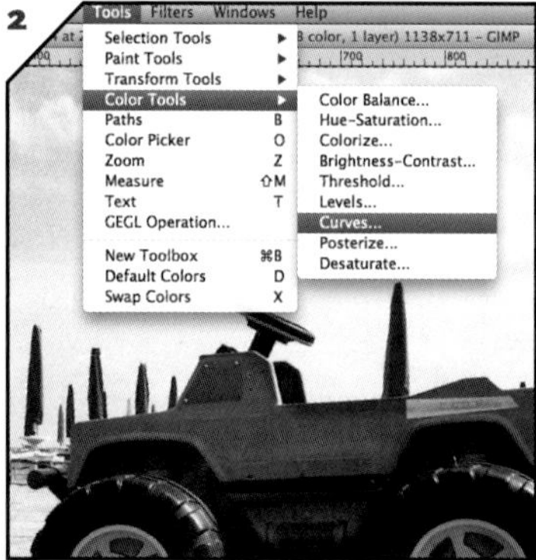
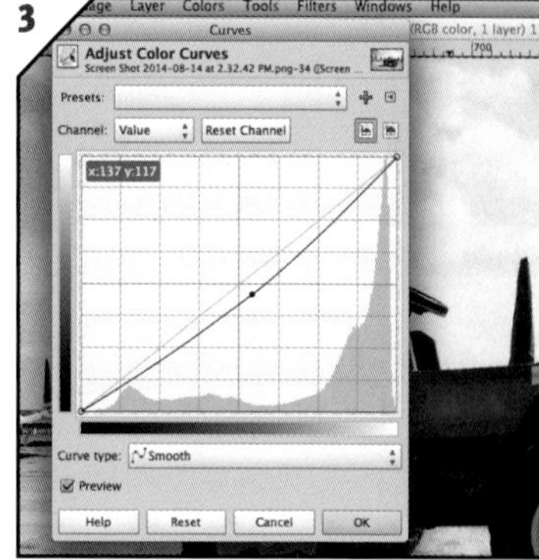

What you need:
- [ ] image-editing software
- [ ] inkjet printer
- [ ] transparencies for inkjet printer

From screen to print

Gum printing is a contact-printing process, so you will need to produce negatives that are the same size as your intended print. Although you can make monochrome gum prints using a single colour and one large-format negative, many practitioners prefer to make tri-colour gum prints, as we have done here, using cyan, magenta and yellow (CMY). This requires a separate negative for each colour, which is done by making a set of colour separations with image-editing software. CMYK colour space produces colour separations for conventional offset printing, but since black ink is not necessary in tri-colour gum printing (where the three saturated primary pigments produce black when mixed together), here

we work only within the RGB colour space in preparing the negatives. The original photograph is inverted to produce a negative and separated into its individual channels. Each of these negatives is then printed onto transparency material using an inkjet printer. For this process, we are using the GIMP image-editing program.

Colour space and resolution

1 Open the image and check that the colour space is set to RGB (Image > Mode > RGB). Then check the resolution by selecting Image > Image Size from the main menu. Your image should have a resolution of 300 ppi (pixels per inch) at the size you intend to print.

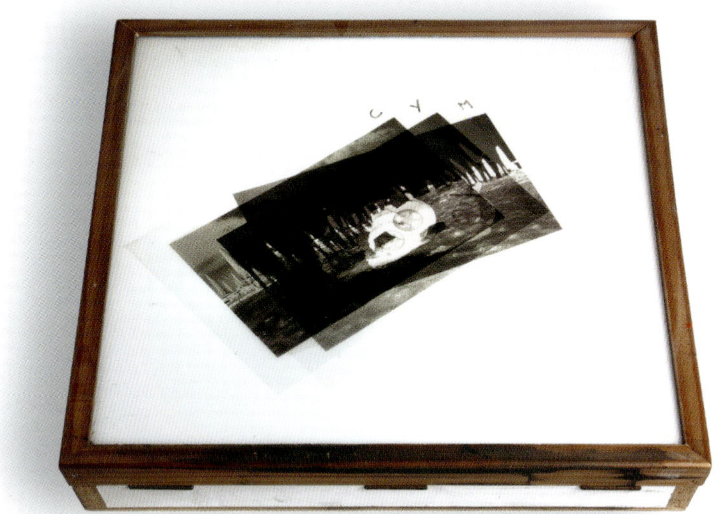

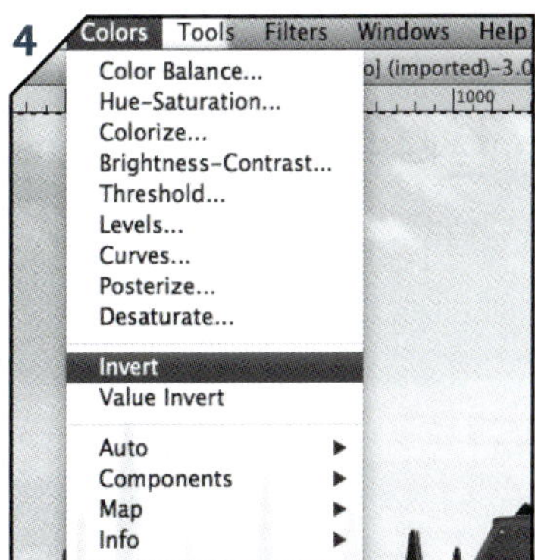

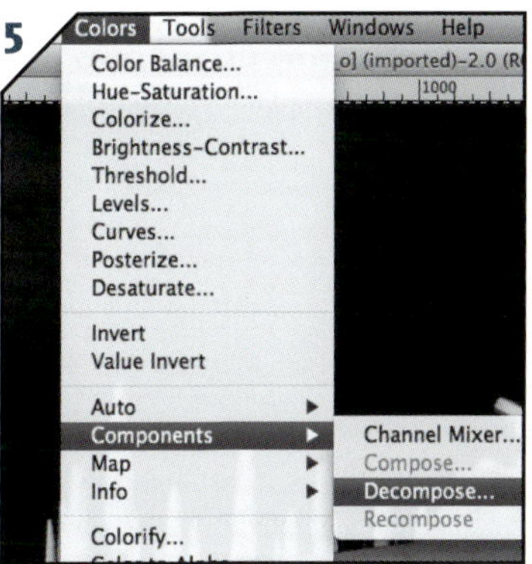

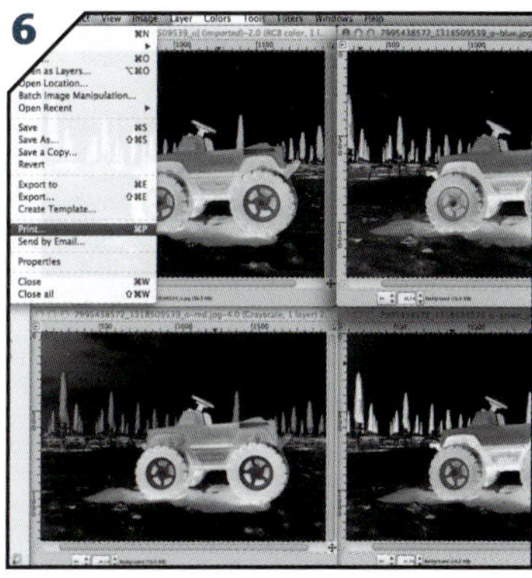

Adjust the contrast

2 & 3 Open the Curves dialogue (Tools > Color Tools > Curves) so you can adjust the contrast of your image. Gum printing is less successful with low-contrast images, so you may need to apply a contrast-boosting S-curve to your image. You can find an abundance of ready-made curves for gum printing online, which you can use as a starting point for adjustments. It is also possible to use Levels to adjust contrast.

Invert the image

4 Change the positive image into a negative by selecting Colors > Invert.

Separate the channels

5 The Channels palette shows the red, green and blue channels: select Colours > Components > Decompose to separate them into individual greyscale images.

Print

6 The three separated colour channels can now be printed onto three separate transparency sheets. Include registration and/or crop marks on the negatives to aid alignment during printing – most printer dialogue boxes allow you to add these. It is also important to label each negative (either before printing or manually afterwards) to indicate the colour it will print:

- Red channel: label C (cyan)
- Green channel: label M (magenta)
- Blue channel: label Y (yellow)

Part II: Gum printing

What you need:

- 2% gelatin sizing solution
- 56 g gum arabic ⚠
- distilled water
- 11 g potassium dichromate ⚠
- 3–5% potassium disulfite ⚠
- pigments (watercolour or dry) approximating the CMY process colours
- glass jar with lid
- dark brown bottle
- heavyweight watercolour / rag fibre etching paper
- contact-printing frame
- large-format negative
- heavy watercolour paper
- UV lamp (optional)
- beakers / measuring cylinders
- scales
- gloves
- non-metallic brush or glass rod (for coating)
- trays for processing

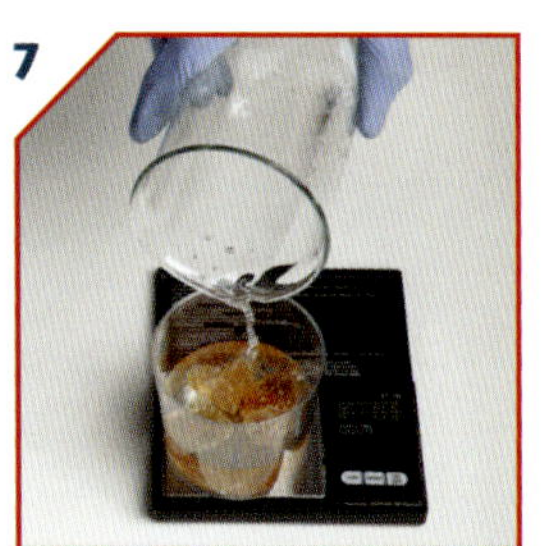

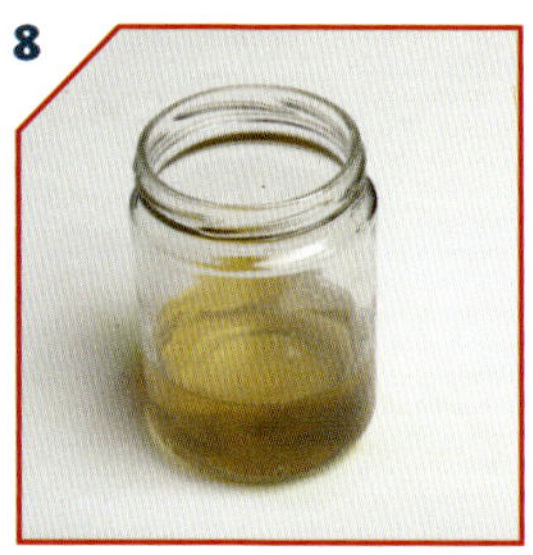

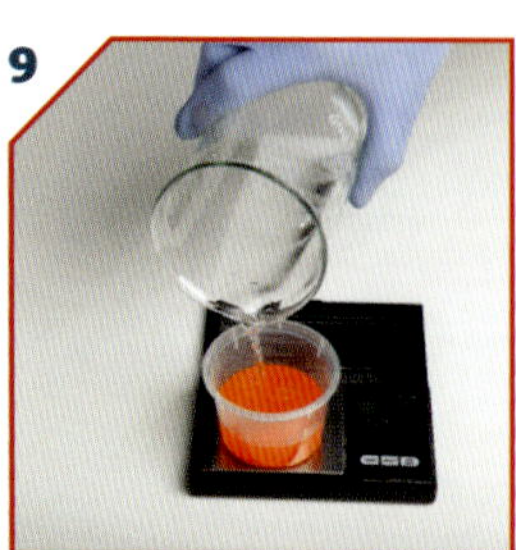

Selecting and preparing the paper

It is important that you choose a paper that can stand repeated soakings, as each colour you print requires the paper to be washed thoroughly afterwards. Although expensive, the best choice is a good grade watercolour or rag fibre etching paper. As the paper will undergo three or more separate printing routines, it needs to be pre-shrunk, so that it doesn't shrink during the printing process. To do this, soak the sheet(s) in warm water for 15 minutes and then in cold water for the same time. Allow the paper to dry before moving on.

Sizing

A light gelatin solution will prevent the heavy paper from absorbing too much pigment. Brush the paper with a thin coating of sizing solution as described in the box on p. 148, and allow to dry.

Prepare the emulsion

7 Working in subdued light, measure 56 g gum arabic (crystal or powdered form) and add distilled water to make up to 100 ml.

8 Mix thoroughly and transfer the gum arabic solution to a jar, which should be sealed and refrigerated.

9 & 10 Prepare a dichromate solution by measuring 11 g potassium dichromate and then adding distilled water to make up to 100 ml. Potassium dichromate is highly toxic and corrosive: it can be fatal if inhaled, and can cause severe damage to skin and eyes, so full respiratory, eye and skin protection must be worn while handling it. Store the finished dichromate solution in a dark bottle.

light-sensitive step

SEE PAGES 226–29

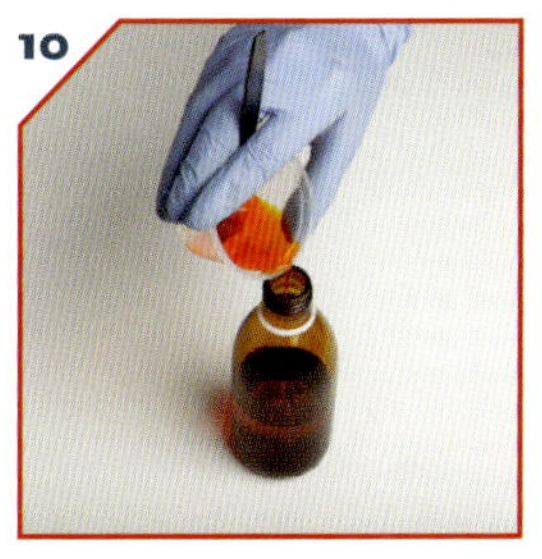
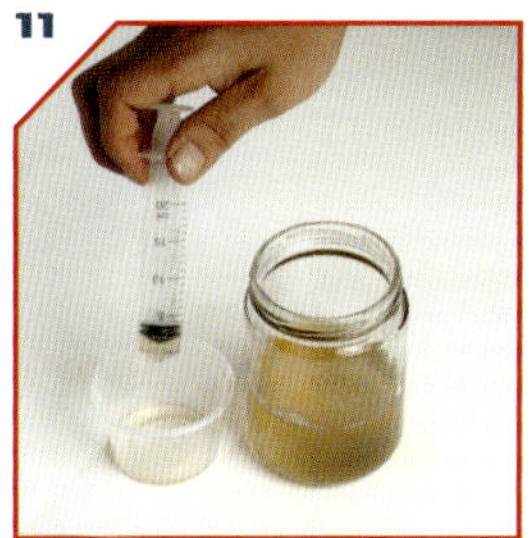
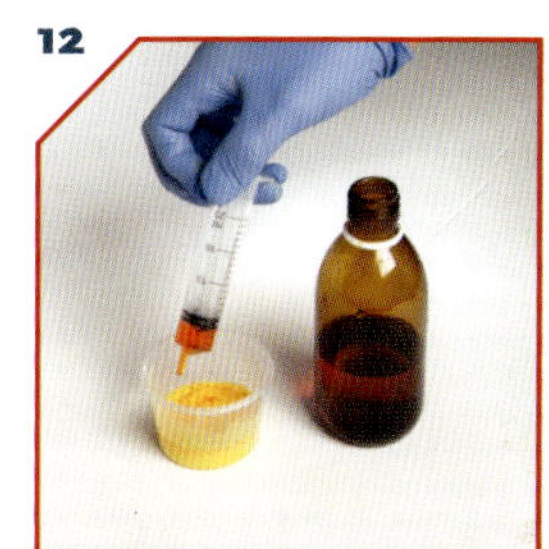
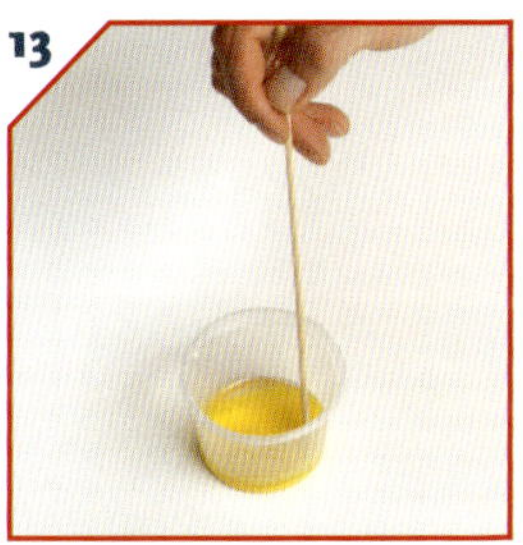
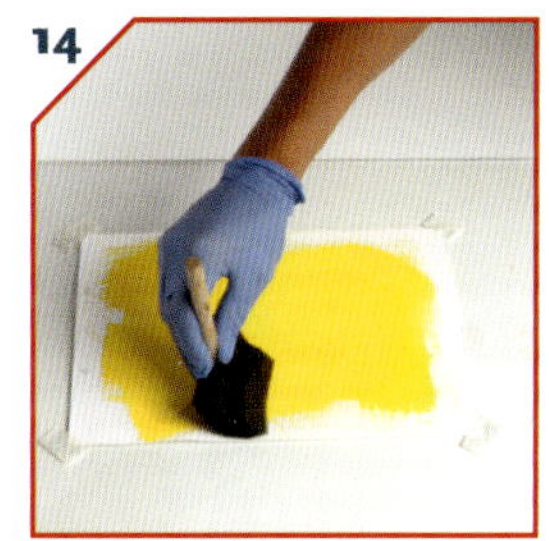
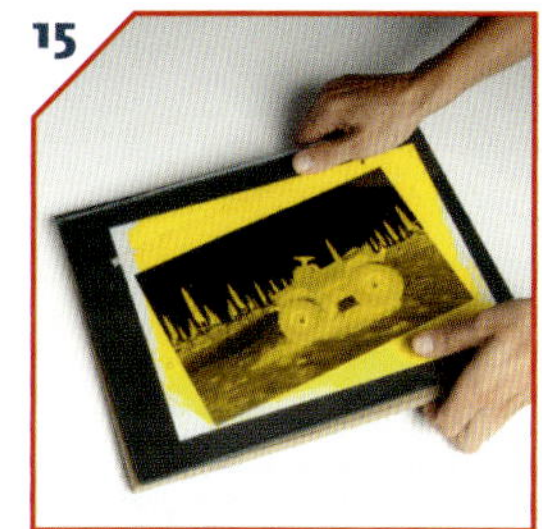

Pigments and colour order

Most gum printers use watercolour paint or dry pigments. Dry pigments are usually cheapest, but liquid paints are easier to mix thoroughly. When it comes to choosing colours, a good starting point – and an accepted combination to best approximate the CMY process colours – is:

- Pthalo blue green shade (PB 15:3)
- Quinacridone rose (PV 19)
- Arylide yellow (PY 97)

Theoretically, process colours should be printed in order (CMY), but many gum printers prefer to print the yellow first and cyan last. This is because the yellow is semi-transparent and tends to leave a soft haze over the other colours if printed last. Conversely, the cyan layer provides the greater part of the tonal structure of the print for many images, so it makes sense to leave it until last. As such, the order in which the colours are printed is typically YMC.

Sensitizing

11 & 12 To prepare each of the three sensitizing solutions for a typical A4-size print, mix together 5 ml gum arabic solution with 1 g of pigment (here yellow) and 5 ml of the dichromate solution.

13 & 14 After mixing the solution, pin or tape the paper to a support or to your work table. Pour the sensitizing solution into the centre of the paper and brush it gently with a sponge brush to cover. A glass rod can also be used for coating the paper.

Drying

Leave the paper taped to the work surface for 3–5 minutes after it has been coated, then hang it up to dry. The paper needs to be dry to the touch before it can be used (test it by placing a finger on the edge).

Loading and exposure

15 Load the paper into the contact-printing frame, making sure there are no creases in either the negative or the paper. Close the contact-printing frame and clamp it shut.

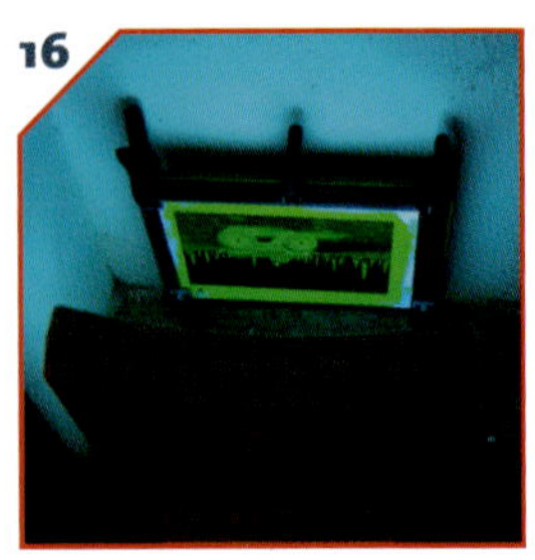

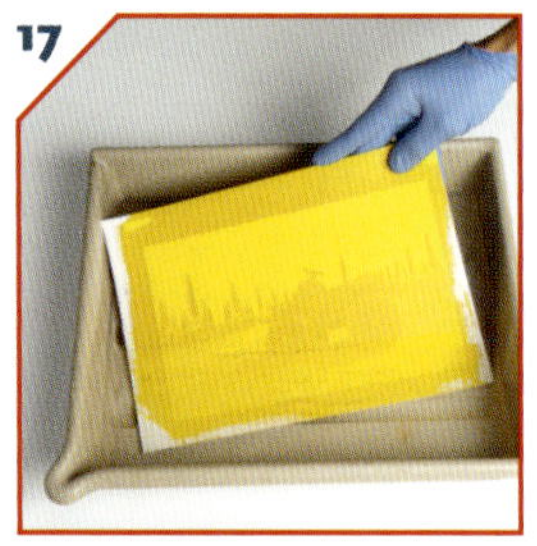

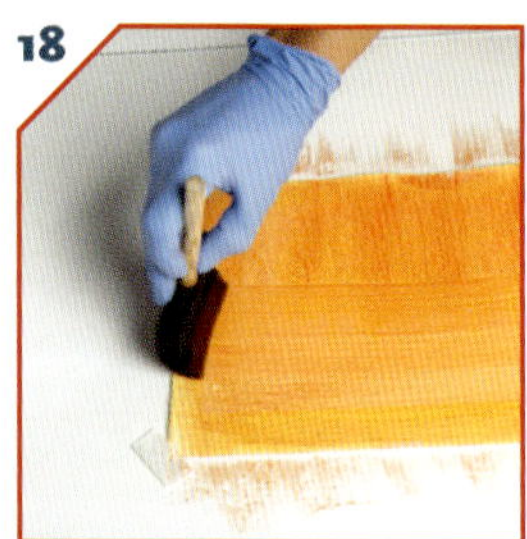

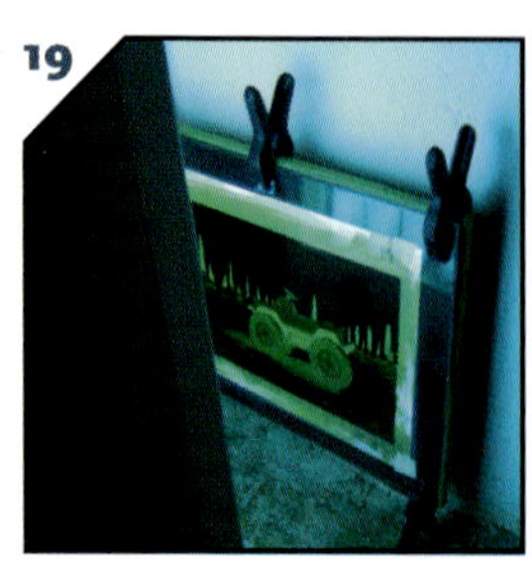

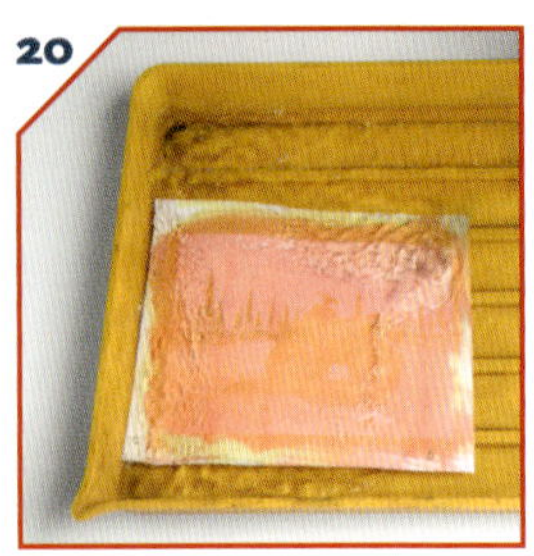

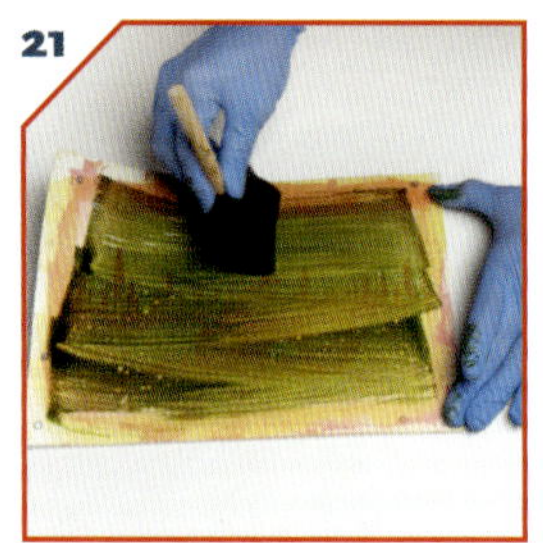

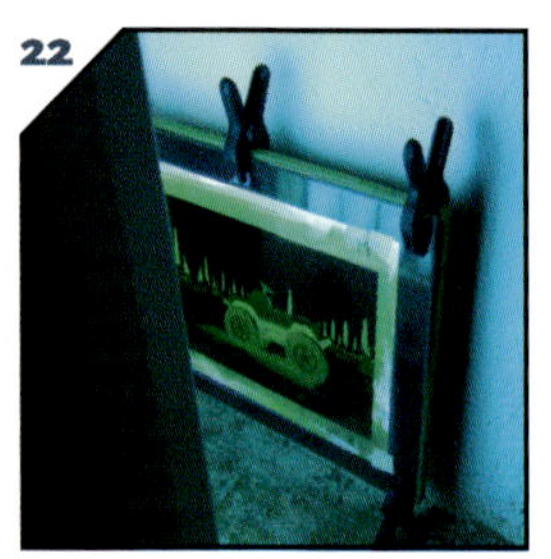

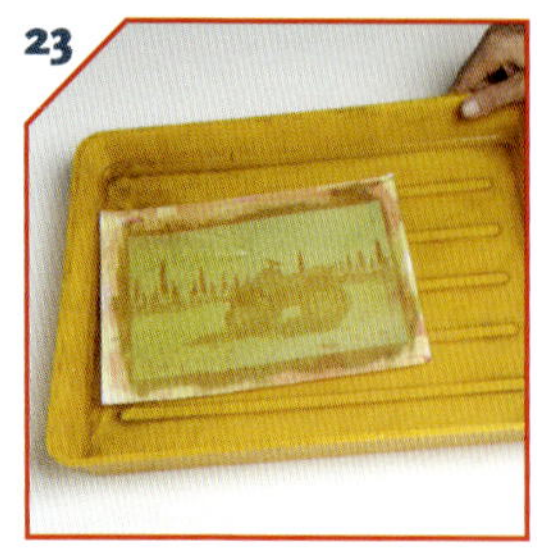

OPPOSITE

Brembo

Beach Tractor (above) and *Beach Tractor* (below), from the series *Monsters on Wheels*, tri-colour gum prints, each 11 × 18 cm (4¼ × 7 in.), 2013

16 Expose the sensitized paper to UV light. Open the back of the contact-printing frame to visually assess the exposure.

Washing

17 Once the image has been exposed, remove the print from the contact-printing frame and place it face up in a tray of water for around 5 minutes. Then, turn the print over so it is face down, and leave it for 10–15 minutes. The gum is very delicate at this stage, so try to avoid rocking the tray. Change the water and repeat the process two or three times to ensure you wash out the yellow/orange dichromate.

Printing additional colours

Before printing the next colour you need to make sure the print is completely dry. While you wait, mix up your next sensitizing solution (in this case magenta) as outlined previously.

18 Tape the paper to the work surface and coat it as before. Allow it to dry thoroughly; then load it into the contact-printing frame, taking care to align the registration marks

on the negative with the corresponding marks on the yellow-printed layer.

19 Expose the paper to UV light. You will need to check exposure periodically, as timing is different for each pigment.

20 Wash the print and allow it to dry. Mix your final sensitizing solution (here, cyan).

21 & 22 Repeat the coating, drying and exposure process with the third colour, again aligning the image carefully when you load it into the contact-printing frame.

23 After the print has been washed and dried, a slight orange stain caused by excess dichromate may remain. To remove this, wash the print one last time in a 3–5% potassium disulfite solution.

Alternative colouring

For this project we've used a colour combination that produces 'realistic' colours. However, you don't have to stick to the CMY process colours – feel free to experiment with alternative combinations!

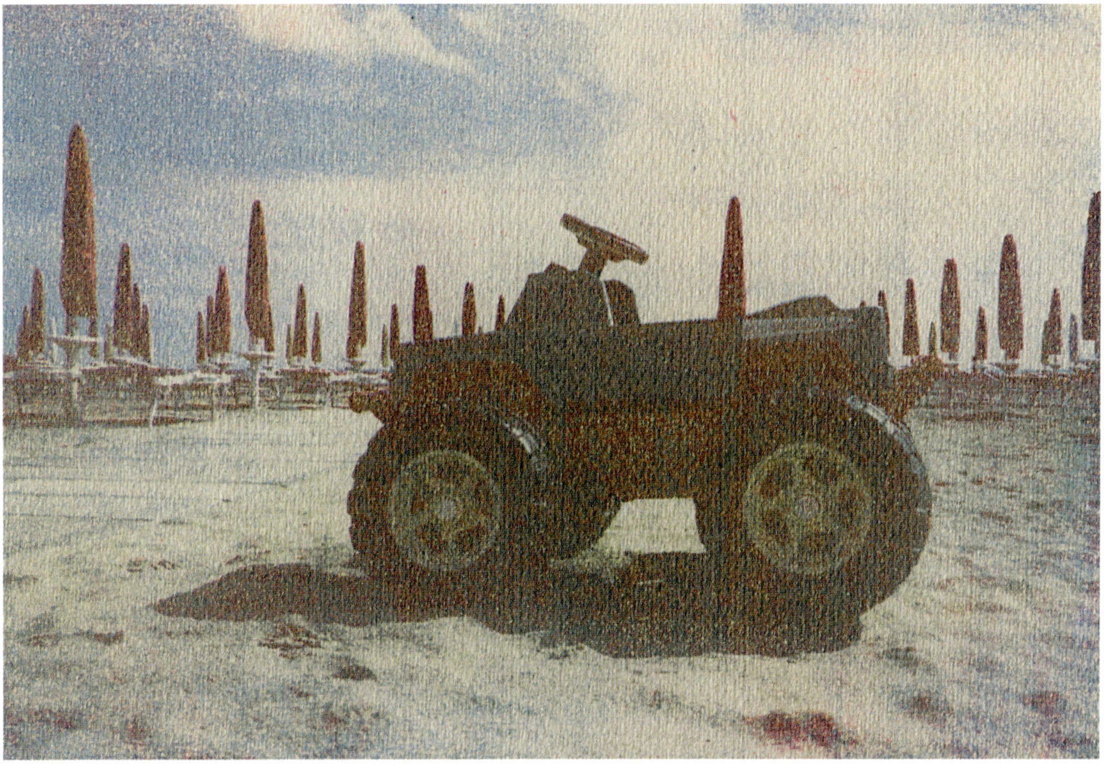

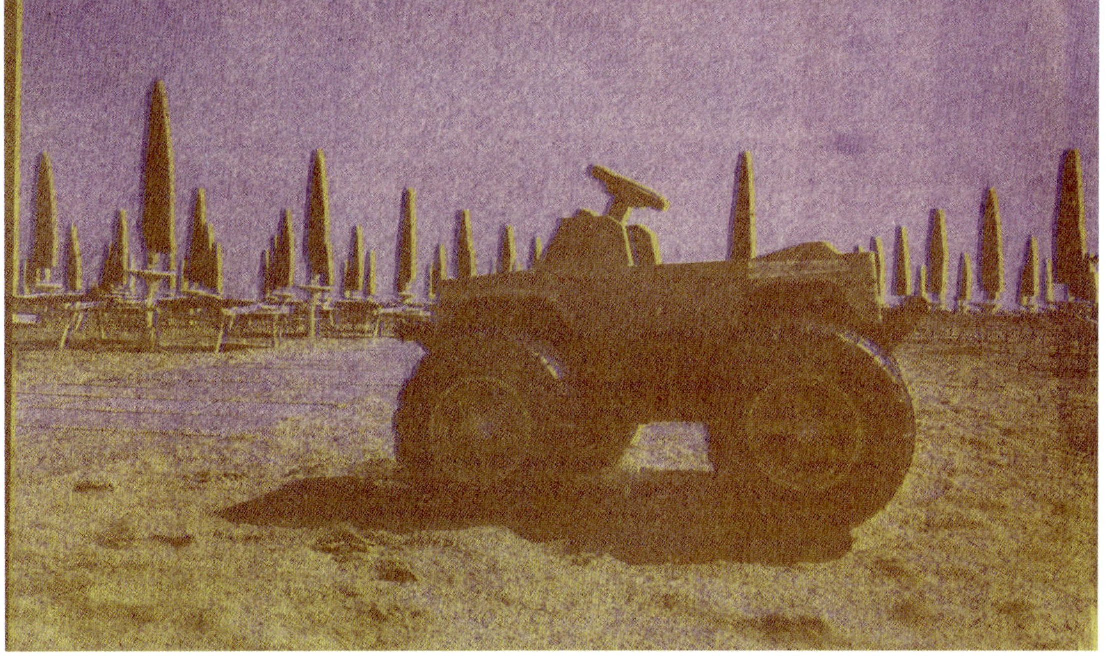

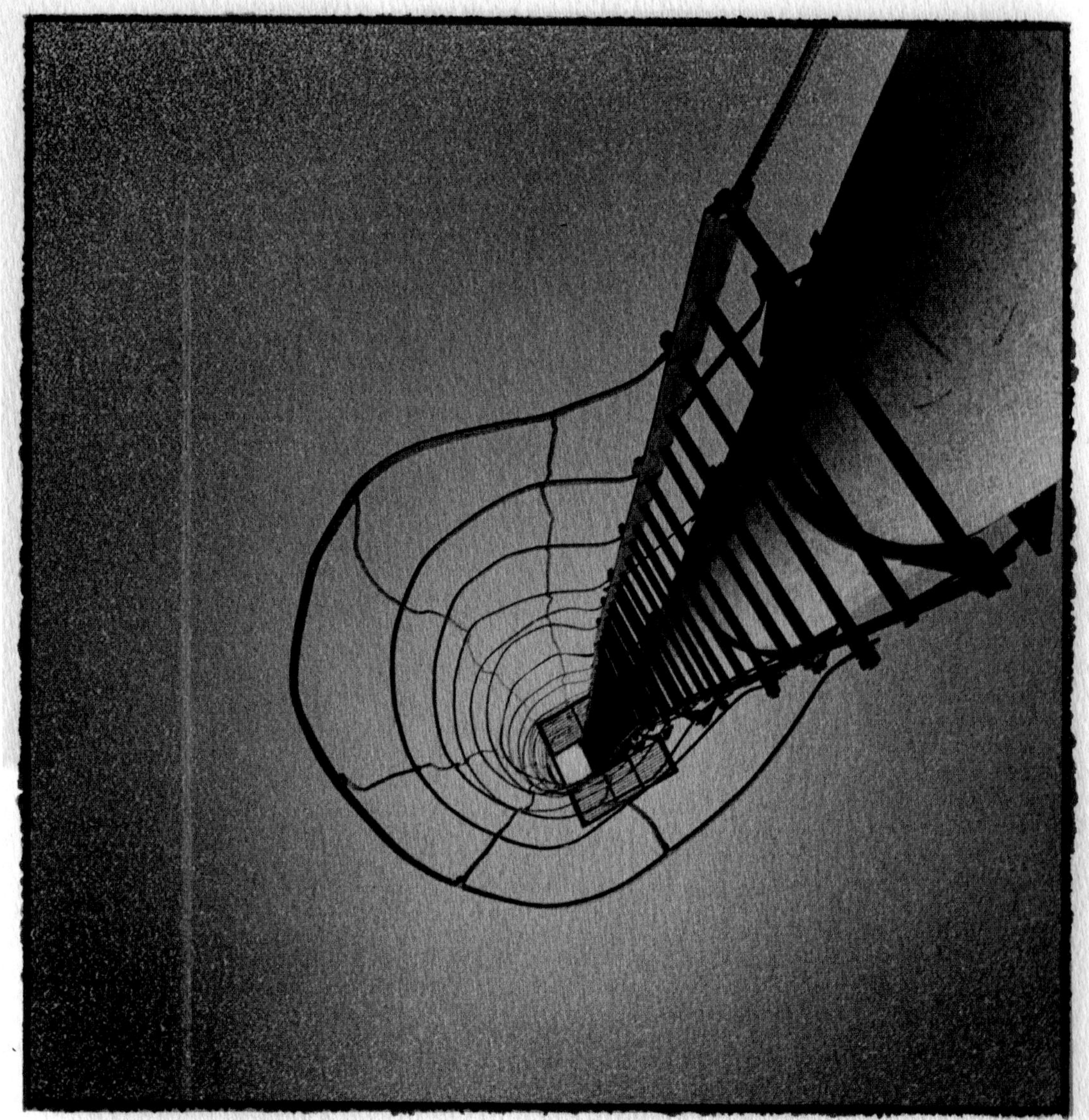

Taras Perun
Annigilator, gum bichromate
print on Saunders Waterford HP
356 gsm paper, 26 × 26 cm
(10¼ × 10¼ in.), 2013

Taras Perun
Untitled, CMY gum bichromate
print, 27 × 19 cm (10⅝ × 7½ in.),
2013

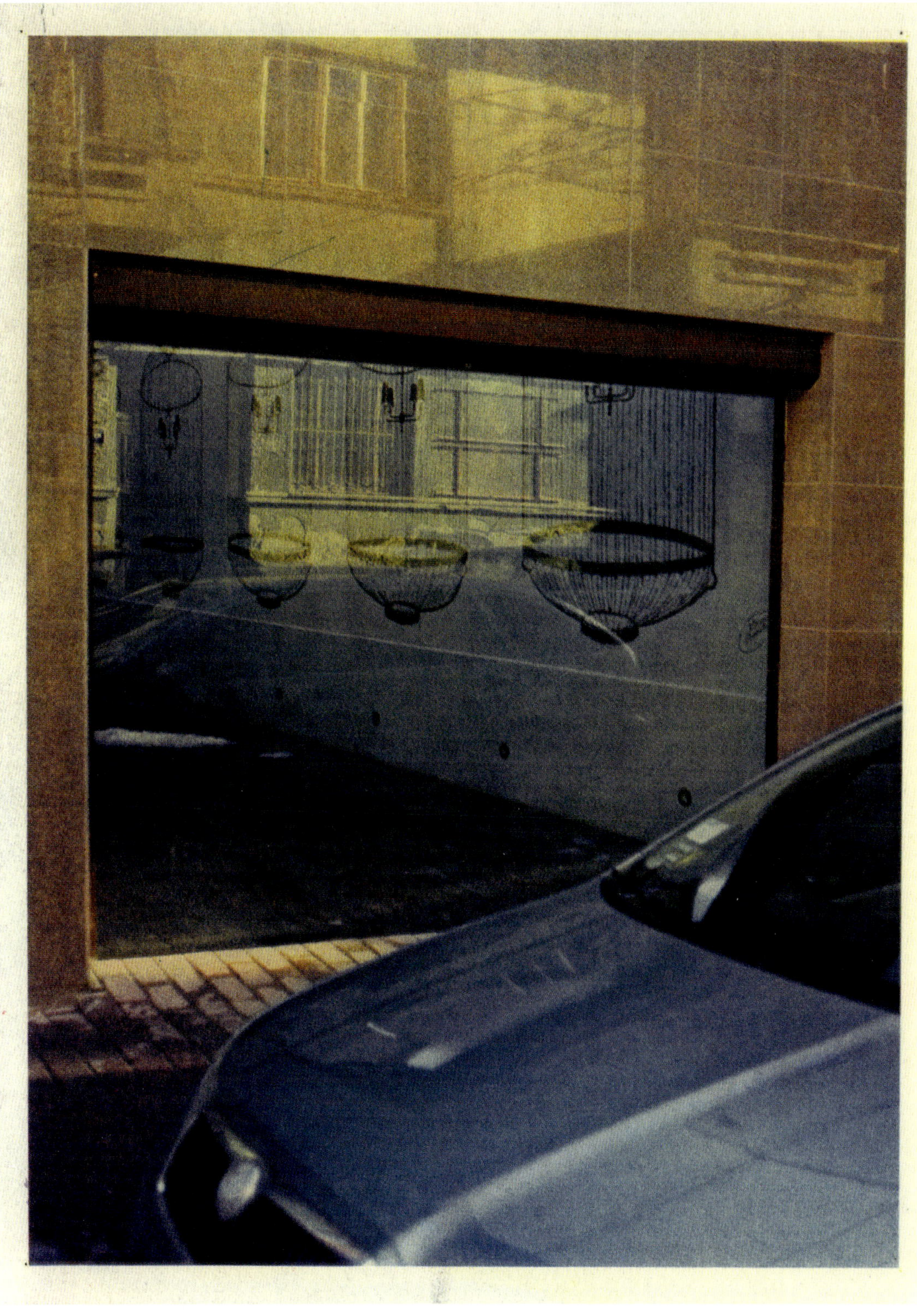

ANTHOTYPE

Anthotypes are one of the most environmentally friendly alternative printing techniques, as the process uses the naturally photosensitive properties of petals, leaves and fruits or roots. It is a fun, non-toxic and relatively simple contact-printing technique consisting of just three steps: making the emulsion, coating and exposure. Even the most sensitive juices yield a weak and narrow tonal range, and images will inevitably fade over time if exposed to light. Here we use beetroot, which, like all flower petals, fruits and vegetables, or other whole plant ingredients, must be blended to a puree to extract its juice; powdered pigment sources such as turmeric, paprika or spirulina can simply be mixed with alcohol to form a paste.

The anthotype process

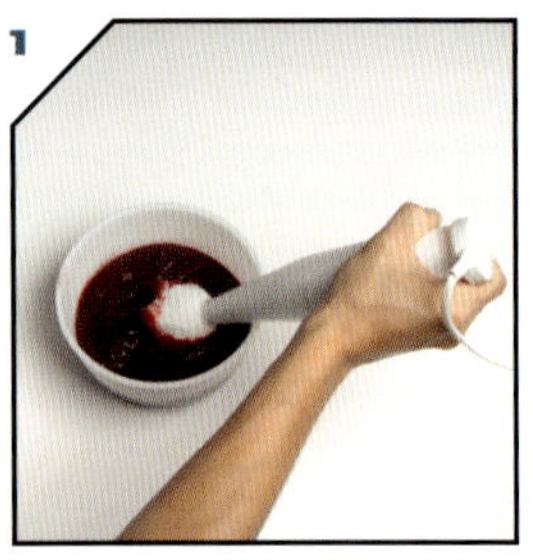
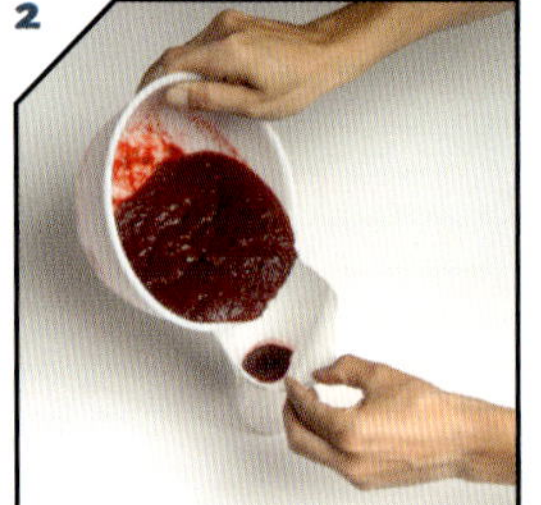
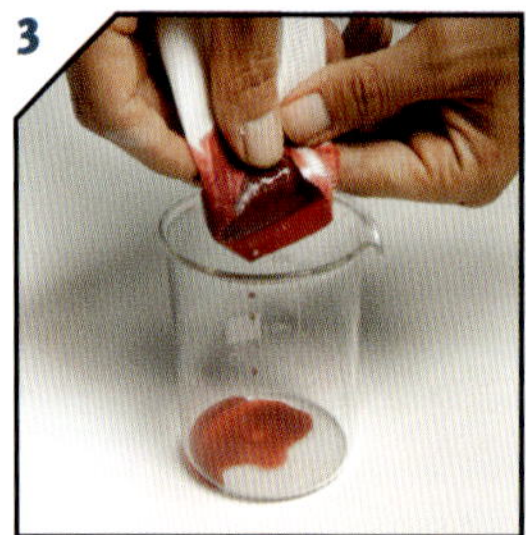
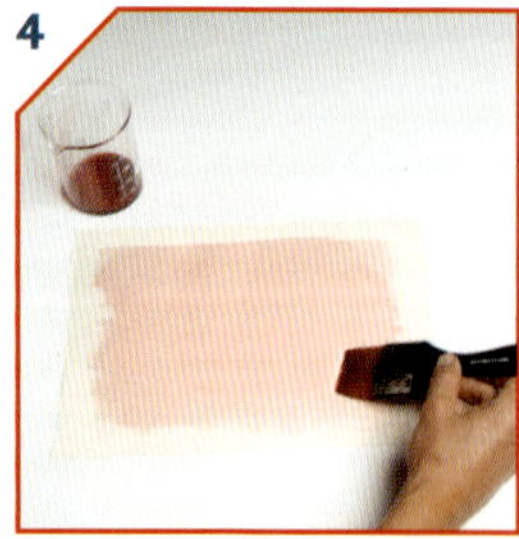

What you need:
- ☐ beetroot or other plant pigment source
- ☐ pestle and mortar or electric food blender
- ☐ bowls
- ☐ distilled water or ethyl alcohol ⚠
- ☐ cheesecloth, coffee filter or cotton cloth
- ☐ contact-printing frame
- ☐ high-contrast positive transparency
- ☐ heavy watercolour paper
- ☐ UV lamp (optional)
- ☐ non-metallic brush or glass rod (for coating)

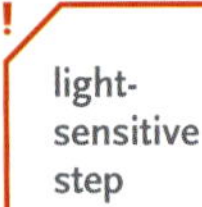

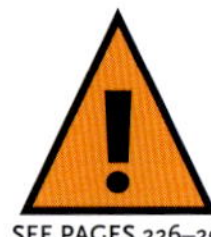

Extracting the emulsion

1 Cut beetroot (or your chosen flower, vegetable or fruit) into small pieces and use a pestle and mortar or electric blender to grind it until you have a dense pulp. Use a small amount of distilled water or ethyl alcohol if the pulp needs dilution. 500 g beetroot will yield enough emulsion to coat 10–15 A4-sized sheets of paper; amounts of other ingredients vary, but be aware that petals and leaves will require very large quantities to produce sufficient amounts of pulp.

2 & 3 Once the pulp is ready, strain it into a small bowl using a cheesecloth, coffee filter or a regular cotton cloth to remove any solids; any impurities will be transferred to the paper and appear in the final print.

Coating the paper

Standard watercolour paper is the ideal substrate for anthotypes. Medium or heavyweight stock is preferred, as the print may need to be exposed for days (or possibly even weeks), depending on the emulsion.

4 Working in subdued lighting, coat the paper with emulsion using a non-metallic art brush or by pouring the emulsion into a tray and 'floating' the paper on top of it. The appearance of the print will be affected by your chosen coating method. Hang until dry.

Prepare the positive transparency

Anthotypes are contact-printed, so you will need a full-sized positive that has been printed on a transparency. Since plant emulsions tend to lighten rather than darken when exposed, a high-contrast

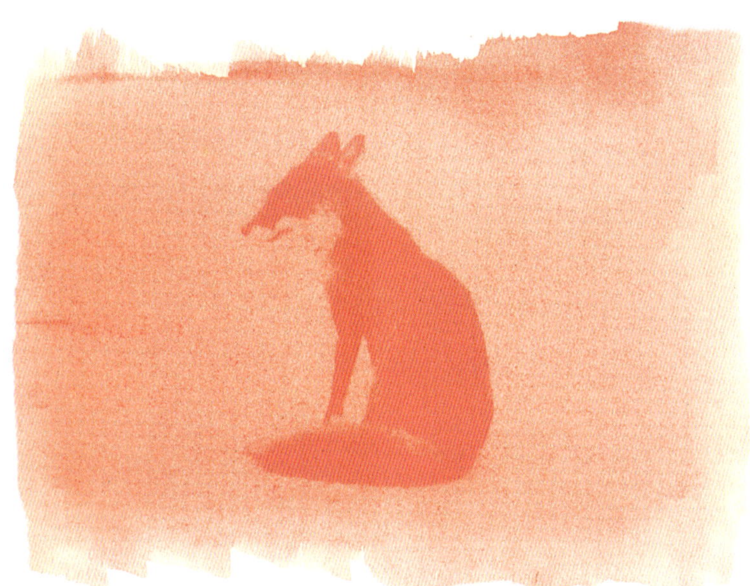

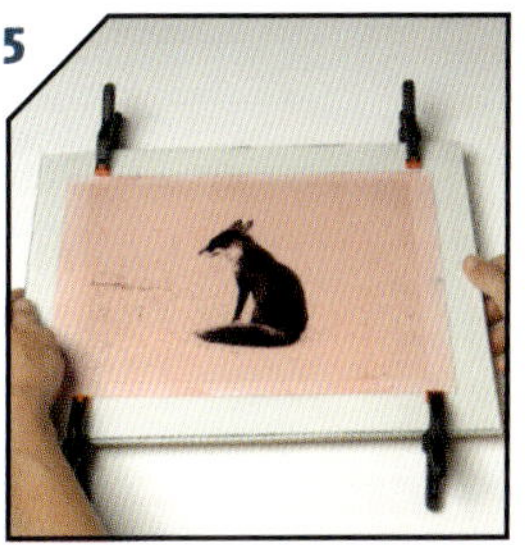

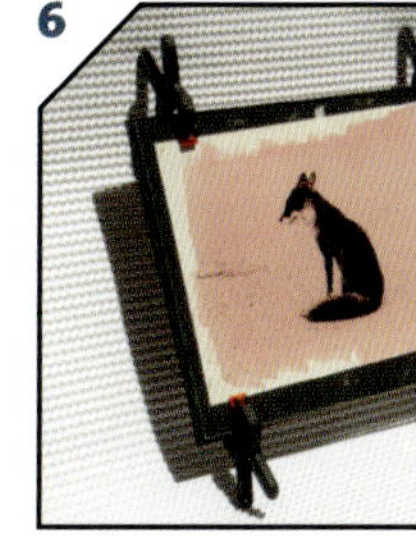

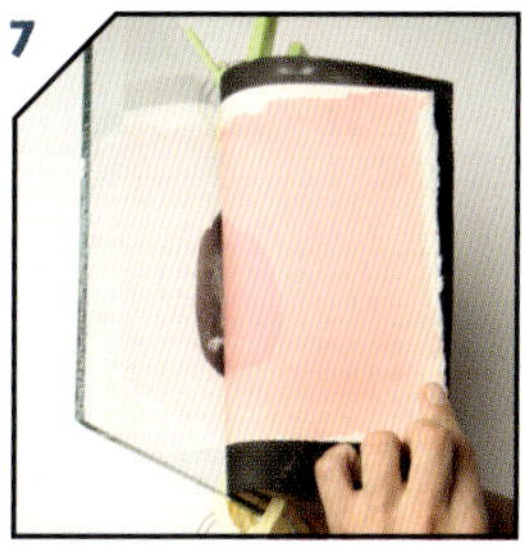

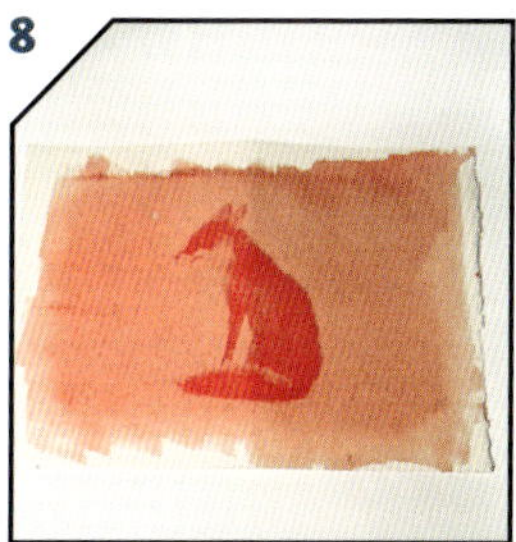

Maurizio Bendandi
La Volpe, anthotype from red
beetroot juice, 21 × 29 cm
(8¼ × 11½ in.), 2013

black-and-white *positive* image, rather
than a negative, needs to be printed
on the transparency. See pp. 132–33 for
instructions on creating large-format digital
transparencies, but do not invert the image.

Loading

5 Load the positive transparency and paper
into your contact-printing frame, making
sure the two are held tight together and
there are no creases or bubbles.

Exposure

6 & 7 Every emulsion will need a different
exposure time: some emulsions need only
a few hours to change colour, while others
might take a few weeks (corn poppies
will produce one of the most sensitive
emulsions). The key is to check your
exposure relatively frequently by opening
up the back of your contact-printing frame.

Fixing

8 There is no development stage with an
anthotype – the process of exposing the
emulsion brings out the image. However,
anthotypes will fade if exposed to UV light,
so it's best to keep finished pieces in light-
tight boxes, or frame the prints behind UV
resistant glass. Alternatively, you can use
an anti-UV spray to coat the paper and
make it UV resistant.

ANTHOTYPE COLOUR RECIPES

by John Dearing

Anthotypes may not deliver a wide tonal range, but the individual colours that can be achieved are as varied as nature's palette. The swatches and colour recipes here are mainly for inspiration: the precise amounts of ingredients needed to produce each anthotype colour can only be determined by trial and error, and even then the resulting shade will vary significantly between batches. Different types and weights of paper stock will also affect the end result.

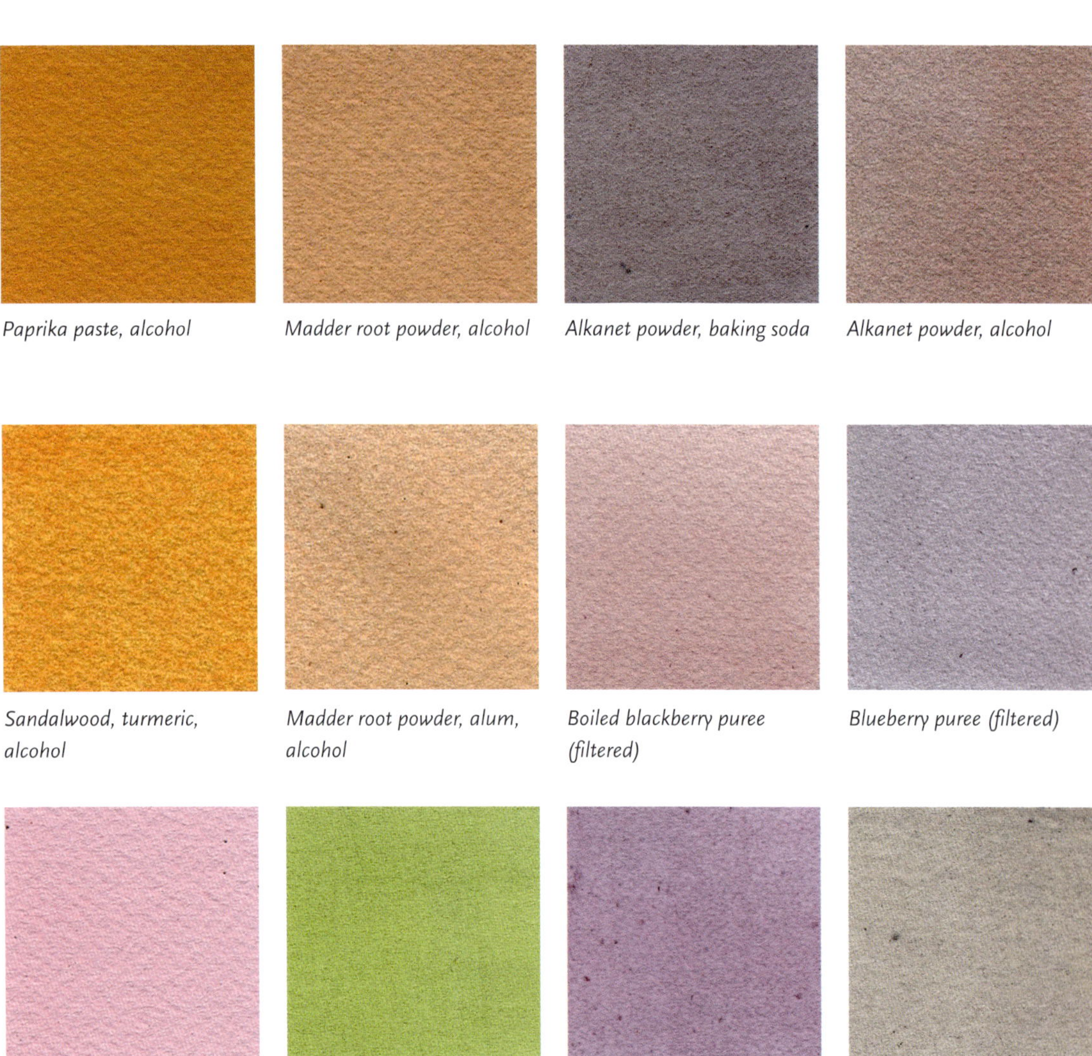

Paprika paste, alcohol

Madder root powder, alcohol

Alkanet powder, baking soda

Alkanet powder, alcohol

Sandalwood, turmeric, alcohol

Madder root powder, alum, alcohol

Boiled blackberry puree (filtered)

Blueberry puree (filtered)

Canned beets

Spirulina powder, alcohol 1:2

Blackberry puree (filtered)

Raspberry puree (filtered), alcohol

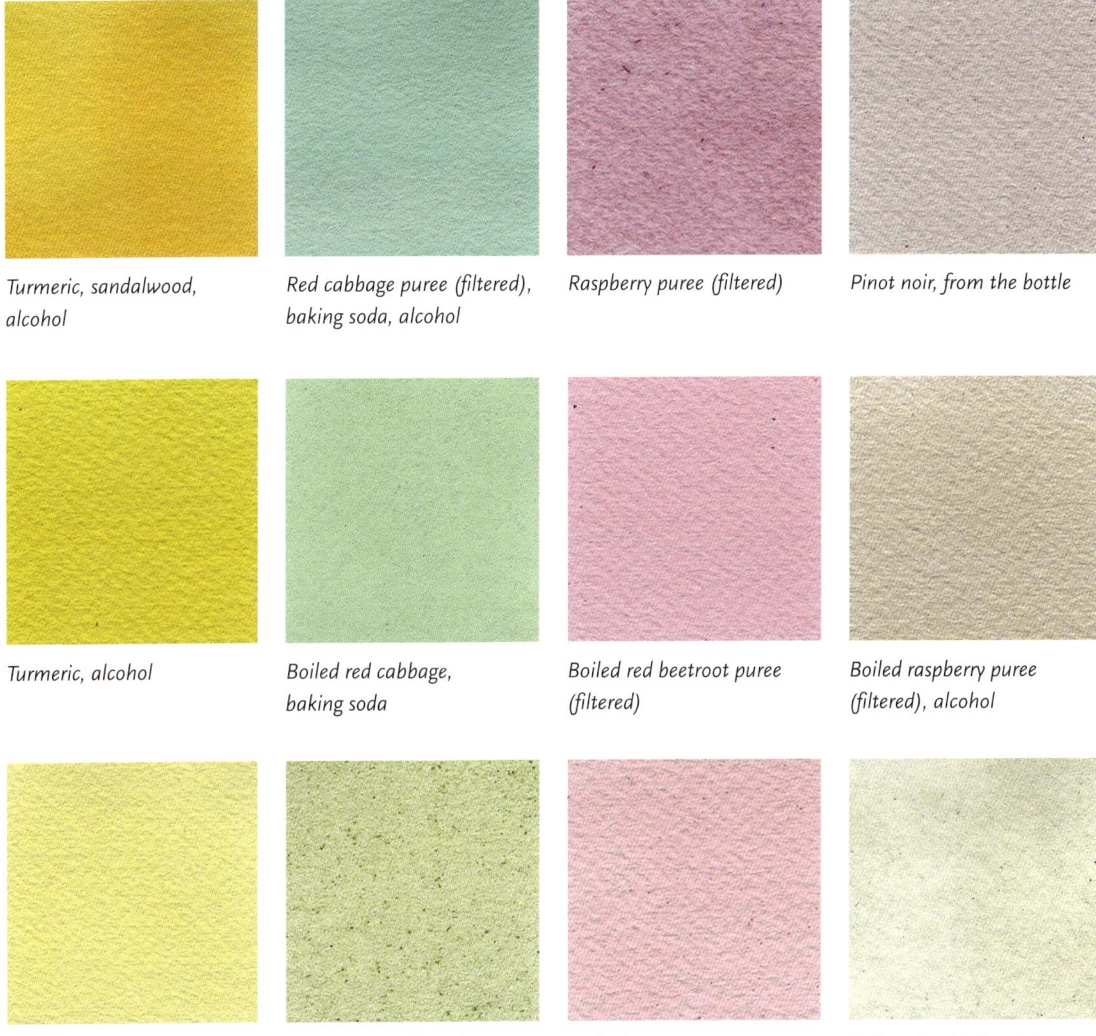

Turmeric, sandalwood, alcohol

Red cabbage puree (filtered), baking soda, alcohol

Raspberry puree (filtered)

Pinot noir, from the bottle

Turmeric, alcohol

Boiled red cabbage, baking soda

Boiled red beetroot puree (filtered)

Boiled raspberry puree (filtered), alcohol

Paprika (filtered), alcohol

Chard puree (filtered), water

Red wine

Boiled chard (filtered), water

CHLOROPHYLL PRINTS

Photosynthetic photography, or 'chlorophyll printing', reproduces images on leaves and grasses by harnessing the photosensitive properties of pigments (primarily green chlorophyll) that are naturally present in the cells of most plants, turning them dark green in the presence of light, or pale in its absence. The process is simple: a positive black-and-white image is printed on a sheet of acetate (or similar transparent medium), loaded into a contact-printing frame with a leaf and then exposed to the sun. The results can be surprisingly detailed and rich in tonal range: contemporary artists such as Binh Danh (overleaf) and Ackroyd & Harvey (see pp. 184–89) are increasingly experimenting with this technique in their work.

The chlorophyll printing process

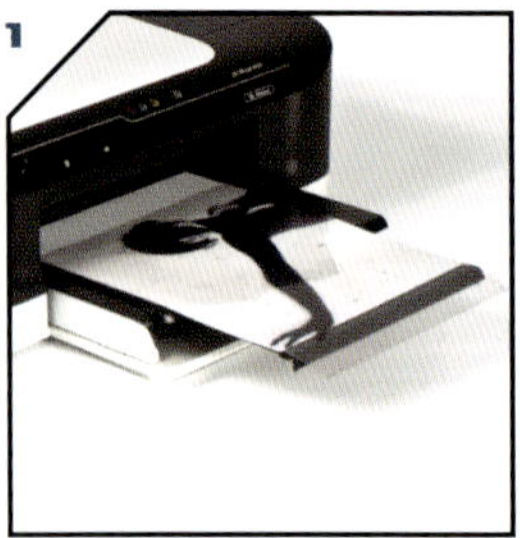
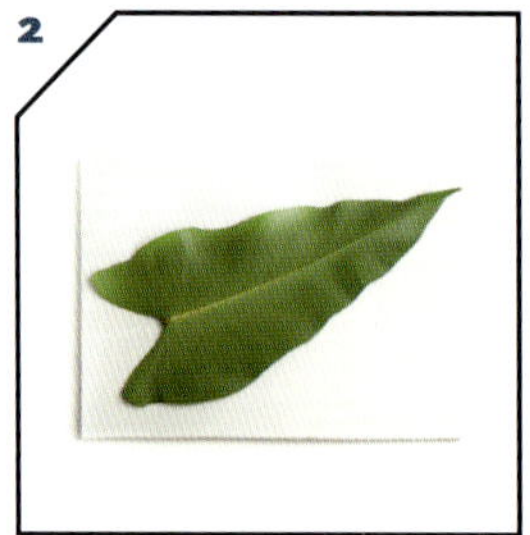
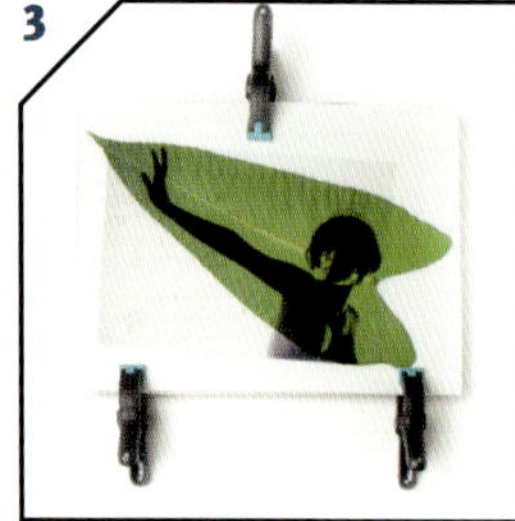
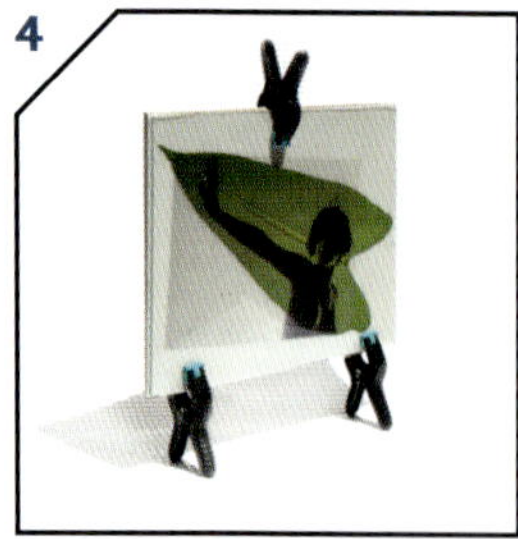

What you need:

- ☐ leaf (the size depends on your transparency)
- ☐ contact-printing frame
- ☐ high-contrast positive transparency
- ☐ UV lamp (optional)

Prepare the transparency

1 A print made on a leaf will have a limited tonal range so the positive image you use must be prepared accordingly. You need to aim for a transparency with maximum contrast, while still retaining detail. See pp. 132–33 for instructions on creating digital transparencies. If you find that the black areas on your printed transparency aren't dark enough, print two sheets and tape them together to increase the density.

Prepare the leaf

2 Leaves come in a variety of shapes and sizes, so it's a good idea to know which image you intend to use when you're picking a leaf to print on. If the leaf isn't flat, press it between two books for a day or two; if it has a solid stem this will need to be removed or sliced to ensure maximum contact with the positive image.

Exposure

3 & 4 Sandwich the leaf and your transparency in a hinged contact-printing frame and expose to the sun. As with most contact-printing techniques that rely on UV light, the exposure time will depend on a variety of factors: open the back of the frame periodically to check the exposure.

There is no processing or fixing stage with chlorophyll prints, and the image will eventually fade. Rephotographing the chlorophyll print is recommended so you have a record of the artefact.

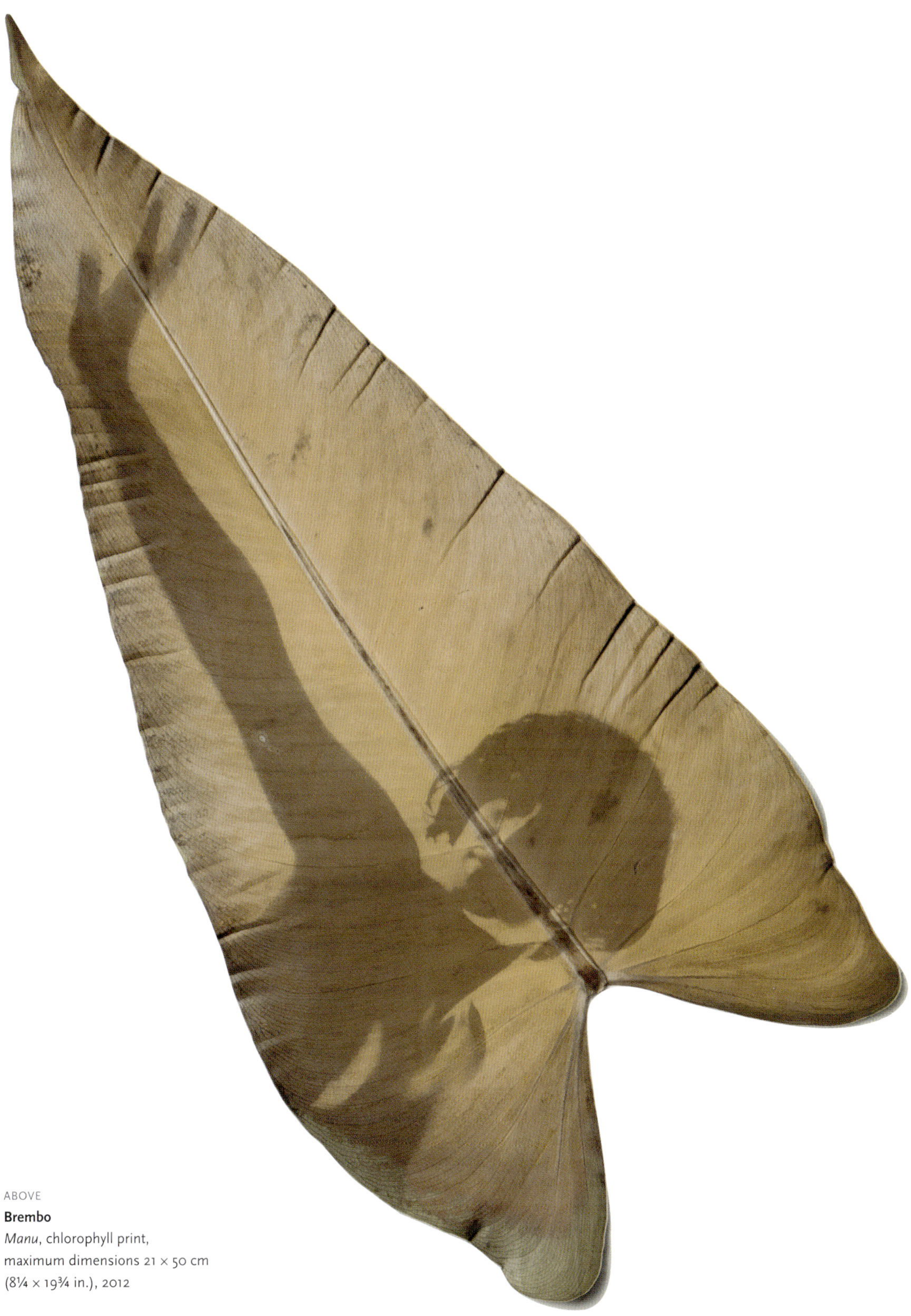

ABOVE
Brembo
Manu, chlorophyll print,
maximum dimensions 21 × 50 cm
(8¼ × 19¾ in.), 2012

BINH DANH

*Profile by Laura A. Guth**

Vietnamese-American artist Binh Danh uses chlorophyll printing to reproduce images of the Vietnam War on tropical plants and grasses, imprinting the memories of the painful conflict on the very jungle that witnessed it.

Binh Danh collects snapshots, newspaper clippings, letters and other artefacts of the Vietnam War and Cambodian genocide, and transfers the images to leaves and grasses, using a chlorophyll-printing technique he developed after seeing parts of his lawn change colour when a water hose was left on it for several days. The final leaf-image is then embedded in resin to preserve it. This technique has important symbolic resonance for Danh because the images are not simply printed onto the surface of the leaves, but become part of the structure of their individual living cells through photosynthesis, evoking both the transformative horror of war and the Buddhist belief that nothing ever truly dies. It is also significant that the images are imprinted in the leaves by the action of the sun, the source of all life. The series *Ancestral Altars* (2005–6) memorializes interrogation mugshots of the more than 14,000 Cambodian men, women and children who were tortured and killed by the Khmer Rouge at a single prison between 1975 and 1979. *One Week's Dead* (2008) is a collection of school-yearbook-style portraits of the 242 young American soldiers who died in one week in 1969, printed on grass. Through these unique photosynthetic portraits, the jungle itself bears witness to the lasting scars of war, and preserves the memory of all those it held in death.

*Adapted from 'Binh Danh: *One Week's Dead*', 2007, <http://binhdanh.com/Projects/1Week/1Week>

OPPOSITE, TOP ROW
Military Foliage, chlorophyll prints and resin, dimensions variable, 2010
Printed on each leaf is a camouflage pattern from a different military organization.

OPPOSITE, BELOW LEFT
The Leaf Effect: Study for Transmission #13, from the series *Ancestral Altars*, chlorophyll print and resin, 33 × 25.4 cm (13 × 10 in.), 2005

OPPOSITE, BELOW RIGHT
James Troy Ralph 21 (above), and *William W. Smith 21* (below), from the series *One Week's Dead*, chlorophyll prints on grass and resin, each 43.2 × 35.6 cm (17 × 14 in.), 2008

RIGHT
Helicopter, from the series *Immortality: The Remnants of the Vietnam and American War*, chlorophyll print and resin, 31.1 × 37.1 cm (12¼ × 14⅝ in.), 2008

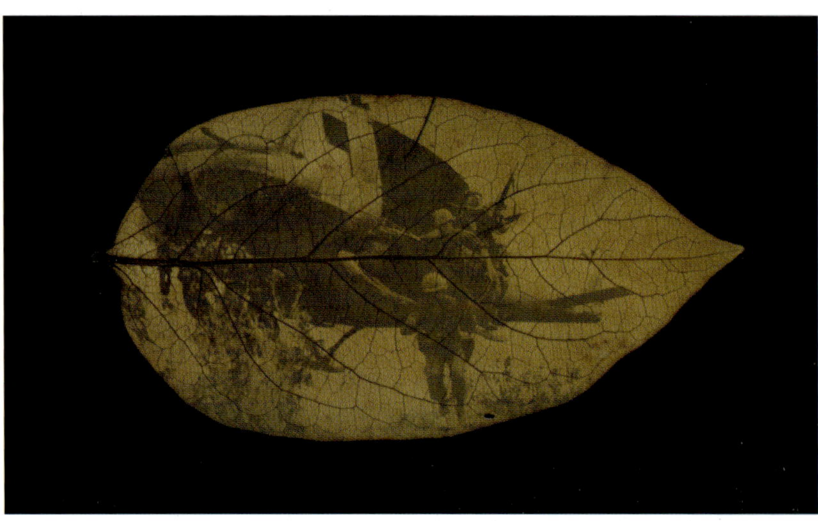

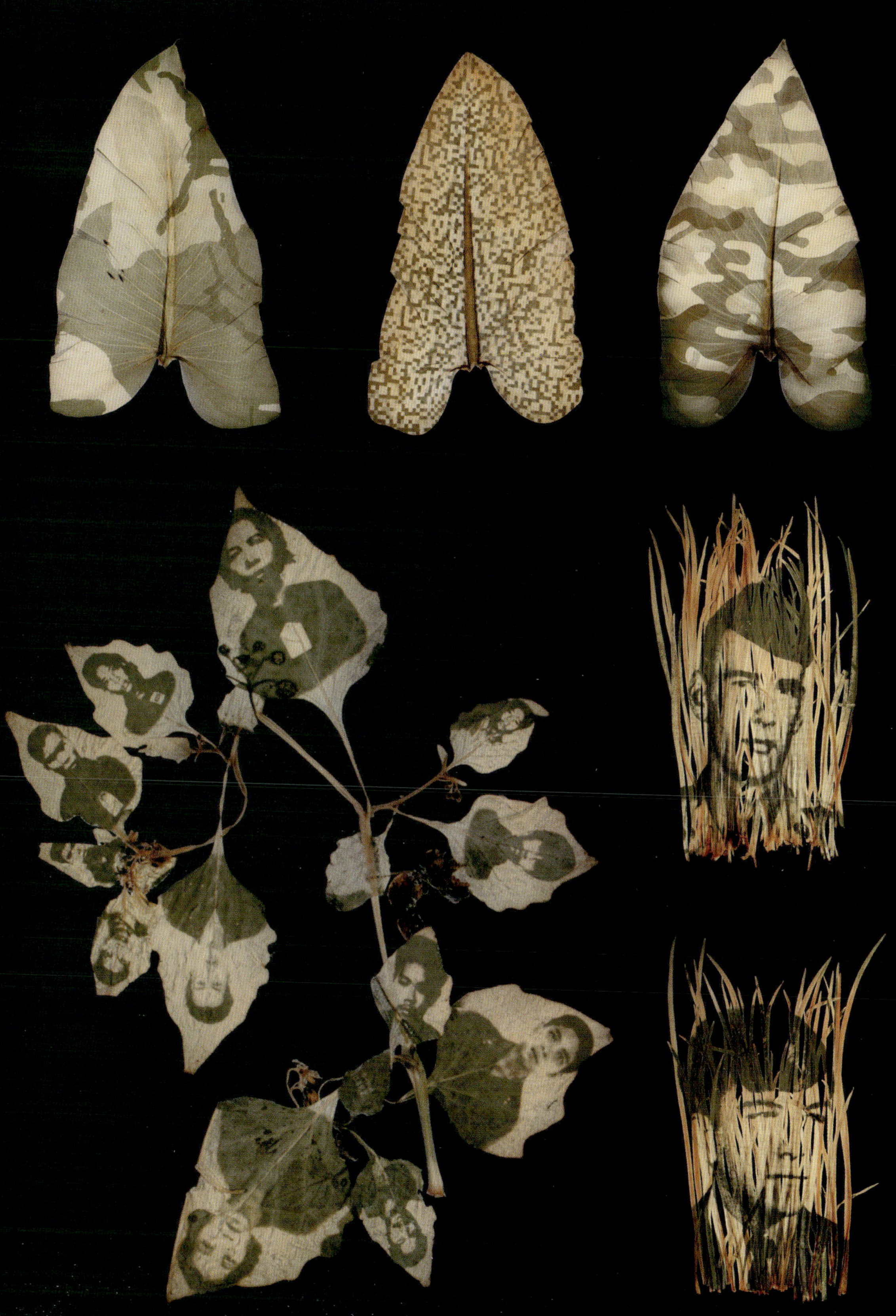

ACKROYD & HARVEY

Interview by Marco Antonini

The work of British duo Heather Ackroyd and Dan Harvey combines photography, architecture and biology, and ranges from large-scale architectural interventions to gallery-sized installations of photographs chlorophyll-printed on grass.

Can you explain the process behind your photosensitive grass images, and how it has evolved over the years?

In a sense we have adapted the photographic art of producing pictures on film to using the light sensitivity of emergent blades of young grass. A tonal range equivalent to that of black-and-white photographic paper is created in shades of yellow and green in the grass. Each germinating blade produces a concentration of chlorophyll molecules depending on the amount of projected light available to it. In complete darkness, the seedling grass grows but no chlorophyll is produced, and other non-light-dependent pigments give it a yellow colour. But once exposed to light in a gallery environment, the grass in the yellow regions seizes the available light and gradually, over hours, changes colour, greening up. Meanwhile, the dark green regions of the grass, exposed to the lower light levels indoors, break down some of their excess chlorophyll. The image begins to resemble an old tapestry, and then slowly fades away.

Early in 1997, we approached scientists Howard Thomas and Helen Ougham at the Institute of Grassland and Environmental Research in Aberystwyth after seeing an article in the *New Scientist* describing their pioneering work with a strain of grass (*Lolium perenne*) that did not senesce in the usual way and lose its green colour when under stress. The colour green is normally volatile and the chlorophyll molecule even more so. So this staygreen grass held promise for a line of inquiry that we had been pursuing for some years in our artistic work. If we keep light levels very low, the dark green regions of fresh grass dismantle their chlorophyll and become susceptible to secondary mould organisms that cause the image to suffer irreversible corruption.

How are the negatives generated and printed onto grass? What kind of optical/ photographic equipment do you use for this?

Testament, image imprinted through controlled production of chlorophyll, grass, clay, hessian, 8 m × 6 m (26 × 19¼ ft), negative 1998, regrown for the exhibition 'Terre Vulnerabili', Hangar Bicocca, Milan, 2010

In our first experiment in 1991, we used ordinary negative film and a domestic 35 mm slide projector to transfer the image to the grass. In 1995, while working on *Reversing Fields* in Germany, we scaled up the projected image to 11 m × 11 m and used a 4 kw projector. The large-format negative was unstable, however, and prone to burning out under the intensity of the beam. On our return to the

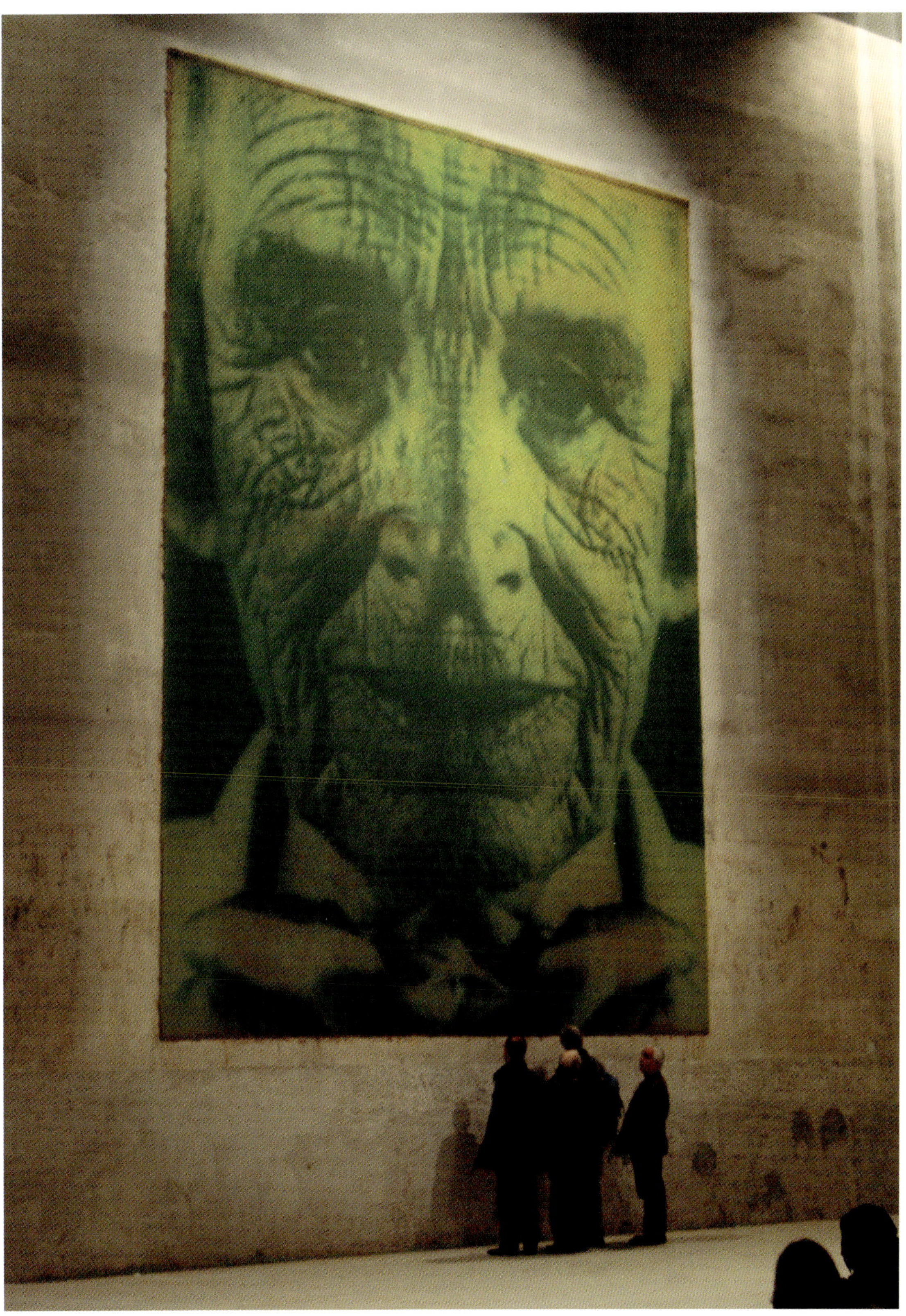

studio we met with Wyatt Enever and he created a specialized negative for us using a random dot pattern in a continuous tone from white to black. This gives the greyscale needed to create a complex image and we use a film base that can withstand heat over many days of projection. In our work we use digital and analogue cameras, and photo retouching software, to achieve the levels of contrast we need.

Can the grass images be preserved, or is their ephemerality fundamental to their artistic significance?

The use of living plants and photosynthesis to create an image invokes a complex set of relationships with regard to time and place. Photography is rendered via an organic matter that is both inevitably bound to decay and disappear, and inherently symbolic of nature's eternal cycles. Additionally, in these grass images domestic portraiture meets the idea of 'landscape', which grass expanses of any form invariably communicate. In the wider body of our work we explore processes of growth, transformation and decay. While we embrace the ephemeral nature of all our materials, somehow the fragility of these chlorophyll apparitions urges us to find a way to preserve them. We justify this conceptually because it follows the established process of exposing, developing and then fixing the image to stabilize the emergent picture, as first conceived nearly 200 years ago by the early pioneers of photography. The ephemerality of our creations has been tempered somewhat by the staygreen

Mother and Child, image imprinted through controlled production of chlorophyll, staygreen grass, clay, 1.8 m × 1.2 m (6 × 4 ft), negative 1998, regrown 2001

Mother and Child, comparative study of conservation properties of staygreen grass and regular rye grass in the artists' studio, 2000

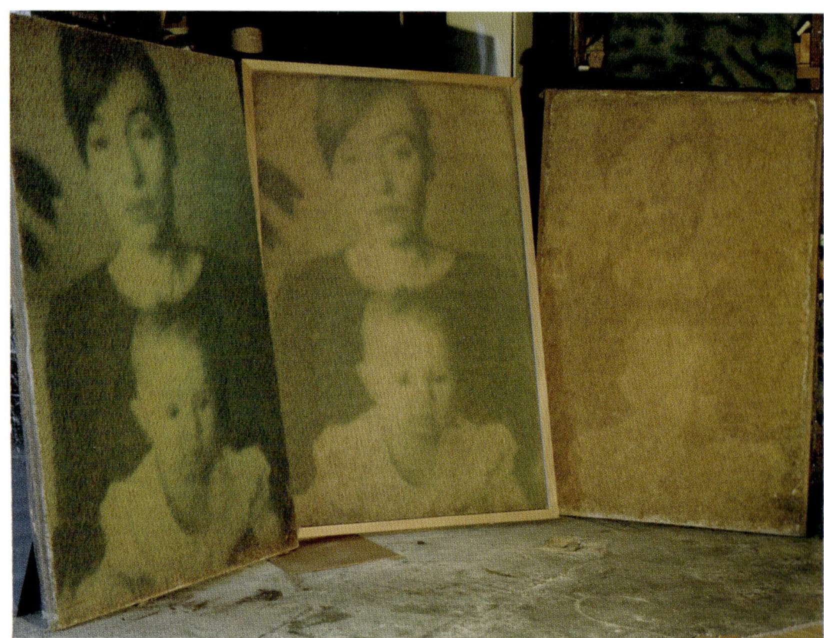

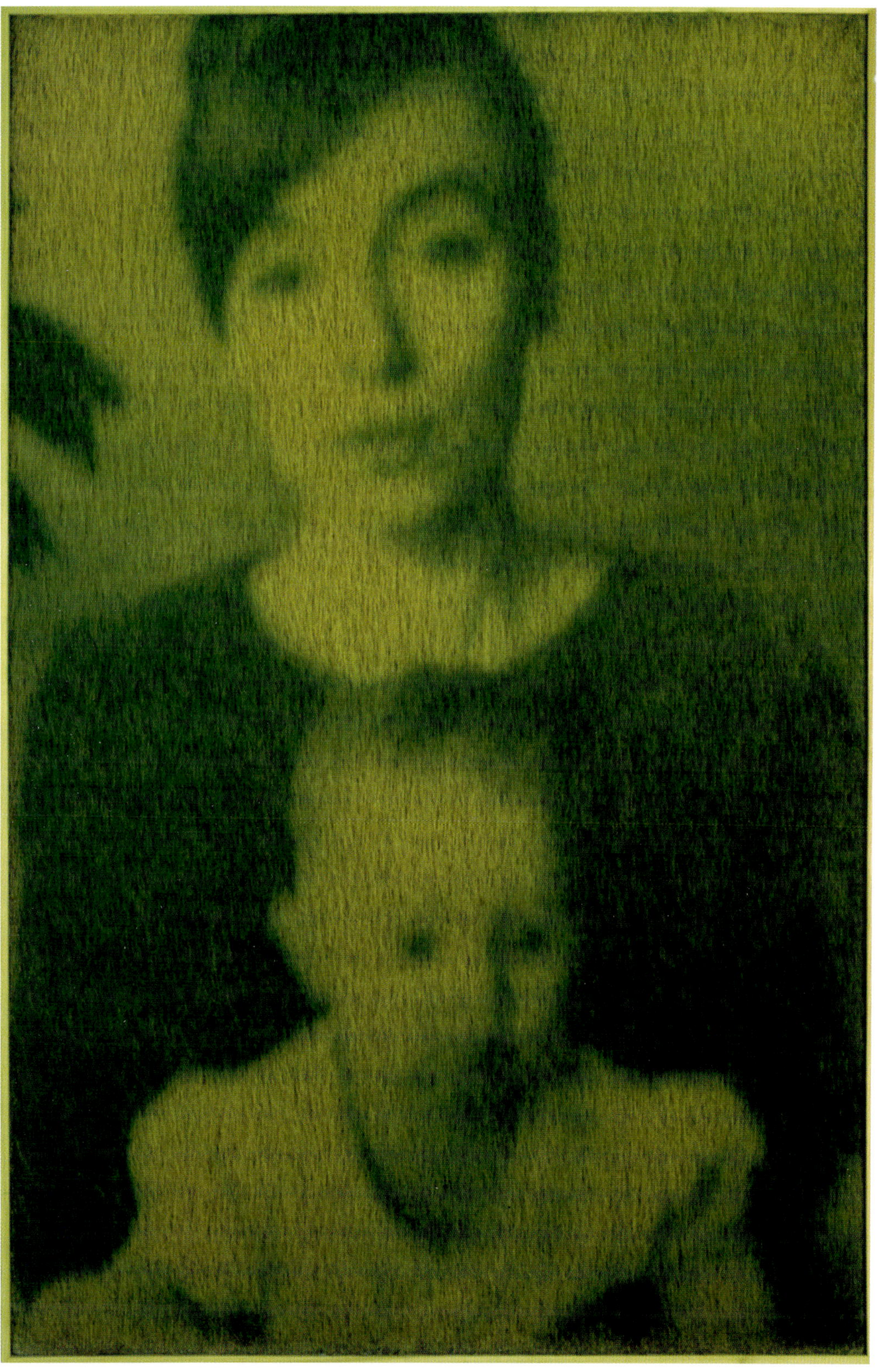

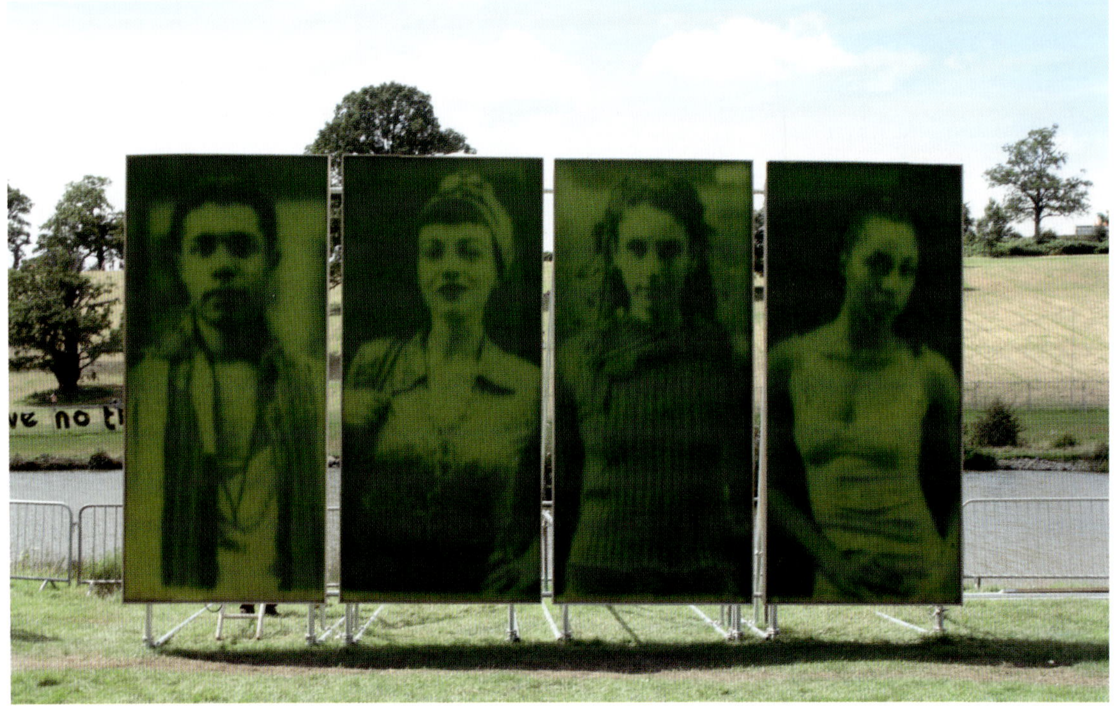

ABOVE
Myles, Basia, Nath and Alesha,
images imprinted through
photosynthesis, seedling grass,
clay, water, installation 3.8 × 7 m
(12½ × 23 ft), for the Art Trail at
the Big Chill festival, Eastnor
Castle Deer Park, Herefordshire,
UK, 2007

grass, which can hold its contrast for a longer period of time after drying, so the fading of the work is no longer exclusively physiological but also pathological, involving the slow bleaching of the dead grass as it decays. Ultimately, however, the image fades and must be regrown on a new piece of grass if it is to be exhibited again. But traditional art forms are similarly ephemeral: museum conservators work to minimize exposure of precious paintings, photographs, textiles and tapestries to light, which can bleach away their pigments, just as it fades our grass images. This was the subject of our exhibition 'Presence' (2001) at the Isabella Stewart Gardner Museum in Boston, where, alongside new artworks inspired by the museum's collection, the first *Mother and Child* grass photograph was brought out of storage and exhibited within view of a freshly grown piece. There is need for debate regarding museum collections policies for objects of finite lifespan, to address the growing schism between those purchased for permanent collections, for which stability is key, and the more idiosyncratic works produced for temporary exhibition.

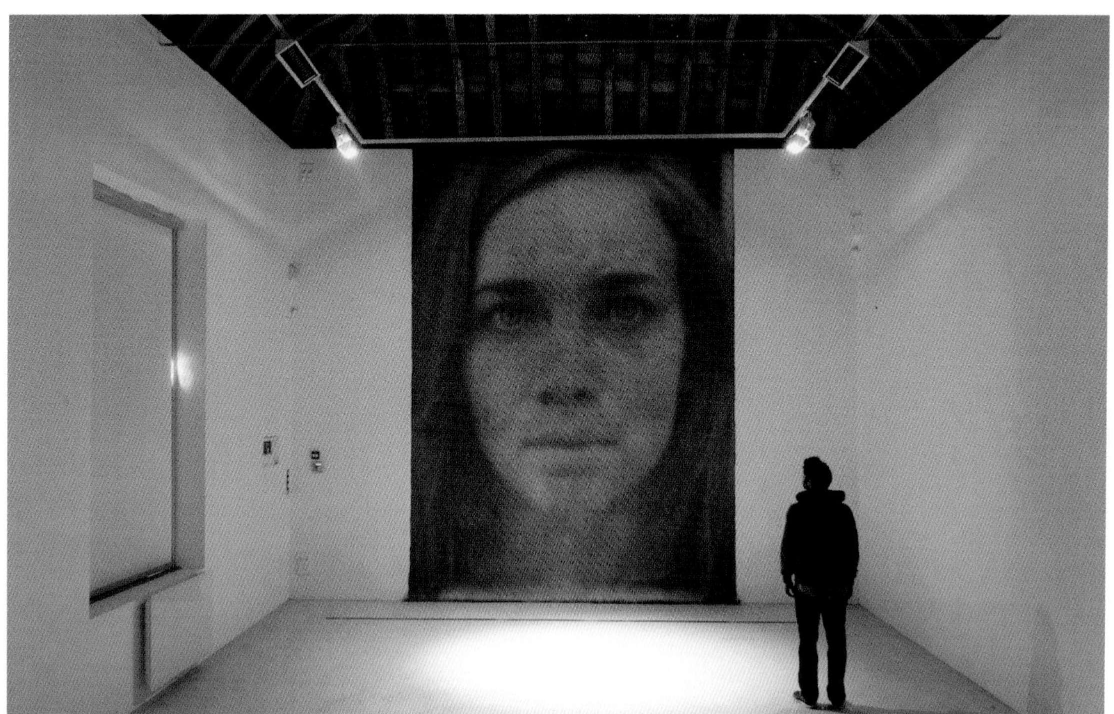

Have you ever considered an integration of your photosensitive grass imaging technique with your architectural projects, or do you see potential for other applications of the process?

Photosynthetic grass images have a limited lifespan in an exterior architectural setting as they will degrade rapidly in sunlight – we used this property intentionally in the images of Myles, Basia, Nath and Alesha that we created as an outdoor installation for the Big Chill festival in 2007. The work was on public view for five days, as the portraits faded away in the sunlight. We have, however, discussed the possibility of exploring three-dimensional photographic works involving photosynthesis.

Face to Face, image imprinted through photosynthesis, staygreen grass, clay; two works, 3.75 × 5 m (12 × 16⅓ ft), Saison Printemps-Été, Domaine de Chamarande, France, 2012

WET-PLATE COLLODION

Collodion was invented in 1851 by Frederick Scott Archer, replacing the slower daguerrotype as the standard portraiture technique and producing beautiful, detailed prints on either glass (ambrotypes, as shown here) or metal (tintypes). While it was originally developed for large-format cameras, both 35 mm SLRs and Polaroid cameras can be hacked to utilize collodion (see Chapter 3). The process is complicated but rewarding. A collodion solution is prepared and applied to a glass or metal plate that is coated and sensitized immediately prior to shooting (this can be difficult in the field). Once developed, fixed and washed, the image on the plate is coated with varnish to preserve it. Japanning or black backing is often applied to glass plates to improve the visibility of the image.

The wet-plate collodion process

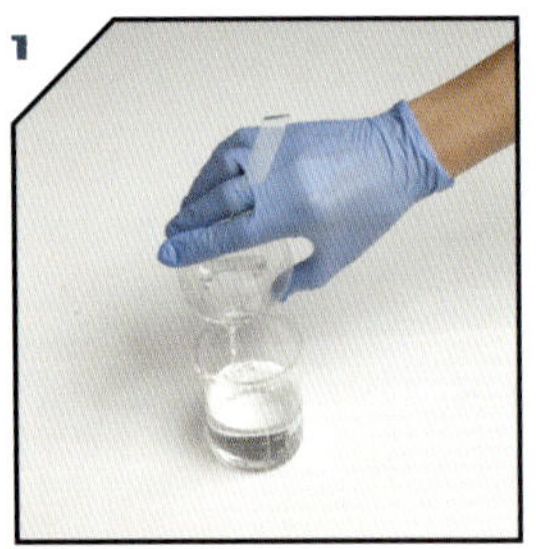 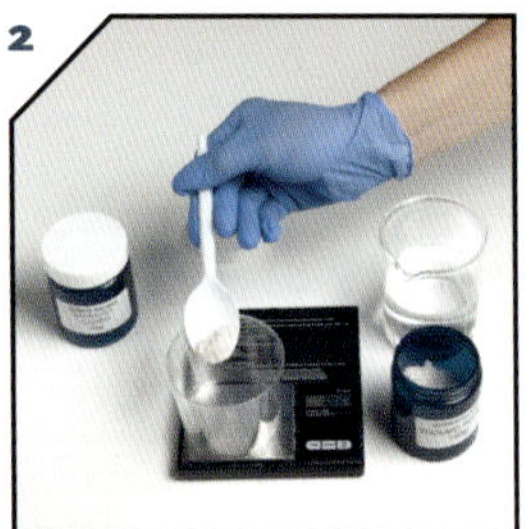 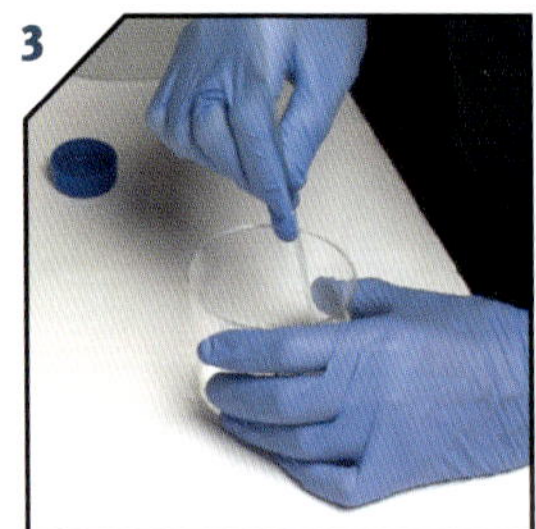 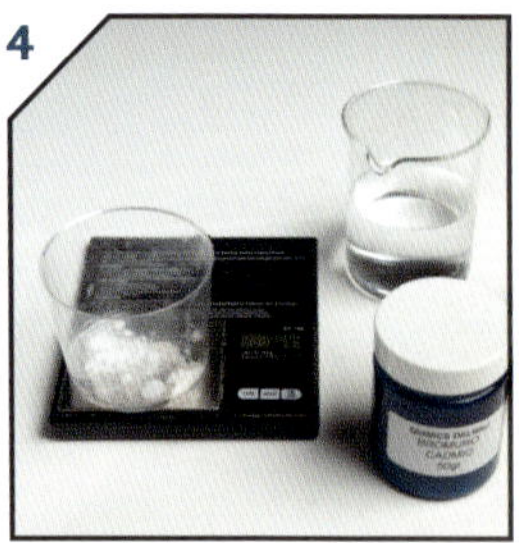

What you need:

- glass (for plates)
- glass cutter
- scales
- measuring beakers and flasks
- vertical sensitizing tray (optional)
- litmus test paper or pH meter
- jar with lid
- cheesecloth or coffee filter
- trays for processing
- black acrylic paint (optional)
- 175 ml ethyl alcohol ⚠
- 2 g potassium iodide ⚠
- 1.6 g cadmium bromide ⚠
- distilled water
- 80 ml plain collodion (a commercially available solution of pyroxylin and ether or alcohol) ⚠
- 80 ml ethyl ether ⚠
- 650 ml ethyl alcohol ⚠
- 24 ml acetic acid ⚠
- 16 g ferrous sulfate ⚠
- 100 g silver nitrate
- 10% solution sodium thiosulfate ⚠
- 57 g gum sandarac
- 47 ml lavender oil

Preparing the collodion

There are many recipes for collodion, but all contain iodide salts and a bromide at roughly 2:1. A solution of only potassium bromide and potassium iodide salts will clear quickly for use the same day, but its shelf life is short. The recipe here rests 2–3 days before use, but lasts for several weeks.

1 Measure 175 ml ethyl alcohol in a beaker.

2 & 3 Weigh 2 g potassium iodide. As potassium iodide is practically insoluble in alcohol, dissolve it in a drop (3 ml) of distilled water (heating the water slightly will also aid dissolving).

4 Measure and add 1.6 g cadmium bromide and mix thoroughly. Cadmium bromide is highly toxic if inhaled, and is also a skin and eye irritant, so ensure

OPPOSITE

Francisco Gómez

Lina V Persson, wet-plate collodion ambrotype, 12 × 8.5 cm (4¾ × 3⅜ in.), 2013

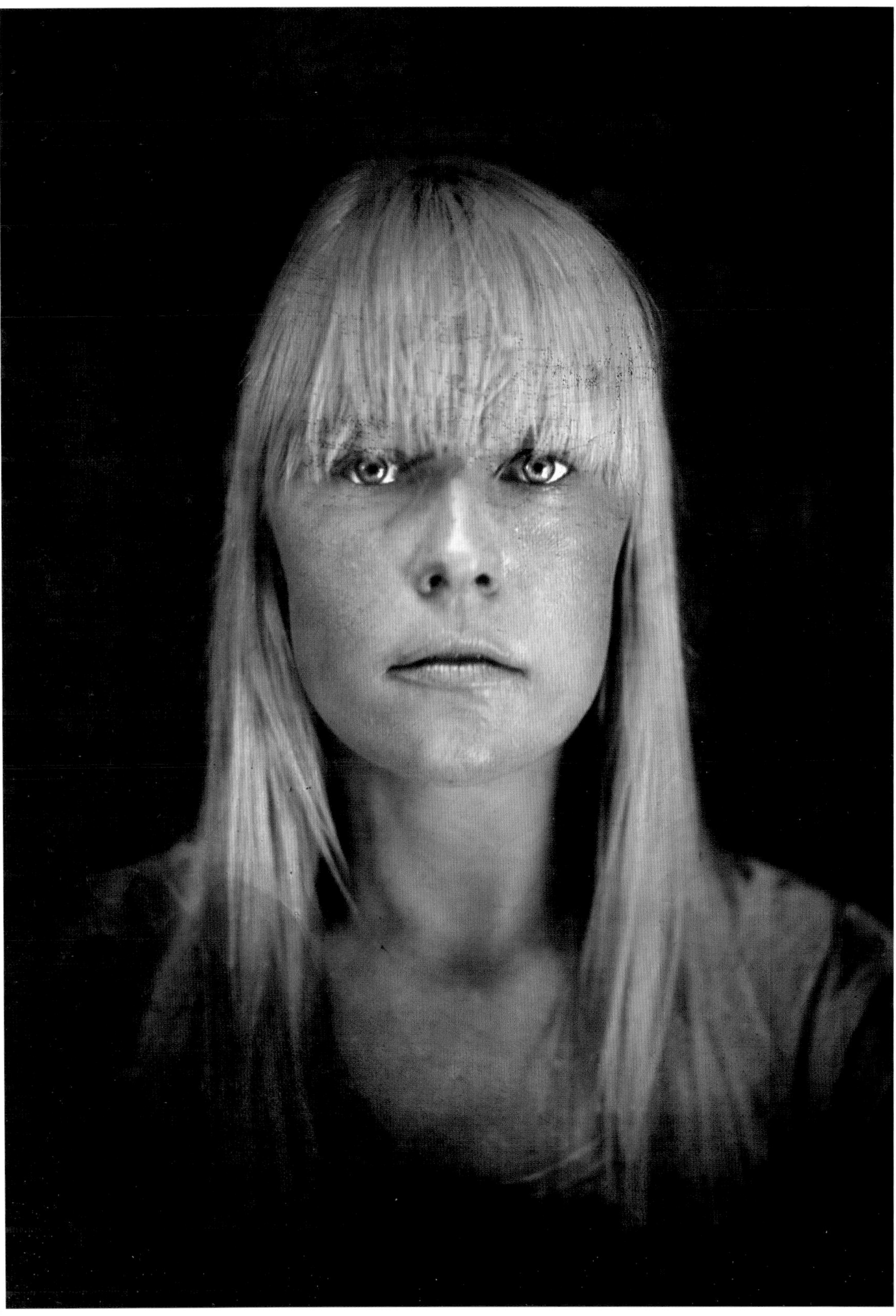

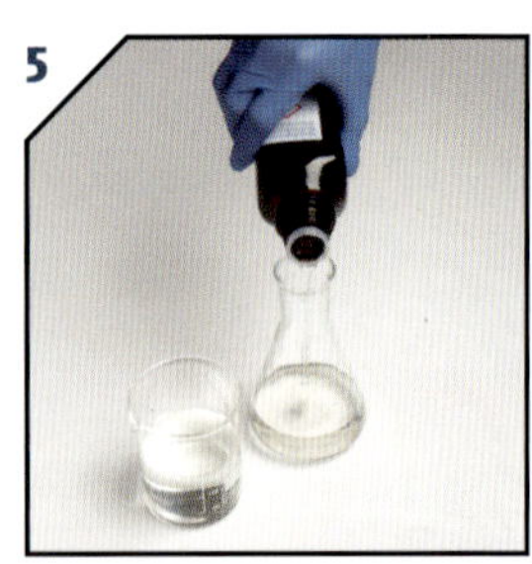
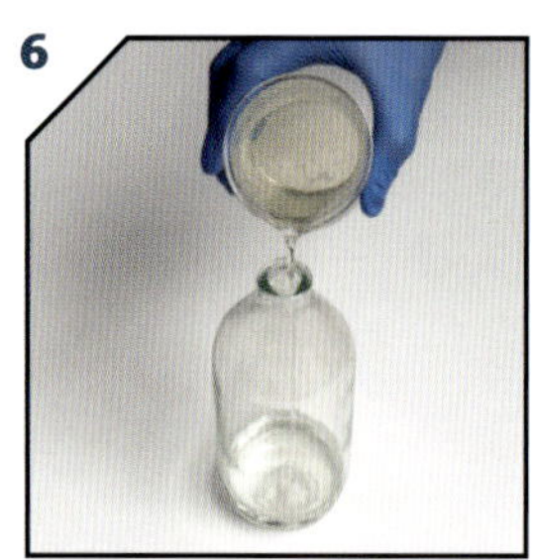
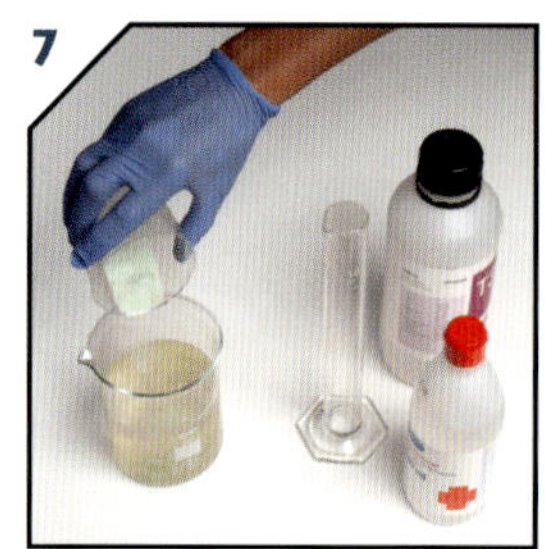
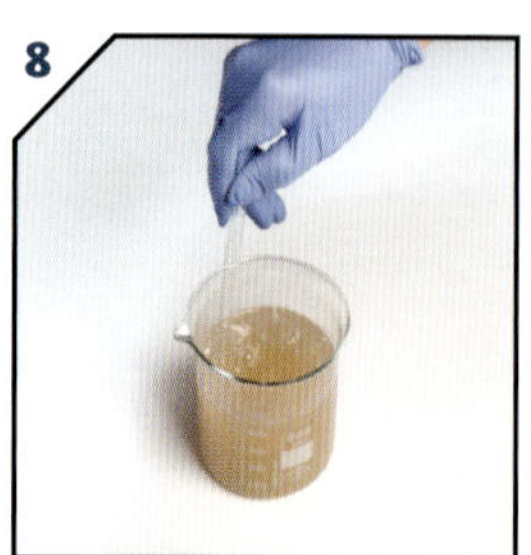

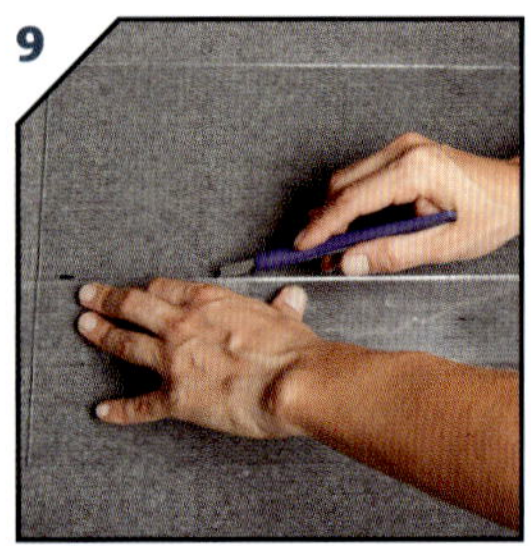
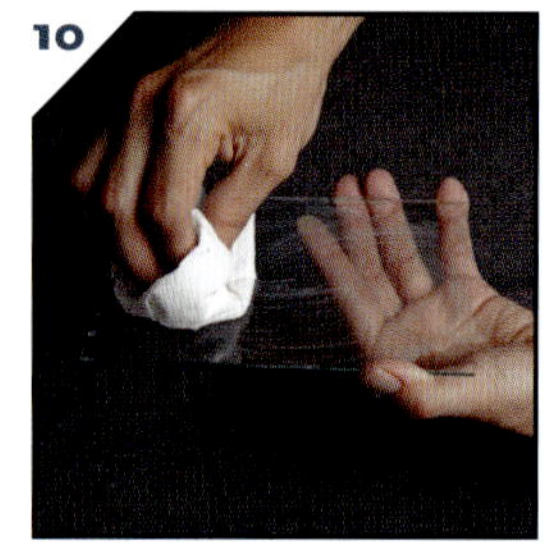
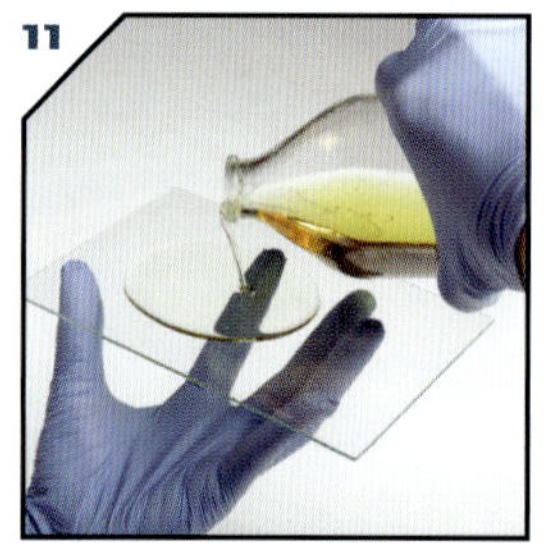
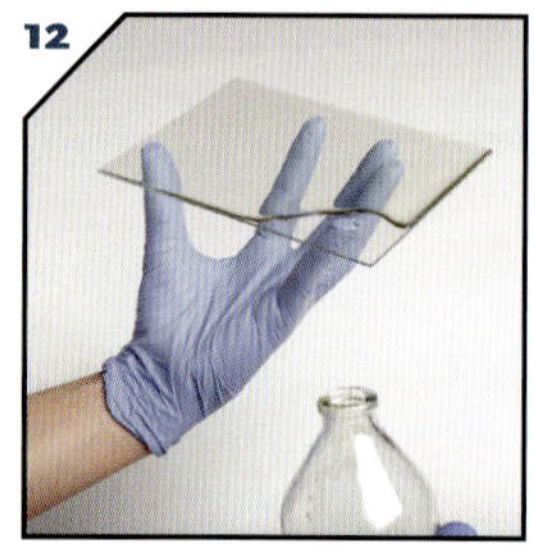

Distilled water test

Not all distilled water is the same: impurities can affect solubility, create precipitates or even form different chemicals that can affect the whole process. To test the purity of the water, add a few crystals of silver nitrate to 20–30 ml into a beaker. If the crystals dissolve and the solution is clear, the water is suitable for collodion use; if precipitates form or the solution turns milky, the water isn't pure enough.

good ventilation and wear a face mask or respirator as well as protective goggles, gloves and clothing while handling.

5 In an separate flask add 80 ml plain collodion and 80 ml ethyl ether. Ether is highly flammable and the fumes are toxic, so be sure to work in a well-ventilated area.

6 Pour this into the first solution (from Step 4) and mix thoroughly. Transfer the mixed solution into a glass bottle and allow it to rest for 2–3 days before use.

Developer

At the same time that you prepare the collodion you can mix the developer. It is worth noting that the developer is sensitive to temperature and humidity: the ratio of acetic acid to alcohol should be increased slightly in hot weather (above 20°C) and decreased in cold weather (below 15°C).

7 To make the developer, take a 500 ml beaker and fill it with 400 ml of distilled water. Add 16 ml ethyl alcohol and 24 ml acetic acid, followed by 16 g ferrous sulfate.

8 Mix or shake until all the iron dissolves – the solution will become brownish in colour. Allow the developer to rest and then

filter any precipitate well. You will need the developer after exposing your plate, so store it in an airtight brown bottle.

Preparing the glass plate

9 Measure the size of the glass plate you need to cut, and mark this precisely on a thin glass sheet. Use a glass cutter to cut the glass down to size.

10 Use a whetstone to de-burr the edges of the glass and then clean the plate. Rinse off any detergent and ensure you don't touch the plate after you've cleaned it: the plate must be completely clean and dry before you apply the collodion.

Applying the collodion

Wet collodion is applied immediately prior to shooting, so you need to set up the camera and have your subject ready before you 'flow the plate'. The 'waiter tray' method shown here is the most popular for coating.

11 Pour the collodion onto the centre of the plate; the puddle should be 2–3 cm from every side of the plate.

12 With the plate resting on your fingertips, spread the collodion by gently tilting the plate. When the glass is fully covered,

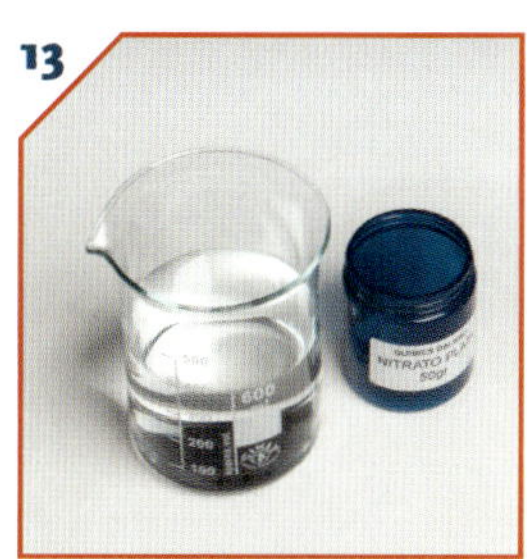
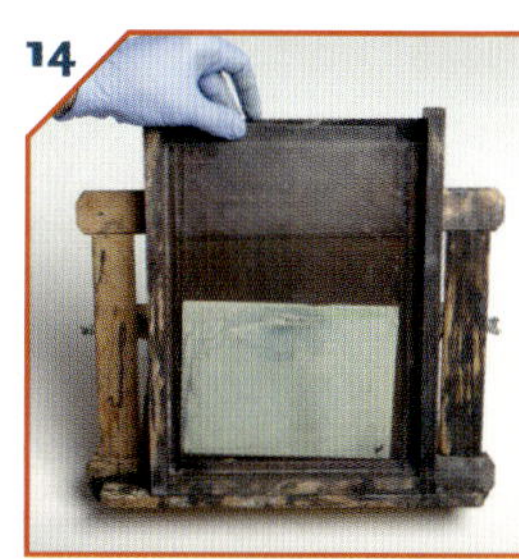
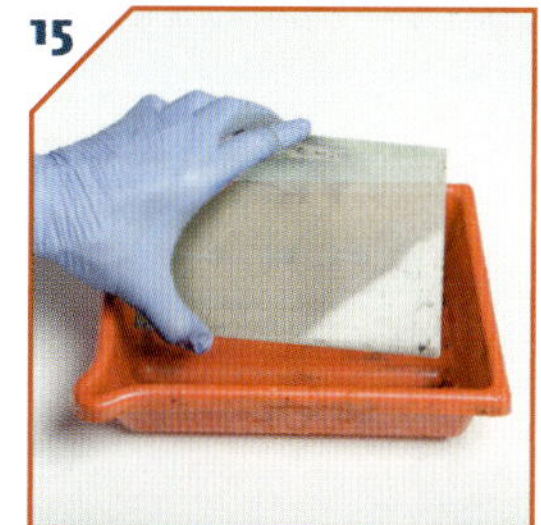
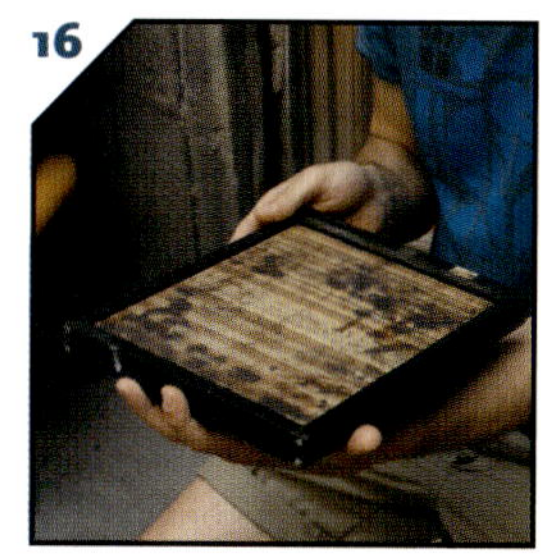
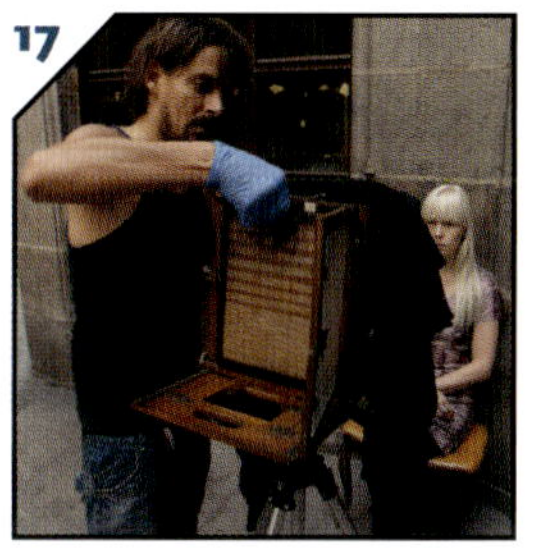
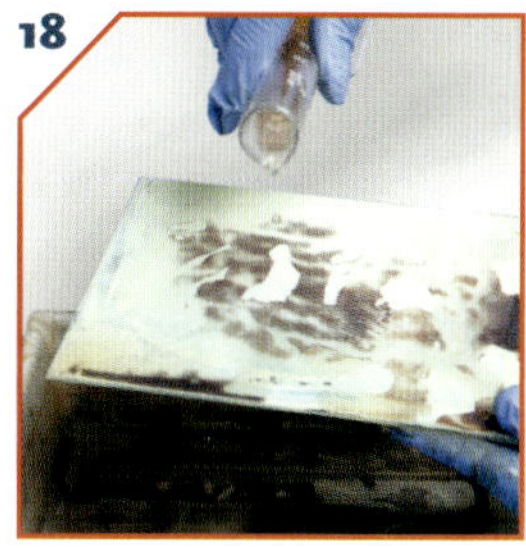
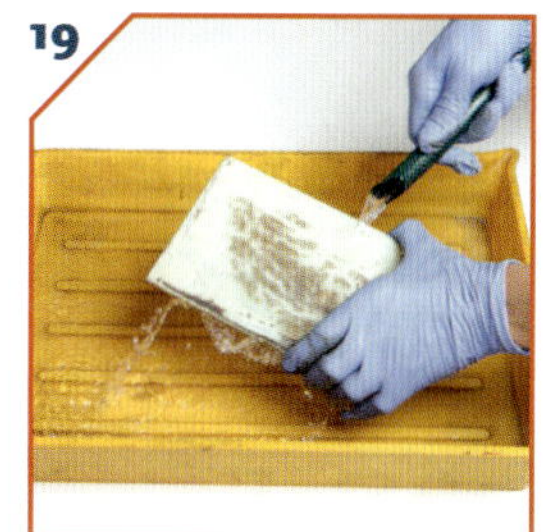
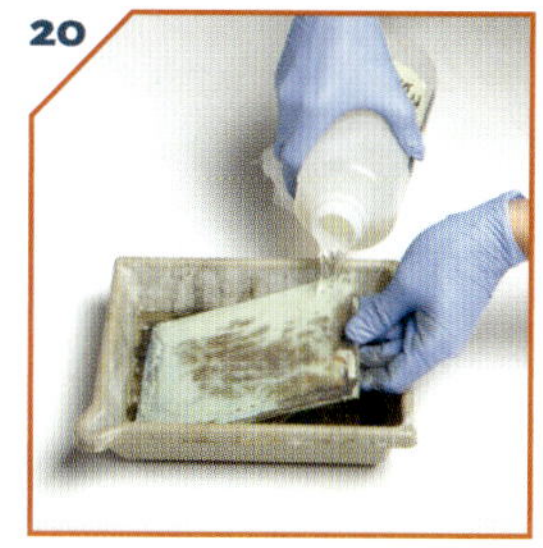

Extending collodion life

As collodion solution ages, it turns reddish. Ageing also increases its contrast, but reduces its sensitivity. To reverse this effect, add 0.7 ml acetone for every 100 ml of collodion. Over a few days or weeks the collodion will gradually turn pale again and contrast will revert to optimal levels.

pour any excess collodion back into the bottle. To ensure the coating is as even as possible, tilt the plate and hold it vertically for about 20–30 seconds while the collodion 'sets'. This is quickly assessed by touching it lightly (at the corner) and making sure no mark is left by your finger. At this point the plate is ready to be sensitized.

Sensitizing

13 The sensitizing bath is a 10% silver nitrate solution (100 g silver nitrate to 1000 ml distilled water). To create a true negative (see 'Variations in sensitizing and exposure', pp. 198–99 for further information), the sensitizing bath will need to be pH neutral (pH=6); a normal 'positive' image requires a slightly acidic sensitizing bath (pH=4–5). The pH of the sensitizing solution can be monitored with litmus test paper or a pH meter. Adjust the pH with drops of nitric or glacial acetic acid.

14 & 15 Working under a safelight, or in a portable darkroom, lower the plate into a vertical sensitizing bath. Alternatively, a small plastic tray can be used for the bath, although it will be harder to lift the plate, so use tongs to lift one edge and be careful not to touch the centre of the plate. Sensitizing takes around 2 minutes. Then remove the

sensitized plate from the bath and wipe the reverse to remove excess fluid.

16 Place the sensitized plate into your plate holder, which will protect it from light until it is inserted into the back of your camera.

17 You are now ready to shoot!

Developing

After shooting your photo, return to the darkroom and develop the plate in a developer bath prepared previously.

18 Cover the plate as quickly as possible (within 2–3 seconds) with developer by holding the plate with one hand above a tray and pouring the developer solution steadily over the plate, moving the developer bottle down the side of the plate as you pour. Agitate the plate while the image develops, which typically takes 10–15 seconds.

19 As soon as the image has developed, pour water onto the plate to stop further development. Once the plate loses its oily appearance, the developer has been washed off completely.

Fixing and washing

20 The fixing bath consists of a 10%

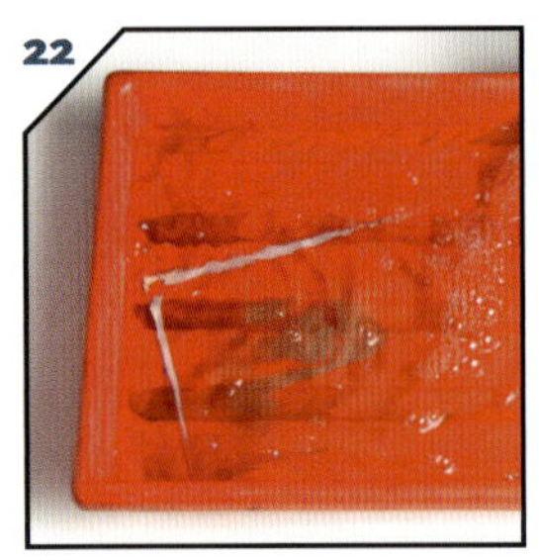

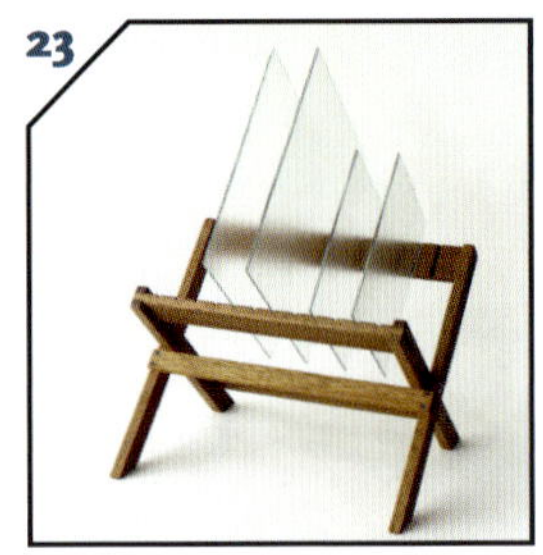

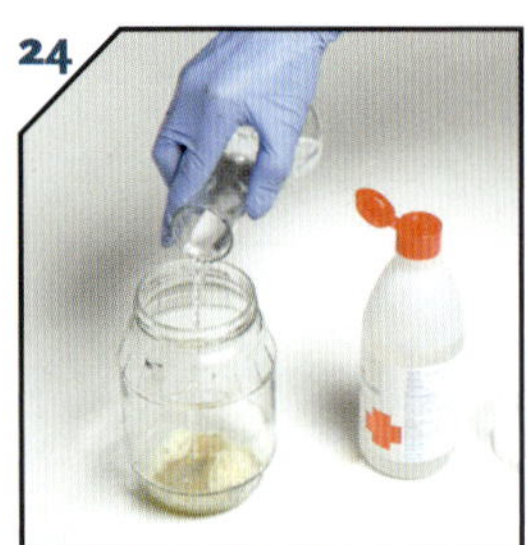

solution of sodium thiosulfate. Pour this generously from the bottle while holding the plate over a tray. A simple rule of thumb is to fix the plate for twice as long as it took the image to develop.

21 Once fixed, wash the plate under running water for 15 minutes, or by using three baths of fresh water.

22 & 23 Finally, rinse the plate with distilled water and place on a drying rack.

Varnish
Varnishing the plate is necessary to protect the image from damage and oxidation (the silver will tarnish over time).

24 To make the varnish, weigh 57 g gum sandarac into a glass jar with a lid and add 415 ml ethyl alcohol. The gum will take a while to dissolve in the alcohol, so fit the lid and shake the jar vigorously.

25 After it is fully dissolved, filter the solution using a cheesecloth or a coffee filter. Do this a minimum of three times.

26 Finally, add 47 ml lavender oil. This should give you a pale yellow or straw-coloured liquid. To compensate for any

evaporation, add 10–20 ml ethyl alcohol. Your varnish is now ready to be used.

27 To achieve optimal coverage, the varnish needs to be applied while the plate is hot. Heat the plate to 40–45°C over a gas flame (on the print side), until it's almost too hot to handle.

28 Using the same method as for coating the plate with collodion, flow the varnish onto the plate, tilting and turning it until you're sure you have covered the entire surface. Pour any excess back into the beaker and allow the plate to dry.

Apply black backing
29 To improve the visibility of the image (optional), mount the finished glass plate over a black paper or felt backing. Alternatively, paint the back of the plate with two layers of black acrylic paint, allowing the first to dry completely before the second is applied.

Variations in sensitizing and exposure
In both tintypes and the standard ambrotype demonstrated here, the images appear as positives, although they are in fact underexposed negatives: the silver exposed areas are lighter than the empty,

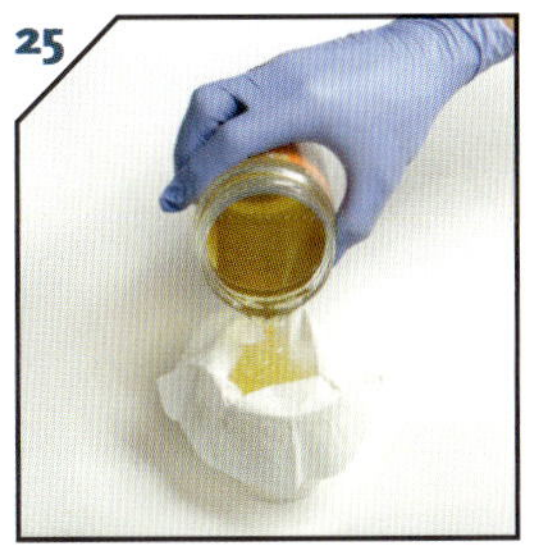

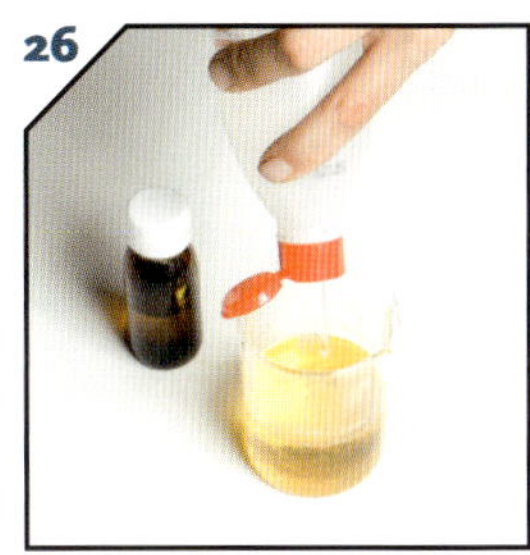

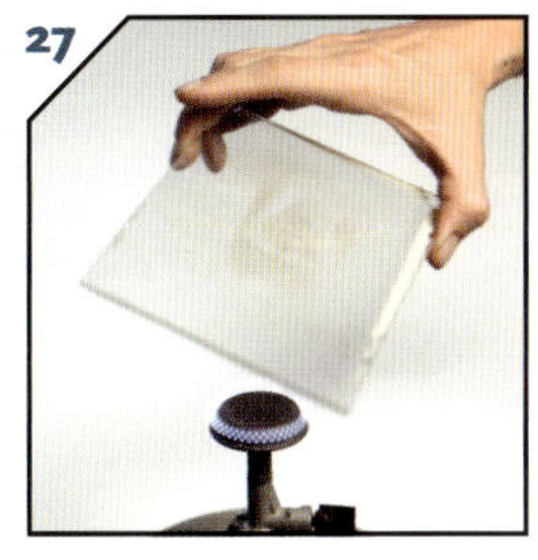

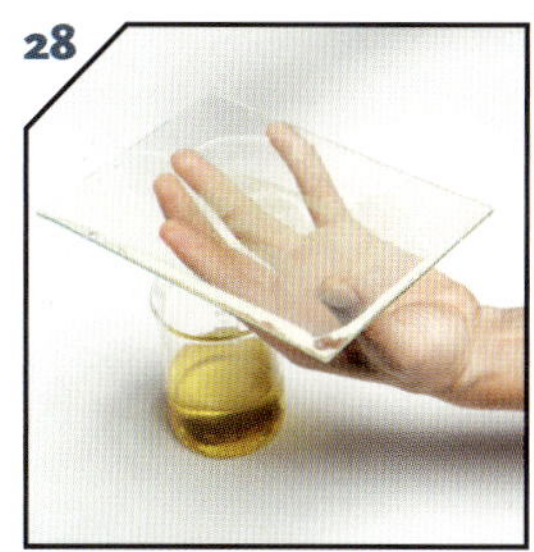

Tintypes

Tintypes are made on thin sheets of iron, or blackened tin or aluminium plates, through the same wet-plate collodion process as ambrotypes. Thin aluminium (for instance, from kitchen foil or drinks cans) is the most widely used material due to its availability and ease of cutting. Cut the plate to the desired size with scissors. Before blackening the aluminium with acrylic paint (japanning), clean the surface to remove any oil or dust and then roughen the metal slightly with steel wool (this will help the paint to stick on the surface). Once the paint is dry, coat, expose and varnish the plate as for ambrotypes.

unexposed areas, and it is this that gives the illusion of a positive. However, with minor alterations the wet-plate collodion technique can be used to create fully exposed negatives in which the silver areas will be darker.

To obtain a fully exposed negative, the acidity of the sensitizing bath should be neutral (pH=6). The plate should then be exposed twice as long as usual (the goal is to overexpose), and developed for 60–90 seconds in a solution containing a reduced proportion of ferrous sulfate. Use this formula for the negative developer:

9 g ferrous sulfate
355 ml distilled water
28 ml acetic acid
18 ml ethyl alcohol

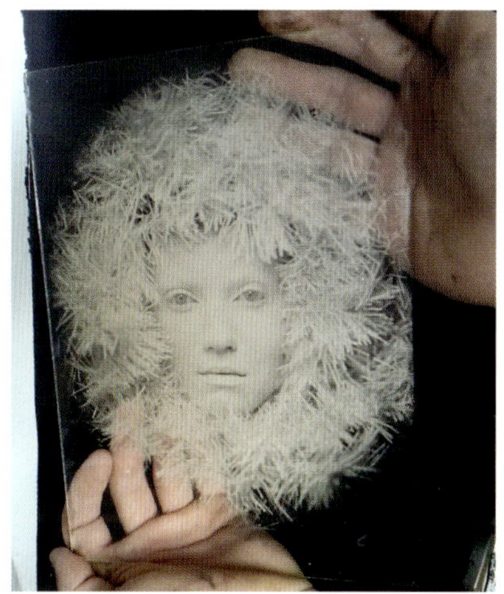

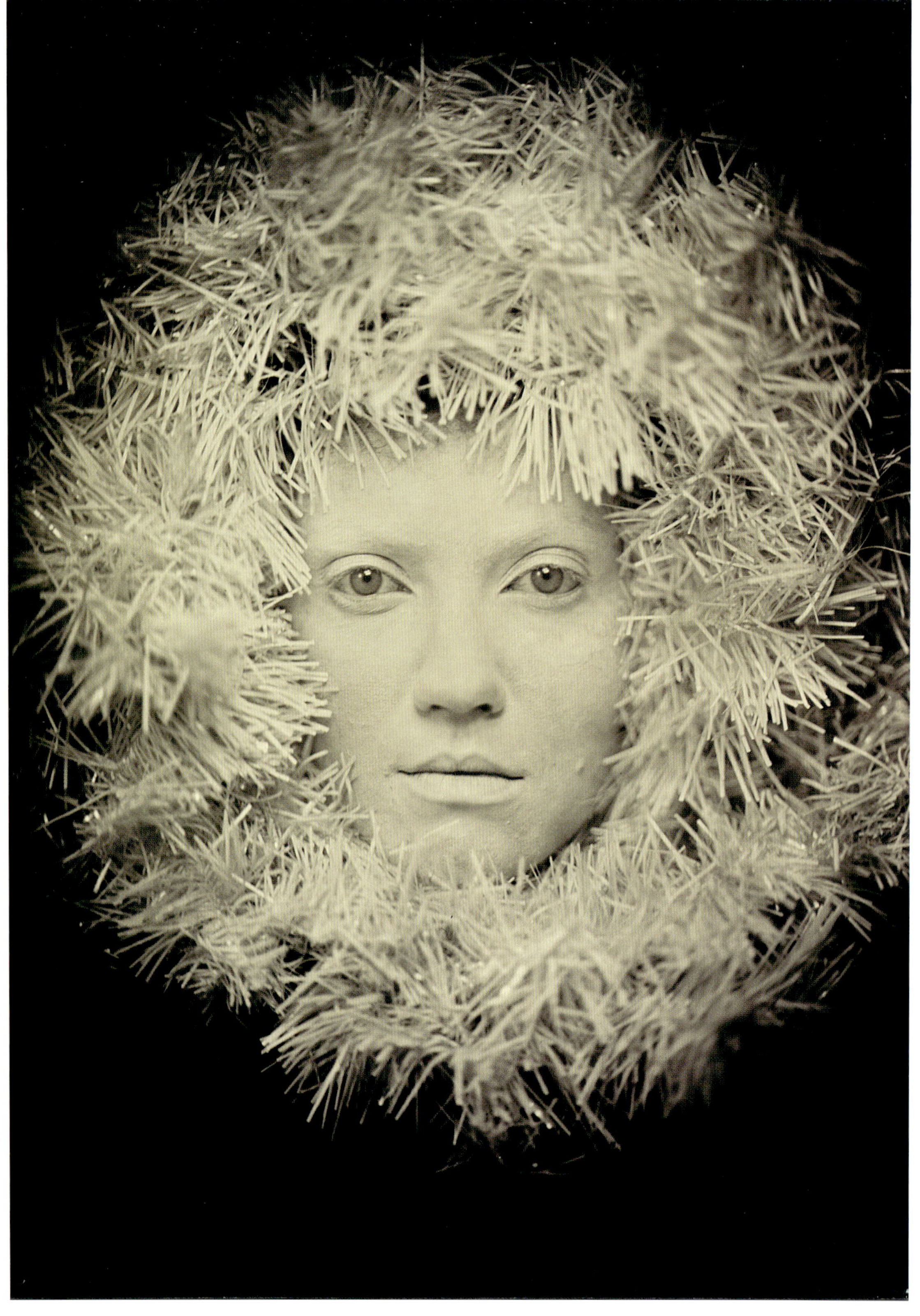

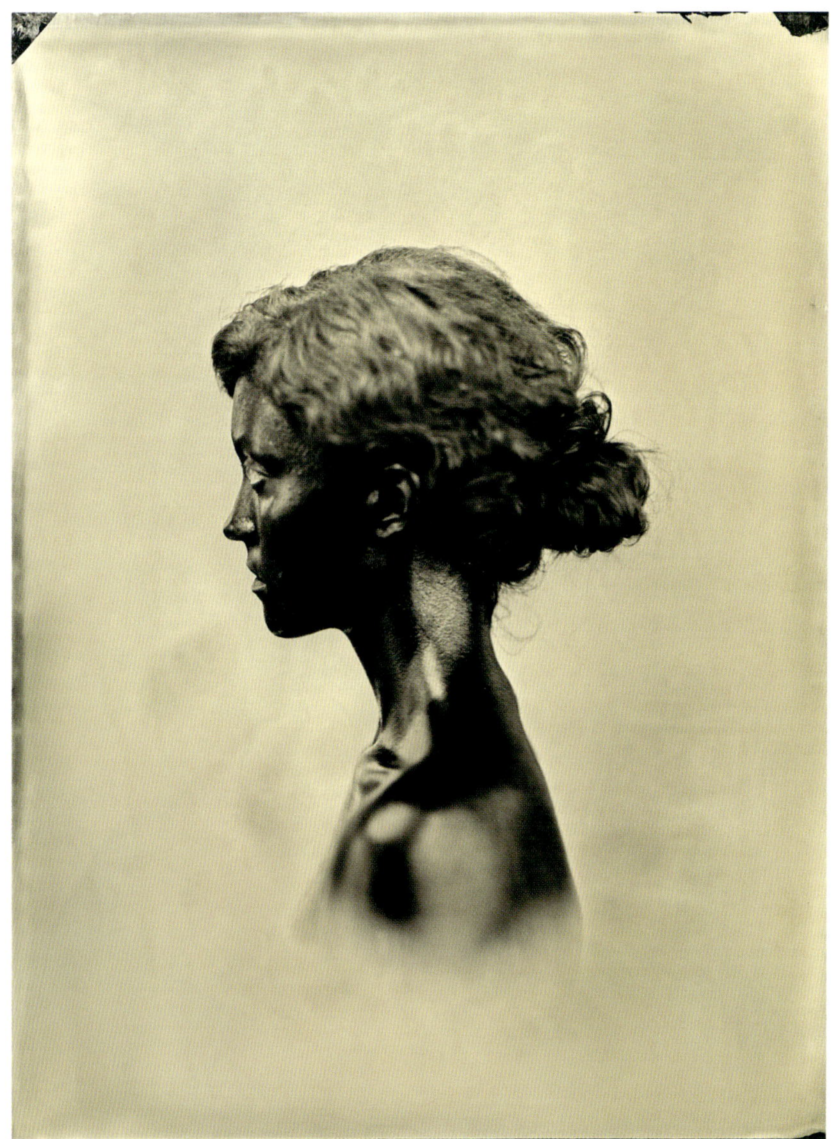

OPPOSITE
Paweł Śmiałek
Dandelion, wet-plate collodion
on clear glass, 24 × 18 cm
(9½ × 7 in.), 2013

ABOVE
Paweł Śmiałek
Kasia, wet-plate collodion
on clear glass, 24 × 18 cm
(9½ × 7 in.), 2013

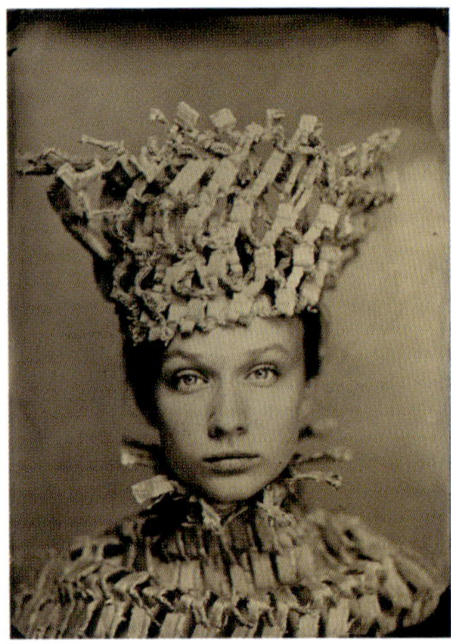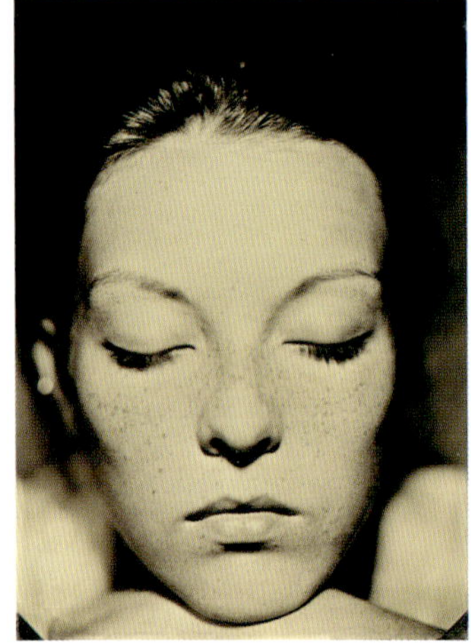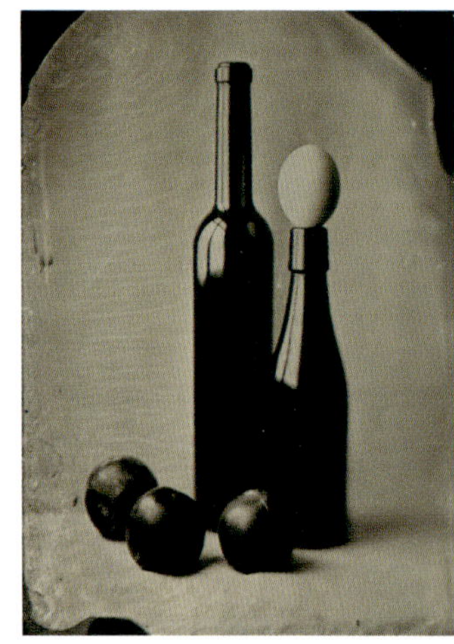

Paweł Śmiałek
Kinga, wet-plate collodion
on aluminium, 18 × 13 cm
(7 × 5 in.), 2013

Paweł Śmiałek
Gosia, wet-plate collodion
on aluminium, 18 × 13 cm
(7 × 5 in.), 2013

Paweł Śmiałek
Still Life, wet-plate collodion
on clear acrylic, 15 × 10 cm
(5¾ × 4 in.), 2013

Paweł Śmiałek
Kasia, wet-plate collodion
on aluminium, 18 × 13 cm
(7 × 5 in.), 2013

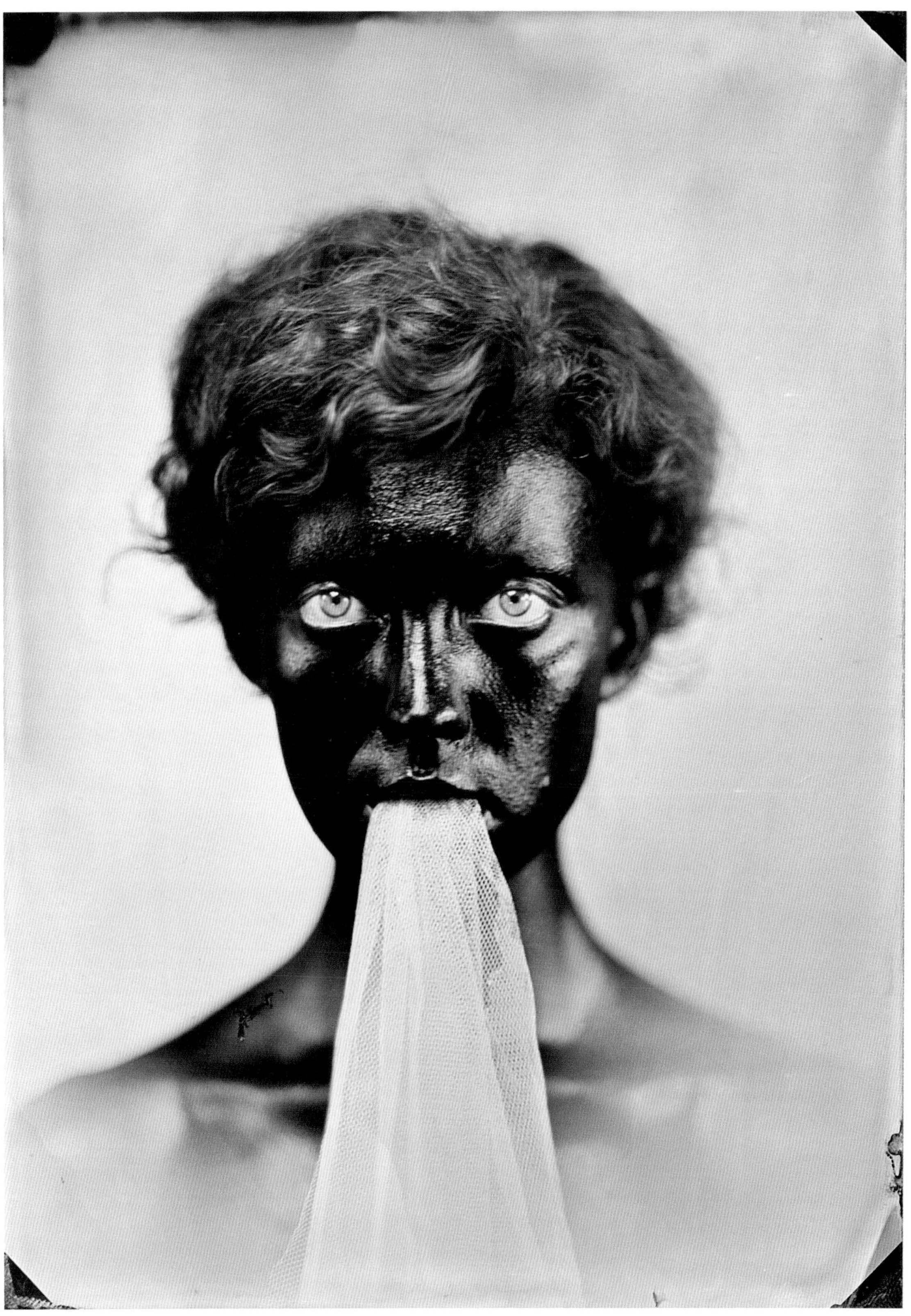

JONI STERNBACH

*Interview by
Simon H. Stevens*

The American artist's series *SurfLand* is a collection of tintype portraits of surfers photographed on beaches around the world.

Using the antique wet-plate collodion process, Joni Sternbach creates one-of-a-kind images that exude ambiguity, timelessness and mystery. Each tintype is prepared on-site. Sternbach pours the liquid emulsion onto the plate minutes before it is exposed; it is then developed on location with the aid of a portable darkbox. The plates are fixed in daylight, allowing the image to be shared immediately with the sitters, forging a relationship with the subject. The large-format camera and extensive gear required brings a performative element to each shoot. *SurfLand* has taken Sternbach to some of the most historic and prized surfing beaches around the world. Part portrait, part landscape photography, it references anthropological images while documenting surf denizens at the juncture between land and sea.

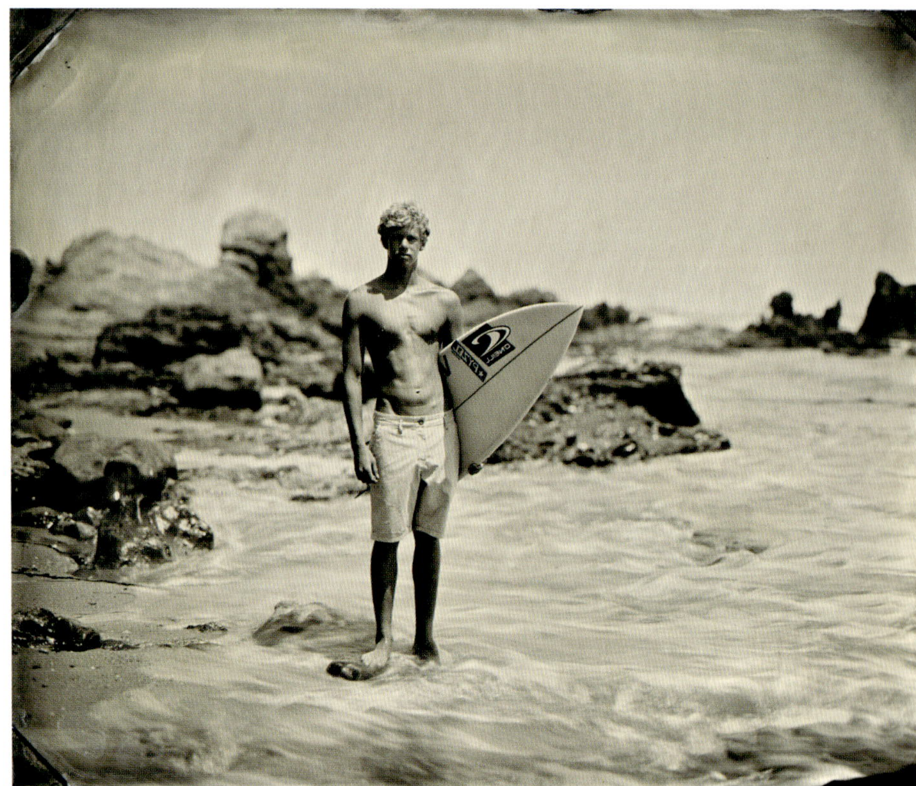

RIGHT

*SurfLand: 27.04.11 #7
John John*, tintype,
20.3 × 25.4 cm
(8 × 10 in.), Orange
County, California,
2011

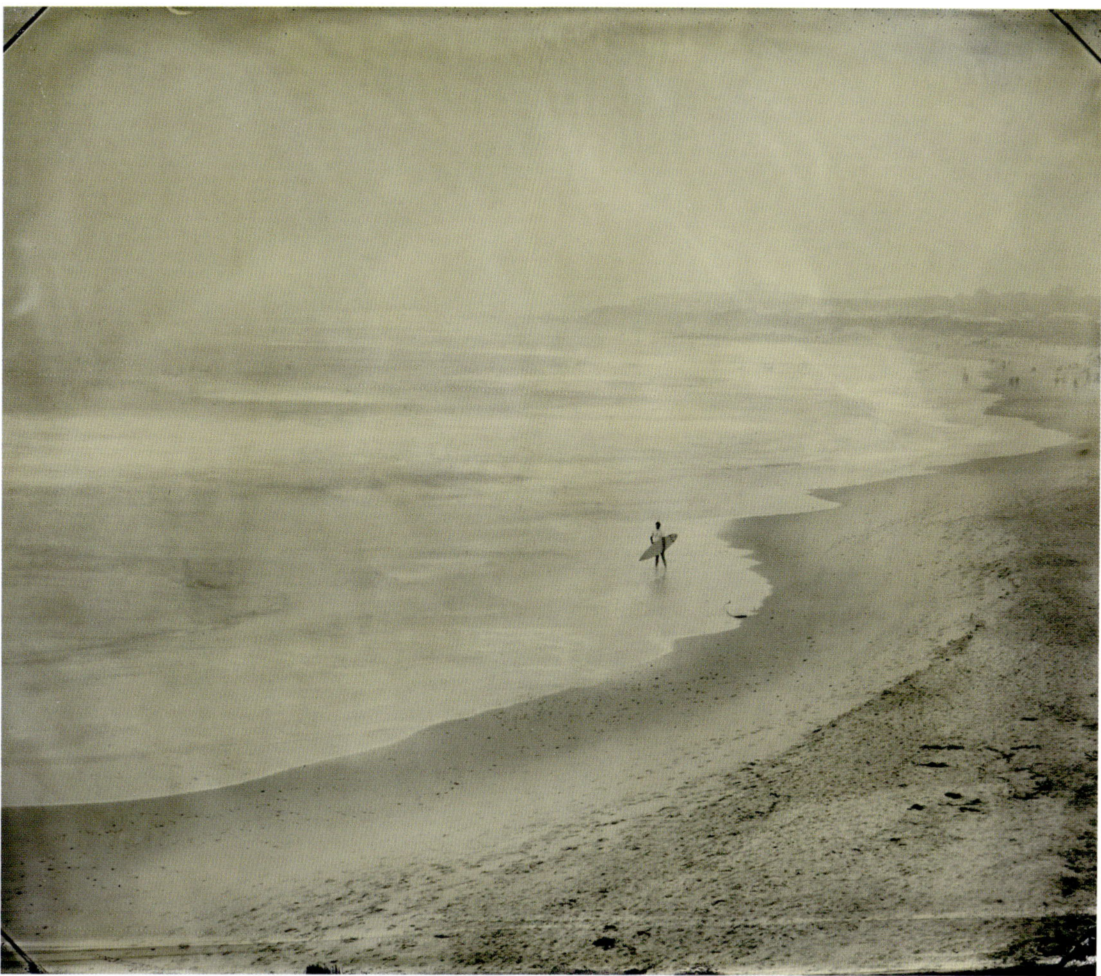

ABOVE
SurfLand: 07.06.12 #4 Lone Surfer,
tintype, 20.3 × 25.4 cm (8 × 10 in.),
Ditch Plains, New York State, 2012

Why did you choose wet-plate collodion for this subject?

I had been working with the medium for several years, making landscapes of distressed and abandoned places. I was looking for a way to use this older medium to say something more contemporary. The process has a generic quality to it that makes everything look old and somewhat the same. Photographing surfers at the water's edge fitted the bill perfectly, creating contemporary portraits that seemed to stand outside time.

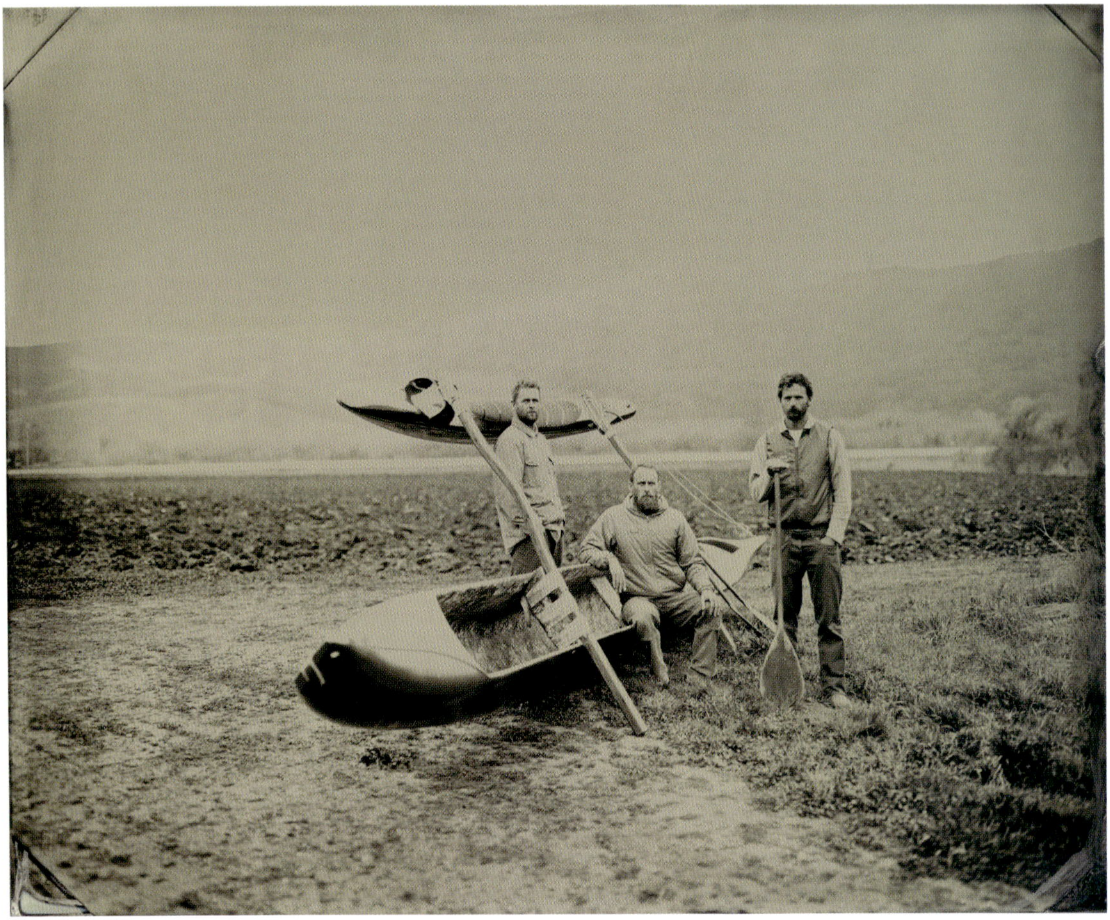

ABOVE
SurfLand: 05.02.13 #8 Malloy Bros,
tintype, 20.3 × 25.4 cm (8 × 10 in.)
Lompoc, California, 2013

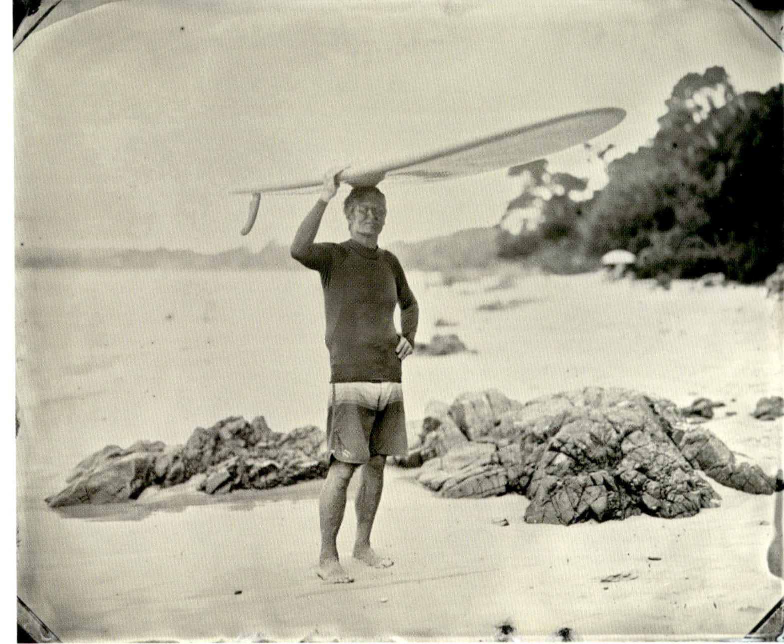

RIGHT
SurfLand: 09.03.11 #3 Rusty,
tintype, 20.3 × 25.4 cm (8 × 10 in.),
The Pass, New South Wales,
Australia, 2011

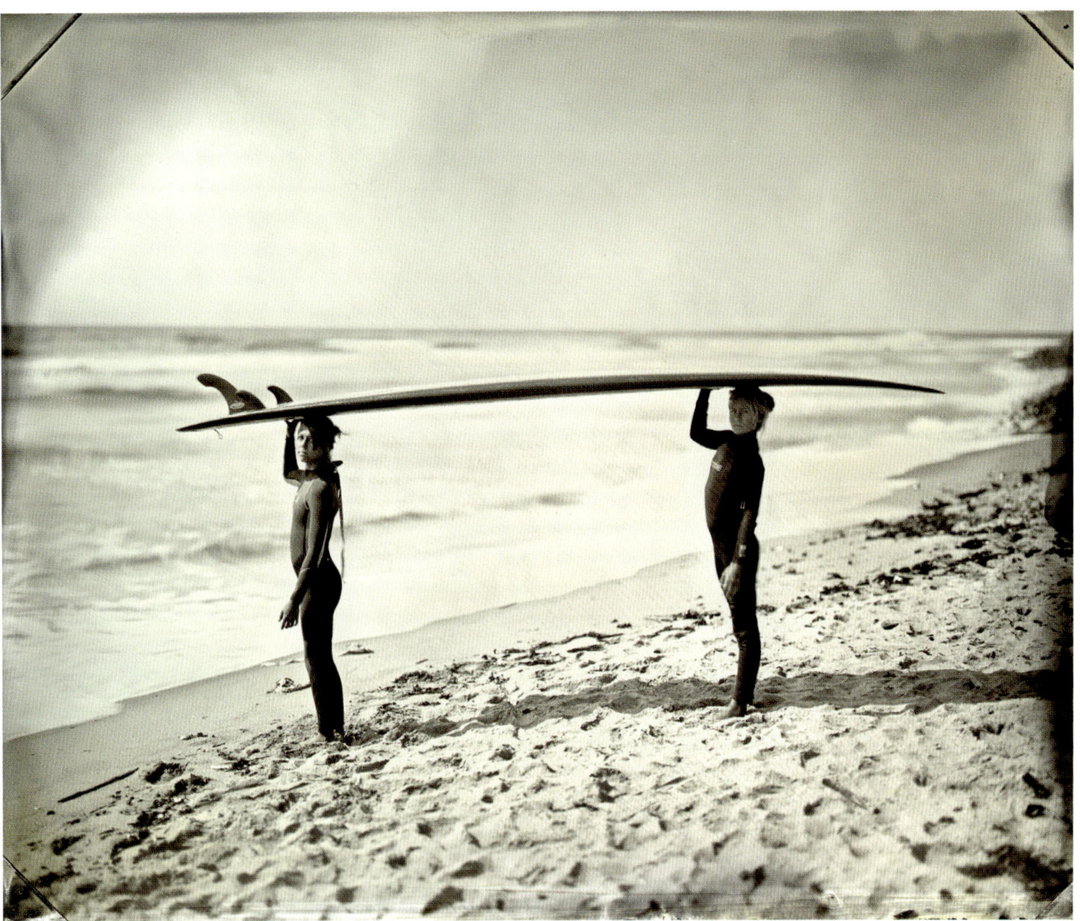

ABOVE

SurfLand: 30.09.06 #6 Minnie & Lulu, tintype, 20.3 × 25.4 cm (8 × 10 in.), Ditch Plains, New York State, 2006

What advantages did this technique give you over, say, normal film or digital?

This technique forces everyone to slow down; it cannot be done very fast. The time spent coating the plate and waiting for it to sensitize is more time spent with my subject. What could be thought of as a chance encounter and conversation can turn into a meaningful connection, an experience on the beach, resulting in a tintype portrait.

Post-Printing Experimentation

Experimentation does not stop once the image is printed: these techniques allow the appearance of finished photographs to be manipulated.

5

ALTERNATIVE TONING FOR CYANOTYPE

Toning is one way that you can change the appearance of a print after development. There are numerous off-the-shelf toners available (and countless others that you can make yourself), each of which will have a different effect depending on the print processes you have used. Here, we experiment with toning cyanotypes, whose distinctive blue colour is commonly altered by this post-printing technique. Many natural and readily available toning agents, including the black tea used below, can be used to colour cyanotypes, as demonstrated by the recipes in the test gallery opposite. Print your photograph in batches to allow multiple opportunties for experimentation!

Toning a cyanotype

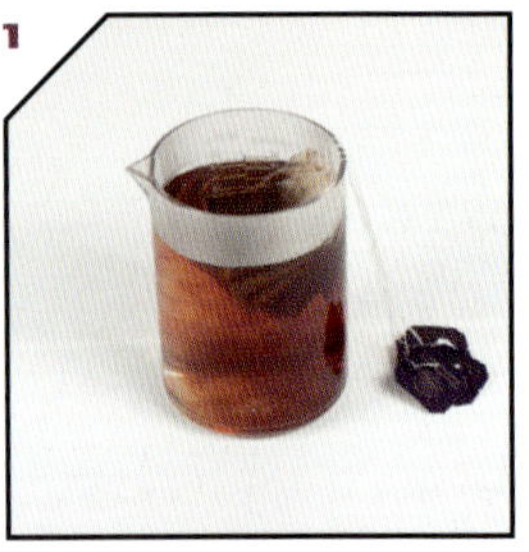
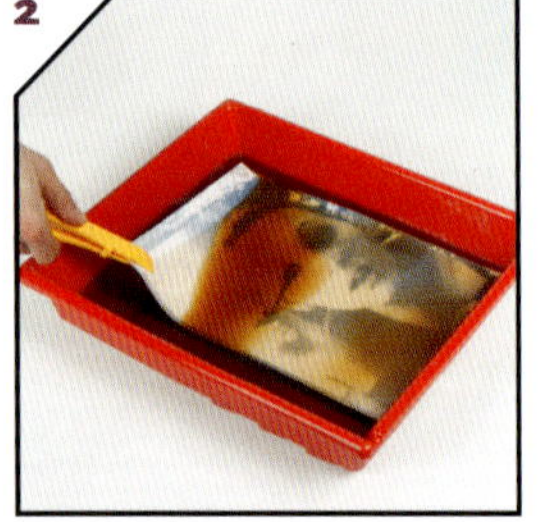
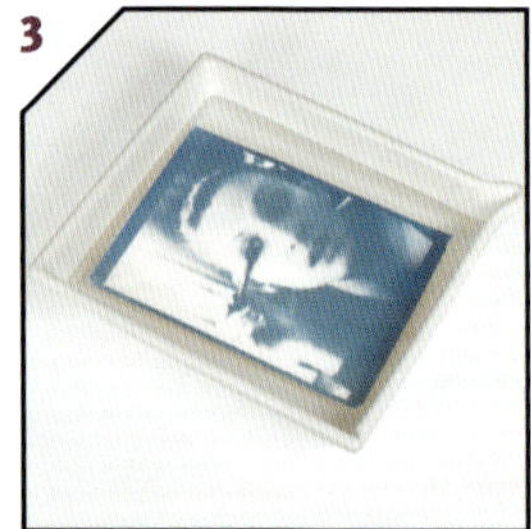
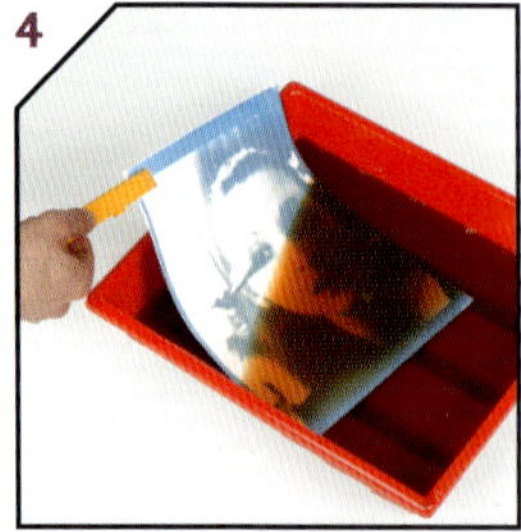

What you need:
- ☐ cyanotype print
- ☐ black tea
- ☐ household ammonia ⚠

Tea toning

1 Tea is a cheap and effective way to shift the colour of a cyanotype print to navy blue or black. Prepare a toning bath with 4–5 bags of black tea – the darkness of the toned result will depend on the strength of the tea toner.

2 Pour the toner into a tray and soak the print, rocking it back and forth. The tannins in the tea react with the iron salts and darken the print. Once satisfied with the visible result, remove the print, wash it thoroughly and hang it up to dry.

Bleaching

3 A second, slightly more complicated method involves bleaching the print before toning it. Start by preparing a bleaching bath consisting of an 8–10% solution of non-detergent, household-strength ammonia and water. Soak the cyanotype print for several minutes, until its blue colour is bleached out. Rinse the print well for at least 10 minutes.

4 Transfer the print to a tea toner bath (as outlined previously). The image will redevelop, but it will be a brown-black colour, rather than the original blue. You can now wash and dry the print as normal.

SEE PAGES 226–29

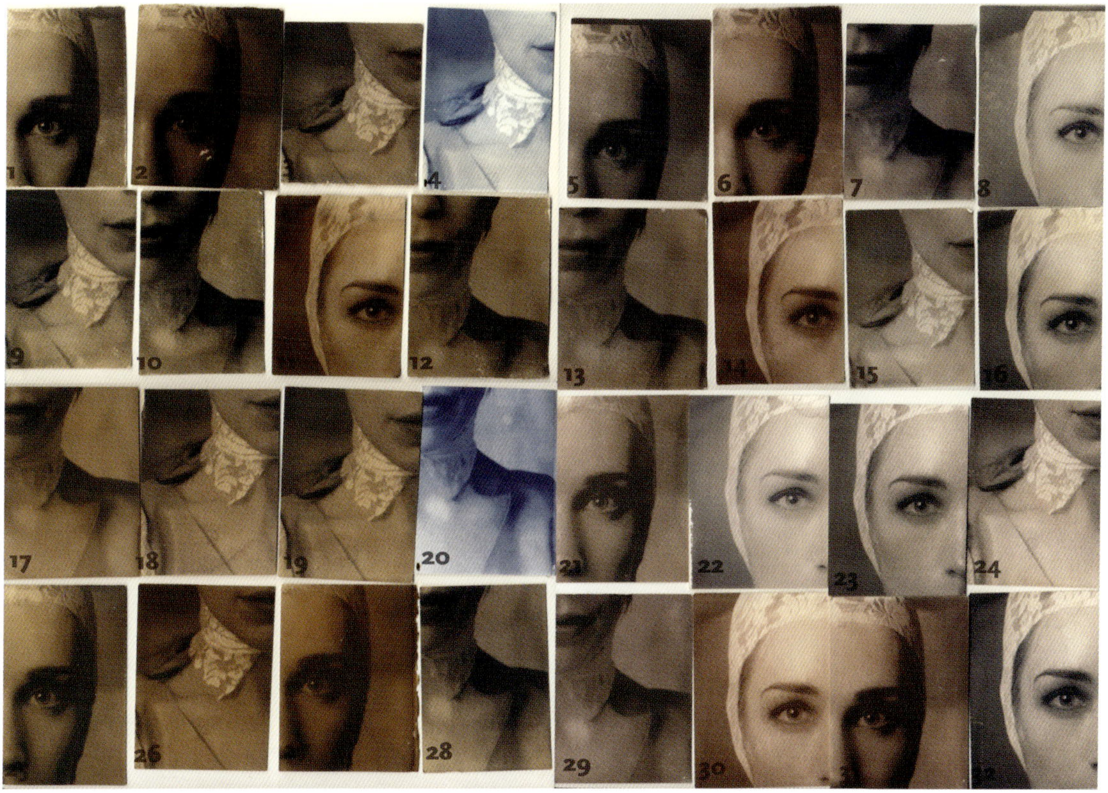

Cyanotype toning tests *by Frank Brouwer*

Bath recipes:

- black or green tea: 5 bags tea brewed in 1 l boiling water, cooled to room temperature
- sodium carbonate ⚠ : 1 tablespoon sodium carbonate dissolved in 1 l water
- ammonia ⚠ : 6 ml household ammonia in 1 l water
- disodium phosphate ⚠ : 15 g disodium phosphate dissolved in 1 l water

⚠ SEE PAGES 226–29

Tests on Simli Japon paper

1. Black tea > Sodium carbonate
2. Ammonia > Black tea > Ammonia > Black tea
3. Ammonia > Black tea
4. Disodium phosphate
5. Ammonia > Green tea
6. Ammonia > Green tea > Ammonia > Green tea
7. Green tea
8. Disodium phosphate > Green tea
9. Black tea
10. Black tea > Ammonia
11. Sodium carbonate > Black tea > Sodium carbonate > Black tea
12. Sodium carbonate > Black tea
13. Sodium carbonate > Green tea
14. Sodium carbonate > Green tea > Sodium carbonate > Green tea
15. Green tea > Sodium carbonate
16. Green tea > Ammonia

Tests on Fabriano Artistico paper

17. Sodium carbonate > Black tea
18. Ammonia > Black tea
19. Black tea > Ammonia
20. Disodium phosphate
21. Sodium carbonate > Green tea
22. Disodium phosphate > Green tea
23. Ammonia > Green tea
24. Green tea > Ammonia
25. Black tea > Sodium carbonate
26. Ammonia > Black tea > Ammonia > Black tea
27. Sodium carbonate > Black tea > Sodium carbonate > Black tea
28. Black tea
29. Green tea > Sodium carbonate
30. Sodium carbonate > Green tea > Sodium carbonate > Green tea
31. Ammonia > Green tea > Ammonia > Green tea
32. Green tea

BLEACHING

Bleaching is the starting point for many toning techniques, as well as for the bromoil process (see pp. 214–15), but it can also be used as a standalone method for altering your photographs. The bleaching solution can be applied either uniformly to the entire print via a bath (see sample image opposite, above) or selectively to smaller areas with a paintbrush, sponge or cotton wool (opposite, below). The process is very simple, but you need to remember that the image has to be re-fixed after you bleach it. You can bleach and re-fix the same print multiple times; just be aware that the more you bleach a print, the grainier and higher in contrast it will become.

The bleaching process

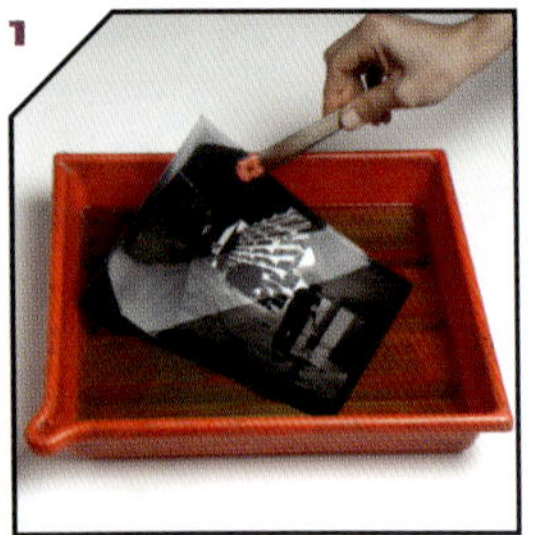
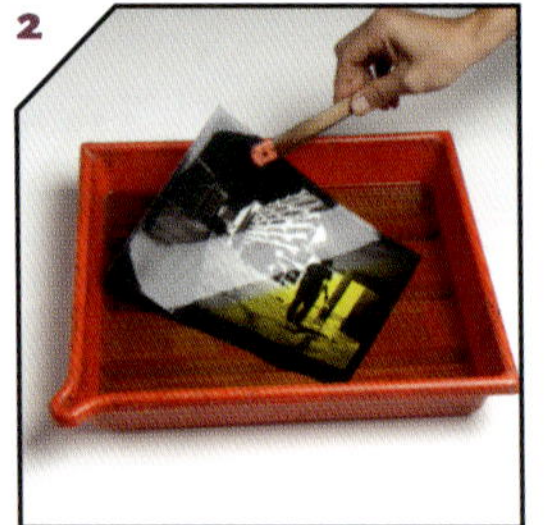
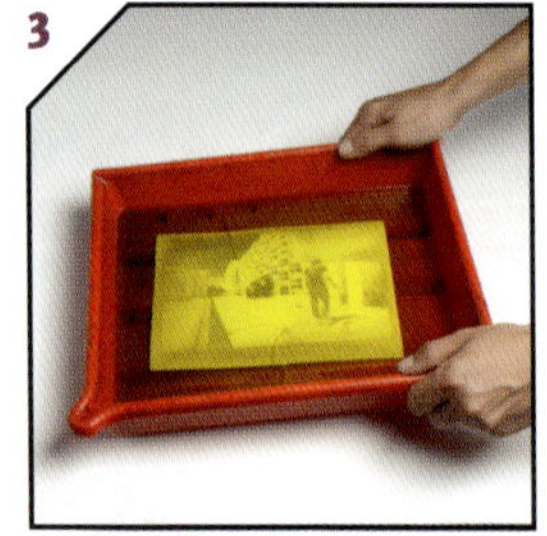
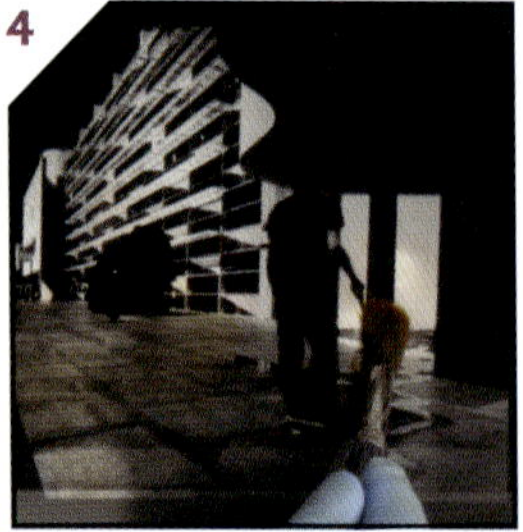

What you need:
- [ ] distilled water
- [ ] 64 g potassium ferricyanide ⚠
- [ ] 30 g potassium bromide ⚠
- [ ] 120 g sodium thiosulfate ⚠
- [ ] paintbrush, sponge or cotton wool (optional)

OPPOSITE

Davide Pellegrini
Summer at the MACBA, bleached (above) and selectively bleached (below) prints, 13 × 18 cm (5 × 7 in.), 2013

SEE PAGES 226–29

Farmer's reducer

In 1883, Howard Farmer invented a chemical compound that would reduce and completely remove the metallic silver from photographic plates and papers. This bleaching solution is very easy to mix yourself. Start by mixing two solutions – A and B – using the following ingredients:

Solution A

250 ml distilled water
64 g potassium ferricyanide
30 g potassium bromide

Solution B

500 ml distilled water
120 g sodium thiosulfate

To make Farmer's reducer, mix 7.5 ml of solution A with 180 ml of solution B, and then add water to make it up to 500 ml.

Bleaching

1 Soak the print in water for 5 minutes to soften the emulsion.

2 To bleach the entire print, transfer it to a bath containing Farmer's reducer, which should be at a temperature of 20–25°C.

3 Rock the bleach bath continually to ensure even bleaching until the print turns a pale yellow-green colour. (Farmer's reducer is a fast-acting solution, so keep a close eye on it.) After the bleach bath, rinse the print for 15 minutes, then fix it in a bath of 10% sodium thiosulfate solution for 5 minutes. Wash thoroughly and hang to dry.

4 Alternatively, Farmer's reducer can be applied selectively to a print with a brush or the like, so that only specific areas are bleached. Rinse, fix and dry as per Step 3.

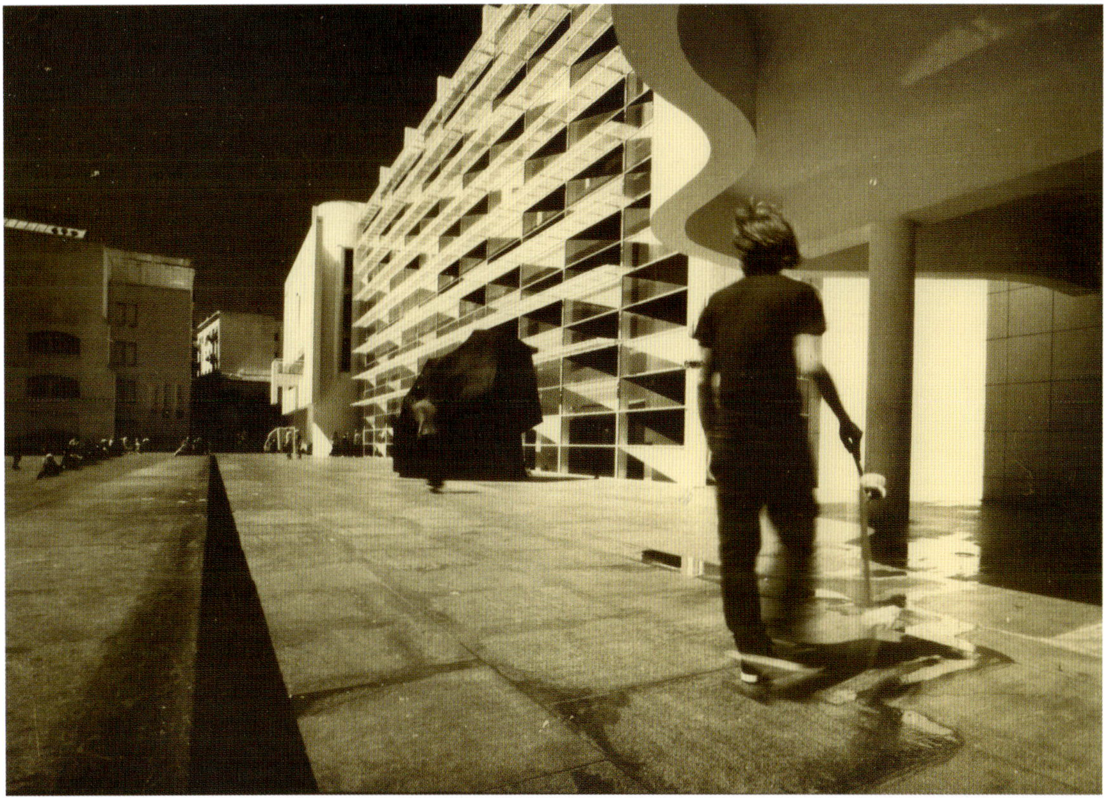

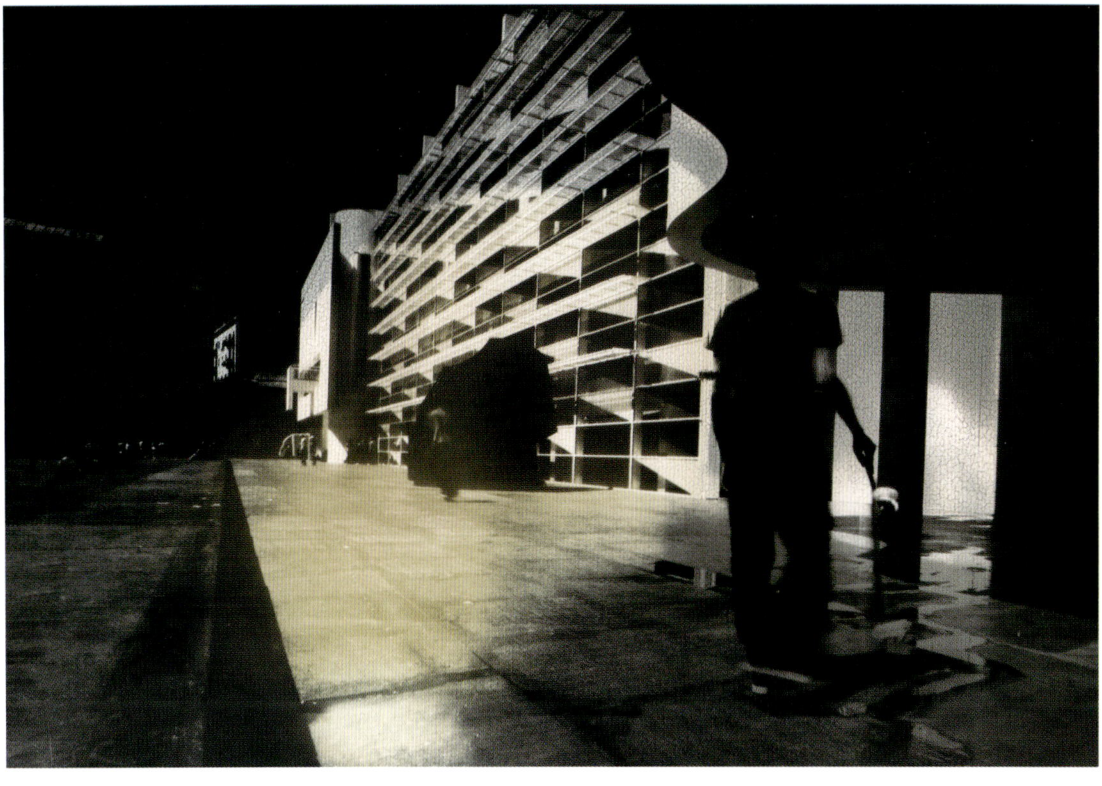

MORDANÇAGE

The mordançage process was invented by Jean-Pierre Sudre during the 1960s, and is based on the earlier bleach-etch technique developed by Paul Liesegang at the end of the nineteenth century. It is a controlled degradation of a black-and-white fibre-based or resin-coated silver print, using repeated cycles of bleaching and redevelopment. The redevelopment creates a part-positive / part-negative appearance in the image, while the bleaching lifts the emulsion away from the paper, allowing it to be manipulated as a separate layer.

The mordançage process

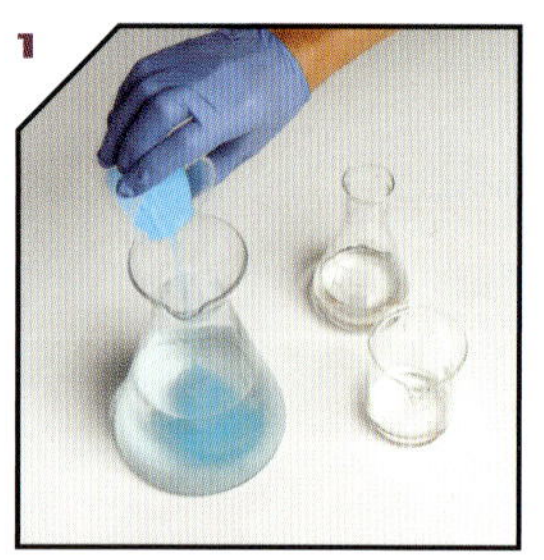
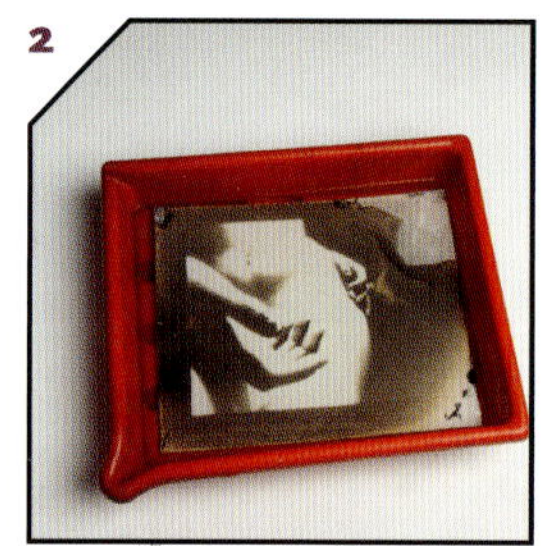
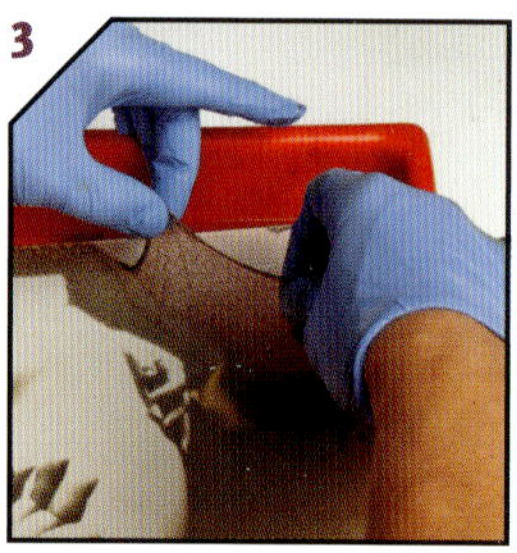

What you need:

- ☐ 10 g copper(II) chloride ⚠
- ☐ distilled water
- ☐ 25 ml 30–35% hydrogen peroxide ⚠
- ☐ 50 ml glacial acetic acid ⚠
- ☐ acrylic spray

The mordançage solution

1 Slowly add 10 g copper(II) chloride to 750 ml distilled water and stir. Add 25 ml 30–35% hydrogen peroxide and 50 ml glacial acetic acid and stir. Add distilled water to make the solution up to 1000 ml (this solution has an indefinite shelf life if stored in an airtight brown plastic bottle).

First bleach

2 Wash a fully processed fibre-based or resin-coated print in the mordançage solution for 3 minutes, followed by a 15 minute wash in water. The black areas of the print should start to lift from the paper.

Redevelopment

Redevelop the print with photographic developer, and then rinse it thoroughly under running water.

Second bleach

3 The second bleach stage is where the most radical changes to your images take place. As the emulsion is 'loose' you can lift entire sections of the print and re-work them or use the mordançage solution to selectively remove more of the emulsion.

Second redevelopment

Redevelop the print for a second time, then transfer it to a stop bath.

Wash

Wash the print for at least 30 minutes. As the emulsion is very fragile at this stage, washing is best done gently in a tray.

Protective coating

When the print is completely dry apply a protective coat of anti-UV non-yellowing acrylic spray.

SEE PAGES 226–29

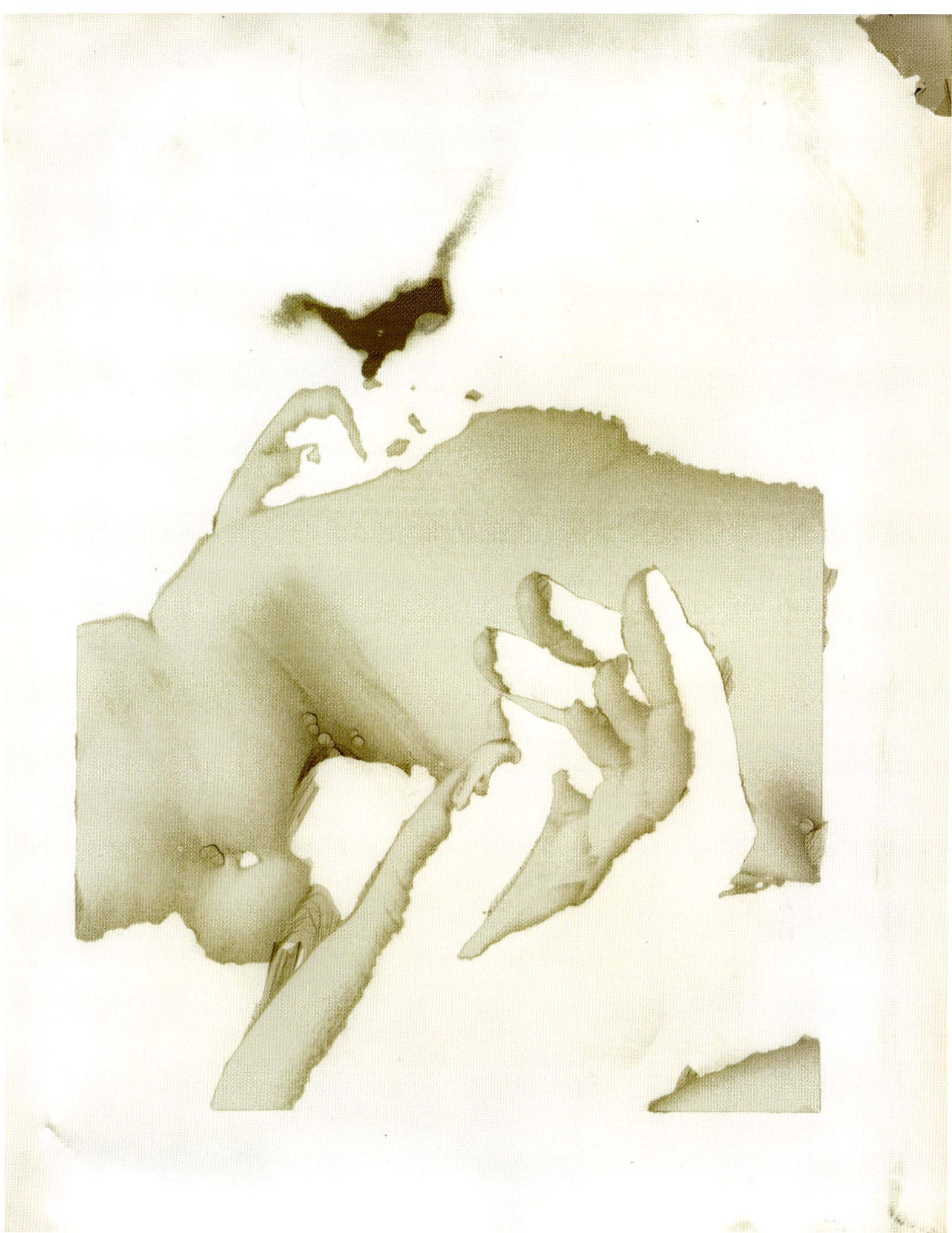

Cristóbal Pereira
Hand, mordançage on fibre-base
matt-finish paper, 25 × 20 cm
(9¾ × 7⅞ in.), 2013

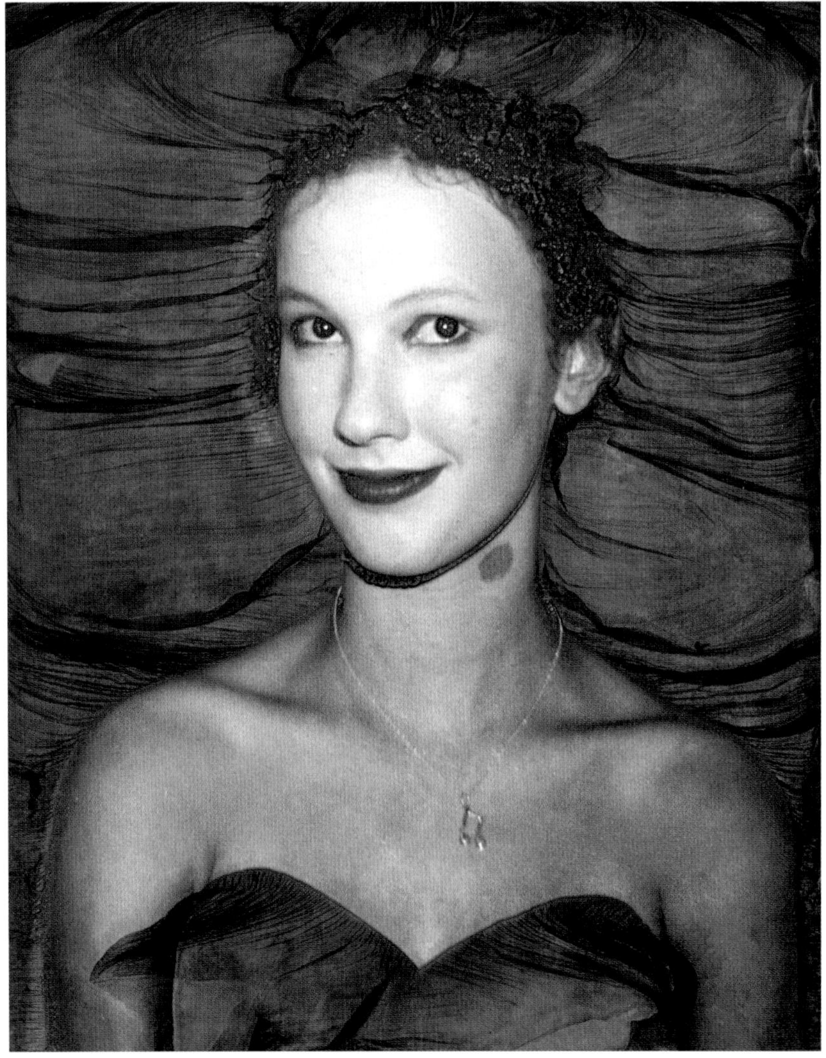

Spiffy Tumbleweed
Maddie, split sepia-toned
mordançage on fibre-base paper,
18 × 13 cm (7 × 5 in.), 2013

David Symonds
The Neophyte, sepia-toned
mordançage of bromide print,
225 × 175 cm (88½ × 68¾ in.),
2001–13
The three component images
(girl, Stonehenge and bird) were
taken over a ten-year period,
then montaged together and
rephotographed. A bromide print
was made and mordançaged,
followed by final toning with an
almost-spent sepia toner.

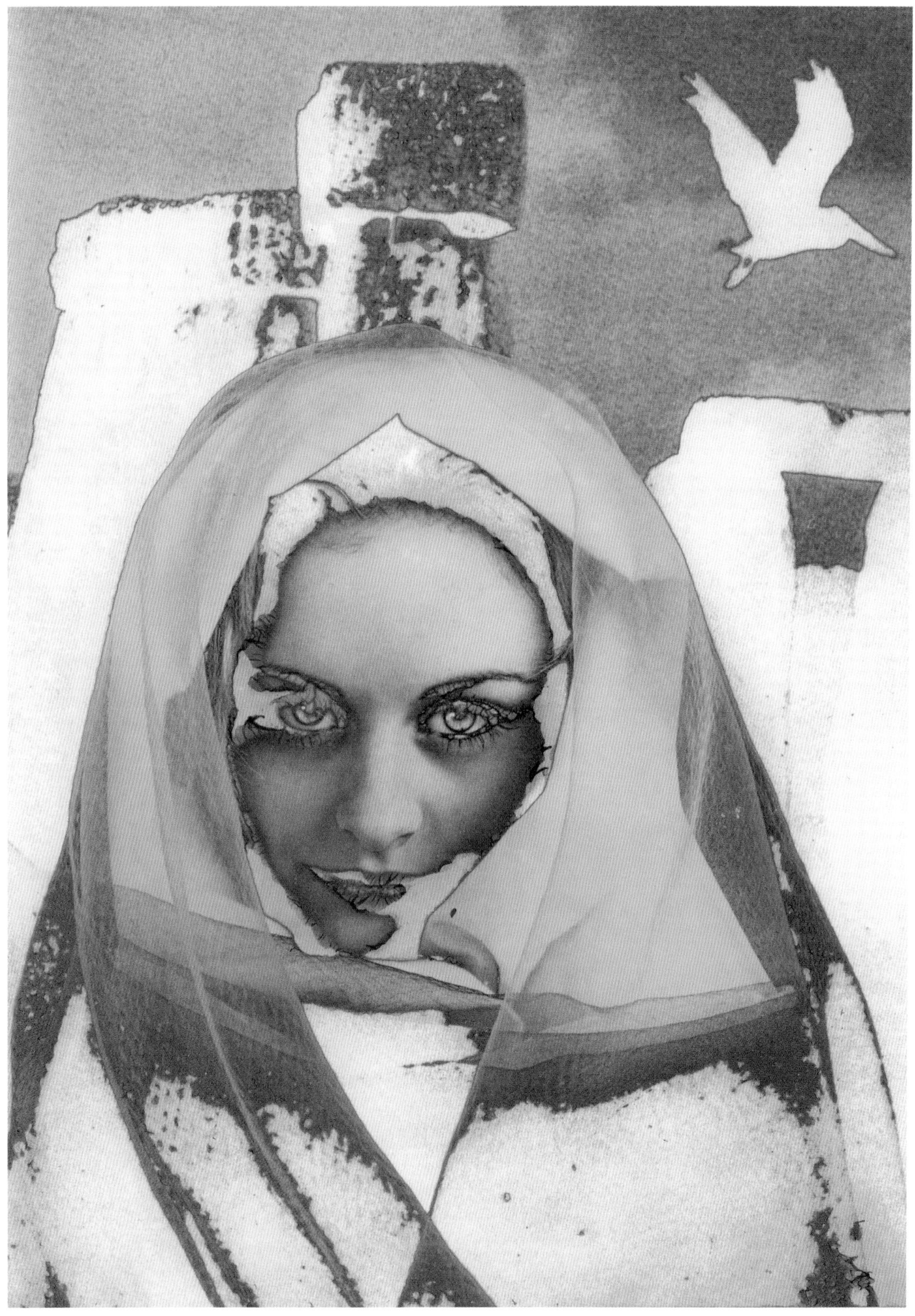

BROMOIL

Bromoil is an early photographic process that takes its name from the bromide papers and oil-based pigments involved. A black and white print on bromide paper is soaked in water, then bleached; finally, oil-based ink is applied manually in successive layers to reveal the image again. This works because the insoluble gelatin in the dark areas of the developed print does not swell in water, allowing it to absorb the oily ink, whereas the soluble gelatin in the lighter areas does swell, repelling the ink. Bromoil can be considered a mix of photography and painting: the final appearance of the print will depend on the brush type, the ink, and the photographer's technique – so no two prints are the same.

The bromoil process

What you need:

- ☐ black and white print on fibre-based bromide paper
- ☐ 50 ml 5% sulfuric acid ⚠
- ☐ 60 g copper (II) sulfate ⚠
- ☐ 60 g potassium bromide ⚠
- ☐ 5 g potassium dichromate ⚠
- ☐ 10% sodium thiosulfate ⚠
- ☐ distilled water
- ☐ black oil-based ink
- ☐ jug (1.5 l)
- ☐ scales
- ☐ blotting paper
- ☐ sheet of glass
- ☐ palette knife, plastic roller and brushes
- ☐ trays for processing

Cristóbal Pereira
Untitled, bromoil, 29 × 21 cm (11½ × 8¼ in.), 2013

SEE PAGES 226–29

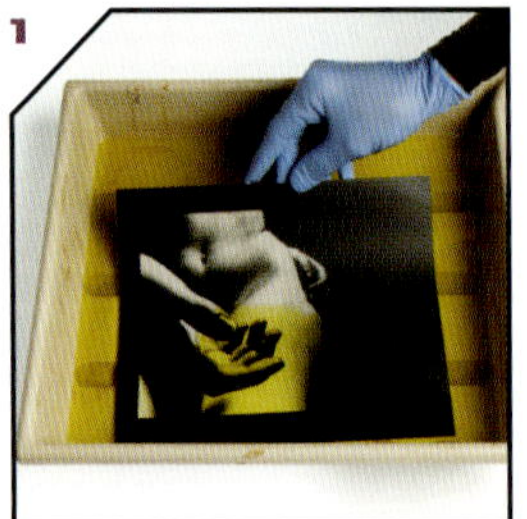
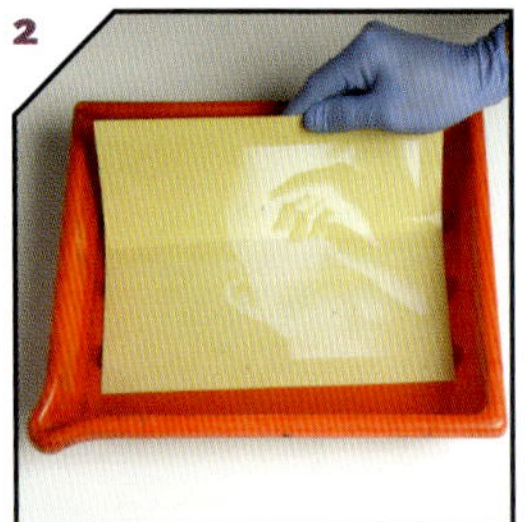
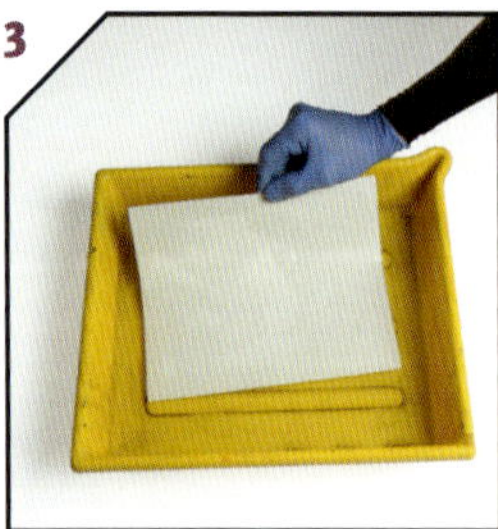

Printing the negative

The starting point for the bromoil process is a black and white print on fibre-based bromide paper. (Many modern papers do not work well for bromoil, as their coating impedes the swelling of soluble gelatine in water, so test beforehand.) Select a negative that is not too high in contrast, and expose it carefully, retaining detail in both highlights and shadows to compensate for the later loss of detail during the inking process.

Bleaching

1 Prepare a bleach-tanning solution using the following chemicals:

50 ml 5% sulfuric acid
60 g copper(II) sulfate
60 g potassium bromide
5 g potassium dichromate

Wearing full skin, eye and respiratory protection, mix acid and chemicals in a 1.5 l jug, then add distilled water to make 1 l of solution. Soak the print in water for 5 minutes, then place in the bleaching solution for 10 minutes. Keep rocking the bleach bath to ensure the print is bleached evenly; it should start to take on a pale yellow-green colour. The bleaching may appear to happen before 10 minutes, but keep the print in the bath for the full time.

Fixing

2 Rinse the print for 15 minutes, then fix it in a bath of 10% sodium thiosulfate solution for 5 minutes.

3 Wash the print for 20 minutes under running water and allow it to dry thoroughly. You now have a 'matrix', which is ready to be inked. A dry, fixed matrix can be kept for a long time before inking.

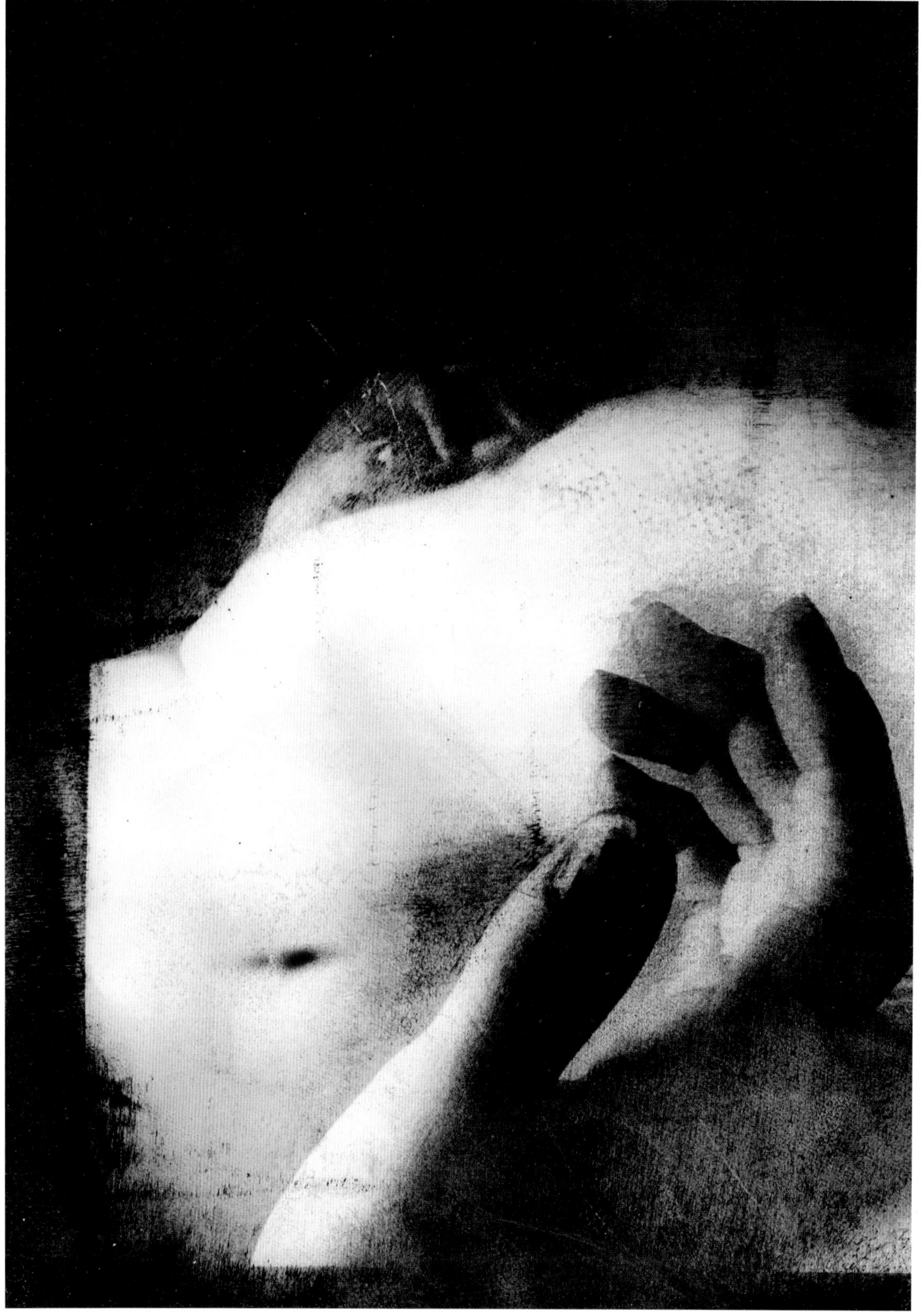

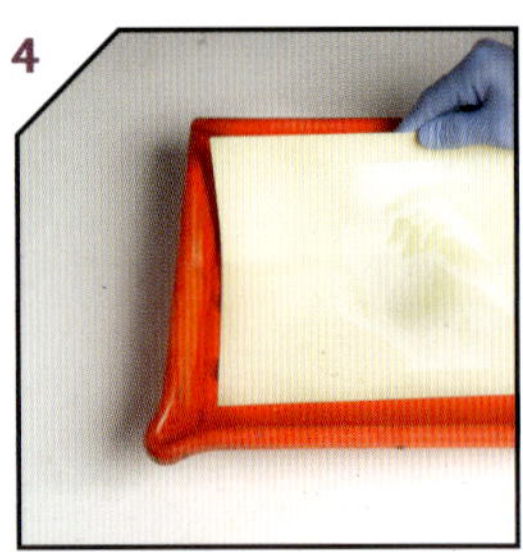 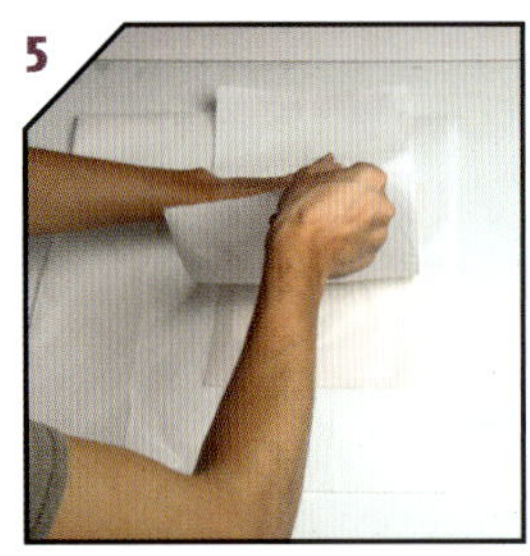 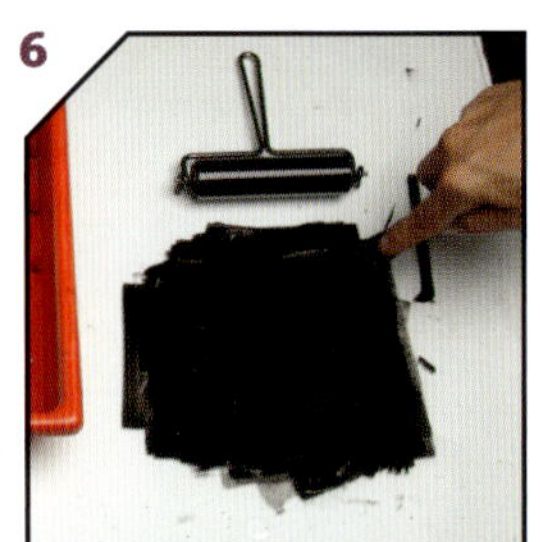 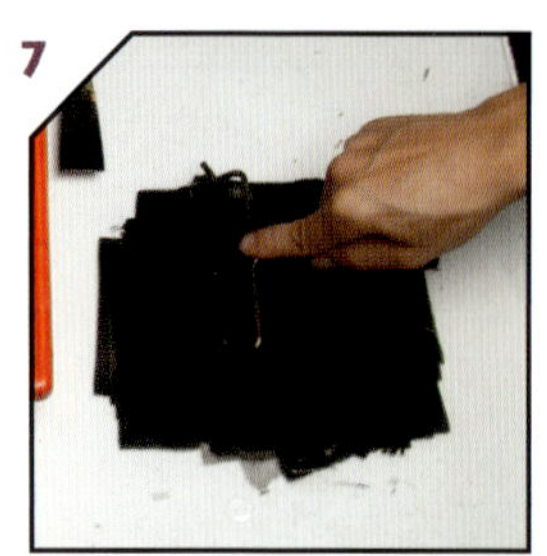

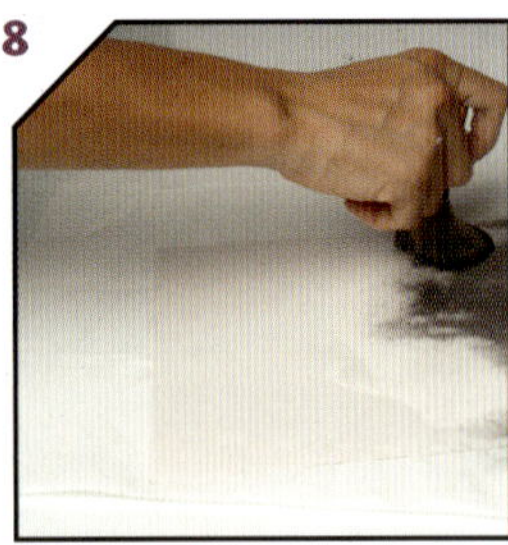 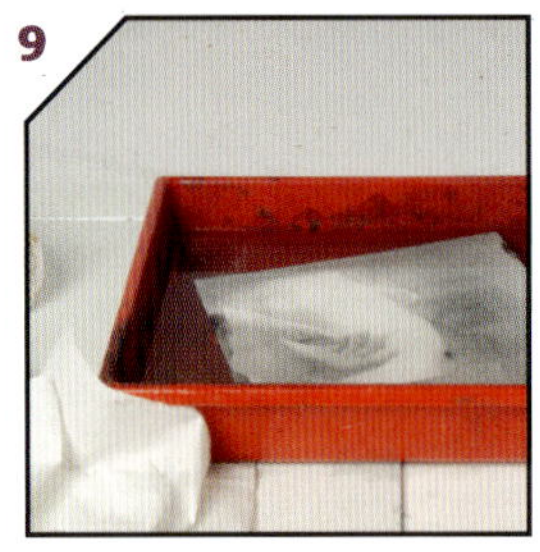 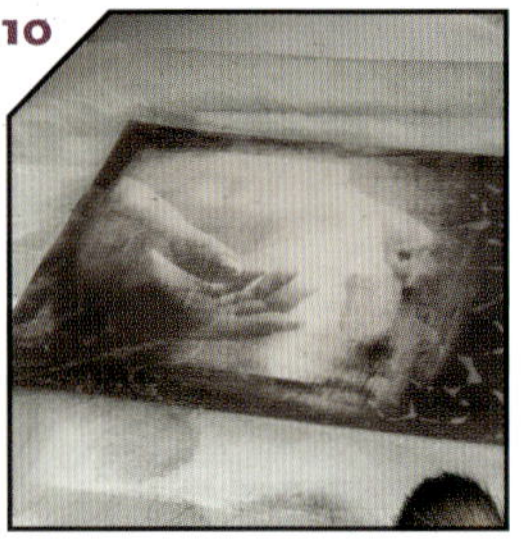 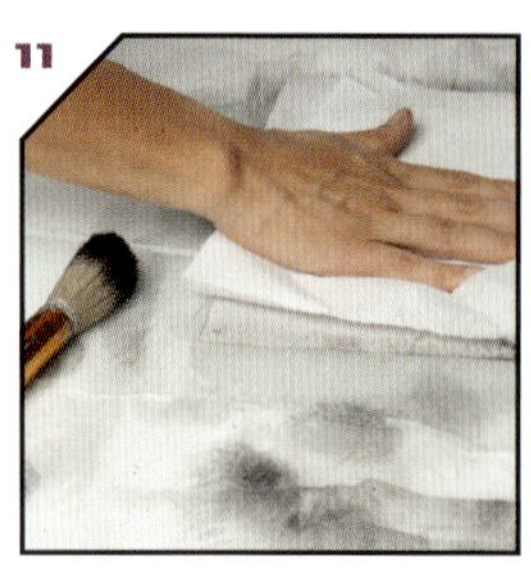

First inking

4 When you are ready to ink the matrix, soak it in water for about 3 minutes.

5 Lay the print between two sheets of blotting paper (or similar absorbent paper). It is important that there are no water droplets left on the print.

6 & 7 Put a very small amount of ink onto the sheet of glass. Spread the ink with a palette knife and then with a plastic roller, until you have created a very thin layer.

8 Load the brush with a small amount of ink and apply it to the print with a 'stippling' action until the print is well covered. Do not worry if the first coat does not reveal much of the image: the matrix should appear 'muddy', with the image faintly visible through the ink.

9 & 10 If the image is completely black after the first inking, don't worry – simply soak the print in a warm water bath (40–50°C, depending on the oiliness of the ink) or use a wet sponge brush to wipe some of the excess ink from the print.

Successive inkings

11 You can re-ink the matrix repeatedly to build up contrast. Shadow areas can be darkened by applying more ink, or you can lighten the highlights using a cotton wool pad soaked in water. Before each successive inking, be sure to dry the surface of the print, as outlined in Step 5. Once you are satisfed with the inking, allow the finished bromoil print to dry.

OPPOSITE
David Symonds
Riders in the Dust, bromoil,
28 × 20 cm (11 × 7⅞ in.), 1999

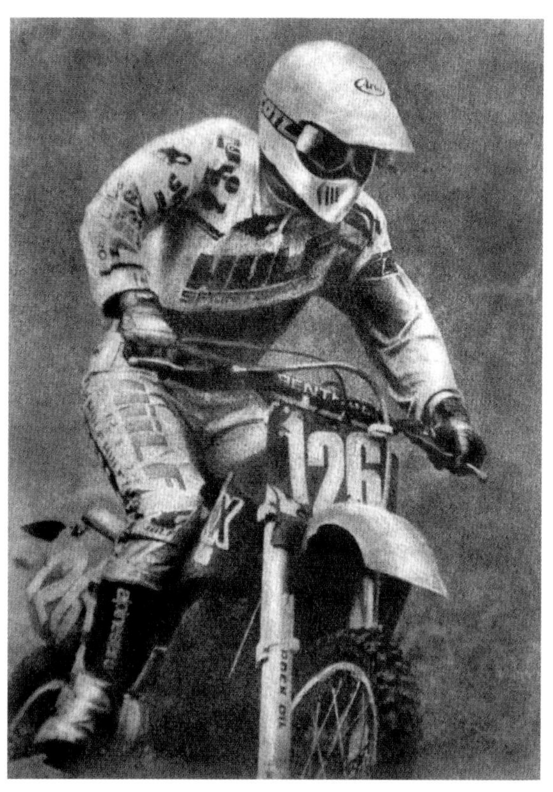

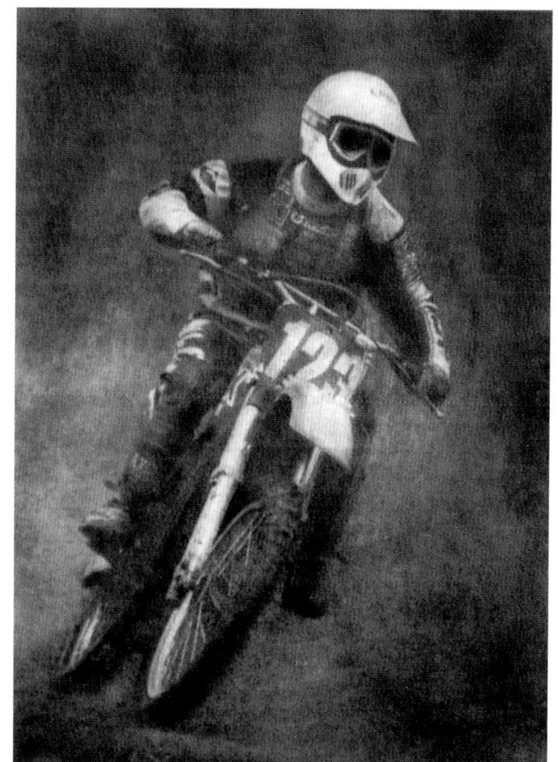

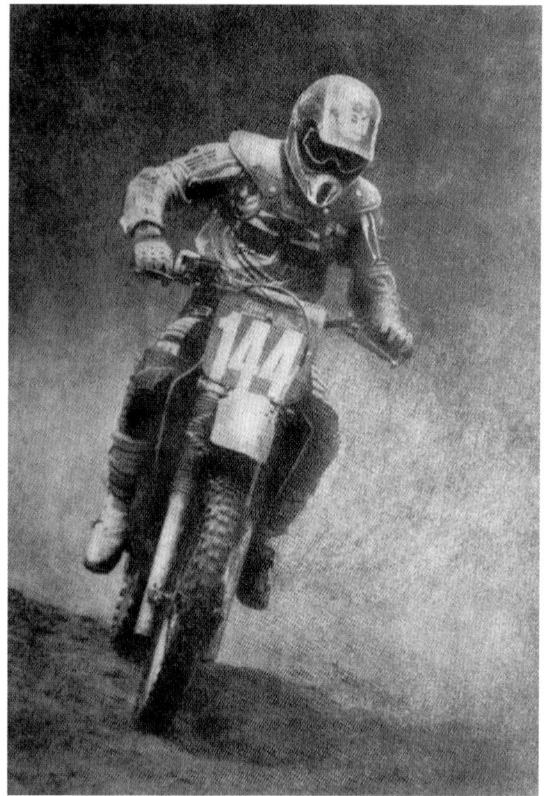

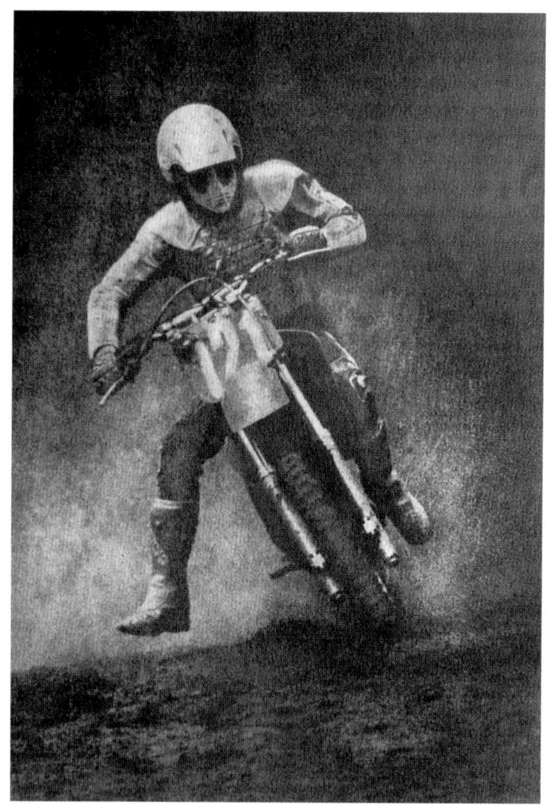

TRANSAQUATYPE

This is a quick and straightforward technique that is capable of transforming even an ordinary inkjet print into a unique, painterly image. The process is simple: a photograph is first printed on copier paper and then wet so that the image bleeds out through the back of the paper, producing dreamlike, washed-out colours and a watery texture. Art photographers can, however, use transaquatype to produce precise, nuanced effects by carefully controlling the amount of water and how it is applied. A related technique is used by artist Matthew Brandt (see interview overleaf), who immerses his finished C-prints in lake water, causing their colours to shift and bleed on the front of the paper.

The transaquatype process

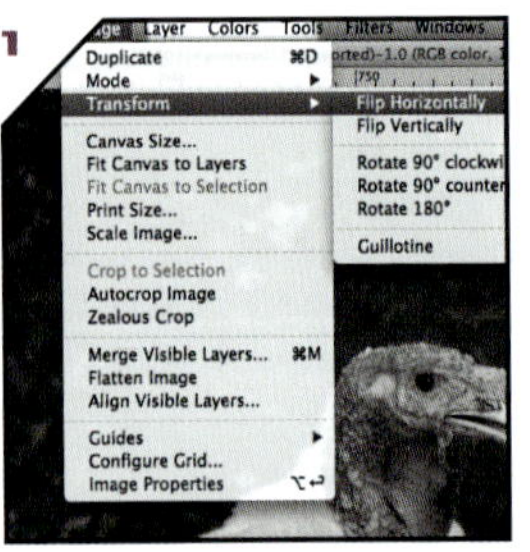

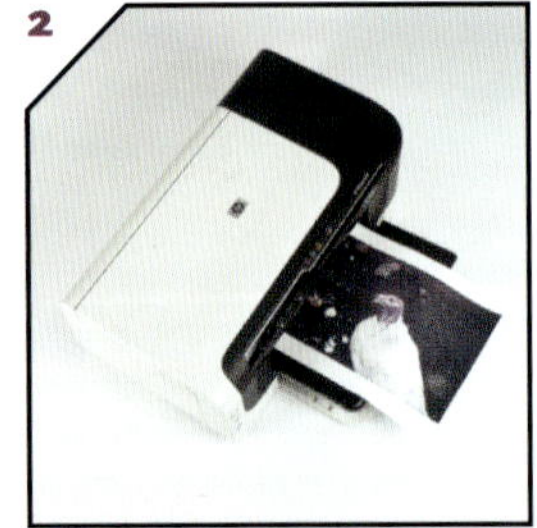

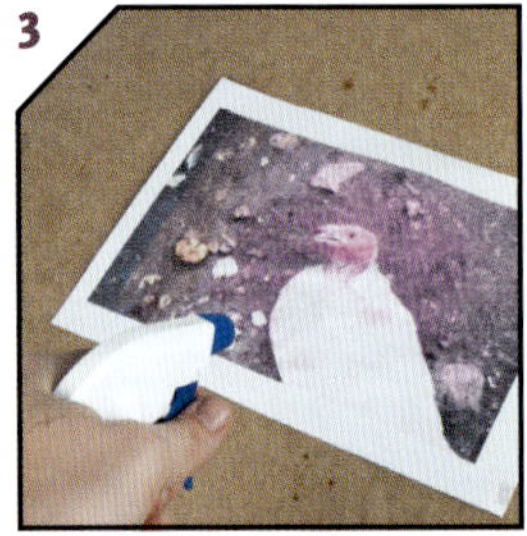

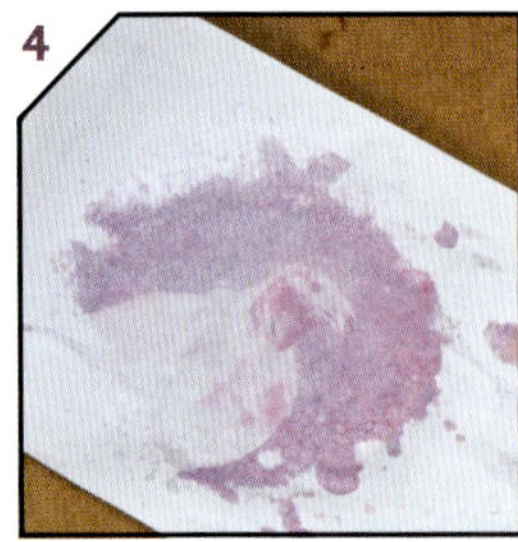

What you need:
- ☐ digital image
- ☐ computer with image-processing software
- ☐ inkjet printer
- ☐ 80–100 gsm paper
- ☐ water
- ☐ spray bottle
- ☐ paper towel or blotting paper

Prepare the print

1 Before you print your photograph, you may wish to flip it horizontally using image-processing software. This is because the final image will be reversed (as you will be viewing it through the back of the paper). Here, we used the freeware program GIMP: choose Transform > Flip Horizontally from the top menu bar.

2 Print your black-and-white or colour image onto 80–100 gsm paper – this is a common weight for photocopier stock. Your paper should not be any heavier than this or the water will settle on the surface of the print and smear the ink, rather than seeping through it.

Apply water to the print

3 Place the print image-side-up on a piece of paper towel or blotting paper. Wet the printed side with a spray bottle, checking periodically to see how much ink is seeping through to the back of the paper.

4 Stop spraying when the image on the reverse of the print attains the desired appearance. Then hang the transaquatype until it is dry.

Variations

There is ample room for experimentation: for example, spraying prints with a diluted alcohol or bleach solution will affect the colours of the print. Bleach will make all colours lighter; alcohol will make them flow and mix together.

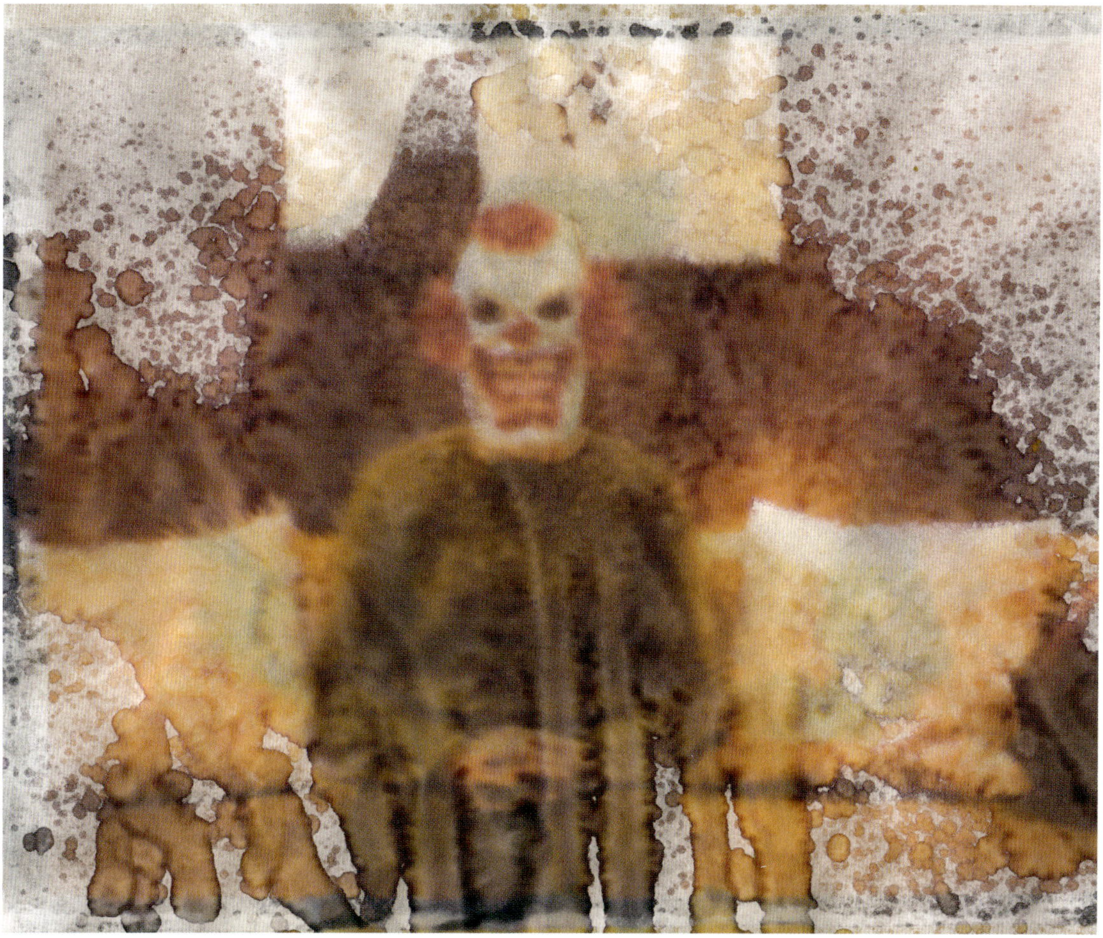

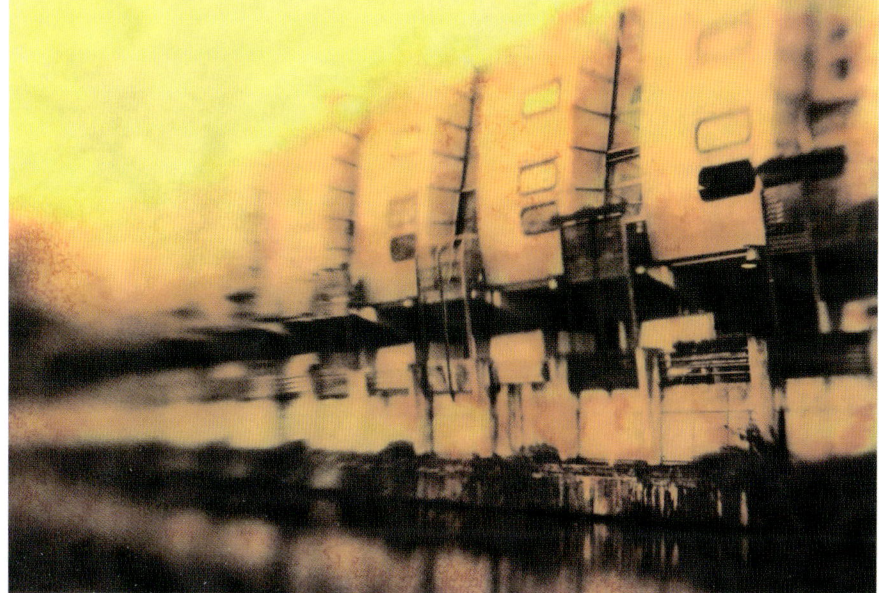

ABOVE
Daniel Meade
Untitled, transaquatype
on standard inkjet paper,
21 × 28 cm (8¼ × 11 in.),
2010

RIGHT
David McNamee
Buildingstransfront,
transaquatype on
standard inkjet paper,
21 × 28 cm (8¼ × 11 in.),
2012

MATTHEW BRANDT

*Interview by
Marco Antonini*

By using liquids, dust, foods or pigments found on-site to develop images and alter his finished prints, Los Angeles-based artist Matthew Brandt establishes an intimate relationship between the subject and the photograph.

I'm interested in your use of substances such as burnt wood, handmade paper, lake water, blood and tears. You seem to be interested in adding a further layer of realism to your image, something beyond the illusion of realism that can be conveyed via conventional photographic technique and materials.

I began incorporating a subject's actual material into the process of producing photographs when I moved back home to Los Angeles from New York and started graduate school at UCLA, studying photography. In order to have a good foundation in the medium, I took it upon myself to learn historical photographic technologies. I began by making salted-paper prints, which I thought had been the first photographic process. (I later learned that I was wrong, but it wasn't a bad place to start.) Now that I was back home in Los Angeles, I was spending time with friends and family who I hadn't seen in a long time, and making photographs while feeling very nostalgic. It made me think closely about the complications of representational photography. I have always been interested in the traces of things, both photographic and physical. I wanted to find some way to collaborate with the friends and family who I had missed, and it seemed logical to use their bodily fluids to produce their own photographic images chemically. It also lessened the burden of representation on me and left more of it up to the subjects themselves: the salted-paper printing process allowed their own chemistry to influence the final image. This idea of using the subject's own material to produce its image has sprung up in other ways in subsequent projects.

Coffee, chewing gum, barbecue sauce: a whole range of food products were used as pigments in the development or finishing processes for your early photographic series. Can you tell us something about the meaning of using food products in your work?

There are different circumstances for using food products in a work. In the project *Taste Tests*, the food/pigment combination stemmed from an interest in the touristic landscape photography of Yosemite National Park. It was a way of describing mainstream taste, in both food and photography. Everyone loves peanut butter and jelly just as everyone loves Yosemite landscape pictures. I printed the same image in different flavours: different strokes for different folks.

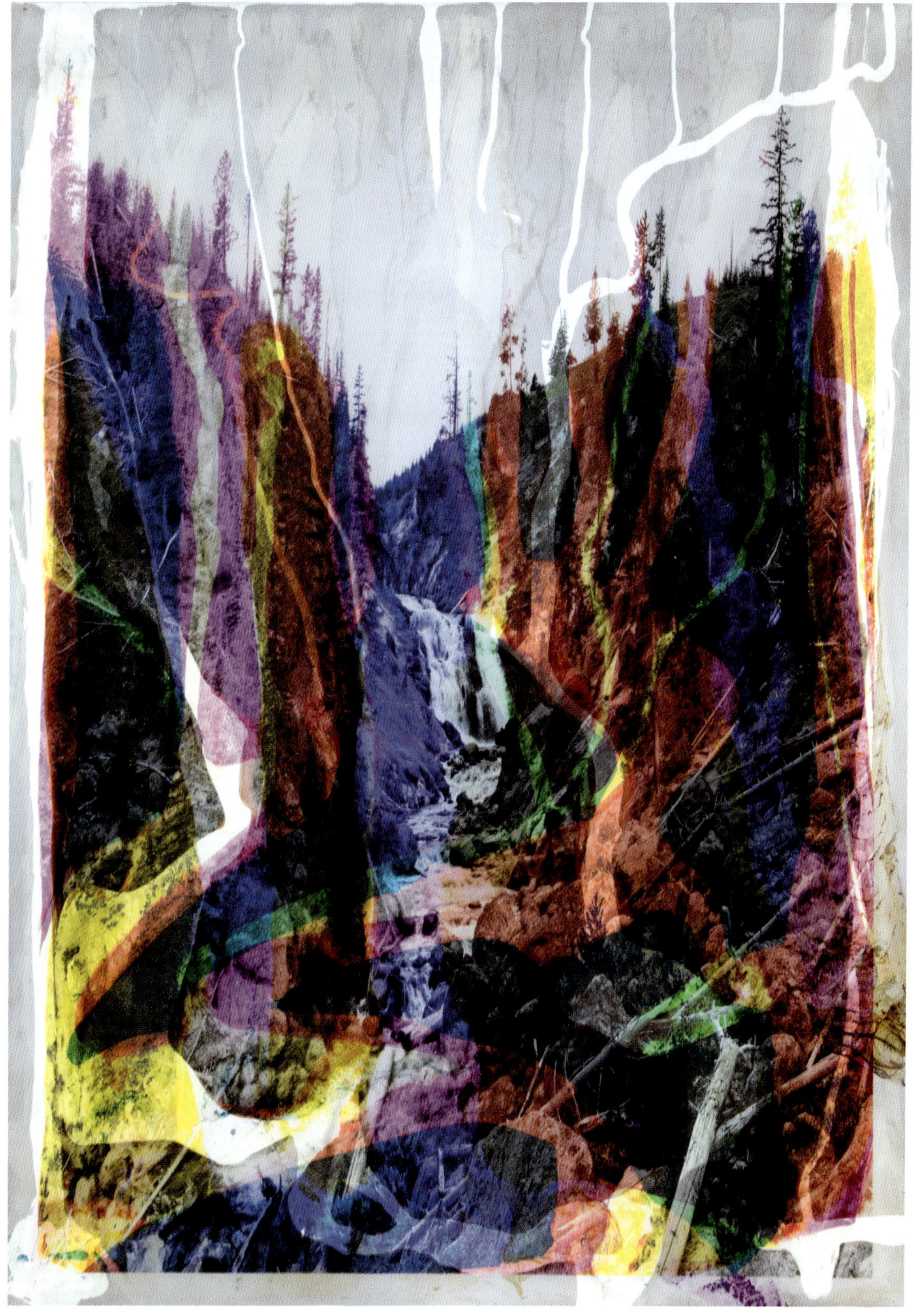

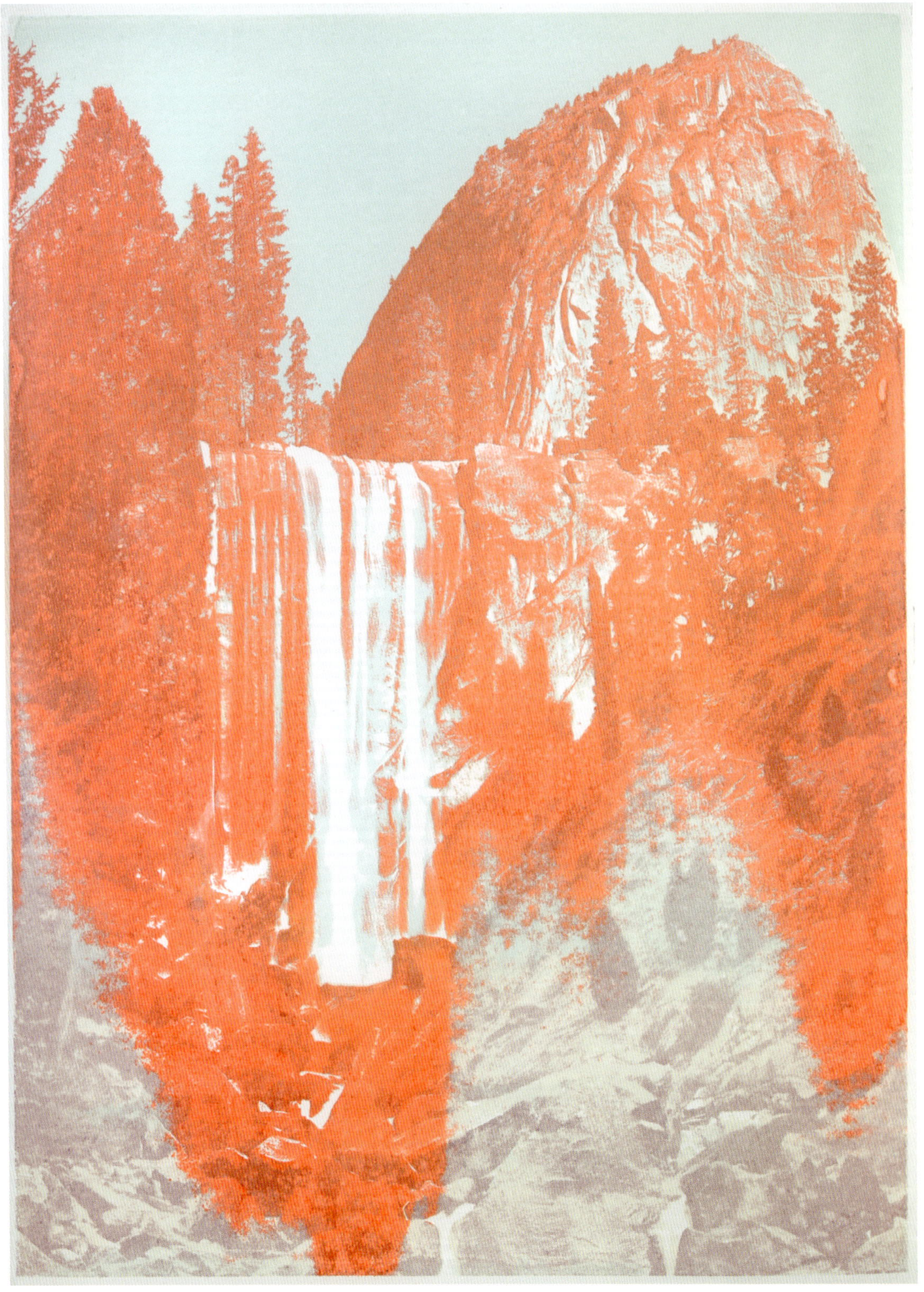

Food is a universal necessity with which we all have particular relationships, and I like this familiarity. When a food product is used as a material for making pictures, for me it carries a status equal to more conventional mediums like silver and gelatin.

Where did you find the materials for your Honeybees *series of gum bichromate prints made from emulsions of dead honeybees? Can you tell us a little bit about the story and motivations behind the project?*

It was during a time when CCD (Colony Collapse Disorder) was all over the media headlines. Honeybees were acting strange, and we didn't know why. I was on the beach in Santa Monica when I noticed hundreds of honeybees sprinkled along the shoreline. Most were dead; a few still in their last twitches. I was a witness to a very surreal moment, and I didn't have my camera. I ended up making a little makeshift box and collecting all the dead bees that I found along the shore. I kept them in that box for over a year before I made my first bee picture.

Your Lakes and Reservoirs *series plays a lot with an idea of controlled decay. Are the prints permanent in their final form? What chemical processes create such spectacular colour effects?*

Bees of Bees 1 (above; detail below) from the series *Honeybees*, gum-bichromate print with honeybees on paper, 152.4 × 254 cm (60 × 100 in.), 2012

Kool-Aid 1 from the series *Taste Tests in Colour*, silkscreen on paper with raspberry lemonade, tropical punch, lemonade and grape Kool-Aid, 101.6 × 76.2 cm (40 × 30 in.), 2012

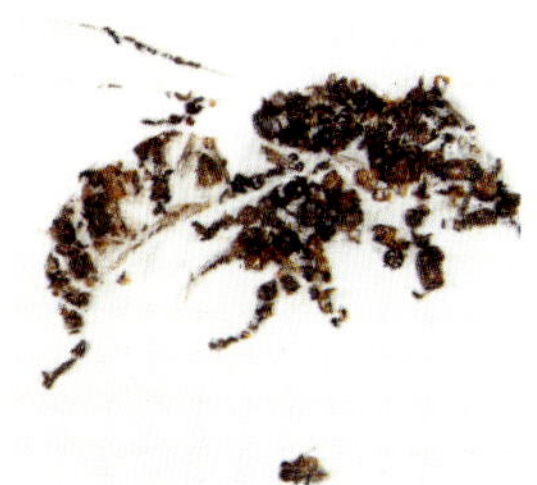

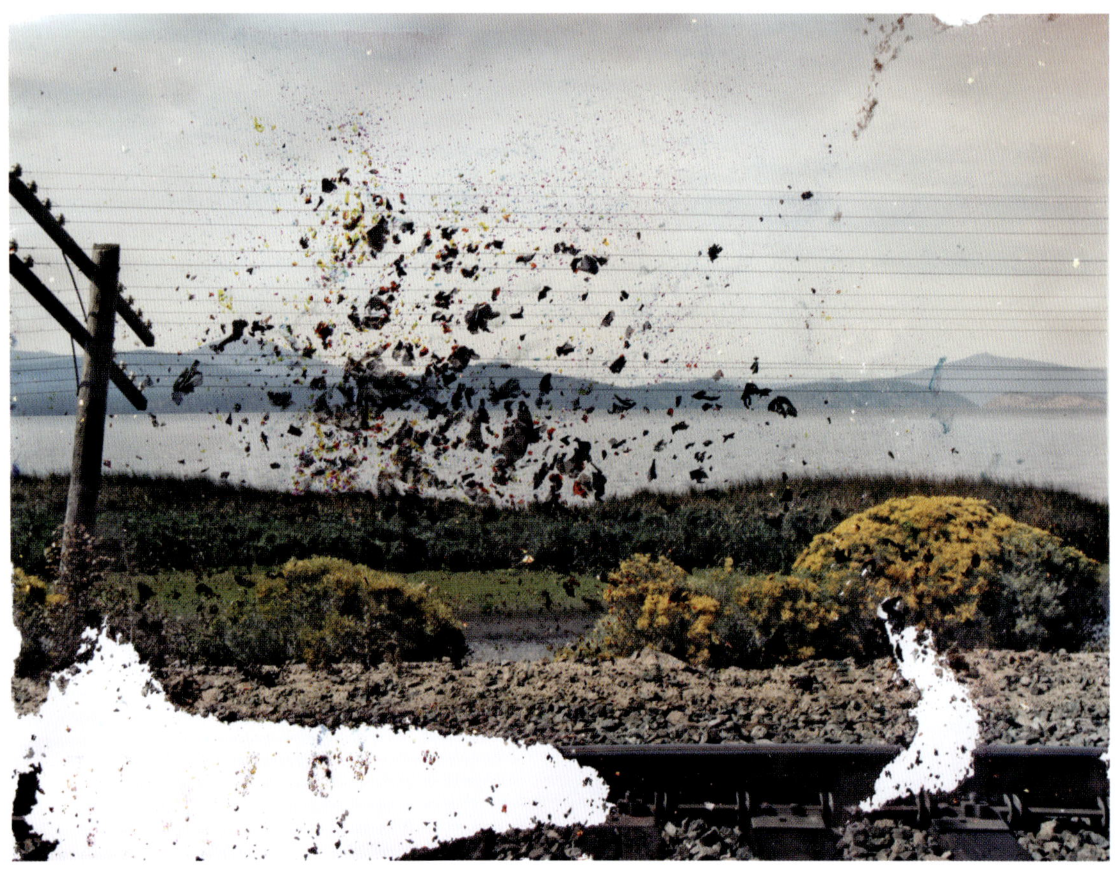

Klamath Lake, OR 2, from the series *Lakes and Reservoirs*, C-print soaked in Klamath Lake water, 76.2 × 101.6 cm (30 × 40 in.), 2009

They are as permanent as any normal colour C-print. They are just ordinary C-prints that have been soaked in the water of the lake or reservoir they depict. The main difference is that the water has rearranged the C-print's inherent colour emulsions. A normal C-print photograph is made up of multiple layers of photosensitive colour emulsions on paper: blue, red and yellow. When the paper is soaked in water, these colours inevitably shift and mix.

Does that process happen in the studio or on location?

It all happens in the studio. I bring back the water from every lake or reservoir that I visit.

Lake Jennings, CA 2, from the series *Lakes and Reservoirs,* C-print soaked in Lake Jennings water, 116.8 × 162.6 cm (46 × 64 in.), 2012

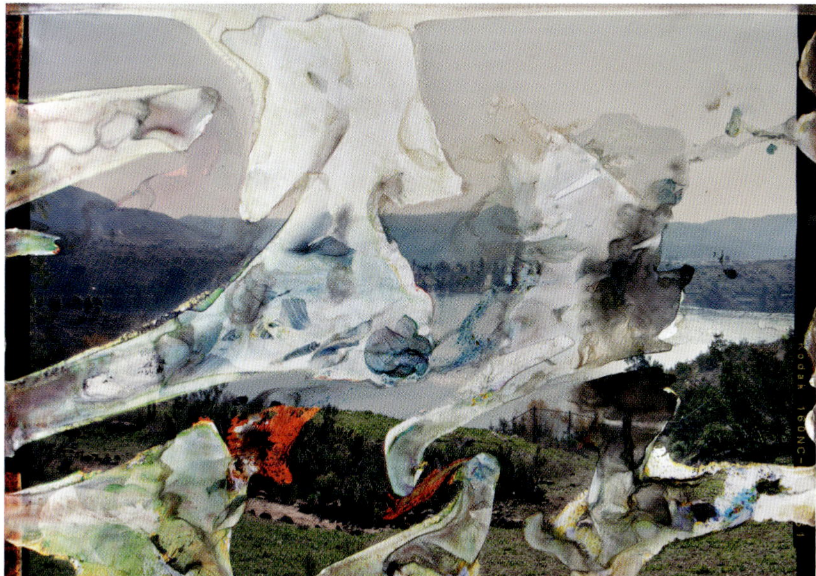

Lewis Lake, WY 2, from the series *Lakes and Reservoirs,* C-print soaked in Lewis Lake water, 76.2 × 101.6 cm (30 × 40 in.), 2012

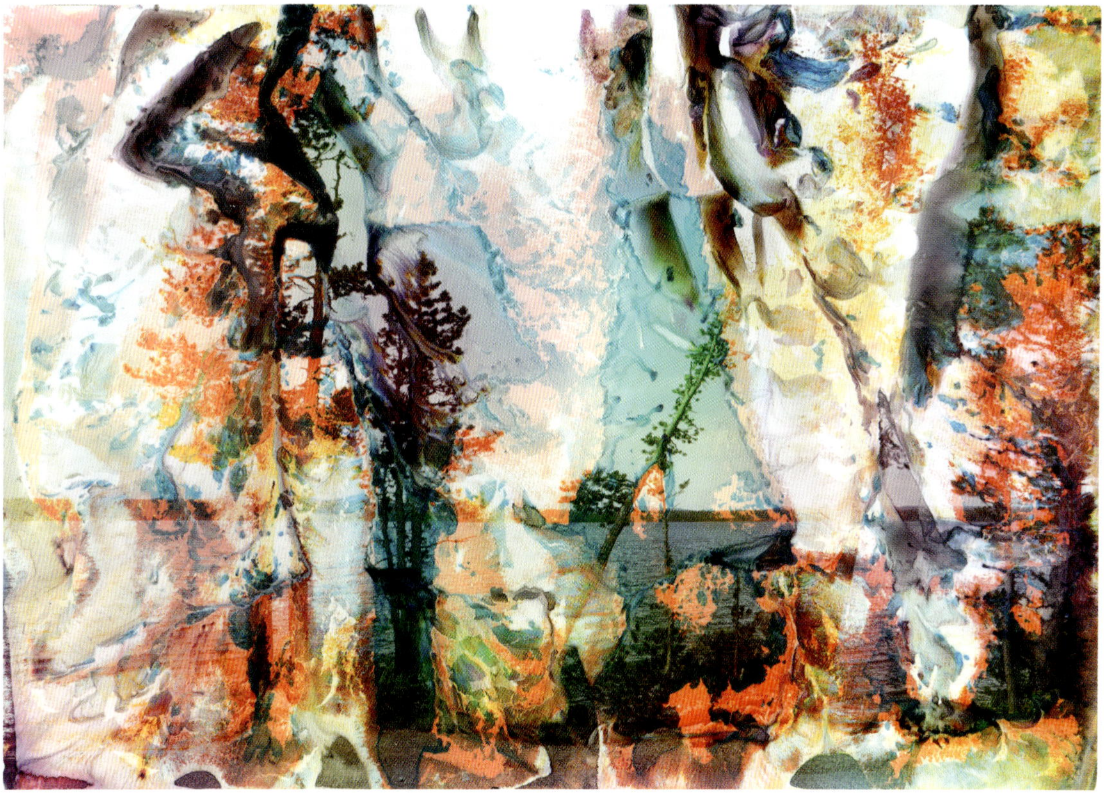

Chemical Safety Information

General precautions

Whenever you work with chemicals you need to be aware of the hazards and safety measures associated with them. The safety information provided in this book is only a starting point and does not supersede the manufacturer's safety instructions, which you should consult in all circumstances before beginning work. It is always recommended that you wear protective gloves, goggles and a lab coat (or similar form of protective clothing) as basic precautions. Additional protective measures may be necessary depending on the chemicals involved.

acetic acid

CH_3CO_2H

Acetic acid (also called *ethanoic acid* or, in its undiluted form, *glacial acetic acid*) is a colourless liquid, categorized as a 'weak' acid. (White vinegar, as used in food, is a very mild form of acetic acid.) Avoid contact with skin and eyes and work in a well-ventilated area. Note that acetic acid can penetrate latex gloves, so nitrile rubber gloves are recommended.

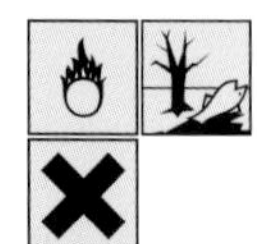

ammonia (household solution)

NH_4OH

Ammonia in pure form (NH_3) is a flammable gas that may explode if heated, cause severe skin burns and eye damage and is toxic if inhaled. In photography, only the diluted form sold as a household cleaning product (*dilute ammonium hydroxide*) is used, typically diluted further with water as a 5–10% solution for bleaching prints (see pp. 208–9). Even in this dilute form it should be used in a well-ventilated area, with full protective clothing (gloves, goggles and lab coat), and disposed of with care, as it is also highly toxic to aquatic life.

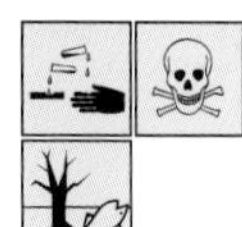

ammonium chloride

NH_4Cl

Ammonium chloride (also called *sal ammoniac*) is a white, crystalline salt compound, widely used in fertilizers, medicines, batteries and as a food additive, among other applications. In the context of this book, it is used in the albumen printing process (see p. 162), although table salt or sea salt can be used in its place. In pure form it is a potential irritant; basic skin and eye protection will suffice.

ammonium thiosulfate

$H_8N_2O_3S_2$

Ammonium thiosulfate comes in a white crystal form and is typically used in photographic fixer. Fixers made using ammonium thiosulfate work faster than formulas that rely on sodium thiosulfate, but a print fixed for too long in an ammonium thiosulfate solution may start to bleach (depending on the paper being used). Ammonium thiosulfate is a potential irritant – basic skin and eye protection will suffice.

ascorbic acid (vitamin C)

$C_6H_8O_6$

Ascorbic acid (also referred to as *L-ascorbic acid*) is perhaps better known as *Vitamin C*, which is one of the main ingredients in Caffenol developer (see p. 130). The crystalline form used for Caffenol developer is white to slightly yellow in colour and in pure form poses a mild irritation hazard to eyes and skin.

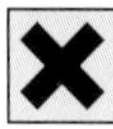

cadmium bromide

$CdBr_2$

Cadmium bromide is a highly toxic cream-coloured crystalline salt used in the wet-plate collodion process (see p. 190). Good ventilation and a face mask are essential, as inhaling the dust or fumes is extremely harmful and signs of exposure, which include flu-like symptoms and pulmonary edema, can be subtle initially. It is also a skin and eye irritant, so wear protective goggles, gloves and clothing. Cadmium bromide is a known carcinogen that may cause cancer at high concentrations or with repeated exposure.

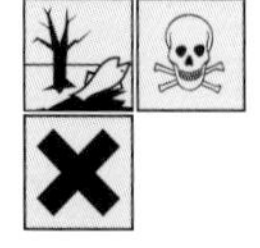

citric acid

$C_6H_8O_7$

Citric acid, another form of *Vitamin C*, is a weak, naturally occurring acid found in a variety of fruits and vegetables, although millions of tonnes a year are now made synthetically using fermentation. As with its fruit-based counterpart, the white crystalline powder can cause eye irritation – if this happens, rinse your eyes immediately with cold water. Citric acid is used in the Vandyke printing process.

copper(II) chloride

$CuCl_2$

Copper(II) chloride is a key ingredient in the mordançage process (see p. 210). It is a light brown powder when it is anhydrous (with all water removed), turning blue-green in colour when it is in a hydrated state. Copper(II) chloride is irritating to eyes, skin and the respiratory system, as well as being very toxic to aquatic organisms: wear protective clothing (including a face mask) and dispose of carefully.

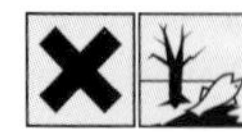

Key to hazard symbols

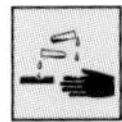 Corrosive

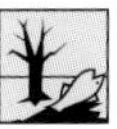 Hazardous to the environment

 Toxic

 Flammable

 Irritant

---

copper(II) sulfate

$CuSO_4$

Copper(II) sulfate (also known as *cupric sulfate*) is a pale grey powder (in its anhydrous form), and one of the ingredients of the bromoil bleach-tanning solution (see p. 214). It is particularly irritating to eyes (less so to skin), and very toxic to aquatic life: the effects on the latter can be long lasting, so care should be taken when disposing of the chemical and its packaging.

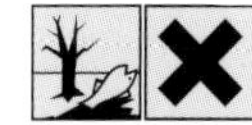

disodium phosphate

Na_2HPO_4

Disodium phosphate is most commonly used as a food additive, but this white, granular or crystalline compound can also be used to bleach cyanotype prints, typically by diluting it to make a 15% solution (see p. 207). Disodium phosphate is irritating to eyes, skin and the respiratory system, so protective clothing and a face mask are recommended.

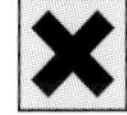

distilled water

H_2O

Distilled water is not a chemical, but it is recommended for many of the printing processes in this book because the distillation process removes residual minerals and chemicals from the water that could otherwise degrade prints over time. As this is 'pure' water, it poses few hazards.

ethyl alcohol

C_2H_6O

Ethyl alcohol (also known as *ethanol*, *grain alcohol* or simply *alcohol*) is essentially the same ingredient that you would find in an alcoholic beverage or sold as rubbing alcohol or surgical spirits. In photography, this colourless liquid is usually employed in a denatured (not for consumption!) form as a solvent to aid chemical mixing. It is highly flammable (both the liquid and its vapour), so do not use around sources of ignition.

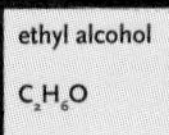

ethyl ether

$(C_2H_5)_2O$

Ethyl ether (or *ether*) is a clear, highly volatile liquid that needs to be handled with care. Not only is it extremely flammable, but it is also toxic through inhalation, contact with the skin or if swallowed. Overexposure can result in blindness or even death, depending on the concentration. As with ethyl alcohol (above), its use in this book is as a solvent, specifically in the wet-plate collodion process (see p. 190).

ferric ammonium citrate

$C_6H_{5+4}Fe_xN_yO_7$

Ferric ammonium citrate (also called *ammonium ferric citrate*, *ammonium iron(III) citrate*, and *ferric ammonium citrate*) is a primary ingredient in both of John Herschel's iron-based printing processes: cyanotype and Vandyke. As the green or red-brown powder can irritate eyes, skin and the respiratory system, a face mask is recommended in addition to basic protective clothing.

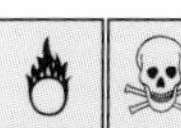

ferrous sulfate

$FeSO_4$

Ferrous sulfate (or *iron(II) sulfate*) is commonly seen as blue-green crystals, which are included in the developer formula for the wet-plate collodion process (see p. 190). It may cause skin irritation and serious eye irritation, so gloves and goggles are essential.

hydrogen peroxide

H_2O_2

Hydrogen peroxide is a clear, colourless liquid, commonly used in bleaching products, especially for hair. It is used in the bleaching solution for the mordançage process (see p. 210). Hydrogen peroxide is corrosive at high concentration and can cause skin irritation and serious eye damage, so standard protective clothing, including gloves and goggles, is recommended. If swallowed, it can cause severe chemical burns internally.

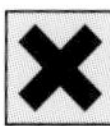 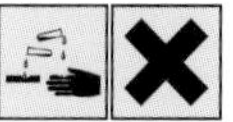

isopropyl alcohol

C_3H_8O

Isopropyl alcohol (aka *2-propanol*, *sec-propyl alcohol*, *IPA*, *isopropanol*, or *isopropyl alcohol*) is a strong-smelling, colourless, highly flammable liquid. It is used in the hardening solution that is applied when double coating paper for albumen printing (see p. 162). The liquid is a serious irritant to eyes, while the fumes can cause dizziness or drowsiness, so wear goggles and work in a well-ventilated area away from sources of ignition.

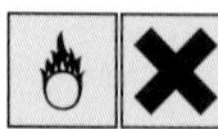

potassium bromide

KBr

Potassium bromide has a long history of use as an anticonvulsant in the treatment of epilepsy, but this ionic salt is also used in numerous photographic formulae (bromoil, some wet-plate collodion recipies, Farmer's reducer, and Caffenol developers, to name a few). As well as being a skin and eye irritant, the dust can also cause respiratory irritation, so a face mask is recommended.

potassium citrate

$KH_2C_6H_5O_7$

Potassium citrate (or *citric acid monopotassium salt*) can be added to the salting/sizing solution of salt prints (see p. 156) to increase print density and give a stronger reddish tone. The white, crystalline powder is not defined as hazardous, although standard safety precautions (gloves, goggles and lab coat) are still advisable.

potassium dichromate

$K_2Cr_2O_7$

Potassium dichromate (also known as *potassium bichromate*) is an extremely toxic and hazardous red-orange salt used in gum printing. It can prove fatal if inhaled. It is a known carcinogen, and may also damage fertility, cause genetic defects, or damage organs through repeated exposure. Contact with skin or eyes may result in severe burns. Respiratory, skin and eye protection and good ventilation are essential. Although not itself flammable, it is an oxidizer that will intensify the burning of other substances, so avoid sources of ignition.

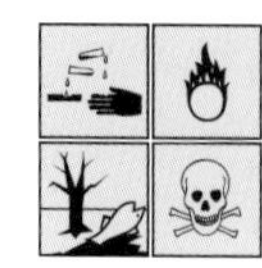

potassium disulfite

$K_2S_2O_5$

Potassium disulfite (also called *potassium metabisulfite* and *potassium pyrosulfite*) is a white powder that can be used to remove the orange stain left by potassium dichromate in the gum printing process (see p. 168). Potassium disulfite is corrosive, so care should be taken to avoid it coming into contact with skin and especially eyes, as the latter can lead to serious damage. Contact with acids releases a toxic gas.

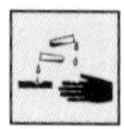

potassium ferricyanide

$C_6N_6FeK_3$

Potassium ferricyanide (or *red prussiate*) is a key ingredient in Farmer's reducer (see p. 208) and also in the cyanotype process (see p. 136). Although the powder is bright red in colour, it reacts with ferrous ions (such as ferric ammonium citrate) to create Prussian blue. Although potassium ferricyanide is not itself listed as 'hazardous', extreme care should be taken to avoid mixing it with acids, as this can release a highly toxic gas.

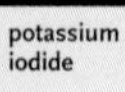

potassium iodide

KI

Potassium iodide is a white salt that is used in numerous photographic processes. When mixed with silver nitrate it produces photosensitive silver iodide, which is one of the cornerstones of photography (see wet-plate collodion process, p. 190). It is both an irritant (to skin and eyes) and harmful if swallowed at high concentrations.

silver nitrate

AgNO$_3$

Silver nitrate is used in creating light-sensitive silver halides, which, combined with gelatin, can be used to coat film, glass plates or other substrates to make them photosensitive. It can cause severe skin burns and eye damage, so protective eyewear, gloves and clothing must be worn. It is also highly toxic to aquatic life, so follow instructions for proper disposal. Avoid proximity to combustible substances, since as an oxidizer it can intensify fire.

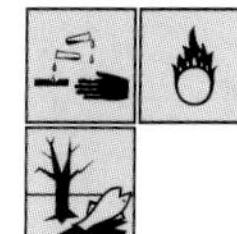

silver(I) oxide

Ag$_2$O

Silver(I) oxide is used in powdered form as part of the argyrotype sensitizing solution (see p. 152). As with silver nitrate (above), it is a strong oxidizer, so should be kept away from combustible substances and sources of ignition. It can also cause serious eye damage, so goggles are essential. Silver(I) oxide needs to be disposed of carefully to prevent it entering the water system, as it is very toxic to aquatic life, with long-lasting effects.

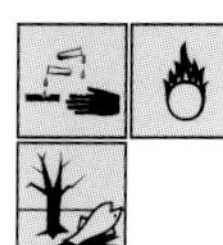

sodium carbonate

Na$_2$CO$_3$

Sodium carbonate (also known as *calcined soda, carbonic acid disodium salt* or *soda ash*) is one of the main ingredients in many Caffenol developer recipes (see p. 130). In this context it is often referred to as *soda crystals* or *washing soda*, as these interchangeable cleaning products are simply sodium carbonate in another guise. Avoid getting the white powder in the eyes, as it is an irritant.

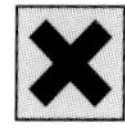

sodium thiosulfate

Na$_2$S$_2$O$_3$

Sodium thiosulfate is widely used as a photographic fixer for both film and paper, and is commonly referred to colloquially as 'Hypo' (from its original name – hyposulfite of soda). It is not regarded as hazardous, but basic safety precautions should still be observed.

sulfamic acid

NH$_2$SO$_3$H

Sulfamic acid (or *amidosulfonic acid*) is one of the ingredients used to make an argyrotype sensitizing solution (see p. 152). The white crystalline compound is an irritant to both skin and eyes, requiring gloves and goggles, and careful disposal is also needed as it is harmful to aquatic life.

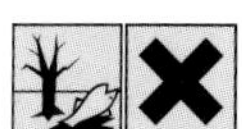

sulfuric acid

H$_2$SO$_4$

Sulfuric acid is usually encountered as a clear liquid, which is highly corrosive and capable of causing severe burns to skin, as well as serious eye damage. It is harmful to aquatic life as well, so disposal needs to be done with care. It is not used excessively in photography, but does form part of the bleach-tanning solution for the bromoil printing process (see p. 214).

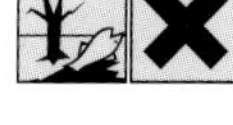

trisodium citrate

Na$_3$C$_6$H$_5$O$_7$

Trisodium citrate (also referred to as *citric acid monosodium salt, sodium citrate monobasic* or *sodium dihydrogencitrate*) can be used as an alternative to potassium citrate in the salt-printing process (see p. 156), to achieve the same result – i.e. increase print density and the reddish colour of the image. As with potassium citrate, it is not defined as hazardous.

FURTHER READING

Anderson, Christina Z., *Experimental Photography Workbook*, Stockholm: AlternativePhotography.com, 2012

The Barnet Book of Photography, London: Elliott & Son, 1898

Barnier, John, *Coming into Focus: A Step-by-Step Guide to Alternative Photographic Printing Processes*, San Francisco: Chronicle Books, 2000

Blacklow, Laura, *New Dimensions in Photo Processes: A Step by Step Manual for Alternative Techniques*, 4th ed., St Louis: Focal Press, 2007

Burkholder, Dan, *The New Inkjet Negative Companion: Digital Negatives Made Easy*, Palenville, NY: Dan Burkholder Photography, 2013 (DVD with printable PDF)

The Caffenol Cookbook & Bible, with contributions from Reinhold G, Mike Overs, Eirik Russell Roberts, John Nanian, Jon Caradies, Gerald Figal, Martin Woll, Dirk Essl and Bo Sibbern-Larsen, Community Spirit Publications, 2012, available at: http://www.caffenol-cookbook.com (accessed 20 August 2014)

Coe, Brian, *A Guide to Early Photographic Processes*, London: Victoria & Albert Museum, 1984

Cowley Malley, Abraham, *Micro-Photography*, London: H.K. Lewis, 1883

Davis, Frederick C., *Making Your Camera Pay*, New York: Robert McBride & Co., 1922

Duchochois, Paul C., *Photographic Reproduction Processes*, New York: The Scovill & Adams Company, 1891

Enfield, Jill, *Photo Imaging: A Complete Visual Guide to Alternative Techniques and Processes*, New York: Amphoto Books, 2002

Eshbaugh, Mark, *Alternative Photography Processes*, Stockholm: AlternativePhotography.com, 2012

Fabbri, Malin, *Anthotypes*, Stockholm: AlternativePhotography.com, 2006

Fabbri, Malin and Gary Fabbri, *Blueprint to Cyanotypes*, Stockholm: AlternativePhotography.com, 2006

Farber, Richard, *Historic Photographic Processes*, New York: Allworth Press, 1998

Fox Talbot, William Henry, *The Pencil of Nature*, London: Longman, Brown, Green & Longmans, 1844

Frontiers of Photography, New York: Time Life, 1972

Greene, Alan, *Primitive Photography: A Guide to Making Cameras, Lenses and Calotypes*, St Louis, MO: Focal Press, 2001

Hewitt, Barbara, *Blueprints on Fabric: Innovative Uses for Cyanotype*, Ft Collins, CO: Interweave Press, 1995

Horning, Beth, 'Radically Recycled Cameras', *Technology Review Magazine*, Cambridge, MA: MIT Press, August 1990

Hinkel, Brad and Ron Reeder, *Digital Negatives: Using Photoshop to Create Digital Negatives for Silver and Alternative Process Printing*, London: Focal Press, 2006

James, Christopher, *The Book of Alternative Photographic Processes*, 2nd ed. Clifton Park, NY: Delmar Cengage Learning, 2008

Keuren, Sarah Van, *A Non-Silver Manual*, 3rd ed., 2004 (self published)

Koenig, Karl, *Gumoil Photographic Printing*, St Louis, MO: Focal Press, 1999

Langford, Michael, *The Darkroom Handbook*, London: Dorling Kindersley, 1981

Nelson, Mike, *Precision Digital Negatives for Silver & Other Alternative Photographic Processes*, 2009 (self published)

Oelbaum, Zeva, *The Natural World in Cyanotype Photos*, New York: Rizzoli, 2002

Reeder, Ron, *Digital Negatives for Palladium and Other Alternative Processes*, 2010 (self published)

Rexer, Lyle, *Photography's Antiquarian Avant-Garde: The New Wave in Old Processes*,New York: Harvey N. Abrams, 2002

Sanderson, Andrew, *Handcolouring and Alternative Darkroom Processes*, Hove: Rotovision Books, 2002

Schewe, Jeff, *The Digital Negative: Raw Image Processing in Lightroom, Camera Raw, and Photoshop*, San Francisco: Peachpit Press, 2009

Scopick, David, *The Gum Bichromate Book: Non-Silver Methods for Photographic Printmaking*, St Louis, MO: Focal Press, 1991

Spence, Ray and Tony Worobiec, *Beyond Monochrome: A Fine Art Printing Workshop*, Minneapolis: Voyageur Press, 2000

Sutton, Thomas, *A Treatise on the Positive Collodion Process*, London: Bland & Long, 1857

Van Monckhoven, Désiré, *A Popular Treatise of Photography*, New York: Virtue Brothers & Co., 1863

Ware, Mike, *Cyanotype: The History, Science and Art of Photographic Printing in Prussian Blue*, London: Science Museum, 1999

Watkins, Derek, *Bromoil: A Foundation Course*, London: Photographers' Institute Press, 2006

Webb, Randall, *Spirits of Salts: A Working Guide to Old Photographic Processes*, London: Argentum, 1999

Webb, Randall and Martin Reed, *Alternative Photographic Processes: A Working Guide for Image Makers*, Rochester, NY: Silver Pixel Press, 2000

Werge, John, *The Evolution of Photography*, London: Piper & Carter, 1890

PHOTO CREDITS

Key to abbreviations:
a=above; b=below; c=centre;
l=left; r=right

Ackroyd & Harvey 185, 186, 187, 188, 189

Bachrat, Ctibor 15b

Baker, Francis 149, 150, 151

Belger, Wayne Martin 60, 61, 62, 63, 64

Bendandi, Maurizio 177

Binh Danh 182, 183

Binvignat Streeter, Loreto 145

Brandt, Matthew 221, 222, 223, 224, 225

Brembo, Luca 39, 163, 173, 181

Brouwer, Frank 207

Capponi, Francesco 47, 48, 49, 50, 51

Cook, Jno 84, 85, 86, 87, 88, 89

Cooper, Alan E. 42, 43, 44

Dearing, John 37, 178, 179

Decam, Édouard 111, 112, 113

The Disposable Camera Project 82, 83

Erdt, Ruth 28, 29, 30, 31, 139

Fabbri, Cesare 102, 103, 104, 105

Figal, Gerald 123al, 123ac, 123ar

Ghidini, Barbara 137, 155

Gioli, Paolo 98, 99, 100, 101

Gómez, Francisco 27, 33, 35, 93a, 121, 191

Guerin, James 68, 69, 97

Hyun, Kwanghun 11, 52, 53, 54, 55

Kamplen, Tony 94, 95, 96

Kossmann, Aaron 79

Krebs, E.V. 157, 166, 167

Kunz, Drew 2, 93bl, 93br

Lewis, Ky 36

Lomography 78, 80, 81

López Calvín, Diego 56, 57, 58, 59

McCaw, Chris 107, 108, 109

Mendez, Michael 37a

Morell, Abelardo 16, 17, 18, 19, 20, 21

Myers, Andrew B. 160, 161

Norton, Cary 66, 67

Onorato, Taiyo & Nico Krebs 70, 71, 72, 73, 74, 75, 76, 77

Paglen, Trevor 125, 126, 127

Pellegrini, Davide 153, 209

Pereira, Cristóbal 147, 157, 211, 215

Perun, Taras 174, 175

Powell, Emma 142, 143

Senkov, Anton 140, 141

Śmiałek, Paweł 196, 197, 198, 199

Sternbach, Joni 200, 201, 202, 203

Symonds, David 213, 217

Tumbleweed, Spiffy 212

Vojnovic, Brana 114, 115, 117, 118, 119

Vuillemin, Eva 139

All photography in the step-by-step
instructions by Cristóbal Pereira and
Gabriele Lungarella unless otherwise
credited.

Binh Danh: all images courtesy of the
artist, Haines Gallery, San Francisco,
USA, and Lisa Sette Gallery, Scottsdale,
AZ, USA

Matthew Brandt: all images courtesy Yossi
Milo Gallery, New York

Chris McCaw: all images courtesy Yossi
Milo Gallery, New York

Taiyo Onorato and Nico Krebs: all
images courtesy of the artists and
RaebervonStenglin, Zurich

ACKNOWLEDG-MENTS

We can safely say that in SHS's three years of operation, *Experimental Photography* has been our most ambitious, challenging and dearest project. What began as an idea stemming from the childhood passion of one of our founding members has now become a reality, thanks to the people who believed in us when others just sneered. A huge thanks goes to Jamie Camplin of Thames & Hudson Ltd, London, for being not only the project's commissioner but also an esteemed guide and help along the way.

We are especially grateful to all the artists who contributed their artwork to the book, and to Marco Antonini and Sergio Minniti, who helped us in selecting and interviewing them. In Barcelona, we are grateful to Francisco Gómez and the people at Taller Milans: Barbara Ghidini, Davide Pellegrini and Giuseppe Sannino. Their passion and dedication to alternative photography exemplified the central role that artistic practice should have in our lives, and were a source of inspiration to follow through with our book. Cristóbal Pereira and Gabriele Lungarella were indispensable for their technical support and photographic prowess. Roberto López, Jose Rios Garaycochea and Mario Dupont kept the crew's morale high during the long days of work in the darkroom.

A huge thanks also goes to Lina V. Persson and Mickia Brangman for their modelling work and their patience: their beauty brought light to a very hectic workspace. Back in Berlin, thanks are due to Maurice Redmond, Katrien Devroe and all the people who helped us during the long working hours in the office.

Finally, a sincere thanks goes to you, the beginning, aspiring or expert photographer who has bought (or are considering buying!) this book. We hope it will continue to foster your interest in the art of photography and inspire you to keep experimenting.

ABOUT THE AUTHORS

Marco Antonini is Executive Director and Curator at NURTUREart, New York.

Sergio Minniti is attached to the Communication and New Technologies department at the IULM University of Milan and is the creator of frankenphotography.com.

Francisco Gómez, born in Buenos Aires, is now lab director at the art-space workshop Taller Milans in Barcelona.

Gabriele Lungarella is Lecturer in Photography at IED Rome.

Luca Bendandi conceived the book at SHS Publishing, Berlin.